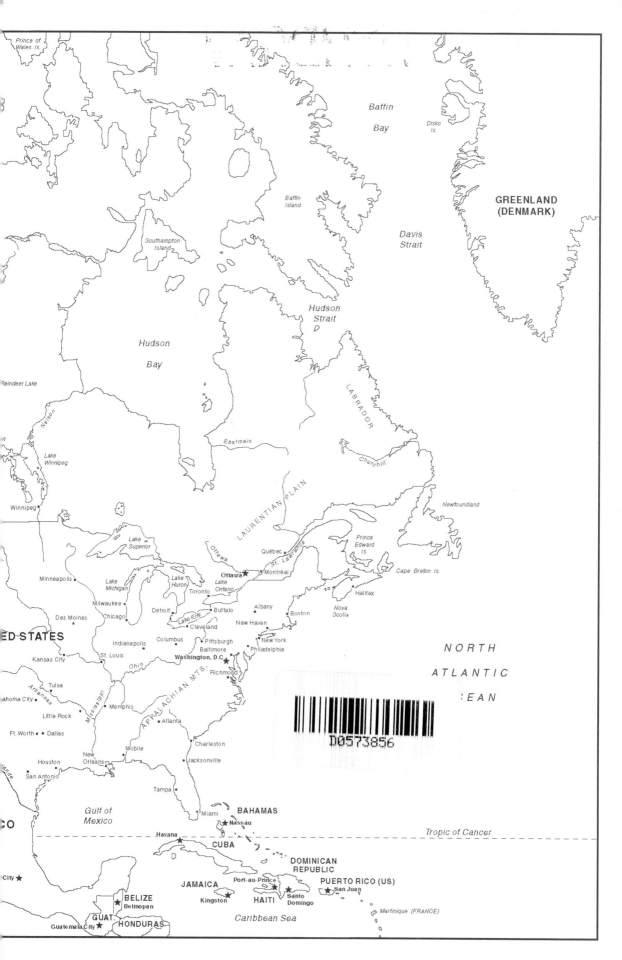

THE GREENWOOD ENCYCLOPEDIA OF
Children's Issues
WORLDWIDE

THE GREENWOOD ENCYCLOPEDIA OF
Children's Issues
WORLDWIDE

NORTH AMERICA AND
THE CARIBBEAN

General Editor
Irving Epstein
Volume Editor
Sheryl L. Lutjens

GREENWOOD PRESS
Westport, Connecticut • London

Library of Congress Cataloging-in-Publication Data

The Greenwood encyclopedia of children's issues worldwide / Irving Epstein general editor.

   p. cm.

  Includes bibliographical references and index.

  ISBN 978-0-313-33614-0 (set : alk. paper) — ISBN 978-0-313-33620-1 (v. 1 : alk. paper) — ISBN 978-0-313-33618-8 (v. 2 : alk. paper) — ISBN 978-0-313-33619-5 (v. 3 : alk. paper) — ISBN 978-0-313-33617-1 (v. 4 : alk. paper) — ISBN 978-0-313-33616-4 (v. 5 : alk. paper) — ISBN 978-0-313-33878-6 (v. 6 : alk. paper)

1. Children—Encyclopedias. I. Epstein, Irving, 1951. II. Lutjens, Sheryl L.

  HQ767.84.G74   2008

  305.2303—dc22   2007031312

British Library Cataloguing in Publication Data is available.

Copyright © 2008 by Irving Epstein

Library of Congress Catalog Card Number: 2007031312
ISBN: 978-0-313-33614-0 (set)
      978-0-313-33620-1 (Asia and Oceania)
      978-0-313-33618-8 (Central and South America)
      978-0-313-33619-5 (Europe)
      978-0-313-33617-1 (North America and the Caribbean)
      978-0-313-33616-4 (Sub-Saharan Africa)
      978-0-313-33878-6 (North Africa and the Middle East)

First published in 2008

Greenwood Press, 88 Post Road West, Westport, CT 06881
An imprint of Greenwood Publishing Group, Inc.
www.greenwood.com

Printed in the United States of America

∞™

The paper used in this book complies with the Permanent Paper Standard issued by the National Information Standards Organization (Z39.48-1984).

10 9 8 7 6 5 4 3 2 1

CONTENTS

CONTENTS

The Six-Volume Comprehensive Index begins on
page 379 of the final volume, North Africa and the Middle East.

PREFACE

Irving Epstein

The decision to publish *The Greenwood Encyclopedia of Children's Issues Worldwide* involved a number of considerations, but was primarily influenced by an understanding that children were deserving of an encyclopedia solely dedicated to a discussion of the quality of their lives. Although there are many sources that compile statistical information and data about the state of children around the world, we believed that by summarizing much of that information in one format, it would be easier for the general public, as well as students, teachers, and policy-makers, to gain a foundational understanding of the challenges the world's children currently confront. However, the difficulties inherent in completing a project of this size and complexity raise larger questions about the ways in which we think about children and childhood in an era of globalization, and it is these questions that I intend to address in the following paragraphs.

To begin with, it should be acknowledged that the *Encyclopedia* is both selective and comprehensive. It is selective, in the sense that we have not been able to adequately cover children's lives in every country or nation-state throughout the world. Due to the prevalence of political, social, and economic conflict and dislocation, it proved impossible to locate experts who had access to the requisite information, and had the time to write about children in certain countries and affected geographical areas. However, the *Encyclopedia* is comprehensive, insofar as all major aspects of children's lives: including educational provision, legal status, family life, health, abuse and neglect, play and recreation, and religious affiliation, are covered within each chapter. Together, the chapters give us a clear picture as to how children are treated and cared for within specific countries and geographical areas, as well as their general quality of life in the twenty-first century. The fact that so many of the chapters within these volumes are co-authored speaks to the penchant for disciplinary specialization that characterizes contemporary academic discourse within the social sciences, a tendency that makes it difficult for a single person to master the many facets of childhood that are covered in the *Encyclopedia*.

It also reaffirms, however, the usefulness of collaboration, in order to better facilitate the framing of a holistic representation of children's lives.

One can certainly raise the issue as to why we need an encyclopedia that is country and region specific in a globalized age. From an organizational and aesthetic perspective, it is reasonable to ask whether this project includes basic redundancies that could be eliminated by adopting a broader, thematic approach. From a conceptual standpoint, it is reasonable to ask whether privileging the nation-state and/or geographic region as a basic unit of analysis makes sense, given the challenges to the long-term viability of the nation-state that globalization tendencies seem to create. My response to both questions is strongly negative, for I believe that issues involving the characteristics of globalization and the nature of childhood can best be understood if they are contextualized. I would therefore reject contentions that an understanding of childhood can be essentialized or that any authentic view of globalization can be formulated through adhering to assumptions that dichotomize the global and the local. By embracing the importance of context, one may indeed at times sacrifice conceptual elegance, and as one reads the various chapters of this volume, no doubt one will find that similar stories are being told in different ways. Certainly, the current legitimacy and long-term viability of certain nation-states and political institutions is implicitly questioned, as the reader learns of their inability to protect children and their complicity in endangering children's lives. Nonetheless, it is doubtful that within our lifetimes, in spite of the growing prominence of transnational influences we associate with globalization, that the nation-state will dissolve as a basic unit of governance, or that our sense of geographical place will no longer have an impact upon our expressions of personal and cultural identity. Therefore, while the importance of globalization influences upon the twenty-first century lives of children must be acknowledged, and while it is clear that our understandings of childhood are informed through cross-cultural comparison and generalization, the *Encyclopedia*'s authors reaffirm the importance of focusing upon the lives of children as they are understood within the regional, area, and nation-state framework.

This being said, there are a number of issues involving the nature of globalization and childhood that can be noted from the outset. First, globalization has been defined according to radically different terms. For some scholars, it has signified the permanent and inevitable ascendancy of empire, be it Western (Fukayama 1992; Huntington 1996), or in reaction to the self-serving nature of that analysis, Asian (Frank 1998). For others, it has signified *both* the triumph of neo-liberal liberalism and the decline of the nation-state as a fundamental organizational unit. Proponents of neo-liberalism, with its embrace of a de-regulated capitalism thriving within an environment of privatization, have associated globalization with these policies; critics point to the resulting the decline and elimination of social services traditionally provided by the state that such policies have promoted. Widespread international institutional neglect and indifference to the needs of children can certainly be viewed in part as a result of these policies.

Regardless of one's political views regarding globalization, its economic dimensions have been characterized by the increasing power of consumption rather than production as a driving economic force. Global consumption patterns are, by their nature, more difficult to chart and are less subject to hierarchical control, than are traditional patterns of industrial production. The fluid nature of global trade created a sense of de-centering that has been observed in other realms too, including the use of technology to create an information age society (Castells 2000), the fluidity with which cultural interactions are transmitted (Appadurai 1996), and the existence of general patterns of flux, mobility, change, complexity, randomness, and contingency (Bauman 2004). The impact of these forces upon the world's children is graphically portrayed within the pages of this *Encyclopedia*. Whether it be through the use of child soldiering, an over-reliance upon child labor and its subsequence denial of basic educational provision, engagement in child trafficking and prostitution, or the promotion of child pornography, often through use of the Internet, children in the twenty-first century are increasingly being defined in global terms as consumable and perishable items, to be used, abused, and then discarded by those who are more powerful.

Globalization theorists disagree as to whether the effects of these trends are irrevocable or whether the trends themselves need be viewed as rigidly deterministic. What is clear though, is that populations in the developing world are becoming increasingly young; 1.5 billion people throughout the world are aged twelve to twenty-four; 1.3 billion live in the developing world (World Bank, 2007). Demographically, a "youth bulge" is predicted, as fertility rates decline. As a result, there will be new pressures for developing countries to integrate their youth into the workforce, encourage more civic engagement, and discourage risk-taking behavior on their part. Most importantly, because of their increasing numbers, youth will have greater opportunities to articulate their own needs within public spaces, to become public self-advocates. The work of UNICEF and other NGOs, in promoting greater child and youth participation in their own affairs, over the past fifteen years, is noteworthy in this regard. The tensions we have noted, between the casual disregard of children's basic needs and the cynical use of children for personal interest and gain, on the one hand, and the increasing recognition of the potential for child and youth advocacy on the other hand, raise even larger questions as to how basic understandings of childhood are being defined and contested in the twenty-first century.

One of the main conclusions one can deduce from a reading of the various chapters of the *Encyclopedia* is that our understandings of childhood express a significant variation as to how childhood is defined, how children develop, and how their interests are protected. Changing biological characteristics associated with childhood and adulthood have had an influence in expanding what it means to be a child in the twenty-first century. In addition, it is clear that notions of childhood are largely social constructions, influenced by such cultural, economic, political, and social factors as the nature of labor markets, demographic trends, the creation and growth of mass education, and the changing notions of patriarchy and family roles and their relationship to the state. No longer can childhood be simplistically expressed as simply a transient state of dependency, defined by the child's relationship to an adult world that she will eventually enter. Instead, it is important to acknowledge the complexity, ambiguity, and malleability that characterize the category we define as childhood.

Archaeologists nonetheless point to the materiality of childhood as being an essential factor in understanding how children have lived their lives, and their emphasis upon the materiality of the child's body (Derevenski 2000, 3–16) has resonance within the pages of this *Encyclopedia* as well. Throughout these volumes, one gains an appreciation as to how children's bodies are abused, violated, harmed, or are in fewer cases protected and nourished. One can find a considerable degree of controversy, associated with how the chronological age of the child is defined, or what constitutes child abuse and neglect, when basic educational provision is satisfactory, or when certain forms of child labor can be considered productive and useful. But, as the chapter authors also emphasize the material nature of childhood, including how children play and negotiate social space, and how they adapt to the conditions around them, they reaffirm the view that it makes sense to examine childhood materiality while acknowledging its ambiguity.

Governments, activists, scholars, and experts have been aided in their efforts to document how children live through their use of the Convention on the Rights of the Child, and as the Convention has indirectly played a significant role in the construct of the categories of analysis within each *Encyclopedia* chapter, it is useful to make a few comments about its utility and the process through which it has been implemented. The Convention itself was adopted by the General Assembly on November 20, 1989 and entered into force on September 2, 1990. Two subsequent protocols have been passed that deal with the sale of children, child prostitution, and child pornography, and child soldiering.

Since its inception, the Convention has become one of the most successful international human rights instruments that have ever been created. Ratified by 192 countries (the United States and Somalia are the only two countries belonging to the UN that have failed to do so), it sets standards as to how children's needs and interests should be defined and articulated. Countries are required to regularly report to the

Committee on the Rights of the Child, a body charged with implementing the Convention, and NGOs are also encouraged to raise questions of concern with the Committee. As a result of this reporting process, member states have improved their data collection mechanisms for assessing the conditions under which their children live; some states have created ombudspersons and national governmental units specifically designed to protect and address the needs of children; others have made a good faith effort to give older children and youth a formal means of articulating their interests through the establishment of youth parliaments and related institutional structures. Indeed, national constitutions now include specific provisions regarding the protection of children. It is undeniable that the nearly universal ratification of the Convention has been accompanied by increased world attention to the plight of children and in that process, children's lives have been saved as their interests and needs are being more clearly articulated (Epstein 2005). It is not surprising therefore, that many of the *Encyclopedia* authors have used information within country reports submitted to the Committee, documenting specific progress in complying with the articles of the Convention, as a basis for assessing the quality of children's lives within the specific country.

The Convention of course is not a perfect document, Scholars have pointed to its contradictory perspectives, with regard to its ambiguous definitions of the chronological age of childhood, contradictory perspectives involving the degree of autonomy that should be afforded the child, the gendered nature of document language (emphasis on child soldiering but not arranged early child marriage, and the lack of attention to the specific challenges girls confront, for example), and its privileging of the protection of children's political rights over economic, social, and cultural rights as major deficiencies. Nonetheless, its importance and influence as an international instrument is beyond dispute, its significance enhanced through the reporting process to which States voluntarily commit themselves and the responses to state reports offered by the Committee on the Rights of the Child.

Although many of the rights enumerated within the Convention replicate those that appear in other international instruments, until the Convention was ratified, the rights of children in particular were merely assumed to fall within larger frameworks that were created for adults. It is perhaps the Convention's greatest strength that it recognizes the fact that children are deserving of rights due their inherent status. This being the case, the rather progressive sections of the document that argue in favor of children themselves exercising their rights to the best of their capabilities makes logical sense. When examining country reports, the Committee operates from a fundamental assumption that the implementation of children's rights cannot be viewed as a voluntary or charitable exercise. Bestowing rights to children is not an act of kindness or generosity; it is a state responsibility to secure, protect, and promote such rights insofar as they are inherently guaranteed to children on the basis of their humanity.

Although the Convention was adopted at a time when the nature of globalization forces was just beginning to be appreciated, its wisdom has stood the test of time at least in one respect. The increasingly harsh circumstances with which many of the world's children must contend, brought about to some degree by the globalization tendencies we have previously described, reinforce the truism that it is becoming increasingly perilous to their own health, safety, and well-being for children to be forced into relying upon adults to defend and protect their basic interests. They are too often the first casualties of poverty, internal conflict and displacement, and illness; the first victims when widespread social suffering occurs. Thus, the need for children to play an increasingly assertive role in defending and articulating their own interests through public advocacy, given the frequent abdication of adult responsibility in this area, is a theme that is strongly expressed within the Convention and is one that has become more salient through the passage of time. It is our hope that this *Encyclopedia* will serve a useful purpose by enhancing understanding about children's lives, the challenges they confront, and the courage they and their advocates express, as they struggle to create a better future during the first decade of the twenty-first century.

ACKNOWLEDGMENTS

The Greenwood Encyclopedia of Children's Issues Worldwide could not have been published without the collective efforts of hundreds of international scholars, a dedicated group of volume editors, and the hard work of the Greenwood Publishing Group editorial staff. Marie Ellen Larcada, who has since left Greenwood, was instrumental in conceiving of the project more than two years ago. But it is acquisitions editor Mariah Gumpert, who through her unlimited patience, laserlike focus, and generous encouragement, is most responsible for the *Encyclopedia*'s completion. My personal gratitude for her efforts is enormous. The task of generating substantive essays about the lives of children in so many countries and regions was extremely complex but was made easier through the hard work of volume editors Laura Arntson, Leslie J. Limage, Sheryl L. Lutjens, Jyotsna Pattnaik, Ghada Hashem Talhami, and Eleonora Villegas-Reimers. Each volume editor contacted numerous experts and convinced them of the importance of the project, worked assiduously with their authors in editing and revising manuscripts, and framed each volume in ways that have insured that the entire *Encyclopedia* is accessible and reader friendly. For their efforts and for the efforts of the chapter contributors, I wish to convey my deepest appreciation.

REFERENCES

Appadurai, Arjun. 1996. *Modernity at Large: Cultural Dimensions of Globalization.* Minneapolis: University of Minnesota Press.

Bauman, Zygmunt. 2004. "A Sociological Theory of Post-modernity." In: *Contemporary Sociological Theory,* Craig Calhoun, James Moody, Steven Pfaff, Joseph Gerteis, and Indermohan Virk, eds. Oxford: Blackwell. pp 429–440.

Castells, Manuel. 2000. *The Rise of the Network Society,* 2nd ed. Oxford: Blackwell.

Derevenski, Joanna Sofner. 2000. "Material Culture Shock: Confronting Expectations in the Material Culture of Children." In: *Children and Material Culture,* Joanna Derevenski, ed. London: Routledge. pp 3–16.

Epstein, Irving. 2005. The Convention on the Rights of the Child: The Promise and Limitations of Multilateralism as a Means of Protecting Children. UNICEF–China, International Forum on Children's Development, October 29–31. 2005. http://www.unicef.org/china/P3_EPSTEIN_paper.pdf.

Frank, Andre Gunder. 1998. *Reorient: Global Economy in the Asian Age.* Berkeley: University of California.

Fukayama, Francis. 1992. *The End of History and the Last Man.* New York: Free Press.

Huntington, Samuel P. 1996. *The Clash of Civilizations and the Making of the New Order.* New York: Simon and Schuster.

World Bank. 2007. *World Bank Report: Development and the Next Generation.* Washington, DC: World Bank.

USER'S GUIDE

The Greenwood Encyclopedia of Children's Issues Worldwide is a six-volume set covering the world's most populous regions.

- Asia and Oceania
- Central and South America
- Europe
- North America and the Caribbean
- Sub-Saharan Africa
- North Africa and the Middle East

All of the volumes contain an introduction to the set from the general editor and a more specific introduction to the volume, written by the volume editor. A copy of the Convention on the Rights of the Child is also printed as an appendix in the North Africa and the Middle East volume. The volumes are divided into chapters organized alphabetically by country or in a few instances by regional name (where countries are grouped together on a regional basis). The following outline includes the sub-sections for each chapter. In a few instances, particularly when information is unavailable or irrelevant to a specific country or region, the sub-section has been eliminated.

NATIONAL PROFILE

The information gathered for this sub-section may include general demographic information, a summary of recent historical and political change within the country or region, a summation of the general challenges that confront the population, and how they might affect children.

OVERVIEW

A discussion of the issues that affect children within the population, highlighting the general state of their welfare and the changing nature of their circumstances.

EDUCATION

A discussion of issues of access, literacy levels, drop-out, opportunities for educational advancement, equity and fairness with regard to socio-economic status, gender, ethnic and religious affiliation, and disability.

PLAY AND RECREATION

A discussion of popular forms of play, children's use of toys and the media, their use of technology, sports, games, and other types of recreation.

CHILD LABOR

A discussion of relevant legislation to protect children, efforts to enforce such legislation, cultural norms, social values, and economic pressures involving the use of child labor, the type of work children are expected to complete, the effects of globalization tendencies upon child labor abuses.

FAMILY

A discussion of relevant family structures, gender roles within the families, demographic trends regarding family size, effects of divorce, inter-generational relationships, effects of poverty and general socio-economic status upon family organization and behavior, rites of passage.

HEALTH

A discussion of issues related to infant and child mortality, vaccination and childhood disease, the general quality of medical care provided to children, access to clean water, exposure to air and other forms of pollution, and relevant sex education programming.

LAWS AND LEGAL STATUS

A discussion of how the country's legal system affects children—what protections they are given under the law, and how legal safeguards are guaranteed. The nature of the juvenile justice system, if one exists, how gang activity is handled, conditions for children and youth who are incarcerated.

RELIGIOUS LIFE

A discussion of prevailing religious practices and their meanings for children, forms of religious training, the role of religious organizations in children's lives.

CHILD ABUSE AND NEGLECT

A discussion including statistics that illustrates the scope of child abuse and neglect within the country or region, types of abuse and neglect and the reasons for their occurrence, and preventative measures that have been taken; how specific issues such as child soldiering, child trafficking, and child pornography are addressed.

GROWING UP IN THE TWENTY-FIRST CENTURY

A discussion summarizing findings from other sub-sections of the chapter while offering assessments as to future prospects as well as what further measures will have to be taken in order to significantly improve children's lives in the immediate and near future.

RESOURCE GUIDE

Suggested readings, relevant video, film, and media sources, web sites, and relevant NGOs and other organizations are listed in this section. Whenever possible, sources are annotated.

MAPS AND INDEXES

A regional map accompanies each volume, and each chapter has its own country or regional map. Each volume includes an index consisting of subject and person entries; a comprehensive index for the entire set is included at the end of the North Africa and the Middle East volume.

INTRODUCTION

Sheryl L. Lutjens

The realities of children in North America and the Caribbean are not the same from country to country, yet there are important similarities that reflect the widespread international concern that the lives of children everywhere be healthy, safe, and productive. Canada, the United States, and Mexico—the North American cases included in this volume—are all large countries in terms of territorial extension and population. Canada has a population of 32.6 million and 3,849,670 square miles; the United States has a population of 299.1 million and 3,717,796 square miles; and Mexico has a 108.3 million population and 756,062 square miles (Population Reference Bureau 2006, 6, 7). The island nations of the Caribbean are smaller. St. Vincent and the Grenadines has 151 square miles, and Cuba, the largest island, has 42,803 square miles. Populations range from less than 100,000 in Grenada, Antigua and Barbuda, and Dominica to 2.7 million inhabitants in Jamaica, 3.9 million in Puerto Rico, 8.5 million in Haiti, 9 million in the Dominican Republic, and 11.3 million in Cuba (Population Reference Bureau 2006, 7).[1]

In addition to distinctions of size, there are also economic, political, social, and cultural differences. GNI per capita ranges from $42,000 (PPP) in the United States (third in the world) and $32,770 in Canada (14th in the world) to $10,560 in Mexico (80th in the world) and $1,660 in Haiti (177th in the world) (World Bank 2007). Language practices vary, for example; Spanish is dominant in Mexico, Puerto Rico, Cuba, and the Dominican Republic; English predominates in many of the Caribbean islands, the United States, and Canada; and French speakers are found in Canada and the Caribbean. Indigenous and creole languages are also spoken. The

---

1. These population estimates are from the Population Reference Bureau and, as with other figures offered in this introduction to the volume, they may differ slightly from those provided by the sources used by chapter authors.

deeper and more intriguing diversities of race, ethnic, and gender relations, economic strategies, and national projects are explained in part by the complex local variations in what are indeed shared histories of colonization (Slocum and Thomas 2003), as well as by the struggles, constraints, and choices in post-colonial development.

The chapters in this volume offer a rich and systematic panorama of the experiences of children in North America and the Caribbean. The countries presented include Antigua and Barbuda, the Bahamas, Barbados, Canada, Cuba, the Dominican Republic, Grenada, Haiti, Jamaica, Mexico, Puerto Rico, St. Kitts and Nevis, St. Lucia, St. Vincent and the Grenadines, Trinidad and Tobago, and the United States. Each country chapter addresses key themes of childhood, beginning with an overview of the country and including education, play and recreation, health, child labor, religious life, law and legal status, child abuse and neglect, and prospects for children into the twenty-first century.

The study of children and adolescents across cultures is a relatively new academic endeavor. With roots in the disciplines of anthropology and psychology, "the cross-cultural study of human development as a recognized field of study with its own definite identity is no more than twenty-five years old. By 1975–1980, a critical mass of studies investigating the psychological development of children and adolescents in a variety of non-Western and Western societies had accumulated" (Gielen 2004, 6). As Gardiner counsels with regard to the possibilities offered in this new area of academic inquiry, contextualization is key; contextualization "refers to the view that behavior cannot be meaningfully studied or fully understood independent of its ecocultural context" (Gardiner 2004, 433). Although explicit comparison is not the objective of the essays here, common issues in the lives of children and adolescents organize the presentation of national patterns and local details, including family structures and parenting practices, educational opportunities, the nature and scope of health care, play and recreation, religion, migrations, and problems of child labor and violence.[2]

New perspectives of children's rights, the global ordering of national and local life, and the resilience of cultures are all part of the contextualization that highlights what is shared and what is specific in the realities of childhood and adolescence.

THE RIGHTS OF CHILDREN

One milestone in the creation of more comprehensive knowledge about children's issues worldwide is the United Nations (UN) Convention on the Rights of the Child (CRC). The CRC is an international

2. One good example of recent efforts is *Teen Life in Latin America and the Caribbean,* an edited volume that includes chapters on Cuba, the Dominican Republic, Haiti, Jamaica, Mexico, and Puerto Rico (Tompkins and Sternberg 2004).

Table 1.
Convention on the Rights of the Child

Country	Date signed	Date ratified
Antigua and Barbuda	March 12, 1991	October 5, 1993
Bahamas	October 30, 1990	February 20, 1991
Barbados	April 19, 1990	October 9, 1990
Canada	May 28, 1990	December 13, 1991
Cuba	January 26, 1990	August 21, 1991
Dominica	January 26, 1990	March 13, 1991
Dominican Republic	August 8, 1990	June 11, 1991
Grenada	February 21, 1990	November 5, 1990
Haiti	January 26, 1990	June 8, 1995
Jamaica	January 26, 1990	May 14, 1991
Mexico	January 26, 1990	September 21, 1990
St. Kitts and Nevis	January 26, 1990	July 24, 1990
St. Lucia	September 30, 1990	June 16, 1993
St. Vincent and the Grenadines	September 20, 1993	October 26, 1993
Trinidad and Tobago	September 30, 1990	December 5, 1991
United States	February 16, 1995	

Source: Office of the United Nations High Commissioner for Human Rights. Status of the Ratification of the Convention on the Rights of the Child.

convention that was adopted into international law by the UN General
Assembly on November 20, 1989. It draws upon previous international
conventions and declarations, reflecting increased attention to the conditions of children around the world (United Nations; Hevener Kaufman
2004). The CRC came into force in September 1990, with 54 articles
that establish child-centered rights and freedoms, the fundamental role
and responsibilities of the family, and the "special safeguards and care"
that children need; according to Article 43, it is monitored by the Committee on the Rights of the Child, composed of ten elected experts of
"high moral standing and recognized competence in the field covered by
this Convention" (Office of the High Commissioner, Convention on the
Rights of the Child). Ratification of the CRC was swift and widespread.
Only the United States and Somalia had not ratified the CRC by 2006.
According to the Campaign for U.S. Ratification of the Convention on
the Rights of the Child, the opposition in the United States fears the
CRC as a threat to the family and national sovereignty alike (Campaign
for U.S. Ratification; Fagan 2001). As Table 1 shows, Canada, Mexico,
and the nations of the Caribbean have all ratified the convention.

The CRC has played a vital role in creating the rules of an international
children's rights regime. In implementing the Convention, the Committee aims to assist governments in bringing national laws and practices into
conformity. The Committee uses a reporting system to assess the conditions of children in individual countries, though "much of the power of

the convention comes from mutual example and pressure from the public and from donor countries rather than a real enforcement power" (United Nations). The system of country reports and Committee responses is only part of an ongoing process of organized discussion, assessment, and reaffirmation of the goals of the Convention. A World Summit for Children was held in September 1990 and the UN General Assembly adopted two Optional Protocols to the CRC in 2000, one increasing the protection of children from involvement in armed conflict and the second increasing protection from sexual exploitation. In 2001, the UN General Secretary issued a progress report entitled "We the Children," and in May 2002 a UN General Assembly Special Session on Children was held with some 7,000 participants, including children. The Special Session produced the "World Fit for Children" document (United Nations Children's Fund, United Nations Special Session).

Other international initiatives support the CRC and the promotion of better lives and full rights for children. The United Nations Millennium Summit in 2000 produced a declaration and eight Millennium Development Goals (MDG) to be met by 2015 (World Bank 2007a); the United Nations Children's Fund (UNICEF) is involved with monitoring the child-specific indicators associated with these goals. The 1990 World Conference on Education for All in Jomtien, Thailand, produced an agreement to universalize primary education and greatly reduce illiteracy by the end of the decade (Education for All—EFA), and follow-up has included the UN Education for All resolution in 1997, the World Education Forum in Dakar in 2000, and the declaration of the UN Literacy Decade (2003–2012) (United Nations Educational, Scientific, and Cultural Organization). Another initiative is the Convention on the Elimination of All Forms of Discrimination against Women (CEDAW) adopted by the General Assembly in December 1979. The International Labor Organization (ILO), an agency of the United Nations dedicated to human and workers' rights, has provided strong support for the CRC with conventions regarding child labor that have the status of international treaties and are thus considered binding.

The ongoing work of the Committee on the Rights of the Child aspires to induce change in the orientation of states and state actors, international and national non-governmental organizations (NGOs), and, as the participation in the Special Session in 2002 shows, in children themselves (Office of the United Nations High Commissioner, Fact Sheet No. 10). Regional organizing and collaboration is a crucial part of the creation of an international legal context that supports and protects children, as the Caribbean states demonstrate. The Caribbean Conference on the Rights of the Child was held in October 1996, promoted by UNICEF and Caribbean Community (CARICOM) and producing a Commitment to Action signed by seventeen Caribbean countries. The Kingston and Bridgetown Accords followed, whereby regional governments agreed upon implementation strategies and committed to a Plan of Action for Early Childhood Education, Care and Development (ECECD) (Williams 2004, 158). CARICOM incorporated these efforts into its Human Resource Development Strategy in July 1997. Progress was assessed at a regional ECECD conference in Jamaica in 2000 and another in Guama in 2002 (Brown 2003). Research on Caribbean children's realities and rights has increased, both in the academy and by policy-oriented international organizations (see Barrow 2001, 2002; United Nations ECLAC 2001; United Nations Children's Fund 2006b).

There are other regional agreements and actions that promote national and international efforts to ensure the health, well-being, development, and protection of children in North America. The Inter-American Court of Human Rights issued an Advisory Opinion in 2002 on the legal status and human rights of children (Pinheiro 2006, 38). With regard to violence against children, the Organization of American States has promoted the Inter-American Convention to Prevent and Punish Torture, the Inter-American Convention on the Forced Disappearance of Persons, the Inter-American Convention on the Elimination of all Forms of Discrimination against Persons with Disabilities, and the Inter-American Convention on the Prevention, Punishment and Eradication of Violence against Women "Convention of Belém do Pará" (Pinheiro 2006, 40).

Regional efforts require the cooperation of states, including active policy making and new legislation if needed, as well as the dedication of human and material resources to meet children's needs. The support of intergovernmental, nongovernmental, and transnational organizations is almost always also needed. In this process, national, regional, and international efforts to improve children's lives are creating new opportunities, helping resolve problems that affect children, and building an invaluable reserve of knowledge about children's lives. In all of this, the commitments and capacities of individual states matter greatly. This is so especially in the unique case of Cuba, whose intended economic and political isolation within the regional and international environments has been pursued persistently by the United States government for more than four decades (Schwab 1999).

Educational opportunities offer a good example of monitoring of progress toward a goal—Articles 28 and 29 of the CRC—that is widely shared and supported. The most recent UNESCO report on Education for All and country performance provides information about improvements in preschool, primary, secondary, and higher education (2007). Regional disparities, in-country differences between the rich and poor or rural and urban children, persistence of some gender disparities despite progress, and variations in teacher training are apparent, though a few countries in Latin America and the Caribbean have achieved the four most quantifiable EFA goals (or are close to achieving them), among them Barbados, Trinidad and Tobago, and Cuba (United Nations

Educational, Scientific, and Cultural Organization 2007, 10). In terms of public spending on education as a percentage of gross domestic product (GDP) in 2002–03, Cuba dedicated 12.3 percent to education, Trinidad and Tobago 3.1 percent, the Dominican Republic 3.0 percent, Mexico, 4.1 percent, and Jamaica 5.2 percent (United Nations ECLAC 2006, 132).

The problem of child labor is another area where improvement is reported. Here, statistics remain only estimates despite the increased attention to discovering, reporting, and eliminating child labor—Article 32 of the CRC—a problem that reflects the multidimensional nature of new standards and goals for children's well-being, opportunities, and success (Weston and Teerink 2005). In the United States, an estimated 3.2 million workers are under the age of eighteen; in Latin America and the Caribbean, an estimated 17.4 million under eighteen work, although the regional rate of decline in child labor has been the best in the world (Child Labor Coalition 2005, 1; and International Labor Organization 2006). One area of special concern is children's involvement in the worst forms of child labor, including activities where they are enslaved, forcibly recruited, prostituted, trafficked, forced into illegal activities or hazardous work (United Nations Children's Fund, Child Protection). Many scholars and activists see child labor as a human rights issue (Weston and Teerink 2005).

Yet even the framing of children's issues—and child labor—as human rights issues is contested by some, using arguments that range from the defense of state sovereignty to rejection of public international law as applicable to private actors to doubts about the very concept of human rights (Weston and Teerink 2005, 6–18). On the grounds of such debate, the importance of state policy and commitments seems clear. In this regard, while the United States shows no signs of moving forward with the ratification of the CRC, it did rejoin UNESCO in 2003 (having left the organization in 1984).

GLOBALIZATION

The creation of an increasingly stronger international children's rights regime is part of the process called globalization. Globalization is a concept or label used to explain relations within the contemporary global order, an order that many see as novel, exciting, and full of promise for a renewed strategy of free-market capitalist development. Globalization is defined in different ways, emphasizing variously economic, political, social, technological, or cultural aspects. Held and McGrew explain that "simply put, globalization denotes the expanding scale, growing magnitude, speeding up and deepening impact of interregional flows and patterns of social interaction" (2000, 4). As Hevener Kaufman and colleagues write in framing a collection of essays on globalization and children:

> Despite many legitimately different definitions of globalization we can construct a working definition that allows a focus on some major impacts of global change on children. Globalization is a process that opens nation states to many influences that originate beyond their borders. These changes are likely to decrease the primacy of national economic, political, and social institutions, thereby affecting the everyday context in which children group and interact with the rest of society. Some of the impacts of globalization on children are therefore normative. Efforts to assess the effects on groups of children must be culturally sensitive. (Hevener Kaufman et al. 2004, 4)

Globalization is in many ways important for contextualizing the lives of children in the United States, Canada, Mexico, and the island states of the Caribbean.

The economic dynamics of the contemporary global order promise that intensified capitalist modernization will be facilitated by freeing domestic markets and orienting development toward competition in world trade. The call to engage the global economy is not entirely new for North America and the Caribbean, however, as history shows involvement since colonization. The forms of present day engagement are characterized by free trade agreements such as NAFTA (North American Free Trade Agreement), which unites Canada, the United States, and Mexico in a commitment to open markets, changes in the preferential trade relationships of Caribbean countries, including the ratification of the Caribbean Single Market in 2006, and the U.S. desire to create an even larger Free Trade Area of the Americas. Also important in neoliberal globalization are the structural adjustment programs demanded of troubled economies by international financial institutions.

Critics of neoliberal globalization point to ongoing inequalities within the still-developing countries of the global south and between them and the developed countries of the global north. Monitoring of the Millennium Development Goals in Latin America and the Caribbean by the World Bank reports that the percentage of people living on less than $1 per day fell from about 9 percent in 2002 to 8.6 percent in 2004, although 47 million people still live in this state of extreme poverty (World Bank 2007d). In North America, the reported share of revenue going to the poorest quintile of the population was 7.2 percent in Canada, 5.4 percent in the United States (where one of every four children lives in poverty), and 4.3 percent in Mexico; in the Caribbean, figures were 4.0 percent in the Dominican Republic, 2.4 percent in Haiti, 5.3 percent in Jamaica, and 5.9 percent in Trinidad and Tobago (World Bank 2007b, 226–232; Pinheiro 2006, 311; and Rodgers 2006). Poverty in both rich and poorer countries affects children and their futures in multiple ways, including its contribution to the problems of child labor.

Critics also identify "structural violence" in the poverty associated with the current phase of global capitalism. Violence does surface in various ways in the present global order, associated with inequalities and other development problems. Worldwide, between 133 and 275 million children witness violence in the home, according to a study prepared in support of the UN Secretary General's Study on Violence against Children. For Latin America and the Caribbean, figures range from 1.3 million to 25.5 million children (Global Initiative to End All Corporal Punishment of Children 2006, 71). While school violence in the United States captures media attention, children in many countries experience the bullying that is part of school violence, see or carry weapons at school, or are involved in fighting. Homicide rates in the Caribbean and North America suggest extensive societal violence (Global Initiative to End All Corporal Punishment of Children 2006, 357–358). Worldwide, fewer than 20 countries have reformed their laws to prohibit corporal punishment in all settings, including the home (though the Committee on the Rights of the Child recommended reform to 130 countries between 1996 and 2006) (Pinheiro 2006, 74).

Violence has consequences. A recent study by the World Bank and the UN Office on Drugs and Crime concludes that economic cost of crime negatively affects development in the Caribbean (2007). Some material costs are direct, including the policing and criminal justice systems, material damages, and counseling and social services required to treat victims and perpetrators (Heinemann and Verner 2006). Heinemann and Verner explored a number of indirect socio-economic costs, categorized as pain and suffering, economic multiplier effects, and social multiplier effects (2006). It is estimated that youth violence in the United States costs more than $158 billion per year in direct and indirect costs.

Structural violence and development difficulties affect health and health care, important issues for children and their well-being. Haiti is the poorest country in the Caribbean and among the poorest in the world. In Haiti there is a high maternal mortality rate, more than one of every ten children die before the age of five, some 5,000 children are born each year with HIV, more than 200,000 children have lost one or both parents to AIDS, and thousands of young girls are enslaved by domestic work in the Restavèk system (United Nations Children's Fund, Haiti; and Haitian Street Kids, Inc.). In the United States, 11.2 percent of children and 19 percent of children in poverty have no health insurance (Samuels 2006). And the HIV/AIDS crisis also creates special issues for children who may be infected, orphaned, and subject to material and familial insecurities associated with the disease. In 2005, there were 1.2 million individuals in the United States and an estimated 58,000 Canadians living with HIV/AIDS (Joint United Nations Programme 2006c, 2006a). In the Caribbean, where prevalence rates are second highest in the world, there are 250,000 people living with HIV, nearly three-quarters of them in Haiti and the Dominican Republic (Joint United Nations Programme 2006b). The countries that have progressed most

Table 2.
Selected Survival Indicators, 2005

Country	Infant mortality	Under-five mortality	Life expectancy (at birth)
Antigua and Barbuda	11	12	–
Bahamas	13	15	71
Barbados	11	12	76
Canada	5	6	80
Cuba	6	7	78
Dominican Republic	26	31	68
Grenada	17	21	–
Haiti	84	120	52
Jamaica	17	20	71
Mexico	22	27	76
St. Kitts and Nevis	18	20	–
St. Lucia	12	14	73
St. Vincent and the Grenadines	17	20	71
Trinidad and Tobago	17	19	70
United States	6	7	78

Source: United Nations Children's Fund (2006a), 102–105.

with controlling and treating HIV/AIDS are the Bahamas, Barbados, Cuba, and Jamaica, in part because of access to antiretroviral drugs. Cuba has an adult prevalence rate of 0.1 percent, Canada a rate of 0.3, and the United States a rate of 0.6 percent; the prevalence rate is 1–2 percent in Barbados, the Dominican Republic, and Jamaica, and 2–4 percent in the Bahamas, Haiti, and Trinidad and Tobago (Joint United Nations Programme 2006a).

Despite striking difficulties in many countries, progress has been made along a number of the basic health measures associated with the CRC and the Millennium Development Goals. Table 2 reports survival indicators for children in the Caribbean and North America in 2005.

CULTURAL PRACTICES AND THE REALITIES OF PLACE

Globalization is also understood in terms of the information technologies that have diminished national sovereignties by speeding up financial transactions and blurring the boundaries of cultural production and distribution. Still, despite the presumed shrinking of an electronically linked world (Wilson 2004), children grow up in homes that are bounded in both time and space. There is indeed movement and change, as families and homes are affected by the flows of information, of cultural products and images, and of people throughout North America and the Caribbean. These flows both conserve and reshape the cultural practices of childhood and gendered family traditions.

The emergence of single mother–headed families is one of the important issues of childhood in the 2000s. The nuclear family ideal still holds quite strong in North America, despite divorce rates, remarriage, and increasing numbers of single parent families. An estimated 550,000 families are headed by single mothers in Canada, while there are 10.4 million single mothers living with children under eighteen in the United States (compared to 3.4 million in 1970) (Statistics Canada; U.S. Department of Commerce 2007). In the Caribbean, especially the Anglophone Caribbean, what anthropologists call matrifocality has strong historical roots and has been reconsidered as an alternative form of family rather than an aberrant version of the class-based nuclear family model imposed with colonialism. In Jamaica, for example, 48 percent of households are headed by a female—the highest in the world according to Williams (2004). Patterns of matrifocality and woman-headed households raise questions about marriage customs and the choice of consensual unions, recast extended families and community in their own terms, and undermine the gendered foundations of the "myth of the male breadwinner" (Nurse 2004; Brown 2003; and Safa 2005). Traditional marriage and gender norms of femininity and masculinity remain important, however, both in creating families and socializing children.

The importance of gender equalities for the well-being of children has been recognized by states, international organizations, and NGOs. This recognition has served to expand the measures used to interpret and assess the conditions of children. The Mothers' Index is one example. The Mothers' Index is prepared by calculating a weighted average of women's health status (lifetime risk of maternal mortality, percent of women using modern contraception, percent of births attended by trained personnel, percent of pregnant women with anemia), mothers' educational status (adult female literacy rate), and children's well-being (infant mortality rate, gross primary enrollments, percent of population with access to safe water, percent of children under five suffering from moderate or severe nutritional wasting). Table 3 shows the international ranking of selected countries in North America and the Caribbean. It is notable that Canada and the United States rank 8 and 11, respectively, followed closely by Cuba as number 13 in the world.

Movements of people have affected the meanings of home and family in North America and the Caribbean. There has long been a northward migratory flow, both permanent and temporary, from the Caribbean and Mexico to the United States and Canada. The diasporas thereby created have many meanings, from the popularization of food and music carried from the homeland to the politically rancorous debates about particular immigrants, language use, and national security. Although many from the Caribbean have preferred to migrate to the United Kingdom, there is a substantial Caribbean-born population in the United States and also in Canada. In 2004, there were 3,323,000 Caribbean-born residents in the

Table 3.
2005 Mothers' Index Rankings (of 110 countries included)

Country	Mothers' Index rank	Women's Index rank	Children's Index rank
Canada	8	9	7
United States	11	15	10
Cuba	13	10	15
Mexico	20	21	27
Trinidad and Tobago	22	19	31
Jamaica	27	34	17
Dominican Republic	33	31	50
Haiti	85	99	74

Source: Save the Children (2005), 40.

United States, as well as 10,805,000 Mexican-born residents. By 2005, 12.1 percent of the U.S. population was foreign-born, and 22.8 percent of the inflow of foreign-born population in 2004 was aged nineteen or younger (Global Data Center, United States: Inflow; Global Data Center, United States, Stock). The remittances sent by permanent or temporary migrants are very important for some countries. In 2004, remittances contributed 52.7 percent of Haiti's GDP, 17 percent in Jamaica, and more than 10 percent in the Dominican Republic. In 2005, Mexico received $21 billion in remittances (Lapointe 2004; World Bank).

The global flows of people are not unidirectional, however. Tourism sends millions to the Caribbean islands and Mexico. Preliminary 2006 estimates of world tourism are 842 million arrivals, 51 million of which were to the United States—the third most popular tourist destination worldwide. In 2005, Mexico ranked number seven with 21.9 million arrivals (ITA Office of Travel and Tourism Industries 2006). Caribbean tourism counted 18.2 million arrivals in 2004, and there were about 20 million cruise ship passengers as well; visitors to the Caribbean spent $21 billion ("Caribbean Tourism Performance in 2004" 2005). Tourism's benefits are accompanied by other more problematic effects, which can include the worst forms of child labor, trafficking, and drugs (Kempadoo and Ghuma 1999).

Migrations, tourism, and the neoliberal economic strategies that inform them as survival tactics in the new global order have ambiguous effects on families, children, and the cultures within which the intimacies of daily life are practiced. It is not just people who move around and between locations and places, however. NGOs with domestic and international roots, humanitarian groups, and other actors in what is called a "transnational civil society" also mark the terrain of work with and for children. Save the Children, for instance, was created as the Save the Children Foundation in England in 1919 (by Eglantyne Jebb, who would write the Children's Charter that was endorsed in 1924 by the League of Nations as the Declaration of the Rights of the Child). Its original work in Europe with children victims of WWI and then WWII was matched with efforts to aid the children of coal miners in Appalachia in the 1930s and the Navajo nation in the northern Arizona blizzard of 1948, and then with international development initiatives. Currently, Save the Children works in Haiti, reflecting its commitment to go where rural poverty is the highest, and also collaborates with three Save the Children Alliance members in Mexico and the Dominican Republic (Save the Children 2007).

NGOs have many roles within the global, regional, and national contexts, including information gathering, agenda setting, and advocacy (Wiseberg 2005, 350–357). As the chapters in this volume report, NGO activity in the countries of the Caribbean and North America is extensive, ranging from XChange, created to work for safe and protective home, school, and community environments for children and youth in Barbardos, Grenada, Haiti, Jamaica, and other countries in the region, to the Red Cross, Soroptomists, and cause-specific organizations working on issues such as family planning, sports and recreation, and HIV/AIDS education and outreach, often with international assistance.

In establishing some local and global landmarks that can be useful in contextualizing the realities of children in North America and the Caribbean that are presented in this volume, it is useful to look for signs of progress and problem solving. The existence of much new information about children and their lives helps greatly on this front, as does the creation of new and better measures for identifying children's issues and their meaning. One such methodology is the Human Development Index (HDI), created in 1990 by Amartya Sen and Mabub ul Haq as an attempt to move beyond simple correlations of economic growth with individual human well-being. The HDI is used by the UN Development Program and reflects a capabilities approach that focuses on the quality of life: longevity (life expectancy), knowledge (adult literacy rate and combined gross enrollment at all three levels of schooling), and standard of living (GDP at Purchasing Power Parity in US dollars). The Human Development Index for 2006 locates countries in the Caribbean and North America in an international ranking, which is presented in Table 4.

Against the backdrop painted by newer and more sensitive assessment tools, the growing body of published research on children, and the theoretical innovations that allow rethinking of old truths, it is indeed possible to explore the realities of what is different and what is shared in the lives of children in the United States, Canada, Mexico, and the island states of the Caribbean. The chapters collected here are important contributions to the foundations of our knowledge about children, each providing the reader with recommendations for key readings on the conditions of childhood in the country under study, visual resources in film, CD, and DVD

Table 4.
**Human Development Index, North America and the Caribbean, 2006
Report**

Country	Rank	Human Development Index value (HDI), 2004
High Human Development		
Canada	6	0.950
United States	8	0.948
Puerto Rico[a]		0.942
Barbados	31	0.879
Cuba	50	0.826
St. Kitts and Nevis	51	0.825
Bahamas	52	0.825
Mexico	53	0.821
Trinidad and Tobago	57	0.809
Antigua and Barbuda	59	0.808
Medium Human Development		
Saint Lucia	71	0.790
Grenada	85	0.762
Dominican Republic	94	0.751
Jamaica	104	0.724
Low Human Development		
Haiti	154	0.482

[a]No ranking is provided by the source; Puerto Rico is often not listed separate from the United States.
Source: United Nations Development Programme (2006), 283–286; and United Nations System-wide Earthwatch, Island Directory, Puerto Rico (United States). http://islands.unep.ch/CSV.htm. Accessed May 4, 2007.

formats a listing of websites that may be consulted, information on relevant international and national governmental and nongovernmental organizations, and a bibliography of sources consulted in preparing the chapter.

SELECTED REFERENCES

Barrow, Christine. 2001. *Situation Analysis of Children and Women in Twelve Countries in the Caribbean.* Barbados: UNICEF Caribbean Area Office. http://www.unicef.org/barbados/SitAn_Final_Report.doc.
———, ed. 2002. *Children's Rights: Caribbean Realities.* Kingston: Ian Randle Publishers.
Brown, Janet. 2003. "Developing an Early Childhood Profession in the Caribbean." pp. 54–73 in *Caribbean Childhoods: From Research to Action; Volume 1: Contemporary Issues in Early Childhood*, Journal of the Children's Issues Coalition, University of the West Indies. Kingston: Ian Randle Publishers.

Campaign for U.S. Ratification of the Convention on the Rights of the Child. CRC Fact and Research, Frequently Asked Questions. http://childrightscampaign .org/crcfacts.htm.

"Caribbean Tourism Performance in 2004." 2005. TravelVideo. TV, January 31, 2005. http://travelvideo.tv/news/more.php?id=A4091_0_1_0_M.

Child Labor Coalition. 2005. "Protecting Working Children in the United States." Washington, DC, June 2005.

Fagan, Patrick F. 2001. "How UN Conventions on Women's and Children's Rights Undermine Family, Religion, and Sovereignty." The Heritage Foundation, Backgrounder, February 5, 2001. http://www.heritage.org/Research/Inter national Organizations/BG1407.cfm. Accessed December 11, 2006.

Gardiner, Harry W. 2004. "Cross-Cultural Human Development: Following the Yellow Brick Road in Search of New Approaches for the Twenty-First Century." pp. 433–442 in *Childhood and Adolescence: Cross-Cultural Perspectives and Applications*. Edited by Uwe P. Gielen and Jaipaul Roopnarine. Westport, CT and London: Praeger Publishers.

Gielen, Uwe P. 2004. "The Cross-Cultural Study of Human Development: An Opinionated Historical Introduction." pp. 3–45 in *Childhood and Adolescence: Cross-Cultural Perspectives and Applications*. Edited by Uwe P. Gielen and Jaipaul Roopnarine. Westport, CT and London: Praeger Publishers.

Global Data Center, Migration Information Source. United States: Inflow of Foreign-Born Population by Age as a Percentage of Total and Sex as a Percentage of Age Group, 1986 to 2003. http://www.migrationinformation.org/global data/countrydata/data.cfm. Accessed October 20, 2006.

———. United States: Stock of Foreign-born Population by Country of Birth, 1995 to 2005 (in thousands). http://www.migrationinformation.org/GlobalData/ countrydata/data.cfm. Accessed October 19, 2006.

Global Initiative to End All Corporal Punishment of Children. 2006. *Ending Legalised Violence against Children, Global Report 2006; A Contribution to the UN Secretary General's Study on Violence against Children.* http://www.nospank .net/globalreport.pdf.

Haitian Street Kids, Inc. Restavèk Fact Sheet—Haitian Child Slavery. http://quicksitemaker. com/members/immunenation/Restavek_Fact_Sheet.html. Accessed October 9, 2006.

Heinemann, Alessandra, and Dorte Verner. 2006. *Crime and Violence in Development: A Literature Review of Latin America and the Caribbean.* World Bank Policy Research Working Paper 4041, October 2006. http://papers.ssrn .com/sol3/papers.cfm?abstract_id.

Held, David, and Anthony McGrew. 2000. "The Great Globalization Debate: An Introduction." pp. 1–45 in *The Global Transformations Reader: An Introduction to the Globalization Debate.* Edited by David Held and Anthony McGrew. Malden, MA: Blackwell Publishers.

Hevener Kaufman, Natalie. 2004. "The Status of Children in International Law." pp. 31–45 in *Globalization and Children: Exploring Potentials for Enhancing Opportunities in the Lives of Children and Youth.* Edited by Natalie Hevener Kaufman and Irene Rizzini. Seacaucus, NJ: Kluwer Academic Publishers.

Hevener Kaufman, Natalie, Irene Rizzini, Kathleen Wilson, and Malcolm Bush. 2004. "The Impact of Global Economic, Political, and Social Transformations on the Lives of Children: A Framework for Analysis." pp. 3–18 in *Globalization and Children: Exploring Potentials for Enhancing Opportunities in the*

Lives of Children and Youth. Edited by Natalie Hevener Kaufman and Irene Rizzini. Seacaucus, NJ: Kluwer Academic Publishers.

International Labor Organization, Department of Communication and Public Information. 2006. Facts on Child Labor—2006. http://www.ilo.org/public/english/bureau/inf/download/child/childday06.pdf.

ITA Office of Travel and Tourism Industries. 2006. World & U.S. International Visitor Arrivals & Receipts. http://www.tinet.ita.doc.gov/outreachpages/inbound.world_us_intl_arrivals.html.

Joint United Nations Programme on HIV/AIDS (UNAIDS) and World Health Organization. 2006a. *AIDS Epidemic Update, December 2006*. Geneva: UNAIDS and WHO.

———. 2006b. Fact Sheet: Caribbean. http://data.unaids.org/pub/EpiReport/2006/20061121_epi_fs_c_en.pdf.

———. 2006c. Fact Sheet: North America, Western and Central Europe. December 2006. http://data.unaids.org/pub/EpiReport/2006/20061121_EPI_FS_NAWCE_en.pdf.

Kempadoo, Kemala, and Ranya Ghuma. 1999. "For the Children: Trends in International Policies and Law on Sex Tourism." pp. 291–308 in *Sun, Sex, and Gold: Tourism and Sex Work in the Caribbean*. Edited by Kamala Kempadoo. Lanham, Maryland: Rowman & Littlefield.

Lapointe, Michelle. 2004. *Diasporas in Caribbean Development: Rapporteur's Report. Report of the Inter-American Dialogue and the World Bank*. Washington DC: Inter-American Dialogue.

Nurse, Keith. 2004. "Masculinities in Transition: Gender and the Global Problematique." pp. 3–37 in *Interrogating Caribbean Masculinities: Theoretical and Empirical Analyses*. Edited by Rhoda E. Reddock. Kingston, Jamaica: University of the West Indies Press.

Office of the High Commissioner for Human Rights. (a). Convention on the Rights of the Child. http://www.unhchr.ch/html/menu3/b/k2crc.htm. Accessed October 9, 2006.

———. (b). Fact Sheet No. 10 (rev.1), The Rights of the Child. http://193.194.138.190/html/menu6/2/fs10.htm. Accessed October 9, 2006.

———. (c). Status of Ratification of the Convention on the Rights of the Child. http://193.194.138.190/html/menu2/6/crc/treaties/status-crc.htm. Accessed October 9, 2006.

Pinheiro, Paulo Sérgio 2006. *World Report on Violence against Children. Secretary-General's Study on Violence against Children*. United Nations.

Population Reference Bureau. 2006. 2006 World Population Data Sheet, p. 7. http://www.prb.org/pdf06/06WorldDataSheet.pdf. Accessed April 1, 2007.

Rodgers, Harrell R., Jr. 2006. *American Poverty in a New Age of Reform*. 2nd ed. Armonk, NY: M. E. Sharpe.

Safa, Helen. 2005. "The Matrifocal Family and Patriarchal Ideology in Cuba and the Caribbean." *Journal of Latin American Anthropology* 10, no. 2:314–338.

Samuels, Christina A. 2006. "More U.S. Children Lacking Insurance." *Education Week* 26, no. 3 (September 13), 12. http://web.ebscohost.com/ehost/detail?vid=8&hid=101&sid=1060c614-63a0-430d-be95-d. Accessed September 27, 2006.

Save the Children. 2005. *State of the World's Mothers 2005: The Power and Promise of Girls' Education*. Westport, CT: Save the Children.

————. 2007. Our History; Creating the Foundation. http://www.savethechildren.org/about/mission/our-history.

Schwab, Peter. 1999. *Cuba: Confronting the Embargo*. New York: St. Martin's Griffin.

Slocum, Karla, and Deborah A. Thomas. 2003. "Rethinking Global and Area Studies: Insights from Caribbeanist Anthropology." *American Anthropologist* 105, no. 3: 553–565.

Statistics Canada. Mother's Day by the Numbers. http://www42.statcan.ca/smr08/smr08_047_e.htm.

Tompkins, Cynthia Margarita, and Kristen Sternberg, eds. 2004. *Teen Life in Latin America and the Caribbean*. Westport, CT: Greenwood Press.

United Nations. Background Note: Children's Rights. http:www.un.org/rights/dpil765e.htm. Accessed October 9, 2006.

United Nations Children's Fund. Child Protection from Violence, Exploitation and Abuse. http://www.unicef.og/protection/index_childlabour.html. Accessed May 9, 2007.

————. Haiti: Country in Crisis. http://www.unicef.org/emerg/Haiti/index+bigpicture.html. Accessed October 9, 2006.

————. United Nations Special Session on Children, May 8–10, 2002. http://www.unicef.org/specialsession/highlights/index.html. Accessed May 20, 2007.

————. 2006a. *The State of the World's Children 2007: Women and Children: The Double Divided of Gender Equality*. New York: UNICEF.

————. 2006b. *Violence against Children in the Caribbean Region: Regional Assessment; UN Secretary General's Study on Violence against Children*. Panama: Child Protection Section, UNICEF Regional Office for Latin America and the Caribbean. http://www.uwi.edu/ccdc/downloads/Violence_against_children.pdf.

United Nations Development Programme. 2006. *Human Development Report 2006: Beyond Scarcity: Power, Poverty and the Global Water Crisis*. Houndmills, Basingstoke, Hampshire and New York: Palgrave Macmillan.

United Nations, Economic Commission for Latin America and the Caribbean (ECLAC). 2006. *Social Panorama of Latin America 2005*. Santiago, Chile, May 2006. http://www.eclac.org/cgi-bin/getProd.asp?xml=/publicaciones/xml/4/24054/P24054.xml&xsl=/dds/tpl-i/p9f.xsl&base=/dds/tpl/top-bottom.xsl.

————. Caribbean Development and Cooperation Committee. 2001. An Evaluative Study of the Implementation of Domestic Violence Legislation: Antigua and Barbuda, St. Kitts/Nevis, Saint Lucia and Saint Vincent and the Grenadines. http://www.eclac.org/publicaciones/xml/0/9910/carg0659.pdf. Accessed January 18, 2007.

United Nations Educational, Scientific and Cultural Organization (UNESCO). Education for All, Background Documents. http://www.unesco.org/education/efa/ed_for_all/background/background_documents.shtml. Accessed May 1, 2007.

———— 2007. *Education for All Global Monitoring Report. Regional Overview: Latin America and the Caribbean*. http://unesdoc.unesco.org/images/0014/001489/148957E.pdf.

United Nations Office on Drugs and Crime and World Bank, Caribbean Region. 2007. *Crime, Violence, and Development: Trends, Costs, and Policy Options in*

the Caribbean. Report no 37820. March 2007. http://siteresources.worldbank
.org/INTHAITI/Resources/Crimeandviolenceinthecaribbeanfullreport.pdf.

U.S. Department of Commerce. 2007. U.S. Census Bureau News. Facts for Features:
Mother's Day 2007. http://www.census.gov/Press-Release/www/2007/
cb07ff-07.pdf.

Weston, Burns H., and Mark B. Teerink. 2005. "Rethinking Child Labor: A Multidimensional Human Rights Problem." pp. 3–25 in *Child Labor and Human
Rights: Making Children Matter.* Edited by Burns H. Weston. Boulder, CO
and London: Lynne Rienner Publishers.

Williams, Sian. 2004. "The Effects of Structural Adjustment Programs on the Lives
of Children in Jamaica." pp. 151–160 in *Globalization and Children: Exploring Potentials for Enhancing Opportunities in the Lives of Children and Youth.*
Edited by Natalie Hevener Kaufman and Irene Rizzini. Seacaucus, NJ: Kluwer
Academic Publishers.

Wilson, Brian. 2004. "Children and the Media." pp. 99–106 in *Globalization and
Children: Exploring Potentials for Enhancing Opportunities in the Lives of Children and Youth.* Edited by Natalie Hevener Kaufman and Irene Rizzini. Seacaucus, NJ: Kluwer Academic Publishers.

Wiseberg, Laurie S. 2005. "Nongovernmental Organizations in the Struggle against
Child Labor." pp. 343–376 in *Child Labor and Human Rights: Making Chil-
dren Matter.* Edited by Burns H. Weston. Boulder, CO and London: Lynne
Rienner Publishers.

World Bank. Latin America and the Caribbean. Fact Sheet. *Close to Home: The
Development Impact of Remittances in Latin America.* http://siteresources.
worldbank.org/INTLACOFFICEOFCE/Resources/RemittancesFactSheet06_
Eng.pdf.

World Bank. 2007a. Global Monitoring Report 2007, website. http://web.wordbank
.org/WBSITE/EXTERNAL/EXTDEC/EXTGLLOBALMONITOR/EXTGO.

World Bank. 2007b. *Global Monitoring Report 2007. Millennium Development Goals:
Confronting the Challenges of Gender Equality and Fragile States.* Washington,
DC: International Bank for Reconstruction and Development/World
Bank http://siteresources.worldbank.org/INTGLOMONREP2007/Resources/
3413191-1176390231604/i-xviii_GMRfm.pdf. Accessed May 1, 2007.

World Bank. 2007c. GNI Per Capital, Atlas Method and PPP. http://DataSitere
sources.worldbank.org/DATASTATISTICS/Resources/GNIPC.

World Bank. 2007d. Regional Highlights, Latin America and the Caribbean. *Global
Monitoring Report 2007: Confronting the Challenges of Gender Equality and
Fragile States.* http://web.worldbank.org/WBSITE/EXTERNAL/EXTDEC/
EXTGLOBALMONITOR/EXTGLOMONREP2007/0,,contentMDK:2125
6825~menuPK:3413287~pagePK:64218950~piPK:64218883~theSitePK
:3413261,00.html. Accessed May 1, 2007.

1

ANTIGUA AND BARBUDA

Christolyn A. Williams and CarolAnn Louise Daniels

NATIONAL PROFILE

Former British colonies, Antigua and Barbuda are part of the English-speaking Caribbean referred to as the West Indies. They gained their independence in 1981. Antigua is situated 61° West longitude and 17° North latitude and is 108 square miles in area. The smaller sister island sister of Barbuda lies thirty miles north of Antigua and is sixty-two square miles in area. Both islands are flat except for one small area on Antigua, which rises to a height of 1,300 feet above sea level. The islands are subject to long periods of drought during the year.

St. John's city and St. John's rural are by far home to the majority of the population. These two parishes alone house almost 60 percent of the population (45,346 inhabitants). The remaining population of 31,540 is found in the other parishes of St. George, St. Peter, St. Phillip, St. Paul, and St. Mary, as well as the island of Barbuda. Women are a majority in all but Barbuda where the male population maintains majority (by some forty-nine males) over the female population (Antigua and Barbuda Summary 2001). The islands are dependent upon tourism, which contributes close to 60 percent of

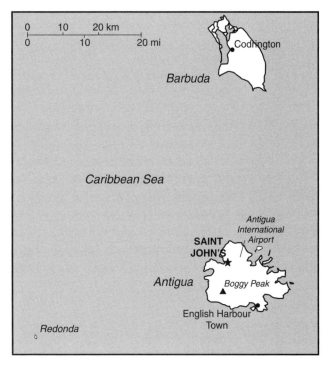

the Gross Domestic Product (GDP). Other major contributors are construction, communications, transportation, and agriculture.

The twin-island nation of Antigua and Barbuda is a multiparty parliamentary democracy. Despite its small size and its dependence upon the tourism and service industries, the socio-economic conditions (status) of the island nation are relatively stable. In 2005, the per capita income was US$10,940. Poverty exists, however, and 12 percent of the population lives at the poverty level (Robert 2006). There are a number of governmental and nongovernmental organizations (NGOs) that provide services to families and children. Families may also receive some support from their religious organization. Poverty alleviation initiatives implemented by the government with support from regional organizations and NGOs have sought to address the basic needs of the most desperate cases. One example is the Management Board of the Organization of American States (OAS) Inter-American Agency for Cooperation and Development (IACD) projects, which approved in 2005–2006 two programs directed at strengthening the agriculture sector. The Agriculture and Tourism Linkages and Agri-Trade Facilitation for Selected Crop and Livestock Commodities programs are designed to strengthen links between the tourism and agriculture sectors. These projects are directed at rural communities and farm families to help them become more competitive and to reduce the high volume of food imports to the islands ("OAS to Assist Antigua"). More localized programs sponsored by the Antigua and Barbuda government provide a small income to every child living in poverty.

Women are the overall majority in Antigua and Barbuda and have been so since the nineteenth century. In a population estimated by the most recent census at 76,886, women number 40,777. Women and girls contribute significantly to the economy of the islands. They demonstrate tremendous academic and social success, completing secondary education in greater numbers than men and boys, and are successful professionals and entrepreneurs. However, their presence in government and politics is not representative of their percentage in the population. In the history of the nineteen-member House of Representatives, only one woman has ever been elected. This woman, Jacqui Quinn-Leandro, was elected in 2004 as a United Progressive Party (UPP) candidate. In addition, the current Speaker of the House, a position filled by the majority party, is a woman, D. Giselle Isaac-Arrindell.

According to UNICEF for the Caribbean region, the family structure in Antigua is dominated by single-parent families. The majority of households are headed by women who have primary responsibility for the care and well-being of children. There are few formal laws that spell out the responsibilities parents have toward their children, but common law recognizes that parents have a duty to care for and provide for their children. Only a small percentage of persons in Antigua and Barbuda experience homelessness. The majority of the population is of African

Table 1.1.
Antigua and Barbuda Vital Statistics 2004–2005

Population mid-2006	Births per 1,000	Deaths per 1,000	Rate of natural increase	Under five years old mortality rate	Total fertility rate	Percentage of population below fifteen years old	Life expectancy		GNI ppp per capita 2005	Percent urban
							M	F		
0.1 of 39 million for region	18	6	1.3	12	2.3	28	69	74	11,700	37

Source: Population Reference Bureau (2006). GNI, Gross National Income; ppp, purchasing power parity.

Table 1.2.
Distribution of Population to Nineteen Years Old

Age group	Male	Female	Total
0–4 years	3,705	3,536	7,411
5–9 years	3,680	3,700	7,380
10–14 years	3,433	3,654	7,087
15–19 years	2,998	3,323	6,321
			28,199

Source: Antigua and Barbuda Summary 2001.
Total population = 76,886. The total number of individuals nineteen years old and younger represents 37 percent of the total population.

descent (Barrow 2001; Antigua and Barbuda Summary 2001; Population Reference Bureau 2006).

There are more than 28,000 children and youth in Antigua and Barbuda. As listed in Table 1.2, this category encompasses the age group from birth to nineteen years old. This group represents 37 percent of the total population of the islands.

Antigua and Barbuda holds membership in a number of regional organizations that focus on political, social, and economic development. These organizations include the Caribbean Community (CARICOM) founded in 1973, the Organization of Eastern Caribbean States (OECS) formed in 1981, and the Caribbean Development Bank (CDB). Because government spending is tied to the GDP, contraction in the tourism sector often results in unemployment and underemployment and a reduction in government-funded services such as health care, education, and social services. This can have a devastating effect on the quality of life for those who depend on government-funded services (Benjamin and Bird 1998). Government agencies whose overall goal is to promote, protect, and meet children's basic needs include the Ministry of Youth Empowerment, the Directorate of Gender Affairs, the Women and Development Program, the Department for Sexually Abused Children, the Child and Family Welfare Center, the Department of Social Improvement, the Health Education Unit of the Ministry of Health and Social Improvement, and the Alliance for Social Well-Being and NGOs such as the Christian Children Fund (CCF) and NGO and the Family and Guidance Center of the Collaborative Committee for the Promotion of Emotional Health in Children (CCOPE).

The Human Development Index (HDI) is used to measure quality of life in countries around the world. The HDI measures three main arenas of human development: longevity, education, and economic standard of living. Antigua and Barbuda falls within the medium range of the HDI index (60), above countries such as Russia, Brazil, and Venezuela. The numbers of births per one thousand is eighteen, while the figure for deaths is six. There is a rate of natural increase of 1.3, and the under-five mortality rate is twelve. A life expectancy of sixty-nine years for men and seventy-four years for women reflects the relatively safe and stable environment of the nation (Population Reference Bureau 2006).

OVERVIEW

The government of Antigua and Barbuda has long ensured that children in the country have access to free education until the age of sixteen. Since 1991, government spending on education has increased to 13.2 percent of GDP. The commitment has been to provide access, equity, and quality education to nationals irrespective of socio-economic status (The EFA 2000 Assessment Reports). The promise of free education for all children irrespective of their race, class, or gender has been a primary concern since the Antigua Labor Party (ALP) took control of the Antiguan state from the British in 1969. The ALP expanded access to education and constructed numerous schools in the period before and after independence in 1981. As a result of having access to free education, many children born to poor parents have been able to improve their social and economic position in the society. Still, there is concern with increasing dropout rates, and a gender performance gap in favor of girls is apparent.

Because of the absence of internal conflict and a largely healthy environment, child mortality rates are very low. The under-five mortality rate is twelve for every 1,000 live births, and the infant mortality rate is eleven. Severe malnutrition is rare. The social and political stability also means that refugees are not a political concern, although Antigua and Barbuda in the past accepted large numbers of persons who sought refuge in the country because of a massive volcanic eruption in neighboring island of Montserrat and political instability in Haiti. As a member of the Caribbean Commonwealth Community, Antigua and Barbuda have also become home to many citizens of other CARICOM countries. Among the largest immigrant populations in Antigua are nationals of Jamaica, Guyana, Montserrat, and Dominica. Nationals from the Dominican Republic are also a significant population in the capital city, St. John's. Many of these Spanish speakers claim Antiguan citizenship as the descendants of Antigua and Barbuda nationals who immigrated to the Dominican Republic during the first three decades of the twentieth century. In addition to CARICOM and other Caribbean nationals, persons from the United States, the United Kingdom, and Asia (in particular China) have established residences and businesses in Antigua. These non-Caribbean expatriates are engaged in establishing businesses on the island or have retired to Antigua because of the political stability and beauty of the islands and the region.

There are no wars between Antigua and Barbuda and any other state, nor have there been internal civil wars or military conflicts in the twentieth and twenty-first centuries. Other than contentious political rallies during election years, the islands have been relatively stable with little social conflict to disrupt the life of citizens and to threaten the safety and security of its children. The political democracies of the eastern English-speaking Caribbean of which Antigua and Barbuda is a part have maintained nondiscriminatory and inclusive policies towards the largely African-descended populations of the region (Benjamin and Bird 1998).

The laws of Antigua and Barbuda provide children and other vulnerable populations with protection against exploitation, slavery, and indentured servitude. Trade unions, formed in 1940, remain an important watchdog against employer abuse and regulate the workplace conditions in Antigua and Barbuda. Juveniles in conflict with the law and the problem of street children are an emerging social and policy problem (U.S. Department of State).

EDUCATION

Education for Antigua and Barbuda nationals is free and compulsory for all children under the age of sixteen, resulting in high levels of literacy across the population. The literacy rate is estimated at 82 percent. Although all children have access to education, its quality is uneven, particularly in the early years. For example, because minimum standards for the operation of early childhood centers are lacking, many centers function without official government monitoring. Moreover, most of the early childhood centers and preschools are privately owned and operated. Because some parents find it difficult to afford the tuition, enrollment rates tend to be low. This means that many children enter the primary system without any pre-primary preparation (Benjamin and Bird 1998; Barrow 2001).

More than 90 percent of children attend primary school. Some children do not attend on a regular basis because of lack of money for uniforms, lunch, transportation, and other costs of education. In 2004, the government instituted a program of free school uniforms for all students in primary and secondary schools, and plans are underway to create a national school meal program through which all children would receive free meals while in school. While some improvements have been made, the education system is still largely unable to meet the needs of children who are disabled or have learning problems. The needs of the most severely disabled are often overlooked, and some disabled adults and children remain hidden in their homes, socially excluded from mainstream society (Barrow 2001).

In Antigua and Barbuda, schools are divided into three administrative zones, not including pre-primary education. The majority of children in schools are enrolled in primary, secondary, and tertiary level institutions. There are some thirty public and twenty-six private primary schools. Education at this level is largely academic. At the secondary level there are some thirteen schools, nine of which are public and four private. These institutions provide both academic and technical and vocational training. The tertiary level institutions include the University of the West Indies School of Continuing Studies, the Antigua State College, and the Hotel Training School.

Special education resources are limited on the islands. Accommodations for deaf and hearing-impaired students have been provided since the 1960s by the Red Cross School, which admits children as young as three years old. Most referrals to the school are from hospitals and in some cases by applications of parents and guardians of deaf and hearing-impaired children. Most disabled students are integrated into regular classes, and more attention is being focused on teacher training to meet their special needs (The EFA 2000 Assessment Reports).

The government also provides some opportunity for vocational training with an emphasis on acquiring skills. Among the poverty alleviation strategies that have been adopted since 2004 is a youth job program. Participants are paid a salary while training through job placements in schools, local industry, and government and private agencies. Vocational education courses are an important part of the education system given the high rates of dropout at the secondary level and a high rate of youth unemployment (Barrow 2001).

Education is also free and compulsory at both primary and secondary levels for nonnationals who have resided in the country for more than three years. However, there are no special programs to teach foreign children in their own language. All students are encouraged to learn English. Nonnationals under the age of sixteen who have resided for less than three years in Antigua and Barbuda are educated primarily through the fee-paying schools. Since the 1990s, enrollments in private or fee-paying schools in Antigua and Barbuda have significantly increased. Currently, they educate more than a quarter of all primary school students. However, most of these fee-paying schools do not educate past the primary level of education (Benjamin and Bird 1998; Barrow 2001).

At the end of their four years of study, students in academic secondary schools are required to complete school-leaving examinations administered by the Caribbean Examination Council (CXC), a regional body that oversees secondary education in the English-speaking Caribbean. Students who pass four or more subjects, including English, can apply for admission to the Advanced level (A Level) program. Academic success in the "A Level" program qualifies students for scholarships to the University of the West Indies.

PLAY AND RECREATION

There are a number of public playgrounds and facilities that have been built through government sponsorship, but these fall short of the demand and tend generally to be facilities for adolescents and adults rather than for children. Access to television is widespread in Antigua and Barbuda. Most households, well over a third, own a television, and considerable children's programming is offered, both local and international. As in other parts of the world, children spend a large portion of their time watching television. Children also have access to computers and the Internet through schools and public libraries. While no figures exist for 2006, growing numbers of households on the island own computers. This has been facilitated by a government policy that offers a tax exemption for personal computers.

All schools in Antigua and Barbuda have some organized sports in which children participate, regardless of racial, gender, or economic group. Schools have an organized sports day when children compete with each other in individual and team sports. The Ministry of Health, Sports, and Youth Affairs attends to youth empowerment, carnival celebrations, and development, and its Sports and Games Department is responsible for organized sports in the public schools. Among the team sports played by children and youth in Antigua and Barbuda are netball, cricket, football, and basketball (United Nations 2004, 50).

Because child labor is not significant in the economy and society, children also have time after school to engage in play. Children in Antigua and Barbuda enjoy their time away from school engaged in leisure activities, both with and without adult supervision. Most participate in recreational activities such as picnics at the beach with family and with church and neighborhood groups. Additional programs include a summer cultural program run by the Ministry of Education and the Ministry of Health. This program emphasizes particular Caribbean cultural forms and it engages children in activities such as arts and crafts, storytelling, chorus speaking, steel band, music, and drama. Because of proximity, the United States has become a major cultural influence in Antigua and Barbuda. Many households have cable network, which allows access to television programs from all across the world, but primarily from the United States. The cultural impact of globalization can be seen and felt, not just in Antigua and Barbuda but also throughout the region.

Other organizations involved with children and youths include the Alliance for Social Well-Being, which was formed in 1993 by the government of Antigua and Barbuda. The objective of this organization is to provide a forum to participate in debates. Youth discussants at these adult-facilitated forums focus on issues such as civic pride, cultural consciousness, and HIV/AIDS. Some 250 youths participate in these annual symposiums (Benjamin and Bird 1998; Barrow 2001).

CHILD LABOR

The Antigua and Barbuda labor code defines a child as someone under the age of fourteen. While child labor is not a significant problem in either urban or rural areas in Antigua, there are a number of existing laws to protect children from child-trafficking, indentured servitude, and economic exploitation. Two laws specifically relate to the protection of children from economic exploitation: the Education Act. No. 7 of 1973, Section 6, and the Antigua and Barbuda Labour Code, Division E, of 1975. The Education Act not only sets the compulsory school age at sixteen but also stipulates that all such persons should not be employed during school hours. No matter the work environment for child workers, the code forbids work during school hours, or for more than eight hours in a twenty-four–hour period. It also restricts the employment of children at night (Benjamin and Bird 1998; Barrow 2001).

In addition to regulating the employment of children under fourteen years old, the labor code also restricts the employment of young people through the age of eighteen. All young persons engaging in work are required to be examined by a medical practitioner who establishes whether the young person is fit for employment. Because of strong enforcement of these laws, there is high compliance among those who employ children and young persons (Benjamin and Bird 1998; Barrow 2001).

FAMILY

The 2001 Census of Antigua and Barbuda indicates that most families are headed by men. Among the 40,777 adult females on the islands, 10,666 women were designated "head of household," compared with 13,872 men. However, UNICEF and other agencies acknowledge "between 31–49% of Caribbean children from birth to 14 years live in homes headed by women" (Family Law Reform in the Caribbean 2002). In addition to the care of their children, these heads of households reported that they care for other individuals such as parents, in-laws (adults and children), grandchildren, and nonrelatives (Antigua and Barbuda Summary 2001).

Few laws in Antigua and Barbuda address the role of parents in guiding their children's lives, but common law does recognize the duty of parents to ensure that their children receive due care and attention. As former British colonies, British common law has directed family relations in Antigua and Barbuda. The law imposes penalties, including imprisonment for parents who neglect their children when they are able to care for them. The state of Antigua and Barbuda is not required by law to assist parents in the raising of children, other than to provide free education and health care. However, there are a number of important statutes that ensure financial support for children in households headed by women. For example, the Magistrate's Code of Procedure, Chapter 255, enables mothers to bring suit against their children's father for financial support. If married, support also extends to women as well. Pregnant women are also entitled to support for expenses, including doctor's fees, and for medical tests and treatment. A father can be named on the birth certificate only if he consents to it. The code denies custodial rights to unmarried fathers (Benjamin and Bird 1998; Barrow 2001).

The laws in Antigua and Barbuda are structured to provide for the financial needs of children and female spouses in cases of divorce and or separation. In such cases, the best interest of the child is given significant consideration. Among the grounds for separation specified by the law are adultery, cruelty, and habitual drunkenness. Children in these households are awarded maintenance by the court. This is generally a maintenance award against the husband and father. In situations where children are physically, emotionally, or sexually abused, or abandoned, the state intervenes to remove them from abusive households and to provide alternate care. There are little or no opportunities for adoption or foster parenting (Benjamin and Bird 1998; Barrow 2001).

Families are multigenerational and intergenerational attachments and obligations are thus at the core of familial relationships. Child rearing is perceived as the shared responsibility of the extended family. However, the overall pattern of parenting tends to reinforce adult control and obedience to parents.

In many households in Antigua and Barbuda, as in much of the Caribbean region where traditional gender roles are practiced, boys enjoy more personal freedom than girls in households. Girls are kept close to home and are expected to perform household duties such as cleaning, washing, cooking, or assisting their mothers or other adults with such chores. Boys in households are often assigned tasks outside the house such as maintaining the yard, taking care of animals, and fetching water where there is no running water piped directly to the household. Women and girls perform a disproportionate amount of domestic work, even when women work outside the home for as many hours as their male spouses and partners. Older girls are expected to take care of younger siblings and relatives. They bathe, dress, and feed these younger brothers and sisters and take them to school or daycare. In single-parent households, older siblings often spend more time overseeing the care of younger children than the parent does, especially in households where the single parent works or is engaged in other activities outside of the home. Parents with alcohol dependency and other drug problems, as well as disabled or sick adults, are especially dependent on older children to run their households and care for younger children. The state provides little in the way of supportive services for these households.

HEALTH

The healthcare and emergency care needs of Antigua and Barbuda nationals are met via the Holberton hospital in the capital and district clinics in the parishes. These clinics provide free immunizations and basic health care, and dental and eye care are provided at low or no cost.

Antigua and Barbuda signed the Convention on the Rights of the Child (CRC) in 1993 and has demonstrated its commitment to the convention by establishing a health policy document that states that "we will continue to pay special attention to mothers and children by implementing the maternal and child health strategy" (Benjamin and Bird 1998, 37–38). Since the 1980s, reported cases of severe malnutrition have remained in the single digits. A 1990s survey showed a 12 percent population with hemoglobin levels below normal. Iron-deficiency anemia has been the most significant micronutrient deficiency in Antigua and Barbuda, and iron deficiency in pregnant women has played a significant role in premature births and stillbirths. The problem of childhood obesity is an emerging concern associated with the growing dependence on junk food and juice drinks. This is attributed to lack of nutritional education and the high fat content associated with fast foods. Children are hospitalized primarily as a result of gastroenteritis, an illness resulting from lack of potable water and an inadequate sewage disposal system. Pit latrines are still commonly used on the island, although the number of households with piped water has increased significantly since the mid-1990s (Benjamin and Bird 1998; Barrow 2001).

Infant and child mortality rates have remained relatively low since the 1990s, and an effective immunization program has provided 97 percent of children with protection from childhood diseases such as measles, mumps, and chicken pox. The under-five mortality rate is twelve and the infant mortality rate eleven for every 1,000 live births. Since 1990 there have been no confirmed cases of polio, measles, or neonatal tetanus; no cases of tuberculosis have been reported since that time. This suggests that the program of immunization is an integral part of protecting children from a range of preventable diseases. Child mortality rates on the island nation are closely connected to medical resources for newborn care. In the mid-1990s, the number one cause of death among infants admitted to Holberton hospital was prematurity. In an effort to reduce the infant mortality rate, the government has invested in the care of newborns, including laboratory facilities, antibiotic availability, and neonatal ventilators (Benjamin and Bird 1998).

Women in Antigua and Barbuda all give birth under medical care at Holberton Hospital and at Adelin, a private medical clinic. In all cases, delivering mothers have full coverage with trained health personnel. Postnatal care is provided both at the hospital and at district clinics distributed throughout the islands. The government has established approximately twenty-seven health clinics and health centers where Antiguans seek care on a daily basis. These health clinics and centers are located in every parish on the islands. In addition to access to parish clinics, follow-up care is also provided by district nurses. Ministry of Health records show that 92 percent of children who attended clinics for follow-up visits were immunized before six weeks of age. Additional follow-up and nutritional assessment is performed for children between one and four years of age and, with parental cooperation, children receive follow-up care until they enter primary school, where scheduled vaccinations and dental care are continued. Although the Ministry of Health has established a rigorous system for postnatal care for mothers and children, this care is underutilized because of the young age of many mothers and because of locations and the time commitment of the postnatal care program (Benjamin and Bird 1998).

Following birth, women receive particular care and consideration through the Maternal Child Health Care Program. Six weeks after delivery mothers are also assessed to ensure that all reproductive organs are back to normal. This examination includes pap-smear tests and examination of the cervix and uterus (Benjamin and Bird 1998). Despite the proactive attitude of the government since the 1990s and a health policy that rigorously promotes health and health care for pregnant women, the *State of the World's Children 2006* reports some 65 cases of maternal deaths in Antigua and Barbuda between 1990 and 2005 (United Nations Children's Fund 2005).

The School Health Program, and others described earlier, target children as well as infants and mothers. The emotional health of children and adolescents is addressed by the Collaborative Committee for the Promotion of Emotional Health in Children. This nonprofit organization provides psychological and support services for children suffering from mental illnesses and for their families. Other agencies provide specialized and professional welfare services to children and families, including the Citizens Welfare Division, sponsored by the Ministry of Health (Pan American Health Organization).

Since the 1990s, more than 50 percent of the population of Antigua and Barbuda have had access to water that was piped into their dwellings. The actual demand for water does not exceed the storage capacity for both surface and ground water, although there are periods of shortage on the island, often the result of prolonged drought. The increase in water storage with the installation of a reverse osmosis plant in 1995 dramatically increased the available water supply and lessens the water shortage even when a prolonged drought occurs (Benjamin and Bird 1998, 45–50). The majority of the population has easy access to clean water; living conditions continue to improve with most people using propane gas to cook (96 percent) and flush toilets linked to septic tanks (71 percent).

Access to clean water and environmental health on Antigua and Barbuda is monitored by the Environmental Health Division of the Ministry of Agriculture, a division of the Antigua Public Utilities Authority (APUA). The water is tested for bacterial organisms and chemical chlorine residue. In addition to testing the water that is distributed by the APUA, private water supplies are all tested. Cisterns and tanks that are used for water storage in private facilities are tested for physical and bacterial quality and a program of disinfection is also undertaken. The water on Antigua is obtained from both surface and ground sources. Surface water includes seawater, desalination, rain, and runoff water in reservoirs. Ground water includes wells (Benjamin and Bird 1998; Antigua and Barbuda Summary 2001; http://www.environmentdivision.info/department/index.htm).

The most serious threat to human health and the environment in Antigua and Barbuda is the increasing growth of chemical manufacturing and the use of pesticides. Persistent organic pollutants (POPs) pose a threat to humans and especially children because they survive in the environment for a long time after their release and are internalized by humans through the air, water, and food. Once internalized, they cause cancer, birth defects, and other system dysfunctions. Although many of these POP-releasing chemicals were banned in 1980, the ability of the chemicals to remain in the air and soil raises concern for the protection of children in Antigua and Barbuda (Ministry of Health/Environment Division). The Environment Division of the Ministry of Works, Transportation, and the Environment has dedicated a web page specifically to educating children around these issues (see http://www.environmentdivision.info/kids/index.htm).

Until recently, children with disabilities in Antigua and Barbuda were largely invisible both to society and to the government. In 1996, a survey was conducted to assess the number of children affected by disabilities, their nature and seriousness, and the services available to them. Disability still carries a social stigma, and many hide their disability or are kept hidden away. These disabilities range from severe cases of cerebral palsy and epilepsy to less obvious problems, such as learning disabilities and emotional or behavioral problems. Although the government provides some services, the care of these children is seen as the responsibility of their families.

Some of the needs of disabled children in Antigua and Barbuda are met by the Child and Family Guidance Center at Holberton Hospital. The Center is run by a local nonprofit organization, the CCOPE. Comprising local professionals, the center was funded in 1987 with the assistance of the Ministries of Education and Health, Sports, and Youth

Affairs. The center offers support to children experiencing emotional problems and physical or emotional abuse, and to those exposed to trauma. The Resource Center for the Handicapped affiliated with the Antigua Council for the Handicapped also provides important services to disabled children and teenagers. Under the supervision of the Ministry of Labor, the center's objectives include improving economic conditions for the disabled. This is done through job training and vocational rehabilitation that ready disabled persons for employment. Among the primary disabilities of those trained by the center are difficulties with walking, retardation, visual impairment, and deafness (Benjamin and Bird 1998).

Services for the visually impaired and blind are provided by the Antigua and Barbuda government as part of a specialized education program at T.N. Kirnon, a private primary school in the capital. Since 1996, services for students have been largely revolving, with faculty from other schools moving back and forth between the public school and the T.N. Kirnon school. Children diagnosed with mental retardation have been served for over thirty years by the Adele School, which was a private institute until 1977 when it was taken over by the government. One of the biggest criticisms of the institution by UNESCO in the late 1990s was the unsatisfactory teacher-to-student ratio. In addition to government funding, the school has benefited from contributions from local businesses and private individuals. These contributions have been used to acquire charts and other audio-visual aids for use of the students (Benjamin and Bird 1998, 122–126).

There has been an increase since the 1990s in the presence and role of NGOs in Antigua and Barbuda. Today, they are organized around a range of issues from food processing, education reform, and community care to care for disabled and the elderly. NGOs play a significant role in raising awareness of social problems, including youth violence and violence against children, as well as education reform. In addition to the thirty-eight NGOs listed as members of the NGO Network of Antigua and Barbuda, many other local and international organizations provide resources for the people and children of Antigua and Barbuda.

In spite of the remarkable strides in health and health care, there is great concern about the increasing number of young people affected by HIV/AIDS. This is especially striking with girls. The increase has been attributed to early initiation into sexual activity (a large percentage of girls are sexually active by the age of twelve), social and cultural norms that condone multiple partners, gender norms that leave women and girls vulnerable and unable to protect themselves, and a cultural pattern of sexual relationships between adolescent girls and adult men. Social taboos also prevent open discussion of sex and sexuality with young people, resulting in unprotected practices and lack of knowledge in relation to sexuality and reproductive health (Benjamin and Bird 1998).

As part of the HIV/AIDS prevention plan, voluntary counseling and testing is available at a number of sites throughout the country. Yet continued stigma and discrimination create a barrier that discourages individuals from seeking care and treatment. There is also a lack of trust in healthcare professionals among adolescents, which results in a reluctance to access health and other services. The national prevention plan includes a school-based AIDS education program, a social marketing program on condoms, and voluntary counseling and testing programs to prevent mother-to-child transmission (UNGASS Report 2005). One of the programs specifically geared to young people twelve years and older is a weekly television program called "Teen Talk."

While the HIV/AIDS Prevention and Control Program in Antigua and Barbuda continues to direct its efforts at education and condom distribution, the growing infection rates in the region have prompted governments to develop a cooperative CARICOM regional strategy to fight HIV/AIDS. This regional organization has sought and gained support from UNAIDS, the joint HIV/AIDS program sponsored by the United Nations (UN). However, the increasing spread of HIV/AIDS underscores the need to strengthen prevention not only for HIV/AIDS but also for sexually transmitted infections (United Nations, Children's Fund 2005; Benjamin and Bird 1998).

The social environment in Antigua and Barbuda is one that is hostile to gay, lesbian, bisexual, and transgendered (GLBT) persons. GLBT youth in Antigua walk a thin line in a society where they are tolerated but might easily become the victims of physical and verbal attacks by strangers and even by members of their own families. The small GLBT community on the island is not very visible, and youths often create their own support networks among similar GLBT youths or with supportive friends and family members. Much of the social stigma and abuse is addressed to gay men and youth who, throughout the English-speaking Caribbean, are called "batty-man." Gay men and boys are often targeted by other youths. Popular reggae singers have promoted homophobia with hate-filled lyrics, which have encouraged audiences to physically attack gay men and others who do not fit the extreme male stereotypes and who are therefore assumed to be gay.

LAWS AND LEGAL STATUS

In Antigua and Barbuda, there are specific laws that provide distinct legal protection for children, some of which predate the UN 1989 CRC. The 1986 Status of Children Act, for example, introduced legislation specifically relating to the status of children. Other laws specifically related to the well-being of children include the 1994 amendment to the Civil Service Regulations. This grants thirteen weeks of maternity leave with full pay for new mothers. In addition, the 1999 Sexual Offences Act raised the age of consent from fourteen to sixteen years of age (United Nations 2004).

One of the most glaring inequalities that existed in Antigua and Barbuda from British colonial rule until 1969 was the distinction between legitimate and illegitimate children. Laws have been reformed to equalize the status of children born out of wedlock with those born in wedlock. While legislation is a step in the right direction, it has not eliminated discrimination against children born out of wedlock. A double standard also persists with regard to the rights and responsibilities of unmarried fathers and mothers.

Caribbean legal systems have attempted to upgrade their juvenile justice systems by establishing family courts. However, such a court has not been created in Antigua and Barbuda. If a child between the ages of eight and fourteen commits a crime and is found guilty, he or she is sent to a home for juvenile delinquents. Boys are sent to the Boys' Training School and girls are sent to the Sunshine Home for Girls, which is run by the Salvation Army. These institutions have primarily been staffed by untrained workers, with few counseling and other rehabilitative resources in place to help young people once they leave the institution. Some child offenders are sent to a detention center in the prison for adults. However, these cases are rare and occur in order to provide protection to these children (Benjamin and Bird 1998).

RELIGIOUS LIFE

The majority of the population of Antigua and Barbuda is Christian. Participation in church is an important avenue of socializing children, and many children also attend church-based schools, at least through primary level. Children begin their lives in the church, being christened as infants. Those children in families that are regular members of a church may also be confirmed or baptized as young teens, a process that signals their membership in and commitment to the church.

Of the approximately fifteen different Christian denominations with followers on the islands, the Anglican and Seventh Day Adventist churches dominate, with 26 and 12 percent of the population, respectively. These are followed by the Pentecostal Church (11 percent), the Roman Catholic Church (10 percent), and Moravian Churches (10 percent). Two other religions practiced in Antigua and Barbuda are Islam and Hinduism, both of which are practiced by less than 1 percent of the population (Antigua and Barbuda Summary 2001).

The laws of Antigua and Barbuda are consistent with the UN CRC in terms of freedom of thought, conscience, and religion. Further, the Antigua and Barbuda Constitution protects children from being made to participate against their will in religious activities other than those of their own religion.

CHILD ABUSE AND NEGLECT

There are a number of laws specifically designed for the care and protection of children. These include the Sexual Offences Act of 1999, the Domestic Violence Act of 1999, and the Childcare and Protection Act of 2003. Although there is a growing recognition of child abuse as a social problem in Antigua and Barbuda, there are no laws to enforce mandatory reporting. There is also little in the way of documentation and information about trends. Child sexual abuse is a source of shame for the family, thus the tendency is to cover up rather than report. However, as a result of recent government efforts people are encouraged to file cases of sexual offences. The government also provides psychological counseling and support for victims of sexual abuse (United Nations 2004).

Parents in Antigua and Barbuda depend heavily on physical punishment to discipline children. Because it is such a deeply ingrained cultural practice, there is little hope that such practices will be formally banned. Nonetheless, there appears to be a growing awareness of the negative effects of corporal punishment and the need for alternative forms of punishment.

There is only one military force on the island, the Antigua and Barbuda Defense Force, and this institution does not recruit children. By law persons cannot join the Antigua and Barbuda defense force or the police force before attaining majority at the age of eighteen. The Defense Force runs a volunteer program of cadets, to which Antiguan high school students are recruited. The cadet program invites both male and female youths between the ages of thirteen and eighteen to participate in drills, survival training, and arms training as part of an after-school program or a month-long summer program. This program facilitates the admission of new recruits into the Defense Force of Antigua and Barbuda.

GROWING UP IN THE TWENTY-FIRST CENTURY

Antigua and Barbuda has made remarkable strides since it gained independence from Britain in 1981. With few exceptions, most children are born healthy and have access to free education and health care, ensuring that their childhood is largely a secure and comfortable stage of life. Children experience no instability from internal conflicts, and there are laws specifically related to their care, protection, and well-being. In spite of the enormous progress made, a number of concerns persist. These include the increasing incidence of HIV/AIDS among young people, lack of participation of young people in matters affecting their lives, and the use of corporal punishment as the primary form of discipline.

As the silent HIV/AIDS epidemic sweeps through the Caribbean, young people and in particular young women between the ages of fifteen and twenty-four are especially at risk of falling victim to this disease. In some Caribbean countries, for example, HIV infection levels are six times higher for fifteen- to nineteen-year-old women than for men. The feminization of HIV/AIDS is particularly alarming given the early age of sexual initiation among girls and the silence around sex and sexuality in most families. This creates a situation where girls are vulnerable to the disease because of a lack of information, and this silence also prevents children from seeking out sexual and reproductive health services. Equally alarming is the refusal of many men to use a condom or to internalize information on the cause of the disease. Many young men continue to believe that HIV/AIDS is a homosexual disease and using condoms is seen as a "sissy" thing to do.

Cultural norms around gender and sexuality further increase the vulnerability of girls to HIV/AIDS. The continued economic dependence of women on men, for instance, often hampers their ability to negotiate safer sex. Poverty and high unemployment among young people mean that girls often look to older men for economic support. For many girls this involves the exchange of sexual favors for either money or basic necessities such as food, clothing, and school books. Thus, even if she perceives herself to be at risk for HIV and other sexually transmitted diseases, a young woman may be unable to practice safe sex behavior if other risks appear more imminent. In other words, poor women and girls may be more concerned with obtaining food, shelter, and safety for themselves than maintaining HIV-protective behavior. While such relationships are not openly condoned, they are not assigned the negative label of prostitution. New sex trends in the region, such as sex tourism and other sex-exchange practices often driven by poverty, also put women at risk for HIV and AIDS (Spooner, Daniel, and Mahoney 2004).

Compounding the risk to women and girls is the practice of multiple sexual partners and the social and cultural repression of same-sex partners. The continuing social and legal repression of same-sex partners drives homosexuals underground, sometimes resulting in bisexual relationships that increase the risk of HIV among women and girls. Behavior change is hindered without consideration of these factors (Kelly and Bain 2005).

The right of adolescents to participate in activities affecting them remains a critical area for improvement in Antigua and Barbuda, as in the rest of the Caribbean. One of the major obstacles to participation lies in the cultural practices where children are perceived as dependent and incapable minors who are the property of their parents. This view of childhood promotes the idea that children, as immature minors, have neither the capacity nor the need to express opinions or to participate in decisions affecting their lives. In Antigua and throughout the rest of the Caribbean, this model is strongly enforced, and the position of most parents and adults is that children are to be seen and not heard. Adults assume responsibility for children, acting and speaking on their behalf (Barrow 2001; Kelly and Bain 2005).

Despite international attempts to change these ideas about children, there is strong resistance from both parents and government against more inclusion of children's opinions and participation in larger family, community, and national decisions. While it is clear that both adults and the government are acting in what they see to be the best interest of children and families, and are committed to socializing and protecting children, their adherence to this model silences children and limits their overall participation. The perception of children as passive beneficiaries of social protection, and also as deviant and disruptive, has increased adult and government use of corporal punishment and the institutionalization of children. Physical punishment of children is widely condoned among adults in Antiguan society. This punishment does not only involve slapping and flogging, but also takes the form of loud scolding (Barrow 2001).

Although efforts have been underway to change the practice of physical punishment in Antigua and other Caribbean societies, there has been great resistance and even a loss of the limited gains of the 1990s. A contributing factor has been the growing public perception that children in Antigua and Barbuda and other Caribbean countries have become more deviant and disruptive. This perception has been strengthened by media sensationalization of crimes committed by young people. In response, a number of programs have been put in place to keep students constructively engaged during after-school hours. However, these programs are few and their contribution towards more active social participation has been limited. In the Situation Analysis of Children and Women in Caribbean Countries, prepared to inform on activities and programs in the 2003–2007 period, UNICEF exposes a Caribbean environment with few examples of projects and programs that are more than mere token responses to international pressure (Barrow 2001).

RESOURCE GUIDE

Suggested Readings

Benjamin, Ernest, and Edris Bird. 1998. *1991–1996 Situation Analysis of Children and Their Families: Consolidating Social Achievements and Meeting the Challenges of the 21st Century. Child Survival, Development and Protection in Antigua and Barbuda*. Bridgetown: UNICEF, Caribbean Area Office. This comprehensive report on Antigua and Barbuda society through 1996 details the experience of women and children and the political, social, and economic structures made available by this small Caribbean nation to provide for this population. Detailed population statistics and socio-economic information are provided in the report.

Daniel, CarolAnn. 2004 "Social Work with West Indian Families: A Multilevel Approach." *Journal of Immigrant & Refugee Services* 2, no. 3/4: 135–145. This article examines the experience of Caribbean immigrants in New York City and the social and economic challenges faced by families in the urban environment. Daniel also addresses the emotional impact of long-term separation on children and the challenges of unification with parents.

Kelly, Michael J., and Brendan Bain. 2005. *Education and HIV/AIDS in the Caribbean*. Kingston, Jamaica: Ian Randle. This study addresses the impact of HIV/AIDS on education in the Caribbean context and outlines for readers lessons to be learned form the global experience. The role of education in AIDS prevention is the primary focus of this work, which looks at how the education sector can play a role in reducing the impact and spread of HIV/AIDS.

Lazarus Black, Mindie. 1994. "Alternative Readings: The Status of the Status of Children Act in Antigua and Barbuda." *Law and Society Review* 28, no. 5: 993–1018. The role of law in the construction of identity in Antigua and Barbuda is analyzed in this article. The focus is the 1986 Parliamentary law that enabled fathers to recognize their illegitimate children and end legal discrimination against such children, who constituted some 80 percent of the population.

Web Sites

Antigua and Barbuda Government, http://www.ab.gov.ag/gov_v2/index.php.

Complete Antigua and Barbuda Summary 2001: Report 2001. July, 2004. Vol. 1, http://www.ab.gov.ag/gov_v2/government/statsandreports/statsandreports2005/complete_census_summary_report.pdf.

Report of the Caribbean Summit for Children on HIV/AIDS, Bridgetown, Barbados, 21–23 March 2004. 2005. Bridgetown, Barbados: United Nations Children's Fund, http://www.unicef.org/barbados/cao_publications_hivreport.pdf.

2005 Common Entrance Passes, http://www.ab.gov.ag/gov_v2/government/statsandreports/statsandreports2005/2005common_entrance_passes.pdf.

UNGASS Report 2005: Antigua and Barbuda, http://www.unaids.org/en/publications/2005ungassreporting/default.asp.

UNICEF, http://www.unicef.org.

UNICEF. At a Glance: Antigua and Barbuda, http://www.unicef.org/infobycountry/antiguabarbuda.html.

Organizations and NGOs

All Saints Community Caring Group
Alphonso Daniel, Vice President
All Saints Road
St. John's, Antigua, W.I.
Phone: (268) 460-2634
Committed to dedicated service for the entire community.

Amazing Grace Foundation
Clarence Pilgrim, Chairperson

All Saints Road, P.O. Box 2142
St. John's, Antigua, W.I.
Phone: (268) 560-1989
Email: amagrac@candw.ag
Web site: http://www.amazinggracefoundation.org
Provides a home and respite care to children with severe disability.

Antigua & Barbuda Association of Persons with Disabilities (ABAPD)
Leslie A. Emanuel, Public Relations Officer
P.O. Box W123, Woods Centre
St. John's, Antigua, W.I.
Phone: (268) 461-7260
Email: info@abapd.org
Provides an environment that enhances and maximizes the opportunity for every person with a physical, mental, intellectual and/or sensory disability.

Antigua & Barbuda Centre for Dyslexia Awareness (ABCD)
Desiree Antonio, President
U.S. Peace Corps Office
P.O. Box 3613, Factory Road
St. John's, Antigua, W.I.
Phone: (268) 560-8168
Email: abcda@actol.net
ABCD's mottos are "To be differently able" and "If they can't learn the way we teach, then we must teach the way they learn."

Girl Guides Association
Caroline McCoy, President
P.O. Box 984, Deanery Lane
St. Johns, Antigua, W.I.
Phone: (268) 460-1285
Email: ab_gga@hotmail.com
The mission of the Girl Guides is to enable girls and young women to develop to their fullest potential, thereby contributing to national, regional, and worldwide development.

Humanitarian Ecumenical Relief Organization (HERO)
Brent B. Emanuel, Director
P.O. Box W325
St. John's, Antigua, W.I.
Phone: (268) 462-1366
Fax: (268) 462-5971
Email: hero@stanfordeagle.com
Web site: http://www.heroantigua.com
HERO, as a cooperative effort of Christian churches in Antigua and Barbuda, seeks to provide moral, spiritual, and financial assistance to persons in desperate circumstances.

National Association for Mental Health
Greta Georges, President
Hope Centre

Nugent Avenue
St. John's, Antigua, W.I.
Phone: (268) 560-2734
To work with the family and friends of people with mental illness alongside professionals; to develop public awareness of mental illness.

The Pan American Health Organization
Web site: http://www.paho.org
Serving as the regional office in the Americas for the World Health Organization (WHO), PAHO has 100 years of experience working to improve health and living standards in the region.

The Professional Organization for Women in Antigua and Barbuda (POWA)
Web site: http://www.powa-anu.org/iwc2004.html
Professional Organization of women in Antigua and Barbuda Resource and Networking organization aiming to empower women.

Soroptimist
Lenore Worrell, Assistant Treasurer
P.O. Box 3161
St. John's, Antigua, W.I.
Phone: (268) 560-0185
Fax: (268) 562-2465
Developmental assistance to women and children in literacy, health, and environment.

Victorious Living Outreach Ministry
Cornelia Michael, President
P.O. Box 477
St. John's, Antigua, W.I.
Phone: (268) 461-0996
To promote positive Christian value amongst youths; to motivate and inspire youths on setting positive goals for the future; to encourage youth participation and concern for the elderly.

Young Women's Christian Association (YWCA)
Cornnelia Michael, President
P.O. Box 477
St. John's, Antigua, W.I.
Phone: (268) 461-0996
The oldest and largest multicultural women's organization in the world committed to eliminating racism and empowering women.

Selected Bibliography

Antigua and Barbuda Summary 2001: Summary Social, Economic, Demographic, and Housing Characteristics. Issued July, 2004. Vol.1 http://www.ab.gov.ag/gov_v2/government/statsandreports/statsandreports2005/complete_census_summary_report.pdf. Accessed July 26, 2006.

Barrow, Christine. 2001. *Situation Analysis of Children and Women in Twelve Countries in the Caribbean.* Barbados: UNICEF Caribbean Area Office. http:// www.unicef.org/barbados/SitAn_Final_Report.doc. Accessed July 26, 2006.

Benjamin, Ernest, and Edris Bird. 1998. *1991–1996 Situation Analysis of Children and Their Families: Consolidating Social Achievements and Meeting the Challenges of the 21st Century. Child Survival, Development and Protection in Antigua and Barbuda.* Bridgetown: UNICEF, Caribbean Area Office,

Daniel, CarolAnn. 2004. "Social Work with West Indian Families: A Multilevel Approach." *Journal of Immigrant & Refugee Services* 2, no. 3/4: 135–145.

The EFA 2000 Assessment Reports: Country Reports. Antigua and Barbuda. http://www2.unesco.org/wef/countryreports/antigua_barbuda/contents .html

"Family Law Reform in the Caribbean." 2002. *Children in Focus* 15, no. 1: 1, 4. http://www.unicef.org/barbados/cao_publications_cifreform.pdf. Accessed October 28, 2006.

Government of Antigua and Barbuda: Members of the House of Representatives. http://www.ab.gov.ag. Accessed November 29, 2006.

Human Development Report 2006: Antigua and Barbuda. http://www.hdr.undp .org/hdr2006/statistics/countries/date_sheets/cty_ds_ATG.htl. Accessed November 29, 2006.

Kelly, Michael J., and Brendan Bain. 2005. *Education and HIV/AIDS in the Caribbean.* Kingston, Jamaica: Ian Randle.

"OAS to Assist Antigua with Agriculture/Tourism Linkages." *OAS Antigua & Barbuda Newsletter.* 2, no. 4. http://www.ckln.org/files/Antigua&BarbudaOAS %20Newsletter%20II.4%20E.doc. Accessed December 26, 2006.

Pan American Health Organization. Antigua and Barbuda, Health Situation Analysis and Trends Summary. http://www.paho.org/English/DD/AIS/cp_028 .htm.

Population Reference Bureau. 2006 World Population Data Sheet. http://www.albany .edu/~yhuang/2006WorldDataSheet.pdf.

Report of the Caribbean Summit for Children on HIV/AIDS, Bridgetown, Barbados, 21–23 March 2004. 2005. Bridgetown, Barbados: United Nations Children's Fund. http://www.unicef.org/barbados/cao_publications_hivreport.pdf. Accessed October 27, 2006.

Robert, Viviennet. 2006. National Report on Higher Education in Antigua and Barbuda. Caracas, Venezuela: IESALC/UNESCO, International Institute for Higher Education in Latin America and the Caribbean. http://www.iesalc .unesco.org.ve/programas/nacionales/antigua%20y%20bermuda/national%20 report%20antigua.pdf.

Spooner, Mary, CarolAnn Daniel, and Annette M. Mahoney. 2004. "Confronting the Reality: An Overview of the Impact of HIV/AIDS on the Caribbean Community." *Journal of Refugee and Immigrant Services* 2, no. 4: 49–67.

UNGASS Report. 2005. Antigua and Barbuda, http://www.unaids.org/en/ publications/2005ungassreporting/default.asp.

United Nations. 2004. Convention on the Rights of the Child 37th Session: Committee Considers Initial Reporting of Antigua and Barbuda. http:// www.hrea.org/lists/child-rights/markup/msg00333.html. Accessed July 25, 2006.

———. 2005. United Nations Children's Fund. At a Glance: Antigua and Barbuda http://www.unicef.org/infobycountry/antiguabarbuda.html.

———. 2005. *The State of the World's Children 2006: Excluded and Invisible*. New York: UNICEF.

United Nations Population and Vital Statistics Report. http://unstats.un.org/unsd/seriesa/031.asp. Accessed October 20, 2006.

U.S. Department of State. Country Reports on Human Rights Practices: Antigua and Barbuda 2001. http://www.terrorismcentral.com. Accessed October 20, 2006.

2

THE BAHAMAS

Elizabeth M. Hunter

NATIONAL PROFILE

The Commonwealth of the Bahamas is an independent nation made up of 700 islands and 2,400 cays that stretch from 50 miles off southeast Florida for some 600 miles, extending almost to Haiti in the Atlantic Ocean. Only thirty of the islands are inhabited, and almost 70 percent of the population resides on New Providence, one of the smallest of the major islands. The capital and principal city is Nassau, on New Providence Island. The climate of the Bahamas is humid and subtropical. The annual rainfall averages 1,200 millimeters, and temperatures normally range between 20°C and 30°C. Hurricanes, fairly common between May and November, have caused severe damage on several occasions (Emergency Disaster Data Base 2006).

The population of the Bahamas is 303,770, with a growth rate of 0.64 percent. The average life expectancy of a Bahamian is seventy-two years. The sex ratio at birth is 1.02 males per female, and in the total population it is 0.96 males per female. Age

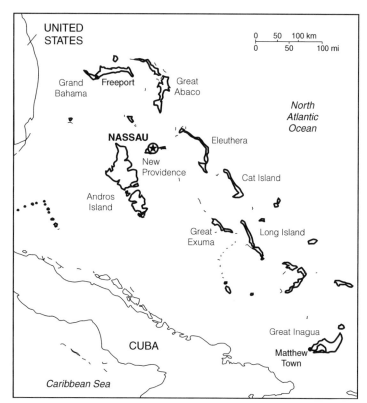

structure statistics indicate that the age group consisting of one- to four-teen-year-olds includes 27.5 percent of the population (there are currently 41,799 males and 41,733 females in this age group). The age group consisting of fifteen- to sixty-four-year-olds includes 66.1 percent of the population (98,847 males and 102,074 females), and 6.4 percent of the population is sixty-five years old and over (7,891 males and 11,426 females). The birth rate in the Bahamas is 17.57 births per 1,000 population. The total fertility rate is 2.18 children born per woman, and the death rate is 9.05 deaths per 1,000 population (Government of the Bahamas, Department of Statistics 2005). In 1990, the infant mortality rate was twenty-two per 1,000 live births, and in 2005 it was thirteen (United Nations [UN] Children's Fund [UNICEF], At a Glance).

In terms of ethnicity, 85 percent of the population is black, 12 percent white, and 3 percent Asian and Hispanic. English is the official language of the Bahamian population, and Creole predominates among Haitian immigrants. The Bahamas' Gross Domestic Product (GDP) in 2005 was $5.8 billion, with a GDP per capita of $18,062, although 9.3 percent of the population lived below the poverty line in 2004 (U.S. Department of State 2007). Labor force statistics for 2005, reported by occupation, show an estimated 5 percent employed in agriculture, 5 percent in industry, 50 percent in tourism, and 40 percent in other services; the estimated unemployment rate was 10.3 percent in 2005 (Central Intelligence Agency 2007).

The female population of the Bahamas numbers 155,896. There were 86,055 women in the labor force in 2004, and of them, 76,560 were employed (9,495 were unemployed) (Government of the Bahamas, Department of Statistics 2005). In 2002–2003, 88 percent of Bahamian girls were enrolled in primary education (UNICEF 2005), and 96.5 percent of the female population could read and write (2003 estimate). With the May 2002 elections, eight of the forty seats in the lower house were held by women (20 percent) and seven of the sixteen seats of the upper house (43.7 percent) (Interparliamentary Union 2007). In 2003, 40 percent of managers and legislators together were women (UN Statistics Division 2006).

Recent studies emphasize the conditions of women as heads of household in the Bahamas. Women are often tasked with the well-being of the family and especially with the responsibilities of parenting. Bahamian women's roles also include extended family obligations, pregnancy, child-bearing and rearing, and supporting the household materially (Hahnlen et al. 1997). In the Bahamas, HIV/AIDS is increasingly a reason for the existence of single-parent families. Between the first reported case in August 1985 and March 2005, 10,187 cases were identified (Thurston 2005). International agencies report a 3.3 percent incidence rate and 6,800 persons living with HIV/AIDS in the Bahamas in 2005, of which 6,500 were aged fifteen to forty-nine; of the 6,500 cases, 58 percent were women (UNAIDS 2006, 309). Women of childbearing age and young women (ages fifteen to forty-four) are the fastest growing population of HIV/AIDS victims (Neely-Smith 2003, 741). Adverse consequences of this dilemma are mother-to-child transmission, declining family welfare, and the breakdown of the family structure, including increasing numbers of orphans.

The government is making strides for the good of children and families. The Ministry of Public Service emphasizes the "people focused–people driven" mission of the government (Government of the Bahamas, Ministry of Public Service 2005). The Ministry of Social Services and Community Development and the Department of Social Services have responsibility for coordination of government actions and policies with regard to children and for monitoring the implementation in the Bahamas of the Convention on the Rights of the Child (CRC) (Office of the UN High Commissioner for Human Rights 2004, 5). Within the Ministry, the Bureau of Women's Affairs and the Department of Rehabilitative Services also oversee state efforts in support of Bahamian families, and in particular for the welfare of women and children (Government of the Bahamas, Ministry of Social Services and Community Development 2005). The Bahamas Department of Social Services' areas of responsibility encompass public assistance, social welfare, old age pensions, indigent and aged persons, care facilities, child protection, self help, and disabled persons. There is also attention to the problem of homelessness. The Urban Renewal Community Policing Project initiated in June 2002 is a comprehensive approach to solving interrelated social problems, including crime, poor housing conditions, unemployment, illiteracy, HIV/AIDS, and homelessness (Dean 2005).

In addition to proactive ministries and agencies, international and domestic nongovernmental organizations, such as UNICEF, the Bahamas Red Cross Society, the Bahamas Association for Social Health, and the Bahamas Crisis Center, work closely with the government in pursuing the welfare of children and their families. Religious organizations also contribute to social development in the Bahamas and have, for example, supported the creation of after-school enrichment programs, hospitals, and the delivery of primary health care. Authorities in the religious community are respected and their views are taken into consideration.

The UNCRC, adopted by the General Assembly of the United

KEY FACTS – THE BAHAMAS

Population: 3 million (July 2007 est.)
Life expectancy at birth: 65.66 years (2007 est.)
Literacy rate: 95.6 percent (2003 est.)
Net primary school enrollment/attendance: 84 percent (2000–2005)
Internet users: 93,000 (2005)
People living with HIV/AIDS: 6800 (2005 est.)

Sources: CIA World Factbook: The Bahamas. https://www.cia.gov/cia/publications/factbook/geos/bf.html. April 17, 2007; UNICEF. At a Glance: Bahamas—Statistics. http://www.unicef.org/infobycountry/bahamas.html. May 1, 2007; World Health Organization (WHO): UNAIDS/WHO Global HIV/AIDS Online Database. "Epidemiological Fact Sheets on HIV/AIDS and Sexuality Transmitted Diseases: Bahamas." http://www.who.int/GlobalAtlas/predefinedReports/EFS2006/index.asp?strSelectedCountry=BS. December 2006.

Nations on November 20, 1989, and ratified by every Caribbean country, serves as a guide for states to set missions and goals for the good of the children and their families. The Bahamas signed on October 30, 1990, and ratified the convention on February 20, 1991. Article 19 of the convention requires governments to take "all appropriate legislative, administrative, social and educational measures to protect the child from all forms of physical or mental violence, injury or abuse, neglect or negligent treatment, maltreatment or exploitation" (University of Minnesota 1989). Article 19 thus states that children should not be hurt in any way and even parents have no right to hurt a child. Article 42 states that all adults and children should know about the CRC; children have the right to learn their rights (University of Minnesota 1989). The Bahamian government has used the convention to orient the efforts of ministries, agencies, and registries with regard to families, women, and children.

OVERVIEW

The CRC affirms that children, because of their vulnerability, need special care and protection; it places special emphasis on the primary caring and protective responsibilities of the family. McCartney reflects upon Bahamian culture and the desire to support the needs of children. "It is important and necessary for the survival of a people that they expose themselves, particularly their children, to the history and culture of their ancestors. This exposure will ensure their successful transition from childhood to adulthood. In this way, they will become proud contributors to the future development of their nation, and by extension, the world" (McCartney 2004, 2).

The history of the islands of the Bahamas precedes the European conquest of Latin America and the Caribbean. When Christopher Columbus encountered the New World on San Salvador in 1492, the Arawak Indians were the only inhabitants. The first English settlements were established during the seventeenth century. In 1781, the Spanish attacked and captured Nassau, claiming the colony. Two years later, the islands came under the rule of Great Britain. The history of the island changed radically as black slaves labored on cotton plantations when Loyalists from the American Revolution migrated to the islands. The emancipation of the slaves transformed island life again in 1834. During the American Civil War, blockade running enriched the economy as did rum running during the prohibition era. During World War II and in the early 1950s, the town of Freeport was established, and offshore banking and a rise in tourism stimulated the economy enormously (Mitchell 1972). The Bahamas became independent on July 10, 1973.

Currently, the Bahamas is organized politically with a parliamentary form of government under the 1973 Constitution. The prime minister is the head of government, and the monarch of the United Kingdom is the titular head of state. There are twenty-one administrative districts. A sixteen-seat Senate and a forty-seat House of Assembly compose the bicameral national legislature.

According to Sullivan, "the Bahamas stands out among the Caribbean nations because of its relative wealth and prosperity" (Sullivan 1991). The Bahamas took in more than $2 billion in 2005 nearly from more than million tourists. International banking and investment management augment the tourist economy, with more than 400 banking institutions from thirty-six countries. The main industries in the Bahamas are tourism, which includes a thriving filmmaking component (Government of the Bahamas, Department of Tourism 2006), banking, e-commerce, cement, oil refining, and transshipment. Presently, Bahamian agriculture includes citrus, vegetables, and poultry, and the national exports are fish and craw-fish, rum, salt chemical, and fruits and vegetables (National Geographic Society 2004). The Bahamian economy is affected by international events and trends, including the drug trade, as well as natural disasters. The United States has played a prominent role as a source of tourism, a partic-ipant in financial activities, and a trade partner (Urwick 2002), and tour-ism was directly and adversely affected by the 9/11 terrorist attack in the United States in 2001. Natural disasters such as hurricanes and storms that carry significant winds also affect tourism and the economy more generally. There have been sixteen hurricanes ("wind storms") with nota-ble repercussions from 1926 to 2005, with some fifty people killed and 3,200 residents left homeless (Emergency Disaster Data Base 2006).

The government of the Bahamas provides free education at the primary and secondary levels. Schooling is compulsory in the Bahamas for children from five to fourteen years of age. The literacy rate for Bahamians aged fif-teen years and older is 95.6 percent (Government of the Bahamas, Depart-ment of Statistics 2005). There has been growth in public secondary and technological schools in recent years. In 1974, the College of the Bahamas was established in Nassau. The College of the Bahamas offers bachelor's degrees and some master's programs in conjunction with other universities, including the University of the West Indies, Florida International Univer-sity, and the University of Miami (http://www.bahamasgov.com).

The CRC stipulates in Article 22 that if children are refugees, they have a right to special protection and help. According to the 2000 Cen-sus, there were more than 38,000 migrants in the Bahamas (residents include citizens from more than seventy countries), with nearly 13,000 of them under nineteen years of age. Estimates are that 30,000 to 40,000 (and perhaps more) undocumented migrants are living in the Bahamas, 85 percent of them Haitians (Office of the High Commissioner 2004; Research and Support Sub-Committee of the National Education Confer-ence 2005, 4). Bahamian policies for children are extended to citizens and both documented and undocumented immigrants. The Ministry of

Social Services and all state agencies are implementing this and other provisions of the CRC, including protection from sexual exploitation and abuse, prostitution, and pornography (Article 34); protection from mistreatment by parents or guardians (Article 19); and protection from labor that is dangerous or interferes with their education (Article 32) (University of Minnesota 1989).

Article 5 of the CRC states that parties shall respect the responsibilities, rights, and duties of parents or, where applicable, the members of the extended family or community as provided for by local custom, legal guardians, or other persons legally responsible for the child, to provide, in a manner consistent with the evolving capacities of the child, appropriate direction and guidance in the exercise by the child of the rights recognized in the CRC. Article 27 states that children have the right to an adequate standard of living, meaning that parents have the responsibility to provide food, clothes, a place to live, and so on. It also states that if parents cannot afford this, then the government should help (University of Minnesota 1989). Though ratified by the Bahamian government and used as the basis in the design of policies and reform efforts, much of the responsibility still falls on women as heads of household to earn the family income, protect and feed the children, and keep the family home intact.

EDUCATION

According to the Bahamas 2004 report to the UN's Committee on the Rights of the Child, "there is no entrenched right to education under the Constitution of the Bahamas" (Office of the High Commissioner 2004, 34). As early as 1878, primary education was made compulsory in the colony, although secondary education remained under the aegis of the church until 1925 and the creation of a public high school (Bahamian History Online). The Education Act of 1962 provided the basis for the present system of education and its purposes. The principle inherent in the act is "pupils are to be educated in accordance with the wishes of their parents, having regard to the available resources and whether it is compatible with the provision of efficient instruction and training" (Office of the High Commissioner 2004, 34). British influences persist, though there has been both a "Bahamianization" and "Americanization" of education since independence (Urwick 2002). A White Paper on Education was published in 1972, primary school teachers were "Bahamianized" in the 1970s, explains Urwick, and a national curriculum was implemented in 1982 (2002).

The schooling system in the Bahamas includes six years of primary education (ages five to eleven), three years of junior high (ages eleven to fourteen), and three years of high school (ages fourteen to seventeen). The Education Act promises that children will have access to state-provided education, though historically such access was not formally guaranteed until the end of the 1960s. As the status report prepared for the 18th National Education Conference in July 2005 explains, only one public secondary school existed and segregation prevailed in private schools (Research and Support Subcommittee of the National Education Conference 2005, 6). Compulsory education through grade nine was instituted, and in 2001 an amendment to the Education Act extended it to grade eleven (age sixteen) (Office of the United Nations High Commissioner 2004, 34).

In 2005–2006, there were 159 public schools and eighty-six private schools in the Bahamas, with 51,146 students enrolled in public schools and 18,538 enrolled in private schools (Ministry of Education, Science, and Technology, 24, 29). Most of the private schools are all-age schools or primary schools. Expenditures in education were 16.9 percent of the national budget (Ministry of Education, Science, and Technology, 28). Private schools, often religious, receive government funding.

Gross enrollment in primary schools in 2005–2006 was 100.2, and it was 87.7 in secondary schools, while net enrollment in primary was 91.1 and in secondary 89.9 (Ministry of Education, Science, and Technology, 28). UN enrollment figures show that at the primary level, 83 percent of boys and 85 percent of girls are enrolled; and at the secondary level 78 percent of girls and 70 percent of boys are enrolled (United Nations Educational, Scientific, and Cultural Organization [UNESCO]). The Ministry's Educational Statistics Digest reports that in 2005–2006, 87.8 percent of teachers were trained, the student/teacher ratio was 16.7 at the primary level and 13.1 at the second level, and 2.9 percent of all students repeated (3.5 percent in primary and 0.7 percent in secondary) (Ministry of Education, Science, and Technology National Examination Results 2005, 28).

The Bahamas educational system uses an examination system to assess learning in grades three and six (the Grade Level Assessment Tests [GLAT]); there is a certification at the completion of ninth grade (Bahamas Junior Certification); an exit examination is administered upon completion of grade twelve. The U.S.-based Psychological Corporation assisted with the creation of the GLAT, although local management was complete by 1998 (Urwick 2002). The exit exam, the Bahamas General Certificate of Education (BGCE), replaced the British General Certificate of Education in 1993 and the Ministry notes positive achievements, including a 90 percent participation rate and increasingly better scores (Ministry of Education, Science and Technology 2005, 2–8; see Urwick 2002).

The expansion of preschool education has been a goal since the late 1980s, although most of what is available remains religious or private. There were three public preschools in 2005–2006 and forty-three schools with preschool units. The government provides access to education for disabled children. In 2005–2006, there were seventeen schools with special education classrooms and ten special education schools (Ministry of Education, Science, and Technology, 24).

Technical and vocational education is also available. Programs exist for the study of construction, food, home economics, management and tourism, business, and electronic and computer studies (Office of the High Commissioner 2004). Higher education was reformed in 1974, expanding access for Bahamian students. Before 1974, higher education consisted of teacher education at Bahamas Teachers College (located in New Providence) and the San Salvador Teachers College (later merged with the College of the Bahamas); C.R. Walker Technical College offered technical education. The Bahamas affiliated with the University of the West Indies in 1964, and in 1973 the Bahamas Hotel Training College was created, followed by the College of the Bahamas in 1974 and the Bahamas Baptist Community College in 1995. "Offshore colleges" established in the Bahamas include College of St. Benedict, University of Miami, Sojourner Douglass College, Nova Southeastern University of Florida, Atlantic College, St. Thomas University (1995–2002), and Omega College (Fielding and Gibson 2005, 5–7).

The 18th National Education Conference identified five challenges for the Ministry of Education, together with the Ministry's response. These areas include institutional capacity for planning and implementation, provision for the educational needs of all students, the pool of local and qualified teachers, better performance by students, and the preparation of students in accord with national economic needs (Research and Support Subcommittee of the National Education Conference 2005). Indeed, steady growth in tourism and the associated boom in the construction industry appear to play a part in the early dropout rates of students in the Bahamas. In 2004, 16 percent of primary school-aged children were not in school (UNESCO), and there is much controversy about the dropout rate for secondary-level students (Smith 2005).

PLAY AND RECREATION

The Bahamian government promotes sports and recreation for children. The Ministry of Youth, Sports, and Housing has divisions that are responsible for Youth Development, National Youth Service, and Athletic and Sporting Development, and the Department of Sports within the Ministry attends to Recreational Programs, Relations with Sporting Organizations, Sports Promotion, the Bahamas Games, the Carifta Games, and the Development of Sporting Facilities (Government of the Bahamas, Ministry of Youth, Sports, and Housing). The Sports Division organizes a variety of programs and competitions, including the Elisha Obed Boxing championship for children ten to eighteen years old, Bahamas Inter-collegiate Sports Association (including basketball and volleyball among other sports), Primary Track and Field Championships, the Community Swim Championship, and the Annual Summer Sports Program (Office of the High Commissioner 2004). Basketball and softball are more popular than cricket (Urwick 2002). The Bahamas sends teams to the Carifta Games, a regional sports competition for youth aged thirteen to nineteen created in 1972. The Bahamas also participates in the international Special Olympics movement that provides sporting opportunities to individuals with intellectual disabilities.

Music is an important part of Bahamian culture and local traditions. The varieties of music characteristic of the islands reflect the influences of African rhythms, the Calypso of the Caribbean, English traditions, and the African American gospel of the United States. The uniquely Bahamian Goombay music—meaning "rhythm" in the Bantu language—is played by "rake and scrape bands." According to the Ministry of Tourism, these bands "have been playing goombay music since the time of slavery, when African slaves had few resources to create musical instruments." "Traditionally, rake and scrape music is used to accompany the Bahamian Quadrille and the Heel and Toe Polka dances—another example of how African and European influences have blended together" (Art/Music/Dance 2007). Other dances include the Jump-In-Dance (with roots in West Africa) (Art/Music/Dance 2007).

Bahamian national holidays include New Year's Day, Labor Day (June 1), Independence Day (July 10), Emancipation Day (the first Monday in August), Discovery/Columbus Day (October 12), and Boxing Day (December 26). The unique Junkanoo national festival is celebrated from December 26 (Boxing Day) to January 1. The carnivalesque Junkanoo parade invites spectators to join in the celebration, marching in dance-like fashion to loud goombay music, whistles, and bells. Junkanoo is more than a parade, however (Rolle 2003). The One Family Junkanoo and Community Organization that formed in 1993 sees it a force for social change, "as an industry that embodies the creativity that will drive the Bahamian economy well into the twenty-first century"—especially important for youth (http://www.onefamilyjunkanoo.org). The government has recently formally committed to encouraging the participation of children in cultural activities, including Junkanoo art, and has created a program for marching bands in inner cities (Office of the High Commissioner, 53). Other state-sponsored cultural activities include the National Dance School, Theatre in the Park programming, the National Arts Festival, and the Summer Dance and Druming Program (Office of the UN High Commissioner 2004).

The government of the Commonwealth of the Bahamas recognizes civic and community organizations that provide social and recreational programming. For example, the Bahamas Chess Federation is involved in education of children through school programs as well as a rehabilitation program in the prison (Bahamas Chess Federation 2005). There are some fifty-five parks and playgrounds in New Providence. The Bahamas Film Commission, a government organization, was established specifically to develop and facilitate film production in the Bahamas. Cable television has been available since 1995, and viewers have access to more than fifty channels from the United States, three from Europe, and one that is national (Urwick 2002). The Bahamas largest Internet service provider supplies residential and commercial subscribers. In 2005, there were 292 Internet users for each 1,000 persons, compared with fifty-five per 1,000 in 2001 (Reuters Foundation 2006).

CHILD LABOR

The Department of Labor is committed to the Declaration of the Fundamental Principles and Rights at Work adopted by the International Labor Organization (ILO) in 1998. The four major areas of the declaration are freedom of association and the right to collective bargaining, the elimination of forced and compulsory labor, abolition of child labor, and the elimination of discrimination in the workplace (International Labor Organization 1998). There are laws to protect children in the Bahamas, and the means exist to enforce them. The Bahamian constitution includes child labor in its section on fundamental rights and freedoms, and other specific legislation regarding child labor has been developed and more recently revised in light of the CRC. The Employment of Children (Prohibition) Act of 1939 prohibited the employment of persons under the age of fourteen ("children") in an industrial undertaking or during school hours. The Employment of Young Persons Act (defined as anyone between twelve and seventeen years old), prohibited employment on a ship (save one employing family members within Bahamian waters) or in night work (Office of the High Commissioner 2004, 7). The Employment Act of 2001 repealed these prior laws, revising them as Part X of the Employment Act.

In 2004, there were 8,635 youth between the ages of fifteen and nineteen years counted as part of the labor force (Government of the Bahamas, Department of Statistics 2005). Some Bahamian children aged five to fourteen do work. The revised Bahamian law allows that a child may be employed as a grocery packer, gift wrapper, peanut vendor, or newspaper vendor (for a period of five years after passage of the Employment Act). Night work for children is still prohibited as it is for young persons, with the exceptions of permissible employment, including hotels, restaurants, food stores, general merchandise stores, and gas stations. Legally, the prohibition of employment during school hours for any person under the age of fourteen years is maintained (Office of the High Commissioner). Work outside of school hours is regulated: a young person may work outside school hours for no more than three hours on a school day; in a school week, for no more than twenty-four hours; on a non-school day, for no more than eight hours; in a non-school week for no more than forty hours (Employment Act 2001). On June 14, 2002, the government ratified the ILO's Convention 182 on elimination of the Worst Forms of Child Labor (U.S. Department of State 2002).

A Rapid Assessment of child labor completed by the ILO in 2002 (Dunn 2002) found a reported 189 cases of children working under conditions of child labor. Of them, 109 (57.6 percent) were involved in such forms of work as assisting in family businesses, vending, and services, 28 (14.8 percent) were related to tourism, and 52 cases (27.5 percent) were associated with the Worst Forms of Child Labor (Dunn 2002). Acknowledging the small and unsystematic sample (157 persons were consulted, including a number of children), the assessment noted that the reported cases "do not necessarily reflect a major child labor problem in the Bahamas, but raise concerns for further research and action" (Dunn 2002, 27). The CRC's concluding observations on the 2005 report of the Bahamas referred in Section 57 to the ILO Rapid Assessment, expressing concern over the possibility of child prostitution and pornography (Office of the High Commissioner 2005).

FAMILY

The legal age for marriage in the Bahamas is eighteen for both women and men. In 1990, the "singulate mean age of marriage" was twenty-seven for women and twenty-nine for men (United Nations Statistics Division 2006). Forty-one percent of households were headed by women in the late 1990s, and in 1993, 72 percent of all births were to single mothers aged ten to nineteen (Nowak 1999, 120). Social problems can also lead to divorce, abandonment, and single heads of household (Government of the Bahamas, Ministry of Health 2005). According to a 1997 ethnographic study of mothering in the Bahamas, "most mothers carried the bulk, if not all, of the responsibility for the well-being of their children, with familial obligations taking significant personal tolls; however, the community, often in the form of extended family, provides informal assistance. The small and relatively safe communities provided a reassuring context in which to raise children, and birthing experiences were also more of a family or community affair. Mothering experiences seemed to vary somewhat by island and the unique circumstances of the community" (Hahnlen et al. 1997).

The Ministry of Health's National Family Planning Policy is a priority goal within the country's overall health policy. There appears to be substantial demand for such services (Government of the Bahamas, Ministry of Health 2005). In 1988, 61.7 percent of women aged fifteen to forty-four used some form of contraception (United Nations Statistics Division 2006). The Ministry of Public health notes that between 1994 and 1995, an average of 246 women had six or more children and that many women have a space of only twelve or eighteen months between children (Government of the Bahamas, Ministry of Health 2005). Abortion is permitted in the Bahamas under very limited circumstances. Abortion is not penalized if the health or life of the woman is at risk (Choike.org 2006). Bahamian women have access to maternity leave of thirteen weeks' duration with 100 percent of their wages paid (United Nations Statistics Division 2006).

An important issue facing families is the HIV/AIDS epidemic occurring in the Bahamas. There are many repercussions for family members of those infected, including erratic school attendance of children because of sickness of a household member, the child's own illness, poverty, the inability to obtain medication, and death in the family (Government of the Bahamas, Ministry of Health 2005). The effects on seropositive women who must maintain a range of traditional gender roles can be very negative (Neely-Smith 2003). Children may wind up orphaned and homeless. A 2005 estimate of Bahamian children from birth to seventeen years of age orphaned by all causes was 8,000 (UNICEF, At a Glance).

The Status of Children Act of 2002 abolished the distinction between children born inside and outside marriage (wedlock) that had previously allowed discrimination on this basis (Office of the High Commissioner, 40). Whether married or not, parents are expected to provide for their children. Cases of children who are neglected, abused, or abandoned are handled by the Child and Family Services Division and its Child Protective Services Unit. Alternative care for endangered children can be arranged, including placement with relatives, foster care, adoption, or institutional homes. At the time of the Bahamas report to the CRC, there were fifteen institutional facilities for children needing substitute family care, some public and some private with government support. Examples are the Elizabeth Estates Children's Home for orphans one to eighteen years old and the Ranfurly Home for Children, a foster home setting for children five to eighteen years old. Adoption is difficult in the Bahamas; domestic adoptions of Bahamian children numbered fourteen in 2001, twenty-two in 2002, and nine in 2003 (Office of the High Commissioner, 17).

The state offers social services for women, children, and families, including food assistance, financial assistance, programs for disabled children and adults, a national lunch program, and education in parenting. There were some 100 trained social workers in the Bahamas in the 1990s and private organizations participate extensively in support of state policies, including the Kiwanis, the Red Cross, the Bahamas Association for Social Health, and others (Nowak 1999, 122).

HEALTH

The 2000–2004 strategic plan of the Ministry of Health identified five principal directions of work: "healthy people; healthy environment; maximized resources; quality service; and healthcare planning." Among the priorities were maternal and child health, adolescent school health, and family planning, as well as HIV/AIDS, disaster preparedness, emergency services, care of elders, and disease prevention and control (Pan American Health Organization). Needed infrastructure for a healthy population is in place. In 2004, 97 percent of the population had access to improved water, and 100 percent of both the rural and urban populations used adequate sanitation facilities (United Nations Children's Fund, At a Glance). Water and sewage services are offered by the Grand Bahama Utility Co. and in the less populated islands, sewage is mainly septic tanks and latrines (Pan American Health Organization). Major hotels and resorts have onsite sewage treatment and disposal systems. In the 1990–2004 period, the Bahamas had 101 physicians per 100,000 population, and there were 667 nurses working in the public sector (Reuters Foundation 2006; Pan American Health Organization); there are currently three public hospitals. The principal causes of death for men in 1996–2000 were communicable diseases, diseases of circulatory system, neoplasms, and external causes; for women circulatory system diseases, communicable diseases, and neoplasms were the principal causes of death (Pan American Health Organization).

Disease prevention is a cornerstone of the approach of the Bahamas Ministry of Public Health. The Ministry of Public Health promotes vaccines as an important way to prevent disease in persons who receive them, and to protect those who come in contact with unvaccinated individuals (Government of the Bahamas, Ministry of Health 2005). The Expanded Program on Immunization that began in the Bahamas in the late 1970s is a cooperative activity with other nations, as well as with the World Health Organization and the Pan American Health Organization. The program initially vaccinated against diphtheria, pertussis, tetanus, polio, measles, and tuberculosis and expanded to include *Haemophilus influenzae* (Hib), mumps, rubella, and hepatitis B. Tuberculosis is controlled in a separate program. Another vaccine offered by the Ministry of Public Health, but not included in Expanded Program on Immunization, is a yellow fever vaccine (Government of the Bahamas, Ministry of Health 2005). Rates of vaccination of children are high (United Nations Children's Fund, At a Glance), and vaccines are available for both immigrant and Bahamian children; the government has announced that immunization for Bahamian children under two years of age will be provided regardless of whether they live in the islands or another country (Government of the Bahamas, Ministry of Health 2005).

The Maternal and Child Health Unit (MCH) was created in 1992 to provide maternal and child health services previously offered by Community Health Services. Established in response to the World Health Organization's call for health for all by the year 2000, the MCH programs include adolescent health, school health, the immunization program, reproductive health and family planning, the Parentcraft program, lactation management, and the Suspected Child Abuse and Neglect Unit (SCAN) (Government of the Bahamas, Ministry of Health 2005). Infant mortality in 2005 was thirteen per 1,000 live births (United Nations Children's Fund, At a Glance).

Rehabilitation services are offered at hospitals, and the government is developing a more comprehensive set of programs for children and youth with disabilities. In 2001, the Ministry of Health established the Neuro-developmental Clinic to offer diagnostic testing for those children and infants considered to be at risk. The Sandilands Rehabilitative Centre provides assistance for developmentally delayed children and youth via its in-patient Robert Smith Ward. There were 675 children and youth aged ten to nineteen with disabilities in the 2001–2003 period, as reported by the Bahamas to the Committee on the Rights of the Child; of them, 258 had learning disabilities, 109 had behavioral disabilities, 122 had vision problems, seventy-three had hearing problems, and 173 had speech problems (Office of the Higher Commissioner, 17).

The Ministry of Health's Adolescent Health Center is a community-based public healthcare facility, created as a pilot project of the MCH program in 1993. It serves adolescents aged nine to nineteen and became self-standing in 1998. Viewing the adolescent "as an important participant in the family unit and the community," the center has a "holistic and team approach to adolescent health and developmental issues" (Government of the Bahamas, Ministry of Health 2005). It offers services for a variety of problems experienced by youth, including sexual molestation, teen pregnancy and parenthood, behavioral problems (such as aggression, suicidal tendencies, and early sexual activity), substance abuse, depression, domestic violence and intrafamily conflict, low self-esteem, depression, and problems of gay, lesbian, bisexual, and transgendered youth (Government of the Bahamas, Ministry of Health 2005).

HIV/AIDS is a serious problem in the Bahamas, where the prevalence rate among those aged fifteen and over was 3.3 percent at the end of 2005 (United Nations Children's Fund, At a Glance). Some 6,800 individuals are living with HIV/AIDS (58 percent of adult cases being women) (UNAIDS 2006, 309). There were a total of sixty-seven children or youth living with AIDS at the end of 2003 (aged birth to nineteen); forty-five were four years old or younger (Office of the High Commissioner, 32). Unlike other countries, transmission in the Bahamas is primarily through heterosexual relations, according to Neely-Smith (2003). Former President Clinton has directed support to the Bahamas (and Rwanda) through his William Jefferson Clinton Foundation's AIDS Initiative, providing assistance with improved national prevention and treatment programs, including the provision of retroviral drugs needed by patients. In his early 2005 trip to the Bahamas, he praised progress made, including a decline in pregnant HIV-positive women from 2.7 percent in 2001 to 1.6 percent in 2004, and the report that there were no new cases of HIV-infected newborns in 2004 (The Body 2005). Deaths were reduced from 250 in 2003 to 140 in 2004. The Bahamas will create a resource center and become a best-practice site for the Caribbean region (Government of the Bahamas, Ministry of Public Service 2005).

In 2001, through its National Health Surveillance Committee, the Ministry of Health altered its approach to food safety. Scientific studies suggested that more emphasis needed to be placed on education in sound food safety methods, rather than whether or not food handlers had any communicable disease. However, food-borne illnesses remain a public health problem in the Bahamas (Government of the Bahamas, Ministry of Health 2005). Regarding the quality of the environment, the Department of Environmental Health Services (DEHS) monitors to ensure air, water, soil, and housing quality, and also monitors hazardous substances. DEHS has developed a comprehensive solid-waste plan for creating sanitary land-fills. The public health laboratories monitor water and food quality.

LAWS AND LEGAL STATUS

As explained in the Bahamas report to the Committee on the Rights of the Child, the Minors Act of 1976 established eighteen years as the age of majority, although specific laws may provide a variation of this general consideration. Eighteen is the age at which citizens of the Bahamas with "full legal capacity" may be registered as voters, though renouncing citizenship cannot be accomplished until the age of twenty-one. The Education Act of 1962 as amended in 1996 defines "child" in terms of compulsory school age (previously fourteen and now sixteen), while the Employment of Children Act of 1939 (revised in December 2001) defines a child as a person under the age of fourteen. The Sexual Offences and Domestic Violence Act of 1991 defines "minor" as a person under eighteen; here, a child under sixteen cannot be considered to consent to intercourse, and a person under fourteen cannot be guilty of rape, procuring, or other sexual offenses. The Children and Young Persons (Administration of Justice) Act explains the age limits on imprisonment or admission to an institution of detention, and prohibits the death penalty for a person under eighteen who commits a homicide. Individuals under the age of fifteen may not marry except under special dispensation (Marriage Act, 1908) and parental (or guardian) consent is needed for marrying before the age of eighteen. A person may be recruited into the police at the age of sixteen (Defense Act, 1979), though the armed forces stipulate the age of eighteen (Office of the High Commissioner 2004, 7–9).

The number of people younger than eighteen years old charged with the commission of a crime (reported to the police) in 2001 totaled 128. Of these, twelve were cases of crimes against persons and 104 of crimes against property, and only three of the cases were young women. In 2002 there were thirty-five crimes against persons, 192 crimes against property, and 148 cases of "other major crime"; fifty-six of the total cases involved a young woman (Office of the High Commissioner, 34–35). Children younger than ten years cannot be held in a detention center of any type. In 2003, fifty-nine boys between the ages of ten and sixteen years were sentenced to the Simpson Penn Center for Boys, and fifty-five girls were sentenced to the Willie Mae Pratt Center for Girls, while thirty males younger than eighteen years old and twenty-eight females were detained in adult facilities (Office of the High Commissioner, 36).

There are a number of state and private sector organizations working with prevention and treatment of youth and child involvement with substance abuse. The Sandilands Rehabilitation Centre admitted 154 Bahamian children seventeen years old and younger in 2003 (Office of the High Commissioner, 39). The government maintains its commitment to controlling drug trafficking and the associated substance abuse by adults and children. It created a Task Force on Drug Abuse in 1984 whose mandate included education of the public. Programs for youth include the Drug-Free Achievers Program, Peer Leadership Program, I'm Special Program for primary-age children, Bahamas Association for Social Health, and Teen Challenge, among others (Office of the High Commissioner 2004, 44–47).

RELIGIOUS LIFE

Religion is a vital part of Bahamian culture, and freedom of religion is provided in the constitution. Christianity is dominant, and the range of Christian and other denominations found in the islands includes Anglican, Assembly of God, Ba'hai Faith, Baptist, Brethren, Christian and Missionary Alliance, Christian Science, Church of God of Prophecy, Greek Orthodox, Jehovah's Witnesses, Jewish, Latter Day Saints (Mormon), Lutheran, Methodist, Presbyterian, Roman Catholic, Seventh Day Adventist, and other smaller denominations (The Bahamas Guide). According to the 2000 census, the three largest religious denominations are Baptist (35.4 percent), Anglican (15.1 percent), and Roman Catholic (13.5 percent), with 8.1 percent Pentecostal, 4.8 percent Church of God, 4.2 percent Methodist, 15.2 percent other Christian, 2.9 percent none or unspecified, and 0.8 percent other (Solcolm House). There are practitioners of Rastafarianism and Hinduism and other South Asian religions, and some Bahamians identify as atheists (U.S. Department of State 2006; Association of Religion Data Archives 2006).

There is no official state religion in the Bahamas, although the Bahamian Christian heritage is expressed in government speeches and cooperation with churches in design and implementation of social policy as well as in the presence of religion as an academic subject in public schools and in the mandatory testing organized by the state (U.S. Department of State 2006). When churches and ministries describe their philosophies for use in the promotion of tourism, they often mention ministry and activities for children. National holidays with a religious basis include Good Friday, Easter Monday, Whit Monday, and Christmas Day.

Children in the Bahamas are protected by the law to have the freedom to choose their own religion. The law permits private associations, the constitution provides for freedom of religion, and the government generally respects this right in practice (U.S. Department of State 2006).

CHILD ABUSE AND NEGLECT

In 2004, there were 520 cases of suspected child abuse reported to the Department of Social Services, 227 of which involved some form of neglect, 162 concerned alleged physical abuse, seventy-two were alleged sexual abuse, and there were forty-seven cases of incest. Concern about abuse is strong and April 2005 was declared Child Protection Month with nationwide programming organized by the Ministry of Social Services, the National Child Protection Council, other advocacy groups, and religious organizations (Government of the Bahamas 2005).

Governmental and nongovernmental organizations address the problem of child abuse, including schools, the police, hospitals, community clinics, and the Ministries of Health and Social Services, especially the Department of Social Services. The Child and Young Persons (Administration of Justice) Act of 1987 establishes that willful assault, ill treatment, neglect, abandonment, or exposure of a child to suffering or injury is an offense leading to a fine or imprisonment (one year) or both. The Sexual Offences and Domestic Violence Act establishes the legal basis for protection of children from sexual exploitation or sexual abuse. The law requires that all persons who have contact with a child they believe to be abused sexually report their suspicions to the police. Failure to comply may bring a fine of $5,000 or imprisonment for two years or both. However, the same reporting requirement does not apply to cases of physical abuse, which healthcare professionals believe occurs quite frequently. The police refer reported cases of sexual and physical abuse to the Department of Social Services, which investigates them and can bring criminal charges against perpetrators. The Department may remove children from abusive situations if the court deems it necessary (Office of the High Commissioner 2004, 48; Government of the Bahamas, Ministry of Social Services 2005). There are stiff penalties for incest and other unlawful sexual activities.

The coordination of efforts to prevent and treat child abuse is organized through the Ministry of Health's Suspected Child Abuse and Neglect (SCAN) Team. Created in May 1999, the program is evidence-based and multidisciplinary. Agencies that are required to report abuse and neglect, and that cooperate in prevention efforts, include, among others, the police, Health Social Services, the Ministry of Education, Adolescent Health Centre, Social Service/Child Protective Services, the Crisis Centre, the Children's Ward of Accident and Emergency, and the Attorney General's Office. Nongovernmental organizations that advocate for children are also involved (Government of the Bahamas, Ministry of Health 2005).

There is concern that sexual abuse has increased since 1991 and the Sexual Offences and Domestic Violence Act. Abuse of disabled children is also gaining more recognition and, as with the protection of all children, efforts are made to raise public awareness. In July 1997, a 24-hour Child Abuse Hotline was created in the Department of Social Services to facilitate reporting (Office of the United Nations High Commissioner 2004, 10–11).

GROWING UP IN THE TWENTY-FIRST CENTURY

Much has been achieved for children, women, and families in the Bahamas in the last thirty years. The government acknowledges that more needs to be done, especially given the standards of the CRC. The nature of the social and economic realities in the Bahamas is changing, part of postcolonial development within the context of globalization. The challenges of change are many. The Bahamas is often used as a gateway for drugs and illegal aliens bound for the United States. Issues like child labor, slave labor, child selling and indentured servitude, child pornography and prostitution do not characterize childhood in the Bahamas, yet they are being monitored. Legal reform to comply with the CRC has heightened awareness of old and newer problems, creating prohibitions and presenting the aspirations of a government that works closely with the organizations of civil society, other Caribbean states, and international institutions in its pursuit of better conditions for women and children. In his remarks in the House of Assembly discussion of a Child Protection Bill in November 2006, Minister of Youth, Sports, and Housing Neville Wisdom promised to introduce a new National Youth Policy in 2007.

RESOURCE GUIDE

Suggested Readings

Barratt, Peter. 2004. *Bahama Saga: The Epic Story of the Bahama Islands*. Bloomington, IN: Authorhouse. Barratt's book combines history and fiction to provide a sweeping and polyvocal narrative of Bahamian history, beginning with the original Lucayan conquest, through the arrival of Columbus and subsequent recolonizations, to independence.

Craton, M., and G. Saunders. 2000. *Islanders in the Stream: A History of the Bahamian People*. Volume Two: *From the Ending of Slavery to the Twenty-First Century*, new ed. Athens, GA: University of Georgia Press. Using a New Social History approach, Craton provides a history of the Bahamas from the emancipation of slaves in 1834 to twentieth century modernization, independence in 1973, and post-independence development. Eschewing the traditional Eurocentric perspective, the author incorporates autobiographies, letters, official and media sources, and travelers' accounts.

Jenkins, Olga Culmer. 2000. *Bahamian Memories: Island Voices of the Twentieth Century.* Gainesville, FL: University Press of Florida. Jenkins, child of Bahamian emigrants to the United States, presents a collection of oral histories that recount—in vernacular—the full range of traditional life in the Bahamas, from folk medical practices to economic and artisan activities.

McCartney, Donald M. 2004. *Bahamian Culture and Factors which Impact upon It.* Pittsburgh, PA: Dorrance Publishing Co., Inc. Donald M. McCartney worked in the Bahamian education system and also as First Assistant Secretary in the Ministry of Public Service for the Bahamian Government. His book provides a reflective cultural and political history of the Bahamas.

Neely-Smith, Shane. 2003. "The Impact of HIV/AIDS on Bahamian Women: A Feminist Perspective." *Health Care for Women International* 24: 738–754. This article uses an "eclectic feminist approach" to explore the impact of HIV/AIDS on women in the Bahamas. It examines women's different roles (caregiver, receiver of care, child bearer, and child rearer), arguing that nurses should empower women and also work toward a transformation of the patriarchal social order that oppresses women.

Nowak, Barbara J. 1999. "Social Work in the Bahamas: A Profession Helps to Build a Nation." *International Social Work* 42, no. 2: 117–126. Nowak's article examines the social work profession in the Bahamas and how it has contributed to nation-building, focusing on social welfare problems, the policy and programs designed to address them, the roles of social work, social work training, and ongoing challenges and issues.

Web Sites

The Government of the Bahamas. About the Bahamas, The Commonwealth of the Bahamas, http://www.bahamas.gov.bs/bahamasweb2/home.nsf/.

Organizations and NGOs

Bahamas Association for Social Health (BASH)
Columbus Ave. Chippingham
P.O. Box SS-5372
Nassau, The Bahamas
Phone: (242) 356-2274
Fax: (242) 356-5252
Created in 1990 "to provide a positive spiritual response to some of the pressing social needs of the Bahamian community."

Bahamas Crisis Center
Dr. Sandra Dean-Patterson, Director
P. O. Box EE-17910
Nassau, The Bahamas
Email: crisiscentre@batelnet.bs
Web site: http://www.bahamascrisiscentre.org
Created in 1982 and previously known as The Women's Crisis Centre, the Crisis Centre is "a registered, non-profit organization that provides services to people who are the victims of physical, sexual and emotional abuse."

The Bahamas Family Planning Association
Valerie Knowles, Manager
37 East Avenue, Centerville
P.O. Box N-9071
Nassau, The Bahamas
Phone: (242) 325-1663
Fax: (242) 325-4886
Email: bahfpa@batelnet.bs
The Bahamas Family Planning Association was founded in 1984 and "is the only
    private organization providing family planning services in the Bahamas." Services
    offered, in cooperation with the government, include contraceptives (including
    Norplant insertions), HIV/AIDS counseling, pap smears, education and aware-
    ness, and other medical services.

The Bahamas Red Cross Society
John F. Kennedy Drive
Nassau, The Bahamas
P.O. Box N-8331
Phone: (242) 323-7370 and (242) 328-4415
Fax: (242) 323-7404
Email: redcross@bahamas.net.bs
Web site: http://www.bahamasredcross.org
The Bahamas Red Cross Society (BRCS) was founded in 1939 under the umbrella of
    the British Red Cross. The Society trains some 500 persons each year in first aid,
    disaster preparedness, and the management of shelters, and also offers emergency
    relief services, including Meals on Wheels, home help service, and a school milk
    program. The BRCS has a Youth Department.

Disabled Persons Organization of the Bahamas
P.O. Box SS 19011
Nassau, The Bahamas
Phone: (242) 325-7475
Fax: (242) 326-2189
Disabled Persons Organization of Bahamas is a National Assembly Member of Dis-
    abled Peoples' International, an international organization dedicated to both equal
    opportunities for disabled individuals and their full participation in families, com-
    munities, and nations.

One Family Junkanoo and Community Organization
#31 West Street
P.O. Box EE-1557
Nassau, The Bahamas
Phone: (242) 328-3786
Email: info@onefamilyjunkanoo.org
The artists that created this organization in 1993 identified the mission of
    "build[ing] Bahamian culture through Junkanoo." "Junkanoo must be seen as the
    'raw material' of the future. Further, the magnetic qualities of Junkanoo and its
    appeal to all Bahamians regardless of superficial differences, makes Junkanoo a
    powerful vehicle for social change, particularly among the youth of our nation."

Special Olympics Bahamas
P.O. Box SS6149

Nassau, The Bahamas
Phone: (242) 323-4671
Fax: (242) 323-3720
The non-profit Bahamas Special Olympics Association is an affiliated member of the
international Special Olympics, an international nonprofit organization active in
160 countries and dedicated to providing sports training and competition to individuals with intellectual disabilities such that they may be physically fit and successful members of society.

Teen Challenge Bahamas
P.O. Box SS-6754
Nassau, The Bahamas
Phone: (242) 341-0613
Fax: (242) 341-0829
Email: tchallenge@coralwave.com
Teen Challenge is a worldwide organization, with 230 centers in 90 countries. The orga-
nization is dedicated to providing "practical solutions to people with life-controlling
problems," notably drugs and alcohol, through religious activity.

Zonta Club of Nassau
P.O. Box N-868
Nassau, The Bahamas
Zonta is a women's service club that created the AIDS Foundation of the Bahamas
in 1992.

Selected Bibliography

Art/Music/Dance. 2007. About the Bahamas, Local Customs, the Islands of the
Bahamas. http://www.bahamas.com/bahamas/about/general.aspx?sectionid=
23148&level=2.
Association of Religion Data Archives. 2006. The Bahamas. http://www.thearda
.com/internationalData/countries/Country_17_1.asp. Accessed April 20, 2007.
The Bahamas Guide. (n.d.) Bahamas Facts and Figures, Religion, Faith and God in
the Bahamas. http://www.thebahamasguide.com/facts/religion.htm.
Bahamian History Online. Personalities in Bahamian Education. http://www
.bahamasnationalarchives.bs/Bahamian_Educators/Educational%20Resources_
Bahamian%20Educators.htm.
The Body: The Complete HIV/AIDS Resource. 2005. "President Bill Clinton Praises
Bahamas for its HIV/AIDS Progress," February 8. http://www.thebody.com/
content/art25416.html. Accessed April 20, 2007.
Central Intelligence Agency. 2007. The World Factbook, The Bahamas. http://
www.cia.gov/cia/publications/factbook/geos/bf.html#Econ. Accessed April 10,
2007.
Choike.org. 2006. Abortion Legislation in Latin America and the Caribbean. October
2006. http://www.choike.org/nuevo_eng/informes/5010.html. Accessed April
20, 2007.
Dean, Stephen, Assistant Superintendent. 2005. "Royal Bahamas Police Target Urban
Renewal." *Gazette* 67, no. 1. http://www.gazette.rcmp-grc.gc.ca/article-en.
html?category_id=55&article_id=104. Accessed April 20, 2007.

Dunn, Leith L. 2002. *The Bahamas: The Situation for Children in the Worst Forms of Child Labor in a Tourism Economy: A Rapid Assessment, December 2002.* Port of Spain, Trinidad: ILO Subregional Office for the Caribbean.

Emergency Disaster Data Base (EMDAT). 2006. Bahamas: Country Profiles—Natural Disasters. http://www.em-dat.net/disasters/Visualisation/profiles/countryprofile.php. Accessed December 5, 2006.

Employment Act 2001. http://www.lexbahamas.com/Employment%20Act%202001.pdf. Accessed April 20, 2007.

Fielding, William J., and Jeannie Gibson. 2005. National Report on Higher Education in The Commonwealth of the Bahamas, prepared for UNESCO, IESALC, May 2005, revised November 2005. http://www.iesalc.unesco.org.ve/programas/nacionales/bahamas/national%20report%20bahamas.pdf. Accessed April 15, 2007.

Government of the Bahamas. 2005. Press Releases: "April to Be Observed as Child Protection Month." http://www.bahamas.gov.bs/bahamasweb2/home.nsf/a2adf3d1baf5cc. Accessed December 8, 2006.

———. About the Bahamas, The Commonwealth of the Bahamas. 2005. http://www.bahamas.gov.bs/bahamasweb2/home.nsf. Accessed December 4, 2006.

———. Department of Labour, The Commonwealth of the Bahamas. 2005. http://www.bahamas.gov.bs/bahamasweb2/home.nsf/vContentW/67925557D9088D0906256ED0007E9C86. Accessed December 8, 2006.

———. Department of Statistics, The Commonwealth of the Bahamas. 2005. http://www.bahamas.gov.bs/bahamasweb2/home.nsf/vContentW/7F1F4F18B3F300C406256ED100726406. Accessed December 4, 2006.

———. Department of Tourism, The Commonwealth of the Bahamas. 2006. Bahamas Film Commission, 2006. http://www.bahamas.gov.bs/bahamasweb2/home. Accessed December 6, 2006.

———. Ministry of Health, National Insurance, and Public Information, The Commonwealth of the Bahamas. 2005. http://www.bahamas.gov.bs/bahamasweb2/home.nsf/vContentW/9BD111B3C248696D8525708100524D38. Accessed December 11, 2006.

———. Ministry of Public Service, The Commonwealth of the Bahamas. 2005. http://www.bahamas.gov.bs/bahamasweb2/home.nsf/vContentW/F1EC04BE893B563D8525716F004F2291. Accessed December 4, 2006.

———. Ministry of Social Services and Community Development, The Commonwealth of the Bahamas. 2005. http://www.bahamas.gov.bs/bahamasweb2/home.nsf/vContentW/FBDC348C7DE5F13806256F0000705889!OpenDocument&Highlight=0,social%20services. Accessed December 5, 2006.

Hahnlen, Nicole C., Mashawn S. Rosado, Kristin A. Capozzi, and Raeann R. Hamon. 1997. *Mothering in the Bahamas: A Student Ethnography.* ERIC Document #ED417004.

International Labor Organization. 1998. ILO Declaration on the Fundamental Principles and Rights at Work. 86th Session, Geneva, June 1998. http://www.ilo.org/dyn/declaris/DECLARATIONWEB.static_jump?var_language=EN&var_pagename=DECLARATIONTEXT. Accessed April 18, 2007.

Interparliamentary Union. 2007. Women in National Parliaments: World Classification, Situation as of 28 February 2007. http://www.ipu.org/wmn-e/classif.htm. Accessed March 30, 2007.

McCartney, Donald M. 2004. *Bahamian Culture and Factors which Impact upon It.* Pittsburgh, PA: Dorrance Publishing Co., Inc.

Ministry of Education, Science, and Technology. The Bahamas National Education Statistics Digest 2005–2006. http://www.bahamseducation.com/Media/Publications/bnsd.pdf. Accessed April 4, 2007.

———. 2005. National Examinations Results. 2005. http://www.bahamaseducation.com/Media/Publications/BGCSE%20Exam%20Results%202005.pdf. Accessed April 1, 2006. http://www.bahamaseducation.com/Resources/Examinations%20&%20Assessments/National%20Examinations%20Results%202005.pdf. Accessed April 1, 2007.

Mitchell, Harold Paton. 1972. *Caribbean Patterns: A Political and Economic Study of the Contemporary Caribbean*. 2nd ed. New York: Wiley.

Moore, James E. 1988. *Pelican Guide to the Bahamas*. Gretna, LA: Pelican Publishing Co.

National Geographic Society. 2004. Bahamas, National Geographic Atlas of the World. 8th ed. http://www3.nationalgeographic.com/places/countries/country_bahamas.html. Accessed December 4, 2006.

Neely-Smith, Shane. 2003. "The Impact of HIV/AIDS on Bahamian Women: A Feminist Perspective." *Health Care for Women International* 24: 738–754.

Nowak, Barbara J. 1999. "Social Work in the Bahamas: A Profession Helps to Build a Nation." *International Social Work* 42, no. 2: 117–126.

Office of the United Nations High Commissioner for Human Rights. Implementation of the Convention on the Rights of the Child; Responses to Issues to Be Taken Up in Consideration of the Initial Report of the Bahamas (CRC/C/8/Add50). http://www.ohchr.org/English/bodfies/crc/docs/AdvanceVersions/CRC.C.RESP.BHS.doc. Accessed April 10, 2007.

———. Committee on the Rights of the Child. 2004. Consideration of Reports Submitted by State Parties under Article 44 of the Convention, Initial Reports of State Parties Due in 1993, Bahamas [5 June 2003]. http://www.unhchr.ch/tbs/doc.nsf/(Symbol)/CRC.C.8.Add.50.En?OpenDocument. Accessed April 10, 2006.

———. 2005. Consideration of Reports Submitted by State Parties under Article 44 of the Convention. Concluding Observations: The Bahamas, March 31, 2005. http://www.ohchr.org/english/bodies/crc/docs/AdvanceVersions/CRC.C.RESP.BHS.doc. Accessed April 10, 2006.

Pan American Health Organization. Bahamas: Health Situation Analysis and Trend Summary. http://www.paho.org/English/DD/AIS/cp_044.htm.

Research and Support Subcommittee of the National Education Conference. 2005. The System of Education in The Commonwealth of The Bahamas. A status report prepared for the 18th National Education Conference, July 3–7, 2005.

Reuters Foundation. 2006. AlertNet: Alerting Humanitarians to Emergencies. Bahamas. http://www.alertnet.org/db/cp/bahamas.htm. Accessed December 6, 2006.

Rolle, James O. 2003. "Art Forms in Junkanoo," December 10. *The Nassau Guardian*. http://www.thenassauguardian.net/print/375312173220402.php.

Smith, Larry. 2005. "Fixing our Failing Schools." The Nassau Institute. http://www.nassauinstitute.org/wmview.php?ArtID=540. Accessed April 20, 2007.

Solcom House. Religion. http://www.solcomhouse.com/religion.htm. Accessed April 20, 2007.

Sullivan, Mark, P. 1991. "The Bahamas." Chapter 2A: General Information, Countries of the World: A CD-ROM Encyclopedia. http://www.highbeam.com/doc/1P1-28383288.html. Accessed December 4, 2006.

Thurston, Gladstone. 2005. Government of the Bahamas. Press Release, "Bahamas a Model in the Fight against AIDS," August 27, 2005. http://www.bahamas. gov.bs/bahamasweb2/home.nsf/a2adf3d1baf5cc6e06256f03005ed59c/58d55 06a80fa2bbf8525706e00554353!OpenDocument. Accessed April 19, 2007.

UNAIDS, Joint United Nations Program on HIV/AIDS. 2006. Report on the Global AIDS Epidemic 2006. UNAIDS, May. http://www.unaids.org/en/ HIV_data/2006GlobalReport/default.asp. Accessed April 10, 2007.

United Nations Children Fund (UNICEF). 2005. *State of the World's Children 2006.* http://www.unicef.org/sowc06. Accessed December 8, 2006.

———. At a Glance: Bahamas. http://www.unicef.org/infobycountry/bahamas.html. Accessed March 29, 2007.

United Nations Development Programme. 2005. Human Development Report. http://hdr.undp.org/reports/global/2005/. Accessed December 5, 2006.

United Nations Educational, Scientific, and Cultural Organization (UNESCO). Institute for Statistics. Education in the Bahamas. http://www.uis.unesco .org/prifles/EN/EDU/countryProfile_en.aspx?code=440. Accessed March 31, 2007.

United Nations Statistics Division, Demographic and Social Statistics. 2006. Statistics and Indicators on Women and Men. http://unstats.un.org/UNSD/ demographic/products/indwm/ww2005/tab5c.htm.

University of Minnesota Human Rights Library. 1989. Convention on the Rights of the Child. http://www1.umn.edu/humanrts/instree/k2crc.htm. Accessed December 4, 2006.

U.S. Department of State, Bureau of Democracy, Human Rights, and Labor. 2002. Country Reports on Human Rights Practices, The Bahamas. http://www .state.gov/g/drl/rls/hrrpt/2002/18318.htm. Accessed December 6, 2006.

———. 2006. Bahamas, International Religious Freedom Report 2006. http:// www.state.gov/g/drl/rls/irf/2006/71447.htm. Accessed April 20, 2007.

U.S. Department of State, Bureau of Western Hemisphere Affairs. 2007. Background Notes: The Bahamas. http://www.state.gov/r/pa/ei/bgn/1857.htm. Accessed April 21, 2007.

Urwick, James. 2002. "The Bahamian Educational System: A Case Study in Americanization." *Comparative Education Review* 46, no. 2: 157–182.

3

BARBADOS

Christine Barrow

NATIONAL PROFILE

The small-island developing state of Barbados is located midway along the chain of Caribbean islands. The flat landscape along with small size, only 432 square kilometers, contrasts with the volcanic mountain terrain of neighboring islands and has facilitated an island-wide, integrated pattern of development. These physical features, combined with a consistent record of stable government and social order, have placed the country among the more developed in the region.

Barbados achieved independence from Britain in 1966 and has adopted a system of parliamentary democracy, with two major political parties and elections under universal suffrage constitutionally due every five years. On the Human Development Index of the United Nations Development Programme (UNDP), Barbados is placed at 31, thereby qualifying for "high human development" status and ranking as the most developed nation within the Caribbean region. A more sensitive indicator is the Commonwealth Vulnerability

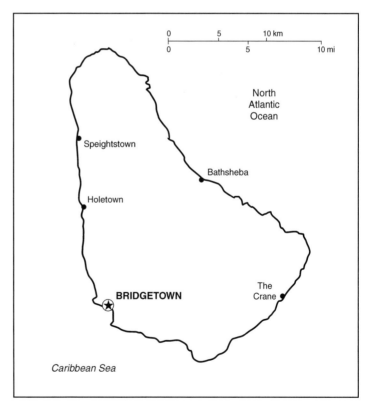

Table 3.1.
Basic Indicators for Barbados

Total population 2006	270,000
Population under age 15, 2004 (% of total)	19.3
Population ages 65 and over, 2004 (% of total)	10.1
Total fertility rate, 2000–2005 (births per woman)	1.5
Life expectancy at birth, 2004 (years)	74.9
Adult literacy rate, 2004 (% ages 15 and older)	99.4
GDP per capita, 2004 (PPP US$)	15,720
Poverty, 2004 (% population living below poverty line)	13.9
Population with sustainable access to improved water source, 2004 (%)	100
Population with sustainable access to improved sanitation, 2004 (%)	100

Source: United Nations Development Programme (2006). GDP, Gross Domestic Product; PPP, purchasing parity power.

Index (CVI) based on a broader range of criteria and assessing vulnerability according to the three critical indicators: lack of diversification, export dependence, and the impact of natural disasters. Significantly, the analysis showed that "small states were systematically more vulnerable than larger countries, irrespective of their incomes" (Easter 1999, 407). Nevertheless, on this scale Barbados was ranked as "higher medium vulnerability" (Easter 1999).

Modern-day Barbados emerged from a heritage of plantation sugar production under slavery to become an economy based on tourism and international services with some contribution from manufacturing and agriculture. However, an estimated 13.9 percent of the population lives below the poverty line (United Nations Development Programme 2006), and the country also experiences the symptoms of social decay that accompany development including increasing crime and violence, much of it related to drug abuse and trafficking, and the appearance of "gangs" of unemployed youths, chronic lifestyle diseases, community and family fragmentation, declining social capital, and social exclusion.

The population has stabilized and the country has entered the final phase of demographic transition with a population of 270,000 in 2006, a reduced proportion of children, and an increasing cohort of elderly persons (see Table 3.1). Residents are predominantly of African and mixed origin with a small group, approximately 4 percent, of European extraction. With a population density of over 600 per square kilometer the country is, however, among the most heavily populated in the world.

During the colonial period, declining mortality rates threatened a population explosion, but migration acted as a safety valve. Critical to population control in the later years of that era was the establishment of the Barbados Family Planning Association in the mid-1950s. This was followed by the passage of the Medical Termination of Pregnancy Act of 1983, under which abortion became lawful. In the three decades up to the 1980s, the total fertility rate per woman declined from 4.2 to 2.1, and today it stands at 1.5. The Barbados record is acknowledged as a model of fertility control in the region. Success has been attributed to the easy access to information and contraceptive distribution, relatively high levels of literacy and education among both men and women, the expansion of employment opportunities, and the absence of strong religious resistance since the country is predominantly Anglican, not Catholic (Nag 1971). But perhaps the most important factor was the positive response to contraceptive use by young women. While their mothers and grandmothers viewed early and continuous child bearing as inevitable and motherhood as their role in life, today's generation are more likely to view early and regular pregnancies as a deterrent to social mobility and a perpetuation of persistent poverty (Handwerker 1989, 112–113).

> **KEY FACTS – BARBADOS**
>
> Population: 280,946 (July 2007 est.)
> Infant mortality rate: 11.55 deaths/1,000 live births (2007 est.)
> Life expectancy at birth: 74 years (2004 est.)
> Literacy rate: 99.4 percent (2004 est.)
> Net primary school enrollment/attendance: 97 percent (2000–2005)
> Internet users: 160,000 (2005)
> People living with HIV/AIDS: 2700 (2005 est.)
> Children living with HIV/AIDS: >100 (2005 est.)
> Human Poverty Index (HPI-1) Rank: 5 (2006)
>
> *Sources*: CIA World Factbook: Barbados. https://www.cia.gov/cia/publications/factbook/geos/bb.html. April 17, 2007; UNICEF. At a Glance: Barbados–Statistics. http://www.unicef.org/infobycountry/barbados_statistics.html. April 24, 2007; World Health Organization (WHO): UNAIDS/WHO Global HIV/AIDS Online Database. "Epidemiological Fact Sheets on HIV/AIDS and Sexually Transmitted Diseases: Barbados." http://www.who.int/GlobalAtlas/predefinedReports/EFS2006/index.asp?str SelectedCountry=BB. December 2006; United Nations Development Programme (UNDP) Human Development Report 2006–Barbados. http://hdr.undp.org/hdr2006/statistics/countries/data_sheets/cty_ds_BRB.html. April 26, 2007; Child Care Board, Government of Barbados.

The Ministry of Social Transformation coordinates and regulates the initiatives of three main agencies: the Welfare Department, the National Assistance Board, and the Child Care Department. The latter provides care and protection for vulnerable children in residential Children's Homes and other centers, supervises and regulates private daycare services, provides counseling and other supports for children in need, and supervises the fostering and adoption of children. With the government assuming this overall responsibility, nongovernmental organizations (NGOs) for children have not been a feature of the Barbadian landscape, the only major one being Parent Education for Development in Barbados (PAREDOS), which provides parenting education and support services.

OVERVIEW

The appearance of childhood as a distinct phase in the life cycle is relatively recent worldwide and even more so in the Caribbean. Under slavery and indentured labor, family life and childhood were virtually nonexistent. Those children that did manage to survive (infant and child mortality rates were extremely high) were earning their keep in agricultural and domestic work from the age of five years. By the time they were ten years old, they graduated to full plantation labor as members of the so-called Third Gang (Beckles 1989).

Gradually over the latter half of the 1800s, education spread to the wider population and children were relocated into a school environment, although child labor persisted illegally for over a century. The social history of childhood in Barbados is still to be researched and documented. But the information we do have reveals the paradox of deplorable social and domestic conditions of family life, along with the positive value of children within the home where they were loved, desired, and the center of attention. A family was empty without children and, for both women and men, parenthood was centered in social identity (Greenfield 1966). In the last two generations or so, adolescence has also emerged as a distinct life-cycle phase. In other words, adult status as experienced through employment, pregnancy, and parenting has been postponed.

On October 9, 1990, Barbados ratified the United Nations Convention on the Rights of the Child (CRC) without entering any reservations, thereby committing the country to all of its stipulations. The CRC seeks not only to ensure children's rights to provisions in health, education, and welfare, and to protection from harm and danger, but it also advances the agenda for children from charity and welfare by advocating for their participation. This is translated into the right to express opinions and to be heard, to freedom of expression and access to information, and to freedom of association. Accordingly, the orthodox construct of children as incapable, passive, and dependent is replaced by one that elevates them to the status of social actors.

Of major importance in child survival and development are provisions in health and education. Between 1951 and 1955, the infant mortality rate in Barbados was reported to be the highest in the region at 132.8 and was attributed to the outdated structure and stigma of public health services (Lowenthal 1957, 460–466). Interventions in hygiene and sanitation and an improved public health system reduced the rate sharply in the years that followed.

The provision and expansion of education, first at the primary level and then at the secondary level, has been a remarkable achievement in Barbados. Coupled with the high level of demand from parents for an education for their children as an avenue to employment and social mobility, this resulted in high enrollment ratios from as early as the 1930s. The Anglican Church played an important role by building and operating primary schools, though their motives might have been somewhat suspect—to reinforce obedience and servitude rather than facilitate the advancement and development of the ex-slave population. By the mid-1960s, the early elite provisions at the secondary level had been expanded by government under the banner of "free secondary education for all" as an independence promise.

EDUCATION

The Education Act, amended in 1992, makes education compulsory for all children up to the age of sixteen years, and Barbados boasts a proud record of near universal coverage for both boys and girls at the primary and secondary levels (see Table 3.2). Today, free education is provided at all levels within the system. Distributed throughout the country, fifteen day nurseries and several preschools have been established by the government at a highly subsidized cost to cater mainly to the children of low-income working women. A range of private facilities for daycare and early childhood education are also available, all of them inspected, licensed, and registered, although they are of varying quality. Primary education is provided privately and also by government. The transition from primary to secondary school is still determined by a screening test—the Common Entrance Examination—despite official and public concern that it traumatizes young children. The exam is known locally as the "screaming test" and labels children as failures at an early age.

Virtually all secondary schools are government-operated, though there is a marked hierarchical distinction in quality and resources between the four so-called top schools with sixth form facilities and those at the bottom of the scholarly ladder. At the tertiary level, there are four main institutions providing academic, technical, and vocational education, including one of the three campuses of the University of the West Indies.

Table 3.2.
Child Indicators for Barbados

Infant mortality rate, 2005 (per 1,000 live births)	11
Child mortality rate, 2005 (per 1,000 live births)	12
Maternal mortality rate, 1990–2005, (per 100,000 live births)	0
Infants with low birth weight, 1996–2005 (%)	11
Children underweight for age, 1996–2005 (% under 5)	6
Births attended by skilled personnel, 1996–2005 (%)	98
Immunization coverage	
DPT (diphtheria, pertussis, tetanus)	97
Polio	91
Measles	93
HepB3 (hepatitis)	92
Net primary school enrollment ratio, 2000–2005 (%)	
Boys	98
Girls	97
Net secondary school enrollment ration, 2000–2005 (%)	
Boys	93
Girls	98

Source: United Nations Children's Fund (2006a).

It is notable that, even at this level, government continues to provide free tuition, despite budgetary constraints and the worldwide trend toward fee payment for tertiary education even in developed countries.

There is, however, a deep concern over gender disparities and the poor academic performance of boys as measured by attrition rates, examination failure, and declining levels of functional literacy. Young black males from the poorer sections of society are most at risk within the system (Layne and Kutnick 2001). Table 3.2 shows the gender imbalance in enrollment rates that has appeared at the secondary level. Violence within schools is also reported to be on the increase. A recent survey conducted with a stratified sample of 521 secondary school students revealed that half considered school to be an unsafe place, almost two-thirds had witnessed a violent incident at school, and 60 percent reported at least weekly fights at school (Barbados 2005).

Education for children with disabilities is provided in special units within mainstream schools and also in specialized schools. Concern has, however, been expressed that the focus has been on providing separate services for children with disabilities, rather than in accordance with a policy of social inclusion in mainstream educational facilities (United Nations Children's Fund 2006b, 13).

In sum, the educational system has pride of place in Barbados as the principal social institution providing the poor with the wherewithal for social mobility and reshaping the rigid race and class stratification of slavery and colonialism. In specific ways, however, the system continues to reflect and even reinforce social inequalities and to marginalize certain sectors of the population, such as those with more severe forms of disability.

PLAY AND RECREATION

Provisions for children's play and recreation in the home, school, and community have been expanded during the last generation. Games and toys are more evident in homes, and children's television programming is slotted on a daily basis during after-school hours and on Saturday mornings, though very few programs are of Caribbean origin. Play parks have appeared in communities and a variety of sporting clubs and organizations have been set up, primarily by private agencies, catering to a wide range of physical activities from tennis to horseback riding, chess to karate. All primary and secondary schools have access to sporting facilities and are mandated to schedule sports and games on their timetables. As students approach examinations, however, the time dedicated to these activities gives way to academic lessons. Of note also is the recent initiative on the part of government known as the Education Sector Enhancement Programme. Designed essentially to prepare young people for the twenty-first century, the program highlights the infusion of information technology into the curriculum.

But the importance of stimulation and play, especially in early childhood, as expressed in the CRC has not penetrated into local cultural constructs of childhood or patterns of socialization and parent–child interaction, especially between parents and their children. Parenting is still defined in terms of care, protection, discipline, and learning. The escalating levels of crime and violence in communities confines many boys and girls to their own homes and yards, and the children of overburdened single parents spend much of their out-of-school time indoors and in front of television and computer screens. In schools, academic activities are given clear priority and many so-called extracurricular activities are squeezed into break and after-school periods. The rhetoric that expresses the link between a healthy body and a healthy mind is often heard, but is yet to be translated into childhood.

CHILD LABOR

In sharp contrast to the past, today's children are protected from child labor, legally and socially (see Table 3.3). Insofar as children do work, this does not take the form of child labor in factory and large-scale commercial enterprises, but there is an established cultural practice, among poorer families in particular, of children helping out in small farm, domestic, and informal sector activities. Summer jobs and assistance with chores are identified as culturally acceptable work for children and are perceived as important to socialization.

FAMILY

The term "matrifocality" or female-centeredness captures the essence of Afro-Caribbean family structure. This characteristic has been variously attributed to African matrilineal patterns, the devastating effects of slavery

Table 3.3.
Age Stipulations by Law for Barbados

Minimum age for leaving school	16
Minimum age for employment	16/18[a]/15[b]
Parental duty to support	18
Age used to define child abuse	16
Age of sexual consent	16
Minimum age for marriage	16[c]/18
Minimum age for criminal responsibility	7/11[d]
Age of majority under penal law	16

[a] Dangerous or unhealthy employment.
[b] Part-time employment.
[c] With parental consent.
[d] Age at which there is refutable presumption that the child is not responsible (the *doli incapax* rule).
Source: United Nations Children's Fund (2005).

on domestic life, high unemployment, and migration among men and, more recently, to dominant patterns of masculinity defining male space as outside the home and family. What it means in effect is that kinship relations are centered on women, that grandmothers, mothers and children form the backbone of the domestic group, and that children are raised within extended family networks of maternal relations encompassing grandparents, aunts, uncles, siblings and half-siblings, and cousins. Not surprising then, are the high proportions of female-headed households in Barbados, estimated to comprise 44.5 percent of the total in 2000 (Barbados 2000).

Also characteristic of these families is the strong and enduring bond between mother and child, in comparison with which conjugal relationships tend to be unstable and short-lived. Marriage is uncommon, with only 22.1 percent of women aged fifteen years and over in marital unions (Barbados 2000) and many women in either "visiting" or "common-law" relationships. In the former, the woman remains in her family home and is visited by her partner. Children are often born to the union, but paternal support, although mandated by law, is usually irregular and inadequate. In the latter, the couple is co-resident and may in later years be married, often as a result of pressure from the children of the union.

From the perspective of childhood, the consequences of this familial pattern are that the majority of children are born out of wedlock and that fathers are absent or play a peripheral role in their lives, whether because they live elsewhere, have migrated, or have denied paternity. Barbados led the way in the Caribbean in passing the Status of Children (Reform) Act in 1979 to abolish "illegitimacy" and mandate unequivocally that all children, whatever the circumstances of their birth, are equal in the eyes of the law. Legislation in the form of the Succession Act was also on the books since 1975 to protect the inheritance rights of children born out of wedlock, as well as the Maintenance Act and Family Law Act to mandate financial support from fathers for children up to the age of eighteen years. Prior to the passage of these acts, the proportion of children labeled as "illegitimate" hovered at around 70 percent and, although there was no social stigma in their communities (Manyoni 1977), as "filius nullius" or the child of no one, they suffered discrimination under the law and in school, the church, and other formal social settings.

The correlate of matrifocality in family life has been described as "male marginality," but there has been a notable enhancement of the ideology and practice of fatherhood within the last generation or so. In contrast to their narrowly defined role in the past, which merely required fathers to provide financial support and occasional heavy-handed authority, today's men are increasingly imaging and practicing fatherhood to include childcare and socialization—"to be there for my children" (Barrow 1998). However, matrifocality also correlates with the phenomenon of the "outside child." Large numbers of children are either born to adolescents and young adults who subsequently separate or are the result of extramarital relationships. They remain with their mothers and are effectively without fathers, many of whom will have formed stable conjugal relationships and co-residential families.

The persistently brittle nature of the conjugal relationship shows up in the escalating divorce rates. The Barbados Family Law Act of 1981 shifted the basis for divorce from fault to mutual consent by stipulating "irretrievable breakdown" as the sole ground. Paradoxically, although there has been an increase in the marriage rate, divorces have also risen and quite significantly. From an average of 5.4 per 1,000 of the population over the last century, the marriage rate rose to an average of 11.5 between 2000 and 2005. Meanwhile, divorce has climbed steadily. From an average of 192 per year during the 1980s, the number has risen during the last ten years (1995–2004) from 393 to 507, with the divorce rate per 100 marriages reaching 15.73 (Barbados, various years). There is some indication that this may correlate with a cultural redefinition of conjugality from the previous emphasis on individual autonomy, a division of labor and place between spouses, and attachment to one's own kin group, to new and more intense expectations of intimacy, romantic love, togetherness, fidelity, and commitment for the future.

In 2004, a total of 352 children were affected by the divorce of their parents. No information on the ages of these children is available, but the fact that in over half of the cases the divorcing wives were under the age of forty-five suggests that significant numbers of the children might be quite young. Although the act gives priority to the interests of children as "the first and paramount concern" during divorce proceedings, a local sociologist refers to the negative impact:

> The major reactions among children of divorce in Barbados vary with age and level of maturity. They run the full range from guilt to anxiety, fear of abandonment, sleeping problems, eating disorders, hyperactivity, withdrawal and physical development regression. These problems are exacerbated by the fact that children are often used as pawns in the divorce proceedings such as when parents take opposite sides in relation to them and refuse to compromise in their interest. (Carter 1994, 36)

HEALTH

Barbados provides free health care, including dental and eye care and prescription medication, for all children up to the age of sixteen years. Much has been accomplished in maternal and child health. As Table 3.2 shows, infant and child mortality and maternal mortality have been reduced to levels on par with developed countries, all deliveries are attended by professionals, low birth weight and underweight children are uncommon, and immunization coverage is high. The provision of antiretroviral drugs for all residents of Barbados who are HIV-positive has cut the mortality rate from AIDS-related infections by half and, therefore, significantly reduced the number of children orphaned by the disease. Additionally, the introduction of an AZT program in 1995 has lowered mother-to-child transmission (MTCT) by 82 percent. However, concerns have been expressed over long waiting periods in public health clinics and the uncaring and judgmental attitudes of many healthcare professionals.

With most serious infectious diseases brought under control, health interventions are giving priority attention to chronic lifestyle problems, such as diabetes mellitus and heart and cardiovascular disease. The child malnutrition of yesteryear has virtually disappeared, but there is today, even among young children, growing evidence of obesity attributable to sedentary lifestyles and the consumption of junk food.

A cause for serious concern is the spread of HIV infection to adolescents. A total of 38 percent of all cases of AIDS has occurred among persons aged fifteen to thirty-four years. Given the relatively long incubation period of the virus before it develops into full-blown AIDS, estimated at anywhere between seven and fifteen years, it is clear that a large proportion of infected persons is contracting the virus during teenage years. Data for adolescents disaggregated by sex reveal an alarming trend among teenage girls. While males carry a higher rate of infection in the overall population, the reverse is apparent within the adolescent cohort. Using the cumulative total since 1984, girls between the ages of ten and nineteen years outnumber boys in that age group by a ratio of 2.2 to 1 for HIV infection and 2.0 to 1 for AIDS cases.

Rates of teenage motherhood have continued to decline and have averaged 16 percent of all births since the late 1980s. However, teenage abortions in the public hospital amount to nearly one-quarter of the total. Rates of teenage motherhood may thereby be reduced, but it is apparent that adolescent girls continue to be exposed to unprotected sex, pregnancy, and HIV infection.

Health and Family Life Education and guidance counseling, including lifestyle information and advice, are provided in all secondary schools and increasingly at the primary level. The result is evident in the high levels of knowledge about health, sexuality, and safe sexual practices within the adolescent population (Carter 2001, 2004). But surveys conducted with adolescents and young persons have also exposed a disconnect between knowledge and practice and alarming evidence of high-risk sexual activity (Barrow forthcoming). In one sample of secondary school students, 33 percent had been sexually active and, of these, 50 percent claimed that sexual intercourse had occurred before the age of thirteen, while 25 percent had been active with more than one partner (Ellis et al. 1990). This and other studies expose subcultural patterns of early experimentation and initiation of sexual activity, short-term relationships and multiple partnering both serial and concurrent, and casual one-night-stand liaisons (Carter 2001, 29; Ellis et al. 1990, 7–8). It has been found, generally, that adolescents who start having sex early are involved with high-risk partners and multiple partners. Early sexual debut is, therefore, a critical risk activity.

Of greatest concern is the prevalence among adolescents of unsafe sexual practice, in this context meaning sex without condom use. Among secondary school children who were sexually active, 63 percent had practiced sex without condoms (Ellis et al. 1990). A more recent survey identified a disturbing proportion (45.8 percent) of young persons aged fifteen to twenty-nine years who admitted to inconsistent condom use, and an alarming 21.9 percent of females who "*never* used condoms" (emphasis in original), compared with 12.2 percent of the males (Carter 2001, 25, 30). This survey took the point further by reporting that condom usage was lowest among those who perceived themselves to be at risk of HIV infection (Carter 2001, 24).

It also appears that public opinion in Barbados is becoming less tolerant of alternative lifestyles and that stigma and discrimination may be growing, especially against men who have sex with men. The recent official recommendations for the decriminalization of homosexuality and also commercial sex work were emphatically rejected in a series of public town-hall meetings across the island. The resistance has been fueled by the growth of fundamentalist religious faiths.

The physical environment of Barbados is generally considered to be healthy and the provision of services such as electricity, transport and communication, garbage disposal, safe drinking water, and sanitation services virtually universal (see Table 3.1). The majority of dwelling units (74.6 percent) are privately owned, public housing is provided for the poor at a heavily subsidized rental rate, and district hospitals provide accommodation for the elderly who would otherwise be destitute. However, there is also evidence of dilapidated housing, especially among the elderly poor.

Public health services are accessible at the nation's central hospital and at polyclinics located across the island. The polyclinics provide a comprehensive program of promotive, preventive, curative, and rehabilitative services that center on children's health and well-being, including the following:

- Maternal and child health
- Family life development programs including family planning
- Ophthalmic and dental care primarily for children
- General medical care including hypertension, diabetes, and STI
- Laboratory, radiological, and pharmaceutical services
- Nutrition

- Community mental health
- Environmental health

Children with disabilities are provided for at the Children's Development Centre, which began as a volunteer organization, but now provides diagnosis, care, and treatment including physical, occupational, and speech therapy and primary health care to over 2,000 children.

LAWS AND LEGAL STATUS

The CRC has no force in law within the jurisdictions of the ratifying countries. Nevertheless, Barbados and other countries of the region had already implemented legal provisions to protect the rights of children. Most significant is the Status of Children (Reform) Act of 1979, mentioned earlier. In Section 3, the act states:

> The distinction at common law between the status of children born within or outside of marriage is abolished, and all children shall be of equal status; and a person is the child of his or her natural parents and his or her status as their child is independent of whether the child is born within or outside of marriage.

Section 6 states:

> This act applies to all children whether born before or after the commencement of this act and to all dispositions and instruments made after such commencement.

Minimum-age legislation to protect children has also been on the books since the colonial period (see Table 3.3). However, much is dated and continues to reflect the days when childhood was hardly recognized in the life cycle. For example, at the young age of eleven years a child is assumed to be criminally responsible.

Substance abuse, mainly of alcohol, marijuana, and "crack" cocaine has become more prevalent with increasing numbers of young men between fourteen and sixteen years appearing before the juvenile court on charges of abuse. If found guilty of this or any other offense, they may be sent to the Government Industrial School, to the compound for boys or that for girls, for up to five years or until they are nineteen years of age. If inmates are over the age of sixteen years and are in breach of the regulations of the school, they may be sent to the adult prison.

A critical point of concern is the slow and piecemeal process of law reform. Caribbean countries, including Barbados, have not drafted a comprehensive code for children and the law remains fragmented into several specific acts. This has prompted the response that "the legislation of the region does not adequately incorporate the 'general principles' recognized in the CRC (such as decisions made in the best interests of the child) nor the 'civil rights and freedoms' of children (such as the right to be heard in decisions affecting them)" (United Nations Children's Fund 2005, 16). Children as children and their rights are not centered in the laws of Barbados, and this has led to the perceptive conclusion that legislation does not focus on

> the ordinary child, but only the abused child, the abandoned child, the student, the school leaver, the 'outside child', the street child, the child prostitute, the delinquent, the child with a disability and so on. As a result most new laws do not address the needs of the whole child but rather a unidimensional child seen from the narrow perspective of some particular concern of society, i.e. ourselves as adults. It is an approach that continues to frame the child as a problem for society rather than an asset with rights to legal protection. Legislators and politicians thus far have not succeeded in putting the child at the center of law reform efforts concerning children. (United Nations Children's Fund 2005, 16)

RELIGIOUS LIFE

Barbados is still considered to be a religious society, with the majority of the population belonging to one of the approximately ninety Christian faiths on the island. The Anglican Church continues to be the largest denomination, though there has been an influx of fundamentalist faiths in recent years. Most children attend church and Sunday school, especially before they are teenagers, and daily Christian prayers and religious teaching are part of the school curriculum.

CHILD ABUSE AND NEGLECT

The children of Barbados and the wider Caribbean start life with a great advantage. They are wanted, loved, and cared for, described as a "joy" and a "precious gift." The notion of an "unwanted child" is alien to Caribbean cultures, and it would still be considered most odd for a woman or a man not to want children.

However, traditional patterns of child discipline have become the focus of official and public concern in recent years, especially since the ratification of the CRC. While the international movement for children abhors the physical punishment of children, local cultural practices continue to favor "beating," "lashing," and "flogging" that "still forms part of the 'tradition' of schools, the judicial system and the home" (United Nations Children's Fund 2006b, 2). Although the language generally overstates the severity of punishment actually administered and today's parents distinguish between the heavy hits of their own childhoods and their preference for "little slaps" and alternative disciplinary methods, several

Table 3.4.
Reported Cases of Child Abuse in Barbados, 1981–2005

Year	Physical abuse	Sexual abuse	Neglect	Emotional abuse	Abandonment
1982–1983	77	28	129	–	53
1983–1984	138	40	361	–	32
1984–1985	225	78	455	–	24
1985–1986	224	93	337	–	23
1986–1987	202	123	322	–	54
1987–1988	246	116	420	–	25
1988–1989	201	120	412	–	20
1989–1990	203	152	382	–	26
1990–1991	385	187	649	–	8
1991–1992	327	152	501	–	11
1992–1993	227	125	553	–	2
1993–1994	173	124	304	10	4
1994–1995	203	106	480	24	6
1995–1996	251	142	447	60	8
1996–1997	218	181	473	78	1
1997–1998	278	185	606	63	0
1998–1999	304	287	477	45	4
1999–2000	241	–	491	69	1
2000–2001	213	197	405	72	–
2001–2002	270	186	611	75	–
2002–2003	303	242	713	112	–
2003–2004	304	231	718	131	–
2004–2005	266	190	565	93	–

Source: Child Care Board, Government of Barbados.

child-rights advocates are pressing for change. They point to the authoritarian nature of the parent–child relationship, the silencing of children, the emphasis in child socialization on obedience and "good manners," and a "property mentality" among parents that allows them to deal with their children as they see fit (Le Franc 2001; Rock 2001).

Official records of child abuse and neglect are notoriously inaccurate. In Barbados, underreporting, of sexual abuse in particular, relates to family shame and denial and the fear on the part of children of the consequences if they reveal the incidents. In this context, in which physical punishment is the norm, cases of physical abuse are also often hidden from officialdom unless they become severe. Nevertheless, the staff of the Child Care Department attests to a growing recognition of the wrong of child abuse and a greater willingness of individuals to come forward and identify cases. Although reporting is not mandatory by law in Barbados, individuals can do so anonymously. This change in atmosphere, rather than any increase in the actual incidence of child abuse may, therefore, explain the official statistics (see Table 3.4). These figures reveal fluctuations in child abuse, but no consistent decline in any category. Among the children affected, there is little distinction between the number of boys and girls in cases of emotional abuse, neglect, or even physical abuse where, in 2004–2005, 45.8 percent were girls. However, girls constitute the overwhelming proportion of victims of sexual abuse, 94.2 percent in 2004–2005.

GROWING UP IN THE TWENTY-FIRST CENTURY

As a small-island developing state, Barbados has accomplished much in the area of economic growth with social development and, in the process, has overcome the historical legacy of slavery, colonialism, racism, and social inequality. The country has a reputation within the region for forward-thinking legal reform, especially in family law, to protect the rights of women and children. In addition, all children have benefited from programs in education, health, and social welfare and, despite the persistence of child abuse including the culturally condoned practice of physical punishment, most are protected from violence, harm, and danger. There remain, however, two principal areas of concern, namely the impact of poverty and the denial of participatory rights.

Children bear the brunt of poverty. Poverty is the greatest obstacle to their survival and wholesome development, hence the insistence by the United Nations Children's Fund (UNICEF) on development "with a human face" (Cornia, Jolly, and Stuart 1988) and that "poverty reduction begins with children" (United Nations Children's Fund 2000). In Barbados, the main indicator of children's vulnerability is food insecurity, followed by the chronic illness of a parent, both of which are closely linked to poverty as a cause and also an effect (United Nations Children's Fund 2006b). Although widespread social destitution is a phenomenon of the past, so-called "pockets" of poverty persist and have multifaceted outcomes for children—from abuse to child labor, to poor health and inadequate education, to adolescent motherhood and single parenting. Children are most at risk when the reach and quality of state social services along with those of NGOs and faith-based organizations are inadequate, when extended family and community social capital shrinks, and when the efforts of families fall short of providing for their needs and rights. Most vulnerable are the children of adolescent mothers who are themselves at risk and parent single-handedly.

From being silent objects of concern, the property of their parents, the beneficiaries of adult benevolence, and minors in need of guidance and control, children have been re-imaged within the CRC as active subjects with a critical voice in their own development. But very few societies have fully embraced this new global construct of childhood. In Barbados, children's rights to participation are yet to be fully realized, and for the region as a whole the Caribbean office of UNICEF has concluded that "children are to be 'seen and not heard', there is little allowance for their point of view, and they are simply expected to adhere to and obey directives from their parents" (United Nations Children's Fund 1998, 35). Play and stimulation are of secondary importance to academic learning and discipline; there is evidence that parents, teachers, and other adults cling to an outdated image of children's incapacity and dependency; and space is provided only for token participation, if at all. At worst, adult fears of escalating child and adolescent delinquency provokes a response that favors increasing control and sanctions, and the active participation of children is interpreted as a threat to the rightful authority of adults. Whether children are sentimentalized as innocent minors or criminalized as deviants, the end result is the denial of their right to participation in decisions that shape their own lives. Small beginnings towards the fuller participation of children are evident in research that increasingly hears and records children's voices (United Nations Children's Fund 2000) and in formal sessions such as Youth Parliaments. The participatory right of children is, however, still to be infused into the local cultural construct of childhood and into everyday practices in the family, school, church, and community.

RESOURCE GUIDE

Suggested Readings

Barrow, Christine, ed. 2001. *Children's Rights: Caribbean Realities.* Jamaica: Ian Randle Publishers. This volume brings together a collection of articles that describe and analyze the situation of children's rights in the Caribbean, giving a frank portrayal of the challenges encountered, including those shaped by cultural factors and poverty, in the implementation of the Convention on the Rights of the Child. Articles from various countries of the region devote attention to a range of pertinent issues, including the law and juvenile justice, health and nutrition, socialization and education, families and parenting. The quality of life of vulnerable groups including children of minority groups and those who are victims of physical and sexual abuse receive special attention.

———. 2001. "Contesting the Rhetoric of 'Black Family Breakdown' from Barbados." *Journal of Comparative Family Studies* 32, no. 3: 419–441. This article reviews, in historical perspective, and challenges the sociological literature that portrays the Afro-Caribbean family using a rhetoric of dysfunctionality and breakdown and, therefore, as responsible for a range of social ills from "unmannerly" children to "abandoned" elderly. Revisiting family and social problems in Barbados in relation to child discipline and abuse, adolescent sexuality and teenage pregnancy, divorce, and care of the elderly, the author proposes an alternative culturally appropriate perspective on family and kinship and more supportive social policy.

———. 2003. "Children and Social Policy in Barbados: The Unfinished Agenda of Child Abuse." *The Caribbean Journal of Social Work* 2: 36–53. After reviewing Barbados' record of achievement in child-centered social policy, the article turns attention to the unfinished business of child abuse, focusing specific attention on physical punishment in child socialization and the sexual abuse of adolescent girls. Noting that both practices are historically and culturally embedded, the recommendation is that the agenda for children move beyond their needs to contest and rethink ideological principles and cultural practices of childhood and adolescence, to re-enter family life and revisit relationships across gender and generation, and to adjust the balance between children's rights and the rights and responsibilities of adult caregivers.

Dicks, Barbara, ed. 2001. *HIV/AIDS and Children in the English Speaking Caribbean.* New York, London and Oxford: The Haworth Press, Inc. This Pan-Caribbean collection of articles on children, adolescents, and mothers presents information and analysis on a diversity of topics from social and demographic factors, knowledge/attitudes/practices, psychocultural factors, residential care, sexual risk-taking, the influence of popular music among adolescents, and policy interventions.

Massiah, Joycelin. 1983. *Women as Heads of Households in the Caribbean: Family Structure and Feminine Status.* Paris: UNESCO. In the Caribbean the incidence of female-headed households is high, constituting between 22 and 47 percent of the total. Demographic data supported by case-study evidence from Barbados confirm that the women who head these households are concentrated in low-paid, low-status occupations with no prospects. Valuable insights are also offered into the composition, problems, and survival strategies of these households. Of concern are the implications for children born and raised in the context of single parenting and poverty.

McDowell, Zanifa. 2000. *Elements of Child Law in the Commonwealth Caribbean.* Jamaica: University of the West Indies Press. This book provides a comprehensive, introductory review of laws relating to children across the Caribbean. With the need for law reform to bring the Caribbean in line with the articles of the United Nations Convention on the Rights of the Child, the author reviews a range of legislation, in both historical and contemporary perspective, in the areas of legitimacy, parental rights and duties, maintenance, succession, custody, adoption, and care and protection.

Web Sites

Barbados Council for the Disabled, http://www.barbadosdisabled.org.bb/.

The Barbados Family Planning Association, http://www.bfpa/.

Parent Education for Development in Barbados (PAREDOS), http://www.bajan.info/parados/.

Organizations and NGOs

Barbados Council for the Disabled
Harambee House
The Garrison
St. Michael
Phone: (246) 427-8136
Fax: (246) 427-5210

Barbados Family Planning Association
Bay Street
St. Michael
Phone: (246) 426-2027
Fax: (246) 427-6611
Email: bfpa@sunbeach.net

Child Care Board (Ministry of Social Transformation, Government of Barbados)
Fred Edghill Building
Cheapside
Bridgetown
Phone: (246) 426-2577 and (246) 429-3961
Fax: (246) 429-3497

Children's Development Centre
Jemmotts Lane
St. Michael
Phone: (246) 427-9514
Fax: (246) 427-7448

National Disabilities Unit
Hastings Towers
Hastings
Christ Church
Phone: (246) 228-2978/88/91
Fax: (246) 228-2979
Email: natdisability@sunbeach.net

Parent Education for Development in Barbados (PAREDOS)
4 St. Clair Gardens, Perry Gap
Roebuck Street
St. Michael
Phone: (246) 427-7777
Fax: (246) 427-0212
Email: paredos@hotmail.com

Selected Bibliography

Barbados. 2000. *Population and Housing Census.* Government of Barbados, Barbados Statistical Service.

———. 2005. *Report on Violence in Schools and Community Survey.* Government of Barbados, Ministry of Education, Youth and Sports.

———. Various years. *Report on the Registration Department.* Government of Barbados, The Registration Department of Barbados.

Barrow, Christine. 1998. "Masculinity and Family: Revisiting 'Marginality' and 'Reputation'." pp. 339–359 in *Portraits of a Nearer Caribbean: Gender Ideologies and Identities.* Edited by Christine Barrow. Jamaica: Ian Randle Publishers.

———. Forthcoming. "Adolescent Girls, Sexuality and HIV/AIDS in Barbados: The Case for Reconfiguring Research and Policy." *The Caribbean Journal of Social Work.*

Beckles, Hilary. 1989. *Natural Rebels: A Social History of Enslaved Black Women in Barbados.* London: Zed Books Ltd.

Carter, Richard. 1994. *Family Disruption and Dysfunction: Divorce and the Use of Social Agencies.* Paper prepared for the International Year of the Family Committee. Barbados.

———. 2001. *Report on the National KABP Survey on HIV/AIDS.* Barbados, Ministry of Education, Youth Affairs and Sport.

———. 2004. *Report on the Secondary Schools Sexual Behaviour Survey, 2003/2004.* Ministry of Education, Youth Affairs and Sports, Division of Youth Affairs, Barbados.

Cornia, Giovanni, Richard Jolly, and Frances Stuart, eds. 1988. *Adjustment with a Human Face.* Oxford: Clarendon Press.

Easter, Christopher. 1999. "Small States Development: A Commonwealth Vulnerability Index." *The Round Table* 351: 403–422.

Ellis, Henrick, et al. 1990. "A Knowledge, Attitude, Belief and Practices Survey in Relation to AIDS amongst Children Ages 11–16 Years Old in Barbados." *Bulletin of Eastern Caribbean Affairs* 16, no. 4&5: 1–12.

Greenfield, Sidney. 1966. *English Rustics in Black Skin: A Study of Modern Family Forms in a Pre-Industrial Society.* New Haven, CT: College and University Press.

Handwerker, Penn. 1989. *Women's Power and Social Revolution: Fertility Transition in the West Indies.* Newbury Park, CA: Sage Publications.

Layne, Anthony, and Peter Kutnick. 2001. "Secondary School Stratification, Gender, and Other Determinants of Academic Achievement in Barbados." *Journal of Education and Development in the Caribbean* 5, no. 2: 81–101.

Le Franc, Elsie. 2001. "Child Abuse in the Caribbean: Addressing the Rights of the Child." pp. 285–304 in *Children's Rights: Caribbean Realities.* Edited by Christine Barrow. Jamaica: Ian Randle Publishers.

Lowenthal, David. 1957. "The Population of Barbados." *Social and Economic Studies* 6, no. 4: 445–501.

Manyoni, Joseph. 1977. "Legitimacy and Illegitimacy: Misplaced Polarities in Caribbean Family Studies." *The Canadian Review of Sociology and Anthropology* 14, no. 4: 417–427.

Nag, Moni. 1971. "Patterns of Mating Behaviour, Emigration and Contraceptives as Factors Affecting Human Fertility in Barbados." *Social and Economic Studies* 20, no. 2: 111–133.

Rock, Letnie. 2001. "Child Abuse in Barbados." pp. 305–329 in *Children's Rights: Caribbean Realities.* Edited by Christine Barrow. Jamaica: Ian Randle Publishers.

United Nations Children's Fund (UNICEF). 1998. *The State of Eastern Caribbean Children 1998: Child Survival Protection and Development in Seven Caribbean Countries.* Barbados: UNICEF, Caribbean Area Office.

———. 2000. *Voices of Children and Adolescents in Latin America and the Caribbean: Regional Survey.* UNICEF, Regional Office for Latin America and the Caribbean.

———. 2005. *The Convention on the Rights of the Child Fifteen Years Later: The Caribbean.* Barbados: UNICEF Regional Office for Latin America and the Caribbean.

———. 2006a. *Women and Children: The Double Dividend of Gender Equality. The State of the World's Children, 2007.* New York: UNICEF.

———. 2006b. *A Study of Child Vulnerability in Barbados, St. Lucia and St. Vincent and the Grenadines.* Barbados: UNICEF Office for Barbados and the Eastern Caribbean, in association with the Governments of Barbados, St. Lucia and St. Vincent and the Grenadines.

United Nations Development Programme. 2006. *Beyond Security: Power, Poverty and the Global Water Crisis.* Human Development Report, 2006.

4

CANADA

Susie Veroff

NATIONAL PROFILE

Canada, from the Huron and Iroquois word *kanata*, meaning "village or settlement," is a confederation of ten provinces and three territories—a vast country stretching across North America from the Atlantic Ocean to the Pacific Ocean and north to the Arctic Ocean, with an area of 3,831,033 square miles (Tremblay 1988). This is slightly less than the area of the United States, its southern neighbor, but Canada has only a little more than one-tenth of its population, at just over 32 million. Children under the age of eighteen constitute 24 percent of this population; 51 percent are boys and 49 percent girls, and 88 percent of children live in an urban setting (Statistics Canada 2006a). Visible minorities in Canada represent 13.4 percent of the total population: Asian (10 percent), black or African origins (2.2 percent), Latino (0.7 percent), and others, including First Nations (0.5 percent). There are two official languages spoken in Canada, English (59.3 percent) and French (23.2 percent), but Italian (1.6 percent), German (1.5 percent), and

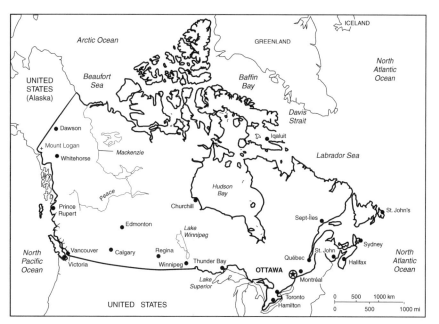

Cantonese (1.1 percent) are of note as well. In 2001, 250,640 people immigrated to Canada. Based on the Canada 2001 Census total population of 30,007,094 people, immigration represented 0.834 percent population growth that year (Statistics Canada 2001a). On a compounded basis, that immigration rate represents 8.7 percent population growth over 10 years, or 23.1 percent over 25 years (or 6.9 million people). Since 2001, immigration has ranged between 221,352 and 262,236 immigrants per annum (Citizenship and Immigration Canada 2005). According to *Canada's Immigration Program* (Dolin and Young 2004), Canada has the highest per capita immigration rate in the world. The three main official reasons given for this are: the social component, Canada facilitates family reunification; the humanitarian component, relating to refugees; and the economic component, attracting immigrants who will contribute economically and fill labor market needs.

Because of changes in the characteristics of Canada's population, particularly the rapidly rising median age, which was 37.8 in 2003 but should reach 41.2 in 2011, Canada has already changed from a child-centered society to one focused on the needs, health concerns, and spending priorities of baby-boomers (Canadian Social Trends 1994). Although Canadian legislation, policy strategies, tax measures, and new and enhanced programs would seem to consistently attempt to ensure the rights, well-being, and optimal development of children in Canada and even abroad, many issues concerning children are still in need of being addressed; for instance, poverty in general, but especially affecting single-parent families (Henripin 2000), Aboriginal children, who are the fastest growing population in Canada, and the increasing and very necessary immigrant population who are major contributors to a healthier demography but who have twice the average poverty as Canadian-born residents (Campaign 2000 2006).

Canada's federal system of government, with constitutional powers shared between the federal, provincial, and territorial governments, and the dual nature of its legal system, encompassing common law and civil law traditions, are two key elements that shape the way government decisions are made. In Canada, all levels of government and First Nations, along with parents, families, communities, and the voluntary and private sectors, play key roles in ensuring the well-being of children. The country's changing demographic profile also shapes the context for government action for children and families. With an average of 1.61 births per woman or 10.78 births per 1,000 population growth (Statistics Canada 2006), the government must pay more attention to the sectors of the population who are contributing to a higher birth rate: Aboriginal peoples and recent immigrants.

Federal, provincial, and territorial governments have acknowledged the need to develop an integrated approach to many issues encountered by children and families; one of these approaches is the National Children's

Agenda (NCA), a cooperative effort by governments in Canada to ensure that all Canadian children have the best opportunity to develop their potential through six important goals: child development; supporting parents and strengthening families; improving income security for families; providing early and continuous learning experiences; promoting healthy adolescent development; and creating safe, supportive, and violence-free communities (Sign On for Canada's Kids 2000).

Although Canada is a wealthy country, one in six children, or 1,071,000 children, still lives in poverty (Campaign 2000 2006). One reason so many children in Canada live in poverty is that the nature of family environments has changed. Although 85.9 percent of children grow up in homes with two parents, 14 percent live in single-parent or lone-parent families that for the most part are led by women and mothers (Department of Justice Canada). Women still tend to gain custody of children after a divorce or a separation. Canada has a divorce rate of 45 percent, one of the highest in the world, and of all single mothers with children, 31.9 percent live below the poverty line (Department of Justice Canada). In 1996, the Prime Minister and provincial Premiers identified child poverty as a national priority and work began by Social Services Ministers to develop an integrated child benefit. The result was the launch of the National Child Benefit (NCB). Single-parent families receive an average of $7,600 in federal monies per year, but working single-parent families have an average income of almost half of the national average, at around $29,485. The increase in daycare costs ($551 a month per child) for most provinces except Québec, which has government-subsidized day care, make the prospect of working seem painfully absurd to many single parents. The employment rate in Canada is 63.1 percent (Statistics Canada 2007), the unemployment rate is 5.9 percent, and there are roughly 12 percent more men employed than women.

Homelessness in Canada is viewed as a serious social problem. Canada is viewed by many as having far too high a number of homeless people, with some of the highest per capita rates of any developed nation (City of Toronto 2000). It is second on the list of countries with the highest homeless population in

---

KEY FACTS – CANADA

Population: 33,390,141 (July 2007 est.)
Infant mortality rate: 4.63 deaths/1,000 live births (2007 est.)
Life expectancy at birth: 80.34 years (2007 est.)
Literacy rate: 99 percent (2003 est.)
Net primary school enrollment/attendance: 99 percent (2000–2005)
Internet users: 21.9 million (2005)
People living with HIV/AIDS: 60,000 (2005 est.)
Human Poverty Index (HPI-2) Rank: 8

Sources: CIA World Factbook: Canada. https://www.cia.gov/cia/publications/factbook/geos/ca.html. April 17, 2007; UNICEF. At a Glance: Canada–Statistics. http://www.unicef.org/infobycountry/canada_statistics.html. April 24, 2007; World Health Organization (WHO): UNAIDS/WHO Global HIV/AIDS Online Database. "Epidemiological Fact Sheets on HIV/AIDS and Sexuality Transmitted Diseases: Canada." http://www.who.int/GlobalAtlas/predefinedReports/EFS2006/index.asp?str SelectedCountry=CA. December 2006; United Nations Development Programme (UNDP) Human Development Report 2006–Canada. http://hdr.undp.org/hdr2006/statistics/countries/data_sheets/cty_ds_CAN.html. April 26, 2007.

the developed world, trailing just behind the United States. One of the most important causes is the unavailability of low-income housing. The 1960s and 1970s also saw an international movement of deinstitutionalization of the mentally ill. Today, up to 40 percent of the homeless have some sort of mental illness. While the years immediately after the Second World War saw a steady decrease in income inequality, this has not been the case in recent years, as the gap between the rich and poor has increased. Despite the booming economy of the 1990s, the very poor saw no real progress in their income or standard of living (Hwang 2001).

OVERVIEW

Canada, being a liberal welfare state, despite a culture of individualism and individual responsibility and reliance on the private market, offers much in the way of assistance to its people with modest but universal social insurance plans that cover health, education, and welfare. A certain dualism between market and state, although fragile, has been maintained to the benefit of Canadian people (Thomas 2000). Canada also has a large nonprofit sector, which is nurtured by the federal, provincial, and municipal governments. This backdrop impacts on the well-being of people in general, but especially on children. Infant mortality in Canada is 5.3/1,000 births, but much higher within the Aboriginal populations. For instance, in Nunavut, the infant mortality rate is 19.8/1,000 births (Statistics Canada 2004). Canada does not engage easily in warfare on an international level. This is partly because of social values and partly because of their small military, but for the most part, Canada has been a fairly safe haven for both refugees escaping from war and people escaping from war-making, such as American draft dodgers of the 1960s and 1970s. Theoretically and legally, children are protected against exploitation in Canada, but much work has to be done to protect vulnerable youth against the underground currents that pull them into unsavory and dangerous contexts that do exist, particularly in urban areas.

EDUCATION

Because Canada has no federal department of education, the provinces and territories are responsible for elementary, secondary, and postsecondary education. Boards of education operate at a local level as authorities of public education. Each of the thirteen education systems across Canada, although similar in general values, reflects a richness and diversity related to geography, culture, and regional history.

Although the government of Canada does not have the primary responsibility for education throughout its nation, it plays a very important supporting role. Several federal government departments have mandates that intersect with education in issues of postsecondary educational funding, human resource development, and official language policy. The federal government also has specific responsibilities related to education for First Nation students at elementary, secondary, and postsecondary levels (Education@Canada 2006).

The Council of Ministers of Education, Canada (CMEC) was created in 1967 to serve as the national voice for education in Canada. Provincial and territorial ministers meet regularly at the CMEC forum to discuss matters of collective interest. CMEC also represents Canadian interests in education with regard to foreign governments and international education, including foreign students studying in Canada. Seven percent of Canada's Gross Domestic Product (GDP) goes to education. Section 23 of the 1982 Constitution Act specifies that education in both French and English is available throughout Canada when the population of children speaking the minority language is sufficient to justify it (Education@Canada 2006).

Education is free and publicly funded for all citizens and permanent residents in Canada from kindergarten until the end of secondary school (grade twelve in English Canada or grade eleven in Québec), basically from age five to age eighteen. In Québec, Cégeps (Collèges d'Enseignement Général et Professionel) are free, preuniversity institutions that serve as a transition between high school and university. Tuition is charged for all other college and university education throughout Canada.

Most schools offer preschool and kindergarten programs that provide pre-elementary education in all provinces and territories. Elementary education, in most provinces and territories, covers grades one to six, and some districts have middle schools or junior high schools for the intermediate level of schooling.

Both academic and vocational curricula are offered at the secondary level. The academic program serves as a potential preparation for the entrance requirements of colleges and universities, whereas the vocational program prepares students to pursue more vocational studies or enter the job market. Diplomas are granted to students who have successfully completed both the required and the optional courses of their program of study.

Postsecondary education in Canada, although the direct financial responsibility of the provincial and territorial governments, receives additional funding from the federal government, research grants, and students' tuition fees. Cégeps in Québec, unique in their form, provide two options for postsecondary study: a general academic program leading to university, or a professional program preparing students for the work force.

Parents who want to educate their own children during any part of their compulsory school years may do so if they conform to the standards, curriculum, and diploma requirements dictated by the provincial or territorial authorities. The same restrictions for home schooling also apply to independent schools.

Public schools try to accommodate special needs students in several ways. Many separate programs exist for physically or mentally disabled students as well as gifted students. Other schools provide strategies for integration of special needs students in regular classrooms. Programs also exist to help newly arrived immigrant children integrate harmoniously into new school situations (Education@Canada 2006).

The Canadian high school graduation rate in 2001 was 75 percent (78 percent for females and 70 percent for males). Diversity among the school-aged population generally increased between 1991 and 2001. From 1991 to 2000, 2.2 million immigrants were admitted to Canada. This is the highest number for any decade in the past century. In 2001, close to three quarters of immigrants lived in just three metropolitan census areas: Toronto, Montreal, and Vancouver. Among these 1990s immigrants, 310,000 were children between the ages of five and sixteen. For many of these children, the first language learned and used at home was neither English nor French. The language skills of children of immigrant parents just entering the school system were weaker than those of Canadian-born parents, but the longer the children lived in Canada, the smaller the gap in performance became, until it disappeared. In fact, in later years, the academic performance of many of these students surpassed that of their Canadian-born counterparts (Worswick 2001).

The school-aged population of Aboriginal students is significant and growing in Canada's Census Metropolitan Areas (CMAs) and in areas outside the CMAs in certain provinces and territories. In 2001, no other Organization for Economic Cooperation and Development (OECD) nation had a higher proportion of its population aged twenty-five to sixty-four with either a college or university degree than Canada (Education@Canada 2006).

Although average undergraduate tuition fees in Canada increased from $2,535 to $3,863 in the years between 1995 and 2005, they remained relatively inexpensive compared with tuition costs in the United States. Despite increases in costs, full-time enrollment at Canadian universities increased by 12 percent between 1992 and 2002, while part-time enrollment decreased 21 percent. The majority of full-time undergraduate students are now women, and their enrollment at the graduate level has almost met the level of men enrolled.

In 2002, 16,500 individuals completed registered apprenticeship programs, which is down 12 percent from 1992. In 2001, the graduation rate for bachelors and first professional degree programs was 31 percent, and graduation rates were higher for women in the humanities and the social sciences. In the physical, natural, and applied sciences, the graduation rate for men remained higher, but the gap narrowed between 1992 and 2001. The graduation rate for men in general dropped by 1 percent between 1992 and 2001 and for women it increased by 10 percent. Sixty percent of graduates in 2001 were women, and the social and behavioral sciences and law were the fields with the most graduates nationwide, closely followed by business, management, public administration, and education.

In 2003–2004 a little over half of all students seventeen years and older were working while attending school. In 2004, the unemployment rate for twenty-five- to twenty-nine-year-olds who had not graduated from high school was at 15 percent compared with 7 percent for university graduates. In 2000, university graduates had 77 percent higher mean earnings than high school-only graduates, while college or trade graduates had only 15 percent higher earnings (Allen, Harris, and Butlin 2003).

Education in Canada is of excellent quality and comparatively inexpensive, but its veritable accessibility is also related to the general economic well-being of families. For many families living on the poverty line, even inexpensive postsecondary education is inaccessible. Although according to statistics, overall literacy levels in Canada are very high (99 percent), grade school teachers are alarmed by the fact that in some Ontario schools, 50 percent of students have not achieved grade three literacy standards, which means that schools and parents need to continue to be vigilant about children's progress in school (Neuman 2003).

PLAY AND RECREATION

According to international guidelines, the majority of Canadian children and youth, aged five to seventeen, are not active enough for optimal growth and development. Canadian girls are less active than boys, with only 38 percent of girls (compared with 48 percent of boys) considered active enough using these guidelines (Public Health Agency of Canada). The average Canadian child watches television for three to five hours a day. A study in the *Canadian Medical Association Journal* showed that obesity in boys had increased from 15 percent to 35 percent between 1981 and 1996 (obesity in girls increased from 15 percent to 29.2 percent) (Tremblay and Willms 2000). Only 766 of 15,800 Canadian schools have been formally recognized for quality physical education on a daily basis. Many children and youth are transported to school and other places because of convenience or for safety reasons, and this also contributes to sedentarism.

Part of the reason for widespread sedentarism is that the availability and diversity of media and technology is overwhelming, and often related to family income and habits. It is rare to find a Canadian family that does not own a television, and even computers and their accessories are commonplace in homes. The issue for parents, teachers, and children is more about learning how to monitor the quantity and the quality of what is offered to children, allowing a healthy balance between experiences that are entertaining and those that are educational.

Several organizations have been preoccupied by these issues and provide guidance. The Media Awareness Network (MNet) is a Canadian nonprofit organization that has been pioneering the development of media literacy programs since its incorporation in 1996. MNet's work is based on the belief that to be functionally literate in the world today—to be able to "read" the messages that inform, entertain, and sell to us daily—young people need critical thinking skills. MNet focuses its efforts on equipping adults with information and tools to help young people understand how the media work, how the media may affect their lifestyle choices, and the extent to which they, as consumers and citizens, are being well informed.

Quality play and recreation opportunities remain vital to the health and personal development of all children and youth. The Canadian Parks and Recreation Association (CPRA), through its members, partners, and allied organizations, has made a commitment to make recreation more accessible to low-income families and their children in Canada. Through the "Everybody Gets to Play" national initiative, CPRA has demonstrated its leadership in addressing this fundamental issue. CPRA endorses the research that clearly demonstrates that recreation interventions are an effective and economical strategy to improve the lives of low-income families and their children. CPRA is committed to increasing awareness and understanding of this important issue and to building partnerships committed to action (Canadian Parks and Recreation Association 2007). The roots of the Canadian public recreation system stem back to the early 1900s when playground programs were provided for underprivileged children—the Playground Movement. Over the years, the focus changed, and in many communities municipal recreation became the domain of the middle class. As a result, many programs are unaffordable to low-income families (Karlis 2004). A Children's Fitness Tax Credit announced by the federal government in 2006 proposes to allow parents to claim a nonrefundable tax credit of up to $500 in eligible fees for the enrollment of a child under the age of sixteen years in an eligible program of physical activity (Statistics Canada 2006b).

Canada, as a geographical entity, offers nearly four million square miles of coastline, mountains, lakes, prairies, and forests, making for an endless adventure center for families that enjoy outdoor sports and activities. The extensive national and provincial parks system provides a structure for many of these activities such as wilderness camping, wildlife observation, visiting historic sites, understanding aboriginal heritage, learning about ecology and conservation, and so on.

Canada also has a history of supporting the arts on many levels—national, provincial, and municipal, and this has an impact on children's exposure to the arts, both as a form of entertainment and as a specific activity for personal development. Almost all of the national and provincial cultural institutions offer activities and special productions for children and youth. An example of this is Assitej, l'Association International du Théâtre pour l'Enfance et la Jeunesse (International Association of Theatre for Children and Young People), the largest association of its kind, representing professional children and young people's theatre in eighty-three countries throughout the world.

CHILD LABOR

In Canada, labor laws have been enacted over many decades dealing with the employment of children and young persons. Factory acts became widespread in the early 1900s. They dealt in part with the employment of children, young girls, and women in the manufacturing sector, and were founded on similar English legislation that had been adopted around 1835 and was applied in Canada. Factory acts set minimum ages for the employment of children, imposed maximum limits on daily and weekly hours of work, and stipulated that no child or woman could be employed where he or she was likely to be permanently injured. Mining laws in some jurisdictions, starting with statutes in Nova Scotia (1873) and British Columbia (1877), also restricted the employment of children in mines. The provisions of these laws, which were amended on several occasions, later became part of employment (or labor) standards acts and occupational health and safety legislation. Most restrictions on access to certain occupations for children are found in these laws today. Many other laws prohibited or regulated occupations in which children and young persons could be employed. As an example, children's protection acts established a minimum age for employment in street trades and the hours during which they would be tolerated. Also, temperance acts, municipal acts, and shops regulation acts often restricted access to occupations (Commission for Labor Cooperation 2006).

Restrictions on the employment of children and young persons can be found in a variety of statutes. The most common are employment standards laws, occupational health and safety legislation, and education acts. Restrictions are also found in an assortment of provisions regulating vocational training, in child welfare legislation, in laws governing establishments where liquor is sold, and other statutes (Commission for Labor Cooperation 2006). It is possible to group the interventions of Canadian legislators, whether in federal, provincial, or territorial jurisdiction, under the three categories described later. There is some overlap between these categories because a number of provisions may serve more than one purpose.

The employment of children and young persons subject to compulsory school attendance is severely limited during school hours. This ensures their presence in school during the crucial years when they acquire basic skills. In New Brunswick, a young person must attend school until graduation from high school or until he/she reaches the age of eighteen. In other provinces and Yukon, compulsory school attendance ends at the age of sixteen (Commission for Labor Cooperation 2006). Several provisions are aimed at preventing the exposure of young persons to occupations or situations that may be harmful to their growth or character. For instance, under Québec's labor standards legislation, no employer may have work performed by a person under the age of eighteen that is disproportionate to

that person's capacity or that is likely to be detrimental to his/her education, health, or physical or moral development. In addition, Québec's
Youth Protection Act stipulates "the security or development of a child is
considered to be in danger where he is forced or induced to ... perform
for the public in a manner that is unacceptable for his age" (Youth Protection Act 1979). In Canada, the approach adopted by the various jurisdictions has been to permit young persons to have relatively broad access to
jobs and work experience, while putting in place measures to protect their
health and safety as well as their normal development, and ensuring that
work does not interfere with the education of children and youth who are
subject to compulsory school attendance.

The labor market for young Canadians aged fifteen to twenty-four has
rebounded sharply from a twenty-one-year low in 1997, thanks to a stronger economy, according to a study published in *Perspectives on Labor and
Income*. The recession at the beginning of the 1990s had a lasting effect on
the youth labor market. By 1997, the employment and participation rates
for this age group were at their lowest point since the mid-1970s. Since
then, employment among these young people has grown at a fast pace,
even faster than among adult workers. Between 1997 and 2004, job creation among youth rose 21.1 percent, the equivalent of 428,000 new jobs.
This compares with a growth rate of just 15.8 percent among adults aged
twenty-five and over. As a result, the unemployment rate among young
people fell from 16.3 percent in 1997 to 13.4 percent in 2004. At the
same time, the proportion participating in the labor force increased from a
record low of 61.5 percent to 67.0 percent. The employment rate
increased 7 percentage points, from 51.5 percent in 1997 to 58.1 percent
in 2004. Although a large increase, this employment rate still does not
match the 63.3 percent peak reached in 1989 (Usalcas 2005).

In particular, the strong economy has benefited young women, whose
job gains have outstripped those of young men, breaking a long-standing
trend. During periods of economic growth, young men have historically
had higher rates of employment than young women. Of the 428,000
new jobs, young women captured 240,000, which was a 24.7 percent
gain from 1997, compared with 188,000 for young men, a 17.7 percent
gain. Also, employment growth was proportionately stronger for teens
aged fifteen to nineteen than for older youth aged twenty to twenty-four
(Usalcas 2005).

The retail trade sector, the largest employer of teenagers, was the driving force behind new jobs for teenagers. Between 1997 and 2004,
employment among teens grew by 192,000, with half of this growth
(97,000) in retail trade. A distant second was the accommodation and
food services sector, where 61,000 new jobs were added. In both sectors,
more jobs went to girls than boys. This is because more women tend to
take jobs as cashiers, salespeople, or servers in food and beverage outlets
(Usalcas 2005).

The illegal trafficking of people does exist in Canada, usually involving the importation of young people from developing countries with promises of legitimate employment and a better life in Canada. Traffickers sometimes try to buy children from their parents or convince parents to send their children away so that they can earn money for the family. Teenagers who have left home are very vulnerable to traffickers. Children and teenagers are most frequently trafficked into the drug or sex trades. The government of Canada is working to combat trafficking in persons both domestically and internationally using the "Protocol to Prevent, Suppress and Punish Trafficking in Persons, Especially Women and Children, Supplementing the United Nations Convention against Transnational Organized Crime" and Bill C-49 in force as of November 2005 (Protocol 2000; and Department of Justice Canada, Trafficking in Persons).

FAMILY

The family environment in which Canadian children grow up has changed dramatically over the past decades. The traditional two-parent family of the fifties is no longer the only significant model of family life. Young children are born into a variety of different family types: married couples and common-law couples (85.9 percent) and lone-parent families (14.1 percent) (Statistics Canada 2002). Some of these are blended families, and the family to which the child is born is not guaranteed to be the family in which the child will spend his or her entire childhood. Family structure is in a constant state of flux. However, most parents of all types seem to understand the importance of the first five years of life and are trying to spend more time with their children than a decade ago (Zuzanek 2001). Due to a low birth rate, family size has changed as well, with 25 percent of Canadian children being only children.

Children who experience parental separation do so at a younger age. Approximately 25 percent of children born after the late 1980s will experience parental separation (Marcil-Gratton 1998). The phenomenon of divorce is a far more complex issue than generally believed. Furthermore, statistics pertaining to divorce are difficult to understand and, as a result, are frequently misinterpreted. Overall, about one-third of all marriages in Canada end in divorce, and the rate is somewhat higher for remarriages. Dissolution rates are even higher among cohabiting couples. Currently, there are no solid predictions of either a sharp decline or a sharp rise in divorce rates in the near future.

Divorce and remarriage are not necessarily in the best interest of the children. It is therefore not surprising that many, albeit not the majority, of children, who suffer serious negative consequences from their parents' divorce and that some of these consequences may last even into adulthood. Divorce can be accompanied by poverty or a significant reduction in financial resources. This factor contributes to the negative effects of divorce on the mother-child family unit and on children's life chances (Ambert 1998).

Canadian family law is an area of shared jurisdiction between the federal and provincial governments. Federal jurisdiction covers marriage and divorce, and provincial jurisdiction includes the certification of marriage and property and civil rights in the provinces. Different marital regimes exist in different provinces and will have different impacts on the outcome of divorce settlements, for instance. There have been many advances for women's equality in relation to property regimes and child support claims. Inheritance laws are enforced according to wills or estate successions, but all children will inherit from their biological or adoptive parents unless the will provides otherwise; if a child is still dependent he or she has first claim on the parent's estate before it is distributed.

Family customs obviously vary in different families and different cultures, and because Canada is a multicultural society, it is very hard to generalize about roles of male and female children in families. Various influences from the media, from school, and from peer pressure may create more equality in male–female roles growing up, or may not. The fact that more mothers are working outside the home may or may not create some change in the way domestic roles or tasks are divided between men and women and between male and female children. The family is a private and individualistically oriented institution. Many couples find parenting a real struggle—41 percent in one Canadian study said it was hard to find time and energy for parenting, and with so many women working the responsibility for family life and for looking after children must be shared by fathers, employers, and childcare providers, not just left to mothers (Adema et al. 2005). Many parents may choose to work for financial security instead of giving their children the time and attention they need for healthy growth and development. Caring and involved fathers need to take a larger part in bringing up their children. Because of time pressures that parents face, many children need other caring adults involved in their lives, such as grandparents, aunts and uncles, neighbors, teachers, coaches, and childcare providers.

Unless governments are willing to give more adequate support to working mothers and fathers in the form of tax credits, family-friendly work places, and financial aid, more and more children will be at risk, meaning they could have problems with school, their physical and mental health, delinquency, and suicide (Hewlett 1992). Canadians have created a social order that, for very good reasons, no longer rewards or restricts on the basis of lineage. Instead, people are acknowledged for their individual accomplishments—educational, professional, financial, athletic, or political. For half a century, Canadian society has valued individual autonomy, achievement, and choice, downplaying the traditional bonds to family, employer, community, and country.

There is a price to pay for individual freedoms and aspirations, and it is often at the expense of family life, marriages, the safety of the streets, relationships with neighbors, and, ultimately, at the expense of knowing what purposes are collectively shared with others. Many Canadian families have entered the new millennium in a state of personal stress, financial indebtedness, perpetual insecurity, and fragile personal relationships. The real question is whether or not the commitments made as a society and culture will serve to acknowledge, support, and reinforce the commitments that individuals are willing to make to one another in the context of family. Although the government of Canada has made helping children and their families a priority of its long-term commitment to a better quality of life through strong income support, employment insurance, parental benefits, tax supports, community-based programs, and research through partnerships with provincial and territorial governments, Canadian society in general must participate in structuring a community that acknowledges families as an important foundation of contemporary life (Glossop 1999).

HEALTH

Canada's universal health system, although at times faltering because of fluctuating budget revisions, remains a stable, high-quality insurance of Canada's commitment to its people's health. Despite pressure from different factions for privatization, the accessibility of health care in Canada is still one of its national keystones. From 1990 to 2000, progress was made in the health of Canadian children, and for the majority of these children, their health remained excellent. Important challenges remain, however, in addressing the most persistent conditions of risk, and acting in other crucial areas to ensure optimal health for all populations of Canadian children. Particular challenges remain in relation to certain vulnerable populations and to Aboriginal children, the child population most at risk for poor health and social outcomes (Grzeskowiak 2005).

Two broadly recognized indicators of child health, and of a nation's health more generally, are the infant and child mortality rates. Canada has shown steady progress in both areas since 1990. First, the child mortality rate has fallen one-third from a rate of 9 per 1,000 to 6 per 1,000; the infant mortality rate has also declined from 6.8 per 1,000 to 5.3 per 1,000, except within Aboriginal populations where the current rate is more than triple that of the Canadian population as a whole. Another important measure, low birth weight, has shown steady improvement over the last decade; over 80 percent of Canadian children are born at a healthy weight (Government of Canada, Health Canada 2002a), and few Canadians are born prematurely. Through a range of programs, the government of Canada remains committed to supporting pregnant women most likely to experience unhealthy birth outcomes, including low birth weight.

Immunization has proven to be an effective and accessible means for the prevention of numerous, potentially fatal diseases. Rates of immunization against diphtheria, pertussis, tetanus, polio, and measles have risen on an average of 90 percent over the past ten years, and these immunization efforts show results (Canadian Institute of Child Health 2000). In Canada, 99 percent of the population has access to safe drinking water and sanitary disposal of sewage. However, even Canadians are not complacent about their clean water as recent outbreaks of *E. coli* in Walkerton, Ontario, illustrate. Collaborative efforts among governments at all levels help address the local environmental needs of communities. Safety of drinking water and sanitary waste disposal has been a particular concern among First Nations communities where certain infrastructures sometimes tend to be lacking (Canadian Institute of Child Health 2000).

Health outcomes among children linked to environmental factors were recently identified as a concern for Canadians, particularly because the majority of children live in an urban setting. There has been an alarming increase in cases of children with asthma over the past ten years, with one in ten children under eighteen being diagnosed with it. There is growing evidence that children's exposure to environmental hazards are different and greater than adults and are linked to most of the leading causes of deaths, illnesses, and hospitalizations for Canadian children (from birth to age eighteen) (Canadian Institute of Child Health 2000). Although some improvements have been made in the levels of toxins in the Canadian environment, this is a global issue that needs coordinated, integrated, and comprehensive research and action to enact important and lasting change.

During the last quarter century, there has been an overall decline in the teenage pregnancy rate in Canada, perhaps reflecting the availability of contraceptives and the increased awareness of the risks of unprotected sex brought about by the AIDS epidemic. Nevertheless, in 1997, an estimated 19,724 women aged fifteen to nineteen gave birth, and a slightly larger number in this age range—21,233—had an abortion (Canadian Institute of Child Health 2000).

Among very young children, chronic conditions are the most prevalent type of disability. In 1986, 90.6 percent of children from birth to four years of age with a disability had some form of chronic health problem, as opposed to a disability based primarily on activity limitation. The single largest group was those affected by heart disease: 15.4 percent of young children with disabilities.

Substance abuse remains an important health issue affecting Canadian children and youth. Although regular use of alcohol among youth is on the decline, tobacco and drug use remains high or has increased. Female rates of tobacco and drug use have dramatically increased and surpassed those of males in the same age cohort (Canadian Institute of Child Health 2000).

Mental health problems are the leading health problems that Canadian children currently face after infancy. At any given time, 14 percent of children aged four to seventeen years (over 800,000 in Canada) experience mental disorders that cause significant distress and impairment at home, at school, and in the community (Waddell et al. 2005). Fewer than 25 percent of these children receive specialized treatment services. Without effective prevention or treatment, childhood problems often lead to distress and impairment throughout adulthood, with significant costs for society. Children's mental health has not received the public policy attention that is warranted by recent epidemiologic data. To address the neglect of children's mental health, a new national strategy is urgently needed. Here, medical experts have used research findings to suggest four public policy goals: promote healthy development for all children, prevent mental disorders to reduce the number of children affected, treat mental disorders more effectively to reduce distress and impairment, and monitor outcomes to ensure the effective and efficient use of public resources. Taken together, these goals constitute a public health strategy to improve the mental health of Canadian children (Waddell et al. 2005).

LAWS AND LEGAL STATUS

According to the Canada Safety Council (1996), most young people in Canada are never in trouble with the law, but the number of criminal charges against young people is expanding. There is a debate as to whether that means there is more crime, or simply more charges being laid. Property crimes are far more common than violent crimes, although the proportion of violent offenses is marginally increasing. Almost half of youth court cases involve property offenses. Canada jails a high proportion of young offenders—higher even than the United States—because the justice system makes comparatively little use of alternate approaches. Young offenders often serve a longer prison sentence than adults for the same kind of offense. (Unlike the adult system, there is no parole for youth.) Aboriginal youth and young people from certain racial and cultural groups and from lower income families are overrepresented in the justice system (Trocmé, Knoke, and Blackstock 2004).

The Youth Criminal Justice Act (2002) clearly spells out both the rights and responsibilities of children under eighteen, the age of legal majority, who have been accused of any criminal act. For instance, the document states that

> communities, families, parents and others concerned with the development of young persons should, through multi-disciplinary approaches, take reasonable steps to prevent youth crime by addressing its underlying causes,

to respond to the needs of young persons, and to provide guidance and support to those at risk of committing crimes; information about youth justice, youth crime and the effectiveness of measures taken to address youth crime should be publicly available; Canada is a party to the United Nations Convention on the Rights of the Child and recognizes that young persons have rights and freedoms, including those stated in the *Canadian Charter of Rights and Freedoms* and the *Canadian Bill of Rights*, and have special guarantees of their rights and freedoms; Canadian society should have a youth criminal justice system that commands respect, takes into account the interests of victims, fosters responsibility, and ensures accountability through meaningful consequences and effective rehabilitation and reintegration, and that reserves its most serious intervention for the most serious crimes and reduces the over-reliance on incarceration for non-violent young persons. (The Youth Criminal Justice Act 2002)

The National Forum on Youth Gangs was convened December 9–10, 1999, by the Solicitor General of Canada and the Minister of Justice and Attorney General of Canada in response to calls from the police community and others who have expressed the need to network and share information and strategies in dealing effectively with youth gangs. The forum brought together more than 120 participants and observers representing police, government, community service agencies, and research institutions to share information and strategies in dealing effectively with youth gangs. Young people themselves were key participants at the forum. Sixteen youth delegates worked together the day before the forum began to develop a report that they presented to the group. They also shared their views with participants throughout the forum.

The forum focused on how the police and the community can work in partnership. In their report and presentation, the youth delegates made specific recommendations to address the needs of youth at various stages of gang involvement. The forum also warns that mainstream youth are not immune from gang life; they require supportive families, communities, and schools, as well as preventative awareness training on issues like gangs and violence. Youth at risk of gang involvement should be targeted for initiatives that are meaningful to them, such as mentoring or skills training. Most importantly, professionals need to reach out to these young people rather than expecting that they will seek out services. Youth who are currently in gangs also require assistance from professionals to limit the harm caused by their lifestyle, such as safe houses and anonymous health care. It is also important that these young people have information about how to exit gang culture so that they may access services when they choose to do so. Risk for gang involvement does not end when a young person leaves a gang. A strong support network and opportunities to develop new skills can help in reentering a mainstream life. The youth delegates also brought some key messages. Young people, particularly those to whom initiatives may be targeted, must be involved in the development of policies, programs, and services. Programs based on a youth-helping-youth model—peer support, peer counseling, and peer education—should be strongly supported. Youth know how to talk to one another and convey key messages, and young people must be actively recruited into programs. Professionals should not assume that youth will access programs simply because they are offered (National Forum on Youth Gangs 1999).

Although a seemingly civilized country, Canada has had many cases of police brutality and outright racism, often in regard to young offenders. In 1994, Dr. Philip C. Stenning prepared a report, *Police Use of Force and Violence Against Members of Visible Minority Groups in Canada*, for the Canadian Centre for Police Race Relations. Stenning conducted a study with 150 inmates (60 whites, 51 blacks, and 39 other non-whites). While Stenning stated that his research does not necessarily reflect police–citizen contacts generally, Smith places its findings within the context of "both the historical treatment of African Canadians and (of) other studies contemporary to and following after" his work. The results, Smith says, "indicate a pattern of treatment that is pervasive within the criminal justice system." Stenning found that police behavior toward African Canadians was less friendly and less polite, that African Canadians are sworn at more often by police (58.8 percent compared to 38.3 percent for whites and 43.6 percent for others) and are subject to racial epithets more often as well (31.4 percent compared to 5 percent for others). In responding to "minor offences," police drew their weapons against African Canadians more frequently than with other groups (25 percent versus 6.7 percent for whites and 6.7 percent for others) (Brown 2002).

RELIGIOUS LIFE

The Preamble to the Canadian Charter of Rights and Freedoms explains that Canada is founded upon principles that recognize the supremacy of God. Canada currently allows believers the religious freedom to assemble and worship without limitation or interference.

According to L. J. Francis (2000), many children lose interest in religious education between the ages of eight and fifteen. Only 36 percent of Canada's children under twelve years of age attend religious services on a monthly basis, although 13 percent went weekly in 1994–1995. That was the finding of the National Survey of Children and Youth, which collected data on more than 22,500 children from newborn to eleven years. Most were accompanied by a parent, usually the mother (Statistics Canada 2001; Francis 2000).

Attendance of religious services varied by geographical region and by religious affiliation. Children in the Atlantic provinces had the highest regular attendance rate, 52 percent, while those in Québec had the lowest at 19 percent. There were no reliable estimates for children in Eastern

Orthodox, Jewish, Buddhist, Hindu, and Sikh faith communities, but apparently children do not always continue to practice the religion of their parents.

Since Canada is one of the most diverse countries in the world in terms of immigration and religious faith, the number of Canadians who reported religions such as Islam, Hinduism, Sikhism, and Buddhism has increased substantially. But how do successive generations of immigrants adapt and transform their inherited or adopted religions in the context of their new country? Peter Beyer's research looks at what happens to the religious faith and beliefs of children of immigrants to Canada. He does this through focus groups and interviews with volunteer students of second-generation Muslim, Buddhist, or Hindu background who attend selected postsecondary institutions in Ottawa, Montreal, and Toronto. Key questions concern how immigrant youth are maintaining or changing religious identities and practices, the nature of their religious involvement, how their views and practices differ from those of their parents' generation, how they see their situation in Canada and in the wider global world, and how religious and other developments in the world at large affect their religious orientations (Beyer 2006).

Canada's approach to religious education has sometimes been criticized as inconsistent. Catholic education public funding is mandated by various sections of the Constitution Act of 1867 and reaffirmed by Section 29 of the Canadian Charter of Rights and Freedoms. More recently however, with a growing level of multiculturalism, particularly in Ontario, debate has emerged as to whether publicly funded religious education for one group is permissible.

CHILD ABUSE AND NEGLECT

The Canadian Incidence Study of Reported Child Abuse and Neglect (CIS) provides national estimates of child abuse and neglect reported to, and investigated by, child welfare services in Canada. The CIS, Canada's only national child maltreatment study, is part of a surveillance program funded and directed by the Public Health Agency of Canada in collaboration with the provinces, territories, and a team of researchers. The CIS-2003 study collected data from a representative sample of sixty-three child welfare agencies across Canada.

The CIS-2003 study indicates that large numbers of children aged from birth to fifteen have been maltreated in Canada. An estimated 235,315 child maltreatment investigations were conducted in 2003 (thirty-eight investigations per 1,000 children). Almost half (49 percent) of these investigations were substantiated (approximately nineteen substantiated investigations per 1,000 children). Unlike the analysis of police-reported data that is based on a narrower definition of child abuse, five maltreatment categories were captured in the CIS study, including emotional maltreatment, neglect, exposure to domestic violence, physical abuse, and sexual abuse. Among substantiated child maltreatment cases (excluding Québec), neglect was the most common form of substantiated child abuse (30 percent), followed by exposure to domestic violence (28 percent), physical abuse (24 percent), emotional maltreatment (15 percent), and sexual abuse (3 percent) (Trocmé et al. 2005).

The CIS study found that most substantiated child maltreatment investigations involved allegations against parents, including biological mothers (54 percent), biological fathers (48 percent), stepfathers/common-law partners (12 percent), or stepmothers/common-law partners (2 percent). Relatives were the next most frequently identified perpetrators (6 percent). Only 3 percent of all cases of substantiated child maltreatment involved nonfamily perpetrators, and less than 1 percent of allegations involved a teacher or another professional working with the child. Biological mothers were considered to be perpetrators in 83 percent of cases where neglect was the primary form of substantiated child maltreatment. The overrepresentation of biological mothers should be interpreted with caution given that 42 percent of these substantiated neglect cases involved lone female-parent families. Biological fathers (36 percent) and stepfathers (9 percent) were considered to be perpetrators in 45 percent of cases of substantiated neglect (Trocmé et al. 2005).

Historical data consistently show parents to be the primary perpetrators of family-related homicides against children and youth. In 2004, 85 percent of victims from birth to age seventeen (twenty-nine victims) who were killed by a family member was murdered by a parent, the same percentage that was reported during the period from 1974 to 2003. Fathers are more likely than mothers to be accused of killing their own children, although the difference is negligible when the child is an infant. The vast majority of spousal homicide incidents involve only one victim. However, between 1995 and 2004, when multiple victims were involved in spousal homicides (7 percent), it was typically the perpetrator's own children who were also killed (Criminal Code of Canada 2007; Canada Evidence Act 2007).

In Canada, child welfare laws require that all cases of suspected child abuse be investigated to determine whether a child is in need of protection. If a child is determined to be in need of protection, the child welfare authorities may respond by, for example, providing counseling and support for the family, removing the child (temporarily or permanently) from the home, or removing the abuser(s) from the home. Criminal sanctions may also apply in cases of sexual or physical abuse.

Since the 1960s, significant steps have been taken to address child abuse in Canada, including, for example, the introduction of mandatory reporting laws, the creation of child abuse registries, changes to the Criminal Code and the Canada Evidence Act (Criminal Code of Canada 2007; Canada Evidence Act 2007), the extension of time limits for laying charges in child sexual abuse cases, and the establishment of child protection agencies run by First Nations. Further, since the landmark reports by Badgley (1984) and Rogers (1990), legislation to address child sexual abuse has been created and efforts to address the sexual exploitation of children are ongoing. Following the 1996 report of the Royal Commission on Aboriginal Peoples, the federal government acknowledged its role in the occurrence of physical and sexual abuse in residential schools, and implemented a community-based healing strategy for Aboriginal communities. (Indian and Northern Affairs Canada 1998).

Given the extent of child abuse in Canada, as well as the complexity of this issue and its enormous impact, effectively preventing, identifying, and responding to child abuse is an enormous but essential task. Addressing this issue requires the ongoing commitment and collaboration of community members, practitioners, and policy makers across Canada. Community supports and services for victims and their families are essential.

The Department of Justice of Canada and its partners—including nongovernmental organizations, provincial and territorial governments, and the private sector—are actively involved in addressing child abuse issues through legal reform, public and professional education, research, and support for programs and services. Some of this work is linked to the department's participation in the federal government's current Family Violence Initiative, which focuses on violence against women and children that occurs in the home (Government of Canada, Health Canada 2002b), while other areas of activity are linked to other initiatives including, for example, the National Children's Agenda, the Aboriginal Justice Strategy, and the National Strategy on Crime Prevention and Community Safety.

GROWING UP IN THE TWENTY-FIRST CENTURY

In Canada, the most pressing issues of the twenty-first century in preparation for a new economy are children and youth, education and knowledge, and health and the environment. To promote these issues, the government of Canada foresees strategies to improve maternity and parental leave benefits, enhance after-tax money for families, the creation of more family-friendly workplaces, the modernization of family law, more generous investments in the National Child Benefit, additional learning opportunities with an expanded School-Net (a partnership with the provincial and territorial governments, the education community, and the private sector, which promotes the effective use of information and communications technologies in learning), and continued special attention to the rights of the child in Canada's foreign policy.

One of the most urgent priorities of Canadian society is child poverty, with special attention to Aboriginal families and other at-risk families such as single-parent families. More coordination between departments and governments will undoubtedly enhance the effectiveness of any of these efforts. Generous social investments that are more broadly based with focus on prevention for all children at risk will eventually contribute to improvement in the well-being of all children and to the elimination of social inequalities in general (Government of Canada 2002).

The Convention on the Rights of the Child recognizes the rights of a young person to have a say in decisions that affect his or her life. Moreover, Canada continues to validate young people by integrating principles of youth participation in initiatives related to community and economic development, youth health, environmental protection, youth justice, sexual exploitation, international development, and the promotion of cultural diversity. It goes without saying that parents and family play the primary role in providing care and nurturing for all children and young people. Whatever support and collaboration different levels of government, municipalities, voluntary sector organizations, professional associations, schools, or the private sector can offer is extremely important in the improvement of children's well-being, rights, development, and ultimate participation into the new millennium. Canada consistently develops and supports policy that gives hope for the present and the future of children and young people and remains a generally progressive and humane nation. This does not mean, however, that there are no obstacles to these noble values. Canada needs, as do other countries, to be vigilant about its participation in globalization, to be clear about the price of their social values, and to pay close attention to seemingly insignificant minority needs. A prosperous and harmonious future lies in the well-being and inclusion of all of a country's citizens; a good place to start is with children.

RESOURCE GUIDE

Suggested Readings

Adema, Willem, Anaïs Loizillon, Elina Pylkkänen, Olivier Thevenon, Maxime Laidique, Elma Lopes, and Mark Pearson. 2005. *Babies and Bosses—Reconciling Work and Family Life, Volume 4: Canada, Finland, Sweden and the United Kingdom.* OECD Publishing. Discusses the challenge of finding a suitable work/family life balance. Many parents and children in Canada, Finland, Sweden, and the United Kingdom are happy with their existing work and care outcomes. However, many others feel seriously constrained in one way or another, and their personal well-being suffers as a consequence. This book discusses the challenge of finding a suitable balance of work and family life and presents comparative studies of work and family reconciliation policies.

Bibby, Reginald. 2002. *Restless Gods. The Renaissance of Religion in Canada.* Toronto: Stoddart Publishing. *Restless Gods* confronts Canadians' misconceptions and myths about religion, spirituality, and themselves. *Restless Gods* reveals the surprising news about religion and spirituality in Canada: Secularization is a myth.

Doob, Anthony, and Carla Cesaroni. 2004. *Responding to Youth Crime in Canada.* Toronto: University of Toronto Press. Doob and Cesaroni present a systematic overview and discussion of many important policy-related issues pertaining to youth crime and youth justice, including the recently implemented Youth Criminal Justice Act. It is a well-written and important corrective to the myths that surround youth crime and youth justice in Canada today.

Howe, R. Brian, and Katherine Covell. 2005. *Empowering Children: Children's Rights Education as a Pathway to Citizenship.* Toronto: University of Toronto Press. In *Empowering Children,* the authors assert that educating children about their basic rights is a necessary means not only of fulfilling a country's legal obligations, but also of advancing education about democratic principles and the practices of citizenship.

Olwig, Karen, and Eva Gullov. 2003. *Children's Places: Cross-cultural Perspectives.* New York: Routledge. Based on in-depth ethnographic research, *Children's Places* examines the ways in which children and adults, from their different vantage points in society, negotiate the "proper place" of children in both social and spatial terms.

Thomas, David, ed. 2000. *Canada and the United States: Differences that Count.* Peterborough, Ontario: Broadview Press Ltd. Political scientists and related professionals—all but one of which are Canadian—point out differences in the archetypal issues of health care, taxes, and guns; social and cultural foundations; institutional structures; and the law.

Nonprint Resources

Blowing the Whistle. 2003. Directed by Sarah Vermette. Tattle Tale Productions. VHS. Vancouver, British Columbia: Moving Images Distribution. This 17-minute video uses interviews with teenaged girls, professionals, shopkeepers, convicted felons, and young men from a Toronto shelter to provide insight and perspective on the causes and consequences of shoplifting.

The Children's Voice. 1994. Directed and produced by Katherine Marielle. Vancouver, British Columbia: Moving Images Distribution. This 30-minute video presents the story of a children's theater group whose goal was to break the cycle of child abuse and domestic violence through the writing and performance of a play based in the children's own lives and concerns.

Fighting for the Family. 1997. Barbara Anderson and Brad Newcombe. Amazon Communications. VHS. Vancouver, British Columbia: Moving Images Distribution. Changing definitions of family are the focus of this 46-minute documentary, which provides profiles of living and parenting arrangements that differ from the traditional nuclear model.

Holding the Sun. 1999. Gumboot Productions, produced with the participation of British Columbia Film, Film Incentive BC, in association with *CBC Newsworld.* VHS and DVD. Vancouver, British Columbia: Moving Images Distribution. Telling the story of Aaron Millar and the Millar family's failed attempt to save him from the schizophrenia that led him to kill his mother, this 39-minute documentary explores mental illness, the healthcare system, and how education and awareness might help prevent such tragedies.

Kingsley: Recognizing the Person. 2002. Directed by Penny Joy. Produced by Peter C. Campbell. Gumboot Productions. VHS and DVD. Vancouver, British Columbia: Moving Images Distribution. The story of Cherry Kinglsey is told in this 47-minute documentary, beginning with her own exploitation as a child prostitute, the personal transformation she experienced, and her successful work in Canada and internationally as an advocate for ending the sexual exploitation of children.

Made in China: The Story of Adopted Chinese Children in Canada. 2000. Directed by Karin Lee. Produced by Shan Tam. VHS and DVD. Vancouver, British Columbia: Moving Images Distribution. *Made in China*, a 47-minute documentary, explores the experiences of Chinese children adopted by Canadian families in Québec, British Columbia, and Newfoundland. Issues of adaptation and hybrid identities are explored.

The Mind of a Child. 1995. Produced and directed by Gary Marcuse. Face to Face Media Ltd. in association with the National Film Board of Canada, Pacific Centre (et al.). VHS. Arcata, CA: Shenandoah Film Productions. This 60-minute documentary focuses on the efforts of Loma Williams, Vancouver School District First Nations education specialist, to develop teaching methods for First Nations students, based on the work of Reuven Feuerstein.

Olivia's Puzzle. 2001. Directed by Jason DaSilva. VHS and DVD. Vancouver, British Columbia: Moving Images Distribution. In this 12-minute short, two seven-year-old girls, Olivia and Reshma, are the focus of a comparison of childhood experiences, hopes, and aspirations in Goa, India, and British Columbia, Canada.

Talk to Me. 1995. Directed by Susanne Tabata. Tabata Productions Associates. In this 45-minute documentary, social justice topics are discussed by British Columbia secondary school students with varied cultural backgrounds (First Nations, Asian, African, Indian, and Asian). The ten students discuss issues of racism, gender equity, class and poverty, homophobia, and immigration and assimilation.

We Don't Live in Igloos: Inuvik Youth Speak Out. 2005. Janet Ip. . This 19-minute documentary challenges stereotypes by presenting the views and values of Inuvik youth, including their own photographs of what they value.

Whose Child Is This? 1994. Produced by Raincoast Storylines Ltd. in co-production with The Canadian Broadcasting Corporation. Directed by Jerry Thompson. VHS. New York: Filmakers Library, Inc. This 48-minute video examines practices of white-family adoption of Native American children that separate them permanently from tribal influences, as well as efforts to find and repatriate these "lost" Native children.

Web Sites

Active Living, http://www.activeliving.ca.

Brighter Futures Family Resource Society, http://www.brighter-futures.ca.

Canadian Centre for Adolescent Research, http://ccar.briercrest.ca.

Canadian Youth Connection Forum, http://www.youth.gc.ca.

Caring for Kids, http://www.caringforkids.cps.ca.

Child Labor in Canada, http://www.cbc.ca/childlabour.

Daycare Bear, http://www.DaycareBear.ca.

Department of Justice Canada, http://www.justice.gc.ca/en.

Education Canada, http://www.educationcanada.cmec.ca.

Gifts in Kind International, http://www.giftsinkind.org.

Ontario Institute for Studies in Education of the University of Toronto, http://www.oise.utoronto.ca.

Statistics Canada, http://www.statcan.ca.

Voices for Children, http://www.voicesforchildren.ca.

Organizations and NGOs

Adoption Council of Canada
Web site: http://www.adoption.ca
Promoting understanding for Canadians of all aspects of adoption for adoptees, birth parents, and adoptive parents and raising awareness of the Canadian children in need of permanent homes.

Big Brothers Big Sisters of Canada
Web site: http://www.bbbsc.ca
Helping in the development of children growing up in primarily lone-parent families through 180 member agencies that provide quality adult volunteer relationships to children across Canada.

Campaign 2000
Web site: http://www.campaign2000.ca
Raising awareness and support for the 1989 all-party House of Commons resolution to end child poverty by the year 2000 through a cross-Canada network of over 80 national, provincial, and community partners.

Canada Safety Council
Web site: http://www.safety-council.org
Providing safety information, education, and awareness for Canadians through 350 national member organizations and 3,000 instructors nationwide.

Canadian Association for Community Care
Web site: http://www.cacc-acssc.com
Serving 1,200 Canadian agencies/organizations providing direct community care services such as Meals on Wheels, home care support, and long-term care.

Canadian Association for Community Living
Web site: http://www.cacl.ca
Confirming human rights for people with intellectual disabilities and to fight for more meaningful lives for people with intellectual disabilities in Canada.

Canadian Association for Health, Physical Education, Recreation and Dance
Web site: http://www.cahperd.ca
Bringing together 900 teachers, administrators, researchers, coaches, students, and others with an interest in the fields of physical education, health, active living, recreation, sport, and dance.

Canadian Association for Young Children
Web site: http://www.cayc.ca
Concerned with the well-being of children, birth through age nine, at home, in pre-shool settings, and at school.

Canadian Association of Family Resource Programs
Web site: http://www.frp.ca
Providing leadership, consultation, and resources to 500 program members and approximately 1,500 nonmembers who care for children and support families across Canada.

Canadian Association of Speech-Language Pathologists and Audiologists
Web site: http://www.caslpa.ca
Representing 3,800 speech-language pathologists and audiologists and supporting their professional development needs through a variety of services, including a national certification program, and championing the interests of people who require speech, language, and hearing services through advocacy activities.

Canadian Child Care Federation
Web site: http://www.cccf-fcsge.ca
Improving the quality of child care for Canada's families through a membership base of 9,000 child care providers across the country.

Canadian Coalition for the Rights of Children
Web site: http://www.rightsofchildren.ca
Promoting the concerns of over fifty national, nongovernmental organizations to ensure the observance, both by governments and individuals, of the rights and freedoms proclaimed in the United Nations Convention on the Rights of the Child.

Canadian Council of Food and Nutrition
Web site: http://www.ccfn.ca
Working toward the nutritional health of all Canadians through a network of some 3,000 key decision makers in the nutrition and health field, including health professionals, academics, government representatives, industry leaders, and media contacts.

Canadian Council on Social Development
Web site: http://www.ccsd.ca
This is one of the largest and most active agencies providing nongovernmental information on social issues, including those of children and youth. Some of their recent publications include: The Progress of Canada's Children for 1999–2000, 2001, and 2002, and can be found at www.ccsd.ca/research.htm.

Canadian Health Network
Web site: http://www.canadian-health-network.ca
The Canadian Health Network (CHN) is a national, bilingual health promotion program The CHN's goal is to help Canadians find the information they are looking
for on how to stay healthy and prevent disease.

Canadian Institute of Child Health
Web site: http://www.cich.ca
Working with governments, educators, and professionals to equip them with the best
in research and programs, and reaching out to families to help with the crucial task
of nurturing, protecting, educating, and empowering our children and youth.

Canadian Mental Health Association
Web site: http://www.cmha.ca
Promoting the mental health of all people for over eighty years.

Canadian Paediatric Society
Web site: http://www.cps.ca
Serving Canadian children and its membership of 2,000 pediatricians by advocating
for the health needs of Canada's children and youth, establishing national standards and guidelines for pediatric care and practice, and providing continuing medical education in pediatrics.

Canadian Parents for French
Web site: http://www.cpf.ca
Valuing French as an integral part of Canada and dedicated to the promotion and
creation of French second-language learning opportunities for young Canadians.

Canadian Parks and Recreation Association
Web site: http://www.cpra.ca
Raising awareness and promoting the importance of quality community leisure services and recreation experiences for all Canadians through the advocacy efforts of
its 3,000 members and hundred of allies.

Canadian Public Health Association
Web site: http://www.cpha.ca
Advocating for the improvement and maintenance of personal and community health
through a membership network of 2,000.

Canadian Teachers' Federation
Web site: http://www.ctf-fce.ca
Ensuring that, as teachers, opinion was heard and taken into account whenever any
authority outside the provincial jurisdiction was considering action that would
affect teachers, or impinge on their work with students.

Canadian Toy Testing Council
Web site: http://www.toy-testing.org
Serving Canada's families through the publication of an annual toy report based on
input from a network of 400 families, evaluators, and advocates who encourage
the design, manufacture, and distribution of toys sensitive to children's needs.

Caring for First Nations Children Society
Web site: http://www.cfncs.com
To provide professional development, research, and liaison services for First Nations who protect and promote the well-being of First Nations children and families by respecting and reaffirming traditional values and beliefs, encouraging innovative and quality child and family service delivery, and empowering the voices of First Nations peoples.

Centre of Excellence for Child Welfare
Web site: http://www.cecw-cepb.ca
The Centre of Excellence for Child Welfare encourages collaborative projects that integrate child maltreatment prevention and interventions across a variety of sectors, including health care, education, justice, and recreation.

Centres of Excellence for Children's Well Being
Web site: http://www.hc-sc.gc.ca/hppb/childhood-youth/centres/index2.html
An initiative of the federal government of Canada. Each centre is focusing on a different issue: child welfare, communities, early childhood development, special needs, and youth engagement. The centres are dynamic "virtual" networks. They link experts in children's health regardless of the region in which they live.

Child and Family Canada
Web site: http://www.cfc-efc.ca
A unique Canadian public education Web site. Fifty Canadian nonprofit organizations have come together under the banner of Child & Family Canada to provide quality, credible resources on children and families on an easy-to-navigate Web site. The managing partner of the consortium is the Canadian Child Care Federation.

Child Welfare League of Canada
Web site: http://www.cwlc.ca
Promoting and protecting the well-being of at-risk children, youth, and their families through a network of 75 service agencies who serve over 500,000 children and their families.

Childwatch International
Web site: http://www.childwatch.uio.no
Childwatch International is a coalition of twenty-nine major academic and other research agencies around the world that focus on children's issues. Their Web site provides a wide range of research and more general information, as well as links to many other websites focused on specific issues.

Family Service Canada
Web site: http://www.familyservicecanada.org
Representing families and family-serving agencies across the country through a network of seventy-five service agencies who serve over 500,000 children and their families.

First Call
Web site: http://www.firstcallbc.org

NORTH AMERICA AND THE CARIBBEAN

A coalition of organizations and community groups that promote legislation, policy, and practice that will enable children and youth to achieve their full potential and to participate in making a better world. They believe that children and youth need first call on society's resources.

First Nations Child & Family Caring Society
Web site: http://www.fncfcs.com
Promoting the well-being of all First Nations children, youth, families, and communities with a particular focus on the prevention of, and response to, child maltreatment.

Girl Guides of Canada
Web site: http://www.girlguides.ca
Challenging girls to reach their potential and empowering them to give leadership and service as responsible citizens of the world.

Go for Green
Web site: http://www.goforgreen.ca
A national not-for-profit organization that encourages Canadians to pursue healthy, outdoor physical activity while being good environmental citizens. One of Go for Green's major programs is Active & Safe Routes to School, encouraging youth and their families to choose walking, cycling, and other active ways to get to and from school. Go for Green identifies and shares community-driven solutions that make a positive contribution to Canadian society.

Home Child Care Association of Ontario
Web site: http://www.hccao.com
Promoting, developing, and supporting home-based child care services for families through licensed agencies.

Hospital for Sick Children
Web site: http://www.sickkids.on.ca
Enhancing the health and well-being of children locally, nationally, and internationally by designing strategies and fostering networks that shape the health outcomes of children.

Invest in Kids
Web site: http://www.investinkids.ca
Ensuring the healthy social, emotional, and intellectual development of young children from birth to age five. Guided by experts in child development and parenting, their research, public education, and professional education initiatives are aimed at strengthening the parenting knowledge, skills, and confidence of all those who touch the lives of Canada's youngest children.

Learning Disabilities Association of Canada
Web site: http://www.ldac-taac.ca
Serving 10,000 families and professionals in every province and territory who work to help those affected by the presence of learning disabilities.

Media Awareness Network
Web site: http://www.media-awareness.ca
Serving the Canadian public school system and all Canadians through an online clearinghouse that provides resources for media education, consumer information, and
background materials on media issues affecting children and youth.

Multiple Births Canada
Web site: http://www.multiplebirthscanada.org
Improving the quality of life for multiple birth individuals and their families in Canada. With an extensive network of local chapters, healthcare professionals, and
organizations, Multiple Births Canada is the source for information on multiple
births in Canada.

Nunavut Inuit Child Care Association (NICCA)
Box 159
Port Inlet, NU X0A 050
Representing children, childcare centers, child development programs and services,
societies, and staff. NICCA will assume the principles of the Inuit Child Care Program and will work to assure that they are employed in Nunavut licensed childcare
centers. These include Inuit-directed, -developed, and -delivered services.

Safe Kids Canada
Web site: http://www.sickkids.ca/safekidscanada
Safe Kids Canada providing the public and professionals with information on
preventing children's injuries.

Sparrow Lake Alliance
Web site: http://www.sparrowlake.org
Raising awareness and promoting the optimal development of all children and youth
through a coalition membership of twelve professions and seven service sectors, as
well as representatives of parent and youth organizations in Ontario.

The Vanier Institute of the Family
Web site: http://www.vifamily.ca
Promoting the well-being of Canadian families through a diverse membership of 500
family lawyers, researchers, professional associations, teachers, libraries, and community groups.

Voices for Children (VFC)
Web site: http://www.voices4children.org
Striving to strengthen public commitment to the healthy development of children
and youth in Ontario. VFC has a vision of citizens working together to communi-
cate the importance of healthy child development and the need for supportive,
family-friendly policies and programs.

Volunteer Canada
Web site: http://www.volunteer.ca
Promoting volunteerism in Canada, strengthening communities, and developing the
capacity of the voluntary sector to engage citizens as volunteers.

Youth Net/Réseau Ado (YN/RA) Ottawa
Web site: http://www.youthnet.on.ca
A bilingual regional mental health promotion and intervention program run by
youth, for youth.

Selected Bibliography

Adema, William, Anaïs Loizillon, Elina Pylkkänen, Olivier Thevenon, Maxime Laidique, Elma Lopes, and Mark Pearson. 2005. *Babies and Bosses—Reconciling
Work and Family Life, Vol. 4: Canada, Finland, Sweden, and the United Kingdom.* OECD Publishing.

Allen, Mary, Shelley Harris, and George Butlin. 2003. *Finding Their Way: A Profile
of Young Canadian Graduates.* Statistics Canada. Catalogue #81-595MIE-
no.003.

Ambert, Ann-Marie. 1998. *Divorce: Facts, Figures and Consequences.* York University,
for the Vanier Institute of the Family, 1998. Ottawa: Vanier Institute of the
Family. Revised 2005. www.vifamily.ca/library/cft/divorce_05.pdf.

Badgley, R. F. 1984. *Report of the Committee on the Study of Sexual Offences Against
Children in Canada.* Ottawa: Ministry of Supply and Services.

Baker, Maureen. 1995. *Canadian Family Policy.* Toronto: University of Toronto
Press.

Beyer, Peter. 2006. *Immigrant Youth and Religion in Canada.* A research project
conducted by and under the supervision of Dr. Peter Beyer. Department of
Classics and Religious Studies, University of Ottawa. http://aix1.uottawa.ca/
~pbeyer/immyouth.htm.

Brown, Maureen. 2002. *We Are Not Alone: Police Racial Profiling in Canada, the
United States, and the United Kingdom.* An Executive Summary of "Crisis,
Conflict, and Accountability," by Charles C. Smith and "In their Own Voices:
African Canadians in the Greater Toronto Area Share Experiences of Police
Profiling." Commissioned by the African-Canadian Coalition on Racial Profil-
ing. http://www.camtraomomg/prg/BTC/docs.CanadianReferences/We%
20are%20Not%20Alone%20-%20Police%20Profiling.pdf.

Campaign 2000. 2006. *2006 Report Card on Child and Family Poverty in Canada.*
http://www.campaign2000.ca/rc/rc06/06_C2000NationalReportCard.pdf.

Canada Evidence Act. 2007. http://laws.justice.gc.ca/en/C-5/.

Canadian Children's Rights Council. http://www.canadiancrc.com/.

Canadian Institute of Child Health; A CICH Profile. 2000. *The Health of Canada's
Children, 3rd edition.* Ottawa: Canadian Institute of Child Health.

Canadian Parks and Recreation Association. 2007. http://www.cpra.ca/e/
index.htm.

Canadian Social Trends: A Canadian Studies Reader. 1994. Vol. 2. Toronto:
Thompson Educational Publishing, Inc.

Central Intelligence Agency. 2006. World Fact Book. https://www.cia.gov/cia/pub
lications/factbook/print/ca.html.

Children and Families at Risk: New Issues in Integration Services. 1998. Center for
Educational Research and Innovation. OECD Publishing (e-book).

Citizenship and Immigration Canada. 2005. http://www.cic.gc.ca/english/pdf/
pub/facts2005.pdf.

City of Toronto. 2000. "The Toronto Report Card on Homelessness." http://
www.toronto.ca/homelessness/2000/index.htm.

Commission for Labor Cooperation. 2006. Guide to Child Labor Laws in Canada. http://www.naalc.org/migrant/english/pdf/mgcanchl_en.pdf.

Criminal Code of Canada. 2007. http://www.efc.ca/pages/law/cc/cc.html.

Department of Justice Canada. Selected Statistics on Canadian Families and Family Law, 2nd ed. http://www.justice.gc.ca/en/ps/sup/pub/selstats2000/chap1 .html.

———. Trafficking in Persons. Legislation (Bill C-49), An Act to Amend the Criminal Code (Trafficking in Persons). http://www.justice.gc.ca/en/fs/ht/bill.html.

Dolin, Benjamin, and Margaret Young. 2004. Canada's Immigration Program, revised. October 2004. Library of Parliament, Law and Government Division. http://www.parl.gc.ca/information/library/PRBpubs/bp190-e.htm.

Education@Canada. 2006. General Overview of Education in Canada. http:// www.education@canada.cmec.ca/EN/EdSys/over.php.

Family Violence Initiative. http://www.phac-aspc.gc.ca/ncfv-cnivf/.

Francis, L. J. 2000. "Youth and Religion." Canada and the World Backgrounder, December.

Glossop, Robert. 1999. "Family Life: Past, Present and Future." Transition Magazine 29, no. 4, Vanier Institute of the Family.

Government of Canada. 2002. National Report–Canada, Ten-Year Review of the World Summit for Children. http://www.phac-aspc.gc.ca/dca-dea/publications/pdf/ children-national-report-e.pdf.

———. Health Canada. 2002a. Healthy Canadians: A Federal Report on Comparable Health Indicators, 2002. Ottawa: Health Canada. http://www.hc-sc.gc.ca/ hcs-sss/pubs/care-soins/2002-fed-comp-indicat/index_e.html.

———. Health Canada. 2002b. The Family Violence Initiative, Five-Year Report. December. http://www.phac-aspc.gc.ca/ncfv-cnivf/familyviolence/pdfs/ Family-Violence-Report-040224.pdf.

Grzeskowiak, Mark. 2005. Healthcare in Canada. http://www.medhunters.com/ articles/healthcareincanada.

Henripin, Jacques. 2000. Les Enfants, la pauverté et la richesse au Canada [Children, poverty and wealth in Canada]. Montréal: Les Éditions Varia.

Hewlett, Sylvia Anne. 1992. When the Bough Breaks: The Cost of Neglecting our Children. New York: Harper Perennial Publishing

Howe, N., and Prochner, L. 2000. Early Childhood Care and Education in Canada. Vancouver: University of British Columbia Press.

Hwang, Stephen W. 2001. "Homelessness and Health." Canadian Medical Association Journal 164, no. 1: 229–233.

Indian and Northern Affairs Canada. 1998. Gathering Strength: Canada's Aboriginal Action Plan. Ottawa: INAC. http://www.ainc-inac.gc-ca/gs/pdf/rprt 98.pdf.

Karlis, George. 2004. Leisure and Recreation in Canadian Society. Ottawa: University of Ottawa Press.

Labor Program, Human Resources and Social Development Canada. October 15, 2006. http://www.hrsdc.gc.ca/en/lp/spila/clli/eslc/minage(e).pdf.

Marcil-Gratton, Nicole. 1998. Growing up with Mom and Dad? Children and Family Instability. Ottawa: Human Resources Development Canada, Applied Research Branch.

Minister of Indian Affairs and Northern Development. 2000. Gathering Strength: Canada's Aboriginal Action Plan, A Progress Report. Ottawa. http://www.inac.gc.ca.

National Forum on Youth Gangs. 1999. http://ww2.psepc-sppcc.gc.ca/Publica tions/Policing/199912_e.pdf.

Neuman, Shirley, Provost, University of Toronto. 2003. Introduction to the Conference [Presented at the Conference *Literacy Policies for the Schools We Need*, at the Ontario Institute for Studies in Education of the University of Toronto, Thursday, November 6]. http://literacyconference.oise.utoronto.ca/papers/provost.pdf.

Protocol to Prevent, Suppress and Punish Trafficking in Persons, Especially Women and Children, Supplementing the United Nations Convention against Transnational Organized Crime. 2000. http://www.uncjin.org/Documents/Conventions/dcatoc/final_documents_2/convention_%20traff_eng.pdf.

Public Health Agency of Canada. Statistics and Public Opinion, Re: Physical Activity Levels and Obesity in Children and Youth (source: Canadian Fitness and Lifestyle Research Institute, 2000 Physical Activity Monitor). http://www.phac-aspc.gc.ca/pau-uap/paguide/child_youth/media/stats.html.

Rogers, Rix. 1990. *Reaching for Solutions: Report of the Special Advisor to the Minister of National Health and Welfare on Child Sexual Abuse in Canada*. Ottawa: Health and Welfare Canada. http://www.phac-aspc.gc.ca/ncfv-cnivf/family violence/archives/html/1reach2.htm.

Sign On for Canada's Kids. 2000. "First Ministers' Communiqué on Early Childhood Development, Ottawa, September 11, 2000." http://www.childcaread vocacy.ca/sock/res/fmcomm.html.

Statistics Canada. 2001a. Census. http://www.statcan.ca/Daily/English/011114/d011114a.htm.

———. 2001b Census: Analysis Series Religions in Canada. http://www12.stat can.ca/english/census01/products/analytic/companion/rel/contents.cfm.

———. 2002. Weddings and Kids Less Popular. October 22. http://www.cbc.ca/news/story/2002/10/22/census_021022.html.

———. 2004. http://www40.statcan.ca/l01/cst01/health21a.htm.

———. 2006. http://www40.statcan.ca/l01/cst01/demo04a.htm.

———. 2006a. "Welcome to Statistics Canada." http://www.statcan.ca/start.html.

———. 2006b. Budget 2006. Ch. 3, Building a Better Canada: Families and Communities. http://www.fin.gc.ca/budget06/pdf/bp2006e.pdf.

———. 2007. Latest release from the Labor Force Survey. http://www.statcan.ca/english/Subjects/.

Stenning, Philip. 1994. *Police Use of Force and Violence against Members of Visible Minority Groups in Canada*. Ottawa: Solicitor General of Canada and Canadian Centre for Police-Race Relations.

Thomas, David, ed. 2000. *Canada and the United States: Differences that Count*, 2nd ed. Peterborough, Ontario: Broadview Press Ltd.

Tremblay, Hélène. 1988. *Families of the World, Family Life at the Close of the 20th Century*. New York: Farrar, Straus and Giroux.

Tremblay, M. S., and J. D. Willms. 2000. "Secular Trends in Body Mass Index in Canadian Children." *Canadian Medical Association Journal* 163, no. 11: 1429–1433.

Trocmé, N., D. Knoke, and Cindy Blackstock. 2004. "Pathways to the Representation of Aboriginal Children in Canada's Child Welfare System." *Social Service Review* 78, no. 4: 577–600.

Trocmé, Nico, et al. 2005. *Canadian Incidence Study of Reported Child Abuse and Neglect, 2003: Major Findings*. Ottawa: Public Works and Government Services.

Usalcas, Jeannine. 2005. "Youth and the Labour Market." *Perspectives on Labour and Income* 6, no. 11. http://www.statcan.ca/english/freepub/75-001-XIE/1110575-001-XIE.html.

Waddell, C., K. McEwan, C. A. Shepherd, D. R. Offord, and J. M. Hua. 2005. "A Public Health Strategy to Improve the Mental Health of Canadian Children." *Canadian Journal of Psychiatry* 5, no. 4: 226–233.

Worswick, Christopher. 2001. *School Performance of the Children of Immigrants 1994–1998*. Statistics Canada. Catalogue no. 11f0019MIE-178.

The Youth Criminal Justice Act. 2002. http://www.justice.gc.ca/en/ps/yj/ycja/explan.html.

Youth Protection Act. 1979, Article 38, Section 1 of Chapter 4. http://72.14.203.104/search?q=cache:wvqWLaF5i-J:142.213.87.17/en/commun/docs/LPJ_.

Zuzanek, Jiri. 2001. "Parenting Time: Enough or Too Little?" *Isuma: Canadian Journal of Policy Research* 2 (Summer): 125–133.

5

CUBA

María Isabel Domínguez,
translated by Sheryl Lutjens

"Children are born to be happy."

José Martí

NATIONAL PROFILE

In Cuban society today, children (birth to eighteen years of age) represent 25 percent of a population of more than 11 million people.[1] This is the lowest proportion in Cuban history. In the 1950s, 1960s, and 1970s, children represented nearly 40 percent of the population; in the 1980s, they were still a third of the population. The sustained rate of decline informs a prediction that by 2020 children will count for approximately 15 percent of the total population (Oficina Nacional de Estadísticas 2006, II.12). This change is a result of low birth rates combined with a continued increase in life expectancy (77.0 years) that is contributing to a rapid aging of the population.[2]

The processes of demographic transition occurring in Cuban society are one part of the larger process of social transformation during the last five decades, transformation that has had a strong impact on the social structure and the composition of families. The principal impact on social structure in Cuba is seen in the radical change in class structure. This change is explained by a concerted redistributive process that substantially reduced economic inequalities as well as by social policies that promoted

My thanks to Claudia Castilla for her assistance in the development of this chapter.

1. In 2005, the number of persons ages birth to eighteen years rose to 2,816,156 to a total population of 11,243,836 (Oficina Nacional de Estadísticas 2006, II.3).

2. Today, the population ages sixty or more years represents 15.8 percent of the total population (Oficina Nacional de Estadísticas 2006, II.3). Estimates are that by the year 2020, this group will represent 21 percent of the population (Oficina Nacional de Estadísticas, 2006, II.12) and by 2030, 30 percent (Oficina Nacional de Estadísticas 2004a, 110).

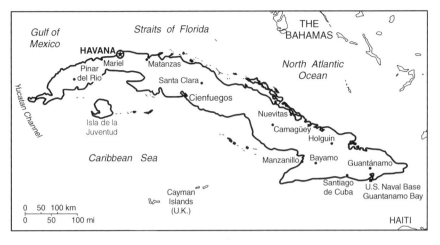

social justice and the eradication of discrimination based on gender, race, geographical location, or any other difference. These changes had a direct effect on the conditions of Cuban families. In the 1950s, the Cuban family was relatively large, with 4.9 members on average (Comité Estatal de Estadísticas 1984, CXXXVI) and a high rural concentration (Comité Estatal de Estadísticas 1984, LXXXOX). Educational levels were very low, with 80 percent of the population not completing the primary level of education (Comité Estatal de Estadísticas 1984, CLXXVII), as was women's participation in the work force and social life. For example, only 11 percent of women were active in the labor force (Tribunal Supremo Electoral 1953, 143).

Only 51 percent of boys and girls between the ages of six and sixteen were enrolled in school during this period (Comité Estatal de Estadísticas 1984, CLXXXVI), and only 25 percent of adolescents between fifteen and nineteen years old finished primary school (Comité Estatal de Estadísticas 1984, CLXXVII). According to the Survey of Employment, Underemployment, and Unemployment undertaken by the National Economic Council between May 1956 and April 1957, some 130,000 children worked for only minimal remuneration.

Improving the situation of children and youth, offering them every possibility for access to education, health, and a dignified life, has been one of the principal priorities of the social policies developed by the Cuban government since the triumph of the Revolution in January 1959. The attention to children and youth has been accompanied by an equivalent focus on women that is understandable given the direct relationship between these groups.

The Federation of Cuban Women, created in 1960, is a non-governmental organization with roots in communities and neighborhoods that represents the interests of women, and at the same time—together with other governmental agencies and social organizations—works to ensure the healthy development of children and youth.

Efforts were thus made to make real women's rights to study and to work. Special improvement and employment plans were created for specific groups of women, such as young women from rural areas and housewives.

As a result of policies such as these, the educational level of Cuban women increased at an accelerated pace.[3] There was also a significant change in the area of women's work outside the home. By 1975 and the United Nations-designated International Women's Year, the figure had already quadrupled, with women's share of the labor force reaching 27 percent (Comité Estatal de Estadísticas 1984, LXIII–LXXII). The proportion of women continued to grow, and by the start of the 1990s it reached 40 percent (Federación de Mujeres Cubanas 1996, 26).

In addition to education and employment, efforts in the area of women's health quite specifically attended to pregnant women, including both the early detection of deformities or genetic problems and the prevention of complications during pregnancy and delivery through the provision of hospital care for nearly all women having children. The attention to the reproductive health of women is accompanied by sex education measures, guaranteed access to contraceptives, and specialized attention (clinical and psychological) to the practice of abortion such that motherhood can be a responsible decision.

These commitments are complemented by legal protections that guarantee women the right to have paternal recognition and maintenance of their children even if the child is conceived outside of marriage, as well as the protection of mothers and their children by the state and society as sanctioned by the Cuban Constitution. The Constitution of the Republic, promulgated in 1976 and modified in 1992, establishes in Article 40 that "the state and society give special protection to children and young people. It is the duty of the family, the schools, the state agencies, and the social and mass organizations to pay special attention to the integral development of children and young people" (Asamblea Nacional de Poder Popular 1992, 21).

All of these policies have contributed to the changing demographic patterns of the population and especially the dynamics of fertility. After the sharp growth that took place immediately after the Revolution (with a high point in the 1964–1965 period), producing a sort of "baby boom" and maintaining high fertility rates until 1972, a sustained decline beginning in 1978 resulted in fertility rates that do not guarantee the replacement of the population. An interesting demographic dynamic in terms of the age structures of the population has, at each point of change, created the principal shifts in social policies.

---

3. During the 1960s and 1970s, the number of male graduates grew 4.76 times, and female graduates increased 12.76 times; in other words, the rate of growth of women graduates tripled the rate for men. For this reason, the proportion of women among graduates of higher education expanded significantly. Before 1959 two of every ten university graduates were women, in 1980 four of every ten were women, and in the 1990s the number rose to nearly seven (Domínguez 2004, 107).

Thus, in the 1960s and the first half of the 1970s, the age distribution was concentrated in children, which obligated social policies to attend rapidly to the demands of this social group. In this stage, the need for childcare centers, primary school teachers, and vaccination and other programs were met with the necessary emergency plans. Already beginning in the 1970s and 1980s, the social demands on state policy shifted to satisfying the needs of the adolescent and youth population. This was the point where huge numbers of students entered basic and higher secondary studies, requiring new emergency plans for the training of teachers for these levels, as well as the extensive construction of educational facilities. Then in the second half of the 1980s, the cohort of youth born in the "baby boom" arrived at working age, creating an expanding demand for employment (Domínguez et al. 1990). In other words, social policy was faced with the challenge of satisfying the widespread demands for basic education, higher levels of education, employment, youth recreation, housing for newly married couples, and childcare centers and primary education for the children of these young couples, all at the same time.

The decade of the 1990s presented the great challenge of conserving social policy at its previous levels, given the severe economic crisis that the country experienced as a result of changes in the international context that accompanied the collapse of the Eastern European socialist camp with which Cuba had maintained is principal economic relations and by the intensification of the economic and financial blockade established by the United States in the early 1960s. Undoubtedly this decade saw the negative effects of crisis in the living standards of the population, which also affected children, requiring a great effort by the state and society as a whole to conserve the successes achieved and to avoid decline in the social standards of education, health, and social well-being.

The current situation is different. Despite the fact that the harmful effects of the blockade continued, Cuba is finding new modes of reinsertion in the international economy and is achieving significant levels of economic growth that have permitted advances in its social programs. For example, during 2006, the gross national product (GNP) grew 12.5 percent, the highest rate of growth achieved by Cuba

---

KEY FACTS – CUBA

Population: 11,394,043 (July 2007 est.)
Life expectancy at birth: 77.08 years (2007 est.)
Literacy rate: 97 percent (2003 est.)
Net primary school enrollment/attendance: 96 percent (2000–2005)
Internet users: 190,000 (2005)
People living with HIV/AIDS: 4800 (2005 est.)
Human Poverty Index (HPI-1) Rank: 6

Sources: CIA World Factbook: Cuba. https://www.cia.gov/cia/publications/factbook/geos/cu.html. April 17, 2007; UNICEF. At a Glance: Cuba–Statistics. http://www.unicef.org/infobycountry/cuba_statistics.html. April 24, 2007; World Health Organization (WHO): UNAIDS/WHO Global HIV/AIDS Online Database. "Epidemiological Fact Sheets on HIV/AIDS and Sexuality Transmitted Diseases: Cuba." http://www.who.int/GlobalAtlas/predefinedReports/EFS2006/index.asp?strSelectedCountry=CU. December 2006; United Nations Development Programme (UNDP) Human Development Report 2006–Cuba. http://hdr.undp.org/hdr2006/statistics/countries/data_sheets/cty_ds_CUB.html. April 26, 2007.

after the triumph of the Revolution and the best in Latin America and the Caribbean in 2006, according to CEPAL. With these economic results, the 2007 state budget will dedicate resources equivalent to 22.6 percent of the GNP to education and public health, four times more than the average in Latin America.

At the same time, low fertility rates sustained over a long period of time, the rising life expectancy of the population, and migratory processes have catalyzed the aging of the population. Such a change in demographic structures favors the actions of social policies accustomed to prioritizing the much higher needs of children and youth whose numerical reduction allowed a shift to a strategy of more differentiated, and in many cases more personalized, attention.

OVERVIEW

At the beginning of the 21st century, a consistent decline in infant mortality rate means that Cuban children benefit from extremely good chances of being born alive, in adequate sanitary conditions, and of remaining healthy. The infant mortality rate in Cuba is about 5 per 1,000 live births, which is the lowest rate in Latin America and locates Cuba among those countries with the lowest infant mortality rates in the world.

Cuban boys and girls develop with free public health services guaranteed, and they have full access to education that is also public and free at every level, with equal opportunities for all children, regardless of gender, race, the economic situation of the family, religious affiliation, or the region of the country in which they live. This equality of opportunity facilitates educational coverage of 99 percent at the primary level and 86 percent at secondary level, with gender parity of 0.99 and 1.03 girls per boy respectively (Oficina Nacional de Estadísticas 2006, XVI.23).

The legal system of the country guarantees the rights of Cuban children to a healthy life and a quality education, to the protection of their families and of society as a whole, and to not be employed in activities that exploit or compromise their physical and moral integrity. Cuba is a signatory to the Convention on the Rights of the Child since January 1990, a mere two months after the approval on November 20, 1989, by the United Nations General Assembly, and to its ratification in 1991.

EDUCATION

Since 1959, education in Cuba has been public and free at every level. Education is compulsory through ninth grade.

For boys and girls of preschool age whose mothers work, there are childcare centers and kindergartens that enroll children between one and five years old. Currently, approximately 17 percent of Cuban children in this age group attend preschool institutions (Oficina Nacional de

Estadísticas 2006, XVI.2). There is also the "Educate Your Child" program for children in this age group. This program was conceived to provide attention to children who do not attend childcare centers, either because their mothers do not work outside the home or because the coverage of childcare centers is still not universal. The "Educate Your Child" program is coordinated by the Ministry of Education and the Federation of Cuban Women, organizing preschool education through informal or noninstitutional methods with the objective of orientating the family to enable it to nurture their child's development with scientifically based ideas and pedagogical methods that correspond to the educational needs of children in this age group.

Primary education has achieved nearly universal coverage for children aged six to eleven (99 percent) and coverage is 96.8 percent at the secondary level (until ninth grade). For the children in the twelve to seventeen years age group as a whole, however, coverage is 86 percent (Oficina Nacional de Estadísticas 2006, XVI. 23).

The upper level of secondary education has two basic modalities: preuniversity education that prepares adolescents for enrollment in high education and technical-professional education that prepares youth for the exercise of a trade or profession, although these youth may subsequently continue with university studies.

Children with physical or mental disabilities also have a guaranteed right to education. They are evaluated by specialists in the Centers for Diagnosis and Orientation, of which there are 193 in all the provinces, and they attend one of the 421 schools of special education that exist on the island. For those children with a physical limitation that means they cannot attend school, there are "traveling" teachers who visit their homes, as well as hospital classrooms for those children who are hospitalized for long periods of time (O. Peñate 2005, 28).

After 2000, social policy was given a new impulse through the creation of what were called "new social programs." An important part of the new social programs is expanding the possibilities for access to a quality education for all Cuban children and youth.

Some of these new programs include the following:

• The large-scale preparation of teachers-in-training for primary education and of comprehensive teachers for secondary education. There was a related change in the conceptions of teaching in basic secondary education (junior high) with the shift from teachers working in specialized subject areas to comprehensive teachers who will cover all areas.

• The reduction in the number of students per classroom, to twenty in primary education and fifteen in basic secondary, in order to provide more personalized attention to students.

• Changes in programs of study with the introduction of computing and audiovisual programs at all levels of education, as well as the guarantee that the program has the needed technology through the provision of televisions, video players, and computers to all schools.

- Creation of Courses of Comprehensive Improvement for youth who neither study nor work, in which students receive remuneration and the opportunity to continue studying in higher education. In the first two years more than 100,000 youth graduated from these courses and, of them, one-third have enrolled in higher education.

- The expansion of higher education to all the localities in the country with the creation of municipal university centers. In the 1950s, only three universities existed in Cuba; in the 1990s, there were fifteen universities and forty-two other centers of higher education in medicine, pedagogical sciences, the arts, sports, and other fields, for a total of fifty-seven university centers (Oficina Nacional de Estadísticas 2004, 306). Currently, there are seventeen universities and another fifty-eight higher institutes in different fields for a total of sixty-five centers of higher education; there are also 3,150 university centers in the different municipalities of the country (Oficina Nacional de Estadísticas 2006, XVI.5). This vision of universalizing higher education has permitted enrollment to increase 3.8 times in only five years, the highest figure achieved in the history of Cuba, and one that ensures that all higher secondary school graduates can enter third-level studies (Oficina Nacional de Estadísticas 2006, XVI.19). Beyond facilitating the expansion of enrollments, the creation of municipal university centers has contributed to the modification of the social composition of the university student body, effectively extending educational opportunities to all sectors of society, in particular youth from the least advantaged social groups.[4]

In addition to institutional delivery of education, the training of children and youth is promoted in other ways. For example:

- Two new television channels with educational programming have been created, and such programs as "University for All" have been introduced to provide specialization in subject offerings, including foreign languages.

- The Youth Computation and Electronics Club Program has been extended to all localities in Cuba in order to develop an informatics culture in each community, with children and youth as a priority. This program has already graduated 150,000 youth in its regular courses. Today there are approximately 600 installations in Cuba's 169 municipalities, with an average growth since its creation in 2000 of eighty-two centers each year (Oficina Nacional de Estadísticas 2006, XIX.13).

---

4. Research findings show an increased presence of children of workers, and of blacks and mestizos in university classrooms (Domínguez and Domínguez 2005).

Without a doubt, education is a right that is guaranteed for children and youth, and they themselves recognize it as such.[5] Education constitutes the biggest category of expenditure in the state budget (in 2005 it reached 25.7 percent of expenditures) (Oficina Nacional de Estadísticas 2006, V.4), but improving the quality of education and making it even more accessible to all Cubans remain ongoing objectives.

PLAY AND RECREATION

Closely linked to the educational system are sports and recreational opportunities for children and adolescents. Physical education is taught throughout the entire educational system, promoting the practice of physical activities and different sports, in which student competitions are held at each level from the local schools up through the national level. For example, in 2005 thirty-six provincial and national level competitions were organized in thirty-six sports specialties with more than 30,000 students competing (Oficina Nacional de Estadísticas 2006, XX.2).

"Interest circles" are organized in primary and secondary schools. Students join these groups according to their diverse interests, which could be scientific, artistic, sports, culinary, and so on, and use play as a means to develop abilities and knowledge in these areas. To the end of development of abilities, there are installations called "Pioneer Palaces." There is still an insufficient number of "Palaces" for all children to attend however.

Student organizations at the primary and secondary levels also develop such activities as the Movement of Pioneer Explorers, Pioneer camping (*campismo*), and other activities and excursions that combine physical activity with learning about nature and the protection of the environment. Children and youth especially like camping and the direct contact with nature it provides, whether it is in the countryside, the beach, or other spots of particular natural interest. As a mode of recreation, families often participate in campismo, although it has a special appeal for youth. Despite the growth of installations for this form of recreation (called "camping bases") and the improvement of general conditions, the demand by youth still exceeds capacity, above all during periods of vacation.

Children can also count on cultural and recreational space in the mass media. Specific radio and television programming is dedicated to children and adolescents, and there is a national production of programs for children.

In Cuba, there exists cinema produced for children that is also expanding. In 2005, seventy-six animated films were produced, a number that is nineteen times greater than the production in 2000 (Oficina Nacional de Estadísticas 2006, XIX.3).

---

5. According to a survey undertaken with adolescents between fourteen and eighteen years of age, 91.7 percent recognized education as one of their principal rights and, in fact, it was the most widely recognized right (A.I. Peñate 2005, 16)

Similarly, there is extensive production of audiovisuals of varied types. The Festival of Audiovisuals for Children and Adolescents is celebrated annually, a project of education for communication based in respect for the creativity and expressiveness of children and their identification with the values that are properly their own. The festival has been accompanied since 1988 by a concurrent theoretical event called "The Audiovisual Universe of Latin American Children" (UNIAL).

At the fifth meeting (1993) of this theoretical event, a network was created with the same name (UNIAL Network), conceived to unify the efforts of individuals and institutions of Iberoamerica that, without any profit motive whatsoever, aim to develop projects that promote the training, from the earliest ages, of more active, critical, and participatory spectators of cinema, audiovisual means of communication, and the world in which they live. Since 1995, the network has convened an international postgraduate course, "The Child and the Image," aimed at educators, researchers, and, in general, any individual interested in audiovisual work with children and youth.

There is also theatrical programming dedicated to children and youth, and some productions have been awarded international prizes. One example is the children's theater group "La Colmenita," composed entirely of children and staging a work that focuses on the integration of children with disabilities. Nevertheless, these offerings are concentrated more in the capital and the other principal Cuban cities, and for this reason special attention is given to the promotion of local initiatives through the Houses of Culture (*Casas de Cultura*) that exist in each municipality, the Workshops of Comprehensive Transformation in Havana City, and the many communitarian projects currently underway throughout the island.

Published work dedicated to children and youth is ample. Of the total number of books and pamphlets published in 2005, 84 percent were textbooks for education, an additional 2.5 percent was dedicated to children's entertainment, and 1 percent was for youth. Although the latter of these percentages might seem rather small, they actually reflect strong growth in publishing for children between 2000 and 2005—that for children grew nine times and for youth eight times, representing a great volume of books (Oficina Nacional de Estadísticas 2006, XIX.2). Magazines for children and youth are published regularly, including *Zunzún*, *Pionero* (Pioneer), *Somos Jóvenes* (We Are Youth), and *Muchachas* (Girls), among others.

In events related to books and reading, such as the International Book Fair celebrated every year in February—and now extended throughout the entire country (the first fairs were only in Havana), sales of children's books are high as is the participation of children in the many activities offered at the fair.

Schools and other cultural institutions work to elevate the taste for reading. Libraries, whether national, provincial, or municipal, have a Children and Youth Room and promote numerous literary competitions.

An effort is being made to increase the production of recorded children's music and to promote musical programs for children, a line of work that has had insufficient attention in recent years. This was a concern for a large number of institutions and specialists because the missing children's songs were substituted by a preference for other songs and styles of rhythm typically considered to be adult, which has little correspondence with the worries, knowledge, and necessary fantasies of children (Pérez 2006, 4; Y. Díaz 2006, 10).

Currently, neighborhood playgrounds, affected by the economic crisis of the 1990s, are also being recuperated as a social space in which boys and girls play, undertake physical activities, and establish social relations with their peers. For example, in Havana City there are 300 children's playgrounds, and efforts are underway to provide better conditions in them as well as to construct new ones (Ríos 2004, 8).

Television is one of the activities preferred by children, and, as noted, Cuban society is experiencing the development of an informational culture with increased access to computing, digital games, and the like. Yet the majority of children actually use their free time to play games and practice traditional physically active sports outside, in the streets and parks, and with the collective participation that is an important component of their socialization.

In this vein, some studies have demonstrated that even though some gender differences exist in the recreational interests of adolescents, young girls preferring artistic and reading options and the boys showing more affinity for sports and active games, in general all adolescents tend to enjoy activities in which they have to "poner el cuerpo" (use their body)—dancing, theater, sports—and have less desire to be passive (Álvarez 2005, 53).

In general, Cuban children and adolescents have many opportunities for the healthy enjoyment of their free time through games, the arts, and recreation, and the major part of these activities are free or offered at a very low cost. Nevertheless, the actual use of many of these opportunities, in particular those that are offered outside the school environment, depend on the possibilities and interests of the family, of levels of education, cultural interests, availability of free time, geographical location, and so on, and this creates a challenge for public policies that aim to expand recreational options and make them increasingly more accessible.

CHILD LABOR

One of the most important actions of the Cuban state in favor of children was the elimination of child labor nearly five decades ago. Legislation establishes seventeen as the age at which working life begins and that only in exceptional conditions may adolescents of fifteen and sixteen years of age be employed (never younger than fifteen years old) in the capacity of apprentices, under the supervision of older workers who act as tutors, and only in certain types of work. For this reason, minors who work (fifteen or sixteen years old) represent only 0.02 percent of workers and constitute 0.3 percent of adolescents in this age group. Moreover, youth of working age between seventeen and nineteen are only 2.7 percent of the work force and 25.6 percent of their age group (Oficina Nacional de Estadísticas 2006, II.3 and VI.8).

The fact that education is compulsory until ninth grade and that both primary and more recently secondary levels of education have a regimen of double sessions, limit the possibility that the family will use children as economic support for the family, whether in agricultural labor or in urban work in the self-employment sector.

Nevertheless, the concept of education that is applied in Cuban schools postulates the importance of linking study and work as a formative element in the creation of capacities such as, above all, the formation of ethical values. In this way, beginning at the secondary level the schools have different modalities for linking the student with productive activities, including the "Schools to the Countryside," the "Schools in the Countryside," and different programs for social and community service. Similarly, in technical-professional education and higher education, adolescents and youth are placed in internships in labor centers associated with the specialty they study. Finally, during periods of vacation student brigades are organized with the voluntary participation of students in a diverse array of socially useful tasks.

These activities are in all cases realized under adequate supervision and have an educational content; in no case is the objective to benefit from the work of children or adolescents.

FAMILY

The families in which Cuban children live today are diverse and do not always correspond with the traditional family patterns. Contemporary families have fewer members (an average of 3.16 members) (Oficina Nacional de Estadísticas 2005, 164); only infrequently will a family have more than two children (a child younger than fifteen is found in only 46.2 percent of family units; of them 66.3 percent have only one child and three or more children are found in a scant 5.5 percent of families) (Oficina Nacional de Estadísticas 2005, 308). There is a high proportion of divorced parents (7 percent of the population is divorced) (Oficina Nacional de Estadísticas 2005, 170), and also a high proportion of families that are recomposed through a new marriage or union of one of the parents. In more than a few cases, children live with their mother only or, to a lesser extent, with their father only (25.8 percent of the heads of household are women) (Oficina Nacional de Estadísticas 2005, 239). And in many cases families live in multigenerational households, sometimes including four generations, in part because the housing deficit—above all in the capital city Havana—necessitates intergenerational cohabitation (40.5 percent of the family units in Cuba are defined as extended or compound, that is, they consist of other persons besides parents and children) (Oficina Nacional de Estadísticas 2005, 309).

Traditional gender roles in the interior of the family are still strong and relegate to the mother the care and education of children, despite the profound social transformations that have catalyzed the transformation of the social role of women. These traditional roles are reproduced in the socialization of boys and girls.

The family, and more specifically women, have the support of the government in the protection of their rights and those of their children. A series of legislative measures and practical actions have favored women, including the following: the promulgation of the Family Code in 1975, which expresses the equality of rights and responsibilities of women and men in the context of the family and their responsibilities with regard to children; the revision of the Labor Code with the objective of eliminating restrictions and prohibitions that affect women; and the approval and implementation of the National Action Plan for Follow-up to the IV United Nations Conference on Women and the creation of governmental commissions needed (M. Álvarez 2000, 83–84), such as the creation within the National Assembly (Parliament) of the Permanent Commission for Attention to Children, Youth and the Equal Rights of Women.

The area of legal protections includes policies regarding motherhood that support women's inclusion in the social sphere. Laws and resolutions grant women paid maternity leave with guaranteed salary and a return to her position for periods of time that have been extended through the years. Law 1263/74 (1974) provided twelve weeks of paid leave (half before and half after the birth of her child), with the possibility of part-time work thereafter. This law was complemented with Resolution 10/91 (1991) that expanded the extent of paid leave to eighteen weeks (six before the birth and twelve after) and the option of extending with a partially paid leave (60 percent of salary) until the child reaches six months or an unpaid leave until the children turns one, if the mother cannot return to her job (Federación de Mujeres Cubanas 1996, 31). Decree-Law 234 of August 2003 reconfirmed the previous conditions but extended the option of a 60-percent paid leave until her child turns one and the possibility that this option can be used by the mother, the father, or another authorized family member (O. Peñate 2005, 25–26).

Since 1987, a program has existed that provides comprehensive social attention to single mothers and minors with social problems, including not only financial assistance through social welfare but also help with job placement for these women, the enrollment of their children in daycare centers and schools with semi-boarding conditions, as well as orientation to help them face their economic difficulties and the psychological and social problems that can be present. In the same way, the program promotes the reestablishing of relations with parents who do not fulfill their obligations, attempting to find them and persuade them to provide both material and affective attention to their children (O. Peñate 2005, 27).

More recently, as a result of two national studies, a program was created in 2003 to attend to mothers of children with severe disabilities. A psychosocial study of persons with disabilities and a psychopedagogical genetic study—both social and clinical—of persons with mental retardation facilitated the decision to turn the labor of mothers who care for their severely disabled children into "employment." In the case of mothers who had previously worked outside the home, they are remunerated at the level of their earlier salary and for housewives, economic measures were defined according to the needs of the family unit. For both groups of mothers, this new form of work comes with all the normal labor rights, including the accumulation of time towards retirement. Those mothers that continue to work are offered the option of a social assistant who will come to the home to care for the child during the hours they are away at work.

For children who are orphaned, help is provided to extended family members to ensure that they are cared for. When this is not possible, there are homes for children without family protection, under the supervision of the Ministry of Education, in which they are provided with maintenance, education, and recreation, as well as the affection of an environment that is as much like a family home as possible (O. Peñate 2005, 27).

HEALTH

The health of the population in general and of children more specifically, together with education, constitute the two principal priorities of the social policies of the Cuban state. The expenditures dedicated to health amount to 17 percent of the total expenditures in the state budget (Oficina Nacional de Estadísticas 2006, V.4).

The efforts in the area of health are reflected in an ongoing reduction in the infant mortality rate. For example, in the last eleven years the decline in infant mortality rate has been on the order of 43.6 percent, which has produced a rate of 5.3 per 1,000 live births at the end of 2006, the lowest in Latin America and in the Americas; only Canada has a lower rate. Cuba is among thirty countries of the world with the lowest infant mortality rates (Peláez, 2007).

The principal causes of death of children less than one year old are perinatal infections such as hypoxia, hyaline membrane disease, and bronchial aspiration of meconial amniotic fluid, as well as congenital malformations and chromosomal abnormalities, infections typical of populations with a high level of development (Oficina Nacional de Estadísticas 2006, XV.20).

This is the result of painstaking attention that begins with the mother, within the frame of one of the most important public health programs in Cuba, the Mother and Child Program. Mothers receive systematic monitoring during the entire pregnancy, which includes not only ambulatory medical attention or admission to the hospital if necessary, but also the possibility to stay in health institutions called "maternity homes" (*hogares maternos*). Maternity homes provide care for pregnant women who are at any type of risk to prevent possible complications; they are attended with such programs as the Early Diagnosis of Genetic Diseases Program and the Reduction of Low Birth Weight Program. These maternity homes fulfill an important function, above all in the most rural and isolated parts of the island. The low infant mortality rates are thus found throughout the entire country, and nine of Cuba's fourteen provinces demonstrate an infant mortality rate lower than the national average, among them some of the provinces with the largest proportion of rural population. It is also important to note as well that, in completing this cycle of care of mothers and children, practically all births are in health institutions with hospital facilities.[6]

After the birth, the mother and child are attended with the Program to Promote Breastfeeding in order to increase this mode of nourishing the child, the Program of Perinatal Development, the Program to Combat Severe Diarrheal Illnesses and Severe Respiratory Infections, the Program for Prevention and Control of Infectious Neurological Syndromes, the Follow-up Growth of Children under Five Years Old, and the National Immunization Program. This last program guarantees the administration of ten vaccinations in the child population to protect against thirteen transmissible illnesses: poliomyelitis, diphtheria, tetanus, pertussis, *Haemophilus influenzae* type B, measles, German measles, mumps, infantile tuberculosis, typhoid fever, meningitis B and C, and hepatitis B (Instituto Nacional de Investigaciones Económicas 2005, 24).

There are other important health programs—attention and prevention—developed by the Cuban state for children and adolescents. These include the National Action Program on Accidents in Minors under Twenty Years Old, the Program for Conscientious Motherhood and Fatherhood, the Program for Responsible Sexual Conduct, the "For Life" Community Program, the Program of Comprehensive Attention to Adolescents, and the "Growing Up in Adolescence" and "My Life Plan" Projects (Audivert and Otazo 2005, 11). State programs are offered to the entire population without any socially based distinction and are completely free.

These health programs are complemented by other community and environmental efforts, such as the National Program for Potable Water

---

6. Even in the most difficult moments of the economic crisis of the decade of the 1990s, hospital births were maintained with a 99.8 percent coverage in 1995 (Federación de Mujeres Cubanas 1996, 89).

that proposed to achieve more extensive coverage and currently guarantees sustainable access to potable water for 95.6 percent of the population: 98.2 percent in urban areas and 87.3 percent in rural zones (Instituto Nacional de Investigaciones Económicas 2005, 65). Related actions include sanitation and vector control, most notably in the Campaign to Eliminate the Aedes Aegyptis mosquito that transmits dengue and yellow fevers.

Cuba works with the collaboration of international organizations and agencies in the implementation of some of its programs, such as United Nations Children's Fund (UNICEF), United Nations Educational, Scientific and Cultural Organization (UNESCO), United Nations Population Fund (UNPF), and the United Nations Development Program (UNDP).

Health programs are also supplemented with communications strategies directed to the education of children and youth for a healthy lifestyle. For example, since 1998 members of UNIAL described earlier have coordinated the "Gemini" Project of education for communication, under the auspices of the UN-HIV/AIDS program and the UNICEF Office. This project organizes efforts to establish a strategy for group work with adolescents in the elaboration and dissemination of audiovisual messages on the thematic of sexually transmitted diseases and HIV/AIDS.

This is an area of health care that has received special emphasis within the programs and policies for prevention and attention to adolescence and youth. The HIV/AIDS epidemic in Cuba has grown slowly since its appearance at the end of the 1970s, and currently the prevalence rate is one of the lowest in the world (less than 0.1 percent of the sexually active population) (Trinquete 2005, 4). This is explained by the existence of specialized services for the population that are universal and free, an effective system of detection that allows for early diagnosis of cases, and a commitment to education, prevention, and comprehensive care that includes clinical, nutritional, and psychosocial attention (Rosabal 2005, 26).

By December 31, 2005, 6,967 cases of seropositive individuals had been diagnosed, of which 41.9 percent became ill with AIDS, and of those 47.6 percent have died. Of the total cases of HIV, 80 percent are men (Rosabal 2005, 24); at the time of diagnosis of their condition, more than 70 percent were between fifteen and twenty-nine years of age, with a concentration in the subgroup aged twenty-five to twenty-nine (Domínguez and Domínguez 2005, 17).

Given that the majority of persons who have contracted HIV have done so through unprotected sexual relations, and that there is a predominance of men who have sexual relations with other men, policy has stressed the importance of disease prevention through education and social communication that modifies the mistaken perceptions of youth (Domínguez and Domínguez 2005).

Cases of seropositive infants are very rare in Cuba, and all are a result of transmission from a mother who has decided to have her child; mother and child are cared for from the gestational stage. The accumulated experience with attention to these children, including the guarantee of adequate health conditions and quality of life, is highly satisfactory (Trujillo and Rodríguez, 2005)

LAWS AND LEGAL STATUS

In the legal field, there is a set of laws and regulations that advocates for the rights and protection of children, enacted even before these were defined in the United Nations Convention on the Rights of the Child. Among the principal laws and regulations are the Constitution of the Republic, the Code of Children and Youth, The Law of Social Security, the Labor Code, the Law of Maternity of the Working Woman, the Penal Code, and others.

Since 1999, the Project of Dissemination of the Rights of Children and Adolescents in Cuba has worked to make known the articles of the convention and to enable social actors who work to promote a legal consciousness in children, adolescents, and the adult population, which will consolidate the process of promoting, developing, protecting, and respecting children and adolescents (Audivert and Otazo 2005, 4). To implement the project, sixteen Centers of Reference on the Rights of Children and Adolescents were created: one with a national scope; three regional centers for the western, central, and eastern regions; and twelve provincial centers (in the remaining provinces). Each reference center relies on multisectorial technical teams coordinated by the Ministry of Justice and its territorial offices. The governmental institutions represented in the technical teams include those attending to education, health, culture, sports and recreation, radio and television, hydraulic resources, work, and social security, among others. Other participating organizations include student organizations, the Federation of Cuban Women, the Commission for Prevention and Social Attention, and research centers such as the Center for Legal Research, the Center for the Study of Youth, and the National Center for Sex Education (Audivert and Otazo 2005, 8).

Despite all the social efforts to guarantee the equality of opportunities for all, there are always children and adolescents that remain in situations of social disadvantage, that find themselves neither studying nor working, and that even fall into antisocial and/or criminal behavior. The Cuban legal system involves different actors in the treatment of these cases, for which it has particular standards. This area of work dates from 1959 and the creation of the Ministry of Social Welfare, one of whose functions was attention to minors who were abandoned or broke the law. This process developed through different stages and in 1986 a decree-law created the System for Attention to Minors, which remains in force today, albeit with some modifications. Among the fundamental objectives of the system was to decriminalize/depenalize minors, taking them out of the traditional legal and penal systems to center attention to them in socio-educative work. This conception of work was, according to the opinion of specialists, based in "the most advanced techniques in the world in relation with the special education pedagogy directed at resolving problems of conduct" (M. Díaz et al. 2006). At the same time, the System of Attention to Minors worked in coordination with Public Health, the family, and other community actors to elaborate a design for attending to minors and the family with a long-term perspective.

One aspect currently under discussion is the age at which majority is achieved. Although the laws establish that full majority is reached at eighteen years of age, the System of Attention to Minors is designed for attention to minors younger than sixteen. The period between sixteen and eighteen requires decisions by the Council of Minors with regard to the placement of youth in centers of reeducation or in penal institutions.

In recent years, the system of reeducation of youth has been strengthened, including the reeducation of those in prison via the creation of university classrooms in these institutions to offer incarcerated youth the opportunity to improve themselves and even to achieve a university-level education.

RELIGIOUS LIFE

The diversity of religious life in Cuba paints a complex picture that is reflected in the different content of religious representations, in the levels of development of religious consciousness, and consequently, in activities and organizational forms (Ramírez Calzadilla 2003, 99).

The religious expressions that exist in the country can be classified according to their origin and content as:

- Christian churches, Catholic as well as Protestant, and among the latter, those representing both the beginning of the Reformation and subsequent development, particular in the United States, whose multiplication of Protestantism into different denominations has been reproduced in Cuba.

- Religious expressions of African origin, shaped according to the religious forms that persons of different African ethnicities who arrived as slaves carried with them, and that evolved according to the living conditions in Cuba.

- Spiritualism, both in the version closest to the European and North American Kardecian tradition as well as the syncretic forms typical in Cuba.

- Expressions associated with different immigrant groups, among which are Judaism and Islam.

- Expressions of Eastern philosophical-religious traditions (Ramírez Calzadilla 2003, 98).

None of the religious expressions has prevailed in making itself the typical Cuban religion (Ramírez Calzadilla 2003, 115).

Nevertheless, the most widespread expression of religiosity is that which the specialists call "popular religiosity," characterized as spontaneous, relatively independent of institutional organization, and expressed at the level of everyday consciousness with a heavy affective content. Popular religiosity is manifested in irregular and occasional practices or elemental norms that are established spontaneously, individually, or in the family grouping, without the constitution of cohesive groups (Ramírez Calzadilla 2003, 102). This popular religiosity is shaped by the assimilation of elements of different religious expressions, in particular those of African origin, spiritualism, and Catholicism (Ramírez Calzadilla 2003, 115).

In this form of religiosity, an important place is occupied by devotion to figures in which the supernatural is personified; these are syncretic figures considered to be miraculous in themselves, rather than mediators before a God. For this reason, they do not have a place within traditional religious systems (Ramírez Calzadilla 2003, 116). This is the case with the Virgin "de la Caridad del Cobre," considered to be the Patroness of Cuba, as well as San Lázaro and Santa Bárbara, among others. Devotion to these figures calls spontaneously upon a larger number of believers than the numbers of any other organized religion or the total of several of them (O. Pérez 2003, 133).

The Cuban Constitution declares that religious institutions are separate from the state and recognizes, respects, and guarantees religious liberty. While religious practice is therefore not officially promoted, different beliefs and religions enjoy equal consideration (Article 8), and children, adolescents, and youth will approach religious belief systems and practices from the everyday perspective of their family and social group.

Research conducted on the participation of the population in festivities of devotion to the miraculous figures mentioned earlier has found that children are about 6.8 percent of the total number of participants (O. Pérez 2003, 134).

With regard to religious rites for children, the most widespread is baptism, which is practiced most by Catholic believers but is also present in other sectors of the population that engage in the popular religiosity mentioned above. To a lesser degree, communion is practiced.

In the 1990s, Cuban society experienced not only the spontaneous growth of religiosity but also an increase in the work of religious institutions and groups (the Catholic Church, Evangelical Churches, expressions of African origin, and others). In this context there was an increase in preaching/proselytizing, work with the young and families, baptisms, and church marriages, among other practices of the populace (Ramírez Calzadilla et al. 2004).

Religious organizations have a space within Cuban civil society and undertake their own institutional activities that include children, adolescents, and youth, although they have no responsibility for fulfilling the needs for education, health, protection for orphaned children, and other activities that the church may assume in other societies. In Cuba, fulfilling these needs is the responsibility of the state.

CHILD ABUSE AND NEGLECT

Given the strength of state policies for the protection of children, adolescents, and youth, institutionalized practices that allow the abuse of children, such as being forced to work or to undertake a type of activity that puts their physical and moral integrity in danger, do not exist. This does not mean that there are no cases of child abuse in the family context or that children do not experience the negative effects of intrafamily violence in general, and violence against women more specifically. The phenomenon of abuse has been substantially invisible and, as the specialists in the subject suggest, it was only in the 1990s that studies of child abuse were undertaken (M. Díaz et al. 2006).

For example, an edited collection by the Center for the Study of Women that included twenty studies about intrafamily violence in Cuba between 1994 and 1999 shows that about 12 percent of the victims of family violence were minors, with a predominance of girls (two-thirds), and the negative consequences are seen in scholarly performance, in family life, and in the community among the sons and daughters of women who were victims of violence. Violence toward children is expressed in terms of abuse (insults, shouting, blows, punishments), inattention, and abandonment (Centro de Estudios de la Mujer 1999, cited by M. Díaz et al. 2006). Other studies undertaken with children admitted to pediatric hospitals have verified the effects of inattention and neglect in the care of children, such as acute diarrheal illnesses, malnutrition, and intoxication due to ingestion of medicines or alcohol (Acosta 2002).

To counteract these tendencies, organizations and institutions exist in the country that direct their work to the protection of minors, such as the Federation of Cuban Women that was founded in 1960 and the National Commission for Prevention and Social Attention created in 1986. At the same time, laws and general welfare dispositions exist that promote the well-being of children at risk of being victims of abuse or negligence. For example, the Penal Code categorizes as crimes such deeds as illegal abortion, abandonment of minors and incapacitated or disabled persons, lascivious abuses, incest, substitution of one child by another, pederasty with violence, corruption of minors, and sale or traffic of minors (Aguilera 2001; González, cited by Díaz et al. 2006).

In 1999, at the suggestion of the Federation of Cuban Women, a series of modifications in the Penal Code took place. The modifications intensified the sanctions for crimes against the bodily integrity and normal development of sexual relations, the family, children, and youth.

Nevertheless, specialists insist on the need for improving the system of collecting and processing statistics, in particular regarding intrafamily violence, and for a system of specialized attention for victims of child abuse.

Work is underway in this area with an emphasis on social education for a nonviolent cohabitation. Currently, the UNIAL network is developing a project, "The Children Say NO to Violence," by means of audiovisual material and television spots whose objective is to stimulate children's reflection and their education with regard to some of the manifestations of violence and to motivate the creativity of minors in the search for non-violent solutions to their everyday problems.

Also underway is the development of an innovative methodology for the prevention of intrafamily violence, called "Living in Families without Violence," whose application offers resources and strategies from social, personal, and familial development perspectives (Durán et al. 2005).

GROWING UP IN THE TWENTY-FIRST CENTURY

Cuban children have entered the new century with a group of basic social guarantees that permit them to arrive in the world healthy, avail themselves of free medical care, have a long life expectancy, enjoy access to quality education, count on identifying for themselves important career choices, and develop in a social context characterized by the security of all citizens. Children in the 2000s are already enjoying in the present— and will have better prospects in the future—the social programs being developed to perfect public policies in all areas (Domínguez 2006).

In addition to these advantages, there are a number of challenges. The first is the reduction in the size of the child population due to low fertility rates. While this does not have immediate effects on today's children, in the medium- and long-term this generational group will have to bear the burden of the expanding population of older persons.

Children also face the challenge of taking advantage of the equality of opportunities provided by existing social programs that are increasingly more differentiated in order to combat the social inequalities that issue from the family situation, such as level of education, socioeconomic standing, racial identity, and geographical locations.

Finally, children also face the challenge of living in a society with a less-developed economy in a world that is increasingly more unequal and polarized, with threats to peace and international stability, and the destruction of the global environment.

Yet without a doubt, in the setting in which they live in the contemporary world, affected by numerous threats and at the same time offering many avenues to a healthy and educated life, Cuban children occupy a privileged location.

RESOURCE GUIDE

Suggested Readings

Álvarez, Mayda. 2000. *Situación de la niñez, la adolescencia, la mujer y la familia en Cuba* [Situation of children, adolescents, women, and the family in Cuba]. Centro de Estudios de la Mujer (CEM) y Fondo de las Naciones Unidas para la Infancia (UNICEF), Havana: Editorial de la Mujer. This report provides an analysis of the situation of children, adolescents, women, and the family based on national statistics.

Audivert, Ana E., and Rubén Otazo. 2005. "El Proyecto de Divulgación de los Derechos de la Niñez y la Adolescencia. Los marcos de la experiencia cubana" [The Project of Disseminating the Rights of Children and Adolescents: The framework of Cuban experience]. *Estudio* (Centro de Estudios sobre la Juventud) 4 (July–December): 4-12. This article offers an overarching vision of the actions undertaken in the Cooperative Project "Disseminating the Rights of the Child," Havana, 2000 and 2004 (unpublished), with the governments of Cuba and Finland and UNICEF, to disseminate information and ensure the fulfillment of what has been established in the United Nations Convention on the Rights of the Child. The article describes the objectives, procedures, achievements, and challenges of the project.

Díaz, Mareelén et al. 2006. *Violencia intrafamiliar en Cuba. Aproximaciones a su caracterización y recomendaciones a la política social* [Intrafamily violence in Cuba, approximations of its characteristics and recommendations for social policy]. Havana: Research Report, Centro de Investigaciones Psicológicas y Sociológicas (CIPS). This report presents the final results of the "Intrafamily Violence" research project, in which the results achieved from numerous years of research on the theme are summarized. Although the vision is focused on the family in a comprehensive fashion, of special importance is the analysis it provides of violence against children and the impact on them of violence among other members of the family, in particular toward women (mothers).

Durán, Alberta, et al. 2005. *Convivir en familias sin violencia. Una metodología para la intervención y prevención de la violencia intrafamiliar* [Living together in families without violence: A methodology for intervention and the prevention of intrafamily violence]. Havana: Casa Editora Imágenes. This book proposes a methodology for the orientation of the family toward the reduction or elimination of violent relations in the family, specifically between adults and children, as the result of the "Living Together in Families without Violence" Project, carried out by the Family Studies Group of the Center for Psychological and Sociological Research (CIPS) under the auspices of the NGO Save the Children. The proposed methodology begins with an innovative element, which is the diagnosis of family violence starting with the very children who are involved.

Peñate Leiva, Ana Isabel. 2003. *La voz de los niños, niñas y adolescentes de Cuba. Evaluación de los avances cognoscitivos de la población infanto-juvenil* [The voices of Cuban children and adolescents: An evaluation of the cognitive advances in the child and adolescent population]. Havana: Research Report, Centro de Estudios sobre la Juventud (CESJ). This report gathers together the advances achieved in the knowledge of children and adolescents with regard to their rights and respect for them, three years after the implementation of the

Disseminating the Rights of Children and Adolescents Project realized in coordination with UNICEF. The report is supported by a comparative analysis of the first assessment done in 2000, in both cases by means of a survey administered to the very children and adolescents. The report, although still unpublished, is available in the Center of Documentation of the Center for the Study of Youth and an article by the author can also be consulted, "La voz de la infancia y la adolescencia cubana desde las investigaciones sociales [The voices of Cuban children and adolescents in social research]." *Estudio* (Centro de Estudios sobre la Juventud) 4 (July–December): 14–20.

Plan Nacional de Acción a Favor de la Infancia y la Adolescencia [The National Action Plan for the Promotion of Childhood and Adolescence]. 2004. Havana. This is the plan developed to organize the follow-up to the United Nations document *A World Fit for Children*.

Nonprint Resources

Full-Length Films

El brigadista [The teacher]. 1977. Directed by Octavio Cortázar. Drama, 35 mm, 119 minutes. Instituto Cubano del Arte e Industria Cinematográficos (ICAIC). This film narrates the experience of a young literacy volunteer who, during the Literacy Campaign of 1961, has left the urban environment to work in a village near the Bay of Pigs. There he copes with experiences that contribute to his maturity.

Como la vida misma [Like life itself]. 1985. Directed by Víctor Casaus. Drama. 35 mm, 107 minutes. Instituto Cubano del Arte e Industria Cinematográficos (ICAIC). A recently graduated actor joins a theater group that is investigating for its next work a preuniversity center where a case of cheating was discovered. The young actor will decide about his future directions.

Madagascar. 1994. Directed by Fernando Pérez. Drama, 35 mm, 53 minutes. Instituto Cubano del Arte e Industria Cinematográficos (ICAIC). A university professor who has lost her capacity to dream faces her adolescent daughter who moves in a fantasy world. The relations between mother and daughter, full of strangeness, incomprehension, and reconciliations, are presented as a necessity if each is to preserve her utopia.

Miel para Oshún [Honey for Oshún]. 2001. Directed by Humberto Solás. Drama, 35 mm, 115 minutes. Instituto Cubano del Arte e Industria Cinematográficos (ICAIC). Paso P.C. TV Televisión Española, Canal + Spain. Reunion and confrontation between a mother and son seven years after he was taken illegally to the United States by his father.

Una novia para David [A girlfriend for David]. 1985. Directed by Orlando Rojas. Drama, 35 mm, 103 minutes. Instituto Cubano del Arte e Industria Cinematográficos (ICAIC). This film tells the story of David, a young man who is preparing to enter the university and shares the camaraderie of friends who practice the conquest of women as a competitive sport. Among prejudices, jealousy, and intrigue on the one hand, and friendship and sincerity on the other, David develops his feelings.

La vida en rosa [Life in pink]. Directed by Rolando Díaz. 1989. Drama, 35 mm, 86 minutes. Instituto Cubano del Arte e Industria Cinematográficos (ICAIC). A group of youth encounters, in a fantasy, images of themselves in their old age. This representation of the future brings them face-to-face with human deceits and misery. They will either accept their destiny or attempt to change it.

Viva Cuba [Long live Cuba!]. 2005. Directed by Juan Carlos Cremata. Drama, Video–DVD. DDC Films LLC, Quad Productions, TVC Casa Productora, Colmenita, and Ingenio. "This is a film that defends the right of children to be taken into account when parents make decisions that affect them," according to Director Juan Carlos Cremata. This feature film has received numerous awards: Cannes Film Festival 2005, Grand Prize Ecrans Juniors, awarded by a jury of children, and First Place for Fiction, Audiovisual Festival for Children and Youth, June 2006, Havana.

Documentaries

Buscando a papá [Looking for Dad]. 1991. Directed by Idelfonso Ramos. Instituto Cubano del Arte e Industria Cinematográficos. 35 mm, 12 minutes. This documentary provides reflections of a group of boys and girls with regard to relations with their parents and the lack of attention associated with divorce.

La entrega de la confianza [Inspiring confidence]. 2007. Directed by Lissette Vila. Instituto Cubano del Arte e Industria Cinematográficos. Videodisk, 13 minutes. Based on the experiences of two seropositive adolescents, this documentary addresses the development of adolescents as activists in the campaign to prevent HIV/AIDS.

Érase una vez [Once upon a time]. 1976. Directed by Constante Rapi Diego. Instituto Cubano del Arte e Industria Cinematográficos. 35 mm, 10 minutes. This film explores activities organized in children's libraries in order to excite an interest in reading.

Eso habría que verlo, compay [You have to see this one, pal]. 1999. Directed by Ian Padrón. Instituto Cubano del Arte e Industria Cinematográficos. Video (Betacam SP), 27 minutes. In this documentary, the creators of Elpidio Valdés, the most popular children's cartoon character in Cuba, view him.

La familia [The family]. 1975. Directed by Idelfonso Ramos. Instituto Cubano del Arte e Industria Cinematográficos. 35 mm, 37 minutes. The process of mass participation in the approval of Cuba's Family Code is presented in this documentary.

Ismaelillo. 1962. Directed by Rosina Prado. Instituto Cubano del Arte e Industria Cinematográficos. 35 mm, 19 minutes. This documentary examines the life of children in a childcare center constructed in a once-marginal neighborhood that has been transformed.

El juego [The game]. 1976. Directed by Idelfonso Ramos. Instituto Cubano del Arte e Industria Cinematográficos. 35 mm, 20 minutes. The importance of games in the physical and intellectual development of children is presented in this documentary.

Pensando en el amor [Thinking about love]. 1980. Directed by Melchor Casals. Instituto Cubano del Arte e Industria Cinematográficos. 35 mm, 13 minutes. This documentary examines problems of adolescent pregnancy, emphasizing the need for greater responsibility on the part of youth.

Primer día de clases [The first day of school]. 1974. Directed by Miguel Fleitas. Instituto Cubano del Arte e Industria Cinematográficos. 35 mm, 10 minutes. This documentary explores the factors that support and impede a child's adaptation to school.

Seño [Teacher]. 1986. Directed by Miguel Torres. Instituto Cubano del Arte e Industria Cinematográficos. 35 mm, 12 minutes. Educators who work in Cuba's childcare centers speak about what they do and how their relationships with children influence their own personal lives.

Sistema penitenciario y reeducación cubano. Menores y jóvenes [The penal system and re-education in Cuba, minors and youth]. 1990. Directed by Lázaro Buría. Instituto Cubano del Arte e Industria Cinematográficos. 35 mm, 13 minutes. The sports competitions organized in the system of re-education for minors are the focus of this documentary, which also provides a short report on two youth who have been re-educated.

Web Sites

Alma Mater digital (dirigida a los estudiantes universitarios) [Alma Mater digital edition (journal directed to university students)], http://www.almamater.cu.

Centro Cultural Pablo de la Torriente Brau [Pablo de la Torriente Brau Cultural Center], http://centropablo.cult.cu.

Centro de Estudios sobre la Mujer [Center for the Study of Women], http://www.mujeres.cubaweb.cu.

Centro de Investigaciones Psicológicas y Sociológicas [Center for Psychological and Sociological Research], http://www.cips.cu.

Centro Nacional de Educación Sexual [National Center for Sex Education], http://www.cenesex.sld.cu.

Centro Nacional de Prevención de las Infecciones de Transmisión Sexual y el SIDA [National Center for the Prevention of Sexually-Transmitted Disease and HIV/AIDS], http://www.bvssida.sld.cu.

Cine Cubano [Cuban cinema], http://www.cubacine.cu.

Derecho Penal [Penal law], http://www.unifr.ch/derechopenal/legislacion/cu.

Instituto Cubano de Amistad con los Pueblos [Cuban Institute for Friendship with the Peoples], http://www.icap.cu/argument/derecho_infancia.html.

Juventud Rebelde (diario de alcance nacional dirigido a la juventud) [Rebel Youth (daily with national distribution directed to youth)], http://www.jrebelde.cubaweb.cu.

Juventud Técnica digital [Technical youth digital journal], http://www.juventudtecnica.cu.

Ministerio de Relaciones Exteriores [Ministry of Foreign Relations], http://www.cubaminrex.cu/Mirar_Cuba.

Oficina Nacional de Estadísticas [National Office of Statistics], http://www.one.cu.

Página Cubana del XVI Festival Mundial de la Juventud y Los Estudiantes [Cuban Page of the XVI World Festival of Youth and Students], http://festival.ujc.org.cu.

Pionero digital (dirigida a los adolescentes) [Pioneer digital edition (journal dedicated to adolescents)], http://www.pionero.cu.

Programa "Educa a tu Hijo" ["Educate your child" Program], http://www.cubava.cu/educa.

Somos Jóvenes digital [We are young people, digital edition], http://www.somosjovenes.cu.

Zunzún digital (dirigida a niños y niñas) [Zunzún digital edition (journal dedicated to children)], http://www.zunzun.cu.

Organizations and NGOs

Asociación de Pedagogos de Cuba [Association of Cuban Educators]
Ave 41 # 3603 Playa, Havana
Phone: (53-7) 202-5420

Asociación "Hermanos Saíz" ["Saíz Brothers" Association]
Ave de las Misiones # 53 Habana Vieja, Havana
Phone: (53-7) 867-0210
Web site: http://www.artejovencubano.cult.cu
Email: ahs@ujc.org.cu

Casa Editora Abril [April Publishing House]
Paseo de Martí # 553 Habana Vieja, Havana
Phone: (53-7) 862-5031
Email: eabril@jcce.org.cu

Centro Cultural Pablo de la Torriente Brau [Pablo de la Torriente Brau Cultural Center]
Muralla # 63 Habana Vieja, Havana
Phone: (53-7) 861-6251
Web site: http://centropablo.cult.cu
Email: centropablo@cubarte.cult.cu

Centro de Estudios Demográficos [Center for Demographic Studies]
Ave 41 # 2003 Playa, Havana
Phone: (53-7) 202-8141

Centro de Estudios sobre la Juventud (CESJ) [Center for the Study of Youth]
Ave de las Misiones # 53 Habana Vieja, Havana
Phone: (53-7) 863-0675
Email: cesj@jovenclub.cu

Centro de Estudios sobre la Mujer [Center for the Study of Women]
Paseo # 260 Vedado, Havana
Phone: (53-7) 55-2779
Web site: http://www.mujeres.cubaweb.cu
Email: cem@ceniai.inf.cu

Centro de Información Cinematográfico [Center of Cinematographic Information]
23 # 1166 Vedado, Havana
Phone: (53-7) 55-2840

Centro de Información para el Deporte [Sports Information Center]
Ave Independencia and Vía Blanca Cerro, Havana
Phone: (53-7) 883-8321
Email: daei@inder.co.cu

Centro de Información para la Educación [Center of Information for Education]
Ave 41 and 14 Playa, Havana
Phone: (53-7) 206-4070

Centro de Investigaciones Jurídicas [Center for Legal Research]
O # 216 Vedado, Havana
Phone: (53-7) 55-3428

Centro de Investigaciones Psicológicas y Sociológicas [Center for Psychological and Sociological Research]
B and 15 # 352 Vedado, Havana
Phone: (53-7) 830-1451
Web site: http://www.cips.cu
Email: ips@cips.cu

Centro de Orientación y Diagnóstico [Center for Orientation and Diagnosis]
San Mariano and Luz Caballero Víbora, Havana
Phone: (53-7) 57-7650

Centro de Referencia Nacional de los Derechos de la Niñez y la Adolescencia [National Reference Center on the Rights of Children and Adolescents]
O # 216 Vedado, Havana
Phone: (53-7) 55-3461

Centro Latinoamericano para la Educación Preescolar [Latin American Center for Preschool Education]
Ave 3ra # 1408 Playa, Havana
Phone: (53-7) 206-6899

Centro Nacional de Educación para la Salud [National Center for Health Education]
I # 507 Vedado, Havana
Phone: (53-7) 55-2557
Fax: (53-7) 830-1047

Centro Nacional de Educación Sexual [National Center for Sex Education]
10 # 460 Vedado, Havana
Phone: (53-7) 55-2528
Web site: http://www.cenesex.sld.cu
Email: cenesex@infomed.sld.cu

Centro Nacional de Información de Ciencias Médicas [National Center of Medical
   Information]
E # 454 Vedado, Havana
Phone: (53-7) 832-4519
Web site: http://www.infomed.sld.cu

Centro Nacional de Prevención de las Infecciones de Transmisión Sexual y el SIDA
   (National Center for the Prevention of Sexually-Transmitted Disease and HIV/
   AIDS]
B and 27 Vedado, Havana
Web site: http://www.bvssida.sld.cu

Federación de Estudiantes de la Enseñanza Media (FEEM) [Federation of Secondary
   Students]
Ave 47 # 2802 Kohly, Havana
Phone: (53-7) 204-1050

Federación de Estudiantes Universitarios (FEU) [Federation of University
   Students]
23 # 502 Vedado, Havana
Phone: (53-7) 832-4610

Federación de Mujeres Cubanas [Federation of Cuban Women]
Paseo # 260 Vedado, Havana
Phone: (53-7) 55-2771
   • Secretaría de Trabajo Social [Secretary of Social Work]
      13 # 760 Vedado, Havana
      Phone: (53-7) 55-2775
   • Esfera de Trabajo Comunitario [Division of Community Work]
      A # 259 Vedado, Havana
      Phone: (53-7) 830-6043

Fiscalía General de la República [Attorney General of the Republic]
Amistad # 552 Centro Habana, Havana
Phone: (53-7) 867-0798

Instituto Central de Ciencias Pedagógicas (ICCP) [Central Institute of Pedagogical
   Sciences]
22 # 112 Playa, Havana
Phone: (53-7) 205-1648

Instituto Cubano de Radio y Televisión (ICRT) [Cuban Institute of Radio and Television, División de Programas para Niños y Jóvenes [Divison of Programs for Children and Youth]
23 # 258 Vedado, Havana
Phone: (53-7) 832-2065
Email: infantiles@tvc.icrt.cu

Instituto Nacional de Deportes, Educación Física y Recreación (INDER) [National Institute of Sports, Physical Education and Recreation]
Ave Independencia and Vía Blanca Cerro, Havana
Phone: (53-7) 54-5000
Web site: http://www.inder.co.cu
  • Grupo de Educación Física Escolar [Student Physical Education Group]
    Phone: (53-7) 57-7054

Instituto Nacional de Seguridad Social [National Social Security Institute] 23 and O Vedado, Havana
Phone: (53-7) 55-0054

Ministerio de Educación (MINED) [Ministry of Education]
17 # 1 Vedado, Havana
Phone: (53-7) 55-2920
  • Dirección de Educación Pre-escolar [Office of Preschool Education]
    Phone: (53-7) 832-2474
  • Dirección de Educación Especial [Office of Special Education]
    Phone: (53-7) 832-2452

Ministerio de Educación Superior (MES) [Ministry of Higher Education]
23 # 565 Vedado, Havana
Phone: (53-7) 55-2314

Ministerio de Justicia [Ministry of Justice]
O # 216 Vedado, Havana
Phone: (53-7) 55-3430

Ministerio de Trabajo y Seguridad Social [Ministry of Work and Social Security]
Dirección de Seguridad Social [Office of Social Security]
23 and P Vedado, Havana
Phone: (53-7) 55-0000

Oficina Nacional de Estadísticas [National Office of Statistics]
Paseo # 60 Vedado, Havana
Phone: (53-7) 830-0000
Web site: http://www.one.cu

Organización de Pioneros "José Martí" ["José Martí" Pioneers Organization]
Ave de las Misiones # 53 Habana Vieja, Havana
Phone: (53-7) 867-0191

Selected Bibliography

Acosta, Néstor. 2002. *Maltrato infantil* [Child abuse]. 2nd ed. Havana: Editorial Científico-Técnica.

Aguilera, Daisy. 2001. "La Violencia intrafamiliar, tratamiento jurídico en Cuba. El delito de asesinato" [The legal treatment of intrafamily violence in Cuba: the crime of murder]. in *Tertulia*. Santa Rosa, CA: Centro de Justicia para Mujeres.

Álvarez, Elcida. 2005. "Adolescencia: Derechos a la cultura e intereses culturales" [Adolescence: The right to culture and cultural interests], *Estudio* (Centro de Estudios sobre la Juventud) 4 (July–December): 50–54.

Álvarez, Mayda. 2000. "Mujer y poder en Cuba" [Women and Power in Cuba]. pp. 77–107 in *Cuba. Construyendo futuro* [Cuba: Constructing the Future]. Edited by M. Monereo, M. Riera, and J. Valdés. Barcelona: El Viejo Topo.

Asamblea Nacional del Poder Popular (ANPP) [National Assembly of People's Power]. 1975. *Código de Familia* [Family Code], Ley # 1289 de Febrero 14 de 1975. Gaceta Oficial Ordinaria de la República de Cuba # 16 de Febrero 15. Havana.

———. 1978. *Código de la Niñez y la Juventud* [Code of Childhood and Youth], Ley # 16 de Diciembre 28 de 1978. Gaceta Oficial Ordinaria de la República de Cuba de Diciembre 29. Havana.

———. 1984. *De la Adopción, los Hogares de Menores y la Familia Sustituta* [On Adoption, Children's Homes, and Foster Families], Decreto Ley 3 76 de Agosto 29 de 1986. Gaceta Oficial Ordinaria de la República de Cuba de Agosto 30. Havana.

———. 1986. *Sobre la Comisión de Atención y Prevención Social* [On the Commission for Attention and Social Prevention], Decreto–Ley # 95 de Agosto 29 de 1986. Gaceta Oficial Ordinaria de la República de Cuba de Agosto·30. Havana.

———. 1987. *Código Civil* [Civil Code], Ley # 59 de Julio 16 de 1987. Gaceta Oficial Extraordinaria de la República de Cuba # 9 de Octubre 15. Havana.

———. 1987. *Código Penal* [Penal Code], Ley # 62 de Diciembre 29 de 1987. Gaceta Oficial Especial de la República de Cuba # 3 de Diciembre 30. Havana.

———. *Constitución de la República* [Constitution of the Republic]. 1992. Havana: Editora Política.

———. 1994. *Decreto-Ley # 151, Modificativo de la Ley de Procedimiento Penal* [Decree-Law #151, Modification of the Law of Penal Procedure]. Gaceta Oficial de la República de Cuba # 6 de Junio 10. Havana.

———. 1999. *Ley # 87 Modificativa del Código Penal* [Law #87 Modification of the Penal Code]. Gaceta Oficial de la República de Cuba # 1 de Marzo 15. Havana.

Audivert, Ana E., and Rubén Otazo. 2005. "El Proyecto de Divulgación de los Derechos de la Niñez y la Adolescencia. Los Marcos de la Experiencia Cubana" [The project of disseminating the rights of children and adolescents: the framework of Cuban experience]. *Estudio* (Centro de Estudios sobre la Juventud) 4 (July–December): 4–12.

Centro de Estudios de la Mujer (CEM) [Center for the study of women]. 1999. *Sistematización de trabajos sobre violencia* [Systematization of works on violence]. Informe [Report]. Havana.

Comité Estatal de Estadísticas (CEE) [State Statistical Committee]. 1984. *Censo de Población y Viviendas 1981* [Census of population and housing, 1981]. Vol. 16. Havana: República de Cuba.

Díaz, Mareelén, et al. 2006. *Violencia intrafamiliar en Cuba. Aproximaciones a su caracterización y recomendaciones a la política social* [Intrafamily violence in Cuba: approximations of its characteristics and recommendations for social policy]. Informe de Investigación, Centro de Investigaciones Psicológicas y Sociológicas (CIPS), Havana.

Díaz, Yimel. 2006. "Nueva colección de música infantil" [New collection of children's music]. *Trabajadores* (Havana), August 28, p. 10.

Domínguez, María Isabel. 2004. "Higher Education in Cuba: Democratization and the Role of Women." pp. 103–122 in *The Challenges of Public Higher Education in the Hispanic Caribbean.* Edited by M. J. Canino and S. Torres-Saillant. Princeton, NJ: Markus Wiener Publishers.

Domínguez, María Isabel. 2006. "Políticas sociales y ciencias sociales en Cuba" [Social policy and social sciences in Cuba]. CD-R *Caudales 2006.* Havana: Editorial Ciencias Sociales (ISBN 959-06-0574-5).

Domínguez, María Isabel, and Deisy Domínguez. 2005. "Percepciones sociales de la juventud sobre el VIH-SIDA en Cuba" [Social perceptions of youth about HIV/AIDS]. *Sexología y Sociedad* (Centro Nacional de Educación Sexual), 11, no. 29: 13–19.

Domínguez, María Isabel, et al. 1990. *Características generacionales de los estudiantes y los desvinculados del estudio y el trabajo* [Generational characteristics of students and youth who neither work nor study]. Havana: Informe de Investigación, Fondos del CIPS.

Durán, Alberta. 1996. *Representaciones de la familia en niños y adolescentes cubanos* [Representations of family by Cuban children and youth]. Havana: Informe de Investigación, Centro de Investigaciónes Psicologicas y Sociológicas.

Durán, Alberta, et al. 2005. *Convivir en familias sin violencia. Una metodología para la intervención y prevención de la violencia intrafamiliar* [Living together in families without violence: a methodology for intervention and prevention of intrafamily violence]. Havana: Casa Editora Imágenes.

Federación de Mujeres Cubanas (FMC) [Federation of Cuban women (FMC)]. 1996. *Las Cubanas: de Beijing al 2000* [Cuban women: from Beijing to 2000]. Havana: FMC.

González, Yamila. (n.d.) *Código Penal y Violencia* [Penal code and violence]. Havana.

Instituto Nacional de Investigaciones Económicas (INIE) [National Institute for Economic Research]. 2005. *Millennium Development Goals. Cuba: First Report.* Havana.

Oficina Nacional de Estadísticas (ONE) [National Office of Statistics]. 2004. *Anuario Estadístico de Cuba 2003* [Statistical Yearbook of Cuba 2003]. Havana.

———. 2005. *Censo de Población y Viviendas Cuba 2002* [Census of Population and Housing in Cuba 2002]. Informe Nacional. Havana.

———. 2006. *Anuario Estadístico de Cuba 2005* [Statistical Yearbook of Cuba 2005]. Havana.

Peláez, Orfilio. 2007. "Cuba con más bajo índice latinoamericano de mortalidad infantil" [Cuba with the lowest indicator of infant mortality in Latin America]. *Granma Internacional Digital.* January 3. http://www.granma.cu.

Peñate, Ana Isabel. 2005. "La voz de la infancia y la adolescencia cubana desde las investigaciones sociales" [The voices of Cuban children and adolescents in social research projects]. *Estudio* (Centro de Estudios sobre la Juventud) 4 (July–December): 14–20.

Peñate, Orlando. 2005. "La protección social de los niños y adolescentes en Cuba" [The social protection of children and adolescents in Cuba]. *Estudio* (Centro de Estudios sobre la Juventud) 4 (July–December): 22–28.

Pérez, Dora, et al. 2006. "Vinagrito naufragó en un barquito de papel (I) [Vinagrito shipwrecked in a paper boat (I)]." *Juventud Rebelde*, February 26, p. 4.

Pérez, Ofelia. 2003. "Religiosidad popular y cambios sociales en Cuba" [Popular religiosity and social change in Cuba]. In *Sociedad y Religión. Selección de Lecturas* [Society and religion: selected readings]. Compiled by Vivian M. Sabater Havana.

Ramírez Calzadilla, Jorge. 2003. "Religión y relaciones sociales en Cuba" [Religion and social relations in Cuba]. pp. 91–117 in *Sociedad y Religión. Selección de Lecturas* [Society and religion: selected readings]. Compiled by Vivian M. Sabater. Havana.

———, et al. 2004. El reavivamiento religioso en Cuba en la década de los años 90s [The religious revivification in Cuba in the decade of the 1990s]. Havana: Informe de Investigación, Centro de Estudios Psicológicas y Sociológicas.

Ríos, Anett. 2004. "Parques infantiles, como el Cachumbambé" [Amusement parks like Cachumbambé]. *Granma*, Julio 31, p. 8.

Rosabal, Alberto. 2005. "Algunos factores sociales asociados a la epidemia de SIDA en Cuba" [Some social factors associated with the AIDs epidemic in Cuba]. *Sexología y Sociedad* (Centro Nacional de Educación Sexual) 11, no. 29: 24–27.

Tribunal Supremo Electoral (TSE), Oficina Nacional de los Censos Demográficos y Electoral [Supreme Electoral Court (TSE), National Office of Demographic and Electoral Censuses]. 1953. *Censo de Población, Vivienda y Electoral* [Population, Housing, and Electoral Census]. Informe General, Havana.

Trinquete, Dixie. 2005. "Adolescentes y VIH/SIDA: ¿Quién dijo que todo está perdido? [Adolescents and HIV/AIDS: who said that everything is lost?" *Sexología y Sociedad* (Centro Nacional de Educación Sexual, La Habana) 11, no. 27: 4–7.

Trujillo, Marlies and Yasmel Rodríguez. 2005. "Mujer—Maternidad versus SIDA: Una reflexión necesaria" [Women—motherhood versus AIDS: a necessary reflection]." *Sexología y Sociedad* (Centro Nacional de Educación Sexual) 11, no. 29: 20–23.

United Nations Children's Fund (UNICEF) 2000. "Convención sobre los Derechos del Niño" [Convention on the Rights of the Child]. In *Los Niños Primero* [Children first]. New York: UNICEF.

———. 2003. *Estado mundial de la infancia 2004* [The state of the world's children 2004]. New York: UNICEF.

6

THE DOMINICAN REPUBLIC

Lilith C. Werner

NATIONAL PROFILE

The island of Hispaniola is divided into two distinct nations: Haiti (independent from French rule since 1804) and the Dominican Republic (independent from Haitian rule since 1844). In the Dominican Republic, children under the age of fifteen represent approximately one-third of the total population of over nine million. The ethnic majority of Dominicans is of a mixed-race ancestry: 75 percent of Dominicans have a European, African, and indigenous American ancestry. The rest of the population is either of European ethnicity (16 percent) or black (11 percent). The Arawaks, Taínos, and Caribs, the indigenous groups of Hispaniola, either became extinct or were almost completely exterminated during the period of Spanish colonial control (Central Intelligence Agency 2006; Axtell 1992).

Hispaniola was where the *Santa Maria* ran aground in late December 1492. Christopher Columbus and his crew set up the first Spanish fort, La Natividad, on the northern part of the island (now Haiti). Although the

Spaniards on Hispaniola were first welcomed and helped by the local cacique, Guacanagarí, it appears that the good will dissipated at some point after Columbus's departure for Spain; when he returned a year later, his men were dead and the fort destroyed (Axtell 1992). Columbus began to enslave the native peoples for labor, thereby founding the encomienda system (this type of system was similar to that of the slave plantation economy found in the South of the United States before the Civil War [Zinn 2003]). The natives of Hispaniola died in large numbers due to the harsh conditions under encomienda enslavement, murder, suicide, or disease such as smallpox. The Spaniards began to import African slaves as replacements (Axtell 1992). Colonial conquest left its mark on contemporary Dominican Republic demography: the forced and willing sexual contacts among European colonizers, indigenous peoples, and Africans created an ethnic majority with a multiracial ancestry. This multiracial ancestry plays an important sociocultural role in terms of the "haves" and the "have-nots." That is, those who are labeled as having a European ancestry are usually found in the upper-SES (socioeconomic status) strata, and those who are determined to be black are usually found in the lower-SES strata. Furthermore, the multiracial majority has a hard time recognizing their African heritage, and there is racism and overt discrimination towards those who are darker. This racial tension heightens when Dominicans interact with Haitians (who have more African ancestry than the Dominicans) (Martínez 2005).

Interestingly, the Dominican Republic does not celebrate their independence day based on the end of hundreds of years of Spanish colonial rule, like most other Caribbean and South American countries. Independence Day in the Dominican Republic is February 27, celebrating the end of twenty-two years of Haitian rule in 1844. This celebration points to the historical tension that still exists between the two nations and cultures that share the island (Martínez 2005).

In 2001, the per capita income in the Dominican Republic was US$2,500. The Dominican economy is primarily service-based, even though it exports goods such as sugar, tobacco, and coffee (United Nations 2005). The overwhelming majority of the population is rural (65 percent), with the rest living in urban areas. In general, the standard of living is a very low one, and many parents cannot provide for the basic needs for their children. Almost 18 percent of the adult population is officially unemployed, and a quarter of all inhabitants live below the poverty level. Because the legal minimum monthly salary of Dominicans is US$142, money sent home from family members working abroad in countries such as the United States, Puerto Rico, and Spain is vital to the national economy. At least three billion dollars (US) are sent back to the Dominican Republic annually (Organisation for Economic Co-operation and Development [OECD] 2003). Because of poor economic conditions since the 1960s, Dominicans have migrated to the United States, Puerto Rico, and Spain. A 2004 report by the U.S. Census Bureau found that

800,000 foreign-born Dominicans live in the United States, and they are the largest immigrant group in New York City (around 100,000). The New York neighborhood of Washington Heights is even known as "Quisqueya Heights" (Quisqueya is the Taíno name for Hispaniola) because of its sizeable Dominican population. The Central Intelligence Agency (2006) estimates that three people out of every thousand migrate from the Dominican Republic annually. While economic conditions improved at the end of the twentieth century, immigrant Dominicans do not generally return home for good.

In the Dominican Republic's population of more than 5.5 million over the age of fifteen, 1.3 million are married, 1.8 million are considered to be living in what are called free unions, 1.8 million are single, and the other 600,000 are either widowed, divorced, legally separated, or separated by mutual agreement (Oficina Nacional de Estadística 2002a). These figures suggest that the ideal of a traditional nuclear family unit composed of married mother and father with children may not be culturally significant in the Dominican Republic (indeed, the lack of roots for the nuclear family model can even be traced back to the era of slavery, when slaves were not allowed to marry). However, given the low numbers of divorced people (121,000 in 2002) compared with 1.3 million who are married, it is likely that once married, divorce is also not culturally accepted, even though it has been legal since 1963. If a Dominican is urban and in a relationship, however, there is a greater likelihood of formal marriage than for a rural Dominican in a relationship. It should also be noted that weddings are expensive events—perhaps too expensive for the majority to afford.

The majority of rural Dominicans are thus considered by the National Statistics Office to be living in free unions (2002a). In addition, the majority of parents are in free union relationships. As domestic partners (and legally married couples), both father and mother share custody of the children. Generally speaking, however, women are often the informal and formal caretakers of the children, regardless of marital or free union status.

KEY FACTS – DOMINICAN REPUBLIC

Population: 9,365,818 (July 2007 est.)
Infant mortality rate: 27.94 deaths/1,000 live births (2007 est.)
Life expectancy at birth: 73.07 years (2007 est.)
Literacy rate: 84.7 percent (2003 est.)
Net primary school enrollment/attendance: 86 percent (2000–2005)
Internet users: 938,300 (2005)
People living with HIV/AIDS: 66,000 (2005 est.)
Children living with HIV/AIDS: 3600 (2005 est.)
Human Poverty Index (HPI-1) Rank: 27 (2006)

Sources: CIA World Factbook: Dominican Republic. http://www.cia.gov/cia/publications/factbook/geos/dr.html. April 17, 2007; UNICEF. At a Glance: Dominican Republic–Statistics. http://www.unicef.org/infobycountry/domrepublic_statistics.html. April 24, 2007; World Health Organization (WHO): UNAIDS/WHO Global HIV/AIDS Online Database. "Epidemiological Fact Sheets on HIV/AIDS and Sexuality Transmitted Diseases: Dominican Republic." http://www.who.int/GlobalAtlas/predefinedReports/EFS2006/index.asp?strSelectedCountry=DO. December 2006; United Nations Development Programme (UNDP) Human Development Report 2006–Dominican Republic. http://hdr.undp.org/hdr2006/statistics/countries/data_sheets/cty_ds_DOM.html. April 26, 2007.

The Dominican government has set up a voluntary national welfare in-surance program. This welfare program is based on contributions from employed citizens and covers health care, unemployment insurance, and pensions. Because of high unemployment and poverty rates, only slightly over 40 percent of the population is able to benefit from this program. Government-provided family financial support is available to unemployed single mothers with unmarried children who are younger than eighteen, or who are younger than twenty-one if a full-time student. If the unem-ployed single mother has a disabled child, there is no age limit at which government assistance is no longer provided (U.S. Social Security Admin-istration 2005). Many social and economic problems affecting women, families, and children are tackled by domestic and international non-governmental organizations (NGOs) in tandem with the Dominican Republic government. Without the assistance of these NGOs, lower-income families and marginalized populations such as the Haitians or Haitian-Dominicans would not receive much needed social and welfare services.

OVERVIEW

Like many other territories that belonged to the Spanish Empire, the political history of the Dominican Republic is tumultuous. At the end of the seventeenth century, Spain ceded the western area of Hispaniola to the French (who had occupied the territory from the beginning of the seventeenth century). The Republic of Haiti was declared in 1804. The Republic of Haiti claimed the entire island in 1822 and occupied the Dominican portion for twenty-two years, until Juan Pablo Duarte forced the Haitians out. The Dominican Republic became independent in 1844, although some seventeen years later it chose to return to the Spanish Empire. After reclaiming status as an independent nation-state in 1865, the Dominican Republic enjoyed self-rule until the American occupation from 1916 to 1924. In 1924, the Dominicans democratically elected their rulers. In 1930, a military coup d'état led by Rafael Trujillo abol-ished democracy, and Trujillo ruled as a dictator until his assassination in 1961. Only in the late 1970s was there a peaceful handover of presiden-tial power, although the peaceful elections that characterized the last quarter of the twentieth century were plagued by allegations of fraud.

Adding to the political troubles of the Dominican Republic were the economic hardships lived by the majority of the nation's residents who of-ten went without basic services, such as water, electricity, or public trans-portation, and who saw the prices of food skyrocket. Economic problems began in 1965, and although there was a decade-long respite under the 1990 economic reforms of President Joaquín Balaguer (president in 1960–1962, 1966–1978, and 1986–1996), the nation suffered a recession and massive banking collapses due to corruption under President Hipólito Mejía (2000–2004) (Ferguson 1999; Doggett and Connolly 2002). The current president is Leonel Fernández. The Dominican Republic still experiences economic difficulties, though President Fernández has promised, on his personal Web site (http://www.leonelfernandez.com), to deliver an economic boom based on technological advances and increases in foreign-direct investment. Resource mismanagement continues to characterize governmental performance (Organization for Economic Co-operation and Development 2003).

The Dominican Republic was one of fifty founding countries that drew up and ratified the charter of the United Nations in San Francisco on October 24, 1945. In doing so, it established its interest in belonging to an international community that desired to promote respect for human rights and basic freedoms, and to help solve humanitarian problems through cooperation and understanding. Even though at that time the country was led by the dictator Trujillo, who failed to implement state policies that would pursue the promulgated goals of the United Nations (UN), the fact that the Dominican Republic was a founding member state means that it has had an historical presence within the international discourse of human rights. Despite the lack of free and fair elections in the Dominican Republic, it was not isolated internationally, nor was it excluded from the ongoing world dialogue in quest of the betterment of humanity since 1945. Indeed, it has participated in the endorsement of several UN declarations that value and aim to fulfill all human potential, adult and child alike.

Many Dominican policy documents reflect the sense of the United Nations' 1948 Universal Declaration of Human Rights (UDHR). Article 26 of the UDHR proclaims the right of all children to a free elementary education. While the UDHR and its articles did not legally bind member states, its guarantee of free schooling to all was included in the national constitution of the Dominican Republic. In 1989, the Convention on the Rights of the Child was ratified by most UN member states, including the Dominican Republic. Article 28 of the Convention provides for the right to a free and compulsory primary education. The most recent initiative of the UN is its Millennium Development Goals of 2000. All 191 member states have committed to attain these goals by the year 2015. Universal primary education is among the Millennium Development goals, and the Dominican Republic has pledged its national efforts to achieve that and other goals.

Dominican state policies manifest the UN human rights discourse, and refer to broad and more specific rights without regard to national citizenship. For example, in the Constitution of July 25, 2002, the Organic Law of Education of 1997, and in the *Strategic Plan for the Development of Dominican Education 2003–2012*, the Dominican Republic promises to create avenues of access to free primary and secondary education for all habitantes (inhabitants) of the country. In making this commitment, formal policies make no distinction between documented residents and undocumented immigrants.

For the past two centuries, the relationship between Haiti and the Dominican Republic has been one filled with tension. Because of the desperate economic situation and civic unrest in contemporary Haiti, the Dominican Republic has experienced a sizeable influx of Haitian immigrants. Current estimates of Haitian immigrants range from 650,000 to one million, meaning that at least 7.5 percent of the total population of the Dominican Republic (a little over nine million as of the Central Intelligence Agency's July 2006 estimate) is Haitian, and the overwhelming majority of them work in the *bateyes*, or shantytowns, and sugar plantations in which decent and humane living and work conditions are not provided (U.S. Department of State 2006). Complicating the integration of Haitians into Dominican society is the fact that many Dominicans hold strong prejudices against Haitians, Dominicans of Haitian ancestry, and other foreigners of dark complexion. The prejudice toward people considered darker is a curious one given that the ethnic background of the majority of Dominicans is that of a mixed-race ancestry. According to San Miguel, many Dominicans have a hard time acknowledging their African descendance (San Miguel 2005).

The issue of discrimination against Haitians and their children is not a new one. In 1996, the National Coalition for Haitian Rights (NCHR) argued before the Inter-American Commission on Human Rights that three distinct classes of Haitians had been created within the Dominican Republic: seasonal migrants, long-term migrant workers without documentation, and children of Haitian workers born in the Dominican Republic. All three groups were subject to institutional discrimination, according to the NCHR (National Coalition for Haitian Rights 1996). In its argument before the commission, the NCHR echoed claims made by the U.S. Department of State that Haitians and Dominicans of Haitian descent were subject to extreme discrimination when trying to officially register their children as Dominican citizens. Even though these children are guaranteed educational services under the law, they are often marginalized from the educational system if they do not have official documentation provided by the state. NCHR stated that children of Haitian descent without an "official" status often experienced bureaucratic resistance or outright rejection when registering for school. (It is important to point out identity cards or birth certificates are not listed as prerequisites to access to the educational system in any of the laws and policies discussed earlier.)

In 2001, the Secretary of Education announced that all children would be allowed to enroll in primary school, whether they had documentation or not. However, in reality, undocumented Haitian children had, and still have, a much harder time enrolling in school than undocumented Dominican children. Any child that is undocumented (i.e., without a birth certificate) is only allowed to enroll at the discretion of each particular school—even Dominican children of Dominican descent. The Dominican primary school enrollment numbers are grim for a nation that considers itself a democracy and aspires to economic development. Only 85 percent of children aged six through thirteen are enrolled, and enrollment rates for secondary school drop 20 percentage points (OECD 2003). If Dominican children are marginalized by lack of access to the educational system, Haitian children are doubtlessly even more marginalized, especially when considering the Dominican cultural prejudice against them. The exclusion of children of Haitian descent is not acknowledged as a challenge faced by the Dominican educational system in any of its current national policy documents.

While the Dominican state has established formal laws and policies regarding the rights of minors, including the Code of the Dominican Minor of 1997, there is very little official oversight ensuring the enforcement of those laws and policies. In 2000, the U.S. Department of Labor's Bureau of International Labor Affairs estimated that 18 percent of Dominican children between the ages of five and seventeen were employed, either willingly or not, and up to 30,000 children were employed in the sex trade. Even though there are laws prohibiting forced child labor and child prostitution, trafficking in children from, to, and within the Dominican Republic remains a serious problem. While there are no official statistics available for children who are homeless, they are the most vulnerable population when it comes to being exploited in the sex trade, forced by adults to beg on the streets, and pushed into a type of bonded labor within other wealthier Dominican households.

EDUCATION

Article 4 of the 1997 Organic Law of Education provides the conceptual framework of the Dominican educational system. It identifies three principles: (a) "education is a permanent and unalienable right of all [and] each person has a right to an education that allows him/her to develop their own individuality and their own socially useful activity ... without any type of discrimination on the basis of race, sex, religious beliefs, socio-economic status"; (b) "everyone has the right to participate in the culture and enjoy the benefits of scientific progress"; and (c) "education shall be based on respect for life, respect for fundamental human rights, adhering to the principle of democratic coexistence, and in the search of truth and solidarity" (Congreso Nacional 1997). The 2003 Strategic Plan for the development of education affirms the educational system's commitment to peaceful democratic coexistence by fostering a mindset within schools that favors a just political and economic order and tolerance of all. The Strategic Plan states that education should be a means to develop the individual and society, a service to the national public interest, and thus the responsibility of all. The plan consists of three volumes: *The State of Dominican Education*; *The Strategic Vision*; and *Implementation, Monitoring, and Evaluation* (Secretaria del Estado do Educación 2003a, 2003b, 2003c).

Dominican citizens themselves have expressed concern over the state of the educational system: in 2004, the NGO Participación Ciudadana surveyed 2,437 Dominicans and found that their number one concern about the nation's future was that of the quality of education, or lack thereof. A 2002 World Development Report (World Bank 2000) devoted to Knowledge for Development emphasized that "knowledge is crucial for development" and argued that education as a form of investment in human capital was a "key ingredient" in the growth and general success of a nation's economy. The Banco Interamericano de Desarrollo (BID) and the OECD both call for increased investments and improvements to education in the Dominican Republic. In 2002, the BID approved a loan of $80 million to improve basic educational services for disadvantaged children in rural and marginal urban areas that would include many Dominican residents of Haitian ancestry.

The 2005 United Nation's Human Development Report found that the Dominican Republic spent 2.3 percent of its gross national product (GNP) on public education between 2000 and 2002. Of this, 46.3 percent was spent on primary education, 18.9 percent on secondary, and 10.9 percent on higher education. The United Nations Educational, Scientific and Cultural Organization (UNESCO) (2005) found the 2.3 percent spent on public education in the Dominican Republic to be the lowest percentage of GNP dedicated to education in all of the 29 countries throughout the Americas.

In the school year 2002–2003, 96 percent of eligible children were enrolled in primary schools. Yet it is worrisome that in that same year only 36 percent of age-eligible children were enrolled in secondary schools (United Nations 2005).

As estimated by the Central Intelligence Agency, literacy rates in the Dominican Republic reach almost 85 percent for those over fifteen. Female and male literacy rates are basically the same (84.8 percent and 84.6 percent, respectively). These rates are considerably higher than their island counterpart, Haiti (an average around 53 percent), yet lower than their neighbors to the north, west, and east (including Turks and Caicos, Cuba, Jamaica, and Puerto Rico). The OECD's 2003 Caribbean Rim Initiative Report states that the Dominican Republic would attract more foreign-direct investment if their workforce became more highly skilled.

Schooling is free and compulsory for Dominicans between the ages of seven and fourteen, and the 1997 Organic Law of Education states that the public system will be grounded in Christian principles. The legal language of instruction is Spanish. However, over 50 percent of Dominican children enter primary school at an age older than legally mandated and fees are often charged. If school fees are not charged, many families cannot afford school uniforms, books, meals, or transportation, thus the doors to an education are essentially shut to poor children. Fewer than

75 percent of those who begin primary school graduate from the final year of primary school. UNESCO attributes this worrisome statistic to the likelihood of forced grade repetition and dropouts. Many schools do not have adequate resources for students (e.g., well-trained teachers, books, or other materials). At least 80 percent of both the primary and secondary teaching force is female. Almost 80 percent of Dominican students are enrolled in public schools, and the rest are enrolled in private schools. There are government-sponsored school breakfast programs in the public school system. Fewer than 50 percent of Dominican students who are of secondary school age are enrolled in school. Of the twenty-nine Americas countries examined by UNESCO, the Dominican Republic ranked twenty-eighth in terms of the net enrollment ratio for secondary schooling. Interestingly, female enrollment in secondary schooling is higher than that of males.

In terms of higher education, there is one public university and many private universities. Because of the relatively high cost of higher education (around $3,600 for a diploma) in relation to annual wages, the majority of Dominicans either cannot enroll or do not graduate from an institute of higher education. Only 17 percent of young people between the ages of eighteen and twenty-four are enrolled in one of the forty institutions of higher education, and the desertion rate fluctuates between 50 and 70 percent.

In terms of education for disabled children in the Dominican Republic, as in other developing countries with high rates of poverty, there is still much room for improvement. Most disabled students' needs are not being met in the classroom, and these students face discrimination within the educational system. A United Nations 2001 report on the Dominican Republic (*Concluding Observations of the Committee on the Rights of the Child, Dominican Republic*) found that not enough is being done to include them in either the schools or the wider society (University of Minnesota 2001). However, in conjunction with the Ministry of Education, the U.S. Peace Corps is attempting to build awareness about students with special needs within the public school system. Part of their awareness-building includes in-service training for teachers about appropriate teaching methodologies for disabled children, as well as creating in-school programs appropriate for these children (U.S. Peace Corps n.d.).

The universal right to an education, which the Dominican Republic has vowed to uphold in both international and national forums, is challenged by institutional racism encountered by Haitian children and Dominican children of Haitian origin. The U.S. Department of State in its 2004 report on human rights practices in the Dominican Republic cites Catholic priests, and various human rights NGOs, such as the Dominican Center for Legal Advice and Investigation (CEDAIL), Participación Ciudadana, Movement of Dominican-Haitian Women (MUDHA), and the Socio-Cultural Movement of Haitian Workers

(MOSCTHA), as having expressed concern for many years over continued discrimination and the exclusion of Haitian children from schools. Bilingual education programs are scarce for Haitian children who do attend school. However, the majority of Haitian children in the Dominican Republic do not attend school, and MUDHA calls attention to the pervasiveness of anti-Haitian sentiment and the denial of human rights to ethnic Haitian women and children within the Dominican Republic (El Movimiento de Mujeres Dominico–Haitiana, 2005).

PLAY AND RECREATION

The Dominican state formally recognizes within national educational policy and law that the child has a right to play and develop her abilities to her fullest capacity. However, it appears that more NGOs than the government itself are responsible for sponsoring recreational activities. In August of 2006, for example, 5,000 teenagers from different areas of the country participated in the *World Vision* National Olympic Games with a theme of "Strike out child's work and delinquency." Prior to these games and since 2004, *World Vision* had subsidized sports activities in the southeast part of the Dominican Republic. Both the Olympic games and other sports activities received funding from the country's Ministry of Sports. The objectives of the Olympic games were to encourage peace and solidarity among different communities, and to allow the children to interact with each other in nonviolent ways.

Playing with toys as infants, toddlers, and children is a necessary part of development that—in stages—fosters creativity, encourages interaction with others, and aids in brain and physical development. The majority of Dominican children—especially poor children—do not have enough toys. At the end of 2004, *World Vision* and the International Advisory Council for Rural Youth (CAJIR), in partnership with the Spanish NGO Fundación Crecer Jugando (Grow Up Playing Foundation) and the National Radio of Spain, distributed over 90,000 Euros worth of toys to children in the poorest areas of the Dominican Republic (*World Vision*).

While there are many television stations available on the island, there are very few programs dedicated exclusively to children. Indeed, radios are more commonly found in lower-income households than are television sets. Regardless of the programming for children, not many children are able to take advantage of it due to the realities of child labor, domestic violence, begging in the streets, lack of electricity for television sets, and so on. Dominicans with a higher SES have access to digital or satellite television programming, thus their children are able to watch more programs dedicated exclusively to them. Less than 10 percent of the Dominican population has access to the Internet, and it is safe to assume that only the higher SES groups in the Dominican Republic are using the Internet on a regular basis.

While most former Spanish colonies are obsessed with soccer, the Dominican Republic's favorite sport is baseball, and many young boys dream of becoming a famous baseball player. (The baseball leagues in the United States hire more players from the Dominican Republic than from any other Spanish-speaking nation.) Unfortunately, many young Dominican boys drop out of school at very young ages to train to become a baseball player and try to get signed by a scout. The majority will never be signed to a team (Public Broadcasting Service 2000).

Merengue music is a form of music native to the Dominican Republic— even though its exact sound origins are still disputed—and it is interwoven throughout formal cultural festivities and informal social parties. It is even part of the individual Dominican's sociocultural identity. Initially rejected by the upper strata of the Dominican Republic until Trujillo became dictator, merengue eventually became the sound accepted and identified in a mainstream way. Today, bachata is a genre of music that is gaining popularity not only in the Dominican Republic, but also throughout the Americas. Much like merengue was perceived by the elites at the beginning of the twentieth century, bachata was first viewed as music for the lower classes because of its rural origins (Hernández 1995).

CHILD LABOR

The Code of the Dominican Minor (1997) regulates children's rights and welfare in the Dominican Republic. This law grants the public agency called the National Council for Children and Adolescents (CONANI) formal powers necessary for enforcing the code and ensuring that children's rights are upheld (Consejo Nacional para la Niñez y la Adolescencia 2005). The government has dedicated 2 percent of the national budget to this national council. Because there are so many areas of need when it comes to children and their rights, 2 percent is insufficient to protect Dominican children. The Code of the Dominican Minor states that there shall be eight years of compulsory education, but does not include any legal language regarding the parental obligation to send children to school.

Child labor has been a serious problem, one that is associated with difficulties of economic development. It has been common for minors to be put on the street to fend for themselves as parents used meager resources to care for younger siblings. Homeless children are frequently at the mercy of adults who gather them together and put them to work begging and selling fruit, flowers, and other goods on the street. In return for their work they are given basic housing. According to a 2006 U.S. Department of Labor report on child labor in the Dominican Republic, 21.6 percent of boys between the ages of five and fourteen were working compared with 7.3 percent of girls of the same ages. The ages at which these children work, the hours they work, and their failure to comply with compulsory school attendance all violate the Code of the Dominican Minor.

The labor code prohibits employment of children under fourteen, and also places limits on the employment of children under sixteen. Children who are between fourteen and sixteen are allowed to work six hours a day. However, child labor still remains an issue because of the low income levels and high unemployment levels of the general population. Parents in both urban and rural areas allow or encourage their children to earn money, thus there are many children under the age of fourteen who work in such places as sugar cane fields, clandestine factories, small businesses, and brothels. Many poor Dominican children accompany their parents to work in the sugar cane fields, and the sugar companies turn a blind eye to their presence. Legally, fines and sanctions may be applied to firms employing underage children. Nevertheless, state employees in charge of investigating agricultural companies' adherence to labor laws also often turn a blind eye when they observe children working in the fields along-side their parents, especially if they are Haitian or of Haitian descent. There are, however, a number of state programs put into place by the Ministry of Labor to combat child labor and exploitation in collaboration with foreign and domestic NGOs, including the International Pro-gramme on the Elimination of Child Labour (IPEC) and the Dominican Republic's Institute for the Family.

When children are forced to work from very early ages and do not receive any substantial formal education or vocational training, their employment opportunities as adults are highly limited. In 2003, the OECD published a Business Environment Report in which the educa-tional level of Dominicans was cited as a weakness by foreign businesses seeking investment opportunities. The Report states that there is a lack of skilled workers and supervisors. Both the BID and the OECD antici-pate that a better educational system, reaching all Dominican residents, would have a positive impact on long-term economic development and the overall well-being of the nation. With support from the BID, the Dominican government is providing a US$10 monthly stipend to poor mothers who keep their children in school (and out of work). The government also provides free school breakfast, nationwide, in order to promote attendance. These benefits are available only to children who are legally permitted to attend school, and it is therefore important that barriers against Dominico-Haitian children be eliminated. While outside international agencies, such as the BID and the OECD, do not specifi-cally address racial or ethnic discrimination in the Dominican educational system, they do call for increased investments and improvements to edu-cation. Despite the 2003 OECD report's criticism of the lack of skilled workers and supervisors in the Dominican Republic, it also states that investors have positive perceptions about the trainability of Dominican workers.

FAMILY

Because of the Dominican Republic's continued political and economic turmoil, in addition to its past as a nation that controlled the lives and relationships of slave families, familial ties are extremely important for social stability within the nation. Indeed, the family is central in the social lives of many Hispanics throughout Central and South America. The role of the male is central in Dominican family life when the male is the head of household. Men are the traditional breadwinners (77 percent compared with 23 percent who are women), and culturally men hold much power over the women and children in the household (Oficina Nacional de Estadísica 2002a). As such, the men can limit their wives' and children's movement to and from the household or even decide whether the children will accompany them to their employment. Yet, 31 percent of Dominican families have a woman as the head of household. Domestic violence is prevalent in lower-SES households with adult males. However, what the advanced countries consider domestic violence against children may not be perceived as such by the Dominicans because corporal punishment is the most commonly used and accepted method of punishing children.

Sex role differentiation is encouraged at an early age and exhibits itself primarily through the differences in parental control over boys and girls. Boys are generally allowed much more freedom than girls. Boys are encouraged to explore and engage in much physical activity. They are not reprimanded if they are not clothed. Expected to be under the supervision of an adult at all times, girls are culturally valued when well behaved, in clean dress, and virgins. The mother–child relationship, regardless of the gender of the child, is a close one in which much physical affection is demonstrated and interest in the child's daily routine is high. This is unlike the father–child relationship, which is a more distant one based on respect and authority.

The law states that when parents in free union arrangements separate, the custody of the children is automatically awarded to the mother. The only reasons for custody not being awarded to the mother would be if the mother were known to have engaged in inappropriate behavior or had social/mental problems. However, the reality is that fathers usually do not have full custody of their children (U.S. Department of State 2004). Although the Dominican Constitution promulgates the principle of equality, discrimination continues to exist in terms of inheritance issues, especially if a single mother living in a rural area has a property claim. This means that there is a greater likelihood that the single mother will lose her property rights to a state claim (Agencia de las Naciones Unidas para los Refugiados 2002).

HEALTH

Health statistics are another crucial indicator of a nation's commitment to providing adequate health care and can bring to light particular health issues that are faced by its citizenry. According to the CIA's *World Fact-book* (2006), the infant mortality rate in the Dominican Republic is 28.25 deaths per 1,000 live births. It is currently ranked eighty-eighth of 225 countries listed within the *Factbook*, well ahead of Haiti (ranked thirty-five, with an infant mortality rate of 71.65), yet behind the rest of their nearest Caribbean neighbors such as Jamaica (ranked 129, with an infant mortality rate of 15.98), Turks and Caicos (ranked 131, with an infant mortality rate of 15.18), Puerto Rico (ranked 160, with an infant mortality rate of 9.14), and Cuba (ranked 185, with an infant mortality rate of 6.22).

In the Dominican Republic, there is a relationship between child mortality and the level of the mother's education. A 2002 Demographic and Health Survey (Oficina Nacional de Estadística 2002b) report revealed alarmingly high rates of child mortality when mothers did not have formal education. However, the child mortality rate has decreased substantially since the 1960s, when almost 160 of every 1,000 children younger than five years old died. There are nearly 40,000 children between birth and age fourteen who have been orphaned by parents who have died from HIV/AIDS and other causes (World Bank 2002). A Human Rights 2004 report states that the Dominican Republic is only second to Haiti in terms of numbers of people infected with HIV/AIDS: around 2 percent of adults are infected with HIV, and rates of infection are increasing faster for women than for men. The report also highlights the social and economic discrimination faced by HIV-positive Dominican women. These women are often blamed for bringing a sexually transmitted disease into the relationship and face the great likelihood of domestic violence (there is a law stating that partners must inform each other of HIV infection). As a condition for employment in many female-dominated sectors (e.g., the tourist or service sectors), women are tested for HIV and can be denied employment if they test positive.

Secondary schools are supposed to provide sexual education. However, given the low rates of secondary school attendance, the fact that the textbook used in the sexual education classes does not encourage condom use, and a male-centered culture already opposed to the use of condoms, stabilizing HIV/AIDS rates in the Dominican Republic has proved to be difficult.

According to 2001 health statistics published by the United Nations Human Development Report, 90 percent of one-year-old children have been vaccinated against tuberculosis and 79 percent against measles. The following vaccinations are offered free to babies: tuberculosis, hepatitis B, polio, measles, rubella, chicken pox, diphtheria, tetanus, whooping cough, and type B influenza (one of the principal causes of meningitis).

In 2001, the Dominican government passed a new social welfare law ensuring universal health care. However, the health system is a combination of private and public subsidization. Every employed Dominican contributes to financing the health system through a sliding-scale percentage of wages. Access to doctors and hospitals is free; however, access to and quality of medical care is not guaranteed. Many NGOs, such as Cáritas International, Patronato Benéfico Oriental, Inc., the Dr. Antonio Cruz Jiminián Foundation, and others, try to supplement the national health care system and provide services to children. As in other developing nations, those citizens who have the financial resources are better able to secure health care for their children and can afford private health insurance and doctors. For the richest 20 percent of Dominicans, the under-five child mortality rate is 26.6 percent compared with 89.9 percent for the poorest 20 percent of Dominicans. The 2001 social welfare law also provided for daycare centers for working class families with children between the ages of forty-five days and five years (U.S. Social Security Administration 2001). In 2002, 93 percent of the population had access to a source of clean water; this is an increase from 86 percent in 1990. Eleven percent of rural children suffer from chronic malnutrition versus 8 percent of urban children (World Bank 2002).

The 2001 United Nations report *Concluding Observations of the Committee on the Rights of the Child, Dominican Republic* (University of Minnesota 2001) expressed concern over a substantial lack of sexual education, health education, mental health education, and substance abuse education in the Dominican Republic, as well as the insufficient availability of counseling services for students. The lack of these programs in schools may have a correlation to the rising rates of sexually transmitted diseases and HIV infections, as well as drug abuse among adolescents.

LAWS AND LEGAL STATUS

According to the Code of the Dominican Minor (Código del Menor Dominicano 1997), a minor is defined as a child from birth to twelve years of age, and is then considered an adolescent until seventeen years of age. The age of majority in the Dominican Republic is eighteen. However, if an individual is younger than eighteen and married, she or he is considered an adult. Once legally considered of age, voting is mandatory. Only those who have national identity documents are allowed to vote. Military recruiters can begin to sign up willing adolescents once they turn sixteen if the country is not at war. If it is wartime, adolescents may be conscripted. In theory, all adolescent military recruits must have formally completed their eight years of compulsory education. Although the Code of the Dominican Minor sets forth specific age groups, when it comes to the justice system, children younger than eighteen years old are often treated like adults.

The Code of the Dominican Minor established a separate juvenile court system with its own legislation regulating infractions by children or adolescents (the code determined that no juvenile may be accused of a crime). It also created a separate police force and an Ombudsperson for Minors. However, the Inter-American Commission of Human Rights (1999) considers that very little has changed with regard to the differentiation of adult and juvenile detainees. There is often no physical separation of adults and juveniles in state-run detention centers or prisons. Because adults and minors continue to be housed together in overcrowded and corrupt prisons, an environment of physical, sexual, and mental abuse is perpetuated on the part of the adults towards the juveniles. In theory, juveniles are supposed to be rehabilitated and educated. More often than not, juvenile delinquents are confined with the adults until past the age of majority because of court system delays. In fact, 70 percent of those incarcerated have not been given a trial or sentenced. Juveniles who are imprisoned often join juvenile gangs (*naciones*) for protection. Due process as understood in the United States does not exist in the Dominican Republic. Even so, under the current administration of Leonel Fernández, there is a reform movement within the justice system, and efforts are being made to address basic human rights violations within the prisons.

RELIGIOUS LIFE

Even though freedom of religion is permitted by the constitution, the Dominican Republic's national motto is "God, Homeland, and Freedom." Legally, the Roman Catholic Bible is supposed to be read by children in public schools, but there are no statistics to indicate the extent to which this law is followed. Sixty-eight percent of Dominicans consider themselves Roman Catholic. Eleven percent are Protestant (including Evangelicals, Mormons, and Jehovah's Witnesses), and others adhere to animistic beliefs. Many Catholics practice a combination of Catholic beliefs and Afro-Caribbean beliefs (known as "santería"). There are also two religious groups that have rising conversion rates, Evangelical Christians and Mormons. While there are no mosques in the Dominican Republic, there are resident Muslims who practice their religion. There are Jewish synagogues and one rabbi, and Buddhism is also practiced (Informe Internacional de Libertad de Cultos 2004). The Haitians on the island practice Catholicism, forms of voodoo, or a combination of both. Although in the general public's eye voodoo may have only an ominous connotation, voodoo is actually a religion of spirits and mysteries as well as a world view (National Geographic News 2002). Much like other former Spanish colonies with a Catholic majority, at least half of the national holidays are Catholic in origin. These include Epiphany/Three Kings Day, Lady of Altagracia Day, Good Friday, Easter, Corpus Christi Day, Lady of Mercedes Day, and Christmas Day. There are, however, very few Dominicans who formally practice their religion or regularly go to mass. Children receive the majority of their religious training through their family networks (Central Intelligence Agency 2006). Another lasting imprint that Catholicism has left on the Dominican Republic is that of homophobia. Being gay and publicly manifesting that sexual identity is generally not culturally accepted.

CHILD ABUSE AND NEGLECT

Child abuse and neglect continues to be a social ill that needs to be addressed in the Dominican Republic. Juveniles and adults are oftentimes incarcerated together. Domestic violence is also prevalent in households where a man and a woman cohabit, and this violence increases the likelihood of physical abuse faced by the children in the household. Many poor parents who live in the *bateyes* take their young children (many under the age of twelve) with them into the sugar fields to work instead of sending them to school. Other children are sent out into the streets to beg, sell trinkets, or work in the sex trade. Haitian immigrant children as young as twelve are brought to the Dominican Republic for the exclusive purpose of the sex trade (U.S. Department of State 2006). The Dominican public agency CONANI states that three out of ten children in Santo Domingo have been sexually abused (Consejo Nacional para la Niñez y la Adolescencia 2005). Because children have been abused by family members or family friends, these crimes often go unreported and unpunished.

While adult prostitution is legal in the Dominican Republic, trafficking in women and children to, from, and within the country is another area of concern for Dominicans and the international community. It is a crime to recruit women and children to prostitute themselves or to make money from their activities. Even though there are laws against human trafficking as well as stiff penalties for those who are caught trafficking, the child sex trade operates throughout the country, and is especially concentrated in tourist areas (International Human Rights Law Institute 2005). Actual statistics are hard to obtain because of the clandestine nature of the trade and because of the Dominican Republic's lack of law enforcement with regard to the sex trade. Between 25,000 and 30,000 minors were estimated to be involved in the sex trade (*El Mundo* 2004). The numbers are sure to be higher because of the difficulty involved in collecting these types of statistics.

The number of women and children involved in the sex trade is proportionally related to the types of educational and employment opportunities available within the society. Because one-third of Dominican households are headed by single women without formal education, viable skills, or lucrative jobs (or legal means to migrate to another country), the sex trade sometimes becomes the only way to make a living and survive. The children in these households, unfortunately, become a population that is even more at risk when they are unduly pressured to join the sex trade. The main agent of trafficking in women and children within the Dominican Republic is the family itself, unlike many other Central American countries where the agents are from outside the family. The Dominican Republic is the only Central American government that has incorporated human trafficking as one of the domestic ills the national agenda is committed to fight against. The Dominican National Commission on the Eradication of Commercial Sexual Exploitation of Children is a governmental agency dedicated to combating this social ill (International Human Rights Law Institute 2005).

GROWING UP IN THE TWENTY-FIRST CENTURY

The availability of formal and public mass education is an important signal of a state's commitment to children and their families. Educational policies may contribute directly to the success of democratization within a society, and schooling is also an important means of socialization that has well-documented effects on the development of children. The Dominican Republic has a long-standing moral commitment to those who reside within its borders and to the international community, with regard to guaranteeing the fundamental human right of access and opportunity to an education. Excluding children, such as poor rural children or children of Haitian ethnicity, from the Dominican Republic's formal guarantees and protections will only have long-term detrimental effects within Dominican society. Uneducated and illiterate children will have a lower quality of life as uneducated and illiterate adults; their income, health, and rates of social and political participation will be negatively affected. These children will become unemployed or underemployed adults who will then look to the Dominican state for welfare and social services, putting a strain on the nation's already limited resources. A limited education or no education as a child and teenager could mean that as adults they could be more easily manipulated by politicians and employers or even disenfranchised without knowing it. Foreign investors from major corporations would likely prefer to do business in other emerging market economies that produce workers with a higher level of training and education.

Yet such unfavorable consequences need not occur. Organizations such as the OECD note that the Dominican work force is "competent, trainable, and cooperative." Other educational policies are being enacted now to ensure that almost 90 percent of the Dominican population will finish primary schooling by the year 2010 (United Nations Educational, Scientific and Cultural Organization 2005). The OECD (2003) recommends several actions that could pave broader avenues of access and opportunity for children in the Dominican Republic. First, the government should increase national spending on public education, create outreach programs to ensure rural and poor children are enrolled in school—regardless of having proper documentation or not, and provide scholarships to low-income students who pursue a university degree. Second, vocational or training programs should be created for those youths who drop out of school. Third, poor parents should be given financial incentives by the government if they send their children to school.

RESOURCE GUIDE

Suggested Readings

Country Review—Dominican Republic (magazine subscription). This is an annual report on the Dominican Republic that provides details about demographics, current events, governmental issues, the economy, and business information. The report also analyzes cultural, societal, political, environmental, and other contemporary issues facing the country. Charts, graphs, and maps are also included. It is published by CountryWatch, a company that provides demographic information on all 192 recognized countries of the world to large media companies.

Gregory, Steven. 2006. *The Devil Behind the Mirror: Globalization and Politics in the Dominican Republic.* Berkeley: University of California Press. In *The Devil Behind the Mirror*, Steven Gregory provides an account of the impact that globalization is having on the lives of Dominicans. He did ethnographic fieldwork in the towns of Boca Chica and Andrés and demonstrates how transnational flows of capital, culture, and people are mediated by contextually specific power relations, politics, and history. He also explores such topics as the informal economy, the making of a telenova, sex tourism, and racism and discrimination against Haitians.

Hernández, Deborah P. 1995. *Bachata: A Social History of Dominican Popular Music.* Philadelphia: Temple University Press. This book explores the history behind the original Dominican music sound of bachata. Bachata has its roots within the 1960s Dominican working class and their oppression; it was rejected by the other classes who found its themes to be vulgar and preferred merengue instead. It also examines how this music, over time, has become accepted by the mainstream music industry.

Howard, David J. 1999. *Dominican Republic in Focus: A Guide to the People, Politics and Culture.* New York: Interlink Books. This travel book provides an in-depth look into the Dominican Republic. It is divided into chapters describing the history, politics, culture, economy, and society of the country.

Pons, Frank M. 1998. *The Dominican Republic: A National History.* Princeton, NJ: Markus Wiener Publishers. This book examines the economic and political continuities between the U.S. military government and subsequent regimes, including the infamous Trujillo dictatorship (1930–1961).

Suárez, Lucía M. 2006. *The Tears of Hispaniola: Haitian and Dominican Diaspora Memories.* Gainesville: University Press of Florida. This book examines four writers (Jean-Robert Cadet, Junot Díaz, Loida Maritza Pérez, and Edwidge Danticat) who were born on the island and eventually left it, and how their autobiographical and fictional pieces bring to light the suffering and injustices experienced by the majority still on the island. Their writings also call for justice for the peoples on the island.

Nonprint Resources

Merengue: Dominican Music and Dominican Identity. Rounder Select Label, compiled and annotated by Paul Austerlits. 1997. CD. This is a music CD that features merengue, a music that is identified with Dominican culture.

Un Pueblo con Alma de Carnaval [A people with a soul of carnival]. Directed by: Fernando Báez. Print Source: Producciones Unicornio, S.A. Calle Pedro A. Lluberes #2, Gazcue, Santo Domingo, Rep. Dom. Email: fernandobaez@ unicorniotv.com. 28 minutes. Not yet available on DVD. Presented at the spring 2006 Film Festival in Chicago, this documentary goes to different villages to film their respective *carnavales.*

Quisqueya en el Hudson: Dominican Music in New York. 2004. Smithsonian Folkways Label. CD. This is a music CD that includes an assortment of Dominican music styles, such as merengue, folk songs, bachata, and the Dominican version of son (an original Cuban sound).

Recuerdos [Memories]. 2006. Not yet available on DVD. Presented at the 2006 summer Latino Film Festival in New York, this is a fictional movie about a romance between two teenagers, one of whom is leaving the Dominican Republic for good.

La República de Baseball: Los Gigantes Dominicanos del Juego Americano [Republic of baseball: The Dominican giants of the American game]. 2006. Directed by Daniel Manatt. Produced by Sports for Development Foundation and Manatt Media LLC. 83 minutes. Not yet available on DVD. Presented at the 2006 summer Latino Film Festival in New York, this documentary examines how Dominicans have come to influence the major leagues in the United States (10 percent of major league players come from the Dominican Republic—a higher percent than players from any other Hispanic nation).

This Is the Dominican Republic. 2005. JVC Productions. 60 minutes. DVD. This is a DVD that shows off the Dominican Republic and its tourist attractions.

Web Sites

Dominicana On Line, http://www.dominicanaonline.org/Portal/espanol/default.asp.

Educando: El portal de la educación dominicana [Educating: the Dominican education web site], http://www.educando.edu.do/educando.

Human Rights Watch, http://www.hrw.org.

International Reports, http://www.internationalreports.net/theamericas/dr/2002/newsocial.html.

Save the Children, http://www.savethechildren.net/dominican_republic/english/what.html.

Organizations and NGOs

La Asociación Pro-Bienestar de la Familia, Inc. (ProFamilia) [Institute for the Family]
Calle Socorro Sánchez #160, Gazcue
Santo Domingo, Dominican Republic
Phone: (809) 689-0141
Fax: (809) 686-8276
Email: info@profamilia.org.do
Web site: http://www.profamilia.org.do/new

Cáritas International, Cáritas Dominicana
C. Coronel Rafael Fernández Domínguez, Esq. 51, Ensanche La Fé
Santo Domingo, Dominican Republic
Phone: (809) 565-7746
Fax: (809) 565-3228
Email: cdrdofna@codetel.net.do
Web site: http://www.caritas.org

Catholic Relief Services
Web site: http://www.crs.org/our_work/where_we_work/overseas/latin_america_
    and_the_caribbean/dominican_republic/index.cfm

Centro de Investigación para la Acción Femenina (CIPAF) [Research Center for
    Feminist Action]
C/ Luis F. Thomen 358, Ens. Quisqueya
Santo Domingo, Dominican Republic
Phone: (809) 563-5263
Fax: (809) 563-1159

Centro Dominicano de Asesoría e Investigaciones Legales (CEDAIL) [Dominican
    Center for Legal Advice and Research]
Av. Los Próceres, GALA
Santo Domingo, Dominican Republic
Phone: (809) 567-9271, ext. 284
Email: lcontreras@intec.edu.do

Clínica Cruz Jiminián [Dr. Cruz Jiminián's Health Clinic]
Av. Jose Ortega Y Gasset No. 90, Cristo Rey
Santo Domingo, Dominican Republic
Phone: (809) 682-9459

Consejo Asesor de la Juventud Internacional Rural (CAJIR) [International Advisory
    Council for Rural Youth]
C. Casado del Alisal 10, Bajo B
28014 Madrid, Spain
Phone: (34-91) 369-0284
Fax: (34-91) 369-0136
Email: oij@oij.org

Direct Relief International
Web site: http://www.directrelief.org/sections/information_center/countries/
    dominican_rep.html

Fundación Crecer Jugando [Grow Up Playing Foundation]
Pasaje Nicolauets, 1
03440 IBI, Alicante, Spain
Phone: (34-96) 655-4980
Fax: (34-96) 655-0275
Email: fundacion@crecerjugando.org

The Inter-American Commission on Human Rights
Web site: http://www.cidh.org

The International Organization for Migration (IOM)
Web site: http://www.iom.int/jahia/jsp/index.jsp
International Programme on the Elimination of Child Labour (IPEC)
Phone: (41-22) 799-8181
Fax: (41-22) 799-8771
Email: ipec@ilo.org
Web site: http://www.ilo.org/public/english/standards/ipec/simpoc

El Movimiento de Mujeres Dominico-Haitiana (MUDHA) [The Haitian-Dominican
    Women's Movement]
Calle Pedro A. Lluberes No. 1, Gazcue
Santo Domingo, Dominican Republic
Phone: (809) 688-7430
Fax: (809) 689-3532
E-mail: mudha@hotmail.com
Web site: http://www.kiskeya-alternative.org/mudha

El Movimiento Socio Cultural Para los Trabajadores Haitianos (MOSCTHA) [The
    Socio-cultural Movement for Haitian Workers]
Calle Juan Erazo No. 39, Villa Juana, Distrito Nacional
Santo Domingo, Dominican Republic
Phone: (809) 687-2318
Fax: (809) 221-8371
Email: mosctha@codetel.net.do
Web site: http://mosctha.redhjacquesviau.org.do

Participación Ciudadana [Citizen Participation]
Calle Wenceslao Álvarez No.8
Santo Domingo, Dominican Republic
Phone: (809) 685-6200
Fax: (809) 685-6631
Email: p.ciudadana@verizon.net.do
Web site: http://www.pciudadana.com

Patronato Benéfico Oriental, Inc. [Eastern Beneficial Patronage]
P.O. Box 326
La Romana, Dominican Republic
Email: laromana@hogardelnino.com

Peace Corps
Web   site: http://www.peacecorps.gov/index.cfm?shell=learn.wherepc.caribbean
    .dominicanrepublic

United Nations Educational, Cultural and Scientific Organization (UNESCO)
Web site: http://www.uis.unesco.org

World Vision
Web site: http://www.worldvision.org

Selected Bibliography

Agencia de las Naciones Unidas para los Refugiados (ACNUR) [United Nations Agency for Refugees]. 2002. *Observaciones Finales del Comité para la Eliminación de la Discriminación contra la Mujer de las Naciones Unidas.* [Final Observations of the United Nations Committee Dedicated to Eliminating Discrimination against Women]. http://www.acnur.org/biblioteca/pdf/1807.pdf. Accessed October 1, 2006.

———. 2006. http://www.acnur.org/motor/index.php?id_seccion=1. Accessed October 1, 2006.

Axtell, James. 1992. *Beyond 1492: Encounters in Colonial North America.* Oxford: Oxford University Press.

Banco Interamericano de Desarrollo (BID) [Inter-American Development Bank]. 2002. *Programa multifase para la equidad de la educación básica–Fase I: Propuesta de préstamo.* [Multi-phase program for basic education equity–Phase I: Loan proposal]. Washington, DC: Oficina de Apoyo Regional de Operaciones.

Central Intelligence Agency (CIA). 2006. *World Factbook: Dominican Republic.* http://www.cia.gov/cia/publications/factbook/geos/dr.html. Accessed October 14, 2006.

Código del Menor Dominicano [Code of the Dominican Minor]. 1997. Santo Domingo. http://www.monografias.com/trabajos14/menordominic/menordominic.shtml. Accessed September 20, 2006.

Congreso Nacional [Nacional Congress]. 1997. *Ley Orgánica de Educación de la República Dominicana* [Organic Law of Education in the Dominican Republic]. Santo Domingo. http://www.educando.edu.do/NR/rdonlyres/3537AB13-B47D-4A9A-BF27-B056C50941AC/0/LeyEdu66_97.doc. Accessed September 4, 2006.

Consejo Nacional para la Niñez y la Adolescencia [CONANI] [National Council for Children and Adolescents]. 2005. *Memoria institucional 2005* [2005 Institutional Report]. http://www.conani.gov.do/Memoria%20CONANI%202005-web.pdf#search='CONANI%20republica%20dominicana'. Accessed September 20, 2006.

Doggett, Scott, and Joyce Connolly. 2002. *Dominican Republic & Haiti.* 2nd ed. Victoria, Australia: Lonely Planet Publications Ptv Ltd.

Ferguson, James. 1999. *The Story of the Caribbean People.* Brooklyn, NY: Interlink Books.

Fernández Reyna, Leonel. http://www.leonelfernandez.com. Accessed November 21, 2006.

General Assembly of the United Nations. 1948. *Universal Declaration of Human Rights.* Paris.

———. 1989. *Convention on Rights of the Child.* New York.

———. 2000. *Millennium Development Goals.* New York.

Hernández, Deborah P. 1995. *Bachata: A Social History of Dominican Popular Music.* Philadelphia: Temple University Press.

Human Rights Watch. 2004. *A Test of Inequality: Discrimination against Women Living with HIV in the Dominican Republic.* http://hrw.org/reports/2004/dr0704/3.htm. Accessed November 23, 2006.

Informe Internacional de Libertad de Cultos. [International Report on the Freedom of Religión]. 2004. Published by the Dominican Republic's Oficina para la Democracia, los Derechos Humanos y el Trabajo [The Office for Democracy, Human Rights and Employment]. http://www.usemb.gov.do/libertad_cultos_2004.htm. Accessed November 23, 2006.

Inter-American Commission on Human Rights. 1999. *Report on the Situation of Human Rights in the Dominican Republic.* http://www.cidh.org/countryrep/dominicanrep99/table.htm. Accessed November 4, 2006.

———. 2000. *Annual Report of the Inter-American Commission on Human Rights 2000.* http://www.cidh.org/annualrep/2000eng/ChapterIII/Admissible/Dom.Rep12.189.htm. Accessed November 5, 2006.

International Human Rights Law Institute. October 2005. *In Modern Bondage: Sex Trafficking in the Americas.* Chicago: DePaul University College of Law.

El Movimiento de Mujeres Dominico–Haitiana (MUDHA) [The Haitian-Dominican Women's Movement]. 2005. *Declaración de la Misión de MUDHA* [Declaration of the Mission of MUDHA]. http://www.kiskeya-alternative.org/mudha/. Accessed October 15, 2006.

El Mundo (Madrid). 2004. "Moldear la Vida de Los Niños de Las Calles de la República Dominicana" [Shaping the lives of Dominican street children]. November 15.

National Coalition for Haitian Rights. 1996. *Statement by the National Coalition for Haitian Rights to the Inter-American Commission on Human Rights Concerning the Situation of Haitian Workers in the Dominican Republic.* New York. http://www.nchr.org/hrp/archive/iach.htm. Accessed October 2, 2006.

National Geographic News. October 21, 2002. "Voodoo a Legitimate Religion, Anthropologist Says," by Brian Handwerk. http://news.nationalgeographic.com/news/2002/10/1021_021021_taboovoodoo.html. Accessed November 23, 2006.

Oficina Nacional de Estadística [National Statistics Office]. 2002a. *VIII Censo Nacional de Población y Vivienda 2002.* [The Eighth National Population and Housing Census 2002]. Santo Domingo. http://celade.cepal.org/cgibin/RpWeb Engine.exe/PortalAction?&MODE=MAIN&BASE=CPVDOM2002&MAIN=WebServerMain.inl. Accessed October 1, 2006.

———. 2002b. *2002 Encuesta Demográfica y de Salud (ENDESA)* [2002 Demographic and Health Survey]. http://celade.cepal.org/cgibin/RpWebEngine.exe/PortalAction?&MODE=MAIN&BASE–DHSDOM2002&MAIN=WebServer Main.inl. Accessed October 1, 2006.

Organisation for Economic Co-operation and Development (OECD). April 2003. *Caribbean Rim Investment Initiative: Business Environment Report on the Dominican Republic.* Paris. http://www.oecd.org/dataoecd/62/21/2635572.pdf. Accessed September 10, 2006.

Participación Ciudadana [Citizen Participation]. 2004. *Estado de la Democracia en la República Dominicana: Informe Ejecutivo.* [The State of Democracy in the Dominican Republic: Executive Report]. Santo Domingo: Centro de Investigaciones y Estudios Sociales (CIES). http://www.pciudadana.com/download/2002–04/Estado_Democracia_Rep_Dom_CIES.pdf. Accessed September 11, 2006.

Public Broadcasting Service. 2000. "The Dominican Comparison: 'Developed vs. Undeveloped Baseball' " from PBS original television program *Stealing Home:*

The Case of Contemporary Cuban Baseball. http://www.pbs.org/stealinghome/ debate/dominican.html. Accessed November 24, 2006.

San Miguel, Pablo Luis. 2005. *The Imagined Island: History, Identity, and Utopia in Hispaniola,* translated by Jane Ramírez. Chapel Hill: University of North Carolina Press.

Secretaria de Estado de Educación [State Secretary of Education]. 2003a. *Plan Estratégico de Desarrollo de la Educación Dominicana 2003–2012: Volumen 1.* [Volume 1 of the Strategic Plan for the Development of Dominican Education 2003–2012]. Santo Domingo. http://www.educando.edu.do/NR/ rdonlyres/3537AB13-B47D-4A9A-BF27-B056C50941AC/0/LeyEdu66_97 .doc. Accessed September 9, 2006.

———. 2003b. *Plan Estratégico de Desarrollo de la Educación Dominicana 2003– 2012: Volumen 2* [Volume 2 of the Strategic Plan for the Development of Dominican Education 2003–2012]. Santo Domingo. http://www.see.gov .do/sitesee.net/plan%20estrategico/Volumen_2.pdf. Accessed September 9, 2006.

———. 2003c. *Plan Estratégico de Desarrollo de la Educación Dominicana 2003– 2012: Volumen 3* [Volume 3 of the Strategic Plan for the Development of Dominican Education 2003–2012]. Santo Domingo. http://www.see.gov .do/sitesee.net/plan%20estrategico/Volumen_3.pdf. Accessed September 9, 2006.

Suprema Corte de Justicia [Supreme Court]. 2002. *Constitución de la República Dominicana* [Dominican Republic Constitution]. Santo Domingo.

United Nations. 2001. *Human Development Report. 2001.* http://hdr.undp.org/ reports/global/2001/en/pdf/completenew.pdf. Accessed September 15, 2006.

———. 2005. *Informe sobre Desarrollo Humano 2005* [2005 Human Development Report]. http://hdr.undp.org/reports/global/2005/espanol/pdf/HDR05_ sp_complete.pdf. Accessed October 8, 2006.

United Nations Educational, Scientific and Cultural Organization (UNESCO). 2005. *Regional Education Indicators Project: Summit of the Americas. Educational Panorama 2005: Progressing toward the Goals.* http://www.uis.unesco .org/template/pdf/EducGeneral/SummitAmericas.pdf. Accessed October 21, 2006.

University of Minnesota Human Rights Library. 2001. *Concluding Observations of the Committee on the Rights of the Child, Dominican Republic.* UN Doc. CRC/C/ 15/Add.150. http://www1.umn.edu/humanrts/crc/dominicanrepublic2001 .html. Accessed October 15, 2006.

U.S. Census Bureau. December 2004. *We the People: Hispanics in the United States: Census 2000 Special Reports.* http://www.census.gov/prod/2004pubs/ censr-18.pdf. Accessed November 19, 2006.

U.S. Department of Labor. 2006. *The Department of Labor's 2005 Findings on the Worst Forms of Child Labor.* Washington, DC: U.S. Department of Labor, Bureau of International Affairs. http://www.dol.gov/ilab/media/reports/ iclp/tda2005/tda2005.pdf. Accessed November 2, 2006.

U.S. Department of State. February 2004. *Country Reports on Human Rights Practices 2003: Dominican Republic.* Washington, DC: Bureau of Democracy, Human Rights, and Labor.

———. March 2006. *Country Reports on Human Rights Practices 2005: Dominican Republic.* Washington, DC: Bureau of Democracy, Human Rights, and Labor.

U.S. Peace Corps. (n.d.) *Where Do Volunteers Go: Caribbean: Dominican Republic.* http:// www.peacecorps.gov/index.cfm?shell=learn.wherepc.caribbean.dominicanrepublic. Accessed November 1, 2006.

U.S. Social Security Administration, Office of Policy. 2005. *Social Security Programs throughout the World: The Americas, 2005*. http://www.ssa.gov/policy/docs/ progdesc/ssptw/2004–2005/americas/dominican_republic.html. Accessed October 14, 2006.

World Bank. 2000. *1999/2000 World Development Report*. http://www.worldbank .org/wdr/2000/pdfs/chap3.pdf. Accessed November 12, 2006.

———. 2002. *Dominican Republic Mortality Rates*. http://siteresources.worldbank .org/INTHNPMDGS/Resources/563114-1112109151438/892594-11134 07069651/DominicanRepublic.pdf. Accessed November 12, 2006.

———. 2006. *Breaking the Cycle of Poverty in the Dominican Republic*. http://web .worldbank.org/WBSITE/EXTERNAL/NEWS/0,,contentMDK:21034305~ pagePK:64257043~piPK:437376~theSitePK:4607,00.html. Accessed November 12, 2006.

———. 2006. *Country Profile*. http://web.worldbank.org/WBSITE/EXTERNAL/ COUNTRIES/LACEXT/DOMINICANEXTN/0,,menuPK:337779~page PK:141132~piPK:141107~theSitePK:337769,00.html. Accessed November 12, 2006.

World Vision. *News Archive–Dominican Republic*. http://www.wvi.org/wvi/ archives/lacro/dominican_republic.htm. Accessed November 10, 2006.

Zinn, Howard. 2002. *A People's History of the United States*. New York: Perennial Classics.

7

GRENADA

M. Gail Sanders Derrick

NATIONAL PROFILE

Grenada is an island nation in the southeastern Caribbean located between the Caribbean Sea and Atlantic Ocean, north of Trinidad and Tobago, and approximately 100 miles from the Venezuelan coast. Grenada is often referred to as the "Spice of the Caribbean" for its cultivation of spices, including nutmeg, cloves, cinnamon, ginger, and mace. Nutmeg was one of the major exports during the twentieth century, providing 20 percent of the world supply ("Grenada Facts"). Grenada is an independent state within the Commonwealth of Nations in the Windward Islands of the West Indies. The Commonwealth of Nations includes the island of Grenada and the southern half of the archipelago known as the Grenadines. Grenada is the largest island in the Commonwealth of Nations, approximately 344 square kilometers with 121 kilometers of coastline ("Grenada Facts"). It is a volcanic, mountainous island with crater lakes and a tropical climate tempered by northeast trade winds. The capital and

largest city is St. George's, and other major towns are Grenville and Gouyave. The island of Grenada is divided into six parishes: Saint Andrew, Saint David, Saint George, Saint John, Saint Mark, and Saint Patrick.

The smaller Grenadines of Carriacou, Petit Martinique, Ronde Island, Caille Island, Diamond Island, Large Island, Saline Island, and Frigate Island are largely uninhabitable and are located north of Grenada ("Grenada, Facts and Figures, Background"). The islands of Carriacou and Petite Martinique have the status of dependency. The administration of the islands of the Grenadines group is divided between Saint Vincent, the Grenadines, and Grenada.

Grenada is not the most developed of the Windward Islands but has progressed steadily over the past twenty years. While not a highly developed tourist destination, Grenada has a low-key and quaint approach, a real appeal for those that have visited the island. Grenada relies heavily on tourism as its main source of revenue. An international airport was finished in 1985 to aid this effort. Construction and manufacturing expansion have also contributed to economic growth.

The devastation caused by Hurricane Ivan in September 2004 and Hurricane Emily in July 2005 has been a major political and economic issue for the government of Grenada. The island has managed to recover with aid and support from international organizations. The tourism industry was particularly hard hit. The majority of visitors used to be from the United States, but now 56 percent are from the Caribbean. Because one in four people are employed by the tourism industry in Grenada, the impact of hurricane damage has been substantial (Saargent 2006). Many hotels, restaurants, and other businesses reopened for the 2006–2007 tourist season. The estimated numbers of tourists arriving on Grenada each year is approximately 110,000 people, and the loss of tourists impacts all segments of island life (Grenada, Facts and Figures).

The 2006 estimated Gross Domestic Product (GDP) was $408 million, the growth rate was 12.1 percent, and the GDP per capita in 2006 was $3,854 (U.S. Department of State 2006). The GDP by area is agriculture (7.7 percent), industry (23.9 percent), and services (68.4 percent). The labor force (1999 estimates) is primarily in the service area (62 percent), followed by agriculture (24 percent) and industry (14 percent). The unemployment rate is 12.5 percent and the population below the poverty line is 32 percent (Central Intelligence Agency). Poverty has likely increased as a result of Hurricanes Ivan and Emily. Many of the previous initiatives to improve incomes, achieve better education and health outcomes, and offer social protection to those in need had just begun to show progress in 1999. The relationship and links between poverty, growth, and employment are addressed through social policies and programs (International Monetary Fund and the International Development Association 2006, 1–6). Grenada is committed to establishing the economic stability needed to rebuild after Hurricanes

Ivan and Emily, as well as to fight poverty as a strategy for social improvement.

Christopher Columbus first sighted the island in 1498 and gave it the name *Conception Island*, and later called it Granada. At the time, the Island Caribs (Kalinago) lived there and called it *knouhogue*. The Spaniards did not permanently settle in Camerhogue. Later the English failed their first settlement attempts, but the French fought the Caribs and conquered Grenada around 1650. Virtually no Caribs and Arawaks survived the French purge at Sauteurs. At one point many Caribs opted not to be captives of the French and leaped to their death near Sauteurs, a present day town in northern Grenada. This resulted in warfare between the Caribs of present-day Dominica and St. Vincent and the Grenadines and the French invaders. The French took control of Camerhogue and named the new French colony Grenade. The colony was ceded to the United Kingdom in 1763 by the Treaty of Paris. Grenada was made a Crown Colony in 1877 ("Grenada's History").

Briefly a province of the West Indies Federation (1958–1962), Grenada became an Associated State of the United Kingdom in 1967. At that point, Grenada became responsible for her own internal affairs and the United Kingdom had responsibility for her defense and foreign affairs. Independence was granted in 1974 under then Premier Eric Gairy, who became the first Prime Minister of Grenada. A coup d'état occurred in March 1979 in protest of Gairy's government, led by Maurice Bishop, the popular leftwing leader of the New Jewel Movement. Welcomed by many on the island and the international community, Bishop's coup was a popular movement. The new government (the People's Revolutionary Government [PRG]) aspired to socialism and attempted many radical reforms that had both positive and negative impacts on the island.

The PRG emphasized the connection of education and health programs, teacher training, and agricultural education to improved social and economic productivity, and pursued improvements in agriculture as a stable industry along with the development of community programs (de Grauwe 1991). There was also a dramatic increase in scholarships offered for university and technical education abroad. The establishment of the Institute of Higher Education supported the government's goals to fast track the offering of higher education. This institute was situated in a large hotel in St George's, which provided space for a campus. These efforts, however, were short-lived given the end of the Revolution in 1983, and the return to a post-colonial government (Bobb-Smith 2005). Imprisonment of political opponents, the abolition of a free press (de Grauwe 1991), Bishop's failure to conduct elections, and his alliance with communist Cuba were not well received by his country's neighbors of Trinidad and Tobago, Barbados, Dominica, as well as the United States ("Grenada History").

Conflicts within the leadership led to the overthrow of the government by the more radical faction on October 19, 1983, Bishop's arrest and subsequent execution, and the establishment of the Revolutionary Council under the short-lived leadership of General Hudson Austin. The island was invaded six days later by forces from the United States and five other Caribbean nations. In 1984, the United States provided Grenada with $48.4 million in economic assistance, and the CIA spent $650,000 to aid a pro-American candidate in that year's election (Bell 2001).

Seventeen members of the PRG and People's Revolutionary Army (PRA) were convicted, fourteen were sentenced to death (subsequently commuted to life imprisonment after an international campaign), and three were sentenced to life imprisonment. These seventeen have become known as the Grenada 17. Amnesty International has stated their continued imprisonment is an injustice. The documentary *Prisoners of the Cold War* explores the idea that the continued imprisonment of the seventeen reflects the post-traumatic state of the island as a whole ("Grenada").

Currently, Grenada is a democratic country with universal suffrage, a well-established parliamentary democracy, free elections, a multiparty structure, equality of access to political activity, and the right to participate in government decision-making. The last elections, held in November 2003, were won for the third consecutive time by the New National Party of the current Prime Minister Keith Mitchell, which currently has a slim 8 to 7 majority ("EU Relations with Grenada").

Most of Grenada's population, more than 80 percent, are descended from Africans brought to the island as slaves by the Europeans. About 12 percent of the population are descendants of the Indian indentured emigration to St. Lucia and Grenada that began in 1855 (U.S. Department of State, Background Note 2006). The racial and ethnic demographics of Grenada are thus 82 percent black, 13 percent mixed black and European, European and East Indian (5 percent), and a trace of Arawak/Carib Amerindian. The population is 53 percent Roman Catholic, 14 percent Anglican, and 33 percent Protestant. The official language is English, and French patois is also spoken ("Facts about Grenada"). French culture is evident in Grenada although less prominently than on other Caribbean islands. French architecture, French family names, and French place names are found on the island, although the island culture is more heavily influenced by African traditions and, to a lesser degree, its Indian heritage. Foods, music, dance, and festivals reveal the influence of this rich cultural heritage.

The estimated population (July 2006) of Grenada is 89,703 ("Facts about Grenada"). The estimated population under eighteen years of age is approximately 33,000 with 9,000 under the age of five, although these numbers vary from different reporting sources. The 2006 World Population Sheet reports that approximately 32 percent of the Grenadian population is under the age of fifteen, and 5 percent are sixty-five years of age and older (Population Reference Bureau 2006). The median age is 21.7

Table 7.1.
Population Demographics

Age	Percentage of total population	Male	Female
0 to 14 years of age	33.4	15,097	14,820
15 to 64 years of age	63.4	30,106	26,764
65 years of age and over	3.3	1,394	1,522

Source: "Facts about Grenada."

years (for males it is 22.1 and for females 21.02) (Grenada, Index Mundi). Approximately 38 percent of the population is considered urban, and 62 percent is considered rural (United Nations 2006). These general population demographics are presented in Table 7.1. As noted, the statistics vary from different reporting sources ("Facts about Grenada").

The population growth rate is 0.2619 percent, the birth rate is 22.3 births per 1,000 live births, and the death rate is 7.17 deaths per 1,000 deaths (Central Intelligence Agency). The infant mortality rate (the number of infants dying before reaching one year of age, per 1,000 live births in a given year) was 21 in 2000 and 17.5 in 2004. The under-five mortality rate (the probability that a newborn baby will die before reaching age five, if subject to current age-specific mortality rates) per 1,000 live births was 26 in 2000 and 21.3 in 2004 (World Development Indicators Database 2006).

According to a report submitted to the Ministry of Education in 2003, there is a large number of single mothers with many children in Grenada. The report indicates that 27.6 percent of Grenadian children lived with their mothers and 14.3 percent lived with their mother and stepfather. Over one-third lived with their mother and father. Nearly half of school children lived in households with more than five persons, and most of them had siblings living elsewhere in Grenada and Carriacou. The "average" father had parental responsibilities in more than one household, and a large number of school children have mothers who have children by men other than their fathers (Kairi Consultants, Inc. 2003, vi).

Nongovernmental organizations and other associations in Grenada provide everything from medical supplies to textbooks. Among the more visible groups are the Rotary Club, Save the Children, Crossroads, Peace Corps, Grenada Education

KEY FACTS – GRENADA

Population: 89,971 (July 2007 est.)
Infant mortality rate: 13.92 deaths/1,000 live births (2007 est.)
Life expectancy at birth: 65.21 years (2007 est.)
Literacy rate: 96 percent (2003 est.)
Net primary school enrollment/attendance: 84 percent (2000–2005)
Internet users: 19,000 (2005 est.)

Sources: CIA World Factbook: Grenada. https://www.cia.gov/cia/publications/factbook/geos/gj.html. April 17, 2007; UNICEF. At a Glance: Grenada–Statistics. http://www.unicef.org/infobycountry/grenada_statistics.html. April 24, 2007.

(GRENED), Programme for Adolescent Mothers, and the New Life Organisation (Countries and Their Culture).

OVERVIEW

Education in Grenada is founded on the belief that it is a basic human need and right, a means of meeting other basic needs, and an activity that retrains and accelerates personal, economic, and social development (World Data on Education 2004). Human resource development, the main goal of the educational process, is seen as the path to the country's prosperity and growth. Every child has an inherent right to an education, which should enhance the development of maximum capability regardless of gender or ethnicity, economic, social, or religious background so that the achievement of personal goals and the fulfillment of all obligations to society may be realized (World Data on Education 2004).

Grenada has one of the highest unemployment rates in the Caribbean (about 15 percent). Unemployment is particularly high among young people and people living in rural areas. The causes of poverty in Grenada are related to historical and economic factors, including the vulnerability of the economy because of the country's small size and its exposure to natural disaster. About 32 percent of all people are poor, and almost 13 percent are extremely poor. Poverty is a predominantly rural problem, driving many young people from family-run farms to look for work in urban areas or abroad. This migration of men leaves many households headed by women (International Fund for Agricultural Development).

Poverty and the limitations of a small island economy affect rural youth, restricting their opportunity to complete schooling or to find employment. Young men in particular feel disenfranchised and participate less at the community level, so it is more difficult to involve them in economic activities. Young people see agriculture as an unsatisfactory employment option unless they have control over family lands. The tourism sector holds much more appeal for them, but they may lack appropriate qualifications and skills (International Fund for Agricultural Development).

While teenage pregnancy appears to be declining in Grenada (from 23 percent in 1980 to 19.7 percent in 1991), it still represents a significant social problem. As elsewhere in the Caribbean, males gain peer status and self-esteem based on the number of women with whom they have sexual intercourse and the number of children they produce. Gender stereotypes limit women's occupational horizons and opportunities (International Fund for Agricultural Development).

Grenada has an active agenda at the local and international levels to address the quality of life for children and women through education and economic security. Child mortality rates have improved as a result of health education programs and international support. Grenada is ranked 108 of 190 countries for under-five mortality. Grenada's rate for under-five mortality dropped from 37 in 1990 to 21 in 2005, and the infant mortality rate (under one year of age) went from 30 in 1990 to 17 in 2005 (United Nations Children's Fund 2006, 103).

Grenadians have mainly emigrated to the Great Britain and Canada. Emigration increased after the 1979 coup. As of 1999, Grenada hosted no refugees or asylum-seekers. However, the country's lack of a national refugee law is a cause for concern as Grenada is likely to see an increase in the number of asylum-seekers due to escalating extra-regional migration and migrant trafficking through the Caribbean. In 1999, the net migration rate was −13.74 migrants per 1,000 people in the population. The total number of migrants in Grenada in 2000 was 8,000. The government views the immigration level as satisfactory, but the emigration level as too high ("Americas, Grenada, Migration").

Grenada has achieved some notable successes in its efforts against HIV/AIDS. However, legal and institutional reform is needed in the areas of: (a) sexual exploitation and abuse, (b) financial provision and support, (c) the juvenile justice system, and (d) access to health care for minors. The most recent data provided through the HIV surveillance unit of the Grenada National AIDS Programme indicate that in 2005 the total number of HIV-infected persons was 272. The figures have risen since 1984, when the first case of HIV was reported. As much as 15 percent of all cases are among young people aged fifteen to twenty-four years, particularly females. This feminization of HIV is consistent with regional and international trends for young women. The impact filters to children who may be left orphaned or without a support system, particularly in the aftermath of natural disasters such as Hurricane Ivan in 2004 (Sealy-Burke, 5).

As a party to the Convention on the Rights of the Child (CRC), the government of Grenada has undertaken the responsibility to protect children from all forms of sexual exploitation and sexual abuse (Article 34). The Convention also creates a legal obligation on the part of the state to provide alternative care with a supportive infrastructure for children who are abused, neglected, or at risk of harm (Article 20).

Grenada's domestic law provides some protection to sexually abused and exploited children, and amendments to the Criminal Code include new sections addressing the issue of incest. Prostitution and other forms of sexual exploitation are addressed, although the issue of pornography is noticeably absent. The Child Protection Act (1998) offers protection to children who are physically, sexually, and emotionally abused, but could be strengthened, according to Sealy-Burke (6).

The number of single mothers with little education, resources from noncustodial fathers, and little public assistance reinforces the need for legislation with regard to financial support. Poverty is significant in Grenada, and 56 percent of the poor are under the age of twenty-five (Sealy-Burke, 7).

EDUCATION

The school system in Grenada consists of four levels: preprimary, primary, secondary, and tertiary. Education is compulsory from primary school through grade ten—or the age of sixteen. The pupil to teacher ratio has remained more or less constant over the years and was twenty-five to one in 2001. Female teachers are in the majority in primary schools. Literacy is defined as the percentage of the population aged fifteen and over with the ability to read and write. In Grenada, the literacy rate is 95 percent for the adult population (U.S. Department of State 2004).

Grenada is faced with high poverty and unemployment, and 64 percent of the population does not have formal education certification. More than 25 percent of students leaving primary school have no access to secondary school education. While the government increased spending on education from 5.3 percent of GDP in 2000 to 6.3 percent in 2002, low teacher qualification remains endemic (United Nations Development Programme).

Preprimary education for children age three to five is offered mainly in small private institutions and is not compulsory. In 2002, Grenada had 106 preschool centers (seventy-four public and thirty-two private). The public centers are fairly equally distributed throughout the country, while twenty-five of thirty-two private centers are located in the parish of St. George's. Primary education for children age six to eleven is compulsory. There are fifty-eight primary schools (forty-one denominational, seventeen government-run).

Secondary education is for children age twelve to sixteen. There is a vocational alternative to this five-year secondary cycle: the skills training centers offer three-year courses, and the vocational training centers have a two-year program. Of the eighteen public secondary schools in Grenada, nine are denominational and nine are government-run.

There are several options for continued study in higher education following the end of the secondary school cycle. These include courses for the General Certificate Examination (GCE), a technical and/or academic level examination at the T. A. Marryshow Community College (TAMCC), teacher education at the TAMCC, and University of West Indies School of Continuing Studies. The University of St. George's is an American offshore campus that recently started offering scholarships to Grenadian citizens.

Children who are eleven years old sit for the Common Entrance Examination (CEE), which selects 40 to 50 percent of the best performers each year for entry into secondary schools. Those who are not selected can continue for another three years in senior-primary sections of primary schools and can sit for the School Leaving Examination (SLE). This exam is administered to students in the fourteen-and-over age group, and allows those who pass a choice of three different options. One option is the opportunity to go into secondary education, joining in form three. Another is the opportunity to access technical and vocational education and training in the centers and community colleges. A third option is certification for successful examinees that have passed in at least four subjects, including the English language, to be eligible for entry into the job market.

At the secondary level as with the primary level, there is an external examination at the end of the course. The examination is either regional in nature (Caribbean Examinations Council) or international, the GCE–Ordinary Level (GCE-O) (Vaillant, Jabif, and Domingo 2003, 8–9).

According to the *State of the World's Children 2007*, the percentage of primary school enrollment for males is 94 percent and for females is 90 percent. At the secondary level, the enrollment for males is 96 percent and for females is 105 percent (United Nations Children's Fund 2006). The number represents the number of children enrolled in a level of schooling (primary or secondary), regardless of age, divided by the population of the age group that officially corresponds with the same level. This is a standard indicator of the level of participation in education. In countries with gross enrollment ratios over 100 percent, there is much under- and/or over-aged enrollment, meaning that many students are above or below the official age for the grade. This may be the result of having to repeat grades or entering school late because of work and/or inability to afford school fees.

At the primary level, the average repetition rate for grades one to six was 6 percent in the early 2000s (two children out of a class of thirty-three). Pupil progression from grade one to grade six is satisfactory; 95 percent complete grade five and enter grade six. At the secondary level, the attrition rate is between 1 percent and 2 percent on average, somewhat lower in the early grades and slightly higher in forms three (middle school) and four (high school). Secondary enrollment has increased steadily since 1996, with an average growth rate of 4.4 percent. Access to secondary education remains low (60 percent of the age group), which means that about half of all young adults do not have any educational certificate. However, girls have consistently gained a much higher number of awards to secondary education, between 55 percent and 60 percent of the total awards. The Ministry of Education recently declared a strategy of expanding access to secondary education in order to make it universal (Government of Grenada 2002, 18–19).

The government's goal of universal secondary education is seen as a path to global competitiveness and domestic economic growth and stability. However, many families lack the resources to support the specific costs associated with attendance at public secondary schools (or private schools). This has particular implications for female-headed households where the head has not been able to find employment. A study conducted with 743 students in secondary schools found that the vast majority of parents and guardians who were in the workforce had a low level of skills. The cost of education compared with low levels of minimum wages poses a significant obstacle for secondary school attendance (Kairi Consultants, Inc. 2003).

Special education is a collaborative effort between the government and nongovernmental and voluntary organizations. Three institutions are involved in the delivery and development of special education, one of which is government-assisted and the other two government-controlled. They include a school for the hearing impaired and two schools for the mentally challenged (World Data on Education 2004).

Wherever possible, attempts are made to incorporate students with special needs into the mainstream system with minor adjustments made to curricular and testing procedures to accommodate them. For example, visually handicapped students are provided alternative adaptive strategies to allow them to sit the CEE. The curriculum is focused on mastery of basic skills in addition to prevocational training and self-help skills (World Data on Education 2004).

A majority of teachers at the preprimary and primary levels are female. The feminization of the teaching profession can be attributed to a number of factors, which include the unattractive salary perceived as inadequate by males and the general attitude that teaching is largely a feminine role, especially when working with young children (World Data on Education 2004).

Grenada has struggled to rebuild after Hurricane Ivan battered the island on September 7, 2004. The storm shut down the island universities and forced medical students to return to the United States. More than 1,000 students were relocated to Barry University in Miami Shores, Florida, and to the New York College of Osteopathic Medicine. Veterinary students were relocated to North Carolina State University, Kansas State, and Purdue University (Ceaser 2005).

PLAY AND RECREATION

Grenada offers a wide array of outdoor activities for both tourists and locals. Grenada is being increasingly discovered by outdoor enthusiasts of all types, including hikers, mountain bikers, birdwatchers, and water lovers. The island offers opportunities for scuba diving, snorkeling, parasailing, kayaking, sailing, and cruising. The diving in Grenada is considered to be some of the best in the Caribbean, with thirty or more dive sites encompassing reefs, wrecks—including the largest shipwreck in the Caribbean—and walls. Tourists enjoy golf, tennis, and the island's black and white sand beaches. Grenada's most famous stretch of sand is the two-mile-long Grand Anse. Unlike other islands, Grenada has made sure that the development is unobtrusive. By law, no hotel on the island can exceed three stories or the height of the palm trees ("Grenada at a Glance").

The last decade and a half has been a period of considerable development in Grenada. While the expansion of the tourist industry has proceeded rapidly, the island nation has taken great care to protect its natural environment. A number of national parks have been developed, and the protection of both the rain forest and the coral reefs continues to be a high priority. One-ninth of Grenada's land mass is preserved in the way of parks, natural sanctuaries, and wildlife preserves. Important are the Grand Etang Forest Reserve and the La Sagesse estuary.

Grenada's surrounding waters offer some of the best sailing and deep-sea fishing in the Caribbean, and the island is one of the important yachting centers in the region. The Annual Spice Island Billfish Tournament held in mid-January each year attracts fishermen from the world over. The Carriacou Regatta, which takes place in August, covers the distance between Grenada and Carriacou, with cultural exhibits, dances, and street parties before and after the race (Sports and Recreation).

The children of Grenada are active and athletic. Rounders is a popular sport similar to baseball. A tennis ball and a cricket bat are used with four bases and scoring is counted in terms of runs. Cricket, soccer (called football), and netball are popular sports on the island. Cricket is played from January to June and during that time there is a game almost every Saturday and Sunday (Sports and Recreation).

The Preparatory Games in June give children aged from four to twelve a chance to take part in athletic competitions. Intercol is a popular annual sporting affair at which secondary schools compete against each other in running, jumping, and other athletic events. Other athletic events include the Grenada International Triathlon in which competitors swim one kilometer, cycle twenty-five kilometers, and run five kilometers. The National Athletic Championship occurs in March and features the top athletes in Grenada (Sports and Recreation).

Grenadians' celebrate many holidays as religious festivals. Corpus Christi in June marks the beginning of the planting season and is observed by a religious procession in the city of St. George's. St. Patrick's Day is celebrated with a street festival featuring local arts and crafts, agricultural products, and food. Easter Monday is celebrated by a kite-flying competition at various locations on the island. At the end of June, there is the Fisherman's Birthday, the feast of Saints Peter and Paul. Priests bless the nets and boats of the fishing fleet. Carnival is celebrated during the second weekend in August and the days preceding the weekend. During this time there are steelband competitions, King and Queen of the Band competitions, calypso contests, parades, singing, and dancing (Sports and Recreation).

CHILD LABOR

The minimum age for employment in Grenada is sixteen years of age as established by the Employment of Women, Young Persons and

Children Act of 1999. The Ministry of Labor enforces child labor laws in the formal economy through periodic checks of employers. Child labor is reportedly not a significant problem in Grenada, although some children help with harvesting and planting in seasonal agriculture. While education is free and compulsory for children between six and fourteen years of age, and despite an overall high enrollment in the primary grades, poverty, poor school facilities, and the need to assist family farming and harvesting have resulted in a 7 percent absenteeism rate among primary school children.

The government of Grenada has addressed the issue of poverty and child labor with programs and strategies for low-income families. In 1990, the government began a school meals program in the island's pre-primary and primary schools, a textbook program, and a program to upgrade the preschools. The school meals program allows children to pay a nominal fee for the daily meal, and the textbook program assists children from low-income families in obtaining the texts needed for education.

The Constitution of Grenada prohibits forced labor and slavery. There are no specific laws that address human trafficking and no reports of child trafficking to, from, out of, or within the country (U.S. Department of Labor 2002).

FAMILY

Grenada is faced with the challenge of migration, particularly by the younger population. It is estimated that with fewer than 90,000 residents on the island, there are at least that same number of Grenada-born people living in other parts of the Caribbean (Barbados and Trinidad) and major cities such as New York, Toronto, and London. Major countries of destination of migrants from Grenada are Canada, Puerto Rico, Trinidad and Tobago, the United Kingdom, and the United States. According to UN Population Division estimates, the foreign-born represented 10.5 percent (10,843) of the total population of Grenada in 2005 (Migration Information Source, Grenada).

Approximately 31 percent of family households were headed by persons sixty years old and older, 53 percent of them by women and 47 percent by males. Among the elderly, 30 percent live alone. In 1996, 8.9 percent of the labor force (38,078 persons) was sixty years old and older, of which 59 percent were men and 41 percent women. There are thirteen homes that care for the elderly (one public and twelve private), and a nongovernmental organization also works specifically with this age group (Pan American Health Organization 1998).

The percentage of Grenadian children from birth through age fourteen living in a household headed by a man and one headed by a woman is equal at 50 percent and 50 percent, respectively. However, the marital status indicates very disparate numbers for single-parent heads of house-hold: male 5 percent and female 37 percent (Barrow 2001, 20).

HEALTH

In Grenada, the birth rate is 22.1 per 1,000 and infant mortality rate is 14.3 per 1,000. Life expectancy is 72 years overall, while the average life expectancy for males is 69.01 years and 75.9 years for females (Central Intelligence Agency). Between 1992 and 1995, there were 119 deaths in children under one year of age, with 48 percent of these deaths occurring within the first day of life. In the same period, twenty-seven children in the one- to four-year-old age group died, and in the five- to nine-year-old age group, sixteen children died. The proportion of low birth weight infants ranged between 9.7 percent and 10.6 percent of total births in the 1992 to 1995 period (Pan American Health Organization 1998).

According to data on the estimated population of children under five years old and the number of first visits to well-baby clinics, more than 80 percent of this age group are seen by trained personnel in the public sector. In 1995, the Ministry of Health instituted a campaign to encourage more breastfeeding. A total of 1,154 infants were seen at age three months, and of these, 397, or 34.4 percent, had been solely breastfed for the first three months of life (Pan American Health Organization 1998).

Total live births have declined over the last decade from 2,096 in 1996 to 1,264 in 2003. The crude birth rate decreased from 21.3 per 1,000 persons in 1996 to 17.9 per 1,000 persons in 2003. The crude death rate has decreased from 8.0 per 1,000 persons in 1998 to 8.7 per 1,000 in 2002. The rate of natural increase fell from 13.4 per 1,000 persons in 1996 to 8.5 in 2002. The total fertility rate over the 2000 to 2003 period averaged 2.5 children per woman of child-bearing age, down from 3.2 children during the 1992 to 1995 period (Pan American Health Organization 2004).

There were twenty-six reported stillbirths in 2003 compared with twenty-one in 2002. The proportion of low birth weight babies was 8 percent to 10 percent of total births between 1996 and 2003. Low birth weight babies were 7.6 percent of total births in 2003 compared with 7.5 percent in 2002 (Pan American Health Association 2004). It is estimated that approximately 78 percent of pregnant women attended prenatal clinics held in community health facilities and were seen primarily by a nurse. Only 5 percent to 7 percent of these women, however, registered their first visit before the twelfth week of pregnancy, while 80 percent of those who attended did so by the sixteenth week of pregnancy or later (Pan American Health Organization 1998).

The older population is primarily affected by diabetes, hypertension, and coronary or cardiovascular diseases and their complications. For persons screened in the district health services from 1992 to 1995, between

8.5 percent and 14.1 percent were diagnosed with diabetes mellitus and between 10.5 percent and 11.7 percent with hypertension (Pan American Health Organization 1998).

Chronic, noncommunicable diseases such as heart disease, stroke, diabetes, hypertension, and cancers have become the main causes of adult mortality and morbidity and represent big expenditure in national health care budgets. Major risk factors to health in the Caribbean are unhealthy eating habits, physical inactivity, obesity, tobacco and alcohol use, and inadequate utilization of preventive health services. An assessment of the meals consumed in four rural communities in Grenada concluded that there was little variety and that diets were deficient in vitamins B and C, carotene, and some minerals (Charles 1998, cited in Barrow 2001). Studies conducted by the Caribbean Food and Nutrition Institute (CFNI) in seven Caribbean countries on diet and all cancer incidences showed a positive correlation with fat intake and a negative correlation with plant and vegetable intake (Pan American Health Association 2004).

Legislation enacted in 1980, currently being reviewed and updated, mandates that all children under thirteen years old must be immunized against diphtheria, whooping cough, tetanus, measles, and poliomyelitis. In 1996, immunization coverage of children under one year old was lower than the expected standard for the country, showing an overall decline compared to previous years—80 percent were immunized against diphtheria, tetanus, whooping cough, and poliomyelitis, and 85 percent were immunized against measles (Pan American Health Association 2004).

The 1991 Census of Population and Housing indicates that 50.2 percent of Grenadians had their water supply piped into their dwellings, another 13.4 percent had water piped into their yards, 7.5 percent had private catchments, and 21.1 percent used public standpipes. The National Water and Sewerage Authority estimates that in January 1994 the percentage of households with pipe connections was about 59 percent, which means that about 85 percent of the population had access to potable water—96.4 percent in St. George's and 76.1 percent in the rest of the country. Fifty-nine percent of households used pit latrines, 33 percent used septic tanks, 3 percent were linked to a sewerage system, and 3.9 percent (more than 850 households) had no toilet facilities. The St. George's Sewerage system was upgraded in 1992, and in 1993 the Grand Anse Sewerage project was put in place (Pan American Health Association 2004).

The Caribbean ranks second to Sub-Saharan Africa as having one of the highest prevalence rates of HIV/AIDS in the world. The First Summit for Children on HIV/AIDS was held in Barbados in 2004 to address the growing concern over the rising incidence in the Caribbean. The report states that 2.3 percent of all those between the ages of fifteen and twenty-four are infected with HIV/AIDS and that most new infections in this age group are reported among young women, an incidence rate three to six times higher than young men of the same age (Caribbean Summit for Children on HIV/AIDS 2004).

A 2006 report prepared by the World Bank stated that Grenada has achieved some notable successes in its HIV response. However, the report explained that more could be done to protect the welfare, safety, and security of children whose lives are affected by HIV and AIDS and suggested that legal reforms are key to improving the protection of children in Grenada who are orphaned or made vulnerable by AIDS (Sealy-Burke). Sealy-Burke also reports that legal and institutional reform is particularly recommended in the areas of sexual exploitation and abuse, financial provision and support, the juvenile justice system, and access to health care for minors. Children affected by HIV/AIDS will continue to be a growing problem as the AIDS pandemic worsens in the region ("The Real Casualties" 2002). The social concerns centered on the loss of a parent(s) affect children's rights to an education, health, and protection from abuse and exploitation along with economic security. National policies and strategies to build and strengthen government, family, and community capacities to provide a supportive environment for orphans and girls and boys infected and affected by HIV/AIDS are currently being implemented ("The Real Casualties" 2002).

One of the most important issues affecting young people's access to medical advice and treatment is the right to seek these services confidentially, without parental consent or notification. In Grenada, there is no legislative or clear policy position with respect to the age at which a child can consent to medical treatment. The abortion discussion poses even more challenges given the current law of Grenada, which still criminalizes abortion (Sealy-Burke, 10).

LAWS AND LEGAL STATUS

The legal system of Grenada is based on English common law. Queen Elizabeth is Queen of Grenada, and Governor-General, Sir Daniel Williams, represents the Crown. Executive power resides with the Head of Government, the Prime Minster. The Prime Minister is appointed by the Governor-General and is generally the leader of the largest faction in the parliament. The branches of government are a Cabinet, currently led by Prime Minister and National Security Minister Keith Mitchell; a bicameral legislature (fifteen-member elected House of Representatives and thirteen-member appointed Senate); and a Supreme Court ("Grenada" 2005, 61). The government and the opposition appoint the senators, while the population elects the representatives (Central Intelligence Agency, CIA: The World Factbook: Grenada Online).

Grenada ratified the CRC in November 1990 and since then has passed several laws incorporating the CRC principles, including the 1991

Status of the Child Act, the 1991 Maintenance Amendment Act, the 1994 Adopter (Amendment) Act, and the 1998 Child Protection Act (Representing Children Worldwide 2005).

The ratification of the CRC, the Convention on the Elimination of All Forms of Discrimination Against Women, and the Inter-American Convention on the Prevention, Punishment and Eradication of Violence Against Women—also known as the Convention of Belem Do Para—have focused on the rights of women and children in the Caribbean countries. Laws to end discrimination against single-women heads of household and children born out of wedlock are a focus of social reform efforts, as are legislative efforts to deal with divorce, matrimonial property, and financial provision ("Family Law Reform in the Caribbean" 2002).

A global study on Violence Against Children was conducted by the United Nations in 2005. This study explores forms, causes, and consequences of violence against children (those under the age of eighteen), and collaborative efforts with UN agencies, nongovernmental organizations, academic institutions, governments, and the public, including children. The 2005 report discusses violence in schools, home and family, communities, institutions, work places, and the legal implications of such violence. The discussions of the delegates point to an overall view of violence against children in the Caribbean as pervasive and on the increase. The increase is attributed to an erosion of family life, negative impact of the media, increased crime, and apathy of law enforcement (Voices of Caribbean Youth 2005). Based on cultural norms, male violence is regarded as normal, and the link between poverty and crime was seen as a major link.

RELIGIOUS LIFE

The population of Grenada is largely Roman Catholic, with estimates ranging from 53 percent to 64 percent of the population. The exception is Petite Martinique, where the population is 98 percent Roman Catholic and 2 percent Seventh-Day Adventist (U.S. Department of State 2004).

An estimated 14 percent to 22 percent of the population adheres to Anglican tradition or other Protestant sects, including Methodists (3 percent) and Seventh-Day Adventists (3 percent). The membership of Seventh-Day Adventists on Grenada is approximately 10,633 (Grenada Conference of Seventh Day Adventists 2006). Other Protestant denominations found in Grenada are Presbyterian, Church of God, Baptist, and Pentecostal. Recently, the Church of Jesus Christ of Latter-Day Saints (Mormons) and the Mennonites have become active on the island.

There are an estimated 625 Jehovah's Witnesses and some 5,000 Rastafarians. There are no mosques, although Muslims, who number about 500, including Muslim foreign medical students at St. George's University, congregate at a small religious center. Well over 60 percent of the population regularly participates in formal religious services, and that percentage rises during major Christian holidays (U.S. Department of State 2004).

The Constitution of Grenada provides for religious freedom and prohibits discrimination based on race, place of origin, political opinion, color, creed, or sex. The government is secular and does not interfere with an individual's right to worship. Nearly all government officials are Christians. The Christian holy days of Good Friday, Corpus Christi, Easter, Whit Monday, and Christmas are national holidays. The government established the Ministry for Ecclesiastical Relations to promote interfaith understanding. This group holds monthly meetings to bring together members from Christian and non-Christian groups, including Bah'ais, Muslims, and Rastafarians (U.S. Department of State 2004).

The Conference of Churches of Grenada, created a decade ago, has become more active in its attempts to facilitate closer relations among various religious organizations. The Christian Forum for Social Action discusses social issues such as drug use, HIV/AIDS, and other social ills. For Independence Day and Thanksgiving church services, most Christian denominations worship together at ecumenical observances (U.S. Department of State 2004).

CHILD ABUSE AND NEGLECT

The Division of Social Services, a department in the Ministry of Housing, Social Services, Culture, and Cooperatives, is responsible for providing counseling and other social services to children and families. The National Coalition on the Rights of the Child (NCRC) was established in 1993 to insure that all levels of the Grenadian population were protected under the law. Through the influence of the NCRC, Grenada passed the Child Protection Act in 1998 and established the Child Welfare Authority, which collaborates with the Division of Social Services. In 2001, Grenada established a crisis hotline for domestic violence, and child neglect and maltreatment (Representing Children Worldwide 2005).

Grenada recently completed an audit on its Child Abuse Reporting Protocol and found that public information, interagency cooperation, and staff training are three key elements essential to maximizing the impact of Child Abuse Prevention, Reporting, and Management Protocols. The audit, commissioned by the Grenada National Coalition on the Rights of the Child (GNCRC) and supported by the United Nations Children's Fund (UNICEF), found that the Protocol could have a much greater impact on child protection practices had the three key elements mentioned above, among others, been strongly established. The Grenada audit report was handed over to the Minister of Social Development by the GNCRC. Grenada, along with St. Vincent, Antigua, St. Lucia, and Dominica, is actively working on improving the national protocols (Grenada Completes Audit; Sealy-Burke).

The 2006 World Bank Report (Section 4), prepared by Sealy-Burke, states that sexual abuse and exploitation present some of the most challenging issues confronting the safety and security of Grenada's children. Young women are particularly at risk, often being victims of incest in the home environment, sexual exploitation, and other forms of sexual abuse. Transactional sex with older men, now commonly referred to as the "Sugar Daddy Syndrome," is reported as becoming widespread. The age difference and youthfulness of the young persons exploited by older male adults makes the negotiation of condom use and sexual boundaries very difficult, according to Sealy-Burke.

The CRC, supported by the government of Grenada along with Grenadian criminal law, seeks to protect children from sexual exploitation and abuse. However, the issue of pornography is not addressed.

Grenada's current domestic law ensures that parents assume financial responsibility for their children and remove distinctions between children born in or out of wedlock. Under the current domestic law, parents are legally obligated to financially support their children. However, children born out of wedlock continue to be disadvantaged because of separate legislative schemes for married and unmarried women. As a result, poor child support is a problem for unmarried mothers (Sealy-Burke).

The Maintenance Act (1991) stipulates no statutory maximums for child support, but actual awards are reported to be very low and tend to stay within close range of the statutory minimum of EC$15.00 (East Caribbean dollars) per week. The Ministry of Social Development does offer a "necessitous programme," which provides a very small number of needy children with limited financial assistance of approximately EC$100.00 per month (EC$2.70 = US$1.00) (Sealy-Burke).

The high number of households headed by women in Grenada (48 percent of all heads of household) and the poverty experienced by these families reinforce the importance of adequate financial support from noncustodial fathers and, where required, public assistance from the state. Nevertheless, court-awarded child support has been described as extremely low, discriminatory of unmarried women with children, and difficult to enforce (Sealy-Burke).

GROWING UP IN THE TWENTY-FIRST CENTURY

The government of Grenada has officially subscribed to the Millennium Development Goals (MDGs) agreed upon world leaders at the Millennium Summit in September 2000. Progress toward these goals is in alignment with many aspects of current policies and strategies for improving the quality of life and standard of living for Grenadian citizens. In the 2005 report entitled *Civil Society Perspectives on Attaining the Millennium Development Goals*, the progress was outlined for each goal (Moses 2005).

Goal 1: Eradicate extreme poverty and hunger

A 1999 Poverty Assessment Survey (Moses 2005, 3) revealed that 32 percent of the Grenadian population was living in poverty, with 13 percent considered to be extremely poor. The annual expenditure of the poor was estimated to be less than EC$3,262—the amount required to purchase the basic requirements of food and other necessities. This finding led the government to initiate accelerated assistance programs, and since then every annual budget has included poverty reduction measures. Examples of these measures are as follows:

- increases in old age pensions;
- assistance for housing repairs;
- assistance for school books and uniforms;
- free water supply to the needy;
- free medicines for the elderly;
- financing for small community projects in rural areas.

Goal 2: Achieve universal primary education

Grenada's literacy rate is 95 percent. Dropouts for the period 1996 to 2000 ranged from 0.8 to 1.3 for boys and 0.5 to 0.8 for girls. At the pre-primary level, consisting of children age three to five years, attendance is 70 percent because a considerable number of parents send their children to school only at the age of five years. Currently, 73 percent of primary school leavers enter secondary schools, and 57 percent of them are girls. A key target of the government's 2002 to 2010 Strategic Plan for Educational Enhancement and Development is the achievement of universal secondary education by 2008 (Moses 2005, 3).

Goal 3: Promote gender equality

Educational data for Grenada indicates that at the secondary and tertiary levels, there are more girls studying than boys. This trend continues up to the university level, which is providing a large number of female professionals for the workforce. Women now occupy senior managerial, administrative, and professional positions in all sectors of the economy. In the teaching profession, for example, there are more female than male teachers, though the percentage has declined from 83 percent in 1994 to 76 percent in 2001.

The proportion of seats in Parliament held by women has risen to 28.5 percent in 2005, up from 17 percent in 2001. The current president of the Senate is a woman, while eight of the thirteen permanent secretaries in government ministries are female. The trends in education are positive; however, other issues such as higher general unemployment among women, domestic violence, and male dominance persist. This goal should be achieved by 2015, according to Moses (2005, 4).

Goal 4: Reduce child mortality

Health care in Grenada has been improving over the last three decades, as successive governments have implemented and supported sound health policies. However, the costs are rising, which has implications for access by the unemployed and indigent. The reduction in the child and infant mortality rate is an indicator of the progress that has been made. Immunization programs have been comprehensive, with 100 percent immunization against measles, mumps, and rubella in effect for children at age one and 95 percent to 98 percent coverage against diphtheria, tetanus, pertussis, and polio. Recently, the coverage was extended to hepatitis B and *Haemophilia influenza* type B. This goal is considered largely achieved (Moses 2005, 4).

Goal 5: Improve maternal health

Maternity health care in Grenada has improved considerably over the past two decades. The current low rate indicates that the goal is largely achieved. This is supported by a record of 100 percent deliveries by trained professionals (Moses 2005, 4).

Goal 6: Combat HIV/AIDS, malaria, and other diseases

Since HIV/AIDS was identified in Grenada in 1984, 265 persons have been diagnosed with the disease and 146 have subsequently died. The prevalence rate of HIV/AIDS is estimated at less than 0.5 percent. While comparatively low, a number of existing factors favor the growth and expansion of the disease. These include the tradition of multiple sex partners, limited use of condoms, early sexual initiation, reluctance to engage in voluntary testing, alcohol and drug use, and the stigmatization of the disease. The infection rate has declined within the past five years. Given the comprehensive strategic plan, implementation of which requires considerable resources, this goal could be achieved (Moses 2005, 4).

Goal 7: Ensure environmental sustainability

In 2003, a National Environmental Strategy for Grenada was developed to ensure that the principles of sustainable development are firmly integrated into national policies and programs. Hurricane Ivan has presented significant challenges since 91 percent of the forest was destroyed, seriously affecting the watershed and an ecosystem that supported fauna and flora, diminishing the protected areas, and undercutting the island's biological diversity. However, this situation has presented an opportunity to enforce new policies and integrated approaches to environmental management.

The proportion of persons with access to safe drinking water is estimated at 99 percent. Access to secure land tenure remains a major problem in Grenada. This is a direct result of the island's early plantation system, when the ability to obtain title was difficult if not impossible. During the last twenty years, the problem of squatting has escalated, particularly in the urban areas. Nonetheless, the achievement of this and other targets under this goal remains possible (Moses 2005, 4).

Goal 8: Develop a global partnership for development

The achievement of the MDGs by small-island developing states like Grenada requires cooperation and assistance from developed countries. Hurricane Ivan has clearly revealed a major vulnerability to natural hazards, which can reverse years of sustained progress. Progress has been made in many areas; however, market access and debt sustainability remain areas of concern (Moses 2005, 4).

Grenada has embraced the MDGs selected targets to achieve between 1990 and 2015. All of the development goals affect children and their future. Grenada continues to address the issues related to generational poverty, educational equity, and opportunity as a means of improving both the social and economic standard of living. The support of international organizations such as the World Bank, UNICEF, and the coalitions established by the Caribbean nations will continue to improve the quality of life in Grenada for children.

RESOURCE GUIDE

Suggested Readings

Adkin, Mark. 1989. *Urgent Fury: The Battle for Grenada: The Truth Behind the Largest U.S. Military Operation Since Vietnam.* Philadelphia: Trans-Atlantic Publications. Describes the 1983 U.S. invasion of Grenada and the political climate, and rivalry between the United States and Cuba. A coup in Grenada, coupled with a perceived threat to American students on the island, provided the United States with an excellent excuse to eliminate a Marxist regime allied to Fidel Castro's Cuba.

Brathwaite, Roger. 2000. *Grenada: Spice Paradise.* London: Macmillan Caribbean. Brathwaite has compiled a book that provides photographic insight into his home island of Grenada.

Russell, Lee. 1985. *Grenada 1983 (Men-at-Arms).* Oxford: Osprey Publishing. On Friday, October 21, the leaders of the six small nations forming the Organisation of Eastern Caribbean States voted to intervene militarily to restore order in Grenada. As none possessed the necessary forces, a request for help was formally presented. The United States, already fearing for its 1,000 or so U.S. citizens present there, decided to intervene.

Sinclair, Norma. 2003. *Grenada: Isle of Spice (Caribbean Guides)*. 3rd edition. North Hampton, MA: Interlink Publishing Group. This beautiful eastern Caribbean island is now visited by thousands of tourists each year. *Grenada: Island of Spice* will give visitors an introduction to the culture and history of the island.

Steele, Beverley A. 2003. *Grenada: A History of Its People (Island Histories)*. London: MacMillan Caribbean. This book provides a detailed chronological historical analysis but focuses especially on the story and everyday lives of its inhabitants from the earliest days of settlement to the overthrow, and execution, of the revolutionary Prime Minister Maurice Bishop in 1981, and beyond.

Nonprint Resources

Exploring Grenada, Spice Island of the Caribbean. 2003. Directed by Sheryl Brakey, SJB Productions. 15 minutes. DVD. *Exploring Grenada* provides a glimpse of the history, culture, and life of a beautiful mountainous island nation in the Windward Islands.

Globe Trekker: Destination Eastern Caribbean Travel Guide. 2004. Pilot Productions, 60 minutes. DVD. Traveler Justine Shapiro starts her journey in Trinidad's capital Port of Spain, for one of the biggest street parties on earth—its world-famous Carnival. She then travels to the laid back island of Tobago, the spice island of Grenada, the remote Carriacou, before continuing north to the lush island of Dominica.

Porthole TV; Grenada: Excursion to "The Spice Island" Tours and Attractions. 2006. Sidney Cohen hosts this episode of Porthole's TV visit to the spice island of Grenada.

Prisoners of the Cold War. 2005. Directed by David Grey. 60 minutes. This documentary tells the story of the Grenada 17. In 1983, the Grenada Revolution collapsed when charismatic Prime Minister Maurice Bishop and others were killed. U.S. forces invaded the island and restored order. This action was condemned by the UN as an infringement of sovereignty. Subsequently, seventeen people were convicted in relation to the killings, via an ad hoc legal process set up and financed by the United States. The seventeen have always protested their innocence, and in 2003 Amnesty International published a report saying they had been the victims of a miscarriage of justice.

Web Sites

Chamber of Commerce, http://www.caribsurf.com.

CIA World Factbook, http://www.cia.gov/cia/publications/factbook.

Government of Grenada, http://www.gov.gd.

Grenada Board of Tourism, http://www.grenadagrenadines.com.

Grenada Community Development Agency (GRENCODA), http://www.grencoda.org.

Grenada Education and Development Programme Inc. (GRENED), http://www.grened.org.

Grenada Information and Relief Efforts, http://www.grenadaemergency.com.

The Grenadian Connection, http://www.grenadianconnection.com/Search/Home.htm.

The Ministry of Education, Grenada, http://grenada.com.

Permanent Mission of Grenada to the United Nations, http://un.cti.depaul.edu/cgibin.

Rotary Club of Grenada, http://www.caribsurf.com.

United Nations Children's Fund (UNICEF), http://www.unicef.org/grenada.

The World Bank, http://worldbank.org.

World Health Organization (WHO), http://www.worldhealth.org.

Organizations and NGOs

Agency for Rural Transformation (ART)
P.O. Box 750
Marrast Hill, St. George's
Grenada
Phone: (473) 440-3440/3915
Fax (473) 440-9882
Email: art@caribsurf.com
Established in 1981 to facilitate agricultural and rural development.

Caribbean Women's Association (CARIWA)
Glebe Street
Phone: (473) 442-1654
Fax: (473) 442-1654
Email: elqueen@caribsurf.com
Established in 1970 to improve the status and condition of women in the Caribbean.

Child Welfare Authority
P.O. Box 1962
St. John's Street,
St. George's
Grenada, West Indies
Phone: (473) 435-0293
Fax: (473) 435-0766
Email: childwelfare@caribsurf.com
Services for children and youth in need of protection.

Grenada Community Development Agency (GRENCODA)
Lower Depradine Street
Gouyave
St. John's, Grenada
Phone: (473) 444-8430/9490
Fax: (473) 444-8777
Email: grenco@caribsurf.com
Exists to provide guidance and support to rural individuals, families, and commun-
ities to improve their quality of life.

Grenada National Coalition on the Rights of the Child
c/o GRENSAVE House
P.O. Box 3594
St. George's, Grenada
Phone: (473) 440-2448/435-0944
Fax: (473) 440-5120
Email: gncrc@caribsurf.com
Works to monitor and implement the Convention on the Rights of the Child nation-
ally in Grenada.

Grenada National Organization of Women (GNOW)
C/O YWCA, Tyrell Street
St. George's, Grenada
Phone: (473) 440-2992
Support network for women in need of assistance from abuse and domestic violence.

Grenada Planned Parenthood Association (GPPA)
P.O. Box 127
St.George's
Grenada, West Indies
Phone: (473) 440-2636
Email: gppa@caribsurf.com
The GPPA provides the population with the knowledge and the means to choose
whether, when, and how many children to have. There is a focus on improving the
health and well-being of women and children. GPPA aims to work towards a bal-
ance between human numbers, human needs, and Grenada's natural resources.

Grenada Red Cross Society (GRC)
P.O. Box 551
St. George's, Grenada
Phone: (473) 440-1483
Fax: (473) 440-1829
Email: grercs@caribsurf.com
The society is committed to helping the vulnerable in Grenada, Carriacou, and Petit
Martinique, believing that it must work at the local level to change the public's per-
ception of the organization as almost exclusively a trainer and provider of first aid.

Legal Aid Clinic and Counseling Clinic (LACC)
St. John's Street
St. George's

Grenada, West Indies
Phone: (473) 440-3788/3785
Fax: (473) 440-4595
Legal aid assistance and services to those in need.

Ministry of Social Development
Ministerial Complex
Botanical Gardens, St. George's
Grenada, West Indies
Phone: (473) 440-7952
Supports and addresses issues related to the needy, elderly, and those who need
    assistance.

National Children's Home (NCH), Guyana Office
Old Fort Road, St. George's
Grenada, West Indies
Phone: (473) 440-2822/6275
Email: nch@caribsurf.com
and
Main Street, Sauteurs
Grenada, West Indies
Phone: (473) 442-9315
National Children's Home assists the government in placing disabled students into
    community schools.

Selected Bibliography

"Americas, Grenada, Migration." Encyclopedia of the Nations. http://www.nation
    sencyclopedia.com/Americas/Grenada-MIGRATION.html. Accessed Febru-
    ary 10, 2007.

Barrow, Christine. 2001. *Situational Analysis of Children and Women in Twelve
    Countries of the Caribbean.* Barbados: UNICEF, Caribbean Area Office.

Bell, P. M. H. 2001. *The World Since 1945: An International History.* London: Hod-
    der Arnold.

Blum, R. W., and M. Ireland. 2004. "Reducing Risk, Increasing Protective Factors:
    Findings From the Caribbean Youth Health Survey." *Journal of Adolescent
    Health* 35: 493–500.

Bobb-Smith, Yvonne. 2005. *National Report on Higher Education in Grenada.*
    Caracas: Venezuela: IESALC/UNESCO, International Institute for Higher
    Education in Latin America and the Caribbean. http://www.iesalc.unesco
    .org.ve/programas/nacionales/grenada/National%20Report%20Grenada.pdf.
    Accessed January 12, 2007.

Caribbean Summit for Children on HIV/AIDS. 2004. Bridgetown, Barbados, March
    23, 2004.

Ceaser, Mike. 2005. "Ivan's Aftermath." *Chronicle of Higher Education* 52 (Septem-
    ber 23): A13. Retrieved Tuesday, October 24, 2006, from the Academic
    Search Premier Database.

Central Intelligence Agency. The CIA World Factbook: Grenada Online. http://
    www.cia.gov/redirects/factbook. p. 11. Accessed September 21, 2006.

————. The CIA World Factbook, U.S. Department of State, Area Handbook of the U.S. Library of Congress, Facts about Grenada, Economy, http://worldfacts .us/Grenada.htm.

Charles, L. 1998. *Grenada Community Baseline Surveys: Final Report.* Barbados: UNICEF/CAO.

Countries and Their Culture. Grenada. http://www.everyculture.com/Ge-It/ Grenada.html. Accessed January 19, 2007.

"EU Relations with Grenada." Europa, European Commission, Development. http:// ec.europa.eu/development/body/country/. Accessed January 18, 2007.

"Facts about Grenada." World Facts Index. http://worldfacts.us/Grenada.htm. Accessed September 21, 2006 and January 18, 2007.

"Family Law Reform in the Caribbean." 2002. *Children in Focus (UNICEF)* 15, no. 1: 1, 4. http://www.unicef.org/barbados/cao_publications_cifreform.pdf.

Government of Grenada. 2002. (February 2002). *Educational Statistical Digest, Past Trends, Present Position and Projections 2008.* Granada Statistical Division and Development Unit, Ministry of Education, pp. 18–19.

de Grauwe, Anton. 1991. "Education and Political Change: The Case of Grenada (1979–89)." *Comparative Education* 27, no. 3: 335–356.

Grenada. 2005. *Military Technology* 29, no. 1: 60–61.

"Grenada." The Grenada 17: The Last of the Cold War Prisoners? Amnesty International. http://web.amnesty.org/library/index/engamr320012003. Accessed March 1, 2007.

Grenada at a Glance. http://www.grenadianconnection.com/Search/Home.htm. Accessed December 1, 2006.

Grenada Completes Audit on its Child Abuse Reporting Protocol. Eastern Caribbean Resources, UNICEF. http://www.unicef.org/barbados/resources_132.htm. Accessed January 19, 2007.

Grenada Conference of Seventh Day Adventists. 2006. http://www.grenadaadven tists.org/Homepage.htm.

"Grenada Facts." National Geographic Online. http://www3.nationalgeographic.com/ places/countries/country_grenada.html. Accessed March 3, 2007.

Grenada, Facts and Figures. ECPAT International. http://www.ecpat.neteng/Ecpat_ inter/projects/monitoring/online_database/countries.asp. Accessed January 8, 2007.

"Grenada, Facts and Figures, Background." Nation Master. http://www.nationmaster .com/country/gj-grenada. Accessed March 3, 2007.

"Grenada History." Commonwealth Secretariat. http://www.thecommonwealth .org/YearbookInternal/145158/history/. Accessed March 3, 2007.

Grenada, Index Mundi. http://www.indexmundi.com/grenada/median_age.htm. Accessed January 12, 2007.

"Grenada's History." http://www.grenadaguide.com/History.htm. Accessed March 3, 2007.

International Fund for Agricultural Development (IFAD). Rural Poverty in Grenada. http://www.ruralpovertyportal.org/english/regions/americas/grd/index.htm. Accessed January 11, 2007.

International Monetary Fund and the International Development Association. 2006. Joint Staff Advisory Note of the Interim Poverty Strategy Paper, Prepared by the Staffs of the International Monetary Fund and the International Development Association, March 31.

Kairi Consultants, Inc. 2003. Final Report, Secondary School Students in Grenada: Improving the Assistance Programmes, June.

Migration Information Source, Grenada. http://www.migrationinformation.org. Accessed January 21, 2007.

Moses, Aaron. 2005. *Civil Society Perspectives on Attaining the Millennium Development Goals (MDGs) in the National Context of Grenada.* Commonwealth Foundation. http://www.commonwealthfoundation.com/uploads/documents/mdg_grenada.pdf. Assessed January 20, 2007.

Pan American Health Organization. 1998. *Health Situation Analysis and Trends Summary, Country Chapter Summary from Health in the Americas, 1998.* http://www.paho.org/English/HIA 1998/Grenada.pdf. Accessed November 22, 2006.

———. 2004. *Grenada Health Situation Analysis, Grenada General Health Situation Analysis 23, November 2004.* PAHO. http://www.cpc.paho.org/%5cfiles%5cDoc Files%5c45_72.pdf.

Pinheiro, Paulo. 2006. *World Report on Violence against Children, Secretary-General's Study on Violence against Children, United Nations.* http://www.violencestudy.org/r25.

Population Reference Bureau. 2006. 2006 World Population Sheet, Section 1. http://www.prb.org/pdf06/06WorldDataSheet.pdf. Accessed January 19, 2007.

"The Real Casualties of HIV/AIDS are ... Children." 2002. *Children in Focus* (UNICEF) 15, no. 1: 4. http://www.unicef.org/barbados/cao_publications cifhiv.pdf.

"Representing Children Worldwide: How Children's Voices are Heard in Child Protective Hearings." 2005. Yale Law School, December. http://www.law.yale.edu/rew/jurisdiction/caribbean/grenada/frontpage.ht. Accessed October 21, 2006.

Saargent, J. 2006. "After the Storm." *Geophysical* 78, no. 3: 34–38. Retrieved October 24, 2006 from the Academic Search Premier Database.

Sealy-Burke, Jacqueline. Protecting Children Affected by AIDS in the Caribbean: Recommendations for Legal Reform in Grenada. Global HIV/AIDS Program, World Bank. http://siteresources.worldbank.org/INTHIVAIDS/Resources/375798-1132695455908/LegalReformRecomm-OVC-GRENADA-July24.pdf. Accessed January 21, 2007.

Sports and Recreation. Grenada to Canada, Cultural Profiles Project, Citizenship and Immigration Canada. http://www.cp-pc.ca/english/grenada/sports.html. Accessed January 19, 2007.

United Nations Children's Fund (UNICEF). 2006. *The State of the World's Children 2007: Women and Children, the Double Dividend of Gender Equity.* New York: UNICEF. http://www.unicef.org/sowc07/report/report.php. Accessed January 19, 2007.

United Nations Development Programme. Country Profiles, Grenada. http://www.bb.undp.org/p2p47p0.html. Accessed January 18, 2007.

United Nations, Department of Economic and Social Affairs, Division for Public Administration and Development Management. 2006. Grenada, Public Administration Country Profile, United Nations July 2006. http://unpan1.un.org/intradoc/images/docgifs/UN.gif. Accessed January 21, 2007.

U.S. Department of Labor. 2002. *The Department of Labors 2001 Findings on the Worst Forms of Child Labor, Trade and Development Act of 2000.* Washington, DC: U.S. Department of Labor, Bureau of International Labor Affairs.

U.S. Department of State. 2004. U.S. Department of State Annual Report on International Religious Freedom for 2004, Grenada, September 2004. http://www.state.gov/g/drl/rls/irf/2004/35539.htm. Accessed March 1, 2007.

————. 2006. Bureau of Western Hemisphere Affairs. 2006. Background Note: Grenada, October 2006. http://www.state.gov/r/pa/ei/bgn/2335.htm. Retrieved Tuesday, October 24, 2006 from the Academic Search Premier Database.

————. 2007. Bureau of Western Hemisphere Affairs. 2007. Background Note: Grenada. http://www.state.gov/r/pa/ei/bgn/2335.htm. Accessed March 1, 2007.

Vaillant, Denise, Liliana Jabif, and Rosario Domingo. 2003. Teacher Training, OECS Education Development Project, Final Report, June 27, 2003. http://wbln0018.worldbank.org/lac/lacinfoclient.nsf. Accessed December 1, 2006.

Voices of Caribbean Youth. 2005. *Report on The Youth Forum and on the Caribbean Regional Consultation on the UN Secretary General Study on Violence Against Children.* p. 13. http://www.unicef.org/barbados/UNICEF_report_Caribbean_youth_perspectives_on_violence.doc.

World Data on Education, Web Edition 2004, Grenada. http://www.ibe.unesco.org/countries/WDE/WorldDataE.htm. Accessed February 11, 2007.

World Development Indicators Database, April 2006. http://devdata.worldbank.org/external/CPProfile. Accessed January 20, 2007.

8

HAITI

Catherine Marsicek

NATIONAL PROFILE

The Republic of Haiti is located in the northern Caribbean Sea, approximately 600 miles southeast of Florida, and just off the southeastern coast of Cuba. It shares Hispaniola with its neighbor, the Dominican Republic, occupying the western third of the island and covering 10,700 square miles. Three-quarters of the country is mountainous, with its highest peak reaching 8,744 feet. Haiti is the second most densely populated country in the Americas, surpassed only by Barbados. The capital, Port-au-Prince, is located in the southeastern part of the country, on the Gulf of Gonaives, and over 1.5 million inhabitants reside in the metropolitan area.

Haiti has had a tragic past, plagued by revolt, civil war, occupation, political instability, poverty, and natural disasters. Haiti won its independence from France on January 1, 1804, becoming the first black republic and the second oldest republic in the Americas, after the United States. Almost immediately, Haiti was engulfed in a civil war that divided the north from the south, and was finally reunified in 1820. Soon after, Haiti pledged substantial monetary payments to France in return for official recognition of its status as an independent nation. From the mid-1800s to 1915, Haiti had twenty-two leaders, but only one finished his prescribed term. In response to this political instability, the United States occupied the country for the next twenty years until 1934. The following decades saw successive military coups and rulers, culminating in the election of François Duvalier in 1957. A shrewd leader made untouchable by the personal security forces that surrounded him, Papa Doc ruthlessly ruled the country until his death in 1971. He was immediately succeeded by his son, Claude Duvalier, or Baby Doc. Lacking the personality cult of his father, Haiti experienced widespread unrest, violence, and rebellion over the next fifteen years until Baby Doc fled Haiti into exile in 1986. Since 1986, Haiti has fluctuated between democratically elected governments and military dictatorships, with only one elected head of state completing his term. Jean Bertrand Aristide, a charismatic priest, was elected with overwhelming popular support in 1990 but was deposed soon after in a military coup and forced into exile. With backing from the United States military, Aristide was returned to power several years later. He was also reelected in 2000 by a wide margin. In February of 2004, after many months of violence and opposition, Aristide again fled the country. Even under the watch of a United Nations Peacekeeping Mission, the violence, including kidnappings, killings, and street protests, continued during the transitional government leading up to the election of René Preval as Haiti's new president in 2006.

Estimates in 2006 put the population at over 8.3 million (Central Intelligence Agency 2006). About 95 percent of the Haitian population is of African descent, with the rest of mixed ancestry, including Caucasian, European, and Middle Eastern. French and Creole are the official languages, but only about 10 percent speak and understand French. About one in eight Haitians has emigrated and now lives abroad, the majority in the United States, but also in Canada, France, and neighboring Caribbean nations.

Haiti is the western hemisphere's poorest and least-developed country. It ranks 153 out of 177 countries on the 2005 United Nations Human Development Index. Haiti suffers from poor infrastructure, few social services, high inflation, a significant trade deficit, the migration of many of its skilled workers, and a severe inequality of wealth. The richest 2 percent of the population controls approximately 44 percent of the national income.

Roughly 80 percent live below the poverty line. The estimated per capita Gross Domestic Product (GDP at PPP [purchasing power parity]) is $1,700. The labor force is close to 3.6 million, but there is widespread unemployment and most workers are unskilled. Roughly two-thirds rely on small-scale subsistence farming for survival, although little of the land is arable because of the mountainous topography and the widespread environmental degradation due to deforestation. The main agricultural products are coffee, mangoes, sugar cane, rice, corn, and sorghum. Other industries include sugar refining, flour milling, and textiles. The GDP in 2005 is estimated at $3.7 billion, while remittances from family members living abroad total over $1 billion (Central Intelligence Agency 2006, under "Economy").

The life expectancy for women is fifty-five years; for men it is fifty-two years. The birth rate is 36 per 1,000 people. The child mortality rate is high and about one in ten die before reaching the age of five. Approximately 42 percent of the population is between the ages of birth and fourteen years (Central Intelligence Agency 2006, under "People").

There is little government-provided support for families and children. National and international non-governmental organizations (NGOs) and religious organizations have been working in Haiti for decades and attempt to fill in where the government has been negligent and ineffective. Because of limited finances and the overwhelming needs in Haiti, the most prevalent approach by NGOs to administering services is crisis intervention, not preventive care.

KEY FACTS – HAITI

Population: 8,706,497 (July 2007 est.)
Infant mortality rate: 63.83 deaths/1,000 live births (2007 est.)
Life expectancy at birth: 57.03 years (2007 est.)
Literacy rate: 52.9 percent (2003 est.)
Net primary school enrollment/attendance: 55 percent (2000–2005)
Internet users: 500,000 (2005)
People living with HIV/AIDS: 190,000 (2005 est.)
Children living with HIV/AIDS: 17,000 (2005 est.)
Human Poverty Index (HPI-1): 74

Sources: CIA World Factbook: Haiti. https://www.cia.gov/cia/publications/factbook/geos/ha.html. April 17, 2007; UNICEF. At a Glance: Haiti–Statistics. http://www.unicef.org/infobycountry/haiti_statistics.html. April 24, 2007; World Health Organization (WHO): UNAIDS/WHO Global HIV/AIDS Online Database. "Epidemiological Fact Sheets on HIV/AIDS and Sexuality Transmitted Diseases: Haiti." http://www.who.int/GlobalAtlas/predefinedReports/EFS2006/index.asp?strSelectedCountry=HT. December 2006; United Nations Development Programme (UNDP) Human Development Report 2006–Haiti. http://hdr.undp.org/hdr2006/statistics/countries/data_sheets/cty_ds_HTI.html. April 26, 2007.

OVERVIEW

Children between birth and the age of fourteen make up over one-third of the Haitian population. Haitian children are in a very precarious situation as they confront poverty, poor nutrition, an inadequate health system, political instability and violence, and a weak education infrastructure. One of the best indicators of a countries' development and status of its children is the death rate before the age of five. One out of ten children dies before the age of five in Haiti, demonstrating the vulnerable situation in which Haitian children live (United Nations 2005, Table 8).

Some of the most pressing children's issues include child labor, lack of educational opportunities, inadequate health care, and neglect. The deep, entrenched poverty along with recent political unrest and health issues, including the AIDS crisis, have taken their toll on Haitian children.

Children are protected through legislation, but the Haitian government has inadequate funds and limited personnel to contend with the magnitude of these issues.

EDUCATION

The state of education in Haiti is bleak. Most Haitians have had no formal education, and only a small minority has gone beyond primary school. Although, by government mandate, education is free and compulsory through the primary school level, a comprehensive and accessible education system has never been developed. Estimated illiteracy levels are very high at 60 percent, and only about 65 percent of school-aged children enroll in school. Most children make it only a few grades, about four, before economic pressure requires them to drop out. Dropout rates are high: 80 percent in the rural areas and 50 percent in the urban areas. Over 40 percent of those who do remain in school are usually three grades behind for their age. About 48 percent of enrollment is female, only slightly less than male enrollment, although girls tend to enroll at a later age than boys. Only 50 percent of the schools offer the full cycle of education (Hadjadj 2000, sec. 3.2–3.10).

Society as a whole values education, as demonstrated by the sacrifices made by families to send their children to school and by the educational reforms of the last few decades, but most Haitians do not have access to it. The Bernard Reform in 1979 set up the National Department of Education and established Creole as the language of instruction for the first four grades; prior to this, instruction was in French, although only 10 percent of the population has a command of French. The 1987 Constitution introduced Creole as an official language alongside French and also confirmed education as compulsory: "primary education is compulsory under penalty of sanctions to be determined by the law. School supplies and teaching aids will be provided by the government for pupils at the primary school level (Article 32-3)" (Haiti 1987). These reforms were designed to increase access to education; however, education remains underfunded and public schools are overcrowded, run down, and ill-equipped. Almost 75 percent of the teachers have neither the appropriate qualifications nor the necessary training required. Instruction in Creole has also been resisted by those middle-class families who see the French language as a status symbol and a means of bettering one's social class.

Government spending on education increased slightly in the 1990s to approximately 1.7 percent of GDP, but it is still significantly less than other low-income countries. This public spending is so inadequate that private financing by religious organizations and NGOs controls approximately 85 percent of Haiti's primary and secondary schools. Private schools charge tuition for attendance, and, with additional costs for school uniforms, books and supplies, this payment is a great burden for most families (Hadjadj 2000, sec. 3.11). These private schools are often as poorly equipped as public schools, especially in the rural areas. Thus, access to education is greatly affected by socioeconomic status and proximity to an urban center. A comprehensive education is by and large a privilege of the upper-middle and upper classes. In 2003, the Haitian government offered a 70 percent subsidy of educational supplies to help alleviate the prohibitive costs of education.

The Haitian curriculum includes all the standard subjects. Memorization is widely used as the method of learning. Discipline problems are rare in class as students treat their teachers with absolute respect, teachers are very strict, and corporal punishment, although illegal, is practiced.

Access to higher education is even more limited. Most eligible youth from affluent families go abroad to study, usually to France or North America. Haiti's most important public institution of higher learning is the University of Haiti in Port-au-Prince. During the years of turmoil surrounding Aristide's departure in 2004, the university was effectively closed and is just now reopening.

PLAY AND RECREATION

The majority of Haitian children must contribute to the family work load and thus do not enjoy a rich recreational life. Leisure time is infrequent, and access to games and toys is limited. Some popular children's games include tag (*lago*), hopscotch (*marelle*), and a dice game using goat's bones (*osselets*). Most schools do not have playgrounds, although many schools organize sports teams. Soccer is a national pastime and children often play soccer, both through organized teams and on the street. There is some government and local support and financing of soccer fields, including the national stadium, *Stade Sylvio Cator*, in Port-au-Prince, which was recently renovated in 2004. Cock fighting is also popular, but one must be eighteen years old to actively participate.

Television is a popular form of entertainment for those who can afford it. Most television programs are imported shows from abroad and often dubbed into French. As most families do not own a set, often local entrepreneurs who do will show a movie and charge a minimal fee for others to watch. In 1997, there were only 4.7 television receivers per 1,000 inhabitants (UNESCO 1999, Table IV.14). Internet cafés are popping up in the larger cities, but connections are slow, fees are relatively high, and most children cannot read and are not familiar with the technology. Storytelling, especially in the form of riddles and singing, is also a popular form of entertainment.

A day is reserved for children during the Carnival season. Carnival culminates the night before Ash Wednesday in a wild party and a parade of floats with large bands playing *rara* music and competing for the crowd's attention. The children's Carnival usually takes place the Saturday before the main event, with an elaborate costume parade winding through the city streets.

CHILD LABOR

It is estimated that 21.8 percent of all children between the ages of ten and fourteen were working in 2002 (U.S. Department of Labor 2004). Most work in the informal economy, in petty commerce, in the markets, in agriculture, and as domestic servants. Many remain in the family household while performing these duties, while others leave or are sent away to work elsewhere. It is customary for a Haitian child, usually around the age of six, to begin serving adults and contributing to the family's livelihood (Smucker and Murray 2004, 13).

Many of the child laborers are *restavèks*, or unpaid domestic servants. A restavèk, meaning "to stay with" in Creole, usually comes from a large, impoverished rural family and is sent to another household to perform domestic chores in exchange for food, shelter, and schooling. Some Haitians see this practice as an avenue to a better life and education, but children are usually sent away to become restavèks following a family crisis. Although data is difficult to gather, it is estimated that anywhere between 100,000 and 250,000 children are unpaid domestic servants (Sommerfelt 2002, 8–9). It is widely reported that many of these children receive no schooling, work long hours, are ill-treated and abused, and sometimes sexually assaulted. Pressure to end the restavèk system has been strong, and there has been a sharp decline among the upper classes due to its social stigma. However, it has increased among the middle and lower classes, in those families that cannot afford to pay a maid and where chores are more difficult because of the lack of modern conveniences such as electricity and running water (Bracken 2006, 23).

The Haitian Labor Code, updated in 1984, establishes the minimum age at fifteen years for industrial, commercial, and agricultural work and at fourteen years for apprenticeships. Additional protection includes: children under eighteen must undergo a medical examination before working in an industry; and children between the ages of fifteen and eighteen must have a work permit for industrial, agricultural, or commercial employment. Legislation was passed in 2003 to increase child protection by prohibiting trafficking and rescinding prior laws that permitted domestic work by children (U.S. Department of Labor 2004). These laws, however, are rarely enforced, as the Ministry of Labor and Social Affairs lacks the personnel and the means to monitor child labor compliance.

There are many faith-based organizations and international NGOs, especially in Port-au-Prince, that play an important role in providing some services for restavèks, namely afternoon schools for domestics and homes for restavèks who have run away. They are also active in the campaign to educate the public on the abuses that children face in the restavèk system.

Haitian children are also recruited by the neighboring Dominican Republic to work as field hands, domestic servants, prostitutes, and beggars. An estimated 2,500 to 3,000 are trafficked on an annual basis (U.S. Department of Labor 2004). These children have no legal rights in the Dominican Republic and, at times, are deported during systematic sweeps to rid the Dominican Republic of illegal immigrants from Haiti (Smucker and Murray 2004, 72).

FAMILY

Children are valued within the family, and both the mother and the father take an active role in child rearing and share responsibilities. On average, each woman will give birth to almost five children, although the fertility rate is higher in the rural areas and lower in the urban areas. Traditionally, especially in the rural areas, children were raised in an extended family setting. These days, however, Haitian families closely resemble the nuclear family, although children are sometimes sent to live with relatives to offer companionship, work, or for educational opportunities. As opposed to restavèks, these children are treated equally within the family unit.

Common law marriage, or *plasaj*, is widespread in Haiti, especially among the lower classes and in the rural areas. Although not legally recognized, it is not considered improper, and men and women often have several plasaj relationships in their lifetimes. Children born from these unions are considered legitimate offspring of both parents and are treated as such. Legal marriage and divorce are becoming more common in the urban areas. Land inheritance is divided equally among all children, regardless of gender. As families are large, this often results in very small plots of land.

Male and female children share many tasks, but it is primarily the girls who do domestic chores and the boys who work outside. Girls carry water, cook, and clean, and boys tend livestock, work in the fields, gather firewood, and unload cargo. As girls age, they may accompany women into the marketplace, as this is primarily a female responsibility. These market women, known as *madam saras*, are not required to share their income with their husbands and are thus often financially independent.

Regardless of socioeconomic status, children have a very strict upbringing and are taught at a young age to respect and obey their elders and authority. Corporal punishment is widely accepted and practiced. Children, especially in rural families, are seen as an economic investment and a security in old age. Childhood is usually short because most children begin working within the family unit around the age of six (Smucker and Murray 2004, 11–12). The government provides no support for families with children, although in 2003 it offered a 70 percent subsidy to help cover educational supplies.

HEALTH

The health situation in Haiti is in crisis, especially for young children. Poor sanitation, limited access to safe drinking water, waste management problems, poor nutrition, and severely inadequate medical facilities are standard. Contributing factors are the rising air pollution problem in Port-au-Prince, considerable poverty, environmental degradation and susceptibility to natural disasters, and lack of state spending for health care.

Haiti is experiencing an AIDS epidemic, with over 5.6 percent of the adult population infected. It has the highest incidence of the disease outside of Africa. AIDS is the leading cause of death in adults (22 percent), and it has greatly affected child and adolescent mortality rates. On an annual basis, 5,000 children are born with the virus. Access to safe drinking water is a major problem, with potable water reaching less than 50 percent of the population in both rural and urban areas. Only about one in two children receive all needed immunizations. About 18 percent of children under the age of five are malnourished, many severely. Violence, especially towards women and girls, is frequent with about 70 percent having been exposed to some sort of violence. There are thousands of orphaned and abused children, many of them living on the streets in perilous situations. Teenage pregnancy is high in girls aged fifteen to nineteen (80 per 1,000) as is the incidence of sexually transmitted diseases in both teenage boys and girls. There are no state-sponsored family health programs. Approximately 7 percent of the population has some sort of disability, half of these being children. There are only 2.5 doctors per 10,000 Haitians, and about 75 percent of all births occur without medical attention (Pan American Health Organization 2003).

Under these circumstances, it is easy to see why the infant and child mortality rates are so high. Estimates in 2006 put the infant mortality rate at seventy-two deaths per 1,000 live births. It is higher for males at seventy-eight per 1,000 than for females at sixty-five per 1,000. In 2004, the World Health Organization (WHO) estimated the child mortality rate (under five years) for boys to be 122 per 1,000 children and for girls to be 112 per 1,000. These statistics reveal that approximately one in ten children die before reaching the age of five, a figure that is three times the average for other countries in Latin America and the Caribbean. And approximately 25 percent of all Haitians will die before reaching the age of forty.

The leading health problem in children from birth to age four is diarrhea, and the primary causes of death are intestinal infections, malnutrition, and respiratory infections. Among children ages five to nine, the leading causes of death are infectious and parasitic diseases, and about 20 percent are considered to be living in a state of vulnerability. The leading cause of death among adolescents from ages ten to nineteen is HIV/AIDS (5.8 percent) (Pan American Health Organization 2003).

The 1987 Constitution, in its chapter on fundamental rights, guarantees that "the State shall be under an obligation to provide all citizens in all territorial communities with the appropriate means to assure the protection, maintenance, and restoration of their health by the establishment of hospitals, heath centers, and dispensaries" (Haiti 1987). In reality, however, the state spends very limited funds on health care. In 2003, the estimated total expenditure on health care as a percentage of the GDP was 7.5 percent. However, almost two-thirds of this (62 percent) was from the private sector, with only slightly more than one-third coming from the government (38 percent) (World Health Organization 2006). The WHO estimates that actual funds spent on health by the government only represent, at best, 1 percent of the GDP, with the rest going towards salaries and administration (World Health Organization 2004, 2). The private sector, including the for-profit sector, NGOs, organizations, foundations, and international organizations, supplement the meager state spending and play a major role in the health system. However, public and private health services still reach only about 60 percent of the population. Many Haitians still rely on traditional medicine, especially in the rural areas, and this receives no supplemental spending (Pan American Health Organization 2003).

LAWS AND LEGAL STATUS

The Haitian Constitution of 1987, in its articles on the family, guarantees protection for all children. Haiti has also ratified many international laws, treaties, and protocols that protect children, including the Convention on the Rights of the Child, the International Covenant on Civil and Political Rights, the American Convention on Civil Rights, and the International Labour Organization Convention No. 29 on Forced Labour.

Haiti has domestic laws that protect children, at least on paper. Chapter 9 of the Haitian Labor Code includes fifteen articles that regulate children in service, including the age allowed to work, the requirements for employing a child, the type of work allowed, the appropriate punishment, mandatory education of children, and so on. This legislation was updated in 2003 to rescind many laws that allowed domestic service by children (U.S. Department of Labor 2004). These laws are rarely upheld, and children as young as five often become restavèks.

The Law of 1961, or the Law of Juvenile Delinquents and Youths at Physical and Moral Risk, regulates the treatment of delinquents between the ages of thirteen and sixteen. This law also established the Court for Minors, which protects and regulates children under thirteen within the legal system. Children under thirteen are not responsible for criminal activity, and the law mandates that the child be monitored, given assistance, or provided schooling depending on the offense and the child's situation.

The Law of 1961 establishes that children between the ages of thirteen and sixteen can be sentenced to rehabilitation and educational centers only.

This law does not allow for the sentencing of children to prison. Article 9 of the Law of 1961 requires access to legal counsel in a timely manner. Article 15 requires the judge to take individual circumstances and the child's personality into consideration before sentencing. This mandates that judges thoroughly investigate a child's background, at times requiring the services of medical and mental health professionals, both of which are mostly lacking. Article 33 prescribes the placement of children in the Centre d'Accueil Duval Duvalier, an educational and rehabilitative center. However, it was disbanded in 1987 with the end of the Duvalier dictatorship, and no alternative center has been established. Article 50 states that children convicted of minor offenses can be returned home or placed temporarily in a rehabilitation center, and Article 51 explicitly allows for children convicted of criminal offenses to be placed in educational or rehabilitative centers instead of imprisoned (Zarifis 2001, 37–40).

Although Haiti is legally bound to uphold these domestic and international laws, they are very rarely enforced. In fact, recent statistics show that children make up about 10 percent of Haiti's growing prison population. No state educational or rehabilitation institution exists since the closing of the Centre d'Accueil in 1987. Most private orphanages and homes for street children do not accept children with criminal backgrounds. Many children are estranged from their home lives, thus home detention is often not an option. Courts are understaffed, and sufficient resources are unavailable to meet all legal obligations. Children as young as eight years old have been confined in prisons with no access to legal counsel. Most minors are detained without counsel for such lengthy periods of time that it extends beyond the period that would be legally permitted for that crime. Children over the age of sixteen are tried as adults, violating the international Convention on the Rights of the Child, which defines a minor as anyone under the age of eighteen. Conditions in Haiti's prisons are deplorable: overcrowded, unsanitary, 24-hour confinement, and lack of health care, adequate nutrition, and clean water (Zarifis 2001, 37–39). Haiti has failed to protect the basic rights of children.

Many children, including a high incidence of street children, are imprisoned following street sweeps to rid neighborhoods of gangs. Since Aristide's departure in 2004, the United Nations Peacekeeping Forces have also taken part in these sweeps as a preventive measure to rid the streets of *chimères*, or armed gangs that pledge allegiance to Aristide. These children have no legal representation, and many are incarcerated for months (Scherr 2005).

RELIGIOUS LIFE

The Haitian Constitution of 1987 grants freedom of religion. The majority of Haitians (80 percent) consider themselves Roman Catholics. In recent years, Protestantism has grown considerably, and now approximately 16 percent practice some denomination of a Protestant faith.

Vodou (or voodoo) is officially practiced alongside Christianity by approximately 50 percent of the population (Central Intelligence Agency 2006, under "People"), although most Haitians believe in many aspects of Vodou. Haitian Vodou combines African, Creole, and Christian beliefs, and was historically the religion of the slaves in Haiti. In 2003, Vodou was designated as an officially sanctioned religion by the Haitian Ministry of Culture and Religious Affairs. Vodou practitioners are encouraged to register with the Ministry in order to be able to legally preside over baptisms, weddings, and other rites of passage.

Religion is an integral part of Haitian life. It is weaved into daily routine, major life transitions, artistic and cultural expression, and the political arena. Children grow up surrounded by religious rites and rituals. Children participate actively and frequently in Vodou rites and imitate adults until rituals become habitual. As children age, their responsibilities become greater, and they are expected to guide and teach younger children (Michel 1996, 290). Major life transitions, such as birth, education, initiation, marriage, parenthood, and death, are marked by religious ceremonies, often including both Vodou and Christian rites. At funerals, for example, family members often participate in Vodou rituals, which are then followed by Roman Catholic rites performed by a priest. The Haitian state recognizes several traditional Roman Catholic feast days as holidays, including Good Friday, Easter Sunday, the Feast of the Assumption, All Saints' Day, All Souls' Day, Immaculate Conception, and Christmas. Vodou holidays are not officially recognized by the state.

Foreign missionaries have had a large presence in and a sizeable impact on Haiti. The Haitian government lacks the finances, infrastructure, and organization to provide basic services. Both national and foreign religious organizations and faith-based NGOs play a significant role in providing education, family planning, health care, disaster relief, and social services, such as orphanages and shelters. The majority of the national organizations are from one of the following denominations: Seventh-Day Adventist, African Methodist Episcopal, Baptist, Methodist, Catholic, and Mennonite (Bowie and Potocky 1998, 84–85). Over 50 percent of the Haitian students in school attend an educational center affiliated with a religious institution, the majority of these being Protestant schools (Hadjadj 2000, sec. 3.2). Vodou leaders also play a significant role in providing for social services. Practitioners are expected to pay their leader a significant sum of money in order to perform rites. This money is also often used to provide education, clothing, and medical services when a practitioner or a member of a practitioner's family is in need.

CHILD ABUSE AND NEGLECT

Within both the family and the educational setting, children have strict upbringings that teach respect towards adults and superiors. Corporal punishment is widely accepted as a means of discipline and is not considered abusive by Haitian standards.

Children who are employed are protected from bodily harm in the form of punishment under the Haitian Labor Code. The code also provides a formal mechanism for reporting this abuse and the fine that will be imposed. However, these laws are rarely enforced, and child domestic servants, or restavèks, are often treated as second-class citizens and publicly humiliated. They experience a high risk of physical, emotional, and sexual abuse. They rarely receive adequate nutrition and health care and are very unlikely to attend school.

Street children and orphans are a considerable problem in Haiti, and their numbers have increased since the economic collapse in the late 1980s. Although statistics are difficult to gather, recent figures estimate that there are anywhere from 5,000 to 10,000 street children in Haiti, the majority of these living on the streets of Port-au-Prince (United Nations Children's Fund 1999; Save the Children, under "Map and Stats"). Children become street children for a variety of reasons, most of these related either directly or indirectly to poverty. The AIDS crisis has orphaned 200,000 children (Library of Congress 2006, 12) and, as orphanages are few, these children often end up on the streets. Restavèk children, once reaching the age of fifteen, must legally receive a salary at the same rate as other domestic servants and are thus often released from service in favor of younger children. Runaways from domestic servitude and poor, rural families seeking a better life also end up on the streets. The recent violence preceding and in the wake of Aristide's departure in 2004 has also contributed to an increase in street children.

Street children are often rounded up in violent state-sanctioned sweeps that are publicized as ways to rid the streets of gang violence and drugs (Kovats-Bernat 2000, 419). These children end up in overcrowded and filthy prisons with no legal representation.

According to Amnesty International, human rights abuses, including those against children, soared during the violence and insecurity in the years surrounding the departure of Aristide in 2004. Kidnappings became common as a means to intimidate and for financial gain. Children were reportedly abducted in order to extort money from their parents. In late 2004 and throughout 2005 and early 2006, there were clashes between the United Nations Peacekeeping Forces and local gangs in which innocent bystanders, including many children, were killed. Many children, accused of being members of armed pro-Aristide chimère gangs, were rounded up and jailed (Amnesty International 2006). There were reports of children being pressured and recruited to join these armed chimère gangs (Amnesty International 2004).

Child abuse is very rarely reported, and penalties for abuse are rarely imposed. Many reasons exist for this, including the wide acceptance of corporal punishment as discipline, the established practice of domestic servitude and other forms of child labor, the institutionalized violence against street children, and the lack of a mechanism and practice in reporting abuse.

GROWING UP IN THE TWENTY-FIRST CENTURY

Haitian children are in a vulnerable state, and the outlook is bleak. The majority of children confront poverty and insecurity almost on a daily basis. This has resulted in stolen childhoods. The state has proven itself ineffective in dealing with the urgent needs of Haitian children in basic health care, social services, education, and protection. The recent political upheaval has also taken its toll, and until the protection of civilians and the rule of law are restored, socioeconomic programs remain a low priority. Although there is a sense of optimism since mid-2006 with the election of a new president, René Preval, continued episodes of violence and the weak economy demonstrate the fragility of the state. With a high projected population growth, Haiti will increasingly find it difficult to maintain and improve basic services unless the economy considerably improves.

Yet, there are small glimmers of hope. More organizations, both domestic and international, are discussing child domestic servitude and are launching campaigns to end the system. Although not yet effective, the practice is becoming increasingly taboo, especially among the upper classes. The international development community and NGOs continue to operate in the country and attempt to fill in the gaps left by the ineffective government. Many of these organizations focus on children and offer needed relief. The Haitian government is increasingly attracting the attention of the international community, thus it will be held more accountable to the laws and protocols that it supports and signs. However, the current situation for children in Haiti is grim, and will continue to remain so until the problems of poverty, limited education and health care, and child labor and abuse are effectively addressed at the state level.

RESOURCE GUIDE

Suggested Readings

Arthur, Charles. 2002. *Haiti: A Guide to the People, Politics and Culture*. New York: Interlink Books. A brief overview of Haiti, including sections on history, society, the economy, politics, religion and culture.

Cadet, Jean-Robert. 1998. *Restavek: From Haitian Slave Child to Middle-Class American*. Austin: University of Texas Press. A compelling first-hand account of a young boy in domestic servitude.

Deren, Maya. 1983. *Divine Horsemen: Living Gods of Haiti*. New York: McPherson and Company. The classic text on Haitian Vodou, thoroughly describing the history, spirits, and ceremonies.

Farmer, Paul. 2006. *AIDS and Accusation: Haiti and the Geography of Blame*. Berkeley: University of California Press. A study of AIDS in Haiti, with first-hand accounts and an emphasis on the cultural attitudes towards the disease.

Hadjadj, Bernard. 2000. *Education for All in Haiti over the Last 20 Years: Assessment and Perspectives*. Kingston, Jamaica: UNESCO. http://unesdoc.unesco.org/images/0013/001363/136393e.pdf. Accessed October 25, 2006. An excellent report on the education system in Haiti, the reforms in the 1980s, and current problems and challenges.

Smucker, Glenn R., and Gerald F. Murray. 2004. *The Uses of Children: A Study of Trafficking in Haitian Children*. Port-au-Prince: United States Agency for International Development, Haiti Mission. An in-depth study of the restavèk situation within Haiti and the trafficking of children to the Dominican Republic.

Nonprint Resources

Children of Shadows. 2001. Produced and directed by Karen Kramer. Erzulie Films. 54 min. Videocassette. An excellent film documenting the child labor situation in Haiti through interviews with restavèks, their caretakers, social workers, and economists.

Once There Was a Country: Revisiting Haiti. 2005. Written and directed by Kimberly Green. Two Tone Productions. 55 min. Videodisc. A documentary that follows healthcare providers and community leaders as they tackle health issues in Haiti.

Port-au-Prince is Mine. 2000. Scripted and directed by Rigoberto López. 57 min. VHS. Les Productions CIDIHCA. A documentary that looks at current conditions in the capital of Haiti, including overcrowding, environmental problems, sanitation issues, and the hopelessness of many of its residents.

They Call Me Dog. 1995. Directed by Frode Hojer Pedersen, United Nations International Children's Emergency Fund. 30 min. VHS. A fictionalized account of a female *restavèk* child working for a family in the city and the treatment that she endures.

Unfinished Country. 2005. Directed by Whitney Dow. Two Tone Productions. 45 min. VHS. A discussion of the events surrounding the 2005 elections.

Web Sites

Amnesty International: Haiti, http://web.amnesty.org/pages/hti-index-eng. An excellent overview on the current human rights situation in Haiti.

Background Notes: Haiti. U.S. Department of State, http://www.state.gov/r/pa/ei/bgn/1982.htm. A good overview of current issues relating to Haiti.

Bob Corbett's Haiti Page. Bob Corbett, http://www.webster.edu/%7Ecorbetre/haiti/haiti.html. A personal Web page of a noted Haitian scholar, which includes a very active listserv on Haiti, bibliographies of materials about Haiti, and links to many academic resources.

Country Profile: Haiti. Library of Congress, http://lcweb2.loc.gov/frd/cs/profiles/Haiti.pdf. A recent overview of the main issues within Haiti, an up-to-date complement to the more extensive *Country Study* also published by the Library of Congress (see below).

Haiti: A Country Study. Library of Congress, http://lcweb2.loc.gov/frd/cs/ httoc.html. An excellent historical overview of Haiti, including sections on history, people, politics, the economy, and culture.

Human Rights Watch: Haiti, http://hrw.org/doc/?t=americas&c=haiti. An independent, non-governmental organization providing in-depth information on current human rights issues in Haiti with archives dating back to 1989.

The World Factbook: Haiti. Central Intelligence Agency, https://www.cia.gov/cia/ publications/factbook/geos/ha.html. A good source for current statistics.

World Health Organization: Haiti. http://www.who.int/countries/hti/en/. An excellent source for up-to-date health indicators, disease outbreaks, legislation, and expenditures.

Organizations and NGOs

Haitian Street Kids, Inc.
5209 Rain Forest Drive
McKinney, TX 75070
Web site: http://haitianstreetkids.com
An organization that focuses on and provides housing for street children, abandoned children, and restavèks.

L'Institut Culturel Karl Lévêque (the Karl Lévêque Cultural Institute)
28, rue Jean Baptiste
Canapé-Vert, HT 6115
Port-au-Prince, Haiti
Phone: (509) 245-4598
Email: ickl@ickl-haiti.org
Web site: http://www.ickl-haiti.org
An organization that promotes consciousness building on a variety of issues, including human rights and education.

The Mercy and Sharing Foundation
201 N. Mill Street, Suite 201
Aspen, CO 81611-1557
Phone: (877) 424-8454, (970) 925-1492
Fax: (970) 925-1181
Web site: http://www.haitichildren.com/index.html
A nonprofit organization founded by a U.S. couple, focusing on the needs of Haitian children.

Réseau National de Défense des Droits Humains (National Network for the Defense of Human Rights)
9, rue Riviere

Port-au-Prince, Haiti
Phone: (509) 245-3486
Fax: (509) 244-4146
Email: rnddh@rnddh.org
Web site: http://www.rnddh.org
An organization that promotes and monitors human rights in Haiti, including issues
    within prisons and the police force.

Saint Joseph's Home for Boys
Michael Geilenfeld
c/o Lynx Air
P.O. Box 407139
Ft. Lauderdale, FL 33350
Phone: (509) 257-4237
A religious-based orphanage for homeless boys that also serves as a hostel for
    travelers.

Yéle Haiti Foundation
P.O. Box 2345
New York, NY 10108
Phone: (212) 352-0552
Web site: http://www.yele.org
An organization founded by Wyclef Jean, a Haitian-born hip-hop artist, concentrat-
    ing on issues of education, health, the environment, and humanitarian assistance.

Selected Bibliography

Amnesty International. 2004. *Haiti: Breaking the Cycle of Violence: A Last Chance for
    Haiti.* June 21. http://web.amnesty.org/library/Index/ENGAMR360382004.
    Accessed October 25, 2006.
———. May 2006. *Amnesty International Report 2006: Haiti.* http://www.global
    policy.org/security/issues/haiti/2006/05amnestyreport.htm. Accessed Octo-
    ber 25, 2006.
Aristide, Mildred. 2003. *L'enfant en domesticité en Haiti produit d'un fossé historique*
    (Child domestic service in Haiti and its historical underpinnings). Port-
    au-Prince: Impr. H. Deschamps.
Arthur, Charles. 2002. *Haiti: A Guide to the People, Politics and Culture.* New York:
    Interlink Books.
Bernat, J. Christopher. 1999. "Children and the Politics of Violence in Haitian Con-
    text: Statist Violence, Scarcity and Street Child Agency in Port-au-Prince."
    Critique of Anthropology 19, no. 2: 121–38.
Bowie, Stan L., and Miriam Potocky. 1998. "Social Service and Health Organizations
    in Haiti: A Resource Assessment." *Social Development Issues* 20, no. 1: 77–90.
Bracken, Amy. 2006. "Haiti's Children Pay the Price of Poverty." *NACLA Report
    on the Americas* 39, no. 5: 22–25.
Central Intelligence Agency. 2006. *The World Factbook: Haiti.* https://www.cia.gov/
    cia/publications/factbook/geos/ha.html. Accessed October 25, 2006.
Desmangles, Leslie G. 1992. *The Faces of the Gods.* Chapel Hill: The University of
    North Carolina Press.

Hadjadj, Bernard. 2000. *Education for All in Haiti Over the Last 20 Years: Assessment and Perspectives*. Kingston, Jamaica: UNESCO. http://unesdoc.unesco.org/images/0013/001363/136393e.pdf. Accessed October 25, 2006.

Haiti. *Constitution de la République d'Haiti 1987* (Constitution of the Republic of Haiti 1987). http://pdba.georgetown.edu/Constitutions/Haiti/haiti.html. Accessed October 25, 2006.

————. *Décret du 24 février 1984 actualisant le Code du travail du 12 septembre 1961* [Decree of February 1984 updating the Labor Code of September 12, 1961]. http://www.ilo.org/dyn/natlex/docs/WEBTEXT/135/64790/F61HTI01.htm#Loi9. Accessed October 25, 2006.

Hatloy, Anne. 2005. "Life as a Child Domestic Worker in Haiti." *Journal of Haitian Studies* 11, no. 1: 11–26.

Kovats-Bernat, J. Christopher. 2000. "Anti-Gang, *Arimaj,* and the War on Street Children." *Peace Review* 12, no. 3: 415–421.

Library of Congress. 1989. *Haiti: A Country Study.* http://lcweb2.loc.gov/frd/cs/httoc.html. Accessed October 25, 2006.

————. 2006. *Country Profile: Haiti.* http://lcweb2.loc.gov/frd/cs/profiles/Haiti.pdf. Accessed October 25, 2006.

Michel, Claudine. 1996. "Of Worlds Unseen: The Educational Character of Haitian Vodou." *Comparative Education Review* 40, no. 3: 280–294.

Minnesota Lawyers International Human Rights Committee. 1990. *Restavek: Child Domestic Labor in Haiti.* Minneapolis: Minnesota Lawyers International Human Rights Committee.

Pan American Health Organization (PAHO). 2003. "Country Profiles: Haiti." *Epidemiological Bulletin* 24, no. 1. http://www.paho.org/english/dd/ais/be_v24n1-haiti.htm. Accessed October 25, 2006.

Save the Children. Canada. *Haiti.* http://www.savethechildren.ca/wherewework/caribbean/haitistats.html. Accessed October 25, 2006.

Scherr, Judith. 2005. "Hope is Fading: Haiti's Children's Prisons." *Counterpunch* October 7. http://www.counterpunch.org/scherr10072005.html. Accessed October 25, 2006.

Smucker, Glenn R., and Gerald F. Murray. 2004. *The Uses of Children: A Study of Trafficking in Haitian Children.* Port-au-Prince: United States Agency for International Development, Haiti Mission.

Sommerfelt, Tone, ed. 2002. *Child Domestic Labor in Haiti: Characteristics, Contexts and Organization of Children's Residence, Relocation, and Work.* Oslo, Norway: The Fafo Institute for Applied Social Sciences.

Suarez, Lucia de las Mercedes. 2005. "The Restavek Condition: Jean-Robert Cadet's Disclosure." *Journal of Haitian Studies* 11, no. 1: 27–43.

UNESCO Institute for Statistics. 1999. *Statistical Yearbook.* http://www.uis.unesco.org/TEMPLATE/html/CultAndCom/Table_IV_14_America.html. Accessed October 25, 2006.

United Nations Children's Fund (UNICEF). 1991. *Haiti Faces Major Education Challenge.* May 20. http://www.unicef.org/newsline/99pr19.htm. Accessed October 25, 2006.

———— 2006. *Child Alert: Haiti.* March. http://www.unicef.org/childalert/haiti/. Accessed October 25, 2006.

United Nations. 2005. *Human Development Report.* http://hdr.undp.org/reports/global/2005/pdf/HDR05_HDI.pdf. Accessed October 25, 2006.

U.S. Department of Labor, Bureau of International Labor Affairs. 2004. *Haiti: Incidence and Nature of Child Labor.* http://www.dol.gov/ilab/media/reports/iclp/tda2004/haiti.htm. Accessed October 25, 2006.

U.S. Department of State, Bureau of Democracy, Human Rights and Labor. 2006. *Country Reports on Human Rights Practices: Haiti.* http://www.state.gov/g/drl/rls/hrrpt/2005/61731.htm. Accessed October 25, 2006.

World Health Organization (WHO). 2004. *Health Action in Crisis.* http://www.who.int/hac/crises/hti/background/2004/Haiti_Nov04.pdf. Accessed October 25, 2006.

———. 2006. *The World Health Report 2006: Working Together for Health.* http://www.who.int/whr/2006/en/. Accessed October 25, 2006.

Zarifis, Ismene. 2001. "Minors in Haiti's Prisons." *Human Rights Brief* 8, no. 3: 37–40.

9

JAMAICA

Rose Davies, Janet Brown, and Sian Williams

NATIONAL PROFILE

The island of Jamaica is situated directly south of Cuba in the Caribbean Sea. Approximately 240 kilometers long and 85 kilometers wide, it is the third largest and fourth most populous of the Caribbean islands. Jamaica experiences a warm tropical climate all year round but is vulnerable to hurricanes between June and October each year. The island has interesting topographical features, including hills, valleys and plains, rainforests, and desert-like conditions.

The people of Jamaica are of mixed heritage with the majority (over 90 percent) being of West African descent. The rest of the population comprises people of Chinese, East Indian, Syrian, Lebanese, and European heritage. English is the official language of education and commerce, but most Jamaicans speak "patois," a Creole derivative of the English, Spanish, and African languages. Jamaica's total population is 2.6 million, of which 49 percent are males and 51 percent are females. Children (defined as birth to eighteen years) account for approximately 37 percent of the total population. Although the number of rural communities exceeds urban and semi-urban centers, nearly 52 percent of the population lives in the urban areas. Jamaica's changing demographic trends

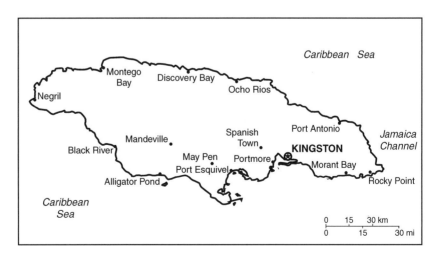

reflect a transition to an aging population as the statistics for recent years show a declining birth-to-fourteen-year age group, an increasing working population (fifteen to sixty-four years), and an increasing dependent elderly age group (sixty-five years onward).

Jamaica is heavily indebted, and almost 60 percent of the annual national budget goes toward debt repayment. The remaining 40 percent only minimally meets the capital expenditure needs of the country and population. Poverty levels have been persistently higher than desirable in Jamaica, where the wealthiest 5 percent of the population accounts for about 46 percent of national consumption, while the poorest 20 percent accounts for less than 7 percent of national consumption. The average unemployment rate for year 2004 was close to 12 percent. Consistently over the years, more males have been employed in the labor force than females (73 percent of males compared with 56 percent of females in 2004), and the unemployment rate for females is approximately twice that for males (16 percent of females compared with 8 percent of males in 2004) (*Economic and Social Survey Jamaica, 2004* 2005).

Unequal access of females to employment in the Jamaican labor market impacts the status of children negatively. The percentage of children living in poverty has averaged over 22 percent in the last five years and has been consistently higher than the 15 percent national incidence of poverty. Child poverty is also associated with the fact that 46 percent of the country's heads of households are single females who are unable to meet the economic needs of their families adequately (*Survey of Living Conditions 2005* 2006). Results from the Profiles Research Project (Samms-Vaughan-cited 2004) in Jamaica indicated that parental stress was strongly associated with children's behavior problems. Jamaican women generally bear the primary responsibility for child-rearing and support, and in many poor, single-female-headed households, parental stress is very high. Male children in particular pose greater challenges to their parents than females. Many boys become wards of the state or join the ranks of the homeless, living on the streets and jeopardizing their health and safety. The number of street children in Jamaica, mostly males, is estimated to be over 6,000 across the island (Leo-Rhynie 2006). Most are dropouts from the primary and secondary school systems.

Poverty levels in the last decade have been trending downward in response to planned government initiatives and interventions. In undertaking these initiatives, the Jamaican government, signatory to the Convention on the Rights of the Child (CRC), has been conscious of the need to meet its obligations to promote and protect Jamaican children's rights to survival, protection, development, and participation. The government's National Poverty Eradication Program (NPEP), established in 1995, works in partnership with private sector and nongovernmental organizations (NGOs; many of these faith based) to improve the quality of existence for poor families and communities. Support is provided through a range of social assistance interventions targeted at households living in poverty, in particular those with children, elderly persons, persons with disabilities, and pregnant and lactating women. Specific assistance is offered in the form of school-feeding programs, school-fee assistance, subsidized medical services, and housing assistance. Other social protection measures include a National Insurance Scheme (NIS) and a National Health Fund (NHF). The more recently established Program for Advancement through Health and Education (PATH) involves cash transfers to families living below the poverty line and a coordinated strategy to ensure that PATH beneficiaries are able to access all other social protection benefits offered under NPEP. The Jamaica Social Investment Fund (JSIF) and the Micro Investment Agency (MIDA) are government agencies established to increase access of poor individuals to small entrepreneurial business endeavors and to community improvement ventures such as establishment of preschool and primary school facilities.

KEY FACTS – JAMAICA

Population: 2,780,132 (July 2007 est.)
Infant mortality rate: 15.73 deaths/1,000 live births (2007 est.)
Life expectancy at birth: 73.12 years (2007 est.)
Literacy rate: 87.9 percent (2003 est.)
Internet users: 1.067 million (2005 est.)
People living with HIV/AIDS: 25,000 (2005 est.)
Human Poverty Index (HPI-1) Rank: 30

Sources: CIA World Factbook: Jamaica. https://www.cia.gov/cia/publications/factbook/geos/jm.html. April 17, 2007; World Health Organization (WHO): UNAIDS/WHO Global HIV/AIDS Online Database. "Epidemiological Fact Sheets on HIV/AIDS and Sexuality Transmitted Diseases: Jamaica." http://www.who.int/GlobalAtlas/predefinedReports/EFS2006/index.asp?strSelected Country=JM. December 2006; United Nations Development Programme (UNDP) Human Development Report 2006–Jamaica. http://hdr.undp.org/hdr2006/statistics/countries/data_sheets/cty_ds_JAM.html. April 26, 2007.

OVERVIEW

Since 2004, the Jamaican government has accelerated the pace of development and implementation of major policies and legislation to strengthen and improve the quality of services to children. These include: (i) passage of the Child Care and Protection Act, with accompanying regulations and standards for the management and monitoring of early childhood institutions. Under this act also, a Registry of Child Abuse and a Child Advocate's Office were established; (ii) passage of the Early Childhood Act and the Early Childhood Commission Act and the subsequent official launch of the Early Childhood Commission as the agency responsible for ensuring a coordinated and integrated approach to delivery of early childhood (birth to eight) programs and services; (iii) passage of the Property (Right of Spouses) Act, which guides the division of property between spouses and some common law unions; (iv) the establishment and strengthening of the Child Development Agency; and (v) development and dissemination of national plans and frameworks for action, such as the National Youth Policy, the National Policy for HIV/AIDS Management in

Schools, the National Framework of Action for Children, the National Plan of Action on Child Justice, the National Integrated Response to Children and Violence, the National Plan on Children Orphaned and Made Vulnerable by HIV/AIDS, and the National Plan on Youth Development. The government has also provided support to NGOs involved in rehabilitation of street children and vulnerable children, such as Children First, Western Society for the Upliftment of Children, the Possibility Programme, Learning for Earning Activity Programme (LEAP), Young Men's Christian Association (YMCA) programs for male dropouts aged twelve to fifteen, and Child Guidance Clinics that provide mental health services for abused, neglected, and vulnerable children.

EDUCATION

All Jamaican children have an equal right to education regardless of gender, religion, ethnic group, or socioeconomic status. This policy is protected by the CRC, to which the government is signatory. Unequal access to education is therefore generally related to other factors, such as poverty or unavailability of services. The Jamaican education system makes provision for individuals from early childhood to tertiary level through a wide network of public and private institutions.

Services for the care and education of children from birth to three years are provided through daycare facilities, which may be purpose-built or redesigned structures as well as private home–based facilities. Daycare provisions for children birth to three years have been inadequate for decades, and presently, only about 10 percent to 12 percent of this age cohort has access to daycare. The private sector is the main provider of daycare services as only six of the estimated 400 daycare centers throughout the island are owned and operated by the government. Daycare coverage in the rural areas is particularly low. Generally, the better daycare facilities are costly and cater to families who are able to pay for the services. Poorer families rely on informal community-based homecare arrangements, which seldom meet the national standards for daycare provision in Jamaica.

Since the last decade, a home-visiting innovation, the Roving Caregivers Program (RCP), has provided early stimulation services in three of Jamaica's fourteen parishes, to children birth to three years living in rural communities not served by any formal early childhood education program. Trained caregivers visit the children and their families in their homes and engage in stimulating developmental activities with the children along with their parents or guardians. Educational toys are loaned to the family for continued interactive experiences between parents and children until the next visit of the caregiver. Findings from research carried out on this program model have shown that it has been very successful in impacting children's development positively (Roopnarine 2005).

This program is now being considered for wide-scale replication in other poor rural Jamaican communities.

Education for three- to five-year-olds is not free, except where offered in government-owned infant schools and infant departments of all-age schools. The private kindergartens and community basic schools charge for service, although the difference in the fees of both types of institutions is significant. The community basic schools, numbering over 2,000, enroll the majority of the children in the three-to-five age cohort (over 80 percent), with the remaining 20 percent shared between the 112 government-owned and 209 privately run institutions across the island. Jamaica has achieved near universal coverage of three- to five-year-olds in early childhood educational institutions (approximately 98 percent) (*Economic and Social Survey Jamaica, 2004* 2005). However, the variation in program quality in the different types of institutions is still cause for concern. Data collected over the last decade have shown repeatedly that children who attend the private and more expensive kindergartens achieve higher scores than their counterparts in the government infant and basic schools, on the Grade One Readiness Inventory (GRI) test administered to all grade one students in the first term of primary school attendance. In this test comprised of four subtests, children are ranked by three categories of achievement: mastery, near-mastery, and nonmastery. The statistics for 2003, which are indicative of the trends over several years, show that only 26 percent of children in basic schools achieved mastery on all subtests compared with 31 percent from the government-owned infant facilities, and 61 percent from private preparatory schools (Task Force on Educational Reform 2004).

Enrollment at the primary level is nearly universal at approximately 96 percent of the children in the six to eleven years of age cohort. The government is the main provider of free primary education for approximately 94 percent of primary-aged children enrolled in 989 primary, all-age, and primary/junior high schools across Jamaica, while the remaining 6 percent of students are enrolled in 196 private fee-paying preparatory schools. As with the early childhood level, the issue of quality and school efficiency is cause for concern. In spite of the high enrollment rate at the primary school level, the actual national attendance rate is much lower, remaining over the years within the 70 percent range. Efforts to institute and enforce compulsory attendance in eight parishes in Jamaica did not result in any improvement in attendance rates.

Three tests are administered to students between primary grades three and six. These are the Grade Three Diagnostic Test, Grade Four Literacy Test, and Grade Six Achievement Test. The scores for 2003 reflect the general trend in student performance on these tests over the years. On the six subtests of the Grade Three Diagnostic Test, 15 percent of the students mastered three to five subtests, 34 percent mastered one to two subtests, and 51 percent mastered none of the subtests. On the 2003 Grade Four Literacy Test, which seeks to identify the children who are at risk of not being literate by the end of primary school, approximately half the number of children achieved mastery and the other half were to varying extents deemed to be at risk of being illiterate on leaving primary school (Task Force on Educational Reform 2004). Students' performance on these two tests over the years indicates that the primary school system is not very efficient at producing the intended educational goals and learning outcomes. The statistics show that by the end of primary grade six, about 30 percent of children are still leaving school illiterate each year. The primary education system has struggled to improve its efficiency levels over the years; however, it has largely failed to achieve the goals of high literacy and numeracy rates among students and also to prepare them to access secondary education.

Secondary level education is provided for children from age twelve to sixteen years through various types of government and private institutions. Schools operated by the government include all-age schools (grade seven to ten); primary and junior high schools (grade seven to eleven); secondary high schools, technical high schools, vocational/agricultural schools, and private high schools (grade seven through eleven or thirteen). Education at the lower cycle of secondary education (grades seven to nine) is offered in all-age schools, primary and junior high schools, and public and private high schools, and technical high schools which also provide secondary education at the upper cycle, that is grades ten and eleven and in many instances through to grade thirteen. The enrollment rate at the lower cycle of secondary education is high, at approximately 98 percent in 2005. The high enrollment rate at this level is indicative of the number of school types offering lower secondary education. The enrollment rate in secondary schools that offer the upper cycle of secondary education is lower at 82 percent, which is not surprising in view of the fact that fewer student places are available in these schools. The variety of school types at the secondary level is also reflected in the differentials in student performance levels.

There is a tendency for many Jamaicans to regard traditional high schools as the only "real" secondary schools. Many of these schools started as private institutions run by a church. Over time respective governments increased their financial support to full grant-aided status. Traditionally, these schools are generally better staffed and resourced, and student performance on national achievement tests is much better than for the other types of schools offering secondary education. However, within the English-speaking Caribbean region, Jamaican secondary school students have shown much weaker performance on the regional Caribbean Secondary Examination Certificate (CSEC) examinations than their regional counterparts, especially in language arts and mathematics. At the end of secondary schooling, many students fail to achieve the requirements to move into higher education or meaningful employment. Inequality of provision at the lower secondary level is a major problem, and equity at this level is still to be achieved.

Postsecondary education and training are offered at multidisciplinary institutions, such as community colleges. The national training agency HEART Trust/NTA provides skills training in a range of vocational areas through its various academies located throughout the island. At the tertiary level, there are three main universities that between them offer a wide range of professional training opportunities. The University of the West Indies (UWI) is the largest and oldest, followed by the University of Technology (UTech), both government-supported. Northern Caribbean University (NCU) is a private, faith-based institution located in one of Jamaica's central parishes. A second small, faith-based university, International University of the Caribbean (IUC), recently started offering a limited range of programs from its location in the capital city of Kingston. A number of foreign universities also offer offshore programs locally. In spite of this, only approximately 15 to 20 percent of the population is enrolled at the university level. Nine teachers colleges and seven training institutions for nursing prepare the majority of teachers and nurses employed in the country's education and health systems. The government pays 80 percent of the cost of tertiary education for the training of teachers and nurses, and its student loan bureau also provides tuition loans to students who cannot afford to pay on their own. Tertiary education in Jamaica reflects the international trend of higher percentages of female participation rates compared with males.

Approximately 10 percent to 12 percent of any population has a disability, and another 10 percent to 12 percent is at risk and in need of assessment and intervention. Between 100,000 and 173,000 Jamaican children have special conditions that require intervention (Task Force on Educational Reform 2004). The 2005 statistics show only a small proportion (6,028 students) enrolled in programs serving the disabled. These facilities include a school for the visually impaired, seven schools for the hearing impaired with four satellite schools, six schools for the mentally retarded, and seven units for the multiple disabled. The units for the multiple disabled are attached to primary, all-age, and junior high schools in six parishes. Satellite units are attached to high schools and primary schools. There are ten private institutions and also home-based programs that provide services throughout the country. The government recently approved construction of a special school on the grounds of one of the teachers colleges, which trains special education teachers. Efforts are also being made to integrate children with disabilities into the regular classrooms. In 2005, twenty-five students with visual impairments were integrated into nine high schools, and special arrangements were made for fifty students with specific challenges to sit the Grade Six Achievement Test. The overall situation with regard to the education of children with special needs reveals inadequacies in provision of appropriate facilities, as well as in the number of trained teachers to provide satisfactory services to these children. The lack of early screening results in many at-risk children being present but remaining undetected in the regular school system. These are the children who frequently become problem cases and are likely to drop out of the school system early.

The Jamaican education system has underperformed at all levels over many years. Not surprisingly, in 2004, responding to social commentary on the state of the Jamaican education system, the incumbent Prime Minister established a special Task Force on Educational Reform for Jamaica, with the mandate to "prepare and present an action plan consistent with a vision for the creation of a world-class education system which will generate the human capital and produce the skills necessary for Jamaican citizens to compete in the global economy" (Task Force on Educational Reform 2004, 5). The Education Reform program aims to systematically reduce weaknesses and improve the quality of education from early childhood through secondary levels of the system. The many recommendations for action include, among others, improving the quality of all school facilities, reducing pupil–teacher ratios, increasing student access to services, improving teacher training and quality of teaching, increasing parent education and involvement, and providing early screening and improved facilities for children with special needs.

PLAY AND RECREATION

In Jamaican society, the importance of play in children's development is not well understood by many adults, including parents and teachers. Although parent education initiatives and improved teacher training in recent years have played an important role in increasingly sensitizing stakeholders and others to the importance and value of play, the provision of adequate and appropriate stimulating play spaces for children has been slow in coming. Research conducted locally (Samms-Vaughan 2004) has shown consistently that especially among poorer families, there are very few, if any, educational toys such as puzzles and playing blocks available for children's use in their homes. Such toys are more likely to be found in the homes of families with higher levels of education and income.

A recently completed comprehensive literature review of Caribbean research on children's play and leisure time (Brown and Williams 2006) highlighted findings from the Profiles Project that the most common leisure activity among 80 percent of six-year-old children surveyed was watching television, in most instances without parents being involved. Most of the children read books at some point in time, but this was not consistent over the period of one month. The survey revealed that "homes had relatively little physical material to stimulate children's development or encourage appropriate play" (Samms-Vaughn 2004, cited in Brown and Williams 2006, 9). Similarly, school environments at all levels of the education system lack adequate play and recreation facilities. Surveys of Jamaican early childhood learning environments have consistently reported conditions similar to what obtains in the homes, that is, a lack of materials to adequately stimulate children, and physical arrangements in most preschool indoor learning environments that do not facilitate effective learning through play (Brown and Williams 2006).

Because planned indoor play opportunities are limited in many homes, Jamaican children tend to spend much of their playtime outdoors, romping and playing tag-like games. Purpose-built playgrounds for children are mostly seen in areas where private businesses or residential communities invest their own resources and time to build them. No special government resources are allocated to provide well-equipped public play parks or playgrounds to encourage children's spontaneous free-play activities. Many Jamaican children, especially from rural communities, have become quite skilled at creating their own toys. The most popular among these are wooden spinning tops called "gigs," as well as pull-along replicas of cars and trucks fashioned from discarded tins and boxes. Also very popular are the roughly hewn wooden go-carts that inspired the historical first Jamaican bobsled team. The local toy manufacturing industry, which was encouraged in the 1970s, declined over the years and was not sustainable because of the influx of imported toys. Today, most of the toys available in the retail sector are imported and too costly for poor families to buy.

School settings at every level usually have some outdoor space designated as playground, but the majority of these provide little or no outdoor play equipment. The emphasis is on encouraging development of more formal competitive sports, such as athletics, football, netball, and the like from as early as the preschool level. For preschools and primary schools, competitive events in these sports are sponsored annually by the business community and mirror the highly acclaimed events at the secondary school level. For decades, Jamaica has been known in international circles to have the most organized approach to the development of athletics at secondary school level. The fact that today Jamaicans have a formidable reputation in world athletics has stimulated interest in protecting this dominance by beginning such preparation from the early childhood stage and ensuring its continuation though the primary and secondary school levels. At the community level, the government, through the special fund Culture, Health, Arts, Sports and Education (CHASE) and the Sports Development Foundation (SDF), helps with provision of play fields and gear to encourage development of group sports such as football, basketball, cricket, volleyball, and similar activities. The amount spent in such infrastructural work in 2005 was approximately J$262 million.

CHILD LABOR

Most Jamaican children grow up routinely sharing domestic chores within and outside the home. In a recent study (Brown 2007), children and parents across classes indicated that children begin home chores early, usually "volunteering" to help in the home with dishes, sweeping, and so on. These chores are formalized by about age six or seven, and both girls and boys were expected to share in home maintenance tasks. Rural children in the sample carried the heaviest loads, particularly boys, who did outdoor farming and other physical tasks in addition to the domestic tasks common to their sisters, such as sweeping the yard and house, washing dishes, washing clothes, cooking, and caring for younger siblings. Children had little say in what chores they were to do; failure to comply with parental expectations in this area is often met with punishment. While some middle-class children receive an allowance, most children cannot expect payment for these tasks. Parents sometimes reward compliant behavior with "treats" or special outings.

While some chores were occasionally described as "male" (usually outdoor) and "female" (usually indoor) tasks, in fact both sexes were called upon to do most tasks within the home from time to time. Middle-class children were often given fewer chores as they approached the exam period at the end of primary school, which largely determines the quality of high school they will attend, and homework and school grades become the focus of parental demand for performance from the children.

A Jamaica Youth Activity Survey in 2002 estimated that 16,240 children, or 2.2 percent of the age cohort between five and seventeen years, were engaged in some form of work for pay, with the majority of those between fifteen and seventeen working an average of 22 hours a week (Fox and Gordon-Strachan 2007).[1] In the more recent 2005 Jamaica Youth Resiliency and Risk Behaviour Survey (Fox and Gordon-Strachan 2007), 5.4 percent of the ten- to fifteen-year-old children had jobs in addition to attending school. This is assumed to be an underestimation when work within the informal sector is considered. Work in the informal sector includes household service, buying and selling, and working in small unregistered and even illegal businesses with little protection from exploitation or opportunities for formal training or advancement. Most of these children are not abandoned or homeless, but they work to increase family income or to support their own school and social needs and are estimated to come from the poorest 20 percent of the population (*Economic and Social Survey Jamaica, 1999* 2000).

Large numbers of working children have given up schooling, or schools have given up on them. The 1998 government statistics show

---

1. This is lower than a 1995 Government of Jamaica/UNICEF estimate 4–6 percent of children age six to sixteen working.

that 22 percent of children in the twelve-to-eighteen age group are out of school; the majority of these are male, and more are from rural than from urban areas. Less than 21 percent of children aged seventeen to eighteen from the poorest quintile of the population remain enrolled in any school, compared with 87 percent from the highest quintile (Williams 2002). Most working children have few skills for earning, and many are illiterate. A 2005 survey of 3,000 in-school children ages ten to fifteen (Fox and Gordon-Strachan 2007) revealed that 9.5 percent were illiterate, 44.9 percent were considered to have basic literacy, and 45.6 percent were functionally literate. Male illiterates outnumbered female by almost four to one. There is a clear link between these realities and the number of young children working or seeking work, as well as with the social problems of crime, drug abuse, teenage pregnancy, and violence.

This pool of out-of-school unskilled teens is of course open to exploitation by adults in the pornography and sex trades, local and foreign. Both young girls and boys have also found that their sexuality can earn income and other benefits to themselves and their families.

Under the Child Care and Protection Act (CCPA) of 2004 (from the Child Care and Protection Act 2004 n.d.), employing a child under the age of thirteen is a punishable offense (fine or imprisonment). The only allowable exceptions for children thirteen to fifteen are when the employment is judged to be sufficiently light and age-appropriate and does not in any way interfere with the child's education or otherwise harm his or her health or development. Such exception permits may be granted for work within the entertainment industry. However, the law specifically forbids employing children in any nightclub for any purpose (e.g., use for immoral purposes, selling liquor or tobacco products). It also can charge adults with causing a child to beg on the street or in any premises, with or without an adult present. The sale of children or their services for any purpose is strictly forbidden by law, with harsh consequences for the trafficker in such cases. As with other provisions of the CCPA, its intentions are ahead of the mechanisms of enforcement and the capacities of the state or NGOs to appropriately provide required care and protection measures.

FAMILY

Jamaican families, when first studied by external as well as local researchers, were most often described as "dysfunctional," even "pathological," because they were viewed through the normative lens of the middle-class European, who saw "family" as father-mother-children under one roof, usually married. In Jamaica, marriage has always been the pattern for the minority middle and upper classes, and only occasionally for the majority, and this often later on in life. Child-bearing most often begins within "visiting" relationships; the mother is young, often still living at home with her mother/family, and her "baby father" visits.

Sometimes these relationships move to firmer ground as a common-law or even married partnership. But a national sample of children at age six indicated that at birth, 50 percent of these children's biological parents were in a visiting relationship, 35 percent in a common-law relationship, and 15 percent were married (Samms-Vaughan 2004). By age six, 40 percent of the children's parents had no relationship, common-law relationships had dropped to 28 percent, 6 percent remained in a visiting relationship, while a few more got married (22 percent). By age sixteen, parents with no relationship rose to 63 percent, common-law relationships were down to 10 percent, and marriage rose to 26 percent, with few visiting relationships remaining. For almost 17 percent, the father figure was now a stepfather or mother's partner. Grandparents served as mother figure for almost 6 percent and father figure for 3 percent. Other relatives served as mother figures (3.6 percent) and father figures (2.6 percent). Migration to earn abroad plays a major role in parent absence.

Households in the urban areas are over 50 percent "female-headed" (slightly less in rural areas), which may signal a single mother with her child(ren), or a grandmother whose offspring and children live with her. This does not mean that men are not in the household, for there may be adult sons, uncles, or boyfriends under the roof and assisting financially, but the woman is de facto household head. A visiting or absent father may be a source of financial help but does not co-reside.

"Child-shifting" is a common experience of many Jamaican families. Child-shifting is the act of informally "giving" a child/children for short or long periods of time to another relative or even an unrelated person to raise, usually with the understanding that this shift is in the best interests of the child, for example, better financial circumstances, nearer to a better school, or because parents are migrating to earn and cannot yet send for the children. This pattern has been common since the exigencies of slavery and its aftermath of privation, and has enabled many children to survive and even do well who might not have otherwise done so (McDonald-Levy 1998).

Data drawn from the 1996 Jamaica Survey of Living Conditions on shifted children indicated that these children were shifted mostly to kin rather than non-relatives, especially grandparents and aunts. Migration and inability to "mind" children (financially) were major causes of shifting. There were no gender differences among the shifted children, and an emphasis was placed on socioeconomic benefits to both parents and children; children most often were moved to richer households with older caregivers. Strong female network ties serve as the main support system for women, especially when fathers are not taking responsibility for their offspring.

But child-shifting is also known to exact a heavy emotional toll on many children, and sometimes a physical one as well, if they are placed with abusive or neglectful substitutes (Ramkissoon 2006). Other studies have extended our understanding of the effects on children of parent–child separation from death, migration, or separation/divorce of parents (Pottinger 2005; Crawford-Brown and Rattray 2001). It was noted that the type of parental loss influenced children's emotional reactions. Those who experienced migration as negative were likely to feel depressed and have suicidal thoughts. Parental break-up or divorce was the greatest predictor of low self-esteem, and sometimes impacted negatively on a child's ability to form secure attachments with others and feel a sense of trust. Reunification with migrant parents also posed problems, especially if the children felt resentment or anger for being left behind. Ramkissoon (2006) confirmed earlier findings that biological parents of shifted children are still perceived to be the main caregivers, even when absent, suggesting that the receivers of children are still expected to provide everyday care and protection, rather than financial resources.

Another long-standing feature of Jamaican family culture is that of multiple partners/families. Perhaps beginning in slavery when marriage of slaves was forbidden and families were routinely wrenched apart, multiple concurrent or serial relationships have resulted in both men and women having children with different partners over time. Sexual activity—and thus child-bearing—generally begins early. Although the fertility rate overall is dropping, more than 11 percent of live births are to girls in the fifteen to nineteen age group (2002–2003 Jamaica Reproductive Health Survey 2002). By the time of educational and/or financial maturity, a young father may have several "baby mothers," and a mother may have several children by more than one father, each proffering hope (however elusive) of greater financial stability. A couple in an eventual stable common-law or married union may thus have one or more children "outside" their current relationship for whom they are actually or nominally responsible. In tight economic circumstances, the needs of "outside children" sometimes become secondary to those within the present union. A corollary of this pattern is that fathers who remain the more common "visiting" partner are sometimes discouraged or even denied access to their children because the mother's new partner is now "stepfather," or because they cannot provide financially, or because the relationship with the mother has broken down. The dynamics of the parent dyad therefore take primacy over the right of the child to know and have access to and relationships with both parents.

Among the findings of a recent qualitative examination of Jamaican parenting styles among middle- and lower-class parents from rural and urban settings (Brown 2007) were the following:

- Corporal punishment is justified on cultural/scriptural grounds as necessary by almost all parents, although some only use it rarely or in "mild" forms.
- Many parents across classes experience high levels of stress, which influence their parenting practices.

- High value is placed on children's obedience, mannerliness, and "respect" for adults and their authority. Across classes, lying and stealing were strongly condemned and the influences of "bad" company feared.
- Children's emotional/social needs are not commonly central to Jamaican parenting, and child participation in family decisions that affect them is usually minimal.
- All respondents described a very real commitment to their children's education as a critical route to future success and opportunities; many of these parents were active within their children's school PTAs and visited the school/teachers regularly. This is often linked to parents' desire that children have more opportunities, or less poverty, or less harsh upbringing than they had.
- Boys are generally afforded greater freedom, particularly outside the house, and somewhat harsher discipline than are girls, although there were exceptions.
- The surveillance and protection of their children, especially girls, was seen as a very important responsibility of parents, particularly within community settings with high levels of violence and poverty.

The parenting styles of the study participants ranged along a continuum of harsh disciplinary regimes and non-negotiable authority at one end, and few rules or limits at the other, either by choice or by virtue of being overwhelmed and "giving up" authority altogether. In between are the majority who use "reasoning *and* beating"—they warn or talk, then use physical punishment that can be either severe or mild, and there is generally more and varied communication between partners and between parents and children with limited physical punishment. Focus groups of children confirmed these patterns, suggesting that although children are unhappy with physical means of punishment, some have incorporated its defense as essential to parenting.

The majority of Jamaican children live in conditions of urban or rural poverty. In these environments, very few have parents who read to them; limited play or reading materials and very few educational toys such as puzzles and playing blocks are in the home. There is lack of systematic supervision of children or routine in homes where parents are frequently absent or are long hours at work, and children are often late to school or play truant in these circumstances (Evans 1989). Children are expected to do regular domestic chores and many are responsible for sibling childcare and supervision (Brown 2007).

The findings from a national study of six-year-olds in Jamaica (Samms-Vaughan 2004) indicated that the five most significant indicators (out of nineteen measured) of child outcomes in early childhood included socioeconomic status, parental education, parental stress, reading books, and the early childhood learning environment (e.g., preschool) outside the home. The implications for parent support needs are apparent, and to date access to parenting support and education programs is very uneven or in some communities almost absent. Health centers, churches, and schools remain the primary sources of support for parents.

HEALTH

Jamaica's health indicators compare very favorably with those of developed and developing countries internationally. Over 86 percent of the population has access to safe drinking water and nearly 100 percent of the population has proper sanitary facilities. Health care is provided through a network of more than twenty-four hospitals, including five specialist institutions and over 348 Type I–V health centers. The designation of Type I–V signifies the capacity and range of services provided at a particular health center. Through a fairly well-organized primary healthcare system, children and their families can access affordable health services at reasonable cost, in spite of the resource challenges faced by many health facilities presently. Poor families who are unable to pay the cost of health care can apply to receive free services under special programs established by the government to assist such families, for example, NHF and PATH. Children and senior citizens are given priority consideration in these instances.

Jamaica's infant and child mortality rate in 2005 was 19.2 per 1,000 live births compared with 24.5 in year 2000. Immunization rates increased steadily during the 1970s as a result of the targeted improvements in primary health care throughout the island. Immunization coverage, which rose to rates of above 90 percent during the 1990s, has shown subsequent decline attributed to the problem of limited resources in the overall health sector. In 2001 the percentage rates of immunization for polio, tuberculosis, and diphtheria/tetanus/pertussis were 96.4, 91.0, and 90.4, respectively. These rates fell sharply in 2003 and 2004 to the 70 percent to 80 percent range but showed improvement for 2005 (94.5, 83.6, 87.5, and 84.0, respectively). The measles-mumps-rubella vaccination rate of 84 percent in 2001 also fell below 80 percent in 2004 but recovered to 84 percent in 2005. The government has indicated its intention to increase immunization prevalence to over 90 percent in the immediate future (*Economic and Social Survey Jamaica, 2004* 2005).

The incidence of HIV/AIDS has continued to increase in the general population in spite of the government's efforts to contain the spread of this disease. An estimated 20,000 children in Jamaica are affected by HIV/AIDS, and approximately 5,000 of these are orphaned. Children in the age range birth to eighteen years account for close to 10 percent of all reported AIDS cases. Adolescent girls ten to nineteen years old are three times more likely to become infected with HIV than boys of the same age. This is due to various factors, such as early sexual initiation involving older infected men, forced sex, and unsafe sexual practices among adolescents. Teenage pregnancy rates are much higher than desired, as adolescents account for approximately 20 percent of all births. Although AIDS is the second most prevalent cause of death among children birth to four years, the incidence of pediatric HIV/AIDS infection among children one to eight years has been trending downward in the last four years because of increased availability of Prevention of Mother to Child Transmission (PMTCT) services and increased testing of pregnant women. In spite of the existence of a national policy on dealing with HIV/AIDS in schools, infected school-aged children continue to experience discrimination and marginalization in their communities and schools. They are also poorly nourished and attend school irregularly (*Economic and Social Survey Jamaica, 2005* 2006)

Table 9.1 provides information on the various conditions that lead to children from birth through nineteen years being seen in accident and emergency units of hospitals. Bites, poisonings, and burns occur most frequently among children five years and under. Assault and motor vehicle accidents also occur quite frequently for this age group but become the leading reasons for seeking hospital treatment among the five to nine and the ten to nineteen age groups. In most instances, males far outnumber females in number of cases that occur. Males ten to nineteen years are also involved in a significant number of incidents involving stabbings and gunshot wounds. The incidence of sexual assault is highest among girls in the five to nine and ten to nineteen age groups (*Economic and Social Survey Jamaica, 2005* 2006).

The majority of Jamaican children are adequately nourished. Prevalence of malnutrition has been trending downward over the years. The

Table 9.1.
Children Birth to 19 Years Seen as Patients in Accident and Emergency Units of Public Hospitals in Jamaica by Condition, Gender, and Age, 2005

Conditions	Under 5 years		5–9 years		10–19 years	
	Male	Female	Male	Female	Male	Female
Burns	267	204	110	94	151	119
Poisoning	283	245	84	52	63	61
Bites	325	206	521	302	577	584
Stab wounds	6	2	29	7	550	199
Gunshot wounds	2	1	4	8	227	52
Blunt injury	228	170	412	239	1528	1225
Sexual assault	10	61	24	131	18	859
Motor vehicle accidents	214	152	400	298	1354	1078

Source: Economic and Social Survey Jamaica, 2005 (2006).

incidence of malnutrition in 2004 was 1.6 percent compared with 3.8 percent in 2003. The latest data on child nutrition provided by the Tropical Metabolism Research Institute (TMRI) show that children are becoming heavier and even obese. In 1966, the average weight of a six-year-old was 19.5 kg compared with 23.2 kg in the 1990s. In 2004, the rate of obesity was 6 percent among preschool-aged children in Jamaica. Weight increase among children is perhaps linked to the rapid growth of the fast-food industry in Jamaica in recent years.

LAWS AND LEGAL STATUS[2]

The first legislation applicable to Jamaica under British rule that acknowledged the state's obligation to protect its youngest and most vulnerable citizens was the Prevention of Cruelty to Children Act (the Children's Charter) passed in 1889 in the U.K. Parliament. Subsequent legislation covered different aspects of child status and child protection (child labor, juvenile justice, sexual offenses against children, etc.). In 1993, Jamaica joined most countries of the world in ratifying the international CRC, which commits countries to ensure a wide range of rights for children. The passing of Jamaica's CCPA of 2004 concluded a lengthy period of consultations with broad sectors of the society, which sought to ensure that the proposed new legislation would preserve all previous elements essential to child protection, incorporate those elements required to comply more closely with the international convention, and reflect Jamaican realities and experience.

The CCPA of (March) 2004 passed after years of consultation with relevant departments of government, NGOs, and many groups and individuals committed to fulfilling the rights of children as outlined in the CRC. The new act also sought to rationalize previous and sometimes contradictory pieces of legislation relating to children or children's welfare, and thus replaced several earlier legislative acts pertaining to children. The act defines "child" as any person under the age of eighteen, except where otherwise stated in a specific clause. The act's preamble asserts that its provisions make paramount the best interests of the child, which is interpreted to take into account these facets of childhood:

- safety
- physical and emotional needs and level of development
- quality of relationship with parents/caretakers and the effect of maintaining those relationships
- religious and spiritual views

---

2. This section draws substantially from two sources: The Technical Working Group for CAMP Bustamante (2006) and Jamaica Ministry of Justice Steering Committee (February 2006).

- level of education and educational requirements;
- views, if age and maturity allow, and situation if decision on interests is delayed.

The principles guiding the interpretation and administration of the new law include the following:

- Children are entitled to be protected from abuse, neglect, and harm or threat of harm.
- A family is the preferred environment for the care and upbringing of children, and the responsibility for the protection of children rests primarily with the parents.
- If a family can provide a safe and nurturing environment for a child with the help of available support services, such support services should be provided.
- Decisions relating to the child should take into account the child's own views when the child's age and maturity allow.
- Kinship ties and the child's attachment to the extended family should be preserved if possible.
- Decisions relating to children should be made and implemented in a timely manner.
- The parents and/or legal guardians are deemed responsible for the care and protection of children; desertion of the family or no residence with the child does not remove this responsibility from either parent.
- The autonomy and integrity of the family unit should be supported, and help provided, with mutual consent wherever possible.
- Services to the child must recognize children's need for continuity of care and stable family relationships, and consider their physical and mental differences.
- Children in conflict with the law have special needs that must be recognized.

The CCPA spells out the legal process and options of the court when reports of abuse are made. Thus, a child is considered legally in need of care and protection if he or she:

- Has no parent or guardian, or whose parent/guardian is unfit to provide care, leaving the child subject to bad associations, moral danger, and without appropriate supervision and control;
- Is cared for in circumstances that are likely to impair his or her physical or mental health or emotional state;
- Is deemed by his/her parents or guardians to be beyond their control and they request the court's placement of the child;

- Has been victim of an offense or attempted offense committed against him or her, including: murder or manslaughter; abandonment or gross neglect; abduction; sexual acts, even if the child consents; assault; rape; any bodily injury; given or sold intoxicating liquor; is in the same household as either the victim or perpetrator of any of the above offenses.

A person convicted of any of the above offenses is liable to a fine and/or imprisonment, with or without hard labor, for periods from two months (common assault) to life imprisonment (carnal abuse of child under twelve, child rape). Fines can range from a maximum of J$1,000 (common assault) to J$1.0 to 1.5 million (cruelty to children, cruelty for monetary gain). Some convictions in Circuit Court can draw fines of even greater amounts, depending on the nature and severity of the offense (e.g., child trafficking).

The law provides legal procedures for removing a child from his/her home if deemed necessary to protect the child, or, alternatively, issuing a warrant for the removal or restriction of access of the person accused of the offense against the child. On hearing the evidence, the court may:

(1) return the child to the home with parents/guardian charged to provide proper care under the supervision of a probation or after-care officer;
(2) place the child with another willing person, relative or not, who is deemed fit, under the supervision of a probation or after-care officer;
(3) place the child directly under supervision of a probation or after-care officer;
(4) remove a convicted offender from the home or refuse access to the child without supervision for a period up to two years;
(5) prohibit contact by a convicted offender with the child's caretaker, if warranted;
(6) require that an offender and/or the children in that person's care receive counseling from a qualified person;
(7) make an interim judgment (any of the above) while further investigations are carried out to ensure the best interests of the child are paramount. Such interim judgments cannot exceed sixty days before a final disposition.

RELIGIOUS LIFE

Jamaica is reputed to have the most churches per square mile in the world. The majority are Christian denominations, namely Anglicans, Methodists, Baptists, Catholics, Presbyterians, Seventh-Day Adventists, Church of God, and a variety of smaller fundamentalist/charismatic religious groups. This latter grouping has the fastest growing church membership in Jamaica today. The non-Christian religious groups in Jamaica include Jews, Hindus, Muslims, Bahais, and the locally founded Rastafarian sect. For the majority Christian population, children are expected to participate in religious life to the extent that their families do.

The religious beliefs of parents and the wider population are a significant influence on attitudes toward and expectations of childhood behavior. The teachings of the church are regarded as a template for what is good versus what is bad child behavior and social habits. Many adherents of Christianity support biblical injunctions such as "spare the rod and spoil the child" and by so doing will justify the use of corporal punishment as a disciplinary strategy. Families who attend church regularly expect children of all ages to accompany them and participate in the various rituals, beginning with infant baptism or "christening." It is strongly believed among devout Christians that infants should be blessed as soon after birth as possible as a form of protecting the child from evil. After infant baptism, children are expected and encouraged to become a part of the church congregation through attendance at Sunday School. Many churches presently provide nurseries for the care of very young infants during adult worship services. Children from preschool age upward attend Sunday School classes where they are tutored in the principles and practices of Christian living through Bible stories exemplifying good moral behavior. By age ten to twelve, children are considered old enough to be included in church life as individual members, and most parents enroll their children in the preparation classes leading to baptism or confirmation, which signals official recognition as an individual church member. The significant symbol of individual church membership is the entitlement to participate in the ritual of Holy Communion.

The church in Jamaica has played a significant role in the education sector. Many public and private schools were founded by different church denominations. Many of Jamaica's basic schools were first founded and are still operated by churches. Initially, they would be established in the church hall until resources allowed for erecting new buildings to house the school facilities. Religious rituals are practiced in most public and private schools, influenced by the incumbent denomination. Worship sessions are held at the start of each school day, and usually involve singing of hymns, reading Bible passages, and saying prayers. Non-Christian students are exempted from participating in Christian worship on request. In addition to the educational services, churches representing many denominations (Salvation Army, Catholic, Anglican, Methodist, United Church, Pentecostal, Church of God, and others) are very active in social service projects and programs, such as skill training for school leavers, health clinics offering primary healthcare to poor families, rehabilitation services for the disabled, orphanages for abandoned children or children whose parents have died from HIV/AIDS infection, and children's homes for boys and girls. Food for the Poor, the largest organization offering support to poor families in Jamaica, is run by the Catholic Church.

Religion is regarded by most Jamaican parents as an important aspect of raising children to become decent citizens. Findings from the Profiles Research Project provide a basis for understanding such a perspective, as church attendance was associated with several positive outcomes and attitudes in children. The research found that there was a very high level of church attendance (over 82 percent attending church two to three times per month) among the children surveyed. This was most evident in the Pentecostal and Evangelical churches, with smaller percentages recorded for the traditional churches (Samms-Vaughan 2004). The research found that children's church attendance was associated with higher spelling scores and arithmetic scores. Attendance at religious services was also associated with children's behavioral strengths, identified as interpersonal and intrapersonal strengths, family involvement, school function, and affective strengths.

CHILD ABUSE AND NEGLECT

Jamaicans take justifiable pride in the historical sacrifices made for their children over generations, and in the achievements that have resulted from these sacrifices. Yet the reported number of children who suffer physical and emotional abuse, neglect, and sexual exploitation within Jamaica testifies to the failure of our collective caring and sacrifice to prevent such travesties. The number of reports are growing. Jamaica's Ministry of Health provides a table (see Table 9.2) indicating the stark rise in violence-related injuries in children between 1999 and 2002.

Additional detail about the nature of these injuries is seen in Table 9.1, which reports more recent information about children (from birth to nineteen years old) seen as patients in accident and emergency units of public hospitals in 2005.

Although the children who attend the ten Child and Adolescent Mental Health Clinics across Jamaica represent only a tip of the iceberg of children in need of counseling and support, the breakdown of child patient visits gives us some picture of the nature of children's problems, many of which are related to situations involving abuse in one form or another. Of approximately 3,000 patient visits (11 months, 2005),

Table 9.2.
Violent Injuries of Children

Violence-related injuries	1999	2000	2001	2002
Children <5 years old	220	319	239	383
Children >5 years old	4,094	6,431	8,183	10,485

Source: Economic and Social Survey Jamaica, 2003 (2004).

3 percent were for physical abuse, 15 percent were for sexual abuse, and 8 percent were for post-traumatic stress disorder (mostly witnessing or experiencing serious acts of violence). The remaining visits related to children with attention-deficit/hyperactive disorder (ADHD), conduct disorders, learning disorders, anxiety disorders, depression, psychosis, adjustment disorders, or substance abuse; many of these conditions can be associated with conditions of neglect or abuse (*Economic and Social Survey 2005* 2006). There are many more children whose suffering goes unnoticed or unreported, and without counseling interventions this often turns into anger or withdrawal; at this point, the child's behavior is often redefined in families as "badness" or "sickness."

In a review of cases in 2002–2003, only 11.7 percent of the perpetrators of violence against children were strangers; 86 percent of child abuse incidents were committed by a relative, friend, acquaintance, or intimate partner (The Jamaica Injury Surveillance System Data 2004). Ninety-eight percent (773) of the 789 victims of sexual assault cases were girls, a female to male ratio of 26 to 1. Violence against children occurred most frequently in homes and in public areas (including on the streets). But the home was especially dangerous for girls, as over half of all violent acts and almost 60 percent of all sexual assaults of girls occurred in their homes (Branche 2004).

In 2005, there were 2,572 children living in state-run or state-supported residential institutions, assigned by the courts upon the death of parent(s) or for abandonment, neglect, abuse, or for behavior problems the parent(s) were unable to control. The Child Development Agency, which is the state's organization for investigating and recommending dispositions of such situations to the court, has launched a strong campaign to increase the number of foster parents for such children with some success, but the numbers assigned to residential care continue to increase. A newspaper headline in early April 2007 noted that 55 children had been abandoned to state care since the beginning of the year (Rose 2007); over 50 percent of these were between birth and six years of age. Conditions of stark poverty, unemployment, mental illness, and young/poor parenting in various combinations are usual push factors in such cases.

A Ministry of Health initiative, supported by the United Nations Children's Fund (UNICEF), established a special unit at Jamaica's one children's hospital (servicing children up to age twelve) dubbed "CAMP," or the Child Abuse Mitigation Project, to tackle suspected cases of child abuse. This pilot provides short-term counseling interventions to children identified at registration or by referral as suspected victims of violence or neglect. Home and school visits are part of this program, as are family counseling and referral to other support services, and the sensitization and training of all levels of hospital staff to identify and refer suspected cases of abuse. Intentions are to replicate aspects of this model in other hospitals and health services island wide. However, the project's effectiveness to date has been limited by the realities of long waiting lists for longer-term public counseling services, high costs of private services, slow processing of cases needing the attention and disposition of the courts, and the dearth of community-based services to support stressed families with individual and group counseling and supervised activities after school and on weekends for children. When CAMP Bustamante was able to successfully link its short-term interventions to other support services, the program recorded successful behavior change within families.

Another disturbing aspect of recorded cases of violence against children is the rising incidence and costs of school-based violence. The Minister of Education cited a J$30 million government cost related to school violence in 2006–2007 fiscal year. Most of these incidents are among peers and involve pencils, stones, knives, and physical fights; some cases of teacher–student violence end up in the hospital and/or court as well. Many children leave homes and communities with high levels of corporal punishment and general violence and enter overcrowded and under-resourced schools where teachers find it increasingly difficult to handle their own stress levels and maintain order. The most disturbing statistics are the rising numbers of children murdered, often as reprisal tokens within internecine gang wars. Over 300 children were murdered between 2001 and 2005; in 2005, the number was 91 (UNICEF 2006). A study on adolescence and violence in Jamaica cites one male high school student as saying: "What I am seeing in modern society now is that nowhere is safe. Yu can be in yuh house, gunman come in, kick off yuh door an' kill yuh. Yu can be at school, dey come shoot up the school and kill yuh. Anywhere yuh be, yu not safe. From a your time fi dead a jus' your time, yuh si me?" (Williams 2002, 227).

Some children try to escape these circumstances by living and working or begging on the streets. Numbers are elusive, but a newspaper article citing a 2002 Ministry of Health survey claimed the number of children who live and work on the streets as nearly 6,500 (although UNICEF figures are a more conservative 2,000–3,000). Although more than 58 percent of the children surveyed said they wanted to return home, for varied reasons those who could actually return home were less than 40 percent (Lewis 2007). Some children work on the streets washing windscreens, or selling produce or other goods for their parent(s) after school hours or on weekends to help pay their school and family expenses. Some are sent, or choose, to beg. Many are physically or sexually abused in hostile street environments. A few government and NGO programs exist to offer re-entry to school and/or greater protection to these children, but the numbers who remain out of reach remain high.

An intersectoral Working Group on Children and Violence has prepared a five-year Plan of Action on Children and Violence (Intersectoral Working Group on Children and Violence 2006), which provides a coordinated and structural approach to issues pertaining to children as victims, perpetrators, and witnesses of acts of violence and abuse. It offers strategies and guidelines to a range of institutions for prevention, treatment, and rehabilitation initiatives. It seeks to reform policies, laws, and standards to strengthen the enforcement of children's rights with regard to violence, to improve access to appropriate and affordable services, to strengthen family and community capacities to address issues of violence and children, to educate the public on children's rights in relation to violence, and to improve coordination of all services working to these ends. This plan of action addresses some of the problems related to implementation and enforcement of the CCPA.

GROWING UP IN THE TWENTY-FIRST CENTURY

With the changing realities of globalization, children of all nations will need to be specially prepared to cope with the complexities of life in the twenty-first century. Levinger (1996) explores the impact of rapid technological innovation on future demands of the workplace and life in general and suggests that individuals will need to be multi-skilled and more socially adaptable to be successful. The twenty-first-century worker will need to place emphasis on employability rather than employment in a highly competitive environment.

As a nation, Jamaica still grapples with many challenges that impact the extent to which its population, and specifically children, are being prepared to meet the expectations of twenty-first-century work and family life. These challenges were outlined in previous sections of this chapter. It is clear from the information provided that advancement in the different facets of children's development has not attained the level of progress desired in some instances.

The government of Jamaica, as signatory to the CRC, has identified the priorities to be addressed in order to increase children's chances of achieving their full developmental potential in becoming ready for life in the twenty-first century. This is critical in light of government's expressed intention to put Jamaica in a position to achieve developed country status by year 2030. *The Economic and Social Survey Jamaica, 2006* (2007) provides an overview of some of the government's plans and programs intended to provide opportunities for children to become healthy, well educated, and well socialized. These initiatives will include, among others:

- Improved child nutrition, which will result from the development and implementation of infant and child feeding policies and programs;
- Increased access to improved basic health care by the vulnerable of the population (includes care and support of children with HIV/AIDS);
- Promotion and protection of the rights of persons with disabilities through improved coordination of a wide range of cross-sectoral issues impacting persons with disabilities;

- Raising the standard of care and education programs at the early childhood level;
- Improved training for staff working in early childhood facilities and residential children's homes;
- Development of a comprehensive parenting policy and parenting education strategy for reaching parents island wide;
- Increased screening and early detection for children from birth through eight years;
- Expansion of school spaces at early childhood through secondary levels to increase access and reduce class size and pupil-teacher ratios;
- Improved early childhood curriculum for children from birth to five years;
- Increased emphasis on the promotion of early literacy and numeracy development;
- Increased provisions for promoting technology readiness in schools;
- Expansion and promotion of the Safer Schools Programme to combat increasing violence in schools; and
- Promotion of the Adolescent Healthy Lifestyles Programme in schools.

Although the above initiatives are not all inclusive, they will address a range of critical activities that will go a long way in providing the appropriate supports children need as they journey into the twenty-first century.

RESOURCE GUIDE

Suggested Readings

Barrow, Christine, ed. 2002. *Children's Rights: Caribbean Realities.* Kingston: Ian Randle Publishers. A compendium of presentations at an academic/research conference on the issues of child rights within the context of the Caribbean. Many of the Caribbean articles cited are relevant to Jamaican experience, and several are specific to Jamaica.

Caribbean Childhoods: Journal of the Children's Issues Coalition
Volume 1: Contemporary Issues in Early Childhood (2003)
Volume 2: Children at Risk (2005)
This research journal is based at the University of the West Indies (Jamaica campus), and the majority of articles in the 2003 and 2005 journal issues concern Jamaican family/child studies.

Caribbean Journal of Social Work, Volumes 1 (2002) through 5 (2006), Lincoln Williams, ed. Covers many articles on Jamaican family life, culture, and community development.

Cherannes, Barry. 2001. *Learning to Be a Man: Culture, Socialization and Gender Identity in Five Caribbean Communities.* Kingston: University of the West Indies Press. This work is a qualitative study of the processes by which male children are socialized in three Caribbean countries: Dominica, Guyana, and Jamaica.

Davies, Rose. 2000. "Investing in Early Education and Development in Jamaica: Perspectives, Problems and Possibilities." *Journal of Education and Development in the Caribbean* 4, no. 2: 75–92. This article provides an overview of the status of the early childhood sector in Jamaica, the relatively low public sector investment, and the resultant poor quality of many preschool services. Suggestions are made for achieving improvements to the sector.

Evans, Hyacinth. 2001. *Inside Jamaican Schools.* Kingston: University of West Indies Press. An ethnography of life in Jamaican school settings that exposes the experiences of those who work and learn in schools and examines how children's identities are shaped in their interaction with others in the school setting.

Leo-Rhynie, Elsa. 2006. *Social Toxins and Our Children: Can the Pollution be Stopped? Environmental Foundation of Jamaica Annual Public Lecture.* Kingston: Environmental Foundation of Jamaica, 18 Norwood Avenue, Kingston 5, Jamaica. This lecture focuses on how children's development is significantly influenced by "social toxins" and proposes strategies for stopping the pollution.

Planning Institute of Jamaica and United Nations Development Programme (UNDP). 2005. *Jamaica Human Development Report 2005.* Kingston: Planning Institute of Jamaica. A collection of papers on several issues related to Jamaica: economy, education, health, culture, and other social issues in the context of globalization.

Samms-Vaughan, Maureen. 2000. *Cognition, Educational Attainment and Behaviour in a Cohort of Jamaican Children.* Kingston: Planning Institute of Jamaica. This document focuses on the impact of socioeconomic status, home and family life, nutrition, and early childhood education on school performance, cognitive function, and behavior.

———. 2006. *Children Caught in the Crossfire.* Kingston: Grace Kennedy Foundation Annual Lecture Series. Grace Kennedy Foundation, 73 Harbor Street, Kingston, Jamaica. This lecture examines the current state of childhood in Jamaica and the many challenges children face as a result of the "crossfire" between the adults in their lives.

Nonprint Resources

Cool Runnings. 1993. Directed by Jon Turteltaub. Walt Disney Productions. 98 min. DVD. This comedy film is directed by Jon Turteltaub. It is loosely based on the exploits of the Jamaican bobsled team at Calgary, Alberta, in the 1988 Winter Olympics. It stars Leon Robinson, Doug E. Doug, Malik Yoba, Rawle D. Lewis, and John Candy.

Life and Debt. 2001. Documentary film directed by Stephanie Black. A Tuff Gong Pictures Production. 86 min. This prize-winning film explores the effects of globalization and neoliberal economic policies on Jamaica and the Jamaican people, contrasting international tourism with the realities of structural adjustment and economic difficulties. Excerpts from Jamaica Kincaid's *A Small Place* and reggae music provide a rich cultural backdrop for the messages of the film. As Director Stephanie Black explained in an interview, "The aim of the film was to clarify, simplify and make visible an essentially invisible subject matter—the impact of economic policies on the day to day

JAMAICA

lives of people whom these policies are ostensibly supposed to benefit but actually don't."

The Rural Family Support Organization (RuFamSo), located in Clarendon, Jamaica, is a nongovernmental entity that provides an educational home-visiting child development program in rural areas of Jamaica. The organization has developed a kit of materials that includes:

1. The Roving Caregivers Early Childhood Home Visiting Programme: Guide for Training Rovers (Compiled by Myrtle Daley)
2. Video: Roving Caregivers Training Video "Play and the Young Child" (22 minutes)
3. Video: "The Making of a Competent Caregiver" (27 minutes)
4. CD: Songs Children Love to Sing
5. Cassette Taped Music: Children's Songs: Have Fun and Learn

35 Years of Child Development in the Caribbean. 1999. CD. Kingston: Dudley Grant Memorial Trust, University of West Indies.

Web Sites

Broadcasting Commission, http://www.broadcastingcommission.org.

Caribbean Child Development Centre, University of the West Indies, http://www.uwi.edu/ccdc.

Child Development Agency, http://www.cda.gov.jm.

Culture Health Arts Sports and Education Fund (CHASE), http://www.chase.org.jm.

Early Childhood Commission, http://www.ecc.gov.jm.

Environmental Foundation of Jamaica (EFJ), http://www.efj.org.jm.

Jamaica Social Investment Fund (JSIF), http://www.jsif.org.

Ministry of Education and Youth (MOEY), http://www.moeyc.gov.jm.

Ministry of Health (MOH), http://www.moh.gov.jm.

Parenting Partners Caribbean, http://www.parentingpartnerscaribbean.org.

Planning Institute of Jamaica. http://www.pioj.gov.jm.

UNICEF Jamaica, http://www.unicef.org/Jamaica.

University of the West Indies, Mona Campus, http://www.mona.uwi.edu.

Organizations and NGOs

Broadcasting Commission
53 Knutsford Boulevard
Kingston 5, Jamaica
Phone: (876) 908-0957
Web site: http://www.broadcastingcommission.org
The Commission has undertaken a leading role in promoting healthy child development and early education, including promoting research, setting standards, and in collaboration with UNESCO, supporting a children's literacy project.

Caribbean Child Development Centre
University of the West Indies
Mona Campus
Kingston 7, Jamaica
Phone: (876) 927-1618
Web site: http://www.uwi.edu/ccdc
The Centre provides a comprehensive database on research on children's issues. It is also the base for the journal *Caribbean Childhoods: From Research to Action*.
Volume 1: Contemporary Issues in Early Childhood (2003)
Volume 2: Children at Risk (2005)
Volume 3: Screening, Referral and Early Intervention (2007)

Child Development Agency
2–4 King Street
Kingston, Jamaica
Phone: (876) 948-2841
Web site: http://www.cda.gov.jm
Jamaica's principal government child development agency, which performs a wide range of functions related to children's welfare and well-being.

Culture Health Arts Sports and Education Fund Ltd. (CHASE)
52 Grenada Crescent
Kingston 5, Jamaica
Phone: (876) 908-3667
Web site: http://www.chase.org.jm
This organization provides funding support for a wide range of projects in the areas indicated. It places special focus on early childhood education and has supported many projects to improve infrastructure of school plants.

Early Childhood Commission
Shop 45, Kingston Mall
Kingston, Jamaica
Phone: (876) 922-9296/7
Web site: http://www.ecc.gov.jm
A recently established agency with overall responsibility for overseeing the comprehensive delivery of early childhood programs and services in Jamaica.

Environmental Foundation of Jamaica (EFJ)
18 Norwood Avenue

Kingston 5, Jamaica
Phone: (876) 960-6744
Web site: http://www.efj.org.jm
A non-governmental organization involved in a wide range of environmental and sustainable development projects. These include a number of early childhood development projects.

Jamaica Social Investment Fund (JSIF)
1c-1f Pawsey Road
Kingston 5, Jamaica
Phone: (876) 906-2869
Web site: http://www.jsif.org
A government-established organization that provides funding support for community development projects aimed at improving the welfare and well-being of the poor.

Ministry of Education and Youth (MOEY)
2 National Heroes Circle
Kingston 4, Jamaica
Phone: (876) 922-1400
Web site: http://www.moeyc.gov.jm
The government ministry with responsibility for all levels of education and youth development.

Ministry of Health (MOH)
2–4 King Street
Kingston, Jamaica
Phone: (876) 967-1100
Web site: http://www.moh.gov.jm
The ministry of government responsible for population health programs and health surveillance.

Office of the Children's Advocate
72 Harbour Street
Kingston, Jamaica
Phone: (876) 948-1134
The children's advocate provides legal representation on children's issues and advises government on legislative reform to safeguard children's interests.

Parenting Partners Caribbean
15 St. Lucia Way
Kingston 10, Jamaica
Phone: (876) 920-4299
Web site: http://www.parentingpartnerscaribbean.org
This Jamaica-based organization provides information on training and projects, such as a regional radio project, for parents in Jamaica and across the region. Also linked to this site are: Caribbean Food and Nutrition Institute (CFNI), Caribbean Support Initiative (CSI), Pediatric Association of Jamaica, and Women's Centre of Jamaica.

Planning Institute of Jamaica
10-12 Grenada Way
Kingston 5, Jamaica
Phone: (876) 906-4463
Web site: http://www.pioj.gov.jm
The Institute's Web site provides access to statistical data and reports on Jamaica, as well as a range of special interest publications, such as the annual survey of living conditions, the annual economic and social survey of Jamaica, studies on parenting, readiness of schools for children, the impact of violence on children, and the range of social and economic conditions affecting children's lives.

UNICEF Jamaica
60 Knutsford Boulevard
Kingston 5, Jamaica
Phone: (876) 926-7584
Web site: http://www.unicef.org/jamaica
UNICEF's office in Jamaica undertakes research, situational assessments of women and children, and projects in cooperation with the government of Jamaica. *Meeting Adolescent Development and Participation Rights: The Findings of Five Research Studies on Adolescents in Jamaica* is a particularly useful resource published in 2002.

University of the West Indies, Mona Campus
Kingston 7, Jamaica
Phone: (876) 927-1660
Web site: http://www.mona.uwi.edu
This Mona Campus Web site provides links to the work of the Institute of Education, Tropical Metabolism Research Institute, Sir Arthur Lewis Institute of Social and Economic Research, and other research centers of the university undertaking work on children's issues such as poverty, migration, and violence. Publications of the University include *Caribbean Quarterly* (Email: cq@uwimona.edu.jm), a journal that regularly explores children's issues. For example, the March 2004 issue (volume 50, number 1) explored HIV/AIDS education in the region with a particular focus on Jamaica.

Selected Bibliography

Branche, C. 2004. *The Jamaica Injury Surveillance System Data*. Kingston: Ministry of Health.

Brown, Janet. 2007. *They Loved Him So Much He Growed: Childrearing and Child Participation in Jamaica*. Rio de Janeiro: Instituto Promundo and Save the Children Sweden.

Brown, Janet, and Sian Williams. 2006. *Childrearing and Cultures: A Literature Review. Research Approaches and Findings on Childrearing and Socialization of Children (Birth to Eight Years of Age) in the Caribbean*. Unpublished manuscript. Bridgetown, Barbados, W.I.: Caribbean Support Initiative.

Crawford-Brown, Claudette P.J., and J. Melrose Rattray. 2001. "Parent-Child Relationships in Caribbean Families." In *Culturally Diverse Parent-Child and*

Family Relationships: A Guide for Social Workers and Other Practitioners. Edited by Nancy Boyd Webb. New York: Columbia University Press, pp. 107–130.

Economic and Social Survey Jamaica, 1999. 2000. Kingston: Planning Institute of Jamaica.

Economic and Social Survey Jamaica, 2003. 2004. Kingston: Planning Institute of Jamaica.

Economic and Social Survey Jamaica, 2004. 2005. Kingston: Planning Institute of Jamaica.

Economic and Social Survey Jamaica, 2005. 2006. Kingston: Planning Institute of Jamaica.

Economic and Social Survey Jamaica, 2006. April 2007. Kingston: Statistical Institute of Jamaica and Planning Institute of Jamaica.

Evans, Hyacinth. 1989, "Perspectives on the Socialisation of the Working Class Jamaican Child." *Social and Economic Studies* 38, no. 3: 177-2-3.

Fox, Kristin, and Georgiana Gordon-Strachan. 2007. *Jamaican Youth Risk and Resilience Behavior Survey 2005: School-based Survey on Risk and Resiliency Behaviors of 10–15 Year Olds.* Kingston: Ministry of Health, USAID, MEASURE Evaluation.

From the Child Care and Protection Act 2004. (n.d.) *Implementation Handbook for Professionals: A Publication of the Child Development Agency.* Ministry of Health, with support of UNICEF and Planning Institute of Jamaica.

Intersectoral Working Group on Children and Violence. September 2006. National Plan of Action on Children and Violence. Kingston: Planning Institute of Jamaica.

Jamaica Ministry of Justice Steering Committee. February 2006. Final Draft, National Plan of Action on Child Justice. Kingston: Ministry of Justice.

Leo-Rhynie, Elsa. 2006. *Social Toxins and Our Children. Can the Pollution Be Stopped?* Kingston: Environmental Foundation of Jamaica.

Levinger, Beryl. 1996. *Critical Transitions: Human Capacity Development across the Lifespan.* Newton, MA: Education Development Center.

Lewis, Taneisha. 2007. "No Night Out for Street Kids." *Jamaica Observer*, April 5. http://www.jamaicaobserver.com/news/html/20070404T230000-0500_12 1358_OBS_NO_NIGHT_OUT_FOR_STREET_KIDS.asp. Accessed April 25, 2007.

McDonald-Levy, Brigette. 1998. *Two Sides of the Same Coin: Child Fostering and Child Shifting in Jamaica.* Masters Thesis, Consortium Graduate School, University of the West Indies.

Pottinger, Audrey. 2005. "Disrupted Caregiving Relationships and Emotional Well-being in School Age Children Living in Inner-city Communities." In *Caribbean Childhoods, Journal of the Children's Issues Coalition*, Volume 2: Children at Risk. Kingston, Jamaica: Ian Randle Publishers. pp. 38–57.

Ramkissoon, Marina. 2006. Descriptions of Child Shifting in Jamaican Children. Draft for publication.

Roopnarine, Jaipaul L. 2005. *The Roving Caregiver Programme in Jamaica: Its Theoretical and Research Foundations and Efficacy.* The Hague, Netherlands: Bernard van Leer Foundation.

Rose, Marshalynn. 2007. "55 Kids 'Dumped' over 11 Months." *Jamaica Observer*, April 15. http://www.jamaicaobserver.com/news/html/20070414T1400 00-0500_121745_OBS_KIDS_DUMPED_OVER_MONTHS_.asp. Accessed April 25, 2007.

Samms-Vaughan, Maureen. 2004. *Profiles–The Jamaican Pre-school Child: The Status of Early Childhood Development in Jamaica.* Kingston: Planning Institute of Jamaica and Environmental Foundation of Jamaica.

Survey of Living Conditions 2005. 2006. Kingston: Statistical Institute of Jamaica and Planning Institute of Jamaica.

Task Force on Educational Reform. 2004. *Jamaica: A Transformed Education System, Report.* Kingston: Office of the Prime Minister.

———. 2005. *Jamaica Early Childhood Care and Development Sector Report, March 2005.* Kingston: Office of the Prime Minister.

The Technical Working Group for CAMP Bustamante. 2006. *Responding to Child Abuse: A Training Resource to Guide Jamaica's Hospitals and Support Services in Responding Effectively to Abused Children and Their Families.* Kingston: Ministry of Health, UNICEF.

2002–2003 Jamaica Reproductive Health Survey. 2002. Kingston: Jamaica National Family Planning Board in collaboration with the Statistical Institute of Jamaica.

United Nations Children's Fund (UNICEF). 2006. *Annual Report (Internal).* The 2007–2011 Government of Jamaica/UNICEF Country Programme.

Williams, Lincoln. 2002. "Adolescence and Violence in Jamaica." pp. 226–280 in *Meeting Adolescent Development and Participation Rights: The Findings of Five Research Studies on Adolescents in Jamaica.* Kingston: UNICEF/UNFPA.

Williams, Sian. 1999. *Sexual Violence and Exploitation of Children in Latin America and the Caribbean: The Case of Jamaica.* Montevideo, Uruguay: Inter-American Institute with Caribbean Child Development Centre, University of West Indies, Mona.

10

MEXICO

Fernando M. Reimers and Felicia Knaul

NATIONAL PROFILE

Mexico is a large, upper/middle-income country. The economy is the fourteenth largest in the world (World Bank 2006). In terms of geographic area, Mexico spans 1,964,375 km² and borders with the United States, Guatemala, and Belize (Instituto Nacional de Estadística, Geografía e Informática [INEGI] 2006a). In 2005, the country included 22,790,188 households and 103,263,388 persons, of whom 30.6 percent are aged birth to fourteen years (INEGI 2006b).

Mexico is a multicultural nation that is home to numerous indigenous groups. Over six million inhabitants speak one or more of the over eighty languages and variant indigenous dialects (INEGI 2006b). The National Commission for the Development of Indigenous People states that these groups of people are divided into sixty-two ethnicities, many of which represent thousand-year-old cultures, languages, and traditions (Comisión Nacional para el Desarrollo de los Pueblos Indígenas 2006).

During the last sixty years, Mexico has been going through profound and polarized demographic and epidemiological transitions. Life expectancy at birth rose from forty years in 1943 to 74.5 in 2006, and the total fertility rate fell from 6 children in 1976 to 2.2 in 2006. Currently, the

annual rate of population growth is 1 percent (Consejo Nacional de Población 2006; INEGI 2006a). While the population is still young—more than 50 percent is currently aged twenty-five or under—the aging process is advancing rapidly. The number of children six years old or younger is declining at an annual rate of just below 1 percent, and the group that is growing rapidly is aged sixty-five and over. In 2000, approximately one in twenty Mexicans was older than sixty-five, while by 2050 this figure will be one in four (Consejo Nacional de Población 2006). This demographic transition represents an opportunity and a challenge; in a decade, most of the population will be of working age and the conditions facing children at present will have a profound impact on Mexican society when today's children constitute the majority of the population.

More than 76 percent of the population lives in urban areas, particularly concentrated in three major megalopolis areas: Mexico City,[1] Guadalajara, and Monterrey. At the same time, the growth—both in number and population—of medium-sized cities has been intense during the last twenty years (INEGI 2006b). However, the rural population continues to represent a great challenge, particularly in terms of the provision of services. The rural areas are highly dispersed, and 72 percent of the 187,938 localities in the country have less than 100 inhabitants.[2] This dispersion is linked to poverty, which in turn is related to geographical conditions that make access to small communities difficult.

Based on advances over the past decades, the country enjoys a more open economic and political system than ever before and is more integrated into the world economy. For example, Mexico has been a member of the North American Free Trade Agreement (NAFTA) and the Organization for Economic Cooperation and Economic Development (OECD) since 1994.

Mexico is a federal republic composed of thirty-one states and the Federal District. The country is a democracy with a presidential system and a division of responsibilities between the executive, legislative, and judicial systems (Secretaría de Gobernación 2006). Both presidential and state-level elections take place every six years. The Mexican political system is one of multiple parties, with the three dominant ones being the Institutional Revolutionary Party (PRI), National Action Party (PAN), and Democratic Revolutionary Party (PRD). A defining characteristic of the Mexican political system was the political transition that took place after the electoral victory of the PAN in 2000. The inauguration of Vicente Fox as president represented both a change of power after more than

---

1. Mexico City includes most of the Federal District. The Federal District has around 8 million inhabitants. The *Zona Metropolitana del Valle de México* extends beyond the limit of the Distrito Federal and covers part of the State of Mexico and one municipality of the State of Hidalgo, and about 20 million people live in the Zona Metropolitana.

2. Authors' estimations based on INEGI 2005b.

seventy years under PRI rule and a move to more transparent electoral processes. The continual process of decentralization to the states that has been undertaken for more than two decades also represents a significant political transition. The states now have substantial margin to pass laws, assign budgets, and organize programs in all sectors and levels of government.

Mexico has one of the highest levels of per capita income in Latin America at 7,411 dollars in 2005.[3] Basic living standards and conditions are also, on average, quite high. In 2005, 88 percent of the 22,261,664 homes registered in Mexico had running water, 85 percent had drainage, and 97 percent had electricity (INEGI 2006b).

Almost 75 percent of the population aged fourteen and over was economically active in 2005, and of these, 63 percent were men (INEGI 2005a). Female labor force participation, while substantially lower than that of men, has increased rapidly over the past four decades, representing one of the key social transitions in Mexico. This rate is now approximately 40 percent (INEGI 2006c). At the same time, women are especially prone to having to manage the double burden of household work and caregiving, alongside their labor market participation (Del Razo Martínez 2003).

Although the country has made important gains in access to services and income per capita growth, poverty rates remain high. In a recent study, the World Bank documents a continual reduction between 1998 and 2004 in the proportion of households living on less than $2 per day from more than 25 percent to almost 15 percent (World Bank 2005). This means that despite improvements, several million families do not earn enough income to cover their basic needs.

At the same time, substantial variation continues to exist in living conditions and economic development between rich and poor, the north and south, and the urban and rural areas. Inequality is pervasive: the richest 10 percent of the population receives over 40 percent of total income, while the poorest tenth receives only 1.1 percent (Tuirán Gutiérrez 2006). There are also deep regional and ethnic disparities and differences in access to basic services. These gaps are usually associated with place of residence and with ethnic status. The National Population Council reports that of the thirty-two federal entities that make up Mexico, three have very high indices of "marginalization" (an expanded measure of poverty that includes income and access to services, as well as literacy and percentage with primary education completed), eight are categorized as high, seven as medium, ten as low, and only four as very low (Consejo Nacional de Población 2005).

Poverty and social deprivation are particularly common among indigenous populations. The presence of these communities constitutes an

3. Authors' calculations based on INEGI 2006d, Consejo Nacional de Población 2005, and Banco de Mexico 2006.

KEY FACTS – MEXICO

Population: 108,700,891 (July 2007 est.)

Life expectancy at birth: 74.5 years (2006 est.)

Literacy rate: 92.2 percent (2003 est.)

Net primary school enrollment/attendance: 98 percent (2000–2005)

Internet users: 18.622 million (2005 est.)

People living with HIV/AIDS: 180,000 (2005 est.)

Human Poverty Index (HPI-1) Rank: 9

Sources: CIA World Factbook: Mexico. https://www.cia.gov/cia/ publications/factbook/geos/mx.html. April 17, 2007; UNICEF. At a Glance: Mexico–Statistics. http://www.unicef.org/ infobycountry/mexico_statistics.html. April 24, 2007; World Health Organization (WHO): UNAIDS/WHO Global HIV/AIDS Online Database. "Epidemiological Fact Sheets on HIV/AIDS and Sexuality Transmitted Diseases: Mexico." http://www.who.int/ GlobalAtlas/predefinedReports/EFS2006/index.asp?str SelectedCountry=MX. December 2006; United Nations Development Programme (UNDP) Human Development Report 2006 – Mexico. http://hdr.undp.org/hdr2006/statistics/countries/ data_sheets/cty_ds_MEX.html. April 26, 2007.

expression of the great cultural wealth and diversity that exists in Mexico. However, largely due to the isolation and geographical dispersion of the majority of their settlements, but also as a result of decades of exclusion, indigenous people suffer from underdevelopment and much lower living standards than the general population. Of the eleven municipalities with a human development index of less than 0.5 in Mexico, eight are communities in which practically the entire population, more than 98 percent, is indigenous. Of the 122 municipalities that score poorly on the human development index, in fifty-five of them more than 95 percent of the population is indigenous; and in thirty-five of these municipalities indigenous people represent between 70 and 95 percent (Comisión Nacional para el Desarrollo de los Pueblos Indígenas 2006).

During the last decades, families in Mexico have experienced transformations reflected in an increase in the percentage of nonnuclear families and an increase in the percentage of single-parent families, most of which are headed by women. In 1970, 80 percent of the families were headed by two parents. In 1997, two-parent families accounted for only 67 percent of all families. The percentage of families headed by women increased from 13 percent in 1960 to 21 percent in 2000 (INEGI 2000b).

OVERVIEW

The national education system is dominated by public institutions, although private educational institutions are also important and cover 8.72 percent of primary and lower-secondary and upper-secondary students (Secretaría de Educación Pública 2006). A total of three years of preschool and nine years of basic education (primary and lower secondary) are constitutionally free and mandatory. The level of educational attainment of the population has increased dramatically as has coverage. The average number of years of education went from 3.4 to 8.1 between 1970 and 2005. Still, more than 40 percent of Mexicans aged fifteen and over have not completed secondary education. Primary school attendance has gone from 65.7 percent to 96.1 percent between 1970 and 2005, and secondary school attendance from 52.6 percent to 82.5 percent (INEGI 2006b).

EDUCATION

Although access to education has increased significantly in Mexico over the last several decades, the low quality and efficiency of the education system, which lead many students to drop out of school before completing the mandatory nine years of basic education, have resulted in a significantly smaller increase in the levels of educational attainment of the economically active population in Mexico than in other OECD countries.

At present, the national education system includes 31 million students, most in primary schools as shown in Table 10.1. During the last three decades, the education priority was to expand access to primary school, which comprised six years of compulsory instruction. From 1970 to 2005, the number of students in elementary school increased 60 percent. In 1993 an education reform expanded compulsory education to nine years. Most recently priority was also given to achieving three years of universal preschool education.

As shown in Table 10.2, relative to the total number of children in the relevant age group, enrollments increased between 1970 and 2005 in preschool (ages three to five) from 8 percent to 70 percent, in elementary school (ages six to twelve) from 92 percent to 97 percent, from 31 percent to 92 percent in lower secondary school (ages thirteen to fifteen), from 7 percent to 42 percent in high school (ages sixteen to nineteen),

Table 10.1.
Number of Students Enrolled at Different Levels of Education in Mexico from 1970, in Thousands

	1970	1975	1985	1995	2004
Total	11,538.87	15,480.58	25,253.79	26,915.64	31,816.90
Preschool	400.13	537.09	2,381.41	3,169.95	4,086.82
Elementary	9,248.19	11,461.41	15,124.16	14,623.43	14,652.87
Lower secondary	1,102.22	1,898.053	4,179.46	4,687.33	5,894.35
Technical high school	33.86	78.38	359.13	387.98	362.83
High school	279.49	607.96	1,538.10	2,050.68	3,185.08
Normal high school (teacher training)	55.94	111.50	64.70	—	—
Normal bachelor (teacher training)	19.03	41.86	126.35	160.03	146.30
Bachelor	252.231	501.251	1,033.08	1,295.04	2,087.69
Graduate	—	—	39.67	77.76	150.85

Source: Instituto Nacional para la Evaluación de la Educación (2006).

Table 10.2.
Gross Enrollment Rates at Different Levels of Education

	Ages	1970	1990	2000	2005
Preschool	3–5	7.92	42.24	51.13	69.54
Elementary	6–12	92.13	97.96	95.47	96.86
Secondary	13–15	31.54	68.05	84.96	91.81
High school	13–19	7.07	22.53	32.83	42.13
College	20–24	13.07	29.35	39.92	23.95

Source: INEGI (2006b) and Secretaría de Educación Pública (2006).

and from 13 percent to 24 percent in college (ages twenty to twenty-four).

Most children begin elementary school at the age of six (69 percent), but a few begin at the ages of five (11 percent) and seven (16 percent).[4] Most children attend preschool for at least one year. In 2004, 21 percent of sixth graders reported that they had attended one year of preschool, 22 percent had attended two years, 26 percent had attended three years, and the rest had attended more years. A new law mandating three years of free and compulsory preschool (passed in 2002) will increase access to this level of education.

Most schools, particularly at the precollegiate level, are publicly funded. Ninety-one percent of all basic education institutions (grades one through nine) are public, and 75 percent of high schools are publicly funded. Funding for education has consistently increased in the last fifteen years; public education spending increased from 3.7 percent of GDP in 1990 to 5.5 percent in 2005. Education spending has also become a greater priority within public spending in general, accounting for 19 percent of total government spending in 1990 and 28 percent in 2005. In spite of this relatively large fiscal effort to fund education, because a large share of Mexico's population is of school-going age, on a per capita basis Mexico spends less per student than most other countries at comparable or higher levels of economic development, as shown in Table 10.3.

Income inequality in Mexico is related to inequality in educational attainment. In 2004, for example, 63 percent of heads of household in the two poorest income deciles had not completed elementary school, compared with only 12 percent of the heads of household in the two richest deciles who had not completed this level of education. Conversely, while only 18 percent of the household heads in the two poorest deciles had completed lower secondary school, 75 percent of the household heads in the two richest deciles had the same level of education. In recent years, in spite of the gradual increase in the levels of educational

---

4. Unless otherwise noted the figures provided in this chapter are authors' calculations based on a random sample survey of sixth graders that was administered by the Instituto Nacional de Evaluación de la Educación in 2004.

Table 10.3.
Per-pupil Spending, by Level, as a Percentage of Per Capita GDP in
OECD Countries (using Purchasing Parity Prices of 2002 in dollars)

Country	Preschool	Primary	Secondary	High School	College[a]
Australia	n/d	17.77	24.29	27.19	30.31
Austria	19.92	22.64	28.03	29.46	25.12
Belgium	14.95	19.16	n/d	n/d	28.08
Canada	n/d	n/d	n/d	n/d	n/d
Czech Republic	15.60	11.89	20.62	20.94	28.42
Denmark	14.59	24.12	24.82	25.14	36.23
Finland	12.31	15.95	25.69	20.23	22.98
France	15.63	17.44	27.09	32.19	25.30
Germany	18.72	17.02	21.25	36.58	24.82
Greece	n/d	18.44	n/d	n/d	21.20
Hungary[b]	22.52	19.55	18.38	23.16	42.12
Iceland	n/d	23.43	24.62	20.21	n/d
Ireland	n/d	11.79	16.08	16.25	21.79
Italy[b]	19.53	25.94	28.96	25.90	n/d
Japan	12.04	19.95	21.55	23.72	n/d
Korea	12.12	17.25	24.45	32.76	n/d
Luxembourg	n/d	21.82	n/d	n/d	n/d
México	15.93	14.23	14.33	23.06	51.38
Holland	16.13	18.21	23.77	20.49	26.13
New Zealand	19.76	19.27	19.29	31.14	n/d
Norway	n/d	18.71	21.28	28.69	n/d
Poland	21.46	n/d	n/d	n/d	33.53
Portugal	21.41	25.43	34.63	36.83	24.16
Slovak Republic	16.13	11.17	13.71	20.44	33.44
Spain	16.25	19.41	n/d	n/d	25.49
Sweden	13.82	24.03	23.80	25.81	26.35
Switzerland[b]	9.92	22.37	26.46	42.26	n/d
Turkey[b]	n/d	n/d	n/d	n/d	60.09
United Kingdom	28.74	17.51	n/d	n/d	30.49
United States of America	21.77	22.24	23.95	26.54	51.31

[a] Does not include spending in research and development.
[b] Includes only public institutions.
Note: n/d, no data.
Source: Organization for Economic Cooperation and Development (2005).

attainment of the population, the gaps in educational attainment separating the richest and poorest groups have grown because the levels of education have increased more among upper-income families. Whereas in 1984 the percentage of household heads without elementary school in the two poorest deciles was three times greater than the same percentage in the two richest deciles (89 percent versus 30 percent), the gap between these two groups became five times greater in 2004 (63 percent versus

12 percent) because the gains in educational attainment were greater for the groups with more income (Bracho 2000; INEGI 2004b).

At the heart of these educational inequalities are the lower opportunities to enroll in schools with quality teachers and to access lower secondary, high school, and college education for children in the lowest income groups, for those who live in rural areas, for those who live in the southern states, and for indigenous groups. The evidence reveals that the stratification of the education system reproduces social stratification in Mexico. Among those older than fifteen years, almost half (47.3 percent) have not studied beyond sixth grade of elementary instruction. Most of these are low-income and indigenous people.

In spite of the fact that since 1993 lower secondary education is compulsory in Mexico, the last census indicates that 58 percent of youth between twelve and fourteen years old have not completed any grade beyond sixth grade of elementary instruction. This is due to the high rates of repetition in elementary school, which cause some in this age group to be still enrolled in elementary school, and also because many students drop out of school before completing lower secondary education. At the elementary level, 9 percent of students drop out before completing this level; at the lower secondary level 20 percent of the students drop out; and 39 percent of the students drop out of high school. While most students attend school until the age of fourteen, there is a precipitous drop after that age, as seen in Table 10.4. While 94 percent of boys are enrolled in school at the age of fourteen, this figure drops to

Table 10.4.

Percentage of Boys and Girls Attending School in 2006 by Age

Age (in years)	Percentage	
	Boys	Girls
12	98	98
13	94	97
14	94	82
15	86	85
16	87	72
17	76	78
18	62	64
19	53	52
20	42	33
21	46	34
22	46	24
23	20	25
24	24	13

Source: Authors' calculations based on data from Instituto Nacional de la Juventud, Encuesta Nacional de la Juventud 2005–2006.

86 percent at the age of fifteen and to 76 percent at the age of seventeen. For girls, 97 percent of whom are enrolled in school at the age of thirteen, the figure drops to 82 percent at the age of fourteen and to 78 percent at the age of seventeen.

Given that the official entry age of elementary school is six years, in theory at the age of fifteen students should have completed the ninth grade of compulsory basic education. Because of high rates of grade repetition in elementary school, in practice only 31 percent of the students aged fifteen have completed nine grades of schooling.[5] Grade repetition is a common experience in Mexico; 23 percent of the sixth graders report that they have repeated at least one grade.[6]

Almost a million youth (930,000) twelve to fourteen years of age do not attend school, representing 14.5 percent of that age group. Exclusion from the last tranche of compulsory schooling is greater for women, for indigenous people, and for those in the south. In Chiapas, for instance, more than 25 percent of twelve- to fourteen-year-olds do not attend school. Among those who speak an indigenous language, 23.4 percent do not attend school, compared with 13.9 percent of those who do not speak an indigenous language. Timely completion rates for elementary instruction are 86.3 percent, but only 72 percent in indigenous schools. Among those who finish elementary school, only 93 percent begin lower secondary school.

There are significant regional differences in educational opportunity. For example, in the southern state of Chiapas, the average level of educational attainment for those aged fifteen to sixty-four is 5.6 years, and the illiteracy rate is 21 percent, compared with Baja California, in the northwest, where average educational attainment is 8.6 years and the illiteracy rate is 3 percent. In the state of Zacatecas, the percentage of school-aged children not enrolled in school among those who do not speak an indigenous language is 10.9 percent, whereas among those who speak an indigenous language, 40 percent do not attend school.

The levels of educational achievement reflected in curriculum-based tests and in international assessments of competencies in math and literacy are low. The results obtained by Mexican students who are fifteen years old in the OECD's Programme for International Student Assessment (PISA), a competency assessment administered in OECD countries in 2000 and 2003, are among the lowest of all countries participating in the study. For example, more than a third of students performed below the minimum level of mathematical competency measured by the assessment, and about a fourth of the students performed below the minimum level of literacy competency measured by the assessment in 2003 (Vidal and Díaz 2004).

---

5. Figures from INEGI 2000b.

6. Authors' calculations are based on data collected in a random sample survey of sixth-grade students administered in 2004 by the Instituto Nacional de Evaluación de la Educación.

PLAY AND RECREATION

As part of Mexico's rich cultural traditions, children's play is common and a widely shared value across most communities. A number of government-sponsored institutions celebrate and maintain traditional games and songs as a means to support the development of cultural identity. Economic demands on families place significant demands on children's time, often limiting the opportunity to play or practice sports. About half of children practice sports, and three in five children play and watch television. Around 25 percent of children have a computer at home, 39 percent have a DVD player, and only 60 percent have ever used a computer.

When asked how they spent their time, 26 percent of sixth graders surveyed in a 2004 study said they took care of siblings, 10 percent cooked meals for the family, 15 percent washed clothes for the family, 46 percent cleaned the house, 9 percent ironed clothes, and 14 percent farmed. In addition, 26 percent of students said that they have a job, and 20 percent received an income for that job. There is a gendered division of children's work and use of free time, as shown in Table 10.5. Boys are more likely to practice sports than girls and as likely as girls to watch television. Girls are more likely to perform household chores, such as cooking for the family, doing laundry, cleaning the house or ironing, and boys are more likely to work in the fields or to hold jobs outside the house. Boys spend

Table 10.5.
How Do Sixth Graders Spend Their Time when Not in School

	Percentage		
	Boys	**Girls**	**Total**
Practice sports	56	37	47
Play and watch television	60	65	62
Take care of siblings	24	28	26
Cook for my family	7	14	10
Laundry for family	8	21	15
Clean house	33	59	46
Iron clothes	5	12	9
Work in fields	17	10	14
Other job	36	18	27
Get paid for work	39	20	30
How many hours a day do you work outside the house			
Up to 2	39	54	45
3	16	15	16
4	14	11	13
5 or more	31	19	27

Source: Authors' calculations based on data from a sample survey administered to sixth-grade students in 2004 by the Instituto Nacional de la Evaluación de la Educación.

Table 10.6.
Age at which Sixth Graders Indicate that They Began to Work

Age of respondent	Percentage		
	11	12	13
Boys			
This year	39	37	38
Last year	27	29	28
Two years or more	34	34	33
Girls			
This year	39	40	38
Last year	32	30	29
Two years or more	29	30	33

Source: Authors' calculations based on data from a sample survey administered to sixth-grade students in 2004 by the Instituto Nacional de la Evaluacion de la Educacion.

more time in work outside the home than girls, and they are also more likely to get paid for the job they perform outside the house.

Children begin to work at an early age, with many beginning at the age of nine or earlier, as shown in Table 10.6. For instance, among boys aged eleven who are in the sixth grade, one third (34 percent) indicate that they began working when they were nine or younger, 27 percent say that they started to work at the age of ten, and 39 percent at the age of eleven. The ages at which children start to work are similar for girls.

There is also a socioeconomic division in how children spend their time as shown by the differences in time use among children who receive the government *oportunidades* (opportunities) scholarships—targeted to extremely poor families—and those who do not receive such scholarships (Table 10.7).

Table 10.7.
How Children Use Their Time by Degree of Poverty—Recipients of Scholarships for Extremely Poor Families versus Nonrecipients

	Percentage		
	Scholarship	No scholarship	Gap (scholarship/ no scholarship)
Practice sports	38	51	76
Play and watch television	54	66	82
Cook for family	14	8	178
Laundry for family	21	12	178
Clean house	50	44	113
Iron clothes	12	7	175
Work in the fields	22	10	220
Have a job	37	22	165

Source: Authors' calculations based on data from a sample survey administered to sixth-grade students in 2004 by the Instituto Nacional de la Evaluación de la Educación.

While extremely poor children are less likely to practice sports than less poor children (38 percent versus 51 percent) and also less likely to watch TV (54 percent versus 66 percent), a significant percentage of all children participate in these activities. There is no difference in the likelihood that children participate in caring for younger siblings. Children from poorer families are more likely to engage in various forms of work at home and outside the home.

CHILD LABOR[7]

According to Article 123 of the Mexican Constitution and the Labor Law, the work of individuals younger than fourteen years old is forbidden, and the work of individuals between fourteen and sixteen years should not exceed six hours per day. All additional rights for adult workers also apply to workers below the age of eighteen. Furthermore, persons under age eighteen cannot work in certain establishments, such as bars. In addition to enacting its own legislation, Mexico has acted as a catalyst for many international agreements and programs designed to combat child labor and has adopted international legislation, such as Convention 182 of the International Labor Organization.

Despite this legislation, for many poor families in Mexico not only are working children an important source of additional income, they are also a substitute for hired help and a vehicle for permitting other family members to go to work, usually at the expense of the child's education and development. Data from a recent survey of youth indicate that among those ten to fourteen years of age, 94 percent of boys only study, 0.4 percent work, 0.8 percent study and work, and 4.8 percent neither study nor work. Among girls of the same age group, 90.2 percent only study, 0.8 percent only work, 0.5 percent study and work, and 8.5 percent neither study nor work. For the fifteen- to nineteen-year age group among boys, 62.5 percent only study, 20 percent only work, 9.4 percent both study and work, and 8 percent neither study nor work; among girls, 63.7 percent only study, 7.2 percent only work, 6.2 percent study and work, and 22.9 percent neither study nor work. Poverty is one of the most important factors that drive children to work, particularly in cases where children do not go to school or work in especially hazardous and often illegal situations. The Instituto Nacional de Estadística, Geografía e Informática (INEGI—National Institute of Statistics, Geography, and Informatics) reports that 21.7 percent of children interviewed said their principal reason for working was because the home needed the extra

---

7. There is no standardized definition of child labor. This section draws on multiple studies, each of which uses slightly different definitions. For this reason, the proportions and absolute numbers are not necessarily comparable. The overall conclusion, highlighted here, are common to all of the studies.

income. An additional 51 percent said that they worked because their family could not afford to hire salaried help (INEGI 2004a).

Child labor is a very heterogeneous phenomenon and includes some forms of labor that are particularly hazardous. Another important and relatively unexplored issue is the gender differences in child work, with a particular focus on domestic labor both within and outside the home. Domestic labor is often a hidden form of work, as it is not counted in many labor force statistics.

According to a recent publication by INEGI, in 2002 almost 2 million Mexican children aged six to fourteen worked in economic activities (all work undertaken in the labor market on either a paid or unpaid basis for at least one hour or one day per week, outside or inside the home). The associated participation rate is 5.3 percent for children aged six to eleven,[8] and 12.2 percent for youth aged twelve and thirteen.[9]

The same study, in addition to other recent publications, undertakes a broader analysis of child labor that includes unpaid domestic work in the home (Knaul 1995; Levison, Moe, and Knaul 2001). In the INEGI study, this includes work undertaken for more than fifteen hours per week. Under this broader definition, there were 3.3 million working children in Mexico in 2002; thus one in every six children worked inside or outside of their homes. This dramatic increase in the figures corresponds to a labor force participation rate of 15.7 percent.

These figures highlight the important gender bias that exists in definitions and analyses of child labor that focus only on economic work and thus miss a large portion of child workers, mostly girls, who undertake domestic work in their own homes. In the case of Mexico, the majority of boys (71.0 percent) work in economic activity, and the majority of girls (73.3 percent) work in domestic activities. Therefore, not including domestic labor, the participation rate for females between six and fourteen is only 5.9 percent and appears much lower than that of males of the same age, at 13.4 percent (INEGI 2000a). Including domestic labor, the female participation rate is similar to that of boys and suggests the need for a very different policy focus.

It is also important to consider the situation of youth below the age of eighteen. Work for more than six hours per day is illegal for youth between the ages of fourteen and sixteen. Still, in 2001, an estimated 375,000 youth were in this category (INEGI 2002). Furthermore, the labor force participation rates for youth are substantially higher than those for younger children. Including domestic work, the participation rate for males aged twelve to seventeen was 35.8 percent, and the participation rate of females was 40.1 percent in 2001 (INEGI 2002).

---

8. This figure is from INEGI 2000a; for the rest of the years mentioned, there is no direct information available on work for children below age twelve, and the figures presented here are based on projections published by INEGI.

9. Estimation based on INEGI 2002.

Child labor is associated with lower school attendance and educational attainment. One-quarter of working children aged six to fourteen do not go to school—a figure that is many times higher than for children in the same age group who do not work. As age increases, the effects of working on dropping out of school become more pronounced. While 8.7 percent of child workers between the ages of six and eleven do not attend school, by the ages of twelve to fourteen this rate rises to 33.7 percent of the working child population (INEGI 2000a). While domestic work is usually regarded as a less dangerous or damaging form of child labor, evidence has shown this not necessarily to be the case as a high proportion of children, mostly girls, who work in their own homes do not attend school (Levison, Moe, and Knaul 2001).

Certain types of child labor are particularly incompatible with attending school. Among them is domestic labor outside the child's home. Long hours and clandestine working conditions contribute to low rates of school attendance. More than 10 percent of working girls aged twelve to fourteen are domestic laborers outside of their home, and only 37.1 percent of these girls also attend school.

Child labor is concentrated in rural and marginal urban areas. It is in the urban areas that some of the most dangerous forms of child labor are present. Urban children work as street vendors, beggars, or offer services such as car-washing on the streets. Mexico City's central market alone employs approximately 14,000 minors between the ages of seven and eighteen, who work as cart-pushers, kitchen help, and vendors, often without pay and for tips only (Robles Berlanga 2000). A recent survey of the 100 largest cities (excluding Mexico City) identified another 114,500 child workers. In addition, this survey found more than 10,000 children under five who work on the street with family members (INEGI 2004a).

Illegal activities associated with child labor, concentrated among children who live on the street, include drug use, robbery, and child sexual exploitation. A 2000 UNICEF report estimated that there were more than 16,000 children working in the sex industry in Mexico and concentrated mainly in popular tourist destinations and border cities that cater to North American sex tourists (UNICEF, DIF, and CIESAS 2000).

In rural areas, child labor is a different phenomenon. Children play an important role in the home and in the fields, and many of these children also attend school. Almost half of working children below the age of fourteen are found in agriculture, and many begin at very early ages (Secretaría de Desarrollo Social et al. 2002; Secretaría de Desarrollo Social et al. 2005).

One group that is particularly at risk is the indigenous child population in Mexico. In 1997, more than one-third undertook economic or domestic work—almost double the national rate of 18.7 percent. Not only do indigenous children take on more work and start working at a younger age, they also face more discrimination at work. The labor participation rate for indigenous children aged six to eleven is 24.2 percent, 1.6 times greater than the national rate of 9.4 percent. Furthermore, school attendance is a particularly important problem for these children, as 16.5 percent of children between the ages of six and eleven who work do not attend school. Gender differences are more pronounced, with a greater number of girls dropping out of school to fulfill their domestic and economic duties. By the age of twelve to fourteen, 40.3 percent of working indigenous girls do not attend school, compared with 28.4 percent of working indigenous boys (INEGI 2004a).

One of the groups in the most severe conditions is day laborers (*jornaleros agrícolas*), many of whom are of indigenous origin. The children of day laborers migrate with their parents in search of work and have little access to a stable school environment. These children have a labor force participation rate that significantly exceeds the national average—41 percent for children between the ages of six and eleven, and 80 percent for youth aged twelve to nineteen. On average, for every 100 day workers over the age of fifteen, there are 24 child day laborers between the ages of six and eleven. Of the total population of child day laborers, 42 percent show some level of malnutrition, 40 percent are illiterate, and 64 percent of children over twelve years of age have not finished primary education (INEGI 2004a).

The government of Mexico operates a number of programs designed to prevent child labor and reduce poverty. One of the most successful is an innovative, integrated social development program called Oportunidades (originally PROGRESA) launched in 1997. One of the aims of the program is to prevent harmful child labor by improving family income and providing incentives for schooling. Oportunidades provides a cash transfer to the mother of the household if her child attends school regularly from grades three through twelve and participates in regular health check-up visits. Recent studies show that for children between the ages of eight and seventeen, the program reduced paid work among boys by 15 to 25 percent, and domestic work among girls by 10 percent (Parker and Skoufias 2000).

There are also a wide range of civil society organizations, both national and international, that undertake direct service projects, advocacy, research, and information dissemination. Often in conjunction with or through government agencies such as the National Program for the Integral Development of the Family (DIF), a multiplicity of projects and programs exists that seek to attend to the needs of specific groups of working children, and in particular, those in especially difficult circumstances.

FAMILY

The responses of sixth-grade students to a questionnaire about their family and life at home provide a glimpse of the structure of the family.

Students were asked how many people lived with them at home. Only 1 percent lived with only one other person, and 6 percent lived with two other persons. Most children lived in homes with three (18 percent), four (25 percent), or five (17 percent) other people, and 30 percent of children lived with six or more other people at home. In terms of the composition of families, 94 percent of children have a mother at home, but only 80 percent have a father at home; 90 percent have siblings at home, 23 percent have grandparents at home, and 20 percent have uncles or aunts at home.

One percent of children do not live with either parent, 1 percent live with their fathers but not with their mothers, 12 percent live with their mothers but not with their fathers, and 85 percent live with both parents. This suggests that, when parents are separated, children are ten times more likely to remain with their mothers than with their fathers. There does not appear to be a relationship between family structure and extreme poverty. The percentage of children receiving the scholarships[10] from *oportunidades*—which are targeted to extremely poor children and constitute a significant policy initiative to support extremely poor families with children—is similar for children in various types of families. Among those who do not live with a father and mother, 33 percent receive the scholarships; among those who live with their father but not with their mother, 30 percent receive the scholarships; among those who live with their mother but not with their father, 29 percent receive the scholarships; and among those who live with both parents, 33 percent receive the scholarships.

HEALTH

In Mexico, as a result of advances in public health (Omran 1971; Frenk 2006b), in the case of both children and adults, the causes of death and disease are no longer dominated by problems associated with low levels of development (infections, malnutrition, and reproductive health), but rather by noncommunicable disease, chronic illness, accidents, and associated risk factors such as smoking and obesity (Frenk 2006b; Frenk, Bobadilla, Sepúlveda, and López-Cervantes 1989). At the same time, there are significant inequalities associated with the transition. The poor have a double burden as they also face the challenges of the diseases of underdevelopment, which are heavily concentrated among these segments of the population (Frenk 2006a).

Progress in child health and hence in meeting the Millennium Development Goals (MDGs) has been significant. In child mortality, Mexico is one of seven among sixty countries that are on track to meet MDG4 and achieve a reduction from 44.9 deaths per 1,000 live births registered in

---

10. Because education is supposed to be free, what they receive is a monthly cash transfer that increases with the grade and an annual transfer for school supplies, such as notebooks, uniforms, etc.

1990 to fifteen in 2015. As of 2005, the country had achieved a level of child mortality of twenty-three, as part of a continual and long-run reduction from 1980 when the level was 64.3. In infant mortality, the level was 51 in 1980, 36.2 in 1990, and 18.8 in 2005, and the neonatal mortality rates were 28.8, 21.9, and 12.9, respectively (Sepúlveda et al. 2006). In the population aged four to fifteen years, for example, the mortality rate has fallen by half in three decades.

The causes of death and disease have changed dramatically, especially among young children. Diarrheal disease, for example, one of the leading causes of death in 1980, has declined dramatically from 1,163 deaths per 100,000 live births to 71 in 2006. Polio, diphtheria, and measles—the three other most common causes of death in 1990—have been eliminated (Sepúlveda et al. 2006).

Another important area of improvement is undernutrition, which has improved in all forms. Between 1988 and 2006, the time span for which data are available, wasting dropped to one-third of its original prevalence, stunting to half, and underweight by two-thirds. Still, anemia and micronutrient deficiencies remain high. In 2006, anemia affected 24 percent, and iron, zinc, and vitamin A deficiency affected 52 percent, 33 percent, and 27 percent of one- to four-year-olds, respectively. There has been recent improvement in anemia, which fell by 15 percent between 1999 and 2006 (Sepúlveda et al. 2006).

A series of public health interventions are at least partially responsible for these improvements. The most important strategies include the Universal Vaccination Program, the Clean Water Program, and the inclusion of oral rehydration salts, all of which have been provided through a proactive, supply-driven approach to the provision of public health services. As of 2006, Mexican children benefit from what has been described as one of the world's most comprehensive immunization programs. In 2004, the coverage was 95.4 percent for one-year-olds (a 1 percent increase from 1990) and 98.2 percent among one- to four-year-olds (an increase of 0.2 percent from 1990).

These healthcare interventions have been complemented and extended through significant poverty alleviation programs. As mentioned earlier, one of the most important is Oportunidades that currently covers about five million low-income households in rural and urban areas—the vast majority of the poor population in Mexico. This program includes an integrated health, nutrition, and education strategy that is tied to financial incentives to families to make decisions that favor the healthy development of their children (Sepúlveda et al. 2006).

In maternal mortality, there has also been significant improvement from a level of eighty-nine deaths per 100,000 live births in 1990 to just over sixty in 2005, which represents a reduction of 29 percent. This has been accomplished through a national strategy for prenatal and postnatal attention, with special emphasis on remote areas of the country and high-risk births. One of the most important recent programs is *Arranque Parejo en la Vida* (Begin Life on an Equal Footing), which was introduced in Mexico during the 2000–2006 administration. In the uninsured population, the proportion of births attended by qualified personal has increased from a level of 69 percent in 2000 to more than 88 percent by the middle of the decade (Sepúlveda et al. 2006). Despite these improvements, reaching MDG6 (combat HIV/AIDS, malaria, and other diseases) implies achieving a level of 22.3 percent, a figure that will not be reached at the current level of decline (Secretaría de Salud 2006).

The successes that Mexico has achieved in many of the basic indicators of child health bring to the forefront the new and complex challenges that are currently being faced. These are associated with specific illnesses, as well as with risk factors and behavior. Mortality is now concentrated in accidents, chronic illness such as cancer, and congenital illnesses, as well as in disability, all of which are more complex and costly to treat (Secretaría de Desarrollo Social et al. 2002; Secretaría de Salud 2006). The principal behavior-related health risks facing adolescents in Mexico are associated with overweight and obesity, alcoholism, drug consumption, accidents, homicide and suicide, and sexually transmitted disease (Secretaría de Desarrollo Social et al. 2002; Knaul and Santos-Burgoa 2006).

An emergent and increasing problem among children and adults alike is overweight and obesity, which are major risk factors for chronic illnesses, particularly later in life. More than 4 million school-aged children are overweight or obese according to data from the National Survey of Health and Nutrition of 2005. Among five- to eleven-year-olds, the prevalence is 26 percent, while in 1999 it was just below 19 percent, suggesting an alarming increase in obesity that affects both boys and girls but has been most pronounced among boys. At the same time, one-third of adolescents also present with overweight or obesity—almost 5.8 million individuals—and there has been a recent increase in obesity in this age group.

Another important area of action for children and adolescents is mental health and addictions. At least in part due to ongoing as well as new health and education programs, many of these risk factors are stable or declining. Between 2000 and 2005, for example, the proportion of adolescent smokers decreased from 9.2 percent to 7.6 percent, which represents a reduction of 25 percent among males and 20 percent among females. In contrast, the suicide rate, which doubled between 1990 and 2004 in the overall population, increased even more rapidly among adolescents and youth eleven to twenty years of age (Secretaría de Salud 2006).

Another set of emergent challenges that are being met with significant programmatic responses are health issues related to sexual activity. Adolescent pregnancy is one of the most important, although rates have been declining in response to reproductive health and education programs directed at this population. The fertility rate among adolescents aged fifteen to nineteen fell by approximately 21 percent between 2000 and 2005 from 60.4 per 1,000 women to 48.8. The rate of use of contraceptives also increased substantially, and data spanning 1976 to 2003 demonstrate an increase in use from 14 percent to 45 percent among sexually active adolescents twenty years old or younger (Secretaría de Desarrollo Social 2006).

Another key issue is HIV/AIDS. Between 2000 and 2004, the prevalence rate in fifteen- to twenty-year-olds fell by almost 25 percent, from 14.8 cases per 100,000 to 11.2 in response to significant national action programs. Furthermore, specific programs have been implemented to reduce transmission during pregnancy including universal, free access to antiretroviral drugs. In addition to prevention programs through education and effective contraception, national campaigns have been introduced to combat the stigma surrounding people both young and old living with the HIV/AIDS and associated with differences in sexual preferences.

LAWS AND LEGAL STATUS

The Mexican Constitution establishes that every child has the right to receive an education, to have necessary medical treatment, and to live in an adequate environment for his or her development and welfare. These rights to education, health, and healthcare are recognized as fundamental and protected in Mexico through a substantial series of laws and institutions. These laws and institutions are complemented by international agreements and treaties such as the Convention on the Rights of the Child (CRC). In addition, this legal framework protects children from various forms of exploitation, supports adoption rights, and establishes the right of children to separate legal process and sanction when they commit crimes.

The central pieces of legislation in Mexico establishing the rights of children are the CRC and the International Law for the Rights of the Child. Mexico is a signatory of the CRC. In the year 2000, a constitutional amendment of Article 4 of the Constitution explicitly included the recognition of the rights of children. The Constitution now states that children have the right to meet their needs of nourishment, health, education, and leisure for their development, and those caring for children have the obligation to meet these rights. The state will provide the necessary conditions to support respect for the dignity of children and their rights. In April 2000, Congress passed the Law for the Protection of Children's Rights. Most Mexican states still have to pass local laws in accordance with this legislative framework in favor of the rights of children.

Mexico also subscribed to the United Nations Declaration of the Rights of the Child, Resolution 1386 passed on November 20, 1959. This declaration, which does not have the force of law, includes rights for children such as special protection and services to support a healthy physical, mental, moral, spiritual, and social development, with freedom and dignity, the right to a name and a nationality, and the right to social security and education. These rights should be recognized for all children without exception or discrimination on the basis of race, color, gender, religion, political views, national or social origin, economic position, birth, or other conditions of the child or of their family.

Mexico is also a signatory to the 1921 International Convention for the Suppression in the Traffic of Women and Children. In accordance with this covenant, the Federal Criminal Code covers the protection of minors, national laws increased the sanctions for child trafficking and sexual exploitation, and a federal law against organized crime increases the sanctions for crimes that use minors, including traffic of minors. The criminal codes of all states—with the exception of Baja California and Chihuahua—include the crimes of corruption and traffic of minors. In 2000, the Mexican state created an interinstitutional commission to eradicate the sexual exploitation of minors.

Mexico subscribed also in 1985 to the UN minimum regulations concerning the administration of justice for minors known as the Beijing Rules. While as with other international covenants this does not have the force of law, national legislation is aligned with the spirit of this covenant.

In spite of the existence of a favorable legal framework to support children's rights, in practice many of these laws are not followed because of the corruption of the judicial and police systems or because of prevailing cultural practices. Because sentencing for crimes committed by minors is less severe than for adults (sentences for minors tend to end at the age of 18), criminal organizations are increasingly recruiting minors.

RELIGIOUS LIFE

While there is no official religion in Mexico, and the Constitution bans clerical involvement in politics, most Mexicans are Roman Catholic. Until 1992, the Mexican state had no formal diplomatic relations with the Vatican. In recent decades, there has been a significant expansion in membership in Evangelical churches. While, in 1950, 98.2 percent of the population older than five was Catholic, in 2000 only 88 percent declared themselves Catholic. The greatest increase in membership in Protestant churches has been in the southeastern states of Chiapas, Campeche, Tabasco, and Quintana Roo. There is a growing presence of the Church of Jesus Christ of Latter Day Saints, with about one million members in the country, predominantly in the major border cities of northeastern Mexico. There is a small Jewish community of about 45,000 members in Mexico. Islam is practiced by a very small number of people, predominantly members of the Arab and Turkish communities, and also by a small number of the indigenous population in Chiapas.

In a recent survey of youth aged twelve to twenty-nine, 45 percent of the respondents declared themselves practicing Catholics, 39 percent declared themselves nonpracticing Catholics, 2.4 percent declared themselves Christians, and 3.5 percent declared themselves indifferent to any religion.[11] Young people differ with regard to the extent to which they perceive that religion addresses their needs. When asked whether they thought that their religion or church had an adequate response to the challenges of family life, 39 percent answered "yes," and 30 percent answered "in part," while 28 percent replied "no." Regarding whether religion or church addressed the spiritual needs of people, the majority said "yes" (53 percent) or "in part" (27 percent), with 16 percent answering negatively. When asked whether they thought that religion had an adequate response to the problems facing youth, 39 percent answered "yes," 30 percent said "in part," and 28 percent replied "no." When asked whether they thought that religion or the church had an answer for the current social problems facing the country, 29 percent replied "yes," 26 percent said "in part," and 41 percent replied "no."

The state has traditionally and constitutionally adhered strictly to separation from the church in particular with regard to education. Among private schools, some have a religious affiliation. Private associations identified with conservative religious groups have in recent decades become more active in challenging public policies, for example, with regard to the introduction of sex education in the national curriculum of instruction, or with regard to health policies supporting contraception and abortion.

The growth of Protestant religions has on occasion led to public expressions of intolerance on the part of some members of the Catholic majority. In 1974, for example, a group of Evangelicals were violently expelled from Chiapas, a Pentecostal pastor was burned in 1997 in Santa Ana Niche in *Estado de Mexico* (the State of Mexico), and in 1998 a group of evangelicals were expelled from Morelos. There are other indications of religious intolerance. A survey administered to adults in the year 2002 revealed that one-third of those interviewed would not accept that a person from a different religion lived in their home (Cox, Jaramillo, and Reimers 2005). There is no evidence of religious intolerance in educational institutions. Only 3 percent of those aged twelve to twenty-nine indicate that they ever had problems in school because of their religion.[11]

CHILD ABUSE AND NEGLECT

In general, young people feel supported by their families, and the majority report positive relations with their parents. According to the Survey of Youth conducted in 2005, only 16 percent of people aged twelve to twenty-nine reported bad relationships with their parents and an additional 13 percent reported occasional poor relationships with their parents, while 70 percent of them reported positive relations with their parents.

---

11. Authors' calculations are from data of the Instituto Naciónal de Juventud, Encuesta Nacional de la Juventud 2005–2006.

Young people reported high levels of violence in families and to a much smaller extent in schools. When asked whether there was violence within Mexican families, 77 percent answered "yes" and 15 percent said "in part," while only 5 percent said there was no family violence. A smaller percentage answered that they had experienced violence within their own family; only 13 percent said "yes," and 18 percent said "in part," with 68 percent of the respondents stating that they had not experienced violence in their family. When asked to what extent they believed that parents physically hit their children to discipline them, 24 percent said to a great extent, 25 percent to some extent, 26 percent said little, and 20 percent said that not at all.

When asked whether there was violence among classmates in the school they had attended, 6 percent reported much violence, 12 percent reported some violence, 30 percent little violence, and 52 percent no violence. When asked about violence from teachers towards students, 1 percent reported much violence, 6 percent some, 15 percent little violence, and 77 percent no violence.[12]

GROWING UP IN THE TWENTY-FIRST CENTURY

A large proportion of the Mexican population is young, and as a result much of the future of Mexico will be shaped by the experiences of these youth as they grow up. Most children are growing up in families that support their development, with access to basic education and health services, and within a framework that guarantees and supports their fundamental rights.

Young people today have unprecedented opportunities relative to those available to their parents and grandparents. As a result, they will be more educated and their knowledge and values will differ significantly from those of older generations. These changes will further support ongoing economic and political development of Mexico.

The central challenges facing youth in the twenty-first century are the challenges of poverty, which place pressures on families that constrain the opportunities for their children. The challenges will be most acute for families in rural areas. Economic dislocations will impact families in numerous ways, in some cases pushing some members of the family to migrate to other parts of Mexico or to the United States. The ultimate effects of these displacements on youth are insufficiently understood at present. Some of the positive effects include the increase in financial and knowledge resources available to families resulting from their ties to migrants. Some of the negative effects include the emotional burdens of separation and the lack of day-to-day support in raising children for those who are separated from their parents.

---

12. Authors' calculations are from data of the Instituto Nacional de la Juventud, Encuesta Nacional de la Juventud 2005–2006.

To the extent that democratic politics further deepens the possibility that the poor and their interests can be represented in the political process and that as a result the poor and their children remain a central focus of concern of national policy, and to the extent that it is possible for Mexican industry to generate sufficiently large numbers of well-paid jobs in more productive areas, the future prospects for youth in the country will improve. Supporting children and their families so that all can develop their talent to high levels is central in making these improvements possible. At present, significant public efforts are aligned towards that goal.

RESOURCE GUIDE

Suggested Readings

Randall, Laura, ed. 2006. *Changing Structure of Mexico: Political, Social, and Economic Prospects.* New York: M.E. Sharpe. This edited volume contains thirty-five articles covering Mexico's economic structures and policies, quality of life and environment, politics, and social and regional structures. Among the specific topics are social development, political participation, tax reform under the Salinas administration, the utilization and management of water resources, Indians and Afro-Mexicans, and approaches to sustainable development in Mexico City.

Red por los Derechos de la Infancia en México [Network for the Rights of Children in Mexico]. 2005. *Infancias mexicanas: rostros de la desigualdad* [*Mexican Childhoods: Faces of Inequality*]. This is a report prepared by the Red por los Derechos de la Infancia en Mexico, a coalition of fifty-eight non-governmental organizations. The report was presented to the UN Committee on the Rights of Children. The report focuses on the multiple dimensions of social and income inequality in Mexico and how those constrain the rights of children. The report combines the analysis of quantitative evidence with testimonials from children documenting the multiple dimensions of inequality among states and municipalities in Mexico. The report examines the lack of implementation mechanisms at the state level to enforce the legal framework supporting the rights of children.

Reimers, Fernando, ed. 2000. *Unequal Schools, Unequal Chances.* Cambridge, MA: Harvard University Press. This edited book contains four chapters focusing specifically on educational inequality in Mexico. These chapters examine the relationship between education and income inequality, the characteristics of extremely marginalized populations, the impact of policies to provide education to indigenous populations, and the impact of a compensatory program to provide education in highly marginalized communities.

———. ed. 2006. *Aprender más y mejor. Politicas, programas y oportunidades de aprendizaje en educación básica en México* [Learning more and better. policies, programs and opportunities to learn in basic education in Mexico]. Mexico, D.F.: Fondo de Cultura Económica. This edited book presents the evaluations of four education programs implemented during the administration of President Vicente Fox Quesada: the program to expand access to three free years of preschool for all children, the program to improve early literacy instruction, the program to foster school-based management, and the program to introduce technology to improve the quality of basic education.

Nonprint Resources

Children of the Street [Niños de la calle]. Produced and directed by Eva Aridjis. This documentary film shot in 2001 features four street children who describe what life is in the streets: their struggles to survive, drugs, the nature of their encounters with the police, and their health challenges. The film also illuminates the tensions in the homes these children left, as some of them return to visit their parents for Christmas.

Granito de arena [Grain of sand]. 2006. Produced by Jill Freidberg. Seattle: Corrugated Films. 60 minutes. http://www.corrugate.org/granito_de_arena/news. This documentary focuses on the teachers' movement in the South of Mexico in favor of local control of education, and resisting the role of the national teachers' union, as well as a number of policies advanced by the federal government that the teachers perceive as threats to their academic autonomy. The film includes interviews with teachers, and covers strikes and protests as well as the occupation of a teacher training college by government security forces.

Los Olvidados. [The forgotten]. 1950. Produced by Luis Buñuel. Ultramar Films. 80 minutes. http://cinemexicano.mty.itesm.mx/peliculas/olvidados.html. The film, considered one of the best movies of Mexican cinema, is about a group of street children in the 1950s. The film depicts how the crimes of these street children lead to problems with the law and to juvenile prison.

El profe [The teacher]. 1971. Mario Moreno (Cantinflas). Directed by Miguel Delgado. Produced by Jacques Gelmar. 117 minutes. In this comedy, the great Mexican comedian Cantinflas represents a very devoted teacher (Sócrates) who decides to move to a rural community. The movie portrays the struggles of teachers in rural areas with local *caciques* and the alliances that are formed among different groups in the town in favor and against public education.

Stolen Childhoods. 2004. Directed and produced by Len Morris and Robin Romano. Galen Films. Vineyard Haven Gala Films, Martha's Vineyard, MA: Romano Productions. 86 minutes. http://www.stolenchildhoods.org. This documentary, narrated by Meryl Streep, about child labor around the world includes a section on child labor of indigenous children in Nayarit, Mexico. This section illuminates how male Huichole workers are paid wages that require labor from their entire families. The film covers in great detail how children working in poverty live in Mexico, India, Indonesia, Kenya, and the United States.

Web Sites

Consejo Nacional de Población [National Population Council], http://www.conapo.gob.mx.

Informe de Gobierno del Presidente Fox [Report of the Administration of President Vicente Fox], http://fox.presidencia.gob.mx.

Instituto Nacional de Geografía, Estadística e Informática [Nacional Institute of Geography, Statistics and Informatics], http://www.inegi.gob.mx.

Instituto Nacional para la Evaluación de la Educación [National Institute for Educational Evaluation], http://www.inee.edu.mx.

Red por los Derechos de la Infancia en Mexico [Network for the Rights of Children in Mexico], http://www.derechosinfancia.org.mx.

Secretaría de Educación Pública [Secretary of Public Education], http://www.sep.gob.mx.

Secretaría de Salud Pública [Secretary of Public Health], http://www.salud.gob.mx.

Organizations and NGOs

Child Rights Information Network
c/o Save the Children
1 St. John's Lane
London EC1M 4AR
United Kingdom
Phone: (44 20) 7012-6865
Fax: (44 20) 7012-6952
Web site: http://www.crin.org
Email: info@crin.org

Instituto Nacional de las Mujeres [National Institute of Women]
Alfonso Esparza Oteo #119, Col. Guadalupe Inn
Delegación Alvaro Obregón
Mexico, D.F., C.P. 01020
Phone: (52 55) 5322-4200
Web site: http://www.inmujeres.gob.mx
Email: contacto@inmjeres.mx
Public autonomous institution in Mexico created in 2001 to advance the rights of
    women through a number of programs fostering nondiscrimination, a fund to finance
    specific development projects, a program to eliminate violence against women, and a
    program to institutionalize gender equitable approaches in government initiatives.

Programa Infancia, Universidad Autónoma Metropolitana [Childhood Program of
    the Universidad Autónoma Metropolitana]
Prol. Canal de Miramontes 3855
Col. Ex-Hacienda de San Juan de Diós
Tlalpan
Mexico, D.F., C.P. 14387
Phone: (52 55) 5673-6088
Web site: http://www.uam.mx/cdi
Email: infancia@correo.uam.mx
A program at the Universidad Autónoma Metropolitana to advance interdisciplinary
    research and education programs to advance the goals of the Convention on the
    Rights of the Child. This program has established a number of interinstitutional
    networks to follow-up programs aimed at advancing children's rights in Mexico.

Red por los Derechos de la Infancia en México [Network for the Rights of Children
    in Mexico]
Av. México-Coyoacán 350
Col. General Anaya

México D.F., CP 03340

Phone: (52 55) 5604-2466 / (52 55) 5604-3239 / (52 55) 5604-2458

Web site: http://www.derechosinfancia.org.mx

Email: buzon@derechosinfancia.org.mx

This is a coalition of sixty-two nongovernmental organizations developing programs in favor of children and adolescents at risk in thirteen Mexican states. This network was established in 2001, although several of the organizations in the coalition began to join efforts in 1995. Information site devoted to child rights with publications, news, and events. Supported by UNICEF, Save the Children.

Save the Children

Web site: http://www.savethechildren.net/alliance/where_we_work/MC/mapMX.html

UNICEF Mexico

Phone: (52 55) 5284-9530

Web site: http://www.unicef.org/mexico/spanish/index.html

Email: mexico@unicef.org

UNICEF has been active in Mexico since 1954; its expansive program in Mexico responds to five-year plans developed in coordination with the consultative council in the country.

Selected Bibliography

Banco de Mexico. 2006. *Directorio de Cuadros y Estructuras de Información* Directory of Tables and Information Structures]. http://www.banxico.org.mx/SieInternet/consultarDirectorioInternetAction.do?accion=consultarDirectorioCuadros&sector=4&sectorDescripcion=Banco%20de%20M%C3%A9xico&locale=es.

Bracho, Teresa. 2000. "Poverty and Education in Mexico, 1984–1996." pp. 248–289 in *Unequal Schools, Unequal Chances. The Challenges to Equal Opportunity in the Americas*. Edited by Fernando Reimers. Cambridge, MA: Harvard University Press.

Comisión Nacional para el Desarrollo de los Pueblos Indígenas de México. 2006. *Informe sobre desarrollo humano de los pueblos indígenas de México 2006* [National Comission for the Development of Indigenous People in Mexico. 2006. Report on the human development of indigenous people in Mexico 2006.] Mexico D.F.: CDI-PNUD. http://cdi.gob.mx/index.php?id_seccion=1916.

Consejo Nacional de Población. 2005. *Índices de marginación, 2005. Colección: Índices Sociodemográficos* [National Population Council. Indices of marginalization, 2005. Series: Sociodemographic Indices]. Mexico D.F.: CONAPO.

———. 2006. *Proyecciones de la población en México, 2000–2050* [Population Projections in Mexico, 2000–2050]. http://www.conapo.gob.mx/00cifras/5.htm. Accessed December 3, 2006.

———. 2006. Instituto Nacional de Estadística, Geografía e Informática, and COL-MEX. *Conciliación demográfica 2000–2005* [National Institute of Statistics, Geography and Informatics and Colmex. Demographic Integration 2000–2005]. Mexico: CONAPO, INEGI, COLMEX.

Cox, C., R. Jaramillo, and F. Reimers. 2005. *Education and Democratic Citizenship in Latin America and the Caribbean*. Washington, DC: InterAmerican Development Bank.

Del Razo Martínez, Lilia M. 2003. *Estudio de la brecha salarial entre hombres y mujeres en México (1994-2001).* Serie: documentos de investigación. Mexico, D.F.: Secretaría de Desarrollo Social. [Study of the wage gap between men and women in Mexico (1994–2001). Series: Research Documents.] Mexico, D.F.: Secretary of Social Development.

DIF, PNUFID, and UNICEF (Desarrollo Integral de la Familia, Programa de las Naciones Unidas para la Fiscalización de Drogras, and UNICEF) 2002. *Estudio de niñas, niños, y adolescentes trabajadores en 100 ciudades.* [Integral Development of the Family, United Nations Program for Drug Control. 2002. Study of working girls, boys and adolescents in 100 cities]. Mexico, D.F.: DIF, PNUFID and UNICEF.

Frenk, Julio. 2006a. "Bridging the Divide: Global Lessons from Evidence-Based Gender Differences in Mexico." In *The Economics of Gender in Mexico: Work, Family, State and Market.* Edited by E.G Katz and M.C. Correia. Washington, DC: World Bank.

———. 2006b. "Health Policy in Mexico." *The Lancet* 368 (September 9): 954–961.

Frenk, J., J. L. Bobadilla, J. Sepúlveda, and M. López-Cervantes. 1989. "Health Transition in Middle-Income Countries: New Challenges for Health Care." *Health Policy and Planning* 4: 29–39.

Gobierno del Distrito Federal, UNICEF, Desarrollo Integral de la Familia-DF. [Government of the Federal District, UNICEF, and Integral Development of the Family-DF] 1999. *Niños, niñas y jóvenes trabajadores en el Distrito Federal* [Boys, girls, and working youth in Mexico City]. Mexico, D.F.: DIF.

Instituto Nacional de Estadística, Geografía e Informática (INEGI). 2000a. *Módulo de Empleo Infantil 1999.* [National Institute of Statistics, Geography and Informatics. 2000a. Module on working children 1999] Aguascalientes: INEGI.

———. 2000b. *XII Censo Nacional de Población y Vivienda.* [XII Census of Population and Homes]. http://www.inegi.gob.mx/est/default.aspx?c=701

———. 2002. *Encuesta Nacional de Empleo 2001* [National Survey of Work 2001]. Aguascalientes: INEGI.

———. 2004a. *El trabajo infantil en México 1995–2002* [Children's work in Mexico 1995–2002]. Aguascalientes: INEGI.

———. 2004b. *Encuesta Nacional de Ingresos y Gastos de los Hogares 2004* [National Survey of Family Income and Expenditures 2004]. http://www.inegi.gob.mx/inegi/contenidos/espanol/prensa/Contenidos/estadisticas/2005/enighs.pdf

———. 2005a. *Encuesta Nacional de Ocupación y Empleo* [National Survey of Occupation and Employment]. Aguascalientes: INEGI.

———. 2005b. *Principales resultados por localidad 2005 (ITER),* [Main results by locality 2005]. Aguascalientes: INEGI, México http://www.inegi.gob.mx/est/contenidos/espanol/sistemas/conteo2005/localidad/iter/default.asp?c=7328

———. 2006a. *México de un vistazo. Edición 2006* [Mexico at a glance. 2006 Edition]. Aguascalientes: INEGI.

———. 2006b. *Conteo de Población y Vivienda, 2005. Resultados definitivos* [Count of Population and Homes, 2005. Definitive Results]. Aguascalientes: INEGI.

———. 2006c. *Mujeres y hombres en México 2006* [Women and men in Mexico 2006]. 10th ed. Aguascalientes: INEGI.

———. 2006d. *Estadísticas Económicas. Producto Interno Bruto Trimestral. Agosto, 2006* [Economic Statistics. Trimestral Gross National Product. August, 2006]. http://www.inegi.gob.mx/est/contenidos/espanol/temas/economicas/intro_economicas.asp?c=125.

Instituto Nacional de la Juventud. Encuesta Nacional de la Juventud 2005–2006 [National Institute of Youth. National Survey of Youth 2005–2006]. http://www.injuventud.gob.mx/main.asp. Accessed December 13, 2006.

Instituto Nacional para la Evaluación de la Educación. [National Institute for the Evaluation of Education]. 2004. *Pruebas de Estándares Nacionales.* [Database of Tests of National Standards].

———. 2006. *Indicadores del Sistema Educativo Nacional 2006* [Indicators of the National Education System 2006]. http://www.inee.edu.mx/images/stories/Panorama2006/01-panorama%202006%20web.pdf

Knaul, Felicia M. 1995. *Young Workers, Street Life and Gender: The Effect of Education and Work Experience on Earnings in Colombia.* PhD Thesis, Harvard University.

Knaul, Felicia, and Carlos Santos-Burgoa, Z. 2006. "Más allá de la sobrevivencia: niñas, niños y jóvenes que viven con enfermedad, grupo prioritario para la inclusión educativa." [Beyond Survival: Girls, Boys and Youth Living with Illness, Priority Group for Educational Inclusión]. Ch. 2 in *Inclusión educativa para niños, niñas y jóvenes hospitalizados: Un análisis basado en el progama nacional de México SIGAMOS Aprendiendo en el Hospital.* [Educational inclusion for hospitalized boys, girls and youth: an analysis based in the national program of Mexico continue learning in the hospital]. Edited by Felicia Knaul, Celia Pérez, María Suárez, and Sonia Ortega. México, D.F.: Fondo de Cultura Económica e Intersistemas.

Levison, Deborah, Karine S. Moe, and Felicia M. Knaul. 2001. "Youth Education and Work in Mexico." *World Development* 29, no. 1: 167–188.

Omran, A.R. 1971. "The Epidemiologic Transition: A Theory of the Epidemiology of Population Change." *Milibank Memorial Fund Quarterly* 49: 509–538.

Organization for Economic Cooperation and Development (OECD). 2005. Education at a Glance. http://www.oecd.org/document/34/0,2340,en_2649_34515_35289570_1_1_1_1,00.html.

Parker, Susan, and Emmanuel Skoufias. 2000. *The Impact of PROGRESA on Work, Leisure and Time Allocation.* Washington, DC: International Food Policy Research Institute.

Robles Berlanga, F. 2000. "El trabajo infantil urbano informal en la Ciudad de México." [Urban Informal Child Labor in Mexico City] *Revista Mexicana del Trabajo* no. 2, second semester: 116–118.

Secretaría de Desarrollo Social, 2006. *Pasos firmes para un major país, Informe Anual 2005, Un México Apropiado para la Infancia y la Adolescencia, Programa de Acción, 2002–2010* [Firm steps for a better country. Annual Report 2005. An Appropriate Mexico for Children and Adolescents, Action Program, 2002–2010]. México, D.F.: Secretaria de Desarrollo Social.

———. 2002. Secretaría de Educación Pública, Secretaría de Salud. *Un México apropiado para la infancia y la adolescencia, Programa de Acción 2002–2010* [An Appropriate Mexico for Children and Adolescents. Action Program 2002–2010]. Mexico: SEDESOL.

———. 2005. Secretaría de Educación Pública, Secretaría de Salud. *Informe Anual 2004. Un México apropiado para la infancia y la adolescencia, Programa de Acción 2002–2010* [Firm steps for a better country. Annual Report 2004. An appropriate Mexico for children and adolescents. Action Program, 2002–2010]. Mexico: SEDESOL.

Secretaría de Educación Pública (SEP). 2006. *Plan Nacional de Educación 2001–2006* [Secretary of Public Education. 2006. National Education Plan 2001–2006]. Mexico, D.F.: SEP.

————. 2006. Dirección General de Planeación y Programación. *Sistema educativo de los Estados Unidos Mexicano, principales cifras ciclo escolar 2004–2005* [General Directorate of Planning and Budgeting. 2006. Education System of the United States of Mexico]. México: SEP.

Secretaría de Gobernación. 2006. *Constitución Política de los Estados Unidos Mexicanos* [Secretary of the Interior. 2006. Political Constitution of the United States of Mexico], updated with the published reform in September 14, 2006. http://www.gobernacion.gob.mx. Accessed December 3, 2006.

Secretaría de Salud, 2006. Salud México 2000–2005, Información para la Rendición de Cuentas [Secretary of Health. 2006. Health Mexico 2000–2005, Information for Accountability]. México D.F.: Secretaria de Salud.

Sepúlveda, Jaime, Flavio Bustreo, Roberto Tapia, Juan Rivera et al. 2006. "Improvement of Child Survival in Mexico: the Diagonal Approach." *The Lancet* 368, December 2: 2017–2027.

Tuirán Gutiérrez, Alejandro. 2006. *La desigualdad en la distribución del ingreso monetario en México* [Inequality in income distribution in Mexico]. Mexico, D.F.: CONAPO.

UNICEF and DIF. 2000. *Programa para la Prevención, Atención, Desaliento y Erradicación del Trabajo Infantil Urbano Marginal* [Program for the Prevention, Attention, Discouragement and Elimination of Child Work in Urban Marginal Areas]. Mexico, D.F.: UNICEF, DIF.

UNICEF, DIF, and CIESAS. 2000. *Infancia robada. Niños y niñas víctimas de explotación sexual en México* [Stolen childhood. boys and girls, victims of sexual exploitation in Mexico]. Mexico, D.F.: UNICEF, DIF, CIESAS.

Vidal, Rafael, and M.A. Díaz. 2004. *Resultados de las Pruebas PISA 2000 y 2003 en México*, Instituto Nacional para la Evaluación de la Educación, México [Results of the PISA tests 2000 and 2003 in Mexico. National Institute for the Evaluation of Education, Mexico].

World Bank. 2005. *Generación de ingreso y protección social para los pobres* [Income generation and social protection for the poor]. Mexico: World Bank.

————. 2006. *World Development Indicators Database*. Washington, DC: World Bank.

11

PUERTO RICO

Ruth Nina Estrella

NATIONAL PROFILE

Childhood in Puerto Rico has many dimensions and is affected by quite diverse social realities. Children are one of the population groups that have experienced major transformations in recent decades. However, looking at the available literature on children in Puerto Rico, there seems to be a very small number of publications dedicated to the topic. This is odd because this population group has been identified as one that most requires attention and effort to satisfy its needs.

Puerto Rico is the westernmost and smallest of the Major Antilles, with a surface area of 9,104 square kilometers. The country also includes the islands of Vieques, Culebra, and Mona, as well as various islets. Puerto Rico is located to the east of the Dominican Republic and to the west of The British Virgin Islands. As part of the decisions made at the close of the Spanish-American War in 1898, Puerto Rico became part of the territory of the United States, but with the status of a colony. In terms of the political relationship with the United States, Puerto Rico became the "Free Associated State of Puerto Rico." This status means that the United States has jurisdiction over every political, social, or economic issue with regard to

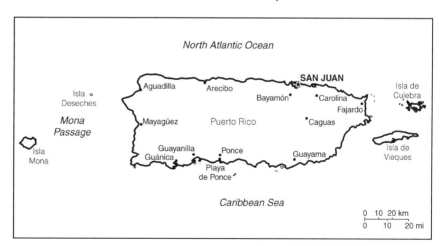

Puerto Rico. The Puerto Rican government is composed of legislative, executive, and judicial branches, and the official language is Spanish.

In 2004, the population of Puerto Rico was over 3.9 million. The Puerto Rican population resident in the United States was more than 4.3 million persons. Puerto Rico is 94 percent urbanized and only 6 percent rural. The annual rate of population growth was 0.47 percent. Life expectancy is 81.77 years for women and 73.67 years for men, with an average of 77.62 years for both groups (Informe del Gobierno de Puerto Rico, 2006). According to the 2000 Census data, the median age is thirty-two years, which means that the Puerto Rico population is primarily an adult population. In terms of race, according to the census of 2000, 80.5 percent of the population self-identified as white, 8 percent as black or Afroamerican, and 2 percent claimed Asian descent.

The 2000 census reports that foreign national residents in Puerto Rico are 3 percent of the total population. This figure reflects a 37 percent growth of the foreign population reported in the 1990 census. There was also a change in the percentage of the resident population of foreign nationals from Latin America. In 1990, 83 percent of foreign nationals residing in Puerto Rico were from Latin America, while in 2000 this figure had grown to 91 percent. The municipalities with the largest concentrations of foreign residents are San Juan, Guaynabo, Bayamón, and Carolina [Informe del Gobierno de Puerto Rico 2006].

Puerto Rico is a society with a variety of family structures, among which the nuclear family model of mother, father, and children predominates. The census estimate of 2000 is that 69 percent of Puerto Rican children live in families composed of married couples (U.S. Census Bureau 2000; Informe de la Oficina del Censo 2006). In addition to

Table 11.1.
Demographic Summary, 2003

Category	Number
Total population	3,878,532
Births	50,803
Deaths	28,356
Child deaths	498
Neonatal deaths	363
Postneonatal deaths	131
Fetal deaths	548
Maternal deaths	7
Marriages	25,236
Marriage rate	7
Divorces	14,225
Divorce rate	5

Source: Departamento de Salud (2003).

married-couple families, there are other family structures in which minors live with a female head of household (no husband or male partner present), grandchildren live with grandparents, or children live with a relative or guardian. Children may also live in reconstituted families (divorced parents remarry and stepparents, stepsisters, or stepbrothers may be present) and homosexual (gay and lesbian) families.

These new family structures demonstrate the multiplicity of socially constructed meanings of "family" and the break with the traditional views of family established by dominant ideologies (Nina 2001). The constructions of childhood and adolescence in Puerto Rico are also based on this changing set of assumptions.

Puerto Rico is composed of seventy-eight municipalities, located geographically in both urban and rural zones. In 2003, 48.1 percent of the population was male and 51.9 percent female (Informe del Gobierno de Puerto Rico 2006). Puerto Rico is considered to be one of the most densely populated areas in the world, with over 1,100 persons per square mile. The average annual family income is US$16,543 per year. Statistics show that in the year 2000, 31.4 percent of Puerto Rican families had an annual income of less than US$10,000 (Colón 2006).

There were 8,418 homeless people in Puerto Rico in 2003. Of these, 152 were minors eighteen years old or younger; the highest numbers are found in the municipalities of San Juan (the capital of Puerto Rico; 37), Ponce (24), Arecibo (25), and Humacao (20) (Departamento de la Familia 2003).

The Administration of Family and Children (ADFAN) of the Department of the Family is the principal government organization in charge of programs for the care, development, and protection of children and teenagers. It also intervenes in cases of adoption, mistreatment, or abandonment of a minor (Departamento de la Familia 2002).

KEY FACTS – PUERTO RICO

Population: 3,944,259 (July 2007 est.)
Infant mortality rate: 7.81 deaths/1,000 live births (2007 est.)
Life expectancy at birth: 78 years (2007 est.)
Literacy rate: 94.1 percent (2002 est.)
Internet users: 1 million (2005 est.)

Sources: CIA World Factbook: Puerto Rico. https://www.cia.gov/cia/publications/factbook/geos/rq.html. April 17, 2007.

ADFAN programs are directed toward the development of the self-sufficiency of individuals and families and promote their active integration in society. Among these programs are the Social Emergencies Program, Family Services for the Disabled, and educational and prevention programs that promote the comprehensive development of children.

OVERVIEW

In 2000, there were 1,092,101 children eighteen years old or younger in Puerto Rico. This represents 29 percent of the entire population (U.S.

Table 11.2.
Population of Children in Puerto Rico by Gender and Age, 2000

Age (in years)	Total	%	Female	%	Male	%
Under 5	295,406	27.1	144,119	13.2	151,287	13.2
5–9	305,162	27.9	305,162	13.6	156,253	14.3
10–14	305,800	28.0	149,816	13.7	155,984	14.3
15–17	185,733	17.0	90,678	8.3	95,055	8.7
Total	1,092,101	100.0	533,522	48.9	558,579	51.1

Source: Consejo Nacional de la Raza (2004) and United States Census Bureau (2000).

Census Bureau 2000). In other words, approximately three of every ten Puerto Ricans are eighteen years old or younger. It is interesting to note that the entire population of children living in Puerto Rico has not increased during recent decades, as has been the case in other countries of the region. The breakdown of population by age groups is shown in Table 11.2.

According to the National Council of La Raza (Consejo Nacional de la Raza 2004), among all municipalities of Puerto Rico, Hormigueros and Mayagüez have the smallest populations of children, while Barranquitas, Loiza, Morovis, and Peñuelas have the largest populations of children. The possible reasons for the lack of growth in the number of children in Puerto Rico are several. These include the following: (1) the general socio-demographic changes in the population pyramid; (2) the transformation of society into a proportionally older one, in terms of age groups; (3) the decline of the fertility rate; and (4) Puerto Rican migration to United States.

In 2003, the total number of live births was 50,803, reflecting a slight decrease compared with 52,871 children born in 2002. Most of these births were in public and private hospitals, and a few were home births. Of the 50,803 live births, 26,191 were male (51.6 percent) and 24,612 (48.4 percent) were female, demonstrating a small difference by sex. The municipalities with fewer births were Culebra (23), Maricao (74), and Las Marías (114). Those with the most births were San Juan (6,467), Bayamón (4,460), and Ponce (2,985). In terms of anomalies at birth, only 443 children had birth defects. The principal problems included urogenital anomalies (3.6 percent), harelip (2.7 percent), muscular and skeletal problems (2.3 percent), and circulatory or respiratory anomalies (2.0 percent) (Departamento de Salud 2003).

With regard to the method of childbirth, of the total number of live births, 53.9 percent (27,360) were born by means of vaginal childbirth and 46.1 percent (23,443) by cesarean section. Nearly 40 percent (39.9 percent) of infants were born with an average weight between six and seven pounds. Of women giving birth, only 182 (4 percent) were younger than fifteen years old, and 8,817 (17.4 percent) were between fifteen and nineteen years old, with the majority of their childbirths being of the vaginal type (Departamento de Salud 2003).

Table 11.3.
Ten Leading Causes of Child Deaths, 2003

Cause of death	Number of deaths	Percentage of deaths
Disorders related to short gestation and malnutrition	194	39.0
Congenital malformations, deformities, and chromosomal anomalies	70	14.1
Other respiratory problems originating in the perinatal period	29	5.8
Bacterial sepsis in newborn	26	5.2
Newborns affected by maternal factors	22	4.4
Other perinatal conditions	22	4.4
Other unspecified respiratory problems	15	3.0
Influenza and pneumonia	12	2.4
Circulatory illnesses	11	2.2
Respiratory difficulty in newborn	10	2.0
Illnesses of the digestive tract	10	2.0
Endocrine, nutritional, and metabolic illnesses	10	2.0
Other causes	67	13.5

Source: Departamento de Salud (2003).

In Puerto Rico, as in other countries, the principal causes of mortality are cancer and cardiovascular illnesses. The total number of infant deaths in 2003 was 518 (1.02 percent) of the 50,803 live births, with a higher number of males (288) compared with females who died (210) (Departamento de Salud 2003). The main causes of infant mortality were short gestation and malnutrition (39 percent). Table 11.3 lists the ten principal causes of child deaths. Considering the stage of life, 363 were neonatal deaths caused by disorders related to short gestation and malnutrition (52.1 percent), while the 131 cases of postneonatal deaths were caused by congenital malformations (19.8 percent), respiratory problems (11.5 percent), and circulatory illness (8.4 percent).

EDUCATION

The Puerto Rican educational system is constituted by four levels of schooling: preschool, elementary, intermediate, and higher education. Over time there has been a consistent pattern of higher enrollments in the public school system than in private schools. In 2004–2005, 81 percent of students were registered in the public schools. The total number of registered students in that school year was 715,978, with 581,150 enrolled in the public school system and 134,828 enrolled in private schools. The largest number of registered students is seen at the elementary level, and the number of students enrolled decreases at each subsequent level of education (Table 11.4).

Table 11.4.
Students in Public and Private School Systems, 2004–2005

		Number		Percentage	
	Total	Public sector	Private sector	Public sector	Private sector
Regular academic services	715,978	581,150	134,828	81	19
Preschool	62,639	40,500	22,139	65	35
Elementary	334,759	273,350	61,409	82	18
Intermediate	165,662	138,050	27,612	83	17
Superior	152,918	129,250	23,668	85	15

Source: Informe del Departamento de Educación (2005).

One of the causes for decreasing enrollments in higher levels of education is student dropout. In the 2001–2002 school year, a total of 2,013 students dropped out of the public school system (Consejo Nacional de la Raza 2004). A comparison of dropouts by gender shows quite similar proportions, with 1,419 males and 1,262 females leaving school. It is at the high school level where the largest number of dropouts is observed, with 1,272 students leaving school out of a total of 93,684 registered high school students. Of students who begin elementary school, 51 percent do not finish high school (Informe del Departamento de Educación 2005). The reasons for this high rate of desertion include the need to work, pregnancy, and the social environment at school (e.g., violence).

Pregnant students present another problem in the school system. The number of student pregnancies has remained consistent in recent years, with the highest rates at the high school level. Table 11.5 shows the number of pregnancies among students in the 1999–2000 and 2001–2002 school terms.

In recent years, school violence, defined in terms of behaviors considered to be violent, has increased by 50 percent. For example, in 2002 1,320 violent situations were reported, and in 2005 reported violent situations numbered 3,038. The main behaviors observed in 2005 were simple aggression (1,563), physical aggression (324), and disturbing the

Table 11.5.
Pregnant Students

	2001–2002	2000–2001	1999–2000
Total	1,356	1,028	1,400
Elementary	5	4	12
Intermediate	244	203	265
Superior	1,037	774	1,112

Source: Departamento de Educación, Servicios Complementarios.

Table 11.6.
Violence in Schools by Educational Level, 2001–2002 School Year

Incidents	School level		
	Elementary	Intermediate	High school
Total incidents	232	361	408
Aggravated assault	15	12	12
Simple aggression	151	205	218
Drugs	0	3	18
Weapons	2	14	17
Threats	18	42	40
Riots	0	0	5
Disturbing the peace	36	84	92
Explosives	2	1	2
Lascivious acts, rape, exhibitionism	8	0	4

Source: Policía de Puerto Rico, Programa de Calidad de Vida Escolar.

peace (341). When school violence is analyzed by level, the statistics show that 408 violent acts were committed in high schools, 361 in intermediate schools, and 232 in elementary schools (Table 11.6). As a response to school violence, conflict mediation programs have been created as a school-level prevention strategy.

PLAY AND RECREATION

In contemporary Puerto Rico, some thirty-five sports disciplines are practiced, among them basketball, baseball, volleyball, swimming, karate, soccer, chess, boxing, and cycling. The most popular are basketball and baseball.

The Department of Sports and Recreation manages programs that are developed specifically for children, such as the Open Intramural School Sports League in which the student body at the intermediate level is offered a high-quality and well-organized sports experience as a preventive measure. The league follows the standards of competition endorsed by the organizations that oversee sports in Puerto Rico as part of the National Sports Plan. Its objectives are to provide a sports milieu that encourages healthy competition and prevents the consumption and abuse of drugs and alcohol. Students at the intermediate level participate in volleyball, softball, cross country, basketball, chess, table tennis, and track and field.

With regard to recreational activities in the home, 97 percent of Puerto Rican homes have at least one television (Meléndez 1989). With approximately six hours of viewing as a daily average, watching television is one of the activities preferred by family members. In terms of the activities and habits of Puerto Rico adolescents, 40 percent visit a fast-food restaurant two or three times a week, 27 percent eat fast food at least once a week, and 9 percent visit a fast-food restaurant every day. Adolescents spend a considerable amount of time watching television. Research shows that 44 percent watch television three or four hours a day, 32 percent watch four to five hours a day, and 24 percent watch six or more hours a day (Oficina del Gobernador para el Fortalecimiento de la Familia 1987). With regard to the Internet, 58 percent of adolescents have access to and use the Internet for entertainment and for school work that requires searching for information. The study of the aspirations and free-time preferences of youth by Arteaga and Arteaga (1999) reported that 93 percent of the youth interviewed hoped to continue with university studies, 62 percent preferred watching television, 38 percent listening to the radio, and 24 percent using the Internet. For 49 percent of the youth in the study, going to the movies was the preferred activity outside the home.

CHILD LABOR

The Constitution of Puerto Rico establishes the basic prohibition against child labor. Section 15 states, "The employment of children less than fourteen years of age in any occupation which is prejudicial to their health or morals or which places them in jeopardy of life or limb is prohibited" (Constitución del Estado Libre Asociado de Puerto Rico 2003). In Puerto Rico, specific laws regarding child labor standards for those under eighteen who do work are similar to state laws in the United States. For example, as of January 1, 2007, the maximum hours of work in non-farm employment for children under sixteen in Puerto Rico is six on a school day—for a combined eight hours of work and school (eight daily and forty weekly); for minors under the age of sixteen nightwork is prohibited between the hours of 6:00 p.m. and 8:00 a.m. Youth aged sixteen and seventeen may work a maximum of eight hours a day and forty hours a week; nightwork is prohibited between 10:00 p.m. and 6:00 a.m. (U.S. Department of Labor 2007).

According to a study of a representative sample of 4,591 youths between thirteen and twenty-six years old, issued in a government report entitled *Profiles and Needs of Puerto Rican Youth,* one of every three (1,582 or 34.5 percent) is working or on a salary (Consultores en Conducta Humana, Inc. 2003). It is important to note that seven of every ten youths interviewed were eighteen or older, which doubled the proportion of the participants that were working. Of the 1,582 youths who identified as working or salaried, 36.7 percent (580) were engaged in professional or administrative work. Another 668 (42.8 percent) worked in the area of services or sales, while 334 youth (21.1 percent) were employed as skilled, semi-skilled, or unskilled workers.

The average (median) monthly income of the 3,362 youths that reported receiving some income was $504 (Consultores de Conducta Humana, Inc. 2003). This reported monthly income is 64.6 percent below the level of poverty established by the U.S. Census for 2002, which was $9,359 for a single person or a monthly income of $780. One of every four youths of the 4,591 in the study reported receiving $250 or less each month (1,190 or 25.9 percent), this being the modal category. One of every ten youths (486 or 10 percent) received between $251 and $500 each month, and one of every thirteen youths (350 or 7.6 percent) had a monthly income between $501 and $750. One of every ten youths (483 or 10.5 percent) in the study reported a monthly income between $751 and $1,000. Only 18.6 percent (853 youths) reported having a monthly income between $1,001 and $5,000. The rest of the youths in the study (1,229 or 26.8 percent) reported having no monthly income whatsoever (Consultores de Conducta Humana, Inc. 2003).

FAMILY

According to the 2000 census, the average size of the family in Puerto Rico is three people. The majority of children live in compound families (69 percent) composed of married couples, and 27 percent live in female-headed single-parent families, as shown in Table 11.7.

More than 44 percent (44.6 percent) of the child population live in homes that are below the level of poverty (Colón 2006). At the same time, 61 percent of families headed by single females live below the poverty line. The municipalities with the highest rates of poverty were Orocovis, Maricao, Las Marías, Lares, Adjuntas, Vieques, and Utuado. According to the distribution among municipalities, it appears that the tendencies of poverty in Puerto Rico are higher in the rural areas (mountains) and lower in the urban areas of the country.

Table 11.7.
Children by Age and Family Type

Age (in years)	Total	Married couple	Male, female absent	Female, male absent
Less than 3	136,211	105,394	5,127	25,690
3–4	99,789	71,470	3,384	24,935
5	51,371	36,490	1,717	13,164
6–11	325,693	225,032	10,684	89,977
12–13	110,125	74,506	3,701	31,918
14	54,899	36,947	1,929	16,023
15–17	157,304	106,142	5,697	45,465

Source: U.S. Census Bureau (2000).

The need for child care in Puerto Rico—that is, care for children aged six and younger when parents are in the workforce—is much lower than in the United States. In Puerto Rican society, cultural practices make it common that a family member, in particular the grandparents, provides the needed childcare when the parents work, and in many homes the grandparents are the principal providers of care for small children.

In 2001–2002, 353 adoptions were granted out of 1,084 applications. Of these, 805 (74 percent) were evaluated, and 279 (26 percent) were left pending. This last number is smaller but nevertheless significant compared with the 451 cases left pending in 1999–2000 and the 399 left pending in 2000–2001. The cities with the most adoptions were Bayamón (80), Arecibo (48), and Caguas (40). The cities with the fewest adoptions were Guayama (11), Humacao (24), and Aguadilla (25) (Departamento de la Familia 2002).

HEALTH

The prevention of infectious diseases in children is organized through the immunization program of the Puerto Rican Department of Health. Successful coverage is one of the major achievements of the Puerto Rican medical community. The immunization program has been so effective that it has reduced significantly many of the most common childhood diseases. Because Puerto Rico is a U.S. territory, its child health programs respond to the Centers for Disease Control and Prevention, to the American Academy of Pediatrics, and to the American Academy of Family Physicians. In Puerto Rico, the immunization program aims to prevent illnesses like polio, measles, diphtheria, whooping cough, rubella (German measles), mumps, tetanus, invasive pneumococcal disease, hepatitis B, chicken pox, and *Haemphilus influenza* type b. The program promotes parental awareness of child immunization schedules according to age. Each child has a record stating when each vaccine is administered, and there are national immunization campaigns. Children must have their appropriate vaccinations in order to enroll in the educational system.

Puerto Rican children present specific health problems, such as obesity and asthma, with higher frequency than in other countries. According to the Department of Health, one-third of Puerto Rican children are overweight (*Primera Hora* 2006). The figures show that 32 percent of the child population between four and twenty-four months of age is in this situation, in contrast with the 10 to 20 percent of the similar child population in the United States. In adolescents between the ages of twelve and sixteen, the problem is seen in a 33.2 percent rate in obesity level I and 14.2 percent in level II. These represent slight to moderate levels of obesity. Among the identified causes of obesity are the absence of a balanced diet (and the related excessive consumption of junk food or fried food), exaggerated portions when eating a meal, and lack of physical activity or sedentary lifestyle. Gender differences have been identified with regard to the obesity problem; girls exceed the measure of body mass (30 percent) more than the boys (25 percent) and, from the age of eight, boys exceed the North American percentages. Currently, a national campaign against obesity is under way.

The second most frequent health problem of children in Puerto Rico is asthma. The Environmental Protection Agency (EPA) reports that Puerto Rico has the highest asthma-related mortality rate in the United States (Rivera 2006). Research has demonstrated that the estimated incidence of asthma in Puerto Rico is 20 percent of the entire population. Also, Puerto Ricans have the highest number of hospitalizations and visits to emergency rooms because of asthma attacks. The Department of Health reports that, in some parts of the island, the situation is worrisome because one in two children visits the emergency room with asthma-related problems annually. The towns with the most cases are Caguas and those in the center region of the country. It is believed that, among the causes or reasons for this high incidence of asthma, there may be a genetic disposition that could incapacitate those who suffer asthma attacks. Although the country does not have the serious problems of air contamination that plague other countries, factors that contribute to asthmatic conditions include high levels of humidity, fungi, mold, cockroaches, mites, the involuntary inhalation of cigarette smoke, pet dandruff, and the inhalation of chemical products used for cleaning that are spilled in large quantities, and other factors found inside children's homes.

Other conditions that are seen as health problems but to a lesser extent are ear infections and developmental disorders. In the latter category, problems of language and the motor system are prominent. Gastroenteritis or intestine and stomach inflammation is a frequent cause for illness, usually caused by a virus or a bacterium.

Another worrisome problem for the medical profession is car accidents and daily life accidents. Car accidents are associated with the failure to use protective car seats or seat belts. According to studies, the majority of car accidents usually occur in a 10-mile radius from home. Other common accidents, excluding intentional habitual injuries, include falls and fractures while in play areas, drowning in swimming pools or wash buckets, and poisoning.

In the 2000 census, thirty-three cases of HIV infections were reported in the birth to nine years age group, consisting of twenty-four males and nine females. These cases comprise 9 percent of the total number of cases of HIV. In the ten to nineteen years age group, 137 cases were reported (sixty males and seventy-seven females), which reflects a slight increase in female adolescents with HIV. Regarding pediatric cases of AIDS, 460 cases were reported in 2006, the principal causes being hemophilic disorder and coagulation (10), mothers infected with HIV (420), blood donation (18), and nonidentified risks (12).

The prevalence rate in Puerto Rico of people with severe mental illness and children with severe emotional disturbances is estimated by the *Federal Register* using the standardized norms of the Center for Mental Health Services. The most recent epidemiological study of children and adolescents in Puerto Rico (Canino et al. 2003), conducted in 2000 with children between the ages of four and seventeen (a total of 856,877) (U.S. Census Bureau 2000), showed that around 16.4 percent or 140,528 children and adolescents fit the diagnostic criteria of mental disorders of the *Diagnostic and Statistical Manual of Mental Disorders*, 4th Edition, Text Revision (DSM-IV-TR; American Psychiatric Association 2000) showing slight to moderate impediments. At the same time, 59,125 children and adolescents, or 6.9 percent, demonstrated the symptoms of severe emotional disturbance. In the fiscal year 2003, 32,521 children with mental health problems were attended by the government services of Administración de Servicios de Salud Mental y Contra la Adicción (ASSMCA, Mental Health and Anti-Addiction Services Administration).

The use of substances is the most alarming sociomedical problem in Puerto Rico, especially in adolescents and young adults. The government considers it to be a matter of public policy, and one with great urgency today. There has been a change in the patterns of substance consumption over the last three decades, including the increasing use of cocaine at the beginning of the 1980s and the use of crack in the 1990s. More recently, there has been an increase in the so-called designer drugs (for example, ecstasy). As part of one of the preventive measures the government has taken with regard to adolescent consumption patterns, it has created the poll program known as Consulta Juvenil 2002 (Moscoso, Colón, Parrilla, and Reyes 2003). Students from fifth grade to high school participate in the poll. Below is a summary of the findings of the most recent poll.

Findings Summary (2002)
Preadolescent–elementary school (fifth to sixth grade)

- The substances most used on a one-time basis were alcohol (34.4 percent), cigarettes (6.1 percent), and inhalants (2.7 percent).
- Sixth-grade students reported more use of cigarettes and alcohol than fifth-grade students.
- Boys reported more use of cigarettes and alcohol than girls.
- Between 1997–1998 and 2000–2002, there was a decrease in the use of cigarettes.

Intermediate school (seventh to ninth grade)

- The substances most used on a one-time basis were alcohol (43.6 percent) and cigarettes (16.2 percent).

- A total of 6.9 percent report having used other illicit drugs, with marijuana (4.3 percent) and inhalants (3.2 percent) the most used.
- There was no significant difference between genders in the use of alcohol and other drugs. Males reported more use of cigarettes than females.
- The use of substances increased with school grade, cigarette use (10.8 percent seventh grade, 24.9 percent ninth grade), alcohol (32.2 percent seventh grade, 60.5 percent ninth grade), and other drugs (5.4 percent seventh grade, 10.1 percent ninth grade).
- Between 1997–1998 and 2000–2002, there was a reduction in the use of cigarettes, alcohol, and other drugs.

High school (tenth to twelfth grade)

- A total of 76.2 percent of high school students reported using alcohol once, and 40.8 percent reported cigarette use.
- A total of 20.7 percent reported having used another illicit drug, with marijuana (19.1 percent) and designer drugs (3.8 percent) the most used.
- The use of substances increased with the school grade, use of cigarettes (34.6 percent tenth grade, 49.7 percent twelfth grade), alcohol (71.6 percent tenth grade, 82.8 percent twelfth grade), and other drugs (16.3 percent tenth grade, 26.9 percent twelfth grade).
- Males reported more use of cigarettes, alcohol, and other drugs than females.
- Between 1997–1998 and 2000–2002, a reduction was observed in the use of cigarettes and alcohol, but not in the use of other drugs.

In Puerto Rico, suicide is the third cause of violent death in males aged fifteen to thirty-four. Between 1990 and 2002, a total of 4,117 cases of suicide were reported, with an average of 343 cases per year. The most recent suicide statistics report that in 2005 a total of 321 persons committed suicide (276 males and 45 females). In terms of the child population, in 2005 there were eleven suicides of youths eighteen years old or younger (nine males and two females). In contrast, during the first half of 2006 there were no reported cases of suicide among children. This can be attributed to the prevention campaigns. Nevertheless, when viewed comparatively, it seems clear that the annual rate of suicide is variable. There were twelve reported cases of suicide among youth in 2004, none in 2003, and eight in 2002. Among the more frequently used methods of committing suicide in this population group was the hanging method, especially in the sixteen- and seventeen-year-old age group, where there were four cases of hanging in 2005. Suicides usually happen in the home (62.9 percent) and in the front yard of the house (19 percent) (Departamento de Policía 2005).

LAWS AND LEGAL STATUS

The government of Puerto Rico has passed legislation creating an array of laws that protect minors. First, the constitution of the Estado Libre Asociado (ELA, which incorporated Puerto Rico as an Associated Free State) recognizes the civil rights of this population group. Among its most important provisions is one stating that every person may receive primary and secondary education free of charge, and another stating that every child has a right to be cared for by his/her responsible adult. Other laws include what is known as Bylaw Number 88 of July 9, 1986, which has been amended several times. Bylaw Number 88 is also known as the Minors Law of Puerto Rico, and it stipulates that minors are to receive care, protection, habilitation, and rehabilitation, and that their well-being in the community will be promoted. This law establishes that education will be free of charge, that minors younger than fourteen will not be employed in any occupation prejudicial to their health or morals, and that the incarceration of a minor younger than sixteen years of age is not permitted. A more recent bylaw is Law 177 of 2003 (Child Protection Law for the 21st Century), which derogates Law 342 of 1999. This law promotes the well-being and comprehensive protection of children. It establishes new policy regarding the protection of minors based on an understanding of the integral development of the child. It provides the state's human and family services agency, Departamento de la Familia (ADFAN, Department of the Family), with the power to offer services in cases of child mistreatment and abuse, to remove children from their families, and to define and impose penalties. The Departamento de la Familia is responsible for the welfare, development, and protection of children and adolescents. ADFAN's programs stress self-sufficiency and promote the active integration of individuals and families within Puerto Rican society. According to the Annual Report of the Department of the Family, 34,259 referrals were received for services in 2002; most of these were referrals for situations involving minors (Table 11.8).

Of the total number of referrals to the Department of the Family, grounds were found for ADFAN intervention in 26 percent (9,785) of cases. This means that three of every ten families referred to the department included minors who were victims or at risk of being victims of mistreatment or neglect by their parents or guardians. Of the total referrals (9,785), 22,340 children were involved. The most common form of mistreatment was negligence (55 percent), followed by multiple forms of mistreatment (19 percent), physical (11 percent), and emotional (10 percent).

Of the minors under the care of the Department of the Family, 997 showed problems of social adaptation, retardation, emotional difficulties, educational shortcomings, and special needs. According to the 2002 Annual Report, 9,555 children were removed from their homes.

Table 11.8.
Referrals Investigated with Cause by Category, Fiscal Years 2000–2001
and 2001–2002

Cause	Minors 2000–2001	Minors 2001–2002
Negligence	8,916	12,376
Multiple	3,129	4,181
Emotional	1,932	2,214
Physical	1,565	2,360
Sexual abuse	1,028	1,151
Exploitation	6	58
Total	16,576	22,340

Source: Departamento de la Familia (2002).

RELIGIOUS LIFE

According to the Constitution of the Free Associated State, freedom of religious expression is guaranteed in Puerto Rico. Although there has been a proliferation of religions, Catholicism predominates; two-thirds of the population is Catholic, and among the remaining population, one-third practice Protestantism, Judaism, and Islam (Román, Silva 2006).

The majority of Puerto Rico's private schools are part of the major religious groups, Catholics and Protestants, and offer Christian education as part of the formal curriculum. There are forty-two Catholic schools in the country, offering classes in religion from the preschool level through high school. These classes serve to instruct students in religion and in moral values and are a requirement for all students enrolled in these schools. These schools also urge that all students comply with religious beliefs in terms of rites such as baptism, first communion, and confirmation, as well as attending mass.

Protestant schools also offer religion classes as part of their academic programs. These classes are a requirement for all students enrolled in the school. The religions that predominate in Protestant schools in Puerto Rico are Disciples of Christ, Methodist, Baptist, and Seventh-Day Adventist. Students are required to attend religion classes from preschool through high school, as well as to be baptized in the church.

CHILD ABUSE AND NEGLECT

According to data from the Department of the Family, in 1999–2000 the child maltreatment rate increased from 1.3 to 2.0 percent (2,000 cases) per month. This would translate to 24,000 cases per year, considering the assumption that for every reported case there are three that remain unreported. Of these 24,000 cases, 38 percent are children under the age of five years.

In the last decade, the problem of violence has assumed increasing prominence in Puerto Rico, including its various manifestations within

Table 11.9.
Homicide by Gender and Age (Victims), 2005

Age (in years)	Male	Female
<10	3	2
10–11	0	1
12–13	1	0
14–15	4	0
16–17	13	1
18–19	46	2

Source: Policía de Puerto Rico (2005).

society: homicide, vandalism in schools, domestic violence, and other sorts of violence. Puerto Rico is considered to hold fifth place in the world in terms of violence, according to Comisión para la Prevención de la Violencia (COPREVI, Commission for the Prevention of Violence 2006). In 2005, there were 766 reported deaths from homicide. In terms of population groups, most victims of minor age were concentrated between the ages of eighteen and nineteen years old, totaling forty-eight victims, of which forty-six were male. This increase was also noticeable in the vital statistics report of 2002, where ninety-one deaths by homicide were reported among minors of eighteen years of age. The fifteen- to nineteen-year-old group presented a rate of 27.2 percent, with eighty-three deaths by homicide. In 1999, there were 115 deaths by homicide in the fifteen- to nineteen-year-old group.

GROWING UP IN THE TWENTY-FIRST CENTURY

In reviewing the current status of children in Puerto Rico, it seems clear that there have been major transformations in their situation since the 1950s. An originally agrarian-based society transformed itself into an industrial society. Today's children increasingly grow up in urban landscapes, enjoying the many benefits that cities offer, as well as the problems of city life. Nevertheless, too little is known about both urban and rural children in Puerto Rico, given the scant research and publishing devoted to the topic. This has important repercussions in the implementation of public policy and for educational and prevention programs that address children and the conditions of their present and future lives.

RESOURCE GUIDE

Suggested Readings

Briggs, Laura. 2002. *Reproducing Empire: Race, Sex, Science, and U.S. Imperialism in Puerto Rico.* Berkeley, CA: University of California Press. Briggs' book uses a gender perspective to examine the history of colonial relations between

Puerto Rico and the United States, focusing on motherhood, prostitution, and family and their ideological construction as part of the U.S. imperial project.

Colón, Linda. 2006. *Pobreza en Puerto Rico. Radiografía del Proyecto Americano* [Poverty in Puerto Rico: an x-ray of the American Project]. San Juan: Editorial Luna Nueva. This text presents a panorama of the political–economic situation in Puerto Rico and the very specific characteristics that mark it. The causes of poverty are analyzed, including the poverty generated beginning with the U.S. invasion of 1898 and the poverty that emerged after the 1950s, with the varied social changes associated with industrialization, urbanism, and modernity.

Consejo Nacional de la Raza [National Council of the People]. 2004. *Nuestros niños cuentan, datos de Puerto Rico* [Our children count: Information from Puerto Rico]. San Juan: Fundación Annie Casey, NCLR. Using the details of the last census conducted in Puerto Rico (the census of 2000), the situation of Puerto Rican children is examined, considering such areas as childhood health, mortality rates, births, and general characteristics of the population (size and family structure, gender, and age). The information is analyzed at both the national and the municipal levels.

Galanes, Luis. 2003. *Los hijos de la infancia. Estudio sobre el embarazo y la maternidad en la adolescencia* [Bearing children during childhood: a study of adolescent pregnancy and motherhood]. San Juan: Editorial Tal Cual. This study analyzes adolescent pregnancy and motherhood from cultural, human, and socio-political perspectives.

Morris, Nancy. 1995. *Puerto Rico: Culture, Politics, and Identity.* Westport, CT: Praeger. Morris analyzes Puerto Rican national identity—its symbols, dynamics, and resilience—in the context of a fifty-year-long U.S. campaign of "Americanization" and the ongoing exercise of political sovereignty by the United States.

Nina Estrella, Ruth. 1996. *Nuestras familias ante un nuevo siglo* [Our families facing a new century]. Río Piedras: Universidad de Puerto Rico. This book is organized as a compilation of works from a variety of disciplines, using such distinctive perspectives as social work, demography, economics, public health, and psychology to present a panorama of the nation's families. The essays analyze the social transformations that have occurred in the family context, transformations that have been made invisible by the state.

Ramirez, Rafael L. 1999. *What It Means to Be a Man: Reflections on Puerto Rican Masculinity.* Translated by Rosa E. Casper. New Brunswick, NJ: Rutgers University Press. This book examines the meaning of machismo and masculinity, analyzes manhood in Puerto Rico, and explores the island's homosexual community.

Rivas Nina, Myrna. 2002. *Los adolescentes y jóvenes en Puerto Rico: En estadísticas; informe final* [Adolescents and youth in Puerto Rico: in statistics; final report]. http://www.Enfasispr.com/evaluación.html. This report presents a general panorama of the situation of adolescents and youth in Puerto Rico, using information on demographics, public health, levels of violence, and education. Leisure time activities are also considered.

Sánchez Korrol, Virginia E. 1994. *From Colonia to Community: The History of Puerto Ricans in New York City.* Berkeley, CA: University of California Press. Originally published in 1983, this edition updates the historical study of the development of the Puerto Rican community in the United States.

Nonprint Resources

Desigualdad y pobreza [Inequality and poverty]. 1998. Río Piedras: CEDME Productions. 60 min. VHS. A documentary on issues of inequality and poverty by Linda Cólon.

El puente sobre el Caribe: el desarrollo económico de Puerto Rico [A bridge over the Caribbean: economic development in Puerto Rico]. 1994. San Juan: Isla Films. 35 min. VHS. This documentary, by Sonia Fritz, examines economic history in contemporary Puerto Rico, including the effects of NAFTA.

Puerto Rico, 500 años [Puerto Rico, 500 years]. 2001. San Juan: Multimedia. 30 min. VHS. With script and direction by Myrian Fuentes, this documentary reviews the general history of Puerto Rico.

Web Sites

Comisión para la Prevención de la Violencia (COPREVI) [Commission for the Prevention of Violence], http://www. coprevi@cayey.upr.edu.

Departamento de Deporte y Recreacíon [Department of Sports and Recreation], http://www.gobierno.pr/DRD/Inicio/Default.

Departamento de Familia [Department of the Family], http://www.familia.gobierno.pr.

Departamento de Salud [Department of Health], http://www.salud.gov.pr.

Gobierno de Puerto Rico [Government of Puerto Rico], http://www.gobierno.pr/gprportal/inicio.

TendenciasPR.com, Datos y estadísticas sobre Puerto Rico y sus municipios [Facts and statistics on Puerto Rico and its municipalities], http://www.tendenciaspr.com.

Organizations and NGOs

Fondos Unidos de Puerto Rico [United Funds of Puerto Rico]
P.O. Box 191914
San Juan, PR 00919-1914
Phone: (787) 728-8500
Web site: http://www.fondosunidos.com

Fundación Chana y Samuel Levis [The Chana and Samuel Levis Foundation]
Ave. Ponce de León #776
2ndo Piso Edificio Principal
Seminario Evangélico de Puerto Rico en Río Piedras
(Postal Box: 776 Ponce De León Buzón #20, San Juan, PR 00925)
Phone: (787) 764-4159
Web site: http://www.diaadia.org/english

Fundación Comunitaria de Puerto Rico [The Communitarian Foundation of Puerto Rico]
Edificio Torre de la Reina
450 Ponce De León Ave.
Suite 203, Puerta de Tierra
San Juan, PR 00907
Phone: (787) 721-1037
Web site: http://www.fcpr.org

Fundación del Banco Popular [Popular Bank Foundation]
Banco Popular de Puerto Rico
P.O. Box 362708
San Juan, PR 00936-2708
Phone: (787) 724-3650
Web site: http://www.bancopopular.com/bancopopular/pages/prspa/bppr-prspa-map
   .jsp

Fundación Puertorriqueña de las Humanidades [Puerto Rican Foundation for the
   Humanities]
P.O. Box 9023920
San Juan, PR 00902-3920
Dirección Física: Calle San José #109, Tercer Piso, Viejo San Juan
Phone: (787) 721-2087
Web site: http://www.fprh.org/index2.html

Iniciativa Comunitaria, Inc. (ICI) [Communitarian Initiative, Inc.]
P.O. Box 366535
San Juan, PR
Phone: (787) 250-8629
Web site: http://www.wecaretoo.com/Organizations/PR/iniciativacomunitaria.html

Proyecto de Niños de Nueva Esperanza [New Hope Children's Project]
Niños de Nueva Esperanza, Inc.
Barrio Esperanza Sabana Seca, Toa Baja, Puerto Rico
Apartado 89
Sabana Seca, PR 00952-89
Phone: (787) 261-4543
Web site: http://www.zonai.com/noticia_main.asp?ZONAI.62842&pos=m&

Salvation Army de Puerto Rico [Puerto Rican Salvation Army]
Cuartel Divisional
306 Ave de la Constitución
Puerta de Tierra
San Juan, PR 00901
Phone: (787) 999-7000
Fax: (787) 999-7072
Web site: http://www.salvationarmypr.org

Selected Bibliography

American Psychiatric Association. 2000. *Diagnostic and Statistical Manual of Mental Disorders DSM IV-TR*, 4th Edition. Washington, DC: APA.

Arteaga and Arteaga (Publicity Agency). 1999. "Como es la Generación Y [What generation Y is like]." *Revista Buena Vida* (August): 78–79.

Canino, G., et al. 2003. "DSM-IV Rates of Child and Adolescent Disorders in Puerto Rico: Prevalence, Correlates, Service Use and the Effects of Impairment." *Archives of General Psychiatry* 61, no. 1: 85–93.

Colón, L. 2006. *Pobreza en Puerto Rico. Radiografía del Proyecto Americano* [Poverty in Puerto Rico: An X-Ray of the American Project]. San Juan: Editorial Luna Nueva.

Comisión para la Prevención de la Violencia [Commission for the Prevention of Violence]. 2006. http://www.coprevi.org. Accessed October 1, 2006.

Consejo Nacional de la Raza [National Council of La Raza]. 2004. *Nuestros Niños Cuentan, Datos de Puerto Rico* [Our children count: statistics from Puerto Rico]. San Juan: Fundación Annie Casey, NCLR.

Constitución del Estado Libre Asociado de Puerto Rico [Constitution of the Free Associated State of Puerto Rico]. 2003. http://www.Lexjuris.com/lexprcont.html.

Consultores de Conducta Humana, Inc. 2003. *Perfil y necesidades del joven Puertorriqueño. Informe preparado por la oficina de asuntos de la juventud* [Profile and needs of Puerto Rican youth: report prepared by the office of youth affairs]. Oficina de la Gobernadora del Estado Libre Asociado de Puerto Rico.

Departamento de Educación, Servicios Complementarios, Programa de Trabajo Social Escolar. Estudiantes Embarazadas, Por Nivel Escolar [Department of Education, Complementary Services, Program of Student Social Work]. Pregnant students, by level of education]. TendenciasPR.com. http://www.tendenciaspr.com/Educación/Tablas/04_embarazo_estudiantes.htm.

Departamento de la Familia [Department of the Family]. 2002. *Informe Annual 2001–2002, Administracion de Familia y Niños* [Annual Report, 2001–2002, Family and Children Administration]. Gobierno de Puerto Rico.

———. 2003. Comisión para la Implantación de la Política Pública para las Personas Reambulantes. Gobierno de Puerto Rico.

Departamento de la Policia, Oficina de Estadísticas [Police Department, Office of Statistics]. 2005. *Infome de Delitos en Puerto Rico (1940–2005)* [Report on Crimes in Puerto Rico (1940–2005)]. http://www.gobierno.pr/PoliciaPR.

Departamento de Salud [Department of Health]. 2002. *Informe de Estadísticas Vitales 2002* [Report of Vital Statistics 2002]. Secretaria Auxiliar de Planificación, Evaluación Estadística y Sistemas de Información.

———. 2003. *Informe Anual de Estadísticas Vitales 2003* [Annual Report of Vital Statistics 2003]. Secretaría Auxiliar de Planificación y Desarrollo, Departamento de Salud, Gobierno de Puerto Rico.

Informe del Departamento de Educación [Digest of Education Statistics]. 2005. Estudiantes Matriculados en el Sistema Educativo de Puerto Rico (2004/05) [Students Enrolled in the Puerto Rican Education System]. TendenciasPR.com. http://www.tendenciaspr.com/Estudiantes_matriculados.htm.

Informe del Gobierno de Puerto Rico [Report of the Goverment of Puerto Rico]. 2006. Tendencias Demográficas de Puerto Rico [Demographic Tendencies in Puerto Rico]. http://www.presupuesto.gobierno.pr/Tomo_I/Referencia/Tendencias.pdf

Informe de la Oficina del Censo [Report of the Census Office]. 2006. Perfil Sociode-mográfico de Puerto Rico, Censo 1990–2000 [Socio-demographic Profile of Puerto Rico, 1990–2000 Census]. http://www.gobierno.pr/NR/rdonlyres/ 442C7575-1184-428A-AD5D-F84953E8A5BE/0/Prensa_Muestra.pdf

Leyes de Puerto Rico, Departamento de Estado, Estado Libre Asociado de Puerto Rico [Laws of Puerto Rico, Department of State, Free Associated State of Puerto Rico]. 2003. http://www. Estadogobierno.pr/leyespr.html.

Melendez, N. 1989. *Los comerciales de televisión y las conductas de tiempo libre* [Television commercials and free time behaviors]. San Juan: Centro de Estudios del Tiempo Libre.

Moscoso, M., H. Colón, I. Parrilla, and J.C. Reyes. 2003. *Consulta Juvenil V 2000–2002, El uso de substancias en los escolares Puertorriqueños* [Youth Consultation V 2000–2002: Substance use among Puerto Rican students]. Bayamón: Universidad Central del Caribe, Departamento de Medicina de Familia y Salud Comunal.

Nina, Ruth. 2001. "La familia Puertorriqueña: diez años de investigación psicológica [The Puerto Rican family: ten years of psychological research]." *Cuaderno no1 de la Red de Estudios de Familia en el Caribe*. San Juan: Proyecto Atlantea.

Oficina del Gobernador para el Fortalecimiento de la Familia [Governor's Office for the Strengthening of the Family]. 1987. La familia Puertorriqueña hoy [The Puerto Rican family today]. Unpublished document.

Policía de Puerto Rico, división de estadística [Puerto Rican police, statistics division]. 2005. http://www.tendenciaspr.com.

———, Programa de Calidad de Vida Escolar, Departamento de Educación; Violen cia en las Escuelas, por Nivel Escolar (Escuelas Públicas Diurnas) [Puerto Rican Police, Quality of School Life Program, Department of Education; violence in schools, by academic level (public daytime schools)]. TendenciasPR .com. http://tendenciaspr.com/Educacion/Tablas/04_Violencia_en_las_escuelas _por_nivel.htm.

Primera Hora. 2006. "Obesidad en los niños, reporte especial [Obesity in children, special report]." October 18, 21–26.

Rivera, E., N. Fernández, A. Torres, and C. Parrilla. 2006. *Análisis de la salud de Puerto Rico: salud mental* [Analysis of health in Puerto Rico: mental health]. Departamento de Salud.

Rivera, M. 2006. Grave incidencia de asma [Serious incidence rates of asthma]. http://www.rcm.upr.edu/Noticias/2006/Febrero/grave_incidencia_de_asma .htm.

Román Silva, A. A. 2006. *El proceso de reclutamiento y selección de ministros en las iglesias evangélicas de Puerto Rico*. Disertación doctoral sometida al Departa-mento de Psicología de la Universidad de Puerto Rico, Recinto de Río Piedras [The process of recruiting and selecting ministers in evangelical churches in Puerto Rico. Doctoral dissertation submitted to the Psychology Department of the University of Puerto Rico, Rio Piedras].

U.S. Census Bureau. 2000. Census; U.S. Census Bureau Data for Puerto Rico. http://www.Census.gov./census 2000/status/pr.html.

U.S. Department of Labor, Employment Standards Administration, Wage and Hour Division. Selected state child labor standards affecting minors under 18 in non-farm employment as of January 1, 2007. Accessed at http://www.dol. gov/esa/programs/whd/state/nonfarm.

12

ST. KITTS AND NEVIS

Hope M. Jordan

NATIONAL PROFILE

Located in the Eastern Caribbean, St. Christopher (St. Kitts) and Nevis, or the Federation of St. Kitts and Nevis, was first explored by Christopher Columbus in 1493 (St. Kitts Tourism 2006). Carib Indians inhabited the islands at that time, and Columbus named the island St. Kitts after Saint Christopher. Prior to the Carib inhabitation, St. Kitts was inhabited by

the more peaceful Arawak Indians (Sharman and Stone 1987). The English and French returned in 1623, and the sugar trade led to early development of the islands. Conflict between the French and the British resulted in British rule in 1783; these English-speaking islands gained independence 200 years later on September 19, 1983. This autonomy has resulted in islands with an excellent reputation with regard to human rights (U.S. Department of State 2006).

The economy of St. Kitts and Nevis is based on tourism and light industry. The sugarcane industry closed down in 2005. Prime Minister Dr. Denzil Douglas

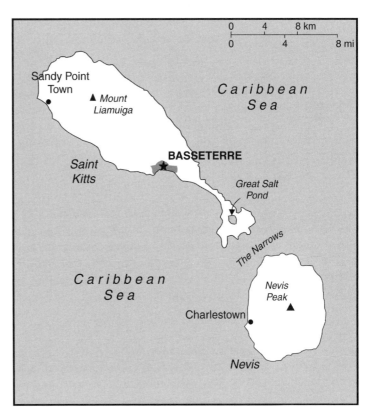

explained in 2006 that the goal of socioeconomic change includes promoting small business, service-oriented tourism, financial services, information communication technology, agriculture, and manufacturing
(Caribbean Net News 2006b).

The two islands have a land territory of 104 square miles. Most of the
population, counted at 39,129, lives on St. Kitts (Encarta 2006). The
populations of both St. Kitts and Nevis are primarily of African descent.
Eighty-six percent of the population is of mixed African descent, another
11 percent of the population is comprised of European descent, and
2 percent of the population is categorized as white. There is also a small
Indo-Pakistani ethnic presence (Atlapedia 2006).

Basseterre is the capital of St. Kitts and Nevis, and Charlestown is the
largest city, with an average temperature of 80°F. The tropical climate
contributes to the tourism industry in these generally mountainous
islands, as do the beautiful beaches, rain forests, dormant volcanoes, and
the famous Green Velvet monkeys. Mt. Liamuiga on St. Kitts is 3,792
feet high, and Nevis Peak on Nevis is 3,232 feet high (Atlapedia 2006;
Encarta 2006).

Tourism contributed $403.9 million to the 2004 Gross Domestic
Product (GDP) and an overall growth rate of 4.9 percent in 2005. The
per capita GDP in 2004 was estimated at $8,600. Though tourism from
the United States was adversely impacted by the 9/11 terrorist attacks,
the industry is recovering and experienced growth again in 2005. Recent
investments to improve facilities and support tourism include the construction of the port at St. Kitts and a new convention center built in
2002. The government encourages foreign investment and the location
of businesses in St. Kitts or Nevis with policies that provide liberal tax
holidays, duty-free import of equipment and materials, and subsidies for
the training of local personnel. These opportunities have resulted in a 5
percent unemployment rate. Good economic performance contributes to
the well-being of children in St. Kitts and Nevis.

The islands' primary export market is the United States, with an annual
average of $60.2 million. Other export markets include Europe, Nether-
lands Antilles, Canada, and Dominica. Machinery, food, electronics, bev-
erages, and tobacco are the primary exports (Infoplease 2005). In 2005,
imports from the United States totaled $192.3 million. Other major
import markets include Trinidad and Tobago, Europe, Canada, and
Japan. The inflation rate rose on average by 3.6 percent in 2005, compared
with 2.3 percent in 2004, and 2.2 percent in 2003. As a member of the
Eastern Caribbean Currency Union (ECCU), the Eastern Caribbean
Central Bank (ECCB) manages and regulates banking (U.S. Department
of State 2006).

In 1999, the United Nations Human Rights Committee on St. Kitts
and Nevis noted that the large number of single-parent families impacts
children. The committee also expressed concern regarding the financial

and psychological impact of "visiting relationships" in single-parent families (with mothers being the primary single parent) and recommended more study be done in an effort to protect children (University of Minnesota 1999). The government promotes the well-being of women and children with such annual events as the Sixteen-Day Campaign for Violence against Women and Children. The United Nations Childrens Fund (UNICEF) reports a problem in the Eastern Caribbean with poverty in households headed by women at 8 percent to 45 percent, depending on the country. Specific information on St. Kitts and Nevis does not seem to be available (United Nations Children's Fund 2006).

> **KEY FACTS – ST. KITTS AND NEVIS**
>
> Population: 39,349 (July 2007 est.)
> Infant mortality rate: 13.74 deaths/1,000 live births (2007 est.)
> Life expectancy at birth: 72.66 years (2007 est.)
> Literacy rate: 97.8 percent (2003 est.)
> Net primary school enrollment/attendance: 94 percent (2000–2005)
> Internet users: 10,000 (2002)
>
> *Sources:* UNICEF. At a Glance: St. Kitts and Nevis–Statistics. http://www.unicef.org/infobycountry/stkittsnevis_statistics.html. April 24, 2007.

The government of St. Kitts and Nevis is a constitutional monarchy with a Westminster-style parliament. This democratic style allows for leadership that is representative of the needs of all people on the islands, including children. Though St. Kitts and Nevis have a very low crime rate, there have been reports of occasional abuse by law enforcement (U.S. Department of State 2000). The legislative branch of government includes an eleven-member senate and an eleven-member popularly elected House of Representatives. The judicial branch (magistrate's courts) consists of the Eastern Caribbean Supreme Court with a high court and court of appeals. There are fourteen parishes and four primary political parties. The St. Kitts and Nevis Labor Party is the current ruling party (U.S. Department of State 2006).

The government provides free health care, which supports the health and well-being of residents, including children, and this care has improved in recent years. Protection from childhood diseases is provided via free vaccinations, and most common childhood diseases have been alleviated on the islands (Country Studies Caribbean Islands 1999).

OVERVIEW

A comprehensive look at St. Kitts and Nevis shows that all children have access to free education (Infoplease 2005). The current infant mortality rate is 14.12 per 1,000 live births (United Nations Children's Fund 2006). Slavery was abolished in 1834 (Guide to St. Kitts 2006). History reveals a relatively peaceful island, free of war for over 125 years providing stability for modern children (History of St. Kitts and Nevis 2004). The United Nations reports that the Caribbean (including St. Kitts and Nevis) experiences significant migratory movement for economic reasons, as well as movement of those seeking protection. The United Nations Human Rights Commission works in this area through Honorary Liaisons and collaborations with the International Organization for Migration (United Nations High Commission for Refugees 2005). The United Nations criticized St. Kitts in 2001 for its lack of legal protection with respect to the rights of children born out of wedlock (Fagan 2001). The Employment of Children Act restricts employment of children under the age of sixteen (Office of the United Nations High Commissioner on Human Rights 1997). A more in-depth look at each of these areas reveals the changing nature of life for children in St. Kitts and Nevis.

EDUCATION

All children in St. Kitts and Nevis have access to a free education, and schooling is compulsory for twelve years, from preschool through grade eleven. At that point, higher education is offered in the form of college/ university or technical schools. The literacy levels are estimated at 98 percent (U.S. Department of State 2006). In 1991, a National Committee on Education was established to investigate issues such as economic trends, management of the system, and teachers' work conditions (Nations Encyclopedia On-line 2006).

In November 2006, the Premier and Minister of Education for Nevis, Joseph Parry, emphasized his government's focus on education. The Minister noted that Nevis needs to focus on education based on test results and asked parents to support the education and behavior initiatives (Caribbean Net News 2006a).

A more recent telephone interview with the Minister of Education Sam Condor and the Secretary of Education Osmond Petty provided the following information regarding the educational system in St. Kitts. The Minister and Secretary confirmed that St. Kitts offers compulsory, free, and public education for all children from kindergarten through grade eleven; the primary level of education includes kindergarten through grade six and the secondary consists of grades seven through eleven. By law, children must attend school, and this education is the responsibility of the state. Students wear uniforms in all schools. Students from lower socioeconomic circumstances are supported with various programs, which may cover a variety of expenses associated with schooling, including testing fees. Among these programs are the Uniform Program, which helps pay for school uniforms; the Text Book Program, which helps pay for books; and the School Feeding Program, which provides meals for students. Children with disabilities are supported by a special unit that attends to them according to their special needs (Condor and Petty, telephone interview 2007).

The Ministry of Education has identified gender as an issue of concern, in that the boys are falling behind the girls in terms of academic performance. Special efforts are being made to identify the cause of this gender disparity in performance and address the needs of the boys in schools. Diversity is not an issue in St. Kitts. The government of St. Kitts works in collaboration with various organizations to support the needs of the students of St. Kitts. These organizations include the Organization of Eastern Caribbean States (OECS), the Caribbean Examination Council, and the United Nations Educational, Scientific, and Cultural Organization (UNESCO). All students at the primary level participate in testing to assess ability and achievement based on the standard curriculum achievement. In grades three through six, the students take the National Test of Standards (assessing basic skills in math, English, social studies, and science). At the secondary level, students participate in subject area testing and all aspire to take various exit exams, including the exit exams from the Caribbean Examination Council. Currently, an interim exam is under development that would also assess job skills and achievements in English and Math (Condor and Petty, telephone interview 2007).

The education system serves the needs of students at all levels of ability, offering three special programs for underachievers. These programs are funded to provide individual academic and technical support to capture and support those not doing as well as expected in school. Many students leave these programs to participate in further technical and university-level studies. These three programs are the Advanced Vocational Education Center (AVED), Project Strong, and Practical Youth Skills (soon to be renamed National Skills) Program. Scholarships for those graduating secondary school include the State Scholar Scholarship (US$25,000 a year) and the Technical Scholarship (US$10,000 a year) (Condor and Petty, telephone interview 2007).

Every school in St. Kitts (K–11) is equipped with computers. Parental involvement is encouraged, as the Ministry acknowledges that those students who do the best in school have family support. The Education Act created an advisory board consisting of parents, educators, teacher union representatives, Ministry of Education representatives, and the private sector. Parents also participate in the Parent Teacher Association (PTA). Many private firms support the school systems with scholarships (Condor and Petty, telephone interview 2007).

PLAY AND RECREATION

Sports are offered for youth on the islands, including cricket, football (soccer), and track. Weather conditions are generally conducive to year-round sports activities. Summer camps as well as art and music activities are also offered for children and youth (Sun On-line 2006). The Minister of Education explained that students on the island especially love outdoor sports (soccer, cricket, net ball, basketball, and volleyball) and, like other students around the world, enjoy video games. St. Kitts sponsors an

Annual Youth Camp through the Ministry of Youth. This residential camp takes place after school is out, and children from the region attend for two weeks. This camp is very popular and meets its capacity every year (Condor and Petty, telephone interview 2007). Recently, the Cable & Wireless corporation created a new sports program called CONECT: Committed to Optimistic National Goals for Each Child Together (Smithen 2006).

CHILD LABOR

The government of St. Kitts and Nevis participated in the 1999 International Labor Organization Meeting, during which it was determined that statistics on the number of children in the labor force were not available. It was noted, however, that children do help their families by working in agriculture and domestic service. There is some concern that they may also be involved in distribution of drugs, pornography, and prostitution. There have been no reported cases of forced or bonded child labor (U.S. Department of Labor 2006).

A minimum working age of sixteen was set by the Employment of Children Ordinance and the Employment of Women, Young Persons, and Children Act. The Employment of Children Ordinance also outlaws slavery, servitude, and forced labor. The national constitution similarly prohibits slavery, servitude, and forced labor (U.S. Department of Labor 2006).

FAMILY

Family life in St. Kitts and Nevis in many ways demonstrates regional patterns, though demography and changes in the gender division of labor are also distinctively local. According to Christine Barrow, children in the Caribbean are valued though often seen as property of their parents. Children are disciplined and taught the value of manners. Girls are often kept home doing cognitive activities, while boys are encouraged to be outside and active. Education is valued and adults are considered to be authorities. Punishment is often preferred over positive encouragement (Barrow 2001). In his report for the United Nations Division of Social Policy and Development, Department of Economic and Social Affairs Program on the Family, Godfrey St. Bernard points out that religion plays a major role in family life in the Caribbean with regard to spousal roles, marriage, child bearing, and socialization of children. Consensual unions persist along with formal marriages, and though common-law and visiting unions traditionally are more prevalent in lower socioeconomic groups, there seems to be a trend in their increase in middle and higher income groups.

The 2001 Survey of Living Conditions in St. Kitts and Nevis, conducted with the support of the Caribbean Development Bank and Kairi Consultants Ltd. and reported in the Economic Commission for Latin America and the Caribbean's *Quality of Life: A Compendium of Selected*

Social Statistics of Five Caribbean Countries (1995–2001), offers useful information about families (Economic Commission for Latin America and
the Caribbean 2001a). In terms of family size, the survey reported the
findings that 10.4 percent of families had only one member and 3.0 percent had ten or more members; 15.7 percent had three, 16.9 percent had
four, and 14.8 percent had five members (Economic Commission for
Latin America and the Caribbean 2001a, 22). Of the 117 cases of elderly
persons living alone in the 2001 survey, 15.4 percent were between the
ages of sixty and sixty-five, 15.4 percent between the ages of sixty-five
and seventy, 18.8 percent between seventy and seventy-four, and 32.5
percent aged eighty or above (Economic Commission for Latin America
and the Caribbean 2001a, 22). The projections of population in the Caribbean show a continued increase of older citizens, attributed to
increased longevity, declining fertility rates, and the return of older
natives to the islands during retirement. An aging population often results
in multi-generational households, which may give grandmothers important roles in the family (St. Bernard 2003).

Although there appears to be a tendency toward the Western model of
the nuclear family with male providers and more working women in the
Caribbean, there continues to be a concern for the marginalization of single mothers (St. Bernard 2003). There are a large number of families
with female heads of household. The 2001 survey reported that 48.3 percent of family households were headed by females and 51.7 percent by
males. The distribution of female-headed households reveals greater proportions at lower income levels. In other words, 65.1 percent of households in the poorest twenty percent are headed by women, compared
with 43.0 percent in the richest twenty percent of households. In terms
of employment, the poorest twenty percent of households also shows
more unemployment among female heads of families (Economic Commission for Latin America and the Caribbean 2001a, 23 and 24).

There is an increase of women in the Caribbean seeking higher education and entering the work force. According to St. Bernard, the trend
leads to a declining fertility rate that correlates with the higher levels of
education among females. Higher levels of female education also increase
the likelihood of women entering the workforce, which may increase the
family income (but also decrease the supervision of children in the
home). These factors contribute to smaller families and a decline in
household size (St. Bernard 2003). Education levels achieved by heads of
household in St. Kitts and Nevis also showed some gender differences
and variations associated with family incomes and economic status. Of
the 969 families surveyed in 2001, 43.3 percent of male heads of household and 42.5 percent of female heads of household had finished secondary education, 25.1 percent of male and 24.4 percent of female heads of
household had achieved only a primary education, and 6.2 percent of
male and 4.6 percent of female heads of households had completed

university level education. Whereas 10.4 percent of women family heads in the wealthiest quintile had a university-level education (compared with 11.2 percent of male heads), none in the poorest three quintiles had achieved this level of education (Economic Commission for Latin America and the Caribbean 2001a, 26).

Globalization and technology also impact families in the Caribbean. The increase of tourism and air travel may have positive economic effects, though recent terrorism threats had an initial negative impact on tourism. Television and internet technologies expose families to other cultures, providing information, socialization, and entertainment. Some studies indicate that growing juvenile delinquency might be linked to television viewing that brings elements foreign to the traditional Caribbean cultures directly into homes (St. Bernard 2003).

St. Kitts and Nevis, as in the rest of the world, is seeing changes in families due to globalization and technology, demographic shifts, higher levels of education, and an increase of women in the work force. Such changes may have both positive and negative effects.

HEALTH

The Ministry of Health is responsible for mobilizing resources to promote the health of the population in St. Kitts and Nevis. The Ministry has specifically targeted infants and children as a priority, including prenatal care. Attention has been turned to the promotion of breast feeding and the reduction of low birth weight babies (Pan American Health Organization 2001). Women who are mothers have been identified as an at-risk group, so programs to support prenatal and postnatal care are increasing on the islands. Childhood malnutrition and infant mortality were issues in the 1980s, but great strides have been made to improve the situation and provide more adequate health care. Thus severe childhood malnutrition is not a problem and mild to moderate undernutrition is decreasing. Breastfeeding is promoted in an effort to improve infant nutrition. Hepatitis B immunizations have been given to children from birth to five years of age since 1995. With widespread immunizations, most childhood diseases have been alleviated (Pan American Health Organization 2001). Young children (under five years old) are primarily hospitalized due to gastroenteritis and acute respiratory infections, as well as internal and external trauma (Pan American Health Organization 2001).

There are three hospitals on St. Kitts and one on Nevis, with additional health clinics and pharmacies throughout the island to provide free health care, prescriptions, and vaccinations to residents (United States Department of State, Bureau of Western Hemisphere Affairs 2006). The current infant mortality rate is 14.12 per 1,000 births and the life expectancy at birth is now seventy years for men and seventy-six years for women (Pan American Health Organization 2001).

The government of St. Kitts and Nevis is committed to improving health services for the vulnerable groups in society by strengthening programs targeted at women and children, the urban and rural poor, the elderly, and the disabled; to pursue an aggressive health advocacy and health promotion program; to continue the organizational reform of the health sector; to implement programs aimed at reducing the incidence and prevalence of chronic diseases, based on morbidity and mortality patterns; and to actively seek international partnerships in health (Pan American Health Organization 2001). To this end the Prime Minister has committed to increasing the portion of the national budget for health care by 5 percent (Pan American Health Organization in Focus 2005).

As in most parts of the world, HIV/AIDS is a health concern that impacts the lives of children. The Prime Minister addressed this issue in 2001 in a statement to a special session of the United Nations. Dr. Douglas stated that the Caribbean is second to Africa in rates of infection and emphasized the devastation this causes in families, along with the need for international support to alleviate the spread of AIDS. He also noted that his country was working with the Caribbean Epidemiological Center (CAREC), the Pan American Health Organization (PAHO), local private-sector organizations, civil society, and persons infected with the disease, and others to implement initiatives in an effort to address the problem of aids (Douglas 2001).

LAWS AND LEGAL STATUS

The UNICEF Office for Barbados and the Eastern Caribbean has overall responsibility for Antigua and Barbuda, Barbados, the British Virgin Islands, Dominica, Grenada, Montserrat, Saint Kitts and Nevis, Saint Lucia, Saint Vincent and the Grenadines, and Turks and Caicos Islands, with an aggregate population of approximately 715,400. Though similar in many respects, each area also has uniqueness with regard to law and legal status of children (United Nations Children's Fund 2006).

According to the St. Kitts and Nevis 1997 report to the United Nations Committee on the Rights of the Child, the age of majority in St. Kitts and Nevis is eighteen years (until 1983 and the passage of the Age of Majority Act it had been twenty-one years). The Juvenile Act establishes expectations with regard to the protection of children; it defines "juvenile" as an individual less than eighteen years old and "young person" as an individual between ages of fourteen and eighteen. An individual may legally marry at the age of sixteen, and the age of sexual consent is over sixteen years. The Juvenile Act specifies eight as the age of criminal liability (Office of the United Nations High Commissioner for Human Rights 1997).

A report from the U.S. Department of State on Human Rights noted that violence against women was a problem, though many women do not file reports. Though law does not restrict the role of women, culture and tradition may limit women's roles. For example, women do not hold as many high level positions as men do. The Ministry of Health and Women's Affairs is promoting change in this area, and training for public officials on issues of domestic violence, sex crimes, and abuse is on-going. The UN Convention on the Rights of the Child has prompted a commitment to the rights or women and children (Office of the United Nations High Commissioner for Human Rights 1997).

RELIGIOUS LIFE

The constitution provides for freedom of religion in St. Kitts and Nevis (United States Department of State 2000). The local phone book records over fifty-seven churches on the island and local residents report their religion to be an important part of life on Nevis and St. Kitts. The primary religion is Christianity, with Anglican being predominant; Evangelical Protestants and Roman Catholics have a minority presence (United States Department of State, Bureau of Western Hemisphere Affairs 2006). There are also small Rastafarian and Orthodox communities. The citizens of St. Kitts and Nevis are tolerant of all faiths, but Christian values and attitudes predominate. The government requires all schools to conduct morning Christian prayers and hymns (United States Department of State 2005).

CHILD ABUSE AND NEGLECT

Domestic violence legislation has been passed in St. Kitts and Nevis, although it had still not been put into force as of November 2001 when the Economic Commission for Latin America and the Caribbean did an evaluative study. Despite the passing of legislation on domestic violence, violence, including child abuse, continues to spread in the Caribbean region. Policy-makers have an ongoing problem obtaining victim profiles, identifying groups at risk, developing intervention programs, and monitoring the effectiveness of violence prevention. The situation is complicated by the social barriers of guilt and shame that inhibit self-identification as well as by a cultural acceptance of domestic violence. Official reports of incest are miniscule, though a strong perception remains that this is indeed a problem in the Caribbean countries studied by the Economic Commission for Latin America and the Caribbean (2001b).

There is a concern that officials cannot respond effectively because children are not allowed to give evidence, teachers and health professionals do not report all cases, and social systems cannot provide quality alternative care. From 1990 to 1994 the number of cases of reported child abuse remained fairly constant (ranging from thirty-two to thirty-seven per year) with a slight drop to 25 reported cases in 1995. The Ministry of Social Development provides counseling services to families who are victims of abuse. The St. Christopher's Children Home offers care for neglected, abused, abandoned, or homeless children. It is estimated that as many as 48 percent of children live with single mothers (Economic Commission for Latin America and the Caribbean 2001b).

GROWING UP IN THE TWENTY-FIRST CENTURY

Conditions for children on St. Kitts and Nevis continue to improve with the current governmental focus on issues concerning women, children, and families as well as the overall improvement of education and the economy. The outlook for children in the twenty-first century is encouraging.

RESOURCE GUIDE

Suggested Readings

Hubbard, Vincent K. 2002. *Swords, Ships, & Sugar: History of Nevis.* Revised edition. Corvallis, OR: Premier Editions International. This short, easy-to-read book provides a basic history of Nevis. The book includes information on the geography, weather, religion, pirates, slavery, and the sugar industry.

Hubbard, Vincent K. 2003. *A History of St. Kitts: The Sweet Trade.* Northampton, MA: Interlink Pub Group, Inc. This book provides a short history of St. Kitts, which was the first British Colony in the West Indies.

Mcdonald Byron, Rupert. 2001. *The Dawn of Statehood in St. Kitts–Nevis–Anguilla.* Bloomington, IN: Authorhouse. This novel provides a history of the first two years of statehood in the British colonies of St. Kitts, Nevis, and Anguilla. Though the novel does use actual events, it also introduces fictitious events.

Permenter, Paris, and John Bigley. 2001. *Antigua, Barbuda, St. Kitts and Nevis Alive!* Edison, NJ: Hunter Publishing, Inc. This book offers a history of St. Kitts and Nevis that takes the reader right to modern St. Kitts and Nevis. It also discusses everything from culture, language, and media to plants, animals, and people.

Sharman, Frank, and Amalia Stone. 1987. *Discover St. Kitts: Columbus' Favorite Island.* Basseterre: Creole Publishing. This colorful book provides insight into the history, geography, and basic lifestyle of the island and people of St. Kitts.

Nonprint Resources

Video Visits—Martinique, St. Kitts & Antigua, and the US Virgin Islands. Questar, Inc. 2003, 81 minutes. DVD. This DVD explores St. Kitts, Martinique, Antigua, and the Virgin Islands. It is narrated by Shari Belafonte-Harper.

Web Sites

Explore St. Kitts–St. Kitts Tourism, http://www.stkittstourism.kn. This site provides video and narrative about St. Kitts. It includes a video tour and discusses topics such as businesses, dining, where to stay, and contact information.

Government of Saint Christopher (St. Kitts) and Nevis official website, http://www.gov.kn.

United Nations Development Programme (UNDP) Human Development Report 2006–St. Kitts and Nevis, http://hdr.undp.org/hdr2006/statistics/countries/data_sheets/cty_ds_KNA.html.

Organizations and NGOs

Caribbean/Latin American Action
1818 N Street, NW, Suite 310
Washington, DC 20036
Phone: (202) 466-7464
Fax: (202) 822-0075

Nevis Teachers' Union
Wakely Daniel, President
Bernella Caines Hamilton, General Secretary
P.O. Box 559
Charlestown, Nevis
Phone: (869) 469-1118/8465
Fax: (869) 469-5663
Email: nevteach@caribsurf.com

Nevis Tourism Authority
Main Street
Charlestown, Nevis
Phone: (869) 469-7550 or 1-866-55-NEVIS
Fax: (869) 469-7551
Email: info@nevisisland.com

St. Christopher Heritage Society
Bay Road
Basseterre, St. Kitts and Nevis
Phone: (869) 465-5584

St. Kitts and Nevis Information Service
Government Headquarters
Church Street
Basseterre, St. Kitts
Contact: Ms. Heather Herbert
Phone: (869) 465-2521 x1039
Fax: (869) 466-4505
Email: infocom@caribsurf.com

St. Kitts Evangelical Association
Dr. Oldain Charles, President
P.O. Box 70
Basseterre, St. Kitts
Phone: (869) 465-2203
Fax: (869) 465-6057

St. Kitts-Nevis Bar Association
C/O Kelsick Wilkin & Ferdinand
South Square Street
Basseterre, St. Kitts

St. Kitts Teachers' Union
P.O. Box 545
Basseterre, St. Kitts
Phone: (869) 465-2004/2096
Fax: (869) 465-1921
Email: stkittsteachersunion@hotmail.com

St. Kitts Tourism Authority
Pelican Mall, Bay Road
P.O. Box 132
Basseterre, St. Kitts
Phone: (869) 465-4040
Fax: (869) 465-8794

Selected Bibliography

Atlapedia Online. 2006. Federation of St. Kitts and Nevis. http://www.atlapedia
.com/online/countries/stkitts.htm. Accessed November 20, 2006.

Barrow, Christine. 2001. *Situation Analysis of Children and Women in Twelve Countries in the Caribbean*. Barbados: UNICEF Caribbean Area Office. http://www.unicef.org/barbados/SitAn_Final_Report.doc.

Caribbean Net News. 2006a. Children to Receive Fair and Equal Opportunities in Education, says Nevis Premier. http://www.caribbeannetnews.com/cgiscript/csArticles/articles/000041/004137.htm. Accessed December 15, 2006.

———. 2006b. St Kitts-Nevis PM calls on young people to tap into the Empowerment Development Fund. http://www.caribbeannetnews.com/cgiscript/csArticles/articles/000033/003369.htm. Accessed November 9, 2006.

Condor, Sam, Minister of Education, and Osmond Petty, Secretary of Education. 2007. Personal telephone interview, January 31. St. Kitts.

Country Studies Caribbean Islands. 1999. St. Kitts and Nevis Health and Welfare. http://countrystudies.us/caribbean-islands/104.htm. Accessed November 5, 2006.

Douglas, Denzil L. 2001. *Statement to the Special Session on the United Nations General Assembly on HIV/Aids, St. Kitts and Nevis*. http://www.un.org/ga/aids/statements/docs/sknE.html. Accessed November 12, 2006.

Economic Commission for Latin America and the Caribbean (ECLAC). 2001a. *Quality of Life: A Compendium of Selected Social Statistics of Five Caribbean Countries (1995–2001)*. http://www.eclac.cl/publicaciones/xml/7/9877/carg0680.pdf. Accessed March 31, 2007.

———. 2001b. Caribbean Development and Cooperation Committee. *An Evaluative Study of the Implementation of Domestic Violence Legislation: Antigua and Barbuda, St. Kitts/Nevis, Saint Lucia and Saint Vincent and the Grenadines*. http://www.eclac.org/publicaciones/xml/0/9910/carg0659.pdf. Accessed January 18, 2007.

Encarta On-line Encyclopedia. 2006. St. Kitts and Nevis. http://encarta.msn.com/encyclopedia_761552904/Saint_Kitts_and_Nevis.html. Accessed November 9, 2006.

Fagan, Patrick F. 2001. How UN Conventions on Women's and Children's Rights Undermine Family, Religion, and Sovereignty. http://www.heritage.org/Research/International Organizations/BG1407.cfm. Accessed December 11, 2006.

Guide to St. Kitts. 2006. http://stkitts-guide.info/past.and.present/history/. Accessed January 20, 2007.

History of St. Kitts and Nevis, History of the Nations. 2004. http://www.historyof nations.net/northamerica/stkitts.html. Accessed January 24, 2007.

Infoplease, St. Kitts and Nevis. 2005. http://www.infoplease.com/ipa/A0107930. html. Accessed January 20, 2007.

Nations Encyclopedia On-line. 2006. Americas St. Kitts and Nevis. http://www .nationsencyclopedia.com/Americas/St-Kitts-and-Nevis-EDUCATION.html. Accessed December 15, 2006.

Office of the United Nations High Commissioner for Human Rights. 1997. Committee on the Rights of the Child. Consideration of Reports Submitted by States Parties under Article 44 of the Convention: St. Kitts and Nevis. http://www.hri.ca/fortherecord1997/documentation/tbodies/crc-c-3-add51 .htm. Accessed December 11, 2006.

Pan American Health Organization. 2001. St. Kitts and Nevis. http://www.paho .org/English/SHA/prflskn.htm. Accessed December 15, 2006.

Pan American Health Organization in Focus. 2005. Caribbean Leaders Endorse Health Recommendations. http://www.paho.org/English/DD/PIN/ptoday 15_sep05.htm. Accessed January 25, 2007.

Sharman, Frank, and Amalia Stone. 1987. *Discover St. Kitts: Columbus' Favourite Island*. Basseterre, St. Kitts: Creole Publishing.

Smithen, Corliss. 2006. "Cable & Wireless Launches CONECT." *Sun St. Kitts and Nevis*, July 20. http://sunstkitts.com/paper/?asknw=view&asknw=view,view &sun=494418078207132005&an=384519088507202006&ac=Local. Accessed December 20, 2006.

St. Bernard, Godfrey. 2003. *Major Trends Affecting Families in Central America and the Caribbean*. Prepared for United Nations Division of Social Policy and Development, Department of Economic and Social Affairs Program on the Family. http:// www.un.org/esa/socdev/family/Publications/mtstbernard.pdf. Accessed March 31, 2007.

St. Kitts Government. 2006. Contact Information. http://www.gov.kn/default.asp? PageIdentifier=49. Accessed December 26, 2006.

St. Kitts Tourism. 2006. Explore St. Kitts: An Experience Like No Other. http:// www.stkittstourism.kn/DiscoverStKitts/index.asp. Accessed November 9, 2006.

Sun On-line St. Kitts and Nevis. 2006. Arts Competition. http://sunstkitts.com/ paper/?asknw=view&asknw=view,view,view,view,view,view,view,view&su n=494418078207132005&an=440129118408192003&ac=Community%20 Calendar. Accessed December 26, 2006.

United Nations Children's Fund (UNICEF). 2006. Country Issues. At a Glance: St. Kitts and Nevis. http://www.unicef.org/infobycountry/stkittsnevis.html. Accessed November 20, 2006 and January 28, 2007.

United Nations High Commission for Refugees. 2005. North American and Caribbean Global Report. http://www.unhcr.org/publ/PUBL/41ab28d70.pdf. Accessed January 25, 2007.

University of Minnesota Human Rights Library. 1999. United Nations Human Rights Committee on the Rights of the Child, Concluding Observations:

Saint Kitts and Nevis. http://www.law.wits.ac.za/humanrts/crc/saintkitts1999
.html. Accessed December 5, 2006.

U.S. Department of Labor, Bureau of International Affairs. 2006. St. Kitts and Nevis
Government Policies and Programs to Eliminate Worst Forms of Child Labor.
http://www.dol.gov/ilab/media/reports/iclp/tda2003/saint-kitts-nevis.htm.
Accessed December 5, 2006.

U.S. Department of State. 2000. Country Reports on Human Rights Practices,
St. Kitts and Nevis. http://www.state.gov/g/drl/rls/hrrpt/2000/wha/
829.htm. Accessed November 20, 2006.

———. 2005. International Religious Freedom Report, St. Kitts & Nevis. http://
www.state.gov/g/drl/rls/irf/2005/51651.htm. Accessed February 24,
2007.

———. 2006. Bureau of Western Hemisphere Affairs. Background Note: St. Kitts
and Nevis Profile. http://www.state.gov/r/pa/ei/bgn/2341.htm. Accessed
November 9, 2006.

13

SAINT LUCIA, SAINT VINCENT, AND THE GRENADINES

Xenobia N. Barrow

NATIONAL PROFILE

Saint Lucia and Saint Vincent and the Grenadines (SVG) are both island nations within the eastern Caribbean region and are members of the Organization of Eastern Caribbean States (OECS). In the chain of islands, both Saint Lucia and SVG are north of Trinidad and Tobago and South America, and south of the island of Dominica. On the east, they are bordered by the Atlantic Ocean and on the west by the Caribbean Sea as part of the Lesser Antilles. The landmass of Saint Lucia is approximately twice the size of SVG, although SVG is more densely populated. While there is a strong history of resistance to slavery in both islands, when independence was attained, it was more realistically a political concession and negotiation made by Britain rather than a war of independence (Knight 1990, 301–302).

The colonial history of both islands is similar in the sense that domination and ownership was largely a political and geographical battle between the British and French empires in the

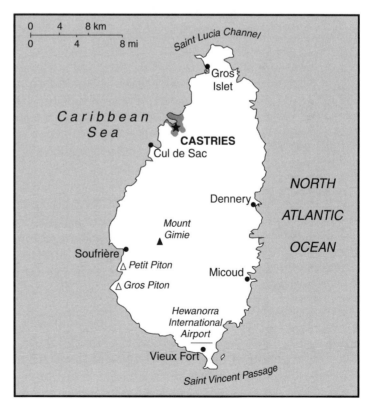

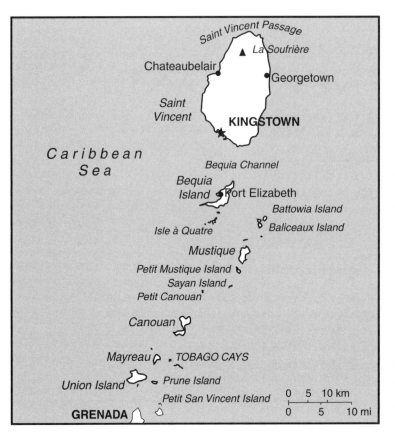

seventeenth and eighteenth centuries. In the late eighteenth century, Britain eventually gained full control over SVG and then similarly in Saint Lucia some thirty years later in 1814 (Knight 1990, 78, 176; Central Intelligence Agency 2007a). Both islands are young in their independence as they were granted autonomy from Britain in 1979, less than thirty years ago. During the West Indian Independence movement, however, Saint Lucia and SVG practiced self-government as Associated States while still under political allegiance to Britain (Knight 1990, 301–302).

The archeological and anthropological research based on cultural artifacts and other excavated materials indicate the presence in the islands of native Indians groups, such as the Ciboneys over 7,000 years ago and the Arawaks in approximately 200 B.C. (Sutty 1993, 6). Today, the majority of the islands' populations are descended from continental Africans who were enslaved during the triangular slave trade, as well as from runaway African slaves during the seventeenth century (Sutty 1993, 10). There is also a European presence from the colonial settlers, and historical miscegenation has increased the population of mixed-race islanders.

In Saint Lucia, the population is approximately 90 percent black, 6 percent mixed descent, 3 percent East Indian, and 1 percent Caucasian (Central Intelligence Agency 2007a). In SVG, the population statistics differ in that there is a much larger percentage of the population that is considered to be mixed race, as well as a small presence of Carib and indigenous populations. Blacks form approximately 66 percent of the population. Nineteen percent are mixed persons, 6 percent are East Indian, 2 percent are Amerindians, and 7 percent are various ethnic groups that have settled in the islands over the years (Central Intelligence Agency 2007b). While research indicates that the European presence in the islands may have occurred before the voyages of Christopher Columbus, the most documented history of Europeans in the islands began with Columbus (Knight 1990, 28). Europeans entered SVG in 1498 on the third voyage of Christopher Columbus in search of gold. The evidence is uncertain, but historians generally tend to believe that Columbus landed in Saint Lucia during his fourth voyage in 1502.

The population of Saint Lucia is approximately 168,458. Slightly less than 30 percent of this population is under fifteen years of age (Reuters Foundation; Central Intelligence Agency 2007a). While the island has natural resources and is rich in minerals, only 6.25 percent of Saint Lucia's land is arable. Much of the country's income is generated by tourism and the related industries. The Gross Domestic Protect (GDP) is $4,800 per capita, and the island is ranked seventy-first on the United Nations Develop-

---

KEY FACTS – SAINT LUCIA, SAINT VINCENT, AND THE GRENADINES

Saint Lucia:
Population: 168,458 (2007 est.)
Infant mortality rate: 12.81 deaths/1,000 live births (2007 est.)
Life expectancy at birth: 74.08 years (2007 est.)
Literacy rate: 90.1 percent (2001 est.)
Net primary school enrollment/attendance: 98 percent (2000–2005)
Internet users: 55,000 (2005 est.)
Saint Vincent and the Grenadines:
Population: 117,848 (2007 est.)
Infant mortality rate: 14.01 deaths/1,000 live births (2007 est.)
Life expectancy at birth: 74.09 years (2007 est.)
Net primary school enrollment/attendance: 94 percent (2000–05)
Internet users: 8,000 (2005 est.)

Sources: CIA World Factbook: Saint Lucia. https://www.cia.gov/cia/publications/factbook/geos/st.html. April 17, 2007; CIA World Factbook: Saint Vincent and the Grenadines. https://www.cia.gov/cia/publications/factbook/geos/vc.html. April 17, 2007; UNICEF. At a Glance: Saint Lucia–Statistics. http://www.unicef.org/infobycountry/stlucia_statistics.html. April 24, 2007; UNICEF. At a Glance: Saint Vincent and the Grenadines–Statistics http://www.unicef.org/infobycountry/stvincentgrenadines_statistics.html. April 24, 2007.

---

ment Programme Human Development Index (United Nations Development Programme 2006). SVG has a smaller population of 117,848 people, and similar to Saint Lucia, just below 30 percent of the population is under the age of fifteen. Ten percent of SVG's GDP comes from the agricultural economy, unlike Saint Lucia where only 5 percent of GDP originates from agro-industry, although Saint Lucia exports larger amounts of crops and produce than SVG. In SVG, over 17 percent of land is arable, and export income is based primarily on crops and natural produce. The GDP is approximately $3,500 per capita, and SVG maintains a Human Development Index rank of 88 (United Nations Development Programme 2006). In general, both islands have a good amount of infrastructure in place to care for children and provide food security, but with the new challenges of poverty, unemployment, and health concerns, investment in existing infrastructure is necessary to support their child populations.

OVERVIEW

SVG has placed a significant effort into developing government infrastructure for social welfare and development. Within the government there is a Ministry of Education, a Ministry of Health and Environment, a Ministry of Tourism, Youth, and Sports, a Ministry of National Mobilization, Social Development, Non-Governmental Organizations (NGO) Relations, Family, Gender Affairs and Persons with Disabilities, as well as a Ministry of Urban Development, Labor, Culture, and Electoral Matters. Children are serviced in a number of capacities through these and other ministries, but the national legal provisions for children outside of the international Convention on the Rights of the Child 1989 (CRC), in both Saint Lucia and SVG, are not as well developed. Through government-sponsored provisions, public assistance is available in SVG for foster children, orphans, and children with disabilities. However, public assistance is minimal, at approximately $60 per month (Eastern Caribbean dollars [ECD]), particularly when the number of female-headed households is high and the income of males in the household is often absent (Sealy-Burke 2006, 5). In addition, the Ministry of Social Development partially subsidizes facilities for rehabilitation and training for persons with disabilities (U.S. Department of State 2006b).

Both islands have made education a priority, but gains generally are more notable at the primary level than at the secondary level. Health and welfare conditions are challenged by the growing HIV/AIDS epidemic in the region. They are also challenged by the onslaught of natural disasters as both islands are situated within the hurricane belt. Exploitative child labor is generally differentiated from work that children perform on both islands, and infringement of child labor standards is generally unheard of in SVG and Saint Lucia, while the abuse of women and children is increasingly being recognized as a social and legal problem. The family structure continues to be based on traditional forms of unions in the Caribbean region; the dynamics of the international economy in addition to the implementation of economic structural adjustment policies have impacted women and children, as well as the income-generating activities that are typically utilized in female-headed households. Religious activities provide a basis for community interactions as well as cultural education and recreation for children in both islands.

EDUCATION

Education has been a national priority in Saint Lucia, particularly at the primary school level. Because the national government seeks to increase its economic independence with less reliance on export-oriented and tourist industries, it has increased education expenditures to develop the national human capital. Before independence, education was largely a function of the dominant churches on the island, such as the Catholic Church (Sheldon). After independence, schools that were organized under the colonial churches were supported by the national government and developed into a system of subsidized education. Preschool education was not practiced in Saint Lucia until the 1970s and was more clearly defined under the authority of the Ministry of Education by the mid-1980s. At least 80 percent of children between the ages of three and five years old now attend preschool in Saint Lucia. In 1998 it was estimated that there were at least 150 preschools and thirty-three childcare facilities on the island, although many women still chose to have family members care for their children (Sheldon).

Primary-school education is mandatory for all boys and girls, and universal education at the elementary stage has been achieved. By 2005, net primary school enrollment of young males was estimated at 99 percent, whereas net enrollment of females was estimated at 96 percent (United Nations Children's Fund, "At a Glance: Saint Vincent and the Grenadines"). Even though there is a 3 percent differential between males and females, it has been noted that females are consistently outperforming males in educational settings across the board. The Common Entrance Exam (CXE) is a mandatory exam at the end of the seventh grade for those students wishing to attend secondary schools in the West Indian islands. The 2002 report on CXE results in Saint Lucia demonstrates that females consistently scored higher on all subject areas compared with males, which resulted in the placement of approximately 356 more female students into secondary schools than males (Office of the Registrar of Examinations 2002).

In addition to lower scores on the CXE for males, net male enrollment in secondary schools in Saint Lucia is generally lower than females. Male enrollment averages around 68 percent, whereas the average female enrollment is 74 percent (United Nations Children's Fund, "At a Glance: Saint Lucia"). The social problems associated with young boys and girls that do not attend high school, such as early pregnancy and increased levels of crime, are thus a concern for government. In 2003, 60 percent of children that took the CXE were placed in various secondary schools across the island, leaving 40 percent of youth in need of alternative forms of education (Social Issues 2004). There is a concern that the common entrance system is in fact exclusive and places a large amount of pressure on children to perform at extremely high levels in order for them to be able to attend high school. The 1997 Saint Lucia Education Act deems it necessary for all students to participate in mandatory education until the age of sixteen years. If a student does poorly on the CXE and is not placed in a secondary school, he or she attends a senior-primary program, which is focused on job-training education for three years of additional schooling (Sheldon). The benefit of such a system is that students have an option of developing skills that allow them to become productive citizens, but there is a stigma associated with attending such programs for children who have not done well on the CXE.

In SVG, the Ministry of Education seeks to provide a high standard of education across the island in all areas, including academic, vocational and technical, athletic, and ethical education. In cooperation with the private sector, the government has sponsored a nonformal skills program for vocational education. The Youth Empowerment Program creates apprenticeship opportunities for children to learn the trades. In 2005, 500 young people were enrolled in the program and earned an estimated $148 per month while in training. There are currently six vocational technology schools on the island (Government of Saint Vincent and the Grenadines).

Community education efforts are also allotted support by the SVG government. For example, there is a specific Community Education Program, which is designed to deliver workshops, training, and lectures on subjects dealing with social welfare and available social services and legal provisions. In addition, the program works with the Ministry of Education to deliver adult and continuing education opportunities, particularly for socially vulnerable parents (Government of Saint Vincent and the Grenadines).

There are approximately sixty-two primary schools in SVG, and one school partially subsidized by the government for special needs children (Government of Saint Vincent and the Grenadines). Under the National Education Act, the government mandates that every child must attend primary school. Primary school education tuition is subsidized by the government, but families must pay through personal funds for food, transportation, and books for their children. For families under the poverty line, at least 37 percent of families, personal funds for education of children are often unavailable (Sealy-Burke 2006, 5, 10). Consequently, universal primary education has not been achieved in SVG. While the net enrollment of males in primary school was 95 percent and the net enrollment of females in primary school was 92 percent between 2002 and 2005 (United Nations Children's Fund, "At a Glance: Saint Vincent and the Grenadines"), the student attrition rate for young boys from the age of five to fifteen years was approximately 39 percent and 26 percent for young girls (Sealy-Burke 2006, 10). Thus retention, rather than enrollment, of children at the primary level of education is a challenge for SVG.

There are twenty-two secondary schools on the island (Government of Saint Vincent and the Grenadines). Net enrollment for boys at the secondary level is 62 percent and for girls it is 63 percent (United Nations Children's Fund, "At a Glance: Saint Vincent and the Grenadines"). The results from the CXE in SVG show a similar trend to that of Saint Lucia. In 2006, 1,376 boys wrote the examination, and 482 passed. On the other hand 1,302 girls wrote the examination and 619 passed. Comparatively, in 2005, 453 of 1,812 boys passed the exam and 723 of 1,572 girls passed (Government of Saint Vincent and the Grenadines). Young girls continue to outperform young boys on the CXE, which translates into more young boys not attending secondary schools. The government must work toward promoting the realization of universal education, and the efforts to expand vocational education must be supported to give those children not in secondary schools valid options for career and educational development.

PLAY AND RECREATION

In SVG and in Saint Lucia, as in the majority of the West Indian islands, cricket and football (soccer) are among the most popular sports and recreational activities for children. With over fourteen cricket leagues in SVG, children and youth can engage in government-sponsored recreational and competitive activities. Government organizations such as the National Sports Council, the National Olympic Association, and the Ministry of Sports all participate in providing recreational and competitive sports opportunities for children (English 2001). Cricket has also been used to capture children's attention regarding national social welfare initiatives that are pertinent to children. For example, the International Cricket Council and international human development organizations have used the popularity of cricket and other sporting activities to promote programs related to children and HIV/AIDS awareness. Children are excited to meet famous cricketers and also gain information on the important social issues that they face (McClean-Trotman 2007).

In Saint Lucia, government-sponsored recreation for children and families has also typically appeared under the form of alternative education, which in turn is often centered on HIV/AIDS prevention efforts. Saint Lucia Family Planning worked with the national government and media to expand the conceptualization of HIV/AIDS education by using a radio soap opera to promote awareness, education, and prevention. The Apwe Plezi program ran for approximately two years and followed the themes typical of any other type of soap opera, except that it focused on issues related to family planning, sexual health, and social development (Vaughan, Regis, and St. Catherine 2000, 148). A national survey conducted to test the benefits of Apwe Plezi found that listeners and fans of the show were more aware of contraceptives, family health, and family planning. Preshow statistics showed that approximately 27 percent of female respondents thought that it was generally acceptable for partners or husbands to conduct sexual relations outside of a monogamous relationship or marriage, regardless of the associated health risks, whereas after the two years that Apwe Plezi aired, that percentage had decreased to 14 percent. Listeners of the show were more likely to work with family planning counselors and had actually adopted family planning methods in their daily lives (Vaughan, Regis, and St. Catherine 2000, 148). Such innovative attempts at educating the national population through media and recreation for families are crucial to Saint Lucia's attempt to develop their human resources and to stem the impact of HIV/AIDS and other health concerns in the future.

Established in 1987, the Saint Lucia School of Music is a world-renowned institution that develops musical and arts activities in the framework of education for children. With two large centers and over four hundred students, the school has afforded young children the opportunity to develop skills and abilities in the performing arts while also engaging in fun activity. The school teaches children from preschool age and engages them in the larger cultural events of the island to develop a sense of community involvement. For example, students from the school participate annually in the internationally known Saint Lucia Jazz Festival (Saint Lucia School of Music).

CHILD LABOR

There are legal prohibitions against the employment and labor of children and minors under the age of sixteen years. The law in Saint Lucia becomes more specific for industrial-related labor where minors under the age of eighteen are prohibited from employment. For infringement of labor laws with regard to children under sixteen, the fine is at least US$3.55 (ECD$9.50) and for children under eighteen in industrial work it is US$8.88 (ECD$24.00) (U.S. Department of State 2006a). At times, child labor laws present obstacles to the informal labor sector, as well as agricultural work and family farming. While there are no reported incidences of child labor law infringement, it is not unusual for children to perform unclassified forms of work, particularly in large families. Children often work as small vendors during market days or in public cultural celebrations. They also tend to work in harvesting crops particularly in the rural areas of Saint Lucia (U.S. Department of State 2006a). Family farmers generally tend to employ immediate family on the farms rather than outsiders. Parents may have many children hoping to provide the human resources necessary to work their land. However, because of increasing trends of urbanization, there is a significant incidence of children leaving rural farms to live overseas or in urban areas (Barrow 1992, 41–49).

In SVG, there are laws that protect children from child labor and exploitation in employment. The child labor that occurs on small family-owned farms, in cottage-industries, and on family-owned banana plantations that produce for the export sector is legally recognized as acceptable forms of child work (English 2001). The government has attempted to provide other opportunities for youth employment to stem the tendency towards exploitative child labor conditions by offering a youth employment program, where youth are given training and job experience within government ministries through one-year internships (U.S. Department of State 2006b).

FAMILY

Over 40 percent of the households in SVG are female-headed households (English 2001). Common-law unions are common between partners, and "visiting unions" and "friending" are frequently found in both islands. Such relationships allow the male to live apart from the female and their children (English 2001). As a result, although men maintain relationships with their children, women tend to bear the majority of the responsibility for child-rearing (English 2001). Women do enjoy some level of equity, as 53.5 percent of women are economically active in the Saint Lucian public sphere (United Nations Development Programme 2006). The rate of female activity as a percentage of male economic activity was 67 percent in 2006 (United Nations Development Programme 2006).

Saint Lucian women working in export industry-related activities in settings such as factories experience high levels of job dissatisfaction and generally report a lower quality of life than those in other sectors of employment. In a 1980s survey, women commented on low salaries that left them with inadequate amounts of money to buy food for their children (Kelly 1987, 37). Some of these female workers were aware of the government's role in the determination of their salaries, particularly those that worked in factories owned by foreign corporations, and believed that the government should assert more stringent policies towards foreign companies operating in Saint Lucia (Kelly 1987, 38). The enabling economic environments of small-island states, which are created by the national government to seek higher levels of direct foreign investments, means that national salaries are set at low rates and taxes on foreign corporations are reduced. As a result, cracking down on corporations to improve women's labor rights is unlikely (Kelly 1987, 89).

Women of female-headed households often reported that they engaged in piecework. These workers are paid based on the amount of pieces they produce according to assigned quotas, which pressure women to work quickly with long hours and no breaks in unsafe conditions (Kelly 1987, 40–42). Because such labor is considered to be flexible, women can be laid off at any time with minimal job security. The flexibility of labor caused psychological stress for women in female-headed households (Kelly 1987, 47–48). In circumstances where the family exists on one income, women are responsible for providing food, housing, and clothing for their children. Women were generally concerned that because of their low incomes, the education of their children would be affected in the long-term even though only approximately one-fifth of women had their children enrolled in primary/nursery schools. Most often, women relied on other female family members to care for children while at work, in addition to neighbors and surrounding community members (Kelly 1987, 80–81).

HEALTH

Saint Lucia's population growth rate is approximately 1.29 percent, with an estimated twenty births per 1,000 persons and just over five deaths per 1,000. The total fertility rate is 2.2 percent, and life expectancy is estimated at seventy-three years of age (United Nations Children's Fund, "At a Glance: Saint Lucia"). Female life expectancy averages approximately 73.9 years while male life expectancy is estimated at 69.3 years of age (United Nations 2006, 338). On a scale of 0 to 1, the probability of survival for children between birth and fifteen years of age has increased from 0.83 probability in the 1950s and 1960s to 0.98 probability in 2002 (United Nations 2006, 338). The crude death rate has also decreased from around 8 percent in the 1970s to 7 percent in 2005. Infants that are born with low birth weight averaged about 10 percent between 1998 and 2005. Generally, infant and child mortality rates have improved significantly through the latter half of the twentieth century (United Nations Children's Fund, "At a Glance: Saint Lucia"; United Nations 2006, 338). National data for Saint Lucia indicates that in the 1950s and 1960s, infant mortality for males was at least 110 deaths for every 1,000 live births and for females 104 deaths for every 1,000 births. By 2002, male infant mortality had decreased sharply to thirteen deaths per 1,000 births, and female infant mortality decreased to fifteen deaths for every 1,000 births (United Nations 2006, 338). Yet the United Nations estimates that the mortality rate for children under the age of five is at least twenty deaths for every 1,000 births. Consequently, international organizations are encouraging the Saint Lucian government to strengthen healthcare provisions in this area (United Nations 2006, 338).

Almost all of the population of Saint Lucia has access to clean water and has been immunized against typically preventable illnesses, such as tuberculosis, diphtheria, polio, measles, and hepatitis. Averages for immunization in these areas fluctuate between 95 percent and 100 percent, and the provision of clean sanitation facilities in both urban and rural areas is just below 90 percent (United Nations Children's Fund, "At a Glance: Saint Lucia"). Malaria was a great concern in the 1980s and 1990s, but with widespread government efforts towards national infant immunization, malaria has been contained in the island in accordance with the International Millennium Development Goals ("Millenium Development Goals" 2004).

The first reported case of HIV/AIDS in Saint Lucia occurred in 1985. The numbers of reported incidences are steadily increasing. By 2003, there were 401 reported cases of HIV-infected victims, with at least 194 persons who had full-blown AIDS. Even though there have been attempts at early intervention and prevention through community-based programming, the rates of infection have continued to grow. By 2005, the Division of Gender Relations notes that there were over 546 reported cases of HIV infection (Division of Gender Relations 2006, 1). The national prevalence rate is approximately 0.12 percent, which is quite low for the region when compared with islands such as Haiti, Trinidad and Tobago, Jamaica, and the Dominican Republic. Under the Ministry of

Health, the Saint Lucia Aids Action Foundation and the Aids Secretariat were created in order to deal with the growing number of AIDS patients (Division of Gender Relations 2006, 1).

The most notable growth of prevalence is in young females between the ages of twenty-five and thirty-four, the segment of the population most likely to be of childbearing age. HIV/AIDS prevalence in this female cohort increases the possibility of mother-to-child-transmission (MTCT). Of all cases, 47 percent of HIV infections occur among females and, although more men than women have died from AIDS, the ratio of deaths among females in the late twentieth and early twenty-first centuries is increasing rapidly. Because of low levels of condom usage, power relations based on gender domination in sexual activity, rape, economic dependency on male partners, poor awareness on sexual education matters, and multiple partnering, women are increasingly affected by HIV/AIDS (Division of Gender Relations 2006, 1).

Saint Lucia has a national program for HIV/AIDS (Jack 2001, 32). With the assistance of the World Bank, the government was able to deliver the National HIV/AIDS Strategic Plan that was created to mitigate the impact of HIV/AIDS from 2005 to 2009. In addition to the strategic approach, a National AIDS Coordinating Council (NACC) was created to encourage and monitor the delivery of the HIV/AIDS plan (Division of Gender Relations 2006, 1).

Although women from the age of twenty-five are most affected, the increasing risk to young girls around the age of fifteen is also of concern. Because of the young ages of first sexual intercourse experience in the island, teen girls generally are more at risk than young boys for new infections. There are children infected by HIV/AIDS, although prevalence rates and statistics are underreported. Children are also orphaned, which heightens their experience of alienation and poverty. There is a national program for the care of children infected by HIV by which children receive public assistance, including a monthly stipend in addition to provisions that allow them to gain care and free medication. The allowance has increased from ECD$60 to ECD$250 (Division of Gender Relations 2006, 4).

The population growth rate in SVG is 0.26 percent. Approximately 26.7 percent of the population is under the age of fourteen. Total fertility rates are estimated at 1.83 births per woman. There are approximately 16.18 births for every 1,000 persons, and 5.98 deaths for every 1,000 persons. Infant mortality rates for children under the age of five are approximately 14.4 deaths for every 1,000 live births. For infant males, the mortality rates are higher than for females; in 2006, the male infant mortality rate was 15.67, while the female infant mortality was 13.08. In general, infant mortality rates have decreased since the millennium. In 1990, infant mortality for children under the age of five was twenty-five deaths for every 1,000 live births (Central Intelligence Agency 2007b).

At 10 percent, the rate of infants born with a low birth weight is the same as in Saint Lucia (United Nations Children's Fund, "At a Glance: Saint Vincent and the Grenadines").

The government of SVG has subsidized a school-feeding program nationally. The school-feeding program seeks to ensure national food security and services to those children in preschool and primary school who are particularly socially vulnerable, whose families are in poverty, and who are at a higher risk for malnutrition and preventable illnesses than other segments of the population. The program subsidizes at least one-third of young children's daily nutrition requirements (Government of SVG). As such, the government has made child nutrition a social welfare priority.

Like Saint Lucia, the government of SVG has made considerable efforts toward ensuring national immunizations against tuberculosis, diphtheria, polio, measles, hepatitis, and other preventable and treatable illnesses. National immunization rates range from 93 percent to 100 percent. Life expectancy in the island is approximately seventy-one years of age, a ten-year increase from the 1970s expectancy rate of sixty-one years of age (United Nations Children's Fund, "At a Glance: Saint Vincent and the Grenadines"). Male life expectancy averages 71.99 years of age and female expectancy 75.77 years (Central Intelligence Agency 2007b).

The prevalence of HIV/AIDS in SVG is actually higher than that of Saint Lucia, although SVG has a smaller landmass and population. The first AIDS case was reported in 1984, one year before the first case was reported in Saint Lucia. In 2002, the prevalence rate was estimated at 1.36 percent in SVG, while it was estimated at 0.83 percent in Saint Lucia (Caribbean Epidemiology Center 2004). In 2004, the number of reported cases of HIV infection was 796 (Sealy-Burke 2006, 2), 250 more cases than those reported in Saint Lucia in 2005.

While MTCT seems to be a growing concern, the government has worked toward mitigating this problem through a program for MTCT. In the early 1990s, when the concern was greatest, approximately 0.5 percent of children were infected by this mode of transmission, and by the millennium, the rate of MTCT had decreased significantly and was 0.1 percent (United Nations Children's Fund, "At a Glance: Saint Vincent and the Grenadines"). SVG shares the concern for women and the HIV/AIDS pandemic. The trend in the island has followed the pattern of the majority of the Caribbean islands in that females have become the most affected population. Annually, females are infected at a higher rate than males in all age cohorts, twenty-five to thirty-five, fifteen to nineteen, and birth to five years of age. In addition, the high rate of teen pregnancies on the island heightens the risk for teen girls and increases the chance that newborn children will become orphaned at an early age. International researchers have termed this trend the "feminization" of HIV/AIDS (Sealy-Burke 2006, 2).

Gains in social welfare and health were impacted by the recent Hurricane Ivan in 2004. Saint Lucia and SVG were affected to a lesser extent than islands such as Grenada. Natural disasters do have negative impacts in that they erode potential gains made by non-governmental and governmental organizations, as well as communities, to alleviate circumstances of poverty and poor health across the board (Sealy-Burke 2006, 3). The SVG Red Cross reported that approximately nineteen homes were lost and forty homes were in need of repairs after Hurricane Ivan. In addition, an estimated 1,000 persons sought accommodation in the twenty-eight shelters that were provided in the island (Red Cross Relief Web 2004).

LAWS AND LEGAL STATUS

In Saint Lucia, the Ministry of Education and Culture, as well as a Ministry of Social Transformation, Human Services, Family Affairs, Youth and Sports, work in coordination with the Ministry of Housing and the Ministry of Health to provide for the social welfare of children. Under the Saint Lucia Civil Code (SLCC), children have significant social protections that are legally enshrined, although enforcement of legal protection is less successful than the delineation of legal measures. The Canadian International Development Agency and the government of Saint Lucia reformed the Saint Lucia Civil Code in accordance with the CRC in 2004. Since 1879 when the code was created, children's rights have increased dramatically as they are considered persons under the law (Family Law Committee 2006, 4–5).

One concern in the SLCC is that the rights accorded to children in relation to their legal status as legitimate—children born into a marriage—are denied to illegitimate children who are not legally under the submission of a parental authority. This may work in favor of or against children, depending on the circumstances; for example, in the case of inheritance laws. Illegitimate children are often denied rights to inheritance, but in terms of support, illegitimate and legitimate children are accorded the same rights (Family Law Committee 2006, 28–31). Illegitimacy is particularly significant in Saint Lucia, according to the research findings from international family-planning perspectives. Traditional Caribbean unions are still prevalent in Saint Lucia, as many couples do not engage in official marriages but opt to cohabit in common-law type unions. Consequently, legal protections are difficult to provide in a context where an average of 85 percent of children, for example, were born outside of legal marriages in 1990s (Vaughan, Regis, and St. Catherine 2000, 148).

In 2005, SVG recognized the problem of social violence against women when it was addressed at the Inter-American Convention on the Prevention, Punishment, and Eradication of Violence against Women. The government of SVG has ratified this convention. In addition, under the Domestic Violence and Matrimonial Proceedings Act of 1984 and the Domestic Violence Act of 1995, women are entitled to protections under the law from domestic abuse (International Women's Rights Action Watch).

The provision of child support for single mothers in SVG is supported by the CRC under Article 27. In terms of national law, the Status of the Children Act created in 1971 also provides for child support and eliminates the previous legal differentiation between legitimate and illegitimate children, which caused both legal and social inequity (Sealy-Burke 2006, 5–6). In reality, illegitimate children are still victims of social inequalities. Mothers of illegitimate children are required to follow different legal procedures to gain support for their children under the Maintenance Act than married mothers who file for support under the Matrimonial Causes Act. Support allocated for illegitimate children is often granted in lower amounts and comes attached with more stringent conditions (Sealy-Burke 2006, 5–6).

RELIGIOUS LIFE

According to a 2001 census, the Central Intelligence Agency reports that 67.5 percent of the population in Saint Lucia are Roman Catholic, 8.5 percent are Seventh-Day Adventist, 5.7 percent are Pentecostal, 2.1 percent are Rastafarian, 2 percent are Anglican, 2 percent are Evangelical, 5.1 percent consider themselves as part of another Christian denomination, and 2.6 percent are other or unspecified. Just over 4 percent report that they have no religious affiliation (Central Intelligence Agency 2007a). The religious practices vary across Christian spiritualism for the most part, but the retention of African cultural traditions as well as indigenous Amerindian spiritualism have historically played a part in the cultural and religious life of Saint Lucia as well as SVG (English 2001). In SVG, the majority of the religious population are Anglican. Approximately 47 percent of the population reports their affiliation to the Anglican Church, while 28 percent are Methodist, 13 percent are Catholic, and 12 percent are Hindu, Seventh-Day Adventist, or practice another form of Protestantism (Central Intelligence Agency 2007b). In general, children are typically well versed in Biblical scriptures, which they learn through attending church services and other activities centered in the church community (English 2001).

The syncretism that has occurred in Saint Lucia and SVG, where there has been a blending and mixture of West African traditions, East Indian cultural practices from the indentured Indians that arrived in the islands during the nineteenth century (English 2001), and European forms of Catholic worship, has resulted in a cultural context where religious and artistic practices have served as educational tools for children. Historically, there have been monthly religious celebrations in Saint Lucia that involve festivals, music, dancing, church services and processions, and so on. Children's play activities as well as the passing down of oral histories and storytelling are often involved in these activities (Crowley 1957, 4–5).

On the weekends and during the evening times, adults traditionally sang folk songs called "ti shaso"—meaning "little songs"—and told traditional stories to school children. Singing activities, music to accompany children's games, and rhyming activities were also typically conducted in English rather than Creole/patois (Crowley 1957, 13–14).

Cultural education and community history were taught through songs and drumming. Through such artistic methods, religious and cultural information about the origins of the African Caplawu nation, the Angol, and the Awandu nations, which were African tribes from which certain segments of the Saint Lucian population claimed their ancestry, were passed down to children. In order to keep cultural traditions alive, dances and rituals such as the Kele and the Kutumba were performed. This type of education was particularly important during the masquerades of Saint Lucia during the Christmas and New Years seasons (Crowley 1957, 8).

Today, children participate in masquerades, and young children are often the most skilled dancers and artists that participate in such celebrations. The community participates in cultural activities by making musical instruments on which children perform, or costumes. Children participate with adults in singing the traditional songs of Saint Lucia and other islands, which are often combined with religious hymns that have been passed down from European religions. While the extent to which community members still integrate indigenous forms of worship and culture into the everyday lives of children is obscure, there is evidence to suggest that tradition continues through the noted importance of dreams and supernatural beings, Moco Jumbies or spirits, which are often depicted with vibrant costumes in festivals and carnivals (English 2001).

CHILD ABUSE AND NEGLECT

The incidence of child abuse is underreported, and the abuse of women goes almost unreported. For example, although violence against women is a recognized social dilemma in Saint Lucia, the family court only tried 34 cases in 2004, and documentation of reported cases in other years is not readily available. The legal system tends to have a hands-off policy toward domestic affairs and generally does not pursue cases of domestic or social violence unless the victim reports them. The victim must file a complaint and must press charges against the perpetrator (U.S. Department of State 2006a). Protection orders can be issued by the court, and the penalty for rape can range from fourteen years imprisonment to life in jail. Under such legal provisions, sexual harassment is illegal but often goes unnoticed, particularly in cases against prostitutes since prostitution is itself illegal and sex workers are typically stigmatized and marginalized from the larger society (U.S. Department of State 2006a).

More knowledge of the abuses against women and children is generally found in the non-governmental sector. In Saint Lucia's capital city,

Castries, an organization named the Saint Lucia Crisis Center began to keep track of reported cases of social violence against women and children. In 2004, nine cases were tracked. Cases involved sexual violence, incest, poverty, homelessness, delinquency in child support payments, alcoholism, drug use, and other social welfare concerns. The organization works with a government-provided shelter, the Women's Support Center, for crisis management, and women's help hotlines (U.S. Department of State 2006a).

In 2005, the U.S. State Department's Country Report on Human Rights Practices documented reported abuses against children in Saint Lucia. There were seventy-five reported cases of sexual abuse, ninety-five cases of non-sexual physical abuse, twenty-nine incidents of psychological abuse, and at least 107 incidents of neglect and abandonment (U.S. Department of State 2006b). It is important to note that the statistics document only reported cases, and real numbers in small-island societies are often difficult to determine, particularly when urban–rural differentials and underreporting are taken into consideration. While children's legal protections are officially in place under the SLCC, instituting social acceptance of the concept of children's rights is often a more challenging task.

The responsible government ministry for such child abuses is the St. Lucian Division of Human services under the Ministry of Health, Human Service, Family Affairs and Gender Relations. Although reporting of sexual abuse has gradually increased from forty-nine reports in 2003 to sixty-five cases in 2004, the division has come under criticism from children's advocates who claim that there are few mechanisms in the welfare system that encourage children and parents to report abuse. In addition, the Country Report indicated that parents in financial difficulty would sometimes accept monetary compensation for agreeing not to report circumstances of abuse to appropriate authorities. Public court cases and statements by legal officials in Saint Lucia are beginning to bring national recognition to the growing problems of sexual assault and of adults engaging in sexual activities with minors; almost half of criminal cases heard in the court are related to sexual violence (U.S. Department of State 2006a).

In SVG, a non-governmental organization the St. Vincent and the Grenadines Human Rights Association (SVGHRA), takes responsibility for ensuring that human rights violations for children and adults are minimal, particularly in the areas of police brutality and other forms of social violence (U.S. Department of State 2006b). The SVGHR has reported to the U.S. Department of State that the conditions of juvenile offenders in prison are unacceptable. Furthermore, there are no juvenile detention centers on the island, and child offenders are imprisoned with adult offenders (Sealy-Burke 2006, 9). There are concerns for health and hygiene, the spread of HIV/AIDS in the facility, and lack of training development while in detention (U.S. Department of State 2006b).

There were sixty-three instances of child abuse handled by the Family Services Department in 2005. These cases were tried in family court, however, as in Saint Lucia, underreporting is still a concern for children who remain in abusive circumstances with limited social advocacy or support mechanisms. While it is socially acknowledged that child abuse, particularly sexual molestation of young girls and boys, is a significant social problem, there are insufficient legal mechanisms in place to deliver justice in such circumstances. While the Juvenile Act of SVG does address child protection issues, as of July 2006 there were no specific provisions in the law that dealt with legalities and due process in sexual or domestic abuse cases (Sealy-Burke 2006). In addition, because the age of consent is as young as fifteen years old, teens above the age of fifteen remain vulnerable to sexual abuse. Furthermore, punishments for abuses of children under that age of fifteen are lenient at best (Sealy-Burke 2006, 8).

The Caribbean Association of Family Research and Action has been active in SVG, facilitating programs and workshops for women and police officers on domestic violence against women and legal interventions. In 2005, seventy-eight instances of rape were reported. Under half of these cases were prosecuted, and forty-seven were assigned for further investigation (U.S. Department of State 2006b). Between 1986 and 1989, researchers noted that at least 75 percent of abusers were a significant other, while 15 percent of abusers were husbands and 10 percent were another male member of the extended family (International Women's Rights Action Watch). Female victims typically ranged from age thirteen to thirty-four. In combination with the non-governmental organizations, the National Committee against Violence under the Ministry of Education, Women's Affairs, and Culture has conducted workshops on social equity and empowerment for women in the island (International Women's Rights Action Watch).

It was noted that, in 2005, 443 cases were brought to the attention of the family courts, but many cases have not been prosecuted (U.S. Department of State 2006b). Non-governmental organizations, such as SVGHRA and Marion House, work with women to encourage reporting of cases and the social empowerment of women and their families. While Marion House provides other social support services for women and children, such as counseling and therapy, there are no official battered women's shelters on the island (International Women's Rights Action Watch).

GROWING UP IN THE TWENTY-FIRST CENTURY

In the twenty-first century, both SVG and Saint Lucia face issues of economic competitiveness as small islands in an international economic system. The welfare of the islands' children depends on the ability of national governments and regional organizations, such as OCES and the

Caribbean Economic community, to navigate the waters of social change and development. Both islands must focus on equipping their populations with skills, abilities, various forms of education, and awareness of social welfare challenges. The current competitiveness and exclusivity of the education system has led to high standards of achievement among a minority of excellent students, but the larger goals of national education must focus on inclusion and achievement across the islands in order to adequately address social, health, and economic concerns.

RESOURCE GUIDE

Suggested Readings

Correia, Maria, and Wendy Cunningham. 2003. *Caribbean Youth Development: Issues and Policy Directions*. World Bank Country Study. World Bank Publications. This World Bank publication focuses on child and youth development as it relates to health, social productivity, and well-being of the surrounding community.

Mohammed, Patricia. 1999. *Caribbean Women at the Crossroads: The Paradox of Motherhood among Women of Barbados, St. Lucia and Dominica*. Mona, Jamaica: Canoe Press, University of the West Indies. Mohammed provides a psycho-social analysis of the experience of family and mothering in St. Lucia. Her book describes the social conditions under which women live and how social circumstances impact their ability to rear children.

Orr, Tamra. 2003. *The Windward Islands: St. Lucia, St. Vincent and the Grenadines, Grenada, Martinique, & Dominica*. Mason Crest Publishers. This is a text intended for children to read about the culture, history, and society of the islands.

Parry, Odette. 2001. *Male Underachievement in High School Education: In Jamaica, Barbados, and St. Vincent and the Grenadines*. Mona, Jamaica: University Press of the West Indies. Parry discusses male performance in the education systems of the West Indies in the context of gender issues, as well as the topic of homophobia in Caribbean society.

Reynolds, Anderson. 2003. *The Struggle for Survival: An Historical, Political, and Socioeconomic Perspective of St. Lucia*. Vieux-Fort, St. Lucia: Jako Books. This text examines the precolonial and colonial history of St. Lucia, as well as the development of the primary commodity export industry and the impact of tourism on the socioeconomic, political, and environmental climate of St. Lucia.

Rubenstein, Hymie. 1987. *Coping with Poverty: Adaptive Strategies in a Caribbean Village*. London: Westview Press. Case studies of St. Vincent and the Grenadines that provide specific examples of how everyday people within the African community of the island employ various mechanisms to cope with conditions of poverty.

Nonprint Resources

Derek Walcott. 1989. By Bill Moyers. New York: WNET. PBS Television Series. In this interview, the Nobel Prize-winning author, poet, and teacher talks about his homeland, St. Lucia, and the importance of language in a formerly colonized society.

Parker, Phillip, and Eli Lilly. 2006. *The Economic Competitiveness of St. Vincent & the Grenadines: Financials Returns, Labor Productivity and international Gap*.

Digital–PDF. Fountainebleau, France: Icon Group International. Parker and Lilly explore issues of international finance and productivity in St. Vincent and the Grenadines that affect the state of the island.

Web Sites

Organization of Eastern Caribbean States, http://www.oecs.org/. Web site for the regional organization that includes information on economic, social, and political developments in the region. Also has information and literature regarding development programs and projects.

Organizations and NGOs

CARE–Centre for Adolescent Rehabilitation and Education
Executive Director, Dr. Karleen Mason
Parish Centre, Micoud Street
Castries, St. Lucia
Phone: (758) 452-7689
Skills Centre in Vigie
Phone: (758) 451-8211
Gros Islet Center
Phone: (758) 450-8179
Anse-La-Raye Center
Phone: (758) 451-4889
Canaries Center
Phone: (758) 452-4144
Type of vocational education setting that accommodates many students who did not pass the Common Entrance Examinations and seek alternative educational settings outside of secondary schools.

Saint Lucia Folk Research Center
Plas Wiches Foklo
Executive Director, Kennedy Samuel
Mount Pleasant
P.O. Box 514
Castries, St. Lucia
Phone: (758) 452-2279/31477
Fax: (758) 451-9365
Mobile: (758) 285-0340
Email: frc@candw.lc
This organization works with educational, social, and cultural institutions to promote cultural education and economic development in the island of St. Lucia.

Saint Vincent and the Grenadines Red Cross
Mr. Jonathan Pitt, President
Mrs. Dora James, Vice President
Halifax Street
Ministry of Education Compound
P.O. Box 431
Kingstown, St. Vincent

Phone: (748) 456-1888
Fax: (784) 485-6210
Email: svgreddcross@caribsurf.com
International organization with national base in St. Vincent and the Grenadines.
  Works in the area of general health and social welfare development, as well as disas-
  ter and crisis management.

Selected Bibliography

Barrow, Christine. 1992. *Family Land and Development in St. Lucia.* Monograph Series
    No. 1. Institute of Social and Economic Research: University of the West Indies.
Caribbean Epidemiology Center. 2004. *Status and Trends: Analysis of the Caribbean
    HIV/AIDS Epidemic, 1982–2002.* CAREC/PAHO/WHO.
Central Intelligence Agency. 2007a. The World Factbook: Saint Lucia. https://
    www.cia.gov/cia/publications/factbook/geos/st.html. Accessed March 29,
    2007.
———. 2007b. The World Factbook: Saint Vincent and the Grenadines. https://
    www.cia.gov/cia/publications/factbook/geos/vc.html. Accessed March 29,
    2007.
Crowley, Daniel. 1957. "Song and Dance in St. Lucia." *Ethnomusicology* 1, no. 9:
    4–14.
Division of Gender Relations. 2006. Gender Aspects of HIV/AIDS: Best Practices in
    Saint Lucia. 2006. http://www.oas.org/cim/XXXIII%20Asamblea%20de%20
    Delegadas/Best%20practices%20HIVAIDS/SAINT%20LUCIA%20%20Best%20
    Practices%20Gender%20and%20HIVAIDS.doc. Accessed April 2, 2007.
English, Sharon. 2001. Saint Vincent and the Grenadines: A Cultural Profile. To-
    ronto: Anti-Racism, Multiculturalism and Native Issues Centre, Faculty of
    Social Work, University of Toronto. http://www.cp-pc.ca/english/stvincent/
    stvincent.eng.pdf. Accessed April 3, 2007
Family Law Committee. 2006. Saint Lucia Civil Code Reform Project: Report of the
    Family Law Committee, July 26, 2006. Canadian International Development
    Agency and the Government of Saint Lucia. http://www.stlucia.gov.lc/docs/
    Report_of_the_Family_Law_Committe.pdf. Accessed March 30, 2007.
Government of Saint Lucia. http://www.stlucia.gov.lc. Accessed April 1, 2007.
Government of Saint Vincent and the Grenadines. http://www.gov.vc. Accessed
    April 1, 2007.
International Women's Rights Action Watch. Country Reports: Saint Vincent and
    the Grenadines. http://iwraw.igc.org/publications/countries/st_vincent_
    and_grenadines.htm. Accessed April 6 2007.
Jack, Noreen. 2001. "HIV/AIDS in Caribbean Children and Adolescents." pp. 23–
    40. In *HIV/AIDS and Children in the English Speaking Caribbean.* Edited by
    Barbara A. Dicks. Binghamton, NY: Haworth Press, Inc.
Kelly, Deirdre. 1987. *Hard Work, Hard Choices: A Survey of Women in St. Lucia's
    Export-Oriented Electronics Factories.* Occasional Paper No. 20. Institution of
    Social and Economic Research: University of the West Indies.
Knight, Franklin W. 1990. *The Caribbean: The Genesis of a Fragmented Nationalism.*
    New York: Oxford University Press.
McClean-Trotman, Lisa. 2007. "England Cricketers Inspire Youths and Support
    AIDS Campaign in St. Lucia." UNICEF. http://www.unicef.org/infoby
    country/stlucia_39155.html. Accessed April 6, 2007.

"Millennium Development Goals: A Global Assault on Hunger and Poverty." 2004. *Social Issues* 4, no. 3 (May). http://www.stlucia.gov.lc/docs/socialbulletin/ SocialIssuesBulletinMDG.pdf. Accessed March 25, 2007.

Office of the Registrar of Examinations. July 2002. Synopsis of the 2002 Common Entrance Examination Results. Ministry of Education, Human Resource Development, Youth and Sports: Educational Evaluation and Examinations Unit. http://www.stlucia.gov.lc/docs/commonentrance2002.pdf. Accessed March 28, 2007.

Red Cross Relief Web. 2004. Caribbean: Hurricane Ivan Information Bulletin No. 3. International Federation of Red Cross and Red Crescent Societies (IFRC). September 2004. http://72.14.209.104/search?q=cache:6XXnRAmIQ6EJ: www.reliefweb.int/rw/RWB.NSF/db900SID/HMYT-64MRU9%3FOpenDo cument+Hurricane+Ivan+-+Saint+Vincent&hl=en&ct=clnk&cd=8&gl=us. Accessed March 30, 2007.

Reuters Foundation. Alertnet: Alerting Humanitarians to Emergencies. http:// www.alertnet.org/db/cp/vincentgrenadines.htm. Accessed March 30, 2007.

Saint Lucia School of Music. http://lcmusicschool.com. Accessed on March 30, 2007.

Sealy-Burke, J. 2006. Protecting Children Affected by AIDS in the Caribbean: Recommendations for Legal Reform in SVG. World Bank-Netherlands Partnership Program.

Sheldon, A. St. Lucia Basic Data. http://www.education.statuniversity.com/pages/ 1294/Saint-Lucia.html. Accessed March 29, 2007.

Sutty, Lesley. 1993. *St. Vincent and the Grenadines.* London: Macmillan Press Ltd.

United Nations Children's Fund [UNICEF]. At A Glance: Saint Lucia. http:// www.unicef.org/infobycountry/stlucia.html. Accessed March 27, 2007.

———. At a Glance: Saint Vincent and the Grenadines. http://www.unicef.org/ infobycountry/stvincentgrenadines.html. Accessed March 27, 2007.

United Nations, Department of Economic and Social Affairs, Population Division. 2006. United Nations World Mortality Report 2005. http://www.un.org/ esa/population/publications/worldmortality/WMR 2005.pdf. Accessed March 22, 2007.

United Nations Development Programme. 2006. Human Development Report 2006. http://hdr.undp.org/hdr2006/. Accessed March 29, 2007.

U.S. Department of State, Bureau of Democracy, Human Rights, and Labor. 2006a. Country Reports on Human Rights Practices 2005: Saint Lucia. http:// www.state.gov/g/drl/rls/hrrpt/2005/61740.htm. Accessed April 4, 2007.

———. 2006b. Country Reports on Human Rights Practices, 2005: Saint Vincent and the Grenadines. http://www.state.gov/g/drl/rls/hrrpt/2005/61741. htm. Accessed April 4, 2007.

Vaughan, P., A. Regis, and E. St. Catherine. 2000. "Effects of an Entertainment-Education Radio Soap Opera on Family Planning and HIV/Prevention in St. Lucia." *International Family Planning Perspectives* 26, no. 4: 148–157.

14

TRINIDAD AND TOBAGO

Carolyne J. White and Yanique Taylor

NATIONAL PROFILE

What are the possibilities for children who live in the cosmopolitan, multiracial, multicultural, and multireligious twin-island nation of Trinidad and Tobago? Children below the age of fourteen comprise 20.1 percent of the total population of just over one million people, and 28 percent of the population is between the ages of ten and twenty-four. The population is approximately 40 percent Indian (South Asian), 37.5 percent African, 20.5 percent mixed, 1.2 percent other, and 0.8 percent unspecified. English is the official language, but Hindi, French, Spanish, and Chinese are also spoken (U.S. Central Intelligence Agency 2006).

Located at the southern end of the Caribbean islands, just off the coast of Venezuela, Trinidad and Tobago includes a total landmass of 1,980 square miles, divided into eight counties. Approximately 96 percent of the country's population resides in Trinidad, and 74 percent lives in urban areas (Pan American Health Organization 2006). The nation is

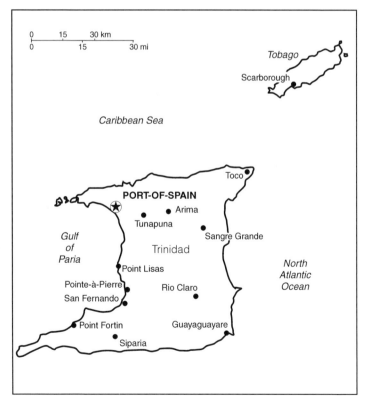

recognized internationally for its central cultural symbols: Carnival, calypso, and steelband.

In 2001, Trinidad and Tobago ranked 49 of 162 countries on the Human Development Index. Nevertheless, continuing inequities include a 12 percent unemployment rate in 2000, 10.2 percent for males and 15.2 percent for females. The government has been committed to addressing inequities through the implementation of universal education and numerous programs to assist children and families. The government has offered HIV/AIDS treatment to all citizens, free of charge, since 2002. Counseling and testing for HIV/AIDS and other sexually transmitted diseases are also offered free of charge. Facilities such as the Eric Williams Science Complex, Cyril Ross Nursery, and the Scarborough Regional Hospital are geared specifically toward pediatric care. The Tobago Youthbuild Programme is a six-month training program that helps young, unemployed people develop useful skills to aid in their development and life-long productivity. Participants are provided with a daily stipend of TT$50 and are offered classes such as customer service, sexual and reproductive health, literacy, food preparation, first aid, and floral arrangement among others. These classes are held at schools and community centers throughout Tobago, as well as the Youthbuild Programme Center, which includes a lecture hall, library and computer room, beauty culture workshop, craft workshop, and kitchen. The program promotes positive social behavior among youth and contributes to crime prevention. Youth Development and Apprenticeship Centres (YDACs) offer youth between the ages of fifteen and seventeen a two-year residential training program where they learn occupational skills such as plumbing, welding, construction carpentry, garment construction, auto mechanics, and computer literacy among others. Participants are paid a monthly stipend of TT$45. The Defining Masculine Excellence Program, offered to males age fourteen and older, uses the examination of the socialization and negative perceptions of males to provide participants with the skills to facilitate personal and group transformation and to help them develop self-esteem and positive attitudes to life. The program is free of charge and offered once a week over an eight-week period. The Adolescent Mothers Programme, located throughout Trinidad and Tobago, aims to service pregnant teenagers, teenage mothers, their children, and partners through support programs such as counseling, daycare services, parenting courses, skills training, health and nutrition education, and teenage pregnancy prevention. Young women between the ages of thirteen and nineteen can take advantage of this service. Early Childhood Care and Education (ECCE) is a noncompulsory program throughout the country that is geared toward the physical, cognitive, and social development of children before they enter primary school. Children between the ages of three and five are eligible. Over 160 ECCE centers have been approved by the Ministry of Education, and educators and parents alike increasingly recognize their value. Parents of children under the age of eighteen who are physically or mentally disabled qualify for the Special Child Grant offered through the Social Welfare Division of the Office of the Prime Minister. This grant is reviewed annually by the Local Social Welfare Board, and provides TT$300 monthly for up to four children per family. Only children who do not receive public assistance are eligible.

OVERVIEW

Many refer to Trinidad and Tobago as a nation in transition from colonialism to postcolonialism with the attendant tensions of social stratification based on race/ethnicity, color, class, nationality, and gender. Eric Williams, the powerful political and intellectual leader of Trinidad and Tobago for twenty-five years, proclaimed in 1944 that "the history of our West Indies can be expressed in two simple words: Columbus and Sugar" (Palmer 2006). Known by the Amerindians as "Iere," or the land of the hummingbird, the island was renamed "La Trinidad or "Trinity" by Christopher Columbus in 1498. The nation has been shaped by many historic developments: the virtual extermination of the indigenous Arawak and Carib population by the Spanish colonizers; British control in 1797 and more than 150 years of domination by French and British planters who embraced slavery; the French, Dutch, and British fights over possession of Tobago and the island changing hands twenty-two times; the emancipation of the African slaves in 1833; plantation owners turning to Chinese, Portuguese, and Syrian/Lebanese indentured servants and then realizing that these workers did not perform in plantation work as their former black slaves had, and looking to recruitment in India that resulted in an influx of over 100,000 Indian indentured servants in 1845; the incorporation of the two islands into the single colony of Trinidad and Tobago in 1888; full independence in 1962 when the nation joined the British Commonwealth; and the continuing effects of globalization (Yelvington 1993; Nurse 1999).

Trinidad and Tobago is one of the most economically prosperous countries in the Caribbean, largely due to rich natural resources of

---

KEY FACTS – TRINIDAD AND TOBAGO

Population: 1,056,608 (July 2007 est.)
Infant mortality rate: 24.33 deaths/1,000 live births (2007 est.)
Life expectancy at birth: 66.85 years (2007 est.)
Literacy rate: 98.6 percent (2003 est.)
Net primary school enrollment/attendance: 92 percent (2000–2005)
Internet users: 160,000 (2005)
People living with HIV/AIDS: 27,000 (2005 est.)
Children living with HIV/AIDS: <1000 (2005 est.)
Human Poverty Index (HPI-1) Rank: 17

Sources: CIA World Factbook: Trinidad and Tobago. https://www.cia.gov/cia/publications/factbook/geos/td.html. April 17, 2007; UNICEF. At a Glance: Trinidad and Tobago–Statistics. http://www.unicef.org/infobycountry/trinidad_tobago_statistics.html. April 24, 2007; World Health Organization (WHO): UNAIDS/WHO Global HIV/AIDS Online Database. "Epidemiological Fact Sheets on HIV/AIDS and Sexuality Transmitted Diseases: Trinidad and Tobago." http://www.who.int/GlobalAtlas/predefinedReports/EFS2006/index.asp?strSelectedCountry=TT. December 2006; United Nations Development Programme (UNDP) Human Development Report 2006–Trinidad and Tobago. http://hdr.undp.org/hdr2006/statistics/countries/data_sheets/cty_ds_TTO.html. April 26, 2007.

petroleum and natural gas. While other Caribbean countries have relied more on tourism, an interest in tourism is only recently being pursued in this nation. The 2005 estimate of the labor force is 620,000 (U.S. Central Intelligence Agency 2006), and it consists of agriculture, manufacturing, mining and quarrying, construction, and utilities and services. Central and south Trinidad are largely agricultural, while much of northern Trinidad appears more modernized with fast cars, satellite dishes, finance houses, offshore drilling, four daily newspapers, email and Internet, shopping malls, and fast-food courts. Home to 4 percent of the nation's citizens, the smaller and more serene island, Tobago, is home to the oldest protected rainforest in the Western Hemisphere. Its south coast is lined with vibrant fishing villages, and the north coast has some of its finest beaches.

When the country declared independence in August 1962, it formed a democratic government consisting of executive, legislative, and judicial branches. In 1980, the Tobago House of Assembly was established to administer that island. In politics, the two prevailing parties replicate specific cultural distinctions. The People's National Movement (PNM) is primarily black, and the United National Congress (UNC) is primarily East Indian. The Chief of State, President George Maxwell Richards, appoints the Prime Minister, currently Patrick Manning of the PNM. This appointment is awarded to the leader of the party with majority seats in the House of Representatives. Prime Minister Manning will be up for re-election in 2008. Those of East Indian descent are represented more in the business environment primarily as entrepreneurs, an outgrowth of the difference in the way they were treated as indentured servants compared to the treatment blacks received as slaves.

As Nurse explains, "The attendant processes of colonization and imperialism created in its wake a new society, a modern culture, one grounded in the logic of capitalist accumulation, social stratification and cultural hybridization—all informed by racial, gender, ethnic and status-based oppression" (1999, 681). The intriguing cultural dynamics of this diverse and fascinating postcolonial nation can be traced in the daily lives of its children.

We look to books, published reports, and personal interviews, and at each juncture we encounter differing versions of reality. It is important to note here that many of the statistics that we reference are contested figures. We have selected the figures we find most credible and provide careful documentation of our sources. In many respects, our efforts to write of this nation are analogous to the efforts of numerous scholars to capture Carnival.

Some claim the seeds of Carnival are located in carnival-like celebrations held by the Amerindians who arrived in "Iere" around 5400 BC, and that these early celebrations were augmented by the practices of invading Europeans. Others argue that it was not until the arrival of the

French Catholic planters in 1783 that Carnival began to take root, while others recognize that most societies have some form of celebration that can be seen as similar to Carnival, a selected time of excess when the normalized rules of public conduct are relaxed. In Trinidad, slaves were forbidden to participate in Carnival until after the 1834–1838 emancipation. From the perspective of the "white elite," this is when Carnival grew "out of control," seemingly contaminated by the "Africanizing" of the festivities by the masses of newly freed slaves (Liverpool 2001). For others (Bakhtin 1984), Carnival is viewed as revolutionary activity that grows out of social conflict. Liverpool writes of Carnival's adaptation and survival as an expression of the cultural identity of Trinidadians, as enactment and navigation of "violent struggle, racism, festivity, oppressive legislation, ethnicity, religious differences, discrimination in education and employment, cultural resilience and creativity, communal work habits and ritualization" (2001, xvi). These processes of active cultural negotiation are seen in the substantial increase of female participation in Carnival and in the creation of what is known today as "Indian Carnival."

There is a similar trajectory within Calypso music. Long embraced as a cultural medium of political critique, pique, and satire, calypso music changes with changes in the lived experiences of residents of Trinidad and Tobago. Today there is an infusion of East Indian presence that creates a blending of jazz, calypso, and parang—a form of Venezuelan-derived Christmas music traditional to Trinidad. There is also a shift to women asserting their right to sing and not just to be sung about. There has also been movement within steelband, or pan as it is called locally, from an African-derived musical form developed among lower-class, urban, dispossessed males, to the increasing involvement of East Indians and their tassa drums, and again an increased entry of women (Stuempfle 1995).

Nurse views Trinidad's Carnival as influenced greatly by the forces of globalization and argues that the exportation of Carnival can be understood as a form of "globalization in reverse" as the overseas carnivals become a basis for "pan-Caribbean identity, a mechanism for social integration into metropolitan society and a ritual act of transnational, transcultural, transgressive politics" (1999, 683). However one interprets Carnival, there is general agreement that, today Trinidad Carnival is unlike carnival in any other place in the world.

EDUCATION

In the 1950s, universal primary schooling was achieved in Trinidad and Tobago, and in 2000 universal secondary schooling was achieved when—for the first time in the country's history—100 percent of primary school students who sat for the Common Entrance Examination (CXC) were placed in secondary schools. The Ministry of Education's stated hope is to solidify the country's status as a developed and progressive nation within the Caribbean and the larger global network (Ministry of Education 2003).

Trinidad and Tobago has a reported adult literacy rate of 98.6 percent (99.1 percent for males and 98 percent for females), and 75 percent of the country's adult population has completed secondary school. Girls' share of enrollment in 2000 was 49 percent at the primary level, 50 percent at secondary, and 54 percent at the university—up from 49 percent in the 1980s. Since its independence in 1962, Trinidad and Tobago has been attempting various reforms through the restructuring of its Ministry of Education to improve the quality and availability of schooling to all citizens. The primary roles of the Ministry of Education are as follows:

- Setting educational policies and strategies;
- Defining curriculum and other norms;
- Overseeing the quality of educational services provided by public- and private-sector institutions; and
- Planning, programming, budgeting, implementing, and monitoring the education system.

The government's commitment to the ministry's fulfillment of these roles is evident in the increase in the proportion of the national budget allocated to the education sector in 2004 to 13.5 percent (Ministry of Education 2004). Even so, total school enrollment has dropped over the past decade, and the dropout rate is estimated at over 18 percent. These figures suggest something is not working well for these students and that other options should be considered. Some assign the decline to socioeconomic factors such as unemployment (Pan American Health Organization 2006).

The current Minister of Education, Hazel Manning, has emphasized her commitment to develop a better education system, arguing that the growth of the country's economy depends on it. The pressing concerns she outlined in 2004 include the lack of provisions for students with special needs, hindrances to the education agenda due to a lack of sufficiently active and positive parental involvement, the need to improve functional literacy rates among adults, and the lower achievement levels of male compared with female students. She also acknowledged the necessity of incorporating technology into the existing curriculum, providing more and better student support services, better teacher education programs, and universal access to early childhood education. A study that surveyed 14,000 primary school students at sixty primary schools identified the following additional problems: sexual abuse, exposure to drugs and drug trafficking, single parenting, and issues relating to HIV and AIDS. To respond, the Ministry has applied Student Support Services including guidance and counseling, special education, and social work for students who have learning and behavioral problems (Ministry of Education 2004).

The educational system demonstrates how Trinidad and Tobago has maintained ties to its British colonial past. To transition between the primary and secondary levels, and from the secondary and postsecondary levels, students must sit for national exams—the CXC and the Ordinary Level Examinations (O'Levels), respectively. Those students not fully ready to enter the university have the option to complete a two-year pre-college program at the end of which they take their Advanced Level Examinations (A'Levels). All of these components are managed by the Ministry of Education under the guidance of the Education Act of 1966.

It appears that the Ministry of Education has given less attention to significant constraints within the educational system that are related to the colonial legacy. For example, the continuing heavy reliance upon national exams fosters a mechanistic and dehumanizing learning environment that minimizes the likelihood that schools will effectively focus upon more meaningful educational goals, such as the cultivation of more culturally responsive and culturally honoring school curriculum, democratic citizenship development, and the cultivation of forms of critical literacy that move beyond mere critical thinking skills to empowering students to critically read and change their worlds (Freire and Macedo 1987; Ellis 2002). Of course, successful implementation of curricular change requires reform in how teachers are prepared (George, Mohammed, and Quamina-Aiyejina 2003).

PLAY AND RECREATION

At the heart of every child's existence is play and recreation. From Carnival to sports and steelband, Trinidad and Tobago provides a rich recreational environment. Home for many of these activities is the largest available open space in the country, called The Queen's Park Savannah and located in Port-of-Spain. The young and old alike can be found at the Savannah, as it is commonly called by locals, exercising, training for a sporting event or marathon, flying kites, playing football or cricket, or just having a nice picnic (http://www.nalis.gov.tt/Places/Places_Queen'sParkSav2.html). Formerly a sugar estate that was purchased and then donated to the city for public use, the Savannah has served many roles in its past life, but now is best known for hosting Carnival events and Independence Day marches.

With the Soca Warriors, Trinidad and Tobago's national football team, qualifying for the 2006 World Cup Final, the importance of sports, particularly football, is evident. The country hosted the 2006 Caribbean Football Union Under-16 Youth Cup, a ten-day tournament where young talent from twenty-eight nations showcased their skills. Similarly, the Queen's Park Cricket Club has organized a youth development program to coach young boys from the age of seven. The club has many notable club members for young boys to look up to, such as cricket great

Brian Lara, who plays on the West Indian Cricket team (http://www.qpcc.com). Through sports, exercise and good health are encouraged in young people. The annual Junior Aerobics Marathon competition was introduced primarily for this purpose. Now in its sixth year, the competition is sponsored by the HCL Group of Companies and is attended by thirty schools and over 100 students. The competition consists of categories in flexibility, choreography, originality, synchronization, and musical interpretation (http://www.triniview.com).

In the spirit of Carnival and steelband, music is also encouraged among youth. Not only do children participate in the revelry of Carnival, but events such as Panorama also allow them to make music. The Panorama Steelband Competition began in 1963 and attracts practically all of the steelbands in the twin islands. Always held on the Saturday night before Carnival Monday in Queen's Park Savannah, the competition introduced a junior category in 1998 to include and encourage young talent under the age of twenty and to allow them the opportunity to partake in this long-valued musical tradition.

In addition, the country's Ministry of Sport and Youth Affairs works with young people between the ages of fifteen and twenty-five and sponsors several annual events that include National Youth Day, Youth Development Awards, Recreational Vocational Camps, Leadership Training Programme, Model United Nations Programme, and a Public Speaking Competition (http://www.nalis.gov.tt/Sport/Sport_YouthDevProg.html).

CHILD LABOR

The country's commitment to develop and provide better education for all its citizens is linked to national child labor initiatives. According to the International Labor Organization's (ILO) 2002 report on their member countries' struggles to eliminate child labor by implementing better policies and enforcing them, Trinidad and Tobago's current Children Act serves to protect children and young people through the age of eighteen. Despite these efforts, the country has many inconsistencies regarding the actual age at which someone is considered a child under national laws. According to the Children Act, a child is anyone under the age of twelve and thus unemployable. Consequently, the Education Act stipulates compulsory schooling up to the age of twelve. However, under the Factories Ordinance, which governs the use of machinery, a child is recognized as being below the age of fourteen and thus not fit to work around or with factory machinery, while a young person is defined as being between the ages of fourteen and eighteen and must be proven medically fit to work (International Labor Organization 2002).

Under the legally binding guidance of the United Nations Convention on the Rights of the Child (CRC) and the four primary principles of non-discrimination, devotion to the best interests of the child, the right to life, survival, and development, and respect for the views of the child, Trinidad and Tobago is taking proactive steps toward establishing a central governing body to oversee issues related to child labor and normalize existing discrepancies in child labor laws. A draft bill by the Ministry of the Attorney General proposed to have a child recognized as anyone under the age of eighteen under the guidelines of the CRC, and the Ministry of Labor and Co-operatives proposed to have the minimum age of employment raised to sixteen. These recommendations have raised concerns regarding delaying employment opportunities for those who may need it (United Nations Children's Fund 2006).

In addition to tackling child labor as one of the top national priorities, the increase in street children and violence toward children—inclusive of physical and sexual violence, sometimes as a result of prostitution—are also issues needing serious attention. These issues all clearly impact child labor in various ways as economic needs push children to engage in particular activities that may be under the radar, making it that much more difficult for the country to accurately assess child labor. Nevertheless, Trinidad and Tobago is forging ahead with a proposed National Plan of Action that seeks to address these problems by identifying government officials and implementing committees to monitor and provide the services needed by this segment of the population. The United Nations Committee on the Rights of Child (2006) strongly recommended that the nation give more attention to improving data collection and increasing resource allocation for children.

FAMILY

Historically, perceptions of family dynamics in Trinidad and Tobago have been distorted by social science research that pathologized these dynamics because they were different from the idealized family structures portrayed by Eurocentric ideology. Since the 1970s, more indigenous perspectives have been honored, and practices that were previously viewed as "dysfunctional" or "promiscuous" have come to be understood contextually; "family instability" is now viewed as "family flexibility" and "adaptability," and widespread family networks are now viewed as importantly related to the poverty and economic marginality that many families face. Today there is evidence of a significant societal shift toward redefining family roles and relationships, a process tied in important ways to the changes in the position of women in the society. Widespread use of birth control has enabled women greater decision-making power about when and how they will mother. Today, women are better able to make choices to balance motherhood, education, and career opportunities. There is also some evidence that young men are redefining fatherhood, assigning it greater importance in their lives, and that couples are moving from patriarchy towards greater equality and togetherness (Barrow 1996). There remains evidence that some people are still blaming families for the increase in gang activity: "Many young people find better comfort in gangs because their families are so disorganized" (Baboolal 2006, 1).

Trinidad and Tobago was among the first of the English-speaking Caribbean nations to adopt domestic violence legislation with the passage of the Domestic Violence Act in 1991. This legislation gave the people the right to go to court to ask for a protection order against a violent or abusive family member (Lazarus-Black 2001). While women in Trinidad and Tobago have a long legacy of working outside of the home, recently there has been a significant increase. For example, from 1990–1995, the number of women in the labor force increased by 21.9 percent compared with a 6 percent increase for men (Ellis 2003).

The National Family Services Division of the Ministry of Social and Community Development is charged with incorporating family programs into the development strategies of Trinidad and Tobago. Their overall goal is to promote, empower, and sustain a community of socially healthy families. The following are among their responsibilities: maintain effective communication with national, regional, and international bodies and organizations concerned with family-related issues; conduct research and collect data about the present situation of families; identify family-related issues and problems; provide guidance for policy formation and program planning; organize counseling and referral for vulnerable persons such as those experiencing family abuse, domestic violence, children at risk, and people housed in institutions or homes managed by the government or nongovernmental organizations (NGOs); and conduct preventative public education programs, such as ongoing sensitization sessions through lectures, workshops, and media programs utilizing popular theatre, role play, group discussions, and distribution of posters, pamphlets, and books. In addition, the government organizes the annual celebration of the International Day of Families, the annual Child Rights Week, and the International Year of Older Persons.

HEALTH

Citizens in Trinidad and Tobago have access to free medical care through public sector healthcare facilities where they can consult with specialist physicians, undergo recommended procedures, and receive free medications. However, they can often incur long wait times and find that drugs are available erratically or not at all. Of course, private health care is also available for those who can afford it.

Life expectancy has been increasing in the nation. The most recent data estimate life expectancy at seventy years. Improvement is also seen in the infant mortality rate, which declined from 110 per 1,000 live births in the 1940s to eighteen per 1,000 live births in 2004. Trinidad and Tobago has well-organized immunization programs with high rates of coverage. According to United Nations Children's Fund data for 2006, 95 percent of children in Trinidad and Tobago are inoculated for measles between birth and the age of one year and 94 percent for diphtheria, pertussis, and tetanus. Polio and DPT immunizations begin at three months of age and yellow fever by two years of age. Improvements in the health of children in Trinidad and Tobago are related to improvements in socioeconomic conditions, environmental conditions, and increased access to child health services.

The unemployment rate among young people under the age of twenty-five is estimated at 38 percent. In most of the Caribbean, this rate is higher among girls than boys. However, in Trinidad and Tobago this trend is reversed. This level of unemployment for young people can cultivate a sense of hopelessness and increase vulnerability to such self-destructive behaviors as increased drug use, spiraling crime, and the high incidence of HIV/AIDS and other sexually transmitted diseases. Government initiatives, such as COSTATT (the College of Science, Technology and Applied Arts of Trinidad and Tobago) and YTEPP (the Youth Training and Employment Partnership Programme) are working to intervene in this situation, working to engage and assist young people in comprehensive training aimed at increasing their chances of returning to school (if they have dropped out) and becoming wage earners or self-employed (John 2004).

The five leading causes of death among young people from fifteen to thirty-four years of age are, in order of frequency, HIV/AIDS, transport accidents, assault, intentional self-harm, and heart disease. The occurrence of HIV/AIDS is predominately among heterosexual couples. Teenage girls outnumbered boys five to one for new HIV infections in 1996. In 1997, the fifteen-to-nineteen age group accounted for 14 percent of all pregnancies. Oral healthcare services are targeted to those younger than fifteen years of age. In the 1970s, the government trained a cadre of dental nurses to educate this group about dental care in schools and clinics (Pan American Health Organization 2006).

Like many developing countries, Trinidad and Tobago has unregulated antibiotic use, misuse, and overuse. There is concern about growing resistance to antibiotics, based in part on the indiscriminate and widespread use of antimicrobials for treating infections, self-medication, incomplete treatment courses, and unregulated use of antibacterial drugs. Recommendations have been made for more stringent regulations, the establishment of a surveillance system to provide information on trends in bacterial resistance, and for continuous education for pharmacists, doctors, and the general public on the consequences of inappropriate antibiotic use (Parimi, Pinto Pereira, and Prabhakar 2002).

LAWS AND LEGAL STATUS

Seeking to bring their national legislation into closer conformity with the provisions of the CRC, in 1998 the government of Trinidad and Tobago appointed a committee of representatives from the Ministry of the Attorney General and the Ministry of Social Development to review all existing laws relating to children. The following five pieces of legislation emerged from the work of this committee.

The Children's Authority Act, No. 64 of 2000

This legislation establishes the Children's Authority of Trinidad and Tobago, which is responsible for investigating complaints of staff, children, and parents of children with respect to any child who is in the care of a community residence, foster home, or nursery.

The Children's Community Residences, Foster Homes and Nurseries Act, No. 65 of 2000

This legislation addresses licensing of children's homes, rehabilitation centers, industrial schools, and orphanages.

The Miscellaneous Provisions (Children) Act, No. 66 of 2000

This legislation amended domestic statutes in a number of areas, including: adoption and citizenship; extending from fourteen to eighteen the age at which a magistrate could impose a custodial sentence on a person found guilty of committing an assault or battery; removing the power of the court to impose corporal punishment against children under eighteen years of age; repealing the act that permitted the minister to commute to a term of imprisonment any unexpired residue of the term of detention of an inmate of the Youth Training Centre who was reported to be incorrigible or exercising a bad influence on the other inmates; requiring parental consent for a child below eighteen years of age to be enlisted into the Defense Force; modified the power of the court to require either parent of a ward of court to pay sums toward the maintenance and education of the ward; and changing the age of offense for selling liquor to a child from under sixteen to under eighteen.

The Adoption of Children Act, No. 67 of 2000

This legislation established an Adoption Board to promote the welfare and protection of children with regard to adoptions.

The Children (Amendment) Act, No. 68 of 2000

This legislation amended a number of sections of the act: changing the definition of a child from under fourteen to under eighteen; providing guiding principles for the rights and responsibilities of children and parents in relation to their children; and empowering the court to commit a child to the care of a relative through age eighteen if the person having custody has been convicted of an offense (Trinidad and Tobago 2003).

RELIGIOUS LIFE

The Constitution of this multicultural and multireligious nation provides for freedom of religion, and the government respects this right in
practice. In 2002–2003, the government gave $420,750 to religious
organizations through ecclesiastical grants. In addition, public holidays
and festivals, supported by the government with financial and technical
assistance, celebrate the religion, heritage, and, culture of each group,
such as Indian Arrival Day, Emancipation Day, Shouter Baptist Day,
Easter, Divali, and, the most well known, Carnival. Examples of the support provided by the Ministry of Culture and Tourism for these festivals
in 2002–2003 included $67,000 for Indian Arrival Day, $131,500 for
Phagwa (Indian Carnival), $25,000 for Divali, and $213,000 for Baptist
Liberation Day. In addition, under a Community Action for Revival and
Empowerment Programme of the Ministry of Community Development
and Gender Affairs, various Hindu organizations were given $7,665 to
support Divali; $7,500 was given to the Orisha Spiritual Community to
support the Annual Rain Festival and $10,000 to support the Annual
Shango Festival; and $1,500 was given to the Pentacostal Assembly for
Christmas celebrations (http://www.ttparliament.org/hansard/house
.2003/hh20030509.pdf 2006).

According to official U.S. statistics from 2000, religious affiliation is
distributed as follows: 26 percent Roman Catholic; 24.6 Protestant (7.8
percent Anglican, 6.8 percent Pentecostal, 4 percent Seventh-Day Adventist, 3.3 percent Presbyterian or Congregational, 1.8 percent Baptist,
0.9 percent Methodist, 1.6 percent Jehovah's Witnesses); 22.5 Hindu;
10.7 percent other (Baha'is, Rastafarians, Buddhists, Jews); 5.8 percent
Muslim; 5.4 percent Spiritual Baptist (sometimes called Shouter Baptists);
0.1 percent Orisha; 1.9 percent Atheists; and 1.4 percent undeclared
(U.S. Department of State 2003). The Jamaat al Muslimeen is the only
religious group known to be closely monitored by the government. This
is because some members of the group attempted a coup in 1990. The
fastest-growing religious groups include the Spiritual Baptists and the
Orisha faith, as well as the American-style fundamentalist Pentecostal and
Mormon religions. The Mormons maintain about thirty foreign missionaries in the country (thirty-five is the maximum allowed by the government), while the Baptists, Mennonites, and Muslims maintain five to ten
foreign missionaries.

Generally, these different religions coexist peacefully and respect each
other's beliefs and practices. This is facilitated by the government's support of the Inter-Religious Organization (IRO), composed of leaders
from most of the religions. IRO promotes interfaith dialogue and tolerance through activities such as cultural and religious exhibitions, study
groups, and publications. IRO also provides a prayer leader for government events, such as the opening of Parliament.

The government subsidizes religious schools and permits voluntary attendance at religious instruction in public schools. This instruction is provided during a special time set aside each week and is taught by representatives from any of the religious organizations. In considering the relevance of religion for the lives of children in Trinidad and Tobago, it is important to recognize the differences between religions that were brought to the islands by European colonizers, Indian and Chinese indentured laborers, and the Orisha religion that comes from Africa. Although African spirituality was viewed as uncivilized and "primitive" by European colonizing forces and was suppressed and outlawed during slavery, a careful review of the philosophy reveals that it is not dualistic (good versus evil, God versus a Devil) as is Christianity. Rather, the Orisha view the universe as benevolent and as containing forces of expansion and contraction that interact in complex ways. Rather than a belief in original sin, there is a focus upon each individual striving to develop a good character through doing good works, and doing the right thing simply because it is right, rather than from a fear of retribution or some future reward. The growth of the Orisha religion is another sign of the transition in the country from colonialism to postcolonialism (Henry 2003).

CHILD ABUSE AND NEGLECT

Definitions of what constitutes child abuse and neglect vary across cultures and over time. According to the Global Initiative to End All Corporal Punishment of Children (http://www.endcorporalpunishment.org), corporal punishment of children has not been legally prohibited in the home, although it has been prohibited in schools as of the 2000 Children Amendment Act (not yet in force). Corporal punishment has been prohibited in the penal system as a sentence but not as a disciplinary measure, and while it is not legally prohibited in alternative care settings, it is prohibited in healthcare and psychiatric institutions as a matter of policy.

There are no reliable data on the extent of child sexual abuse in Trinidad and Tobago. Statistics are collected on convictions for sexual offenses involving children (Table 14.1); however, these figures do not include the numbers of reported cases, nor do they address the problem of underreporting (Jones 2006).

A survey in 1995 into the nature and extent of child prostitution, child pornography, and the trafficking of children in Trinidad and Tobago did not lead to any definitive findings on the extent of child prostitution. It did, however, reveal the following:

- Children and adolescents are involved in prostitution and pornography
- Prostitution is more prevalent among females than males

Table 14.1.
Number of Convictions for Sexual Offenses

Population	2000	2001	2002
Females under 14 years	67	109	103
Females 14–16 years	79	82	129
Males under 16 years	—	5	6
Adopted minor	20	1	20
Total	166	197	258

Source: Office of United Nations High Commissioner for Human Rights (2003), 458.

- There is a market of business and tourist visitors for teenage prostitution
- The commercial sexual exploitation of children and adolescents in Tobago appears to be mainly associated with the tourist industry
- While there was no evidence of a connection to the drug trade, drug use is one of the factors involved in child prostitution
- Economic hardship and adverse social and domestic conditions are cited as the main reasons children became involved in prostitution (Office of United Nations High Commissioner for Human Rights 2003, 458–459).

Like other forms of domestic violence, sexual offenses against children are underreported. Children do not disclose sexual abuse for a number of reasons. These reasons include powerlessness and low status of children within families and society generally, fear that they will not be believed, concern that they will be blamed, shame, uncertainty, and anxiety about the consequences of disclosure, threat of violence, or concern about the effects on the wider family. Trinidad and Tobago is battling increasing levels of violence (domestic violence, gender-based violence, community violence, school violence, child-on-child violence, gang-violence, interpersonal violence, institutional violence, and violence arising out of poverty, desperation, and destitution). The sexual abuse of children is not simply a "domestic" issue; it must be understood within the wider societal context in which it occurs, and strategies to prevent abuse and deal with its effects must target not only the victim, but also the perpetrator, the family, and the wider society. While professionals are able to recognize the signs, risk factors, and effects of abuse, the services to treat the problem are not widely available, and the infrastructure for the assessment and prevention of risk is as yet underdeveloped in Trinidad and Tobago.

GROWING UP IN THE TWENTY-FIRST CENTURY

As it looks to the future, issues of globalization, technological change, and the emergence of new-work organization based on the development of a knowledge- and skills-based society are high on the national agenda in Trinidad and Tobago. Emphasis is being placed upon using NGOs, CBOs (community-based organizations), FBOs (faith-based organizations), and other youth organizations such as uniformed groups (cadets and girl guides) and councils in schools and communities to focus upon leadership development among youth. These groups work to empower young people by equipping them with positive values and experience using their knowledge and skills to solve problems, make decisions, develop negotiation and conflict management skills, and enhance their communication skills.

Attention is also being given to ensuring that the legal framework is sensitive to the needs of young people, enforcing laws designed to protect young people, remove inequalities within the socioeconomic system, improve health care for young people, and increase the level of employment among young people, and promoting culture and sports as mechanisms for employment and income generation for young people.

The religious institutions are being asked to play an active role in developing the moral fiber of young people and to highlight the efforts made to support the family, the schools, and the community as they promote youth development (George 2006).

Trinidad and Tobago's development, including the country's growing interest in tourism, will also determine the future for the nation's children. Ecotourism may prove to have great potential, given the natural splendor of the islands. There are more than 430 species of birds, some 600 species of butterflies, and thousands of flowering plants, including 700 different types of orchids. There are over ninety varieties of mammals and fifty-five species of reptiles, including endangered leatherback turtles that return to the islands' beaches from March through August each year to lay their eggs. Speyside, on Tobago's north end, is one of only a few locations in the world where divers can swim with wild manta rays. However, in order to maximize the future of tourism, the country must resolve growing problems with violent crime and transportation. The road system is not well suited for the volume of cars, so traffic is a worsening problem and traffic fatalities a significant issue. There is no mass transportation system, although a plan for light rail transport has been announced.

Development may not be simply an economic equation as the early name of Iere, "land of the hummingbird," suggests. For the indigenous Taino people who met Christopher Columbus in 1492, the hummingbird was a symbol of the spreading of life on the earth. How different this nation may have been had Columbus and others been able to listen to and learn from indigenous peoples how to sustain life instead of seeking to control and/or destroy. An approach to public planning with more focus upon how we define and sustain life, more focus upon bringing people together as happens during Carnival and through calypso and steelband, may better serve the needs of children.

One example of potential change may be found in the reforms implemented in Bogotá, the capital city of Colombia, under the leadership of former-Mayor Enrique Peñalosa. Peñalosa subverted the common paradigm of building cities primarily for businesses and automobiles and put children first. He promoted a vision that gave priority to public spaces by restricting private car use, building many hundreds of kilometers of sidewalks, bicycle paths, and pedestrian streets, as well as greenways, more than 1,200 parks, and a new, highly successful, bus-based transit system. These changes have clear environmental benefits, and, more importantly, they mediate feelings of hopelessness among the people by actively promoting social equity and happiness. In addition, with more people interacting in public space, crime has significantly decreased, and economic development has been enhanced. In Peñalosa's words, "our goal was to make a city for all the children. The measure of a good city is one where a child on a tricycle or bicycle can safely go anywhere. If a city is good for children, it will be good for everybody else" (Walljasper 2004). These sentiments are echoed by Ken Ramchand, who spoke the following words to the Trinidad Senate in 2005: "We are whoring after a shiny El Dorado made up of the crumbs from the plates of the conquistadors, but the gold we seek is all around us. The gold is our environment; ours to cherish and to nurture for ourselves, our children, and our children's children" (Bratt 2006).

RESOURCE GUIDE

Suggested Readings

Ellis, Patricia. 2002. *Citizenship Education in Small States: Trinidad and Tobago.* London: Commonwealth Secretariat Publications. This booklet highlights challenges of citizenship in the multiethnic, multicultural, and multireligious nation of Trinidad and Tobago and outlines programs directed at promoting citizenship education.

Harney, Stefano. 1996. *Nationalism and Identity: Culture and the Imagination in a Caribbean Diaspora.* Kingston: University of the West Indies. Drawing upon novels by Trinidadians and European-based scholarship on theories of nationalism, this book provides a significant contribution to the field of Caribbean cultural studies and postcolonial theory.

Klass, Morton. 1991. *Singing with Sai Baba.* Boulder: Westview Press. This book offers commentary on the emergence of a religious movement in Trinidad and Tobago centered on the adoration of Sathya Sai Baba, a South Indian holy man, recognized as God. This movement primarily involves Trinidadians of South Asian descent.

Liverpool, Hollis. "Chalkdust." 2001. *Rituals of Power & Rebellion: The Carnival Tradition in Trinidad & Tobago 1763–1962.* Chicago, IL: Research Associates School Times Publications/Frontline Distribution Int'l Inc. This book provides a well-researched, critical study of the African roots of Trinidad Carnival. Data sources include ethnographic and archival materials.

Mason, Peter. 1998. *Bacchanal! The Carnival Culture of Trinidad.* Philadelphia, PA: Temple University Press. This book is a reflection upon Carnival as far more than simply an event; rather the author argues that Carnival is a powerful cultural phenomenon that defines the country and its people.

Meeks, Brian. 2000. *Narratives of Resistance: Jamaica, Trinidad, the Caribbean*. Kingston: The University of the West Indies Press. This book offers hard-hitting analysis of contemporary social, political, and intellectual resistance to domination in Caribbean societies.

Ministry of Education. 2004. *National Report on the Development of Education in Trinidad and Tobago*. http://www.ibe.unesco.org/international/ICE47/English/Natreps/reports/tobago_scan.pdf. Accessed October 27, 2006. The most recent report from the Trinidadian Ministry of Education, this document provides a detailed accounting of new initiatives, as well as progress that is being made toward realizing national educational objectives.

Moodie-Kublalsingh, Sylvia. 1994. *The Coca Panyols of Trinidad*. New York: St. Martin's Press. This book provides an engaging and intimate oral history of Spanish-speaking Trinidadian peasants known as Panyols.

Palmer, Colin A. 2006. *Eric Willams & the Making of the Modern Caribbean*. Chapel Hill: The University of North Carolina Press. This book offers a hybrid between biography and political/intellectual history. It begins with an analysis of Williams's ideas on colonialism and ends in 1970 with the Black Power–inspired February Revolution.

Scher, Philip W. 2003. *Carnival and the Formation of a Caribbean Transnation*. Gainesville: University Press of Florida. This book explores the significance of Carnival for identity formation for Trinidadians both at home and abroad through the movement of this cultural celebration into new spaces, including Brooklyn, New York City, London, and Toronto.

Stuempfle, Stephen. 1995. *The Steelband Movement: The Forging of a National Art in Trinidad and Tobago*. Philadelphia: University of Pennsylvania Press. This book illuminates parallel negotiations between different ethnic groups, socio-economic classes, and social organizations within the steelband movement and the building of Trinidad and Tobago.

Yelvington, Kevin A. 1993. *Trinidad Ethnicity*. Knoxville: The University of Tennessee Press. This edited volume traces the ethnic and cultural history of Trinidad and suggests the nation's important contribution to broader understandings of the relationship between race and class and how ethnicity becomes politicized.

Nonprint Resources

Further information can be found at http://www.search.co.tt/trinidad/movies/index.html

The A Word. 2005. An independent video documentary by Lisle Waldron and Brianne LaBauve. While women's health rights improved over the years in Trinidad and Tobago, abortion remains a taboo and controversial subject socially, politically, and religiously. This documentary explores this sensitive subject, not simply to determine whether it is right or wrong but to determine whether the legal sphere of the country serves or disserves women's rights on this issue.

At Sea. 2006. Director Neisha Agostini. 25 min. Set in the small fishing village of Parlatuvier in Tobago, *At Sea* pulls viewers into the simple lives of fishermen and their families. The intricacies of the fishing lifestyle are explored offering interesting parallels to our everyday lives.

Barrel Children. 2006. Cara E. Weir. 24 min. This documentary offers a firsthand look at the impact of immigration on children left behind by a mother seeking a better life for her family. But soon both she and her children realize that the costs far outweigh the benefits for them all.

Calypso Dreams. 2003. Geoffrey Dunne and Michael Horne. 90 min. At the heart of Trinidad and Tobago's culture is the legacy of Calypso, which is explored in this film through the more famous Calypsonian performers of the country, including Lord Pretender, Lord Kitchener, and The Mighty Sparrow, among others.

Hosay Trinidad. 1999. John Bishop and Frank J. Korom. 45 min. A multicultural and multiethnic film, *Hosay Trinidad* examines the cultural and religious celebration of Shi'ite Muharram rites on the island of Trinidad.

A Loss of Innocence. 2006. Director Jenine Mendes-Franco. 21 min. An examination of child labor and other abuses against exploited children within the Caribbean using interviews with political and social workers as well as the children involved.

Web Sites

Trinidad & Tobago Express, http://www.trinidadexpress.com.

Trinidad and Tobago News, http://www.TrinidadandTobagonews.com.

Trinidad *Guardian* newspaper, http://www.guardian.co.tt/news9.html.

"What's Going On?" Episode on HIV/AIDS in Trinidad and Tobago (for children), http://www.un.org/works/goingon/whatsgoingon.html.

Organizations and NGOs

The Empowerment Society of Trinidad and Tobago
Web site: http://www.estt.org/INDEX.HTM
Formed in 2001, this nonprofit, nongovernmental organization (NGO) serves to promote the improvement of human welfare and the environment by addressing current problems on its own or by collaborating with other established organizations that share a similar goal.

Friends of Tobago AIDS Society (FOTAS)
Web site: http://www.fotasonline.org
The organization is a registered nonprofit whose purpose is exclusively charitable and educational. The mission of the organization is to provide financial, medical, professional, and other resources for persons infected with and affected by HIV/AIDS through already established local organizations geared toward serving this population.

SERVOL
Web site: http://www.estt.org/FRIENDS.htm
SERVOL is labeled as one of the most successful NGOs in Trinidad and Tobago. This organization serves to empower underprivileged communities by targeting its programs to the development of children ranging from newborns to the age of nineteen. SERVOL recognizes that, to develop successful programs, one must

address self-esteem issues and "work with" rather than "teach" persons within the community. This group has established projects such as the Special School that serves mentally challenged children between the ages of six and seventeen.

The United Nations Development Programme (UNDP)
Web site: http://www.undp.org.tt
The UNDP has been a presence in Trinidad and Tobago since 1961, helping the country foster its own resolutions for national and global development challenges. During its early development between 1961 and 1970, UNDP aided the country in its discovery of oil and gas, two of its greatest resources to date. At the core of the UNDP's support, which includes policy advice on issues like human security, economic and regional integration, and development of the nonenergy sector, is their work to ensure that knowledge and skills are passed along to nationals so that progress achieved through collaborative programs will not be impeded or eradicated in the future.

Women Working for Social Progress
Web site: http://www.peacewomen.org/contacts/americas/trinidad/tri_index.html
An affiliate of Peace Women, the Women's International League for Peace and Freedom, this organization's goals include campaigning and raising consciousness on the situation of women and man–woman relations through a number of activities, which include public education programs, advocacy, and public awareness campaigns. Such campaigns include workshops and training sessions on issues such as domestic violence, antiracism, and sexual harassment.

W. R. Torres Foundation for the Blind
Web site: http://www.torresfoundation.org
This organization's mission is to promote the educational, cultural, and social development of blind people in Trinidad and Tobago in an effort to bring about independence, career opportunities, and overall life enhancement. Since its inception in 1998 in honor of Wilfred Robert Torres, a blind and well-respected citizen of Trinidad and Tobago, the foundation has amassed several impressive achievements, such as introducing the first reading and shopping service for the blind through their Community Volunteer Network (CVN) program and establishing the first scholarship fund for blind citizens of Trinidad and Tobago.

YMCA (Young Men's Christian Association)
Web site: http://www.ymcatt.org/
Geared toward building strong children, families, and communities, the Trinidad and Tobago YMCA offers programs and services that help in achieving this goal such as vocational classes, after-school care, and day camp services. The organization's Youth Outreach Department focuses on community outreach, addressing issues such as rights of the child, violence, and of course HIV/AIDS.

Selected Bibliography

Baboolal, Yvonne. 2006. "Increased Gang Activity Likely, Warns Criminologist Deosaran." *The Trinidad Guardian*, November 30. http://www.guardian.co.tt/news9.html. Accessed November 30, 2006.

Bakhtin, Mikhail. 1984. *Rabelais and His World.* Translated by Helene Iswolsky. Bloomington: Indiana University Press.

Barrow, Christine. 1996. *Family in the Caribbean: Themes and Perspectives.* Kingston, Jamaica: Ian Randle Publishers.

Bratt, David E. 2006. "Paradigm Shift." *The Trinidad Guardian.* November 28. http://www.guardian.co.tt/news9.html. Accessed November 30, 2006.

Ellis, Patricia. 2002. *Citizenship Education in Small States: Trinidad and Tobago.* London: Commonwealth Secretariat Publications.

———. 2003. *Women, Gender and Development in the Caribbean: Reflections and Projections.* New York: Zed Books.

Freire, Paulo, and Donald Macedo. 1987. *Literacy: Reading the Word and the World.* South Hadley, MA: Bergin and Garvey.

George, June, Jeniffer Mohammed, and Lynda Quamina-Aiyejina. 2003. "Teacher Identity in an Era of Educational Reform." *Compare* 33, no. 2: 191–206.

George, Wesley. 2006. "Empowering Youth." *The Trinidad Guardian.* November 24. http://www.guardian.co.tt/news9.html. Accessed November 30, 2006.

Henry, Frances. 2003. *Reclaiming African Religions in Trinidad: The Socio-Political Legitimation of the Orisha and Spiritual Baptist Faiths.* Jamaica: The University of the West Indies Press.

International Institute for Vital Registration and Statistics (IIVRS). 2001. "Organization and Status of Civil Registration and Vital Statistics in English-speaking Countries in the Caribbean." Report prepared for the Pan American Health Organization and condensed into an article in *Epidemiological Bulletin,* 24, no. 3, September 2003. http://www.paho.org/English/DD/AIS/be_v24n3 Civ_reg_vit_stats.htm. Accessed November 2, 2006.

International Labor Organization. 2002. *The Effective Abolition of Child Labor.* Cornell University. http://digitalcommons.ilr.cornell.edu/cgi/viewcontent.cgi ?article=1002&context=child.

John, Sandra. 2004. *Youth, Unemployment and the Caribbean Information Society: A Challenge and an Opportunity.* Report prepared for the Economic Commission for Latin America and the Caribbean Subregional Headquarters for the Caribbean, Caribbean Development and Cooperation Committee.

Jones, Adele. 2006. *Tackling Child Sexual Abuse.* St. Augustine, Trinidad and Tobago: The University of the West Indies. http://www.sta.uwi.edu/uwiTo day/2006/chldabs.asp. Accessed November 5, 2006.

Lazarus-Black, Mindie. 2001. "Law and the Pragmatics of Inclusion: Governing Domestic Violence in Trinidad and Tobago." *American Ethnologist* 29: 388–416.

Liverpool, Hollis "Chalkdust." 2001. *Rituals of Power & Rebellion: The Carnival Tradition in Trinidad & Tobago, 1763–1962.* Chicago: Research Associates School Times Publications/Frontline Distribution Int'l Inc.

Mason, Peter. 1998. *Bacchanal! The Carnival Culture of Trinidad.* Philadelphia: Temple University Press.

Ministry of Education. 2003. *Education Policy Paper (1993–2003).* National Task Force of Education (White Paper), Executive Summary. http://www.nalis .gov.tt/Education/EducPolicy_Sum.html. Accessed October 27, 2006.

———. 2004. *National Report on the Development of Education in Trinidad and Tobago.* http://www.ibe.unesco.org/international/ICE47/English/Natreps/ reports/tobago_scan.pdf. Accessed October 27, 2006.

Nurse, Keith. 1999. "Globalization and Trinidad Carnival: Diaspora, Hybridity and Identity in Global Culture." *Cultural Studies* 13: 661–690.

Office of the United Nations High Commissioner for Human Rights, United Nations Committee on the Rights of the Child. 2003. *Second Periodic Report of the Republic of Trinidad and Tobago: Convention on the Rights of the Child*, *June 2003*. http://www.unhchr.ch/html/menu2/6/crc/doc/report/srf-trinidad&tobago-2.pdf.

Palmer, Colin A. 2006. *Eric Williams: The Making of the Modern Caribbean*. Chapel Hill: University of North Carolina Press.

Pan American Health Organization. 2006. *PAHO Basic Health Indicator Data Base Regional Core Health Data System: Trinidad and Tobago*. http://www.paho.org/English/DD/AIS/cp_780.htm. Accessed November 10, 2006.

Parimi, Neeta, Lexley M. Pinto Pereira, and Parimi Prabhakar. 2002. "The General Public's Perceptions and Use of Antimicrobials in Trinidad and Tobago." *Revista Panamamericana de Salud Public* 12, no. 1. http://www.scielosp.org/scielo.php?script=sci_arttext&pid=S1020-49892002000700003. Accessed November 13, 2006.

Stuempfle, Stephen. 1995. *The Steelband Movement: The Forging of a National Art in Trinidad and Tobago*. Philadelphia: University of Pennsylvania Press.

Trinidad and Tobago. Ministry of the Attorney General, Human Rights Unit. 2003.

United Nations Children's Fund (UNICEF). 2006. At a Glance: Trinidad and Tobago. http://www.unicef.org/infobycountry/trinidad_tobago_statistics.html. Accessed November 10, 2006.

United Nations Committee on the Rights of Child. 2006. *CRC 44th Session: Trinidad and Tobago*. http://www.hrea.org/lists/child-rights/markup/msg00392.html. Accessed June 7, 2006.

U.S. Central Intelligence Agency. 2006. The World Factbook 2006. http://www.cia.gov/cia/publications/factbook/geos/td.html. Accessed January 4, 2007.

U.S. Department of State. 2003. International Religious Freedom Report 2003. http://www.state.gv/g/drl/rls/irf/2003/24523.htm. Accessed November 12, 2006.

Walljasper, Jay. 2004. "Cities of Joy." *Making Places Newsletter*. http://www.pps.org/info/newsletter/november2004/november2004_joy. Accessed January 4, 2007.

Yelvington, Kevin A. 1993. *Trinidad Ethnicity*. Knoxville: University of Tennessee Press.

15

THE UNITED STATES

*Angela A. A. Willeto, Doreen E. Martinez,
and Mary Ann E. Steger*

NATIONAL PROFILE

In the United States, children under the age of eighteen years are approximately 25 percent of the nation's 300 million citizens. This percentage represents a decrease when compared with the "baby boom" era of the 1950s and 1960s. At present, slightly under half of children are girls, and just over half are boys. The child population includes white Americans (59 percent), Latinos (19 percent), black or African Americans (15 percent), Asians (4 percent), and American Indians and Alaskan Natives (1 percent) (Kids Count 2006b). Although the United States was founded on principles of justice and equality, the benefits of being a child are not enjoyed by all. More children are living in poverty (17.6 percent) than any other age group, and children are approximately 39 percent of the country's homeless population. Forty-two percent of homeless children are under the age of five, and it is estimated that the homeless youth population (minors living on the streets) is between 500,000 and 1.3 million (National Coalition for the Homeless 2005). In a country with a very high standard of living, poor families with children, especially those that are homeless, may not be able to provide adequate food and shelter for their children, much less provide for their

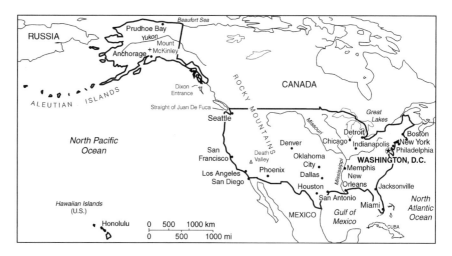

overall well-being. The only recourse for many of these families is to turn to the thousands of food pantries, soup kitchens, and emergency shelters that are found in U.S. communities across the nation.

There are significant income differences between married families with two parents and those with a single parent. Married couples with children have median incomes more than twice the amount of male- or female-headed households with children; this pattern is consistent among white, black, and Latino families, although black and Latino families have significantly lower median incomes than all types of white families (U.S. Bureau of the Census). Because of high divorce and out-of-marriage birth rates and increasing cohabitation trends, almost a third of children live in single-parent families. Moreover, these numbers vary along racial/ethnic lines. Only 15 percent of Asian and 23 percent of white children have single parents compared with 35 percent of Latino, 47 percent of American Indian/Alaskan Native, and 64 percent of black children (Kids Count 2006a). In cases of divorce, the rights of a mother to her children have varied over time, as have the rights of children. Historically, men had control over their wives and children, but this changed in the nineteenth century when the doctrine of tender years was established. Under this doctrine, the belief was that the interests of young children and girls were best served by being with their mother, as long as her fitness was established. As a result, mothers were usually awarded custody of the children, especially if they were girls. Currently, custody decisions are based on what is seen to be in the best interests of the child, and mothers are not automatically awarded sole custody as they were in the past, even though mothers still receive sole physical custody in a majority of cases (Walker, Brooks, and Wrightsman 1999, 79–86).

The government response to children's issues is affected by the fact that both the national government and the fifty state governments have the power to make policy that impacts children. Moreover, the power of the national and state governments is divided among legislative, executive, and judicial branches. The result is that policy makers located in various parts of government may be in serious disagreement over what is best for the nation's children. American Indian and Alaskan Native children are in a unique situation in relation to the federal government because of sovereignty rights, treaty obligations, and congressional legislation. As of 2005, the federal government officially recognizes 562 American Indian and Alaskan Native nations, tribes, bands, and organized communities, and this recognition carries with it an obligation to protect tribal lands and resources and to provide programs and services to Native American communities (Wilkins 2007, 21). It is important to note that each group of Indigenous Peoples, both recognized by the federal and state governments and not recognized, has its own culture and traditions to pass on to their children. Another layer of government is found at the local level and includes city, county, and school district governments. In addition, there are thousands of nongovernmental organizations (NGOs) located in all parts of the country that are concerned with children's issues, and these groups, along with religious organizations and churches, support families in a variety of ways by providing basic needs and a range of social services. The numerous organizations that advocate for children's interests do not necessarily agree on what these interests are, and this difference is reflected in their positions on policies and programs. Some advocacy organizations work to nurture children by improving the inadequate state of their lives; others work to give children the right to decide what is good for themselves (Walker, Brooks, and Wrightsman 1999, 46–51).

Government concern for families with children was evident in the early 1900s when the first mothers' pension laws were passed by a few states. These laws provided cash payments for mothers so that children could remain in the family home in the case of a father's death, desertion, or imprisonment. The federal government started supporting families in a major way with the passage of the Social Security Act of 1935, which provides guaranteed benefits to various groups of qualified citizens, including the elderly, the unemployed (Unemployment Compensation), and their dependents. In addition, the legislation created a small entitlement program called Aid to Dependent Children, which targeted benefits to poor families with children and grew into a much larger program called Aid to Families with Dependent Children (AFDC). In the 1950s and 1960s, the number and type of social programs were increased to include the Disability Insurance Program, which provides cash to disabled workers who are no longer able to engage in gainful employment and the spouses and children of these disabled workers; Medicare, which provides health benefits to the qualified elderly and disabled; Medicaid, which provides health benefits to low-income families and the elderly poor; the Food Stamp program, which provides assistance in purchasing food items to low-income families and the elderly poor; and the Supplemental Security Income (SSI) program, which is a guaranteed income program for the aged, disabled, and blind (Haskins 2001, 10–11).

In 1996, the major entitlement program for poor families with children, AFDC, was abolished and replaced by a nonentitlement block grant program called Temporary Assistance for Needy Families (TANF), which is part of the Personal Responsibility and Work Opportunity Reconciliation Act (PRWORA). Under TANF, states use federal block grant money to implement a welfare reform program that is created by state welfare agency personnel, which produces considerable variation in eligibility requirements and cash assistance amounts across the states. All state TANF programs impose a 60-month lifetime limit on the receipt of benefits funded by block grant money, and these programs are structured to move mothers off of welfare assistance and into a job as quickly as

KEY FACTS – UNITED STATES

Population: 301,139,947 (July 2007 est.)
Infant mortality rate: 6.37 deaths/1,000 live births (2007 est.)
Life expectancy at birth: 78 years (2007 est.)
Literacy rate: 99 percent (2003 est.)
Net primary school enrollment/attendance: 92 percent
    (2000–2005)
Internet users: 205.327 million (2005)
People living with HIV/AIDS: 1,200,000 (2005 est.)
Human Poverty Index (HPI-2) Rank: 16

Sources: CIA World Factbook: United States. https://www.cia.gov/
    cia/publications/factbook/geos/us.html. April 17, 2007; UNICEF.
    At a Glance: United States–Statistics. http://www.unicef.org/
    infobycountry/usa_statistics.html. April 24, 2007; World Health
    Organization (WHO): UNAIDS/WHO Global HIV/AIDS Online
    Database. ''Epidemiological Fact Sheets on HIV/AIDS and
    Sexuality Transmitted Diseases: United States.'' http://www.who
    .int/GlobalAtlas/predefinedReports/EFS2006/index.asp?strSelected
    Country=US. December 2006; United Nations Development
    Programme (UNDP) Human Development Report 2006–United
    States. http://hdr.undp.org/hdr2006/statistics/countries/
    data_sheets/cty_ds_USA.html. April 26, 2007.

possible, without much consideration given to the quality or the salary of the job. The federal legislation gives Native American nations and tribes the flexibility to tailor tribal TANF programs to their communities by defining their own work activities and work participation requirements, time limits, and eligibility requirements. For example, some tribal TANF programs allow recipients to participate in work activities that help strengthen community ties and preserve cultural traditions; others encourage recipients to pursue an education and count this as a work activity. These alternative types of work activities would not count as work in most state-run programs. Actually, the administrators of tribal TANF programs have to exercise considerable flexibility in their program designs so that they can begin to address the very high rates of poverty and unemployment found on most American Indian reservations.

OVERVIEW

In these times, U.S. children have lower infant and child mortality rates than in the recent past, but racial and ethnic disparities exist, with American Indian/Alaskan Native and African American children having higher mortality rates than others. For a variety of reasons related primarily to family income levels, childhood experiences vary significantly. Many children are well cared for and have many opportunities open to them, but some grow up in poverty, are victims of neglect and abuse, have no access to health care, do not have a decent place to live, and go to bed hungry. All children, however, have the opportunity to attend public schools at the primary and secondary levels, and many children are exposed to a structured curriculum from preschool (ages three or four) through high school. While war may affect U.S. children in various ways, they must be eighteen (legal adults) to join the military.

Some children come to the United States as refugees and immigrants, either with family members or alone, and face a number of obstacles, especially if they lack the necessary documents for legal residence. Currently, there are an estimated 1.8 to 5 million children living in unauthorized migrant families, and their ability to remain in the country with their families is a contentious public policy issue. It is estimated that the children of immigrants, both documented and undocumented, will represent a quarter of all children by 2010 (Urban Institute 2006; Passel 2006). Another serious issue is the trafficking of children within or into the country for use as sex slaves. Recent legislation makes it illegal to force a person to engage in commercial sex acts and provides some protection for immigrant victims of sex trafficking, such as special visas, medical care, and shelter services. In addition, law enforcement officials have the ability to prosecute violent sex crimes committed against children by citizens and legal permanent residents of the United States, and these officials cooperate with the United States Attorney's Offices, the Federal Bureau of Investigation (FBI), the National Center for Missing and Exploited Children, and the Central Intelligence Agency (CIA) to find victims and punish traffickers.

EDUCATION

In the United States, education is primarily a state and local government matter, and there is substantial policy and funding variation across the school districts found in the fifty states. All states, however, have compulsory education laws, which in most states require school attendance for children between the ages of five and sixteen. As an alternative to the public schools, parents may send their children to private schools, which charge tuition, or provide home schooling, and some states allow parents to use charter schools, which are publicly funded yet separate from public schools. Funding for the public schools comes from state and federal government sources, but local property taxes are, by far, the largest source of funding. Because of this, schools in districts with high property tax bases have more resources available per student than schools in districts with low property tax bases. So, while there is universal access to public education at the primary and secondary levels, the quality of the educational experience can vary significantly.

The education of Native American children has been an issue since the 1800s, and government-run day and boarding schools and federal funds to encourage public school attendance did little to provide a quality, culturally relevant education for these children. In the 1960s and 1970s, Native Americans were given more control over their children's education than they had in the past through congressional legislation, especially the Indian Self-Determination and Educational Assistance Act of 1975, which enabled tribes to operate their own schools and provided funds for bilingual and bicultural programs, culturally relevant teaching materials, and other resources. Although improvements were made, much remains to be done (O'Brien 1989, 241). Another problem affecting the quality of the education experience of Native American children is the low level of public funding many tribal schools receive. This problem is most serious for schools located on reservation lands that are a part of the millions of acres held in trust by the federal government. Schools located on trust lands lose property tax revenues because local property taxes are not paid on trust land property.

Reading test scores are considered a good measure of literacy and overall academic achievement by educators, and these scores are regularly reported for fourth and eighth graders in the nation's public schools. Although the test scores for all students have increased over the last fifteen years, differences emerge when the results are broken down by gender and race or ethnicity. Girls have higher scores than boys, and white and Asian/Pacific Islander children significantly outperform American Indian/Alaskan Native, Latino, and African American children in that order (Forum on Child and Family Statistics 2006b). Another marker of academic achievement is the high school diploma. While the vast majority of U.S. youths earn high school diplomas, high school dropout figures (8 percent) show that secondary school completion is not universal. These dropout rates vary by race or ethnicity, with Latinos having the highest rate (15 percent) and Asian/Pacific Islander youths having the lowest rate (3 percent) (Kids Count 2006a).

Disabled children have universal access to a free public education through high school, and federal law mandates that the educational experience of these children must take place in the least restrictive environment. Even with this legislative mandate in place, more than 40 percent of students with disabilities do not receive high school diplomas (National Council on Disability 2004). Teens in the United States do not have access to a free and universal higher education system, but they do have a number of choices, some of which are more accessible and affordable than others. The choices include two-year public community colleges, public and private four-year colleges and universities, tribal colleges, professional schools, and technical institutes. Some institutions are highly selective in admissions policies while others are not, and some private schools are much more expensive than public schools. Financial aid, although limited, is available in the form of guaranteed loans, scholarships, work study, and PELL grants for low-income students. Consequently, access to quality higher education is affected by a number of factors, one of which is the income level of the student's family.

PLAY AND RECREATION

The number and array of play and recreational activities available to U.S. children is astounding and includes physical education classes in primary and secondary schools, organized intramural and extramural school sports, informal recreational activities with family members and friends, activities sponsored by local governments and recreational organizations, such as Young Men's Christian Associations (YMCAs), and the activities focused on children at private athletic clubs. Local communities have parks, sports fields of numerous types, tennis courts, and swimming pools; additionally, school and community recreational facilities provide opportunities for indoor/outdoor sports and play activities.

Many but not all play and recreational activities sponsored by school districts, local governments, and community organizations are open to both girls and boys, but this was not the case until a national policy, referred to as Title IX, opened up opportunities for girls to participate in athletic activities in 1972. Title IX made it illegal to exclude girls from participating in any educational program or activity that received federal funds. Since that time, there has been a significant increase in the amount of funding and support given to girls' athletics in the nation's public schools. It is estimated that 2.4 million high school girls now participate in interscholastic sports (U.S. Department of Education 1997).

Native American children have access to the same play and recreational activities as other children do, and some Indigenous children are taught the games of their ancestors. One example is the game of stickball, which is popular today among the Choctaws and other Indigenous Peoples living in the eastern part of the United States. Several centuries ago, stickball games were treated as ceremonies or rituals and were played to settle disputes and to reinforce clan and tribal solidarity (O'Brien 1989, 8). To encourage the physical fitness of disabled children, the national government's Office on Disability collaborates with disability-based organizations across the country to link disabled children with mentors who offer training and guidance on how to become physically fit. Children with intellectual disabilities have the opportunity to participate in the sports training and competition that is offered in local communities by the Special Olympics, a nonprofit organization that works with over half a million special athletes in the United States.

In spite of the many opportunities for play and recreation open to children, increasing numbers of children and teens are engaging in sedentary activities, such as watching television and playing computer games, rather than physical activities. Multiple television sets in a home are common, and some children and teens have access to a large number of television channels through basic cable, digital cable, or satellite programming. In addition, many children have video game consoles, DVD players, and handheld gaming devices. Even with parental control over what children watch and the games they play, many children are exposed to content that is inappropriate for their age because of the abundance of media outlets. If children are not supervised in their use of the Internet, they run the risk of being the victims of those who use the Internet for illegal activities. The studies on television viewing report that, on average, children spend about 20 hours or more each week watching television, which is more time than is spent in any other activity besides sleeping. During this time they see tens of thousands of commercials, including 1,000 to 2,000 ads for alcohol each year (Health Systems 2004). Economic competition for children's attention in the commercials is pervasive and permeates television viewing. Children are targeted by the toy and fast-food industries, which spend billions of dollars each year on advertising specifically directed at young people. Fast-food chain restaurants offer incentives, such as playgrounds, contests, clubs, games, and free toys. These incentives are often tied to popular music, movies, television shows, and professional sports leagues and reinforce the focus on children as consumers. Some marketing involves products linked to movies and video games considered inappropriate for both young children and teens because of the extensive violence in the content of the movies and games (Media Awareness Network 2006).

The health impact of the sedentary child's lifestyle is a concern for public health officials and the U.S. public, especially since growing numbers of the nation's children are overweight. For many decades, the President's Council on Physical Fitness and Sports has encouraged and promoted the development of physical fitness and sports participation for children of all ages. Council members advise the president through the Secretary of Health and Human Services and act as the catalyst for fitness and sports activities in partnership with interested parties in the public, private, and nonprofit sectors. Children, including disabled children, who engage in a sixty-minute physical activity program five days a week for six weeks are eligible for a Presidential Active Lifestyle Award, and, once that is achieved, they can strive to earn the President's Challenge Award by engaging in extra physical activities for longer periods of time. In contrast, cuts in federal and state funding have significantly reduced sports and physical activities in many public schools. Historically, children and teens had some kind of physical activity, such as recess or gym class, every day. Today, these classes may be limited to a few times a week. Reducing the amount of time each week that young people engage in physical activities may impact the health of these children, especially if they do not have access to extracurricular physical or sports activities.

CHILD LABOR

Beginning in the mid-1800s, reformers argued that child labor harmed the health and welfare of the nation's children. The first child labor laws were passed in states in the early 1900s, and the Fair Labor Standards Act (FLSA) became law in 1938. Initially, the emphasis was on educating young laborers. These efforts were then reinforced by state compulsory school attendance laws. The FLSA sets age limits for specific types of work, especially work considered too hazardous for young workers, and specifies occupational and hour restrictions for workers less than sixteen years old. The minimum age for nonagricultural workers is sixteen; those who are fourteen and fifteen may be employed less than full-time if working does not interfere with their schooling, and children under fourteen may be paid for tasks on a part-time, irregular basis. In agricultural work, children under sixteen working on farms owned or operated by a parent are exempted from FLSA rules, as are youths who have reached the age of sixteen. Federal and state governments promote compliance with child labor regulations through investigations and enforcement, but violations exist. Violators are fined up to $10,000 for each violation leading to death or serious injury, and criminal sanctions may occur after a second conviction (U.S. Department of Labor 2000). Young workers are protected against discrimination in the workplace on the bases of race and color, national origin, sex, and religion under Title VII of the Civil Rights Act of 1964. Title VII applies to employers with fifteen or more employees and covers federal, state, and local governments. It also applies to employment agencies and labor organizations.

Compliance with FLSA regulations is particularly important in hazardous occupations, and these include agriculture, construction, landscaping, operating heavy equipment, and door-to-door and street selling. Young people working in these areas run the risk of serious injury (or death) from equipment rollovers, falls, exposure to dangerous pesticides, sexual assaults, and the like. At times, national labor advocacy groups and labor unions join forces to protect youth workers in hazardous jobs. In 2005, the Department of Labor (DOL) was criticized for issuing new child labor regulations that allow youths at ages fourteen and fifteen to operate and clean deep fryers and grills and youths at ages sixteen and seventeen to load paper balers and compacters. Under the old regulations, such jobs were prohibited for young people in these age groups. A DOL settlement with Wal-Mart also was criticized, and, again, the criticism was aimed at the failure to protect young workers from hazardous jobs. Besides a fine, the retailer was assured that future inspections would be announced, but critics wanted the government to conduct unannounced inspections and to force Wal-Mart to provide distinct employee badges to young workers, so they would not be called upon to operate hazardous equipment (Child Labor Coalition 2005).

Children and youths are employed by many types of industries, both agricultural and nonagricultural. In rural areas, young people who do farm work are usually teens on their own or dependents of farm workers, but some children as young as four or five work alongside their parents in the fields. The lack of enforcement of FLSA standards results in some children and teens working very long hours for six or seven days a week in peak harvesting seasons (Human Rights Watch 2000). In cities and towns, young people sixteen and older can work in all industries, as long as the job is not classified as a hazardous one. Children under the age of sixteen can work less than full-time in offices, grocery stores, retail stores, restaurants, movie theaters, amusement and baseball parks, or gas stations.

Those who are age thirteen or younger can baby-sit, deliver newspapers, or work as actors or performers (U.S. Department of Labor 2006). Besides legal employment, some children are forced into illegal work in the sex industry and trafficked as sex slaves. Children and teens living on the streets in the United States run a substantial risk of becoming victims of this commercial sex exploitation, and the risk extends to girls, boys, and transgender youths. A research study in 2001 estimated that 200,000 to 300,000 children each year are at high risk of being forced into illegal sexual activities (Child Labor Coalition 2003). Additionally, low-wage or sweatshop factories owned by U.S. companies but located outside the nation's borders may benefit from the forced labor of children. Anti-sweatshop organizations, especially those operating on university campuses in the United States, have been actively engaged in efforts to ban products from companies using sweatshop labor, which often includes children.

FAMILY

In recent decades, a number of factors have affected the roles of male and female children in the family, and these include changing family structures, working parents, and the rise of the feminist movement. These changes are reflected in the media, which now show girls as well as boys engaging in a broad range of physical, intellectual, and group endeavors. Since half of all current marriages now end in divorce, there is concern over the impact divorce has on children. The ideal situation is to have children grow up in a home with parents who have a healthy, loving relationship. When this is not the case and divorce occurs, children may suffer material losses and psychological distress. For example, when divorced mothers retain custody of their children, they often have less income than they had when married, and this may affect their children's material well-being. However, it is also true that many married couples, especially those of color, are already struggling financially because of the differences in income across racial lines. The psychological impact of divorce on children is less straightforward. Some argue that children are resilient and recover in a matter of years, while others argue that the devastating effects of divorce affect children into their adulthood. Inheritance customs and laws also affect the material well-being of children. Under state laws, when a parent dies, the surviving spouse and dependents receive equal parts of the estate. In cases of divorce, children are acknowledged as the legitimate children of each parent for purposes of inheritance. State laws favor children born to married parents, but children born to unmarried parents are eligible to receive the inheritance from a deceased parent as long as the person acknowledged the children as his or hers, either in writing or by their conduct, and contributed to the children's maintenance for a reasonable period of time prior to the parent's death (Social Security Administration).

Because the U.S. population lives longer lives now than they did in the past, children have ample opportunities to form relationships with grandparents and, possibly, great-grandparents. On the other hand, the obsession with youth that is prevalent in mainstream U.S. culture may prevent the formation of intergenerational relationships and lead to an increase in the age segregation that already exists (Riley and Bowen 2005). Yet the numbers of intergenerational households are growing, and millions of grandparents are the primary caregivers for their grandchildren, especially in households where parents work or are not living with their children (U.S. Bureau of the Census 2003a).

There is a severe income gap between the rich and the poor in the United States, and this gap has implications for the nation's children. Since 1980, increases occurred in the percentages of children living in families categorized as extremely poor (up to 7.2 percent in 2004) and those living in high income and very high income families (up to 29 percent and 12.9 percent, respectively, in 2004), and decreases occurred in the percentages of children living in families in the below poverty, low income, and median income categories. Families of all racial and ethnic backgrounds are represented in these economic categories, but many more white and Asian families are in the privileged economic categories than are Latino, African American, American Indian and Alaskan Native children (Forum on Child and Family Statistics 2006c). In general, the children in privileged families have many opportunities open to them and promising futures, while the children of families living in poverty face obstacles rather than opportunities and futures that are filled with risks.

A number of government programs exist to offer some help to children living in poor and low-income families, and the major programs include TANF cash assistance, childcare support for TANF recipients and working poor families, medical coverage under Medicaid and State Child Health Insurance programs, housing assistance through public housing and rent assistance programs, Supplemental Security Income benefits for disabled children, and the Food Stamp program. Parents who are poor, yet work and pay federal income taxes, can benefit from two tax credit programs. The first is the Earned Income Tax Credit (EITC), which is a refundable personal income tax credit that pays benefits to workers based on family size and the amount of income that they earn. Working poor taxpayers who qualify may use the credit to offset their tax liability or receive it as a lump sum payment as a tax refund. The second is the Child Tax Credit (CTC), which is a conditionally refundable tax credit available to low- and middle-income families with incomes below specific thresholds. What is amazing is that the subsidies provided to families by the CTC and the EITC are considerably larger than the entire federal budget for children and family services programs (excluding health care) administered by the Department of Health and Human Services (Burman and Wheaton 2005).

The high school or secondary school years mark the transition from childhood to young adulthood for many U.S. teens. These years include various events, such as homecoming activities and junior and senior proms, and culminate in the graduation ceremony, which is a significant rite of passage in young people's lives. Other activities may occur during these years that are not viewed favorably by parents, school officials, and the broader community, and these include illicit drinking, experimenting with drugs, and sexual behavior. A socially accepted marker of independence from parental control for many teens is learning to drive and getting a driver's license, and those who have the resources may have their own cars (Hoffman 2002). Rites of passage also include cultural and religious ceremonies and events that mark the passage from childhood to young adulthood, and some examples of these are Jewish bar or bat mitzvahs, Latin American girls' fifteenth birthday celebrations (*quinceañeras*), and Native American puberty ceremonies.

HEALTH

Racial and ethnic differences persist in infant and child mortality rates. Although the overall infant mortality rate was 6.9 deaths per 1,000 live births in 2003, the rate for black children was twice that number, and the rate for Asian/Pacific Islander children was only a bit over half the rate for all infants. The national death rate for children ages one to fourteen was twenty-one deaths per 1,000 children, and, again, Asian/Pacific Islander children had the lowest rates, while American Indian/Alaskan Native children had the highest rates at thirty deaths per 1,000 children (Kids Count 2006a). According to the Centers for Disease Control and Prevention, the leading causes of death among children and teens include accidental deaths, malignant tumors, suicide, homicide, heart disease, birth defects, influenza and pneumonia, respiratory distress or disease, and cerebral hemorrhages. Many children receive a range of vaccinations in infancy and childhood, and the immunization rates, while not universal, range from 73 percent to 94 percent across the nine vaccines commonly given to children (Forum on Child and Family Statistics 2006a). These vaccines include protections against the following bacterial or viral diseases and conditions: diphtheria, hepatitis A and B, meningitis, pneumonia, arthritis, influenza, measles, hearing loss, neurological disability or loss of a limb, mumps, seizures, brain disorders, ear infections, blood infections, polio, diarrhea and dehydration, excessive bleeding, breathing difficulty, and chickenpox (Children's National Medical Center).

It is important to note that children are considered more susceptible to toxins in the environment than adults. This may be due to the fact that children eat more food, drink more water, and breathe more air in proportion to their body size when compared with adults, which increases their exposure to toxins. In the United States, an estimated 3 to 4 million children, primarily children of color, live within a mile of a hazardous waste site and, consequently, may be exposed to toxic substances and be in high-risk categories for health problems. In addition, children who live in the older and poorer residential areas of cities may be exposed to toxic levels of lead leeching from pipes and plumbing fixtures. Another health danger facing children is chronic disease, and, currently, asthma is one of the most common and serious chronic diseases affecting the nation's children. The American Lung Association reports that 6 million children have been diagnosed with asthma, and this number represents a significant increase over the last decade (Centers for Disease Control and Prevention 2006). A more positive sign for children's health is that drinking water across the nation has improved over the years due to national, state, and municipal regulations and regular testing.

Health care in the United States is very expensive, and access to health care is a major problem for children in low-income and poor families. Moreover, health insurance coverage varies among families with different racial or ethnic backgrounds. Employer-sponsored or private-sector insurance covers only 56 percent of white children, and less than a fourth of American Indian/Alaskan Native children have this coverage. Two federal government programs target low-income families, Medicaid and the State Children's Health Insurance Program (SCHIP), but the coverage provided varies by state and leaves large numbers of children uninsured. In 2002, the proportion of uninsured children in the total child population was 11.6 percent or 8.5 million children. Latino children were more likely to be uninsured (22.7 percent) compared with white (11.1 percent), black (13.9 percent), and Asian children (11.5 percent). In addition to Medicaid and SCHIP medical coverage, some Native American children are covered by the national government's Indian Health Service (IHS), but even with this extra coverage 25 percent of these children remain uninsured. Families who do not have private or government health coverage for their children may be forced to take their children to hospital emergency rooms, and a few of these families may be able to use the medical services provided by the relatively small number of free health clinics operating in some communities (U.S. Bureau of the Census 2003b; Garrett and Yemane 2006).

Disabled children, including those who suffer from serious mental disorders, had better chances of being covered by the disability benefits offered through the Social Security Act in the past than they do at the present time. In 1996, a very restrictive definition of a disabled child was written into the PRWORA, and, as a result, this landmark piece of social legislation dramatically reduced the number of children who qualified for SSI disability benefits. Under PRWORA, a child is disabled only if there is a medically proven physical or mental disability that results in marked and severe functional limitations and is expected to cause the death of the child or last more than twelve months. Although deprived of the income assistance, disabled children who lost SSI benefits because of this law do continue to receive medical coverage under the Medicaid program (Rodgers Jr. 2006). In addition, many children with mental health disorders do not receive adequate care. Public and private insurance plans may not cover mental illnesses, and there may be a lack of affordable service providers in the child's community. Moreover, some families fear losing custody if they seek help from government agencies in caring for children with mental health disorders. A 2003 government report concluded that desperate parents were placing their children into state child welfare or juvenile justice systems with the hope that these children would receive the mental health treatment that they needed. The report, however, also documented the inadequate and inappropriate care found in the juvenile justice system and the fact that less than one-third of the children in out-of-home care provided through the child welfare system received the mental health care that they needed (Children's Defense Fund).

A problem facing the nation's young people is teen pregnancy, which is viewed by many as a serious social issue. In 1998, the nation's teen birth rate, at 52.1 births per 1,000 teens, was the highest rate among the world's twenty-seven richest nations. The rates have fallen in recent years, and the decreases are thought to be the result of lower rates of teen intercourse, the increasing use of contraceptives, and steady rates of abortions. Yet racial and ethnic differences exist. In 2003, Latina teens had the highest rate of teen births and Asian/Pacific Islander teens had the lowest rate, and the birth rates for African American teens showed the most significant decrease from the rates of the early 1990s (Martin et al. 2005). An issue facing some girls is female genital mutilation (FGM), a term that refers to a number of traditional practices that involve the cutting of female genitals. The procedure is usually performed upon girls who are between the ages of four and twelve as a rite of passage. The extent to which FGM is currently practiced in the United States is unknown, but the Centers for Disease Control and Prevention estimated that there were 168,000 girls and women with or at risk for FGM in 1990. In 1996, Congress defined the practice of FGM as a federal criminal offense unless it was necessary to protect the girl's life, and, as of 2004, sixteen states had legislation instituting criminal sanctions for the practice (Center for Reproductive Rights 2004).

There is support for school-based sexuality education that teaches young people about ways to protect themselves from sexually transmitted diseases, HIV/AIDS, and unintended pregnancy, and it is found among the medical, scientific, public health, religious, and educational communities and in public opinion polls of parents and voters. In spite of this support, government funding primarily supports the teaching of abstinence-only-until-marriage in public schools. Gay, lesbian, bisexual, and transgender (GLBT) youth, although a smaller population in schools across the county, suffer discrimination and harassment because of their sexuality and are considered more at risk of being harmed by their classmates than heterosexual students, according to the Sexuality Information and Education Council of the United States (SIECUS). This organization reports that over 75 percent of the country's students reside in states where "sexual orientation and identity are not protected classes under the law," so these students lack legal protection from discrimination and harassment (Sexuality Information and Education Council of the United States).

LAWS AND LEGAL STATUS

The definition of childhood in the United States has changed over time. During the nineteenth century, fourteen was generally accepted as the age limit of childhood. The limit was raised to sixteen and, then, to eighteen in the twentieth century. This age standard is vital in determining juvenile court jurisdiction and the legal age for such things as marriage, working, voting, and joining the military. In some areas, uniformity is provided by national legislation, but in other areas, the legal status of children varies from state to state. In 2005, the Supreme Court abolished the execution of children convicted of murder and argued that executing offenders under the age of eighteen violated the prohibition of cruel and unusual punishment that was provided by the Eighth Amendment to the Constitution. Also, recent lower federal court decisions have helped ensure the safety and well-being of gay, lesbian, bisexual, and transgendered youth in school environments. In contrast, custody decisions for children whose parents divorce are decided in state courts. Generally, custody is awarded to one parent, with whom the child lives most of the time, but divorced parents may share custody of their child in a joint custody arrangement in which the child spends an approximately equal amount of time with both parents.

Segments within U.S. society hold very different views on the nature and breadth of children's rights. Moreover, Supreme Court decisions have not clearly specified these rights. A document that does clearly define children's rights is the Convention on the Rights of the Child, which was adopted by the United Nations in 1989 and set minimum standards for rights that protect the well-being of children. These standards are contained in the forty-one substantive articles of the convention that extend "civil, political, economic, social, cultural, and humanitarian rights to children" (Walker, Brooks, and Wrightsman 1999, 30). While the United States Ambassador to the United Nations, Madeleine Albright, signed the document in 1995, the treaty has not been ratified by the U.S. Senate. The United States joins Somalia as the only two members of the United Nations who have not ratified the convention. There is no simple explanation as to why the treaty has not been ratified by the Senate, but one reason may be that some policy-makers and advocacy organizations see the convention as a threat to national sovereignty and the parent–child relationship (Walker, Brooks, and Wrightsman 1999, 30–38). In order for ratification to occur, the provisions of the Convention on the Rights of the Child must be evaluated as to their compatibility with existing law and practice at both the state and federal levels of government. This evaluation, however, is open to interpretation by government officials who may or may not view the convention as appropriate for the United States.

When young people are arrested for violating the law, the arrests are usually for arson, vandalism, and motor vehicle theft. In most cases, young violators come under the jurisdiction of the juvenile justice system, which was established in 1899. The system is based on the assumption that young people are different from adults in their ability to make sound judgments, to understand the impact of their actions, and to realize the ramifications of engaging in criminal behavior and committing criminal acts. Consequently, juvenile courts operate somewhat differently than courts handling adult cases. For example, the juvenile's identity is maintained in files that are highly confidential and kept from the public. Under federal law, seventeen is the legal limit for juvenile status in the criminal justice system, but states have the authority to impose different limits. Within the juvenile justice system, disagreement exists over whether the emphasis should be on rehabilitating juvenile offenders or on protecting the community from these offenders. This disagreement leads state officials to question whether to use resources to build additional detention facilities so that more juvenile offenders are off the streets or to focus on teaching skills to these offenders so that they will not return to criminal behavior in the future. If officials choose the latter, the results of prevention and rehabilitation programs may not be realized for years after the programs are started, which makes this choice difficult to pursue (Juvenile Justice FYI).

Another behavior that causes concern among parents, law enforcement officials, and society in general is participation in youth gangs. The popular belief seems to be that all gangs promote and engage in violent behavior, but research exists that shows this belief is an exaggeration. The research also shows that gang members come from a variety of social class and ethnic group backgrounds and are found in both urban and rural areas. Youth gangs are not a new phenomenon and emerged around the time that the United States was experiencing an influx of European immigrants at the beginning of the twentieth century. Today, there is no consensus on what constitutes a gang or why young people join gangs, but some explanations emphasize the need to have a peer group and a sense of belonging and empowerment (Shelden, Tracy, and Brown 2001). Currently, the United States has a considerable amount of gang activity, especially in large cities. According to the results from the National Youth

Gang Survey, an estimated 731,500 gang members and more than 21,500 gangs were active in the United States in 2002, and every city with a population of 250,000 or more reported the presence of youth gangs (U.S. Department of Justice).

RELIGIOUS LIFE

The separation of church and state is a long-recognized constitutional principle in the United States, but defining the boundary between the two has never been easy. While religious education is not allowed in public schools, except when it is presented from a neutral, academic perspective, the boundary between church and state in the public schools is frequently tested in court cases that challenge the treatment of religious holidays, religious displays, and prayer in school. Private religious elementary and secondary schools, which include religious instruction in the school day, are an alternative to the public system, but these schools charge tuition and are unaffordable for many families. Children who do not receive religious instruction in their schools can attend instructional sessions held at their places of worship, either in conjunction with religious services or at a regularly scheduled time.

While Native American children may learn the doctrines and dogmas of mainstream religions, they also may be taught to respect the traditions and ceremonies of their ancestors. Although traditional practices vary among the many groups of Native Americans, Indigenous belief systems are based, in part, on the perception that the land itself is sacred. Consequently, many ceremonial practices of Native Americans are site-specific and follow instructions passed from one generation to another. The sites where ceremonies are held are considered sacred ground. Yet, conflict occurs when sacred sites are located in national parks, monument areas, or places used by the general public for recreational purposes (rock climbing and skiing, for example). These conflicts between tribal, federal, and state governments may need to be settled in the federal court system (Wilkins 2007, 9).

Religious rites of passage that children experience include baptisms, confirmations, bar or bat mitzvahs, puberty ceremonies, and initiation rites. Two examples of puberty or female coming-of-age ceremonies are the Navajo Kinaaldá and the Apache Sunrise ceremony in which a four-day set of rituals is used to ascribe an identity to the girl that transforms her into a woman. All types of religious ceremonies are considered important events in children's lives and involve the young person's parents or guardians, relatives, and, oftentimes, extended family members. In addition, there are numerous organizations with religious roots that have an influence on the lives of children. One nationwide organization is the YMCA (Young Men's Christian Association), which was created more than 150 years ago to serve as a place for bible study and prayer to counter the influence of life in the streets. In recent decades, local YMCAs offer a range of activities, including sports activities, to foster the development of the whole child or young adult. Another nationwide organization is the YWCA (Young Women's Christian Association), which had its start in the United States in 1858. The YWCA has its roots in the Christian faith but is "sustained by the richness of many beliefs and values" (YWCA USA). Currently, local YWCAs engage in two hallmark programs—racial justice and the economic empowerment of women—and provide a range of social services that meet women's needs (child care, rape crisis intervention, domestic violence assistance, and job training, for example). Some local YWCAs also provide health and fitness programs for women (YWCA USA). Other examples of organizations with religious foundations include the Boy Scouts and Girl Scouts of America and the Salvation Army, and numerous other organizations with religious affiliations exist to promote the spiritual and moral development of children and teens.

CHILD ABUSE AND NEGLECT

The Children's Bureau of the Department of Health and Human Services tracks and reports on cases of child abuse and neglect through the National Child Abuse and Neglect Data System (NCANDS), which is based on information from cases of children who were investigated or assessed by state child protective service agencies. The 2004 report estimates that 872,000 children were victims of various types of abuse in that year, and an estimated 1,490 children died due to abuse or neglect. More than 80 percent of these fatalities were children younger than four years old. As in many other areas of children's lives, differences based on racial or ethnic background exist. Among all victims, children who were African American, Pacific Islanders, and American Indians or Alaskan Natives had the highest rates of victimization at 19.9, 17.6, and 15.5 per 1,000 children of the same race or ethnicity, respectively, compared with white, Latino, and Asian children, who had rates of victimization at 10.7, 10.4, and 2.9 per 1,000 children of the same race or ethnicity, respectively (U.S. Department of Health and Human Services 2004). The care of abused or neglected children is the responsibility of government at all levels, especially state child protective service agencies, and children's advocacy groups play an important role. Adequate funding is always a problem. National legislation provides some funding for victims of family violence, and this funding usually supplements existing community efforts to provide temporary shelter, counseling, transportation, emergency childcare assistance, and health care referrals for victims. Some maltreated children are placed in state-run foster care, where they live with adults who serve as substitute parents. Foster-care children tend to be from poor families, and nonwhite children are overrepresented in this population. For example, in 2003, African American children were less than 15 percent of the total child population, but they comprised 35 percent of the foster care population (Congressional Research Service 2005).

The maltreatment of Native American children has a long history and came to the government's attention when a 1930 congressional investigation into abuse in boarding schools reported the deaths of students from abuse and lack of care. Currently, tribal nations have programs that provide information, support, and assistance to victims of child sexual abuse, and federal laws also address the problem. The Indian Child Welfare Act (ICWA) works to reduce the number of victims of abuse or neglect placed in non-Indian adoptive and foster homes and to provide placements in homes that reflect American Indian traditions and culture. The Indian Child Protection and Family Violence Prevention Act mandates the reporting of suspected abuse to the appropriate authorities so that further abuse can be prevented. The effectiveness of these efforts is compromised by inadequate funding and the ongoing tension between the power of government agencies and the sovereign status of tribal nations (Center on Child Abuse and Neglect 2000).

Those who are convicted of murdering children face the death penalty, and a small number of states allow the death penalty for certain sex crimes (rape or sodomy) involving young children, even though legal scholars question the constitutionality of such laws. In recent decades, steps were taken to remove child sex offenders from their communities permanently or for long periods of time and to subject them to surveillance when living in communities. Parents who mistreat their children risk losing custody, but some rulings terminating parental rights are overturned if a court decides that the due process rights of parents were violated.

Children are not forced into the military in the United States, and only men living in the country, ages eighteen through twenty-five, must register for selective service. Although joining the military is voluntary and only for men and women eighteen and older, public high school students are targeted by military recruiters. Moreover, recruiters have the legal right to get student at-home contact information from high school administrators.

GROWING UP IN THE TWENTY-FIRST CENTURY

The future of children growing up in the twenty-first century in the United States will definitely be affected by issues associated with family income level and the child's racial or ethnic background. Currently, many more white and Asian children are living in families with high or very high incomes than are Latino, black, or Native American children. Moreover, the percentages of families categorized as extremely poor and those categorized as high or very high income have increased in the last several decades, creating a significant income gap between rich and poor families. In general, black and Latino families have significantly lower median incomes than white families. Also, the fact that more Latino, Native

American, and black children are growing up in single-parent families than are Asian and white children is significant because two-parent married families have much higher median incomes than single-parent families. Similar racial disparities are found in other areas of children's lives. American Indian, Alaskan Native, and African American children have higher mortality rates than children with other racial or ethnic backgrounds. White and Asian children outperform Native American, Latino, and African American children in reading tests, and Latino children have higher school dropout rates than other children. Many of these patterns have existed for decades and are likely to continue well into the twenty-first century.

Although a plethora of government programs have been created to deal with problems that affect the lives of children, the programs that currently exist do not adequately cover the pressing needs of children growing up in families that are low-income or poor. For example, the TANF program has pushed a large number of single mothers with children off of the welfare rolls and into the low-wage and part-time labor force. This has the effect of reducing the ranks of the welfare poor and increasing the ranks of the working poor, but does not necessarily improve the lives of the children living in these families. Another example is Medicaid and the SCHIP, which were both designed to meet the health needs of low-income families. Even with these programs, there are significant numbers of children growing up without health insurance coverage, and these children are found in poor, low-income, and even middle-income families. Not all families are covered by government programs, and many low- or middle-income working parents cannot afford the health coverage that may be available to them at their place of work.

Since the 1980s, the thinking behind government's response to the economic and social welfare needs of poor and low-income families has shifted ideologically. Policy makers no longer consider the so-called social services safety net an entitlement for families who are in need. Instead, those who seek help from government programs are expected to pull themselves out of poverty on their own with a small amount of temporary assistance and without the benefits provided by a broad and permanent system of social and economic supports. If this ideology persists well into the twenty-first century, the well-being of children living in poor and low-income families will remain in danger.

RESOURCE GUIDE

Suggested Readings

Corsaro, William A. 2004. *The Sociology of Childhood*. 2nd ed. Thousand Oaks, CA: Pine Forge Press. This academic text explores children's rights and changing demographics and contains many examples of children's behaviors and play activities that are illustrated in charts and photographs that capture the complexity and diversity of children's lives.

Duncan, Greg J., and P. Lindsay Chase-Lansdale, eds. 2001. *For Better and for Worse: Welfare Reform and the Well-Being of Children and Families.* New York: Russell Sage Foundation. This edited volume examines the changes brought about by the Personal Responsibility and Work Opportunity Reconciliation Act of 1996, and looks at the impact welfare reform is having on the well-being of children in low-income families. The chapters include academic perspectives and empirical studies on the links among employment, family dynamics, and child development.

Lareau, Annette. 2003. *Unequal Childhoods: Class, Race, and Family Life.* 2nd ed. Berkeley: University of California Press. This book explores the argument that class makes a difference in the lives and futures of children in the United States. It draws upon the in-depth observations of black and white middle-class, working-class, and poor families to demonstrate differences in the child-rearing approaches of parents from these income classes.

Pardeck, John T. 2006. *Children's Rights: Policy and Practice.* 2nd ed. Binghamton, NY: Haworth Press. This book describes the most significant laws and policies in the United States that protect the rights of children. It is written as an information source and advocacy tool for families and professionals who are fighting for the fair treatment of children.

Walker, Nancy E., Catherine M. Brooks, and Lawrence S. Wrightsman. 1999. *Children's Rights in the United States: In Search of a National Policy.* Thousand Oaks, CA: Sage Publications. The authors of the book argue that the lack of a national policy on children's rights is a major obstacle to ensuring that the best interests of children prevail. They believe the United Nations Convention on the Rights of the Child should be the foundation for such a national policy and analyze the rights of children in six policy areas from this perspective.

Wilkins, David E. 2007. *American Indian Politics and the American Political System.* 2nd ed. Lanham, MD: Rowman & Littlefield Publishers. The author starts with the fact that American Indians are separate and sovereign peoples with histories that predate the American republic and recognizes the unique political, economic, cultural, and moral rights and powers exercised by tribal nations. He analyzes the internal dynamics of American Indian governments and politics and examines the relationships of these governments with the states, the federal government, and other relevant actors.

Nonprint Resources

Barbie Nation. 1998. New York: New Day Films. 53 min. VHS. The 53-minute video tells the story of the cult of the Barbie doll, telling the Barbie stories of diverse men, women, and children.

Born to Buy: Advertising and the New Consumer. 2005. Dallas: LeCroy Center for Educational Telecommunications. 60 min. Videodisc. The videodisc explores the changing world of children's consumer culture, with special emphasis on the role of marketing and its connection to popular culture.

Dying to Be Thin. 2004. Boston: WGBH Video. 60 min. Videodisc. The videodisc goes behind the statistics of eating disorders to examine the deadly battle girls wage as they strive for impossible beauty.

Girlhood. 2003. Brooklyn: Moxie Firecracker Films. 82 min. Videodisc. This documentary tells the story of the dramatic journey of two teenagers through the juvenile justice system and back out to the streets of East Baltimore.

Girls Like Us. 1997. New York: Women Make Movies. 60 min. VHS. The documentary explores female teenage experiences of sexuality and pregnancy and exposes the impact of class, sexism, and violence on the girls' dreams and expectations.

Juvenile Justice. 2001. Alexandria, VA: PBS Video. 90 min. VHS. The video explores whether children who commit serious crimes should be tried as juveniles or adults.

Juvies. 2004. Pacific Palisades, CA: Chance Films. 90 min. Videodisc. The videodisc focuses on twelve young lawbreakers and delivers an unblinking look at the juvenile justice system.

Kinaaldá: A Navajo Rite of Passage. 2000. New York: Women Make Movies. 57 min. VHS. The video explores Kinaaldá, a four-day coming-of-age ceremony for Navajo girls ages eleven to fourteen.

Méndez vs. Westminster: For All the Children. 2002. Huntington Beach, CA: KOCE-TV Foundation. 27 min. Videodisc. The videodisc presents information on a 1943 court case that set an important legal precedent for ending segregation in the public schools.

Merchants of Cool. 2001. Alexandria, VA: PBS Video. 60 min. Videodisc. The videodisc investigates the ways in which marketing firms assess the tastes, attitudes, and aspirations of teens in the United States so that Hollywood and Madison Avenue can craft tailored versions of teenage life in movies, television, music, and advertising.

Our House: A Very Real Documentary about Kids of Gay and Lesbian Parents. 1999. New York: Cinema Guild. 57 min. VHS. The video presents interviews with five families from New York, Arkansas, Arizona, and New Jersey describing their experiences of living in households led by gay and lesbian parents.

The Return of Navajo Boy. 2000. Chicago: Jeff Spitz Productions. 52 min. VHS. The video documents the family reunion of a Navajo man who was taken from his family as a child by missionaries forty years before.

Song of Our Children. 2005. Boulder, CO: Landlocked Films LLC. 58 min. Videodisc. The videodisc is a documentary about the inclusive education of kids with special needs.

Stolen Childhoods. 2003. Vineyard Haven, MA: Galen Films. 86 min. Videodisc. The videodisc is a documentary on child labor, in which the story is told in the words of laboring children, their parents, and the people working daily to help them.

When the Bough Breaks. 2001. New York: Filmakers Library. 58 min. VHS. The video looks at children coping with their mothers' incarcerations and illustrates the policy gaps between the judicial and social service systems that are supposed to serve these children.

Web Sites

Center for Law and Social Policy, http://www.clasp.org.

Center for the Advancement of Responsible Youth Sports, http://hdcs.fullerton.edu/knes/carys/resources.htm.

Child Abuse Prevention, http://child-abuse.com.

Child Development Research, http://www.cdwire.net.

Child Labor Coalition, http://www.stoplabor.org.

Child Stats, http://www.childstats.gov.

Child Trends, Inc., http://www.childtrends.org.

Family Support America, http://www.familysupportamerica.org.

Generations United, http://www.gu.org.

Human Rights Watch, http://www.hrw.org.

Institute for Women's Policy Research, http://www.iwpr.org.

Kids Count, Annie E. Casey Foundation, http://www.aecf.org/kidscount.

National Center for Health Statistics, http://www.cdc.gov/nchs.

National Child Welfare Resource Center on Legal and Judicial Issues, http://nccan ch.acf.hhs.gov/pubs/rcslist/cbttan/rclji.cfm.

National Committee to Prevent Child Abuse, http://www.childabuse.org.

National Fatherhood Initiative, http://www.fatherhood.org.

National Institute on the Media and the Family, http://www.mediafamily.org.

National Resource Center for Family Centered Practice, http://www.uiowa.edu/~nrcfcp.

Pew Research Center, http://people-press.org.

Resource Center for Adolescent Pregnancy Prevention, http://www.etr.org/recapp.

Safe Kids Worldwide, http://www.safekids.org.

Sweatshop Watch, http://www.sweatshopwatch.org.

United States Bureau of the Census, http://www.census.gov.

Urban Institute, http://www.urban.org.

Welfare Information Network: Teen Parents, http://www.ssc.wisc.edu/irp.wrr/teenparents.htm.

Welfare Reform Network, http://www.welfareinfo.org.

Organizations and NGOs

Administration for Children and Families, United States Department of Health and
    Human Services
370 L'Enfant Promenade SW
Washington, DC 20201
Web site: http://www.acf.dhhs.gov

American Civil Liberties Union
125 Broad Street, 18th Floor
New York, NY 10004
Web site: http://www.aclu.org

American Humane Association
63 Inverness Drive East
Englewood, CO 80112
Phone: (303) 792-9900
Fax: (303) 792-5333
Web site: http://www.americanhumane.org

Child Welfare Institute
111 E. Wacker Drive, Suite 325
Chicago, IL 60601
Phone: (312) 949-5640
Fax: (312) 922-6736
Web site: http://www.gocwi.org

Child Welfare League of America
440 First Street, NW, Third Floor
Washington, DC 20001
Phone: (202) 638-2952
Fax: (202) 638-4004
Web site: http://www.cwla.org

Children's Defense Fund
25 E Street NW
Washington, DC 20001
Phone: (202) 628-8787
Web site: http://www.childrensdefense.org
Email: cdfinfo@childrensdefense.org

Children's Rights, Inc.
330 7th Avenue, 4th Floor
New York, NY 10001
Phone: (212) 683-2210
Fax: (212) 683-2240
Web site: http://www.childrensrights.org

National Campaign to Prevent Teen Pregnancy
1776 Massachusetts Avenue NW, Suite 200

Washington, DC 20036
Phone: (202) 478-8500
Web site: http://www.teenpregnancy.org

National Center for Children in Poverty
215 W. 125th Street, 3rd Floor
New York, NY 10027
Phone: (646) 284-9600
Fax: (646) 284-9623
Web site: http://www.nccp.org

National Center for Mental Health and Juvenile Justice
Policy Research Associates
345 Delaware Avenue
Delmar, NY 12054
Phone: 1-866-9NCMHJJ (toll-free)
Fax: (518) 439-7612
Web site: http://www.ncmhjj.com
Email: ncmhjj@PRAINC.COM

National Child Welfare Resource Center for Family-Centered Practice
Hunter College School of Social Work
129 East 79th Street
New York, NY 10021
Phone: (212) 452-7053
Fax: (212) 452-7475
Web site: http://www.cwresource.org

National Clearinghouse on Child Abuse and Neglect Information at Child Welfare
    Information Gateway
Children's Bureau/ACYF
1250 Maryland Avenue SW, Eighth Floor
Washington, DC 20024
Phone: (703) 385-7565 or (800) 394-3366
Web site: http://childwelfare.gov

National Indian Child Welfare Association
5100 SW Macadam Avenue, Suite 300
Portland, OR 97239
Phone: (503) 222-4044
Fax: (503) 222-4007
Web site: http://www.nicwa.org

Office of Juvenile Justice and Delinquency Prevention
United States Department of Justice
810 Seventh Street NW
Washington, DC 20531
Phone: (202) 307-5911
Web site: http://ojjdp.ncjrs.org

Prevent Child Abuse America
500 N. Michigan Avenue, Suite 200
Chicago, IL 60611
Phone: (312) 663-3520
Fax: (312) 939-8962
Web site: http://www.preventchildabuse.org
Email: mailbox@preventchildabuse.org

Selected Bibliography

Birdseye, Debbie Holscla, and Tom Birdseye. 1996. *What I Believe: Kids Talk about Faith.* New York: Holiday House.

Burman, Leonard E., and Laura Wheaton. 2005. "Who Gets the Child Tax Credit?" *Tax Notes,* October 17. http://www.urban.org/UploadedPDF/411232_child_tax_credit.pdf. Accessed May 1, 2006.

Center for Reproductive Rights. 2004. Legislation on Female Genital Mutilation in the United States, November 2004. http://www.crlp.org/pdf/pub-bp/fgm/dwsusa.pdf. Accessed May 22, 2006.

Center on Child Abuse and Neglect. 2000. History of Victimization in Native Communities, March 2000. http://devbehavpeds.ruhsc.edu/assets/pdf/pmm. Accessed May 22, 2006.

Centers for Disease Control and Prevention. 2006. Asthma's Impact on Children and Adolescents, May 2006. http://www.cdc.gov/asthma/children.htm. Accessed July 12, 2006.

Charnov, Iaine. 2000. "Kinaaldá." http://www.vibrani.com/Kinaalda.htm. Accessed July 7, 2006.

Child Labor Coalition. 2003. Alert: Stop and Report the Trafficking and Exploitation of Children and Youth. Press release. http://www.stopchildlabor.org/pressroom/trafficking.html. Accessed June 16, 2006.

———. 2005. "Activists: Stop Child Labor at Wal-Mart Now," and "Bush Department of Labor Not Protecting America's Young Workers." Press releases, February 16, 2005. http://www.stopchildlabor.org/pressroom. Accessed June 16, 2006.

Children's Defense Fund. The Barriers: Why Is It So Difficult for Children to Get Mental Health Screens and Assessments? http://www.childrensdefense.org/childwelfare/mentalhealth. Accessed May 9, 2006.

Children's National Medical Center. Immunization Dictionary. http://www.dcchildrens.com/dcchildrens/advocacy/pdf/Immunization_Dictionary.pdf. Accessed August 24, 2006.

Congressional Research Service. 2005. Race/Ethnicity and Child Welfare. Memo, August 25. http://www.cwla.org/programs/culture/memo050825race.pdf. Accessed May 22, 2006.

Forum on Child and Family Statistics. 2006a. Childstats.gov. America's Children 2006: Health. http://childstats.gov/americaschildren/hea.asp. Accessed July 17, 2006.

———. 2006b. America's Children: Education, Table ED3.B, Reading Achievement. http://childstats.gov/americaschildren/xls.ed3b.xls. Accessed July 24, 2006.

———. 2006c. America's Children: Child Poverty and Family Income. http://childstats.gov/americaschildren/econ1b.asp. Accessed July 17, 2006.

Free the Slaves and Human Rights Center, University of California, Berkeley. 2004. Hidden Slaves: Forced Labor in the United States, September 2004. http://www.hrcberkeley.org/research/hiddenslaves.html. Accessed June 28, 2006.

Garrett, Bowen, and Alshadye Yemane. 2006. "Racial and Ethnic Differences in Insurance Coverage and Health Care Access and Use: A Synthesis of Findings from the *Assessing the New Federalism* Project." *The Urban Institute*, April 2006. http://www.urban.org/UploadedPDF/311321_DP06-01.pdf. Accessed May 9, 2005.

Goodluck, Charlotte T., and Angela A. A. Willeto. 2001. *Native American Kids 2001: Indian Children's Well-being Indicators Data Book*. Portland, OR: National Indian Child Welfare Association.

Haskins, Ron. 2001. "Liberal and Conservative Influences on the Welfare Reform Legislation of 1996." In *For Better and for Worse: Welfare Reform and the Well-being of Children and Families*. Edited by Greg J. Duncan and P. Lindsay Chase-Lansdale. New York: Russell Sage Foundation. pp. 9–34.

Hays, Sharon. 2003. *Flat Broke with Children*. New York: Oxford University Press.

Health Systems. 2004. Your Child, July 2004. University of Michigan. http://www.med.umich.edu/1libr/yourchild/tv.htm. Accessed June 14, 2006.

Herrick, John H., and Paul Stewart. 2004. *Encyclopedia of Social Welfare History in North America*. Thousand Oaks, CA: Sage Publications.

Hoffman, Lynn M. 2002. "Why High Schools Don't Change: What Students and Their Yearbooks Tell Us." *The High School Journal* 86: 22–37.

Human Rights Watch. 2000. Fingers to the Bone: United States Failure to Protect Child Farmworkers, 2000. http://www.hrw.org/reports/2000/frmwrkr. Accessed June 21, 2006.

Juvenile Justice FYI. Juvenile Justice System. http://www.juvenilejusticefyi.com/index.html. Accessed August 17, 2006.

Kids Count. 2006a. Kids Count Data Book Online: Race and Child Well-being. http://www.aecf.org/kidscount/sld/auxiliary/race_child.jsp. Accessed July 12, 2006.

———. 2006b. Kids Count Data Book Online: Child Population by Gender and Child Population by Race. http://www.aecf.org/kidscount/sld/compare_results.jsp?i=690 and http://www.aecf.org/kidscount/sld/compare_results.jsp?r=710. Accessed July 12, 2006.

Lindenmeyer, Kriste. 1997. *A Right to Childhood: The U.S. Children's Bureau and Child Welfare, 1912–1946*. Chicago: University of Illinois Press.

Martin, J. A., B. E. Hamilton, P. D. Sutton, S. V. Ventura, F. Menaker, and M. L. Munson. 2005. "Births: Final Data for 2003." *National Vital Statistics Report* 54.

Media Awareness Network. 2006. Media and Internet Resources. http://www.media-awareness.ca. Accessed June 16, 2006.

National Coalition for the Homeless. 2005. Why Are People Homeless? NCH Fact Sheet #1 and Homeless Youth, NCH Fact Sheet #13, June 2005. http://www.nationalhomeless.org/publications/facts/html. Accessed May 15, 2006.

National Council on Disability. 2004. Improving Educational Outcomes for Students with Disabilities, May 17. http://www.ncd.gov/newsroom/publications/2004/pdf. Accessed July 26, 2006.

O'Brien, Sharon. 1989. *American Indian Tribal Governments*. Norman: University of Oklahoma Press.

Passel, Jeffrey S. 2006. The Size and Characteristics of the Unauthorized Migrant Population in the U.S. March 7. http://pewhispanic.org/files/execsum/61.pdf. Accessed August 28, 2006.

Riley, Lesley D., and Christopher Bowen. 2005. "The Sandwich Generation: Challenges and Coping Strategies of Multigenerational Families." *The Family Journal: Counseling and Therapy for Couples and Families* 13: 52–58.

Rodgers, Harrell R., Jr. 2006. *American Poverty in a New Age of Reform.* 2nd ed. Armonk, NY: M. E. Sharpe.

Sexuality Information and Education Council of the United States. Lesbian, Gay, Bisexual, Transgender, and Questioning (LGBTQ) Youth. http://www.siecus .org/policy/LGBTQ_FS.pdf. Accessed May 22, 2006.

Shelden, Randall G., Sharon K. Tracy, and William B. Brown. 2001. *Youth Gangs in American Society.* 2nd ed. Belmont, CA: Wadsworth.

Skye, Warren. 2002. "E.L.D.E.R.S. Gathering for Native American Youth: Continuing Native American Traditions and Curbing Substance Abuse in Native American Youth." *Journal of Sociology and Social Welfare* 29, no. 3: 117–135.

Social Security Administration. SSR 68-73: Section 216(h)(2)(A). Relationship–Child Born Outside of Marriage–Rights of Inheritance from Father. http:// www.ssa.gov/OP_Home/rulings/oasi/53/SSR68-73-oasi-53.htm. Accessed August 16, 2006.

Thorne, Barrie. 1993. *Gender Play: Girls and Boys in School.* New Brunswick, NJ: Rutgers University Press.

Urban Institute. 2006. Children of Immigrants: Facts and Figures, May 2006. http://www.urban.org/UploadedPDF/900955_children_of_immigrants.pdf. Accessed May 29, 2006.

U.S. Bureau of the Census. Historical Income Tables–Families, Tables F-10 and F-10D. http://www.census.gov/hhes/income/histinc/f10.html. Accessed July 14, 2006.

———. 2003a. Grandparents' Day 2003. Press Release, August 25. http:// www.census.gov/Press-Release/www/2003/CB03-FF13.pdf. Accessed July 25, 2006.

———. 2003b. Health Insurance Coverage in the United States, September 2003. http://www.census.gov/prod/2003pubs/p60-223.pdf. Accessed May 9, 2006.

U.S. Department of Education. 1997. Title IX: 25 Years of Progress, July 1997. http://www.ed.gov/pubs/TitleIX/index.html. Accessed June 7, 2006.

U.S. Department of Health and Human Services, Administration for Children and Families. 2004. Child Maltreatment 2004. http://www.acf.hhs.gov/pro grams/cb/pubs/cm04. Accessed May 11, 2006.

U.S. Department of Justice, Office of Juvenile Justice and Delinquency Prevention. National Youth Gang Survey: 1999–2001. http://ojjdp.ncjrs.gov/publica tions/PubAbstract.asp?. Accessed August 7, 2006.

U.S. Department of Labor. Youth Rules! When and Where Is Your Teen Allowed to Work? Press Release. http://www.youthrules.dol.gov/newsroom/rm1894.pdf. Accessed June 16, 2006.

———. 2000. Report on the Youth Labor Force: Child Labor Laws and Enforcement, Chapter 2, November 2000. http://www.bls.gov/opub/rylf/pdf/ chapter2/pdf. Accessed June 1, 2006.

Waksler, Frances Chaput. 1996. *The Little Trials of Childhood and Children's Strategies for Dealing with Them.* Washington, DC: Falmer Press.

Walker, Nancy E., Catherine M. Brooks, and Lawrence S. Wrightsman. 1999. *Children's Rights in the United States: In Search of a National Policy.* Thousand Oaks, CA: Sage Publications.

Wilkins, David E. 2007. *American Indian Politics and the American Political System.* 2nd ed. Lanham, MD: Rowman & Littlefield Publishers.

YWCA USA (Young Women's Christian Association). Eliminating Racism, Empowering Women. http://www.ywca.org/site/pp.asp?c=djISI6PIKpG&b=281372. Accessed August 24, 2006.

BIBLIOGRAPHY

RESOURCES

Baker, Maureen. 1995. *Canadian Family Policy*. Toronto: University of Toronto Press.

Barrow, Christine, ed. 1996. *Family in the Caribbean: Themes and Perspectives*. Kingston, Jamaica: Ian Randle Publishers.

———. 2002. *Children's Rights: Caribbean Realities*. Kingston, Jamaica: Ian Randle Publishers.

Bottoms, Bette, Margaret Bull Kovera, and Bradley D. McAuliff, eds. 2005. *Children, Social Science, and the Law*. Cambridge University Press.

Conway, M. Margaret, David W. Ahern, and Gertrude A. Steuernagel. 2004. *Women & Public Policy: A Revolution in Progress*. 3rd ed. Washington, DC: Congressional Quarterly Press.

Ellis, Patricia. 2003. *Women, Gender and Development in the Caribbean: Reflections and Projections*. New York: Zed Books.

Fass, Paula S. 2006. *Children of a New World: Culture, Society, and Globalization*. New York: New York University Press.

Fass, Paula S., and Mary Ann Mason, eds. 2000. *Childhood in America*. New York: New York University Press.

Fletcher, Todd V., and Candace S. Bos, eds. 1999. *Helping Individuals with Disabilities and their Families: Mexican and U.S. Perspectives*. Tempe, AZ: Bilingual Review/Press.

Frenk, Julio. 2006. "Health Policy in Mexico." *The Lancet* 368 (September 9): 954–961.

Goodluck, Charlotte T., and Angela A. A. Willeto. 2001. *Native American Kids 2001: Indian Children's Well-Being Indicators Data Book*. Portland, OR: National Indian Child Welfare Association.

Government of Canada. 2002. *National Report–Canada, Ten Year Review of the World Summit for Children*. http://www.phac-aspc.gc.ca/dca-dea/publications/pdf/children-national-report-e.pdf.

Hevener Kaufman, Natalie, and Irene Rizzini, eds. 2004. *Globalization and Children: Exploring Potentials for Enhancing Opportunities in the Lives of Children and Youth*. Seacaucus, NJ: Kluwer Academic Publishers.

Hodgson, James F., and Debra S. Kelley, eds. 2001. *Sexual Violence: Policies, Practices, and Challenges in the United States and Canada*. New York: Praeger Publishers.

Howe, R. Brian, and Katherine Covell. 2007. *A Question of Commitment: Children's Rights in Canada*. Waterloo, ON, Canada: Wilfrid Laurier University Press.

Interparliamentary Union. 2007. Women in National Parliaments: World Classification, situation as of 28 February 2007. http://www.ipu.org/wmn-e/classif.htm.

Jack, Noreen. 2001. "HIV/AIDS in Caribbean Children and Adolescents." pp. 23–40 in *HIV/AIDS and Children in the English Speaking Caribbean*. Edited by Barbara A. Dicks. New York: Haworth Press Inc.

Kachur, Jerry L. 2000. "Northern Dreams: Schooling and Society in Canada." pp. 53–66 in *Education in a Global Society: A Comparative Perspective*. Edited by Kas Mazurek, Margret A. Winzer, and Czeslaw Majorek. Boston, London: Allyn and Bacon.

Kelly, Michael J., and Brendan Bain. 2005. *Education and HIV/AIDS in the Caribbean*. Kingston, Jamaica: Ian Randle,

Lareau, Annette. 2003. *Unequal Childhoods: Class, Race, and Family Life*. 2nd ed. Berkeley: University of California Press.

Levison, Deborah, Karine S. Moe, and Felicia M. Knaul. 2001. "Youth Education and Work in Mexico." *World Development* 29, no. 1: 167–188.

Pardeck, John T. 2006. *Children's Rights: Policy and Practice*. 2nd ed. New York: Haworth Press.

Pinheiro, Paulo Sérgio. 2006. *World Report on Violence against Children. Secretary-General's Study on Violence against Children*. United Nations.

Save the Children. 2007. *State of the World's Mothers 2007: Saving the Lives of Children under 5*. Westport, CT: Save the Children. http://www.savethechildren.org/publications/mothers/2007/SOWM-2007-final.pdf.

Schneider, Dona. 1995. *American Childhood: Risks and Realities*. New Brunswick, NJ: Rutgers University Press.

Tompkins, Cynthia Margarita, and Kristen Sternberg, eds. 2004. *Teen Life in Latin America and the Caribbean*. Westport, CT: Greenwood Press.

Torres, Carlos, and Octavio Pescador. 2000. "Education in Mexico: Sociopolitical Perspectives." pp. 67–76 in *Education in a Global Society: A Comparative Perspective*. Edited by Kas Mazurek, Margret A. Winzer, and Czeslaw Majorek. Boston, London: Allyn and Bacon.

United Nations Children's Fund (UNICEF). 2005. *The Convention on the Rights of the Child Fifteen Years Later: The Caribbean*. Barbados: UNICEF Regional Office for Latin America and the Caribbean

———. 2006. *The State of the World's Children 2007: Women and Children, the Double Dividend of Gender Equality*. New York: UNICEF.

———. 2006. *Violence against Children in the Caribbean Region: Regional Assessment; UN Secretary General's Study on Violence against Children*. Panama: Child Protection Section, UNICEF Regional Office for Latin America and the Caribbean. http://www.uwi.edu/ccdc/downloads/Violence_against_children.pdf.

United Nations Development Programme. 2006. *Human Development Report 2006: Beyond Scarcity: Power, Poverty and the Global Water Crisis*. Houndmills, Basingstoke, Hampshire and New York: Palgrave Macmillan.

United Nations Office on Drugs and Crime and World Bank, Caribbean Region. 2007. *Crime, Violence, and Development: Trends, Costs, and Policy Options in the Caribbean*. Report no 37820. March 2007. http://siteresources.worldbank.org/INTHAITI/Resources/Crimeandviolenceinthecaribbeanfullreport.pdf.

Walker, Nancy E., Catherine M. Brooks, and Lawrence S. Wrightsman. 1999. *Children's Rights in the United States: In Search of a National Policy.* Thousand Oaks, CA: Sage Publications.

NONPRINT RESOURCES

And the Dish Ran Away with the Spoon. 1992. Banyan Limited/BBC. Directed by Christopher Laird and Anthony Hall. 49 minutes. VHS and DVD. Made in Trinidad and Tobago, this film documents the domination of Caribbean television by U.S. and French programming.

Black & White in Exile. 1997. Produced and directed by Ray Blanco. 162 minutes. This documentary explores thirty years of Caribbean migration to the United States, focusing on Cuban and Haitian exiles and white and African American residents.

Caribbean Eye. 1988. A series of thirteen television programs focusing on culture and history in the Caribbean, each approximately 30 minutes. Produced by UNESCO and Banyan, Caribbean Eye "represents a pioneering effort in regional television and is the first documentary series about the Caribbean." Programs titles include: Community Celebrations (Other Caribbean Festivals); Survivors; La Musique Antillaise; Pan Caribbean; Dramatic Actions; Talk and More Talk; Independent Voices; Women in Action; Caribbean Carnivals; Visionaries; The Games We Play; Soca; Film Caribbean.

Children of Shadows. 2001. UNICEF. Produced by Karen Kramer, with partial funding by UNICEF. 54 minutes. VHS. This documentary examines the life of Restavèk children in Haiti.

A Closer Walk. 2003. Worldwide Documentaries. Robert Bilheimer. 85 minutes. VHS. Narrated by Glenn Close and Will Smith, this film documents the realities of the global HIV/AIDS epidemic.

Fighting for the Family. 1997. Vancouver, British Columbia: Moving Images Distribution. Barbara Anderson and Brad Newcombe. Amazon Communications. VHS. 46 minutes. A documentary that explores changing definitions of family.

Girls Like Us. 1997. New York: Women Make Movies. 60 minutes. VHS. The documentary explores teenage sexuality and pregnancy and the impact of class, sexism, and violence.

Integrate or Perish. 2003. University of West Indies-Caricom Project. VHS. A three-part television and radio documentary based on *Integrate or Perish: Perspectives of Leaders of the Integration Movement,* edited by Kenneth O. Hall (Ian Randle Publishers).

Life and Debt. 2001. Directed by Stephanie Black. A Tuff Gong Pictures Production. 86 minutes. A prize-winning documentary that explores the effects of neoliberal globalization on Jamaica.

A Loss of Innocence. 2006. Director Jenine Mendes-Franco. 21 minutes. Made in Trinidad and Tobago, this documentary examines child labor and child exploitation in the Caribbean.

Mexico Close-Up. 2000. Maryknoll World Productions. 28 minutes. Part 1 of this documentary focuses on a family in Ciudad Juárez, Chihuahua; part 2 focuses on a 13-year old Mayan girl who survived the 1997 Acteal massacre in Chiapas.

Our House: A Very Real Documentary about Kids of Gay and Lesbian Parents. 1999. New York: Cinema Guild. Videocassette. 57 minutes. A documentary that examines families headed by gay and lesbian parents in the United States.

Portrait of the Caribbean. 1991. Series producer Jenny Barraclough. 370 minutes. A seven-program documentary series that examines the social and cultural history of the Caribbean. Programs include: Iron in the Soul (slavery); Out of Africa (African influences); Paradise; La Grande Illusion (French influences, Martinique); Worlds Apart (indentured labor, China, India); Following Fidel; Shades of Freedom (new Caribbean identity).

Stolen Childhoods. 2004. Galen Films, Romano Productions. Directed and produced by Len Morris and Robin Romano. 85 minutes. VHS and DVD. Narrated by Meryl Streep, this documentary about child labor worldwide was filmed in eight countries, including Mexico and the United States.

Talk to Me. 1995. Tabata Production Associates. Directed by Susanne Tabata. 45 minutes. In this documentary, social justice topics are discussed by ten diverse secondary students in British Colombia, Canada (First Nations, Asian, African, Indian, and Asian).

35 Years of Child Development in the Caribbean. 1999. CD. Kingston: Dudley Grant Memorial Trust, University of West Indies

United Nations Children's Fund (UNICEF). Video/Audio. http://www.unicef.org/videoaudio/index.html.

Viva Cuba (Long Live Cuba!). 2005. Directed by Juan Carlos Cremata. VHS and DVD. This award-winning drama ''is a film that defends the right of children to be taken into account when parents make decisions that affect them,'' according to Director Juan Carlos Cremata.

WEB SITES

Caribbean Child Development Centre, University of the West Indies. http://www.uwi.edu/caribecd/About_Us/ccdchome.htm.

Cáritas Internationalis. Who We Are. http://www.caritas.org/jumpCh.asp?idUser=0&idChannel=6&idLang=ENG.

Child Rights Information Network (CRIN). Caribbean: Latest Resources. http://www.crin.org/reg/subregion.asp?ID=6.

———. Mexico: Latest Resources. http://www.crin.org/reg/country.asp?ctryID=142&subregID=7.

———. North America: Latest Resources. http://www.crin.org/reg/subregion.asp?ID=9.

Children International. Hompage. http://www.children.org/home.asp?sid=CA2CA41C-0B8F-49B4-8070-E73C1B301881.

Childwatch: International Research Network. What Is Childwatch International? http://www.childwatch.uio.no/what_is_cwi/index.html.

ECPAT International (End Child Pornography and Trafficking of Children for Sexual Purposes). http://www.ecpat.net/eng/index.asp.

International Labour Organization. International Programme on the Elimination of Child Labour (IPEC). http://www.ilo.org/public/english/standards/ipec/simpoc.

Safe Kids Worldwide. http://www.safekids.org.

Save the Children. http://www.savethechildren.net/alliance/where_we_work/MC/mapMX.html.

United Nations Children's Fund (UNICEF). At a Glance: Haiti. http://www.unicef.org/infobycountry/haiti_contact.html.

———. UNICEF, Canada. http://www.unicef.ca/portal/SmartDefault.aspx.

————. UNICEF, Eastern Caribbean Office. http://www.unicef.org/barbados.

————. UNICEF, Mexico. http://www.unicef.org/mexico.

United Nations Educational, Cultural and Scientific Organization (UNESCO). http://www.uis.unesco.org.

United States, Central Intelligence Agency. *CIA World Factbook.* http://www.cia.gov/cia/publications/factbook.

United States Fund for UNICEF. http://www.unicefusa.org/site/c.duLRI8O0H/b.25933/k.8DDD/US_Fund_for_UNICEF__US_Fund_for_UNICEF.htm.

The World Bank. http://worldbank.org.

World Health Organization (WHO). http://www.worldhealth.org.

INDEX

ABOUT THE EDITORS AND CONTRIBUTORS

EDITORS

IRVING EPSTEIN, Professor of Educational Studies at Illinois Wesleyan University, has published two edited volumes, *Chinese Education: Problems, Policies, and Prospects* (1991), *Recapturing the Personal: Essays on Education and Embodied Knowledge in Comparative Perspective* (2007), and served as an associate editor of the *Comparative Education Review* from 1988 to 1998. His interests include Asian education, educational policies involving street children, and issues of social theory.

SHERYL L. LUTJENS, Ph.D. in Political Science, teaches Comparative Politics, Latin American Politics, Public Administration, and Feminist Theory and Politics at Northern Arizona University (Flagstaff, Arizona), where she served as Director of Women's Studies from 2002 to 2006. Her published research includes *The State, Bureaucracy, and the Cuban Schools: Power and Participation* (Westview Press 1996), the co-edited *Rereading Women in Latin America and the Caribbean: The Political Economy of Gender* (Rowman & Littlefield 2002), as well as articles and chapters variously focusing on women, children, education, the state, and politics in Cuba, women and politics in the United States, and U.S.–Cuba academic relations.

CONTRIBUTORS

CHRISTINE BARROW is Professorial Fellow, Sir Arthur Lewis Institute of Social and Economic Studies, University of the West Indies, and was Deputy Principal at the Barbados Campus from 2002 to 2005. Her research interests and publications in Caribbean social development have emphasized family and gender ideologies and systems, child rights and development, sexualities, reproductive health, and HIV/AIDS.

XENOBIA N. BARROW is currently a doctoral student at the University at Albany, SUNY in the Department of Latin American and Caribbean studies. She conducted Masters Research on institutions and the social welfare of AIDS orphans in Uganda at Carleton University, in Ottawa, Ontario. Her current research interests are in the condition of HIV/AIDS in island states, as well as literary, visual, and performing arts education for development in the Caribbean.

JANET BROWN, M.S.W., was head of the Caribbean Child Development Centre of the University of the West Indies in Jamaica for almost twenty years. The center focused on training, advocacy, and research in early childhood development and parenting education/support. She now works as an independent consultant in these areas.

CAROLANN LOUISE DANIELS holds a Ph.D. in Social Welfare and is currently an assistant professor at Adelphi University. Dr. Daniel has published several articles on the topics of social work education, multiculturalism, and Caribbean immigrants in the Diaspora. Her research interests include HIV prevention and cultural competence, immigrant incorporation, and race and professionalization.

ROSE DAVIES, Ph.D., has over thirty years working experience at different levels in the early childhood field. She is currently a tenured senior lecturer at the School of Education, University of the West Indies, with responsibility for development, monitoring, and quality assurance for early childhood preservice teacher education. She has published in refereed journals.

M. GAIL SANDERS DERRICK is a professor at Regent University in Virginia Beach, Virginia. Her research interests include autonomous learning, self-efficacy, and motivation. She received the 2007 Distinguished Alumni Award from Virginia Wesleyan and the 2007 Gary J. Confessore Award for Scholarly Achievement at The Autonomous Learning World Caucus.

MARÍA ISABEL DOMÍNGUEZ, Ph.D. in Sociology, coordinates research on youth in the Center for Psychological and Sociological Research, and is Senior Professor and Researcher at the University of Havana. She has published in Cuba, the United States, Spain, and other countries, and is currently a member of the CLACSO Working Group on Youth, the Executive Committee of the Latin American Sociology Association, and the Cuban Academy of Sciences.

ELIZABETH M. HUNTER, Ed.D., is Director of Research on Learning and faculty member in the School of Education at Regent University. She researches, writes, and produces scholarly creative works that include instructional video and documentary film as an ongoing examination of special needs students, providing content to graduate students nationally and internationally.

HOPE M. JORDAN, Professor of Education at Regent University, has over twenty-five years of experience in both K–12 and higher education. Dr. Jordan has written several grants, books, and articles. An academic background in psychology, general education, special education, administration and supervision, and organizational leadership provides her with a broad perspective of education from various levels.

FELICIA KNAUL, a Canadian resident in Mexico City, is Senior Economist at the Mexican Health Foundation and Director of the "Health and Competitiveness" program. She has held senior government posts in Mexico and Colombia, worked for several international development organizations including the World Health Organization, and sits on the Consultative Council of UNICEF Mexico and the Mexican Council on Competitiveness board. She holds a Ph.D. in Economics from Harvard University and has published in the fields of health, education, and children in difficult circumstances.

CATHERINE MARSICEK is the Curator of Latin American and Iberian Collections at the University of New Mexico. Her research interests include library and information issues, particularly in the Caribbean. She has been instrumental in the development of the Digital Library of the Caribbean, a new online library of Caribbean materials.

DOREEN E. MARTINEZ, Ph.D., is Assistant Professor of Women's Studies at Northern Arizona University. Her career focuses on cultural epistemology. This interest is born out of her own mixed ancestry that is Mescalero Apache, Mexican, and Pennsylvania Dutch. Her intellectual commitments are focused on the meanings individuals and communities make with their cosmological understandings and cultural practices.

RUTH NINA ESTRELLA, Professor in the Department of Psychology at the University of Puerto Rico, received a Ph.D. in Social Psychology from the National Autonomous University of Mexico. Her areas of research include the psychology of couples, sexuality, and adolescents. She coordinates the Network of Family Studies in the Caribbean-Atlantea Project.

FERNANDO M. REIMERS is the Ford Foundation Professor of International Education and Director of Global Education and of International Education Policy at Harvard University. His current research focuses on the impact of education policy on literacy instruction and democratic citizenship education. More information about his academic work is available at http://gseacademic.harvard.edu/~reimers/.

MARY ANN E. STEGER is Professor of Political Science at Northern Arizona University. Her publications focus on social welfare policies, including the Temporary Assistance for Needy Families (TANF) program, Medicaid, and the Food Stamp program, Native American land and resource issues, and several environmental policy areas.

YANIQUE TAYLOR is a doctoral student in the Urban Systems Program at Rutgers University, Newark. Her research interests include issues of educational equity and educational interventions designed to increase parental advocacy within urban schools. Her dissertation research explores the experiences of Caribbean students who migrate to the United States for postsecondary education.

SUSIE VEROFF, born in Michigan, lives in Montréal, Canada. She is a teacher and an artist specializing in painting, printmaking, and photography. She earned a doctoral degree in Human and Organizational Development from The Fielding Institute (1996), and has since founded La Espiral Rota, a group that promotes artistic expressions of immigrant artists.

LILITH C. WERNER is a current Ph.D. candidate at Loyola University, Chicago. Her dissertation research focuses on global pressures, national educational policy, and local school reform initiatives in Spain and the United States. She also works for the Chicago Public School system.

CAROLYNE J. WHITE is Professor and Chair, Department of Urban Education at Rutgers University, Newark. Her recent publications include book chapters in N. K. Denzin and M. D. Giardina, eds., *Qualitative Inquiry and the Conservative Challenge*, and D. Macedo and S. Steinberg, eds., *Handbook of Media Literacy*.

ANGELA A. A. WILLETO is Associate Professor in the Department of Sociology and Social Work at Northern Arizona University. Professor Willeto is an enrolled member of the Navajo Nation and a former Spencer Fellow who has published in the area of Navajo educational achievement and American Indian/Alaska Native children and family well-being.

CHRISTOLYN A. WILLIAMS was born in Antigua and Barbuda and migrated to the United States as a young adult. Dr. Williams is Associate Professor of History at Westchester Community College, the State

University of New York (SUNY), where she teaches courses in African, Caribbean, Latin American, and African American history. She received a PhD in history at The Graduate School and University Center of the City University of New York in February 2007.

SIAN WILLIAMS, M.A., has worked as a children's theater director, teacher, youth worker, legal aid adviser, policy officer, and services manager in the United Kingdom. Since 1993, she has lived and worked in Jamaica where she specializes in providing technical assistance to Caribbean governments in early childhood policy and programming

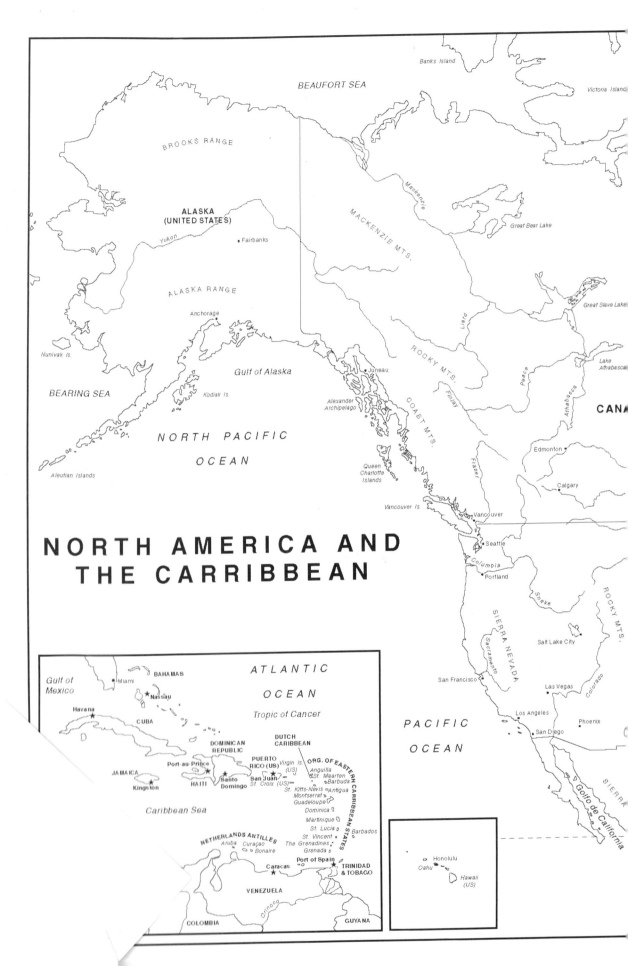

NORTH AMERICA AND
THE CARRIBBEAN

BEAUFORT SEA

Banks Island

Victoria Island

BROOKS RANGE

Mackenzie

ALASKA
(UNITED STATES)

Great Bear Lake

Yukon

• Fairbanks

MACKENZIE MTS.

ALASKA RANGE

Anchorage •

Great Slave Lake

ROCKY MTS.

Peace

Lake
Athabasca

Nunivak Is.

Gulf of Alaska

• Juneau

CAN

Kodiak Is.

Alexander
Archipelago

COAST MTS.

Finlay

Fraser

Athabasca

BEARING SEA

NORTH   PACIFIC

OCEAN

Queen
Charlotte
Islands

Edmonton •

Aleutian Islands

Vancouver Is.

• Vancouver

Calgary

• Seattle

Columbia

• Portland

Snake

ROCKY MTS.

SIERRA NEVADA

Salt Lake City

Sacramento

San Francisco •

Las Vegas

Colorado

Los Angeles •

Phoenix

PACIFIC

OCEAN

• San Diego

SIERRA

Golfo de California

Caribbean inset

Gulf of
Mexico

• Miami

BAHAMAS

★ Nassau

ATLANTIC

OCEAN

Tropic of Cancer

Havana ★

CUBA

DOMINICAN
REPUBLIC

DUTCH
CARIBBEAN

JAMAICA

Port-au-Prince

Kingston ★

HAITI

PUERTO
RICO (US)

San Juan
St. Croix (US)

★ Santo
Domingo

Virgin Is.
(US)

ORG. OF EASTERN CARIBBEAN STATES

Anguilla
★ St. Maarten
• Barbuda
St. Kitts-Nevis • Antigua
Montserrat ◊
Guadeloupe ◊
Dominica ◊
Martinique ◊
St. Lucia ◊
St. Vincent ◊
The Grenadines •
Grenada ◊

Barbados ◊

Caribbean Sea

NETHERLANDS ANTILLES
Aruba ◊ Curaçao ◊
◊ Bonaire

Port of Spain ★

Caracas ★

TRINIDAD
& TOBAGO

VENEZUELA

Orinoco

COLOMBIA

GUYANA

Honolulu

Oahu

Hawaii
(US)